THE RIVER COTTAGE **MEAT** BOOK

HUGH FEARNLEY-WHITTINGSTALL

WWW.RIVERCOTTAGE.NET

PHOTOGRAPHY BY SIMON WHEELER

HODDER

First published in Great Britain in 2004 by Hodder & Stoughton
An Hachette Livre UK company

First published in paperback in 2008

1

A CIP catalogue record for this title is available from the British Library

ISBN 978 0 340 82638 6

Design by Paddy Cramsie at etal-design.com
Typeset in Frutiger and Melior

Photography by Simon Wheeler (email: simonwheeler@onetel.net.uk)

Printed and bound in Italy by L.E.G.O. SpA

Hodder & Stoughton policy is to use papers that are natural, renewable and recyclable products and made from wood grown in sustainable forests. The logging and manufacturing processes are expected to conform to the environmental regulations of the country of origin.

Hodder & Stoughton Ltd
338 Euston Road
London NW1 3BH

www.hodder.co.uk

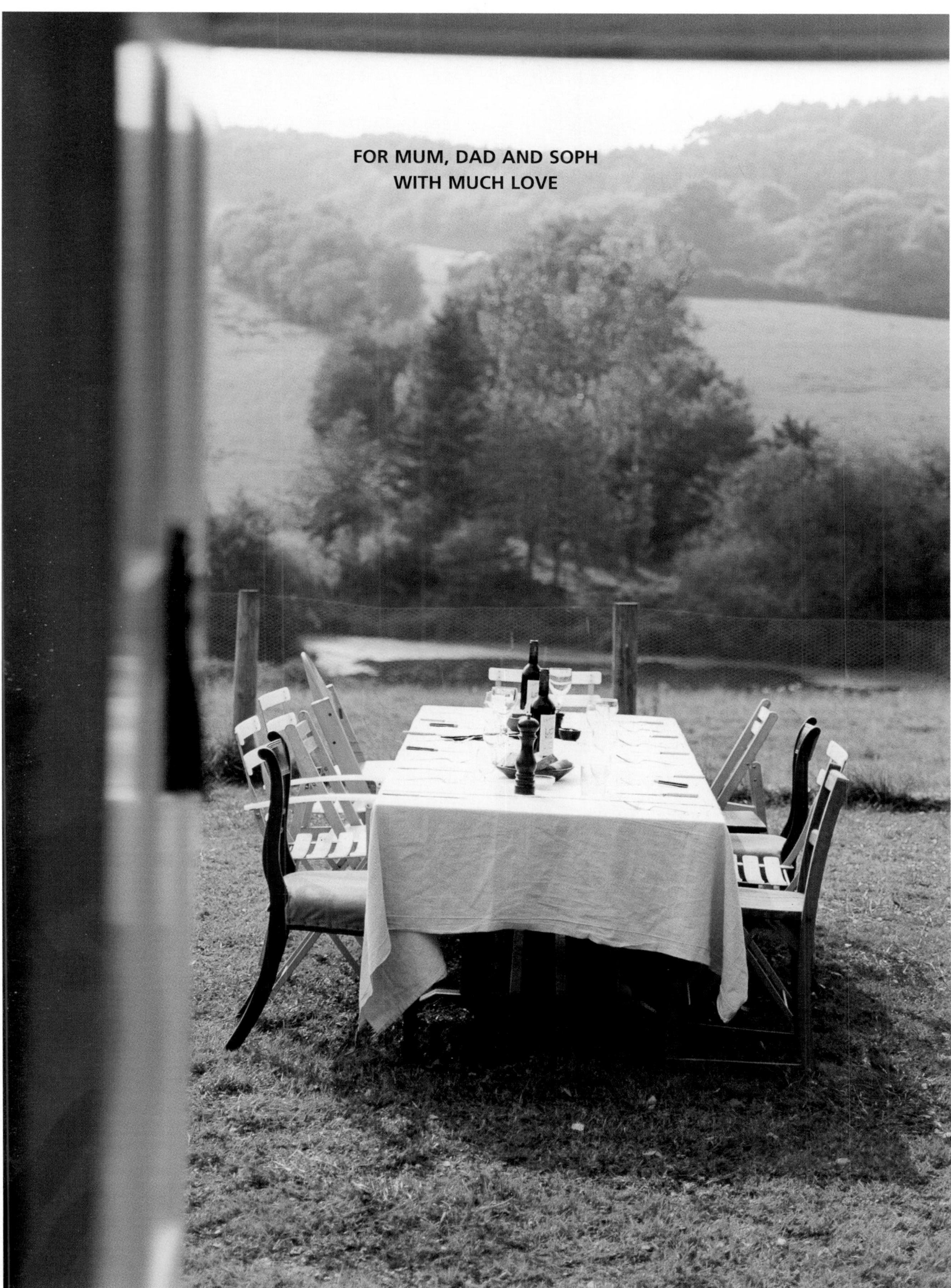

FOR MUM, DAD AND SOPH
WITH MUCH LOVE

TRADITIONAL ENGLISH
MUTTON
FROM OUR OWN FARM.
TENDER AND FULL OF FLAVOUR.
PRICES £
SHOULDER 4·00 /kg (1·81/lb)
LEG. 5·00 /kg (2·27/lb)
CHOPS 5·00 /kg (2·27/lb)
BREAST 2·50 /kg

CONTENTS

INTRODUCTION

I believe that the way we produce and use meat requires radical reform. This book contains, among other things, my personal views on how positive change might be achieved. I'm delighted to say that I am not the only one championing a return to some of the older, more holistic values of meat production and cookery. There are a good number of chefs, writers and commentators, and also hundreds of farmers and meat producers, who care passionately about these issues. But ultimately the only person who is going to make any significant difference to the way meat is produced, sold and cooked is you – the consumer. So it's you I'm after, and your habits I hope to change.

There are already thousands of people who are trying to shop for and cook meat in a more thoughtful way. If you are one of them, I hope this book adds a little to your commitment to good meat, as well as your understanding and enjoyment of it. But if I may be allowed to be unabashedly honest about my ambitions, what I really want to do is help to change those thousands into millions. And this book is one gesture towards that ambition.

Cooking is a daily drama, still staged to some degree in almost every home. One of my jobs as a cookery writer is to make sure that every episode has a happy ending – and, with a bit of luck, a happy beginning and middle as well. I want you to enjoy cooking, eating, and feeding your friends, because I believe these are among the higher pleasures and privileges of our short time on the planet. I hope this book will help you and your loved ones to walk away sated and contented from many a fine meal.

I've written this book because I believe that meat, at its splendid best, helps us achieve this sense of shared contentment perhaps better than any other food. But I've also written it because of my feelings about meat eating at its worst: an ignominious expression of greed, indifference and heartlessness.

After eating badly produced, badly butchered and badly cooked meat, you may be left thinking, if you are prone to such thoughts, 'You mean an animal died *for that.*' I hope this book will mean that in the future you have such thoughts rarely, if at all.

I like to argue, and I like to digress, and I like to take some time cajoling my readers to consider and, I hope, embrace my theories about food. But what I'm saying in this book is not really very complicated. As an exercise for my own benefit, I tried to boil it down to a few bullet points. When I did so, it seemed to make sense – and even to be worth reproducing. So here it is – my 'meat manifesto', if you like, expressed as a series of questions and exhortations to you, the reader. Do feel free to answer back ...

My Meat Manifesto

• Think about the meat that you eat. Is it good enough? Good enough to bring you pleasure every time you eat it? Could it, should it, be better? Are you among the millions of consumers putting pressure on farmers to produce mountains of cheap meat of dubious quality, by dubious means? Perhaps it would make sense to spend a little more on it, a little less often. Or to buy cheaper cuts of better meat.

• Think about the animals from which the meat that you eat comes. Are you at all concerned about how they have been treated? Have they lived well? Have they been fed on safe, appropriate foods? Have they been cared for by someone who respects them and enjoys their contact with them? Are you *sure*? Perhaps it's time to find out a bit more about where the meat you eat comes from. Or to change to a source that can reassure you about these points.

• Where do you get your meat? Might there be a different way of buying meat that works well for you, that could guarantee better quality and give you a cleaner conscience? Could you shop locally, buying direct from the people who actually farm the animals that produce the meat? Or could you use a butcher who can tell you where all his or her meat comes from, and get special things for you when you want them?

• Think about the way you cook meat. Do you respect it? Do you do it justice? Would you like to understand a little more (or even a lot more) about what happens when you roast a joint or a bird in a very hot oven, or when you simmer meat slowly, for hours, with subtle flavours. To discover the remarkable difference that resting roast meat, for fifteen minutes or more, before carving it will make to its texture, and therefore its taste? A few small adjustments to your cooking habits could bring big benefits.

• Are you adventurous with meat? Do you explore the different tastes and textures of the various cuts, particularly the cheaper cuts, and of offal? Could you save money *and* eat better by doing so? There may be all kinds of recipes, not complicated, not expensive, that could breathe new life into your meat cooking and bring more excitement and satisfaction at mealtimes to you, your family and the friends you like to entertain.

• Are you thrifty with meat? That's not the same as mean. Being creative with leftover meat means getting more from it. If anything, you're making it more generous to you and, in so doing, paying greater tribute to the animal that has died to provide it.

• Finally, if you accept that there is any moral content at all in the way we treat animals, then you must accept that there is a moral dimension in your dealings with meat. Please think about it, don't shirk it.

1. MEAT AND RIGHT

1. MEAT AND RIGHT

I have been thinking and reading a lot about meat recently. I have also been cooking and eating somewhat more of it than I usually do. I have visited meat-producing farms, particularly here in the West Country, and tasted their products. And I have been inside broiler houses, pig units, abattoirs, supermarkets, butcher's shops and farm shops.

This kind of research is only right and proper, you would think, given that I'm setting out to write a book about meat. But trying to increase my knowledge of the subject is just a part of what I've been up to. As well as researching into all areas of the meat industry, I have also been trying to shake off my preconceptions and think about meat from first principles. A food that many millions of us take for granted is riddled with complex issues – issues of health, economics and environment, not to mention, of course, taste. But also, undeniably, issues of right and wrong. When thinking about the role meat plays in our lives and how to improve it, it is not enough simply to search for the facts. We must also consider our choices, and examine our consciences.

So there are two fundamental questions that I would like to consider at the very beginning of this book. Why do we eat meat? And is it right, morally, that we do?

Our Carnivorous History

Most meat eaters never really ask themselves these questions. That fact in itself sheds some light on the issue. Unthinkingly, we are carnivores. And historically, we are carnivores. For hundreds of thousands of years we have hunted animals, and for tens of thousands we have farmed them, so that we can eat their meat. It is likely that we were meat eaters throughout that period of our development when our moral capacity could be said to have evolved. There is continuity in our meat eating and it is, in some deep-rooted, even hard-wired, way, natural.

In eating meat, then, I am doing what comes naturally. But that's not enough to resolve the moral dilemma. In order to be an untroubled carnivore I need to persuade myself not merely that it's been okay for my ancestors to eat meat for the past several millennia but that it's still okay for me today.

Things change. We continue to evolve, and so does our relationship with the animals with whom we share the planet. For a long period of evolutionary history, our primate ancestry was primarily, or even exclusively, vegetarian. Today our cousins, the gorillas and orang-utans, survive – indeed, thrive – without a scrap of meat in their diets. On the other hand, our closer relatives, the chimpanzees, do hunt for meat, usually killing other monkey species or even cannibalising other chimp troupes.

So why has the human primate hung on to the meat-eating habit? Why indeed, argues the vegetarian, who sees abstention from meat as a mark of moral progress.

Why not mark the ascent of civilised values by abandoning a wholly uncivilised historical habit? Some carnivores in search of absolution may try to argue that meat is essential for human survival – though, when pressed, they will usually moderate the claim to 'essential for good health'. Others have a tendency to become quite vociferous in defence of their carnivorous ways and, on the basis that attack is the best form of defence, you may hear them argue that vegetarians are pallid, pasty-faced types, who are missing something good in their diets. All they are really observing, though, is that ours is a meat-eating culture essentially hostile to vegetarians – some of whom, through ignorance and lack of support, manage their diets badly.

Pro-meat arguments based on habit, health or survival, persuasive though they may feel to their protagonists, do not really bite on a pragmatic level, let alone in the realm of pure ethics. At best, they establish the self-evident fact that the human race is, and has long been, meat eating. But we carnivores must also concede that, in all but a few extreme environments, meat is not essential for human survival or even for good health.

The real problem with these arguments is that they are often born of a gridlocked antagonism between meat eaters and vegetarians, who each feel the need to defend themselves against the implied criticism of the other's position. They miss the moral nitty-gritty by a wide margin because the issues at stake have become almost tribal: two groups feeling mutually threatened, throwing sticks and bones. This is an unhappy, contaminated forum in which to conduct a reasoned moral discussion.

Present and Future Choices

Any useful moral discussion about eating meat has to focus on the choices we have as individuals today. It must take the world as we find it, but also take seriously the possibility of improving it. As Socrates said, 'The unexamined life is not worth living.' But the introspective exercise is only worthwhile if we embrace the possibility of acting on our conclusions. So what must we examine to reveal the moral nature of our meat-eating ways? And if we can shed light on this difficult area, how must we then act?

It seems obvious to me that the morality of meat eating lies in the factual details of our relationships with the animals we kill for food. It is what we do to them that counts. There is the simple fact that we plan and carry out their slaughter. And, in the case of farmed animals, there are the more complex interactions through which we manage and control almost every aspect of their lives from birth to death. From where do we draw the moral authority to bring about their deaths? And what is the moral status of the means and methods we use to run their lives?

Perhaps the easiest answer to the first question, and historically one of the most enduring arguments in defence of meat eating, is the religious one. It's okay because God says it's okay – not in so many words, of course. This has its variations in different religions but the Christian version involves a fairly crude citing of the scriptures: 'Let them [humans] have dominion over every living thing that moves upon the earth' (Genesis 1:28). This, along with an Old Testament God's ready acceptance of animal sacrifice, is grouped with the observation that Jesus apparently never spoke out against meat eating. Together, these biblical references are interpreted as a general approbation for the notion that it's acceptable to slaughter animals for food.

Personally I don't think that's good enough. But then I would argue that any religious defence of meat eating is *per se* not a moral one. The (mis)interpretation of scripture has been used as justification for some of the most appallingly cruel and immoral acts of history, and continues to be to this day. Questionable interpretations of the edicts of your religion are no excuse for killing innocent people. So why should they excuse killing innocent animals?

A related argument, which may or may not sidestep the obvious pitfalls of religious observance, is that all animals, or at least the ones we use for food, are simply outside the moral framework. That because they are not themselves moral beings, their welfare is not an issue. Or, put another way, because they have no soul, they have no status. They are no better and no worse than machines, and we can do with them what we want. This was the view taken by the Cartesian scientists in the seventeenth century, who pioneered vivisection and dismissed the cries of the animals they cut up as 'no more than the sound of breaking machines' (and they called this 'The Enlightenment'!).

In a post-Darwinian world, where our biological links to the rest of the animal kingdom are clear and the differences between 'them and us' have been demonstrated to be merely quantitative, few would own up to such a view – at least not without regressing to some sort of theological justification. There is no doubt whatever that you can cause pain and suffering to a pig or a chicken, as you can to a mouse or a gorilla, and there is no doubt that you can, in much the same sense as we use the words for our own species, make them 'happy' or 'unhappy'. Of course they are in our moral sphere.

Yet when we look at industrial meat production (and I will be doing so in detail shortly) and consider the miserable lives of animals in the factory-farming system, it is hard not to be reminded of the Cartesian vivisectionists. How can the people who work in these units, and the people who own them, run them and profit by them, reconcile their work with their consciences? Only, one imagines, by diminishing or denying the sentience of the animals concerned, and thereby abolishing their moral status – or by simply not thinking at all.

At the opposite end of the moral spectrum is a group with a very different creed, which again may or may not be grounded in religious faith. It believes that all life is sacred, that animal suffering equates to human suffering, and that to kill any animal for any reason – except perhaps self-defence – is wrong. Even if we

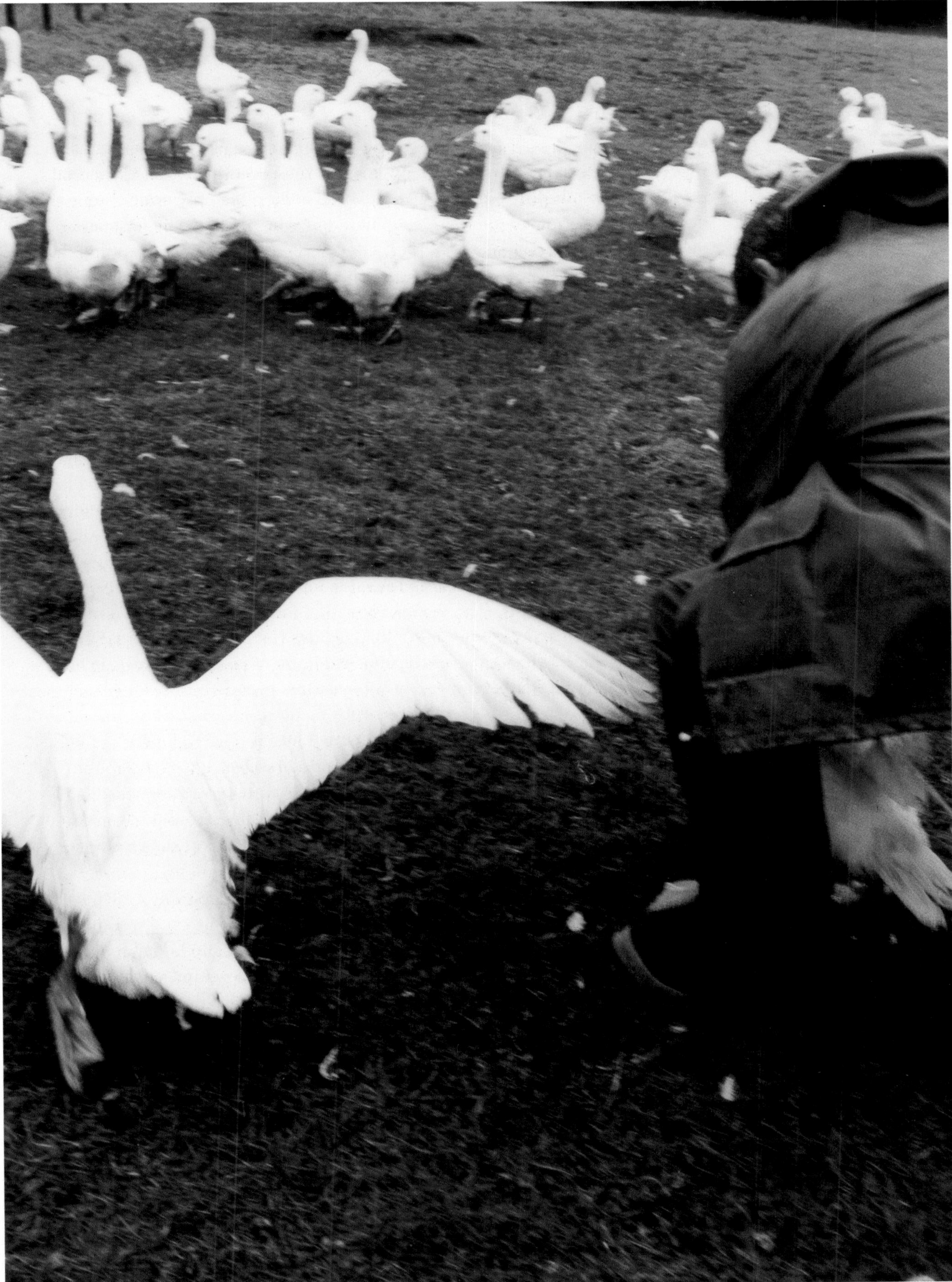

have an instinct to kill for meat, we have evolved to a point where we can deny that instinct, without detriment to our health. And because we can, we should. For those who take this position, a strict vegan code is the only option. As a moral choice it may be something (relatively) new, but why not be at the vanguard of human moral development?

I find this a fairly sympathetic proposition – certainly a lot more compelling than the opposite, Cartesian extreme. The commitment to eliminate the pain and suffering of animals at the hands of humans has to be morally superior to the commitment to ignore it.

The Limits of a Vegetarian Utopia

So why do I not simply embrace this view and become a vegetarian? Because in the end I feel this position also turns out to be simplistic. To maintain that we can live in complete harmony with the rest of animal kind is naive. It misunderstands the nature of our connections with other species, and amounts to another form of denial of our shared moral sphere, albeit better intentioned than the Cartesian one.

The undeniable fact is that any species' pursuit of its interests will always have an impact on the rest of the planet's life – the fox impacting on the chicken population, the flea on the cat, the beaver on the forest, and the sheep on the grass. Living in a bubble, where one's individual actions (let alone those of one's entire species) have only a benign effect, or none at all, on other living things, is not an option. Such moral purity simply doesn't exist.

It is true that of all species, humans exert the biggest, and scariest, influence on the rest of the planet. There is barely another species that is unaffected by our presence. But we must be clear that vegetarian humans are no exception. In pursuit of their goals they, too, affect the balance of nature. They may claim they affect it for the better, that their relationship with the rest of the world's animals is morally superior to the meat eater's. But the truth of such a claim is not self-evident; it needs examination.

Of all the creatures whose lives we affect, none are more deeply dependent on us – for their success as species and for their individual health and well-being – than the animals we raise to kill for meat. I'm talking about common domestic livestock – poultry, pigs, cows, sheep and goats. We control almost every aspect of their lives: their feeding, their breeding, their health, their pain, or freedom from it, and finally the timing and manner of their death. We have done so for hundreds of thousands of years, to the point where their dependence on us is in their nature – evolutionarily hard-wired. With these physical controls come moral responsibilities. Their suffering, or lack of it, their animal happiness, or animal misery, are down to us.

This dependency would not be suspended if we all became vegetarians. If we ceased to kill the domesticated meat species for food, then these animals would not revert to the wild (even assuming, if 'the wild' means 'land unaffected by man', that there is still such a place to be found on the planet). The nature of our relationship would change but the relationship would not end. We would remain their custodians, with full moral responsibility for their welfare.

So what happens to these animals in a vegetarian Utopia? We are not going to eat them, but they remain in our charge. We could consign them to 'reservations' – wildlife parks where the wildlife isn't wild. Tamelife parks, perhaps? But we could hardly abandon them to their own fates – at least not if we are genuinely concerned about their welfare. If we are not to be guilty of great cruelty, we would still have to manage the populations, by veterinary means for their good health and by culling to avoid population booms and consequent starvation. And wouldn't the managers of these parks want to minimise the suffering of old and diseased animals by 'putting them down' humanely? Then what happens to the corpses of the deceased? Do we bury them? Are we allowed to feed them to our cats and dogs, or have they become vegetarian, too? Or should they just be composted to produce fertiliser for the vegetarian agriculture that is now feeding us? But then wouldn't we sort of end up eating them anyway?

Meanwhile, how does our new food-growing landscape look and feel? An agriculture that cultivated only fruit and vegetables would create intense pressures on the environment. The organic system of farming, which depends for its success on an integration of arable and livestock systems, and the use of natural animal manures to replenish the soil, would be among the first casualties. The hedgerows and coppices that define our landscape and support the biodiversity of the countryside are integral to a mixed farming economy, but would soon become redundant in the vegetarian landscape. And why should farmers, who will always (and rightly) expect some profit for their toils, preserve the redundant?

The hard-line proposal for a vegetarian future rejects such questions as beside the point. It accepts the inevitability of the population crash in domesticated livestock, and the radical realignment of the landscape, as necessities for the good of the cause. Better to have no animals than animals we kill for food. But what does this really mean? Better to be indirectly responsible for their death than directly? Better to have their blood on our hands only metaphorically, not literally?

The Morality of Killing Animals

Such determined adherence to the vegetarian cause, at whatever cost, only brings us back to the irreducible, absolute moral position with which we started: that killing animals to eat them is always, and absolutely, wrong. Once the vegetarian position is reduced to this fundamentalist tenet, it becomes hard to counter rationally. But you can have an intuitive objection to such a moral absolute. Who says it's wrong? What makes it wrong? It doesn't strike *me* as in any way obvious that killing animals is, in itself, morally wrong. *Particularly* if we are killing them for food. We are not outside the natural order of things. And if we don't kill them for food, then somebody else, or something else, will.

That may sound trite, but it is an important point in this discussion. That animals kill other animals for food is a fact of nature. That all animals will eventually die is another. A less obvious fact is that, of all the available deaths an animal can face in the wild, the most common, and probably the least traumatic, is death at the hands of another animal who wants to eat it. 'Dying of old age' barely exists in nature. An animal suffering from injury or illness is likely to be killed by a predator before it finally succumbs to weakness or disease. And it will be eaten by something – the jackal, the vulture or the maggot.

Humans and the animals they raise for food do not operate outside this natural sphere. We kill animals for food that would otherwise die another death. We are not taking life from the immortal. There are differences, though, between ourselves and the other potential killers of our livestock. One is that we tend to kill animals that are in the prime of life, whereas other predators favour the young, the weak and the sick. But our preference for the healthy isn't a moral perversion: every predator would prefer a healthy animal to a diseased one, if it could catch it. And by killing animals before they begin to degenerate or get sick, we are arguably minimising their pain and suffering, not increasing it.

Another difference is that we are, uniquely among meat eaters, not compelled to kill animals for food (although, as I have argued above, our ancestors probably had an irrefutable instinct to hunt prey). Another way of putting this is that we are the only predatory species with the capacity to refrain from doing what comes naturally. But does that mean that we should refrain? Not necessarily. After all, if the fate meted out by humans to the animals they kill for food is no worse, or perhaps demonstrably better, than that on offer from other potential killers, then isn't it morally preferable?

As it happens, the way in which we kill animals for food is quite different from that of other predators. We don't chase them down, and tear them to death with our teeth and claws. We don't crush them to death, or swallow them alive. We corral them into groups, load them on to lorries, prod and poke them into a reasonably orderly queue, and then shoot them in the head with something called a captive bolt gun. (We also do a little hunting – mainly with guns. But I'm saving that moral debate for Chapter 8, Game.)

It is ironic, and also fairly astonishing, that the killing methods of many non-human predators are considered such a fascinating aspect of the natural world that films displaying them in graphic detail, often replaying the process several times in slow motion, are considered to be at the classy end of prime-time entertainment, fit for children as well as adults. Whereas the final moments of human predation of our farmed livestock are considered too disturbing and shameful to be made available even for information. In fact, such limited footage as does exist has often been filmed undercover, and is more likely to be used to fuel the rage of the militant vegetarian than to educate us dispassionately about the way our meat is made.

There is no doubt that Western society is very confused about death – both human and animal death. Human death as dramatic entertainment in movies and on television has, like animal-on-animal predation, never been more familiar. Yet the human act of killing animals for food, once familiar to most of society, has now become so shameful that those who condone it – by eating meat every day – are entirely protected from thinking about it. Food animals are killed and their meat is cut up and packaged far from human eyes. By the time meat reaches the consumer, its animal origins have been all but obliterated.

This is the reason I have decided to illustrate this chapter with a sequence of photographs showing a pair of my North Devon beef cattle being taken to slaughter (see overleaf). Along with my photographer, Simon Wheeler, I was present throughout the process – I loaded them up, drove them myself, unloaded them, watched them wait, watched them queue and watched them die. Then I watched them being skinned and sawn in half. I'll admit it was somewhat shocking to see such an unfamiliar process in full, unexpurgated detail. But I'm glad I witnessed it, and I'm happy with the decision to show Simon's pictures here.

Including the sequence in this book somehow seems fair to both sides of the debate. First of all, to remind all carnivores that there is no meat without the death of a warm-blooded, sentient animal – and that those who eat meat must take responsibility for these deaths. And at the same time, to ask vegetarians to consider at just what point of the slaughter process they believe that cruelty and suffering are taking place. Or, put another way, how exactly would they prefer these animals to die – given that immortality is not an option.

Of course, I can't vouch for all abattoirs or all slaughtermen. But I can say that, when practised by a group of sympathetic professionals (as the men and women at my local slaughterhouse undoubtedly are), the slaughter process does not seem to me to cause much suffering. Compare it to almost any other conceivable death for a farmed or wild animal – predation, starvation, drowning, disease – and it stacks up as certainly no worse, and probably a lot better, than any of them. It isn't pretty, and it doesn't compare for excitement with a cheetah running down a gazelle, or a killer whale snatching seals from a beach. But there is something about it that perhaps should inspire a kind of admiration: the notion of an intelligent social creature using its brain and its technology in an attempt to maximise the efficiency and minimise the cruelty of its predation.

That's not to say that there is no room for improvement. We should be constantly striving to make the slaughter of our farm animals as painless and stress free as possible. But what I witnessed at the slaughterhouse did not make me feel angry, or sick, or guilty, or ashamed – either for myself or for any of the people working there. In fact, it made me feel that, whatever is morally questionable about the way we treat our livestock (and there is plenty to be concerned about, as we shall see) happens not so much in the way we bring about their death but at almost every stage of our dealings with them prior to those final minutes.

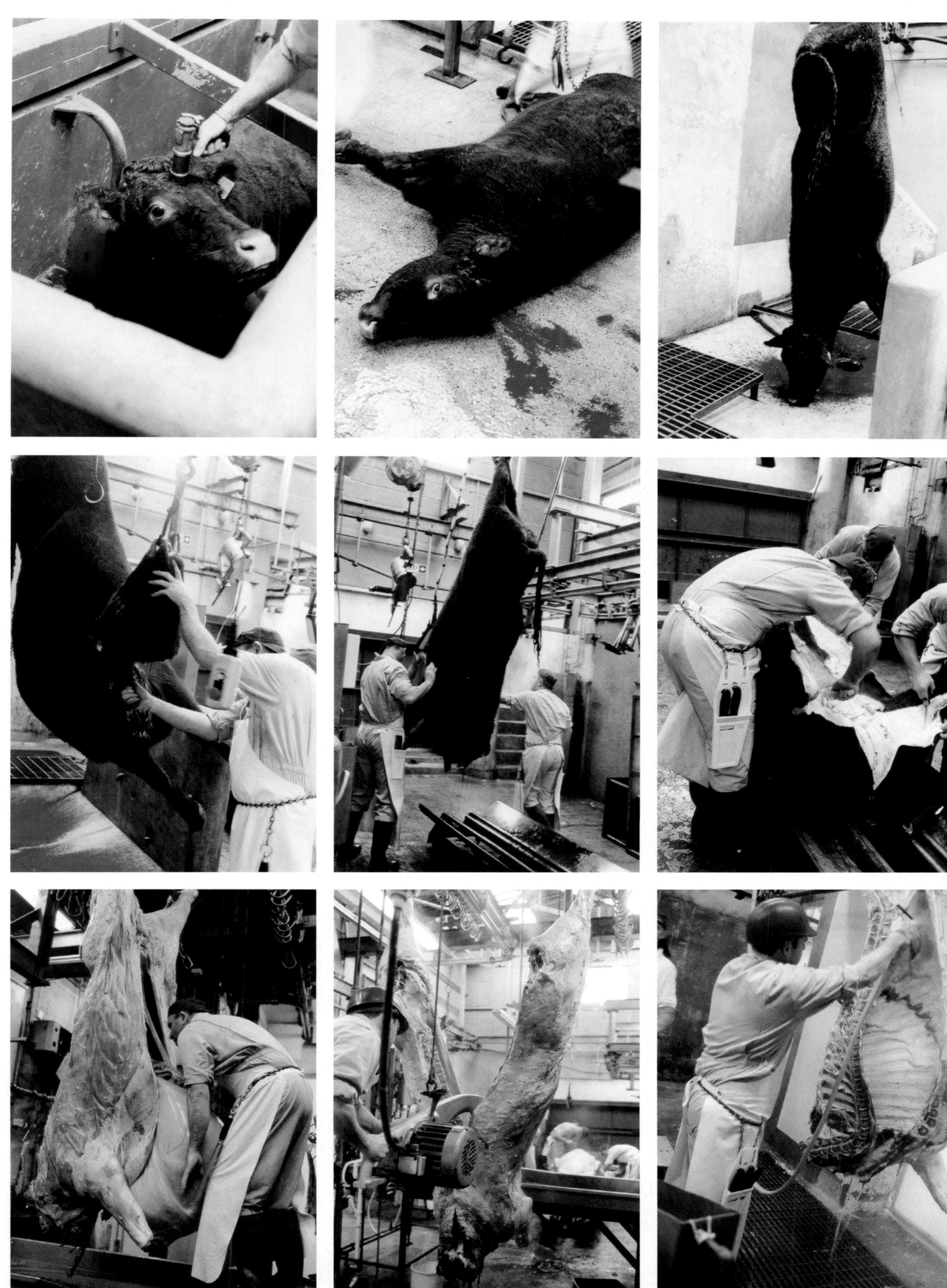

500 Kg

The Symbiosis of Domestication

Of course, it is not only the death of our farm animals over which we have such complete control. It is also their birth, and their life. We breed them and we feed them; and after we kill them, they feed us. In this sense, the relationship is undeniably symbiotic. And such is the success of the symbiosis that, along with ourselves, our sheep, cattle, pigs and poultry are among the most 'successful' species on the planet – at least in crude terms of overall population and global distribution. Should they be grateful?

It is true that this particular symbiotic contract is biologically unusual. Elsewhere in nature, abstention from eating your symbiotic partner is usually a vital part of the deal. The contract here seems a little one-sided, if indeed it is any kind of contract at all. Did these animals have a choice? It can be argued that – in an evolutionary sense, at least – they did. After all, not all the wild animals that our ancestors killed for food became domesticated. Can it perhaps be argued that those that did, chose their evolutionary fate?

This is the controversial but compelling thesis that Stephen Budiansky puts forward in his brilliant book, *The Covenant of the Wild* (HarperCollins, 1992). He argues that the evolution of the process of domestication was largely consensual – though he is at pains to emphasise that the notion of individual consent, which plays such a vital role in the human moral and legal sphere, should not be confused with the symbiotic cooperation of a species over evolutionary time.

Budiansky believes that consensual domestication began when certain species of wild animals became 'camp followers' of human settlements – increasingly dependent on hand-outs of waste food and leftovers. Then came the cultivation of fodder crops specifically for keeping the animals close and fattening them for improved eating. And finally, as the symbiosis embraced full domestication, the livestock received protection from predators, assistance in bearing young, and even rudimentary healthcare. It is interesting that enclosure – i.e. restricting the free movement of the animals with either temporary or permanent barriers – comes historically very late in the day, if at all. In other words, the regular removal and slaughter of their companions has done nothing, over time, to deter our livestock from going along with the arrangement that is domestication.

The results of hundreds of thousands of years of domestication of livestock are populations of many millions of animals who neither know nor want anything else. They do not crave wildness, or the freedom of their ancestors. They accept the way things are. And they thrive under these terms. Premature slaughter is not the best part of the deal but it is, nonetheless, part of the deal.

Ultimately I find the notion of the symbiotic contract persuasive. I believe that, under the terms of this arrangement, farm animals can be healthy, contented and even, at least in a sense that suits their species, fulfilled – for the duration of their short lives. And I believe that these short, domesticated lives are, on balance, better than no life at all.

And so I continue to eat meat. I allow myself to be party to the killing of animals for food, because I have thought about it and concluded that meat eating is, on balance, morally acceptable human behaviour.

The Contract of Good Husbandry

But that isn't the end of the discussion. In fact, it is just the beginning. These arguments, I am aware, are nothing if not fragile. For a start, they demand that we embrace, not reject, the moral status of the animals we farm for food. They embody the notion of a contract with our farm animals that is not God-given, but man-made. The contract is not absolute, but conditional. And it is open to frightening levels of abuse.

The critical point is that we may claim the moral authority to kill animals for food only on the basis that we are offering them a better deal in life than they would get without our help. This means, among other things, better health, better survival rates, less pain, less stress, more comfort, suitable food and plenty of it. These are our promises. And they come with a huge set of responsibilities. There is a word that expresses the good farmer's sense of these responsibilities – husbandry. It's an excellent word, because it also acknowledges the contractual nature of the arrangement. It's an arrangement for the benefit of both parties. The farmer will be a good husband to his animals. In return for the living they provide him, and the food they put on the table, he will look after them.

But what happens when the husbandry is not good? When animals suffer pain and stress at our hands? When their quality of life is no longer a clear improvement on the alternatives? When terrible but preventable diseases rip through the populations of our food animals, causing them to suffer and die? When healthy animals are killed not for food, nor even for the protection of their kin, but for crude economic reasons outside of the contract?

A Cynical Breach of Contract

We need to address these questions urgently because, as anyone who cares to look can see, farming today is guilty of all this and more. The vast majority of our food animals are now raised under methods that are systematically abusive. For them, discomfort is the norm, pain is routine, growth is abnormal and diet is unnatural. Disease is widespread and stress is almost constant.

We have battery laying hens in wire cages so small they can't turn round. We farm broiler chickens indoors for our fast-food restaurants and supermarkets, in such close confinement and such huge numbers that premature deaths counted in the millions are considered the industry norm. We raise millions of pigs who never see daylight, soft ground or even straw, but only strip-lighting, steel and concrete. We keep cattle indoors not for months but for years, bedded on their own excrement and given drug-laced feeds – the only way to stave off the diseases that would inevitably invade such intensive systems. Sheep, who may even be lucky enough to have lived outside, are then herded into trucks to be driven for days, without food or water, to their slaughter.

This isn't husbandry. It's persecution. We have completely failed to uphold our end of the contract. In the face of such abuse, the moral defence of meat eating is left in tatters.

I am keen to do whatever I can to change this state of affairs. If I do nothing, then I feel I can no longer claim any credible moral justification for my meat-eating habits. So what can I do? I can write this book for a start. I can speak out, here and elsewhere, to try and raise levels of indignation about the way things are currently done, and encourage appropriate action to change them.

It shouldn't be too hard. The cruel practices I have mentioned have been increasingly publicised, and clearly do not have popular support. Numerous polls and surveys indicate that the vast majority of the public object to them and would like to see them banned. So surely they soon will be? Won't they?

The Consumer Holds the Key

Not just yet, it seems. Because the same moral majority of the pollster's high street becomes the immoral majority, or at least the apathetic majority, once they get behind the wheels of a shopping trolley. They continue to buy the products they are so quick to condemn. So these appalling, abusive practices, it turns out, do have popular support – albeit that the supporters are in denial (it seems that nothing suppresses the exercise of conscience as effectively as the words, 'Buy one, get one free'). But there's no getting away from it: if you buy something, you support the system that produces it.

In the face of such apathetic meat eaters, I have a lot of respect for vegetarians who are morally motivated. They may or may not believe that killing animals for food is always wrong. They may or may not be able to put forward a consistent vision of a meat-free world. But at least they feel sufficiently strongly about the practices of industrial farming to take a clear stance and change the way they shop and eat. That impresses me.

Personally, though, I think there is a better way to change things. I think we should certainly change the way we shop – and boycott the products of those who do not look after their farm animals, who have effectively reneged on the deal. But I believe there is a positive vote to be cast as well as a negative one. And I think it is best exercised by buying the meat of those who practise good husbandry, who continue to embrace the notion of a contract with their meat animals, and who do all they can to uphold it, honourably, morally and responsibly.

They are in a minority, and have been for a long time now. But their numbers are growing once more, and I dare to hope they may yet gain the ascendancy, so that good husbandry will become the rule, and not the exception.

My job, in the rest of this book, is to help you find these people and their good meat. And then to cook it – with all due respect for the animals from which it comes.

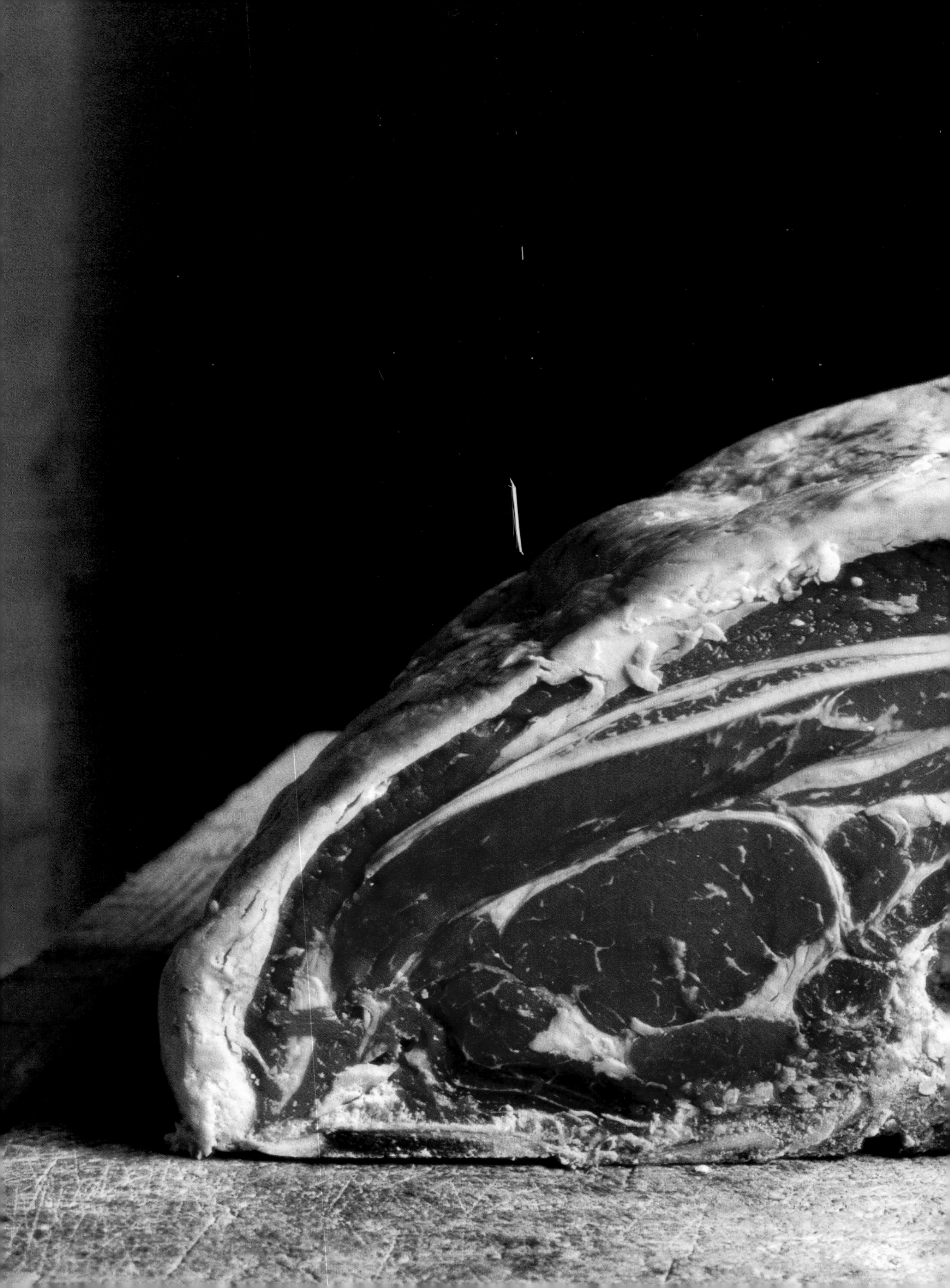

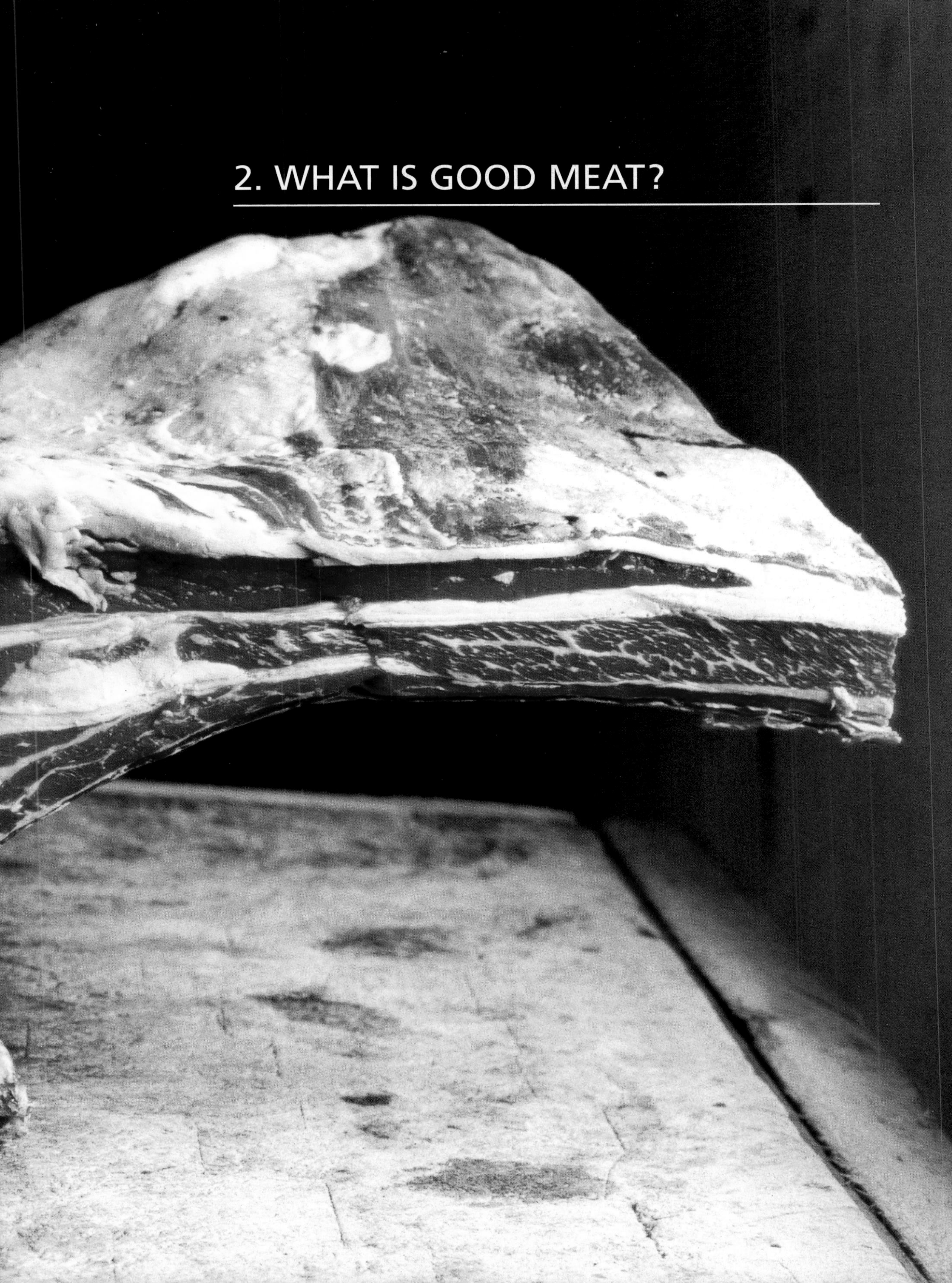

2. WHAT IS GOOD MEAT?

2. WHAT IS GOOD MEAT?

This entire book is based on the argument that meat should be something precious, always to be savoured, never to be squandered. If that's the cook's attitude – your attitude – then every time you sit down to eat a piece of meat will be a mood-enhancing moment. It may not be earth shattering – though let's hope that once in a while it is. But it should, at the very least, always be a net gain – a ladder, not a snake, in the ups and downs of another busy day. That's what mealtimes are for. And that's what meat, more than any other food, should bring to our table.

To achieve this happy state of affairs as often as possible, there are two things that will help enormously. The first is to know from the outset that you have in your hands the very best raw materials. The second is to have the knowledge and skills to use them well. The next seven chapters deal mainly with the first of these tenets, and the rest of the book mainly with the second. It's true that this section is rather more concerned with theory than with practice. And if you're the kind of person I was as a student, you may be tempted to skip the theory and get straight to the practice (I could never write the formula for the experiment where you add sulphuric acid to sugar, but I knew that I liked the smell).

But I hope you'll give theory a chance. Read and percolate. Apart from anything else, knowing what good meat is, in the raw state, adds an extra dimension of pleasure to both your shopping and your cooking, because good meat is a pleasure to find, a pleasure to handle and a pleasure to cook with. Get the good meat habit and the sense of anticipation and excitement about what you are going to cook will always outweigh any anxiety that it might go horribly wrong. This is the confidence trick that means ninety-nine times out of a hundred that you will succeed triumphantly.

Good and Bad Meat

The reality, unfortunately, is that most of the raw meat in our shops is of pitiable quality. The reason for this is simple: we appear to be happy to buy poor meat, so poor meat is what they keep giving us. As long as it's cheap, we don't complain. And as long as we can load it in the trolley without flinching at the price, we don't ask awkward questions either – such as where it came from, what it was fed on, how it lived and how it died, how it was stored, cut and packed, what was added, and how far it travelled. Yet it's the answers to these questions that tell us whether what we have in front of us is worth taking back to the kitchen. And all too often it's those answers, not the price, that should really make us flinch.

I don't mind how many times or in how many ways in this book I make the point that good meat shouldn't be cheap; that cheap meat is, more often than not, ethically tainted, of untraceable origin and dubious quality. And to those who play the socio-economic card, saying what about the poor, they'll never be able to afford your fancy, organic, rare-breed meat from pampered farmyard pets (an argument frequently used by government to justify the massive subsidies and legislative support for intensive farming), I say don't peddle that hypocritical line to me. Flooding the market with cheap meat would be an obtuse way of tackling poverty and dietary privation in a civilised Western country. Hardly anyone in the West is suffering from problems associated with too little meat, whereas millions are not getting enough fresh fruit and vegetables and wholegrain cereals to maintain good health. Principally what's needed is the education to understand that these, along with a modest amount of good meat (and not a mountain of cheap burgers and pies made out of meat recovered mechanically from slaughterhouse slurry), are the foundation of healthy eating.

It is debatable whether the mass market for cheap meat was ever created out of any sense of social responsibility or welfare. But even if it was, such good intentions have long since been corrupted in the industry. Today the driving force of intensive meat production is the search for profit. The millions of factory-farmed, protein- and water-injected, deep-frozen chicken portions that are sold each week are not going to families on the breadline. They're being processed, prepared and packaged to disguise the horrors of their production, and going, via the supermarkets, to busy mothers who are conned into thinking that this is healthy, nutritious food for their families.

In the end, cheap meat is a false economy. This is because meat is a food for which quantity is never a substitute for quality. Once you have tasted a really good barbecued burger, of the kind I describe on page 398, I suggest you'd never be tempted to swap it for half a dozen Big Macs. Similarly, a fat frozen chicken from an intensive production system, swollen by its unnatural appetite and drug-laced feed and injected with water, will taste so pulpy and bland that you could eat every last scrap of it without ever encountering the real taste of roast chicken. By contrast, a couple of slices off a slow-grown, corn-fed organic bird, along with a trickle of the tastiest chicken gravy you've ever made, should leave you very satisfied, with the promise of some delicious cold cuts and a hearty soup to come.

Personally I think it would make sense for almost all of us to pay more money for less meat, of better quality. I'd go further and say we should be ready to pay twice as much money for half as much meat – from animals that have lived infinitely better lives.

If circumstances dictate that you need to be very careful when budgeting your food shopping, then a good understanding of real meat, and how to make best use of the bargain cuts, will save you far more in the long term than counting the pennies on a kilo of economy mince or a bumper pack of factory-farmed chicken thighs (I shudder at the thought). As I hope to demonstrate at some length in the last chapter of this book, a little good meat can go a surprisingly long way in terms of both nutrition and the pleasures of the table. ('Meat thrift', I will argue, is as much about kitchen creativity as it is about good home economy.)

In the end, for most of us it's a question of priorities. Do we want to feed our family with real fresh food, including meat of traceable provenance and genuine quality? Everyone's instinct must surely be to answer 'yes' to this question. Yet we seem all too ready to save pennies on food so we can spend pounds on cars, clothes and computer games. This tendency has to be worth a rethink.

If you feel there is room for improvement in the quality of the meat you eat, and you're ready to change your habits, then I urge you to do just that. This chapter and the next are intended to help you by improving your understanding of good meat – what it is, where it comes from, and how you can get hold of some.

What is Meat?

Meat, good or bad, is of many kinds, and what is understood by the word may vary considerably from culture to culture. For me, the cultural relativity of the 'what is meat?' question is one of the things that makes travel so fascinating. I've eaten whale blubber and cow's udders in Japan, giraffe and crocodile in Africa, insect larvae and tapir in Brazil, cock's combs and donkey in France, and rooks and squirrels in England. I've never eaten dog but I would try it – provided I felt the animal had been well treated before slaughter (an assurance that, sadly, you'll struggle to find in the cultures where dog is regularly eaten).

In a perfect world, poor husbandry and unnecessary cruelty, along with endangered status, would be the only taboos that keep a given animal off the human menu. The remaining issue is how far up the evolutionary tree you can go before the anthropomorphic question of 'how like us' a creature is produces an uncomfortable feeling in the mind, or a queasiness in the stomach. Again, this will depend on your culture – it's the reason we in the West won't countenance the eating of primates, dolphins and elephants. But other cultures may have no such scruples.

I shan't probe this fascinating moral grey area much further here – though I plan to in the future – except to say that it should at least inform the way we think about, and care for, our own culture's traditional meat livestock. We should never forget, for example, that a pig is a smart, gregarious creature, not unlike a dog in its wants and needs.

So in the rest of this book I'm principally going to be talking about what we conventionally understand by the term in the UK – i.e. the flesh of commonly farmed mammals and birds, plus their best-known wild relatives that we regularly hunt for food. I'll spare you the horses, dogs, owls and frogs for the time being.

However, I would like to challenge your assumptions about meat in another way. The British meat culture has shrunk dramatically in the past fifty years or so. Much ground has been lost in terms of the holistic appreciation of all that our meat animals have to offer. The cheapening of meat, in both the literal and metaphorical sense, has engendered a laziness in its use that is disingenuous and insulting to the animals from which it comes. Knowledge of the appropriate and appetising use of the many different cuts is on the wane.

I want to help reverse that trend. So in this book, 'meat' will include some parts of the animal you may not have tried before. I'll be describing and offering recipes for many less familiar cuts, and all but the most obscure offal. I will also mention, if only briefly, some of our wildlife and semi-wildlife, which most people never think of eating. Much of what we call 'game', and some of what we call 'vermin', is both plentiful and delicious, so why not? To my mind, these are all meats that deserve your attention – not just on paper but in the kitchen.

The mission to find good meat, of any kind, is not without challenges. But it is, dare I say, exciting, and ultimate success is hugely rewarding. If, for example, you have never tasted real mutton, or slow-grown pork, or properly finished, well-aged beef from a suckler herd, or a good roast grouse with all the trimmings, or a pigeon pâté, then you are in for a treat of revelatory proportions. It makes me almost jealous just to think about it.

There are two rather obvious phases in the production of meat that determine its ultimate eating qualities, and they are perhaps best considered separately. The first phase, which I have discussed briefly in the context of ethics in the previous chapter, is what happens to the animal when it is alive – this is the responsibility of the farmer. The second is what happens to the carcass after the animal has been killed – this is the responsibility of the slaughterhouse, the butcher/retailer and the cook (you). First things first, and I'll begin by considering how the life of an animal affects the meat you get from it.

Good (and Bad) Farming

Quality and ethics are inextricably linked in the production of good meat, and the point of contact is what we call 'good husbandry'. This resonant phrase describes the art and science of responsible livestock farming. As we might expect, good meat comes from animals that are healthy and in prime condition at the moment they are killed. The most basic responsibility of the farmer – adequate husbandry, if you like – is to maintain the health of his or her livestock. Poor husbandry will produce scrawny, sick creatures (not to mention quite a lot of dead ones), which in turn will produce poor meat that may even be hazardous to human health. Surely you would expect that even the most intensive systems of agriculture deliver their livestock to slaughter in a reasonable state of health? And if that's the case, then you might begin to wonder on what the objections to such farming practices are founded. It all depends what you mean by health ...

Of course, the health of a farmed animal may be assessed from many different perspectives. The vet inspecting a carcass at the abattoir will have different priorities from the farmer who delivered it alive, and the organic farmer will take a different view of the health of his or her animals from the intensive farmer. But it seems obvious to me that good health maintained by minimum intervention, based simply on providing a creature with all that its body and instinct naturally demand, is a sounder kind of health than that maintained by the routine feeding and injection of chemical and medical supplements to try and prevent a whole host of problems associated with a lifestyle that is far from natural.

Herein lies the critical difference between extensive (generally outdoor) and intensive (generally indoor) farming of livestock for meat. Intensive farming is interested in high yields and accelerated growth. The strategy is to raise huge numbers of stock in confined and highly controlled spaces. Unquestionably the stock densities in these environments are not conducive to good health. A great deal of intervention is therefore required to prevent disease, and indeed a high mortality rate. This means routine inoculation against all kinds of diseases – a cocktail of medicines to keep the bugs at bay.

The unnaturally fast rates of growth can be achieved by the routine use of drugs, by special additive-laced feeds that would never be the animals' diet of choice, and by selective breeding of the strains of livestock that go into the systems (in the future, transgenic technology – i.e. genetic modification – will have an increasing role to play in achieving these ends).

There is one particular aspect of intensive farming, a consequence of the above strategies, that is not as widely known about as I feel it ought to be. There are always casualties (i.e. premature deaths) in farming. Inevitably, the more aggressively, or intensively, a given production system is run, the higher the casualty rate will be. In most intensive farming systems, even high numbers of such deaths are regarded not merely as an occupational hazard but as a calculable factor to be built into the business plan. 'Acceptable' mortality rates are expressed in percentages. In the case of intensive broiler houses (poultry being raised for the meat industry), these acceptable mortality rates can be as high as 30 per cent. In intensive pig farming they range from about 5 to 15 per cent.

As you would hope, animals that die prematurely on a farm are not allowed to be sold into the human food chain (though through unscrupulous and quite revolting practices, they often are). Such deaths should therefore, in theory at least, be uneconomic – the ultimate sanction for good husbandry. But in intensive systems (we may be talking about 3,000-5,000 pigs or 20,000-30,000 chickens in a single building), such deaths are simply 'allowed for' – an inevitable consequence of the system working at full tilt.

If up to 30 per cent of the animals produced within a system die prematurely, it seems reasonable to question the true health of the stock that survives to slaughter age and is then sold into the market. It appears that within intensive systems, 'healthy' is defined simply by the achievement of a marketable weight and the fact that the animals are alive when they reach the abattoir. Even abnormalities such as tumours, and defects such as broken legs, may not exclude an animal from the production line, and the supermarket shelf.

A more illuminating approach is to use behaviour, rather than mere survival, as an indicator of health. It's a pretty good rule of thumb that if an animal is behaving abnormally it is, at the very least, severely stressed, and therefore more susceptible to disease. And even if it is so dosed up that it can't get 'conventionally' sick, it can often still summon up a heart attack (the main cause of premature mortality in intensively farmed pigs, for example).

When livestock is reared within intensive systems, all sorts of abnormal behaviours come to light. Bored cows fattened indoors will rub itches against walls, posts and each other until they become gaping, festering wounds. Pigs become aggressive, fight each other, and develop a disturbing tendency to chew each other's tails (sometimes tearing them off). The imaginative preventative measure here is the routine amputation of piglets' tails shortly after birth. Chickens also fight, quite often to the death – so cutting off their beaks minimises damage to the skin and flesh of quarrelsome birds. But it doesn't prevent the most fatal form of aberrant poultry behaviour – an apparently suicidal rush of thousands of birds into a spectacular pile, in which most of the birds will suffocate to death. These smothers, as they are called, account for the dramatic figures in poultry industry mortality – but as long as they stay the right side of 50 per cent there's still money to be made. (Some plants even have a sideline in mincing and desiccating the dead birds, then selling them for pet food or fertiliser.)

So, most intensively farmed livestock can be said to be 'healthy' only in a very limited, even perverted, sense of the word. One thing is for sure: neither the living conditions of these creatures, nor the food they eat, nor the rate at which they grow, nor their general behaviour and habits, are anywhere close to what nature intended for them. We should hardly be surprised if the flesh on their bones at the time they go to slaughter is not quite natural either.

To paint a contrasting picture of traditional extensive livestock farming is not exactly hard. The adjective 'happy' is more than a little anthropomorphically loaded. But I don't think it's too much to say that a good extensive livestock system aims to keep its animals at least contented. However, my point is not that the sun always shines as cockerels crow from the gatepost, lambs skip through the meadow, cows called Buttercup mellifluously chew the cud, and pigs romp and root through leafy Arcadian glades. Extensively farmed animals will, from time to time, get cold, muddy, sore and sick. Occasionally they will get pushed around and prodded, by the farmer or the vet, and then they may get confused and stressed, for a while. But they will nonetheless spend almost all of their time – with a bit of luck, day after unmolested day – doing what cows, sheep, pigs and chickens freely choose to do.

It would also be unfair not to point out that old-fashioned extensive, outdoor livestock farming can be very badly practised, resulting in all sorts of health problems, much suffering, and many unwanted deaths among its livestock. But there will always be an important qualitative difference between traditional extensive systems and modern intensive ones. Such problems in extensive farming generally arise through laziness and ignorance, wilful abuse, or near-criminal negligence. Theoretically, at least, such malpractice can be rooted out, condemned

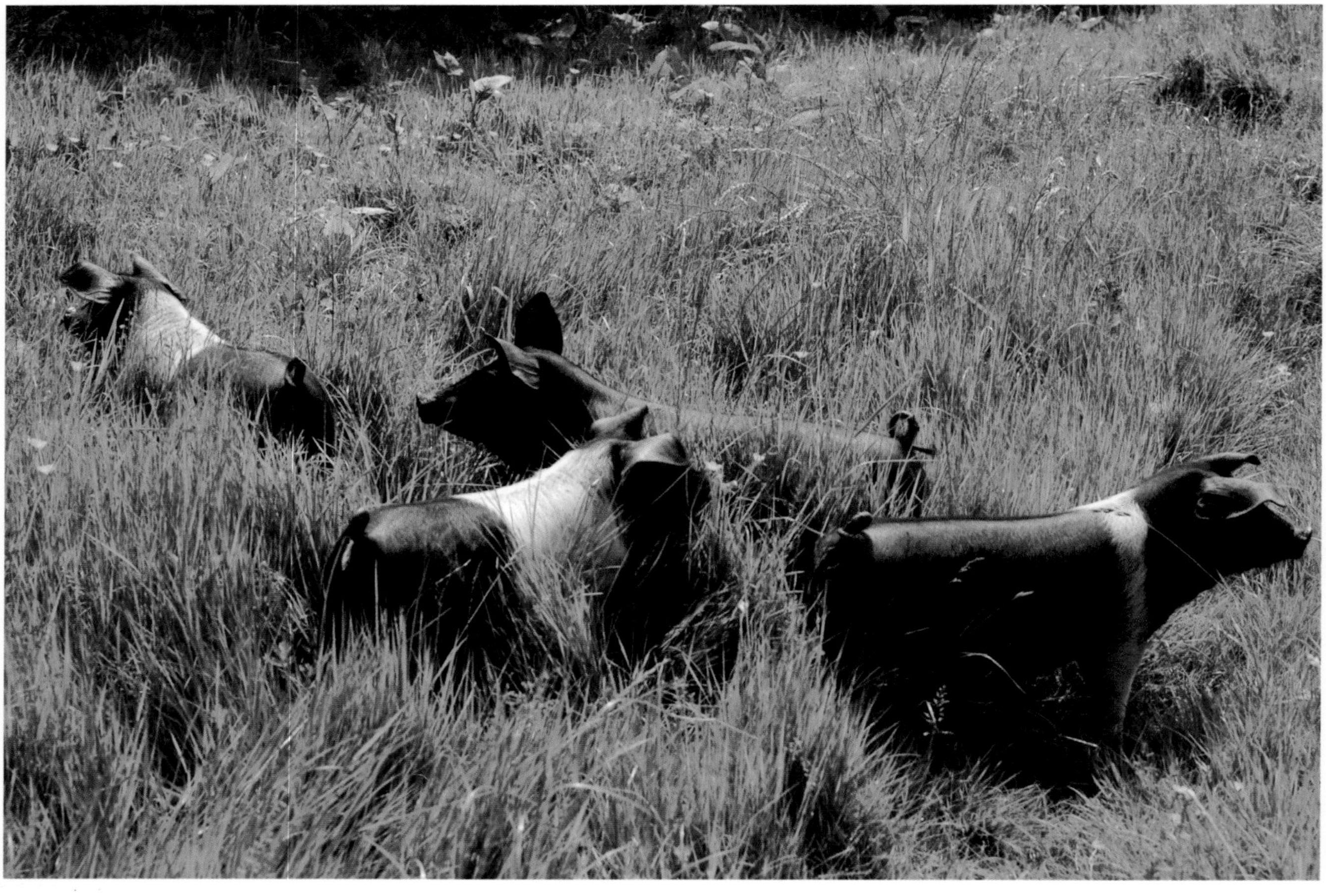

and prosecuted. Whereas in intensive farming, the misery is built into the system, masked in secrecy, and more or less protected by law.

There is some kind of safeguard too, in that the financial margins of extensive farming are very different from those at the intensive end of agriculture. High losses cannot be simply factored into the equation. The economics are such that really shoddy extensive meat farmers do not tend to stay in business long. The fact that each individual animal is economically significant means that traditional extensive practices have an intrinsic motivation for good husbandry. The need to ensure a high survival rate and deliver a well-fattened animal at the abattoir for the best available price is a pretty good incentive to take care of your stock.

The real perversity is that somehow intensive farming has become the norm. Since meat described as 'real' or 'organic' is now marketed as something special, we may be inclined to think of it as newfangled. In fact, good organic meat is as old as farming itself. It's special because it is the product of good farming practice, proven to be sustainable over centuries. It's special because it's not furtive, corrupt, obfuscated, and pursued behind closed doors, but public, unashamed and open to inspection – as wide open, in fact, as the green fields on which the contented animals who produce it wander and graze.

Good (and Bad) Eating

The moral implications of this stark contrast in farming practice are clear enough, and I've discussed them at length in the previous chapter. But since quality is the issue here – the search for good meat – you will probably want to know what the effects of these differences are on the eating quality of the resulting meat. Of course, taste is a subjective thing. But what is beyond dispute is that meat produced by intensive farming is very different in character from the slow-grown meat of extensive systems, and that's true of pork, beef, lamb and poultry.

A discussion of the general eating qualities of meat, and in particular the salient differences between intensively and extensively farmed products, should perhaps start with a discussion of one of meat's vital constituent parts, the ever-controversial and much misunderstood substance known as fat.

Fat

Fat gets a bad press. Because few of us actually want to be 'fat', and because the consumption of 'fat' (the noun) has been identified as one possible cause of people becoming 'fat' (the adjective), fat the substance has been effectively demonised. Yet fat has a critical role in brokering the flavours of meat – not just meat, in fact, but many of our favourite foods. That's why we put butter on our bread, beef fat in our Christmas pudding and grated cheese on our pasta.

The critical thing is that many flavour-bearing molecules are soluble in fat but not in water. In addition, the flavourful substances incorporated into otherwise dry foods are far more effectively absorbed by the taste buds when combined with or accompanied by fat. It's more or less a straight function of time. Fat effectively slows down the progress of the aromatics over the tongue and across the palate – a sensation you may even be conscious of when you are eating chocolate, for example – giving them more time to appreciate and enjoy the taste experience.

This is why traditionally our 'treat' foods, such as biscuits, cakes, chips and chocolate, have always been laced with generous helpings of animal fats. Nowadays, of course, there are alternatives of vegetable origin. But it's interesting that even these supposedly 'healthy' alternatives are routinely transformed, by the industrial process known as hydrogenation, into a state where they far more closely resemble, and behave like, animal fats (effectively they are transformed from flowing liquid-type fats, or oils, to hard-setting fats). It may seem a pretty pointless exercise, given that the end results, of which no chemical equivalent exists in nature, are certainly no healthier, and some say more damaging, than butter, lard, suet and the hard animal fats.

It is clear, then, that fat is critical to the flavour and texture of the meat of which it is a part – both in general terms and as the medium responsible for the distinctive tastes of different meats. It has even been shown that if every trace of fat is removed from both a piece of beef and a piece of mutton (one of the most strongly flavoured meats), it is almost impossible to distinguish between them.

In most meats, most of the fat is present as an external layer, immediately beneath the skin. This 'subcutaneous' fat is valuable to the consumer and the cook in several respects. Firstly, it is a reasonable indicator that the animal from which it came was in a good state of health. Secondly, it allows meat to be properly hung and matured (see below), as a good covering of fat protects a carcass from bacterial infection. Thirdly, it keeps the meat moist and well lubricated while it cooks – especially protecting a roasting joint from drying out in the fierce heat of the oven.

Marbling

As well as this obvious and highly visible layer of fat, there is also a more subtle presence of fat in most meat – as threads that run between and through the muscle meat. This latter type of fat, known to butchers and gourmets as marbling, is a reliable indicator of quality and entitles you to expect good flavour. Really good marbling will occur only in meat that has grown slowly and reached a reasonable maturity. This means it is present only marginally in pork and lamb, both of which are generally killed at less than six months old. But in the case of beef, good marbling is, for the aficionado, pretty much the holy grail (see the picture opposite, and further discussion on page 73). It's also something you will encounter, with great pleasure I hope, should you choose to explore the much underrated mature sheep meat, mutton (see page 94). In both cases marbling is a cook's godsend, and a near guarantee of succulence and tenderness, since it means the meat will be lubricated from within as it cooks and maximum flavour will be delivered when the meat is chewed, as subtle but vital traces of fat are delivered to the palate.

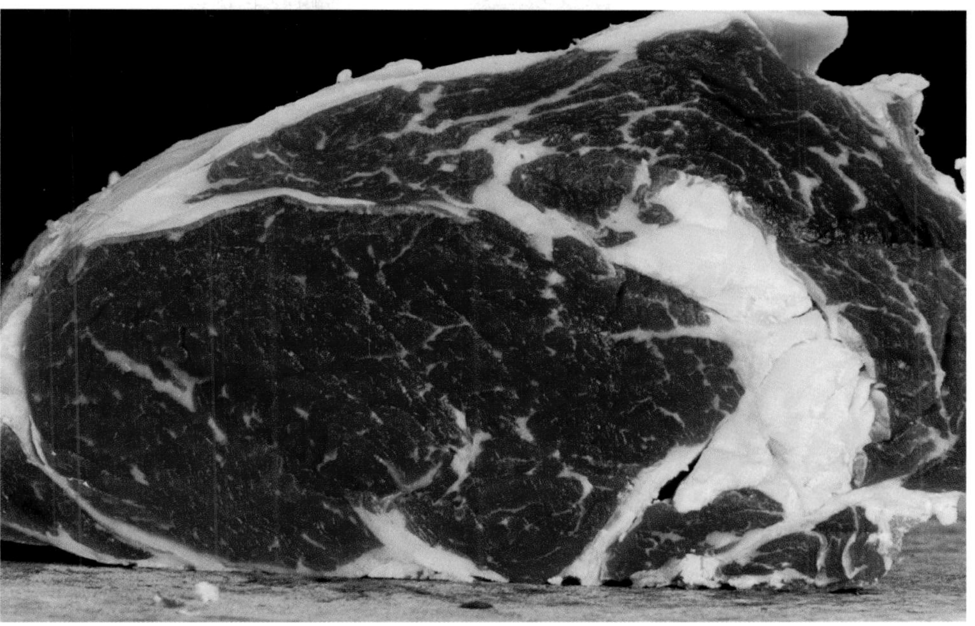

Despite the indisputable contribution of fat to the eating quality of meat, something that all good butchers know in their hearts, the meat industry has for decades been working systematically to minimise, or eliminate, the presence of fat. Because of our cultural 'fear of fat', it is regarded as far easier to market lean meat to a 'health-conscious' public.

It is fair to say that a generous layer of external fat, as well as good marbling, occurs in meat that grows naturally, slowly, and predominantly out of doors (the primary function of subcutaneous fat being to insulate the animal against cold weather). It follows naturally (or unnaturally) enough, that the industrial production of meat, in intensive indoor systems at a speeded-up rate, is well suited to the production of lean (I would say artificially lean) meat. Certain feeds, and feed additives such as antibiotics, steroids and hormones, are routinely used in intensive systems, both to speed up the development of muscle (lean meat) and to inhibit the development of fat. Whilst the supposed dangers of a high-fat diet are discussed *ad nauseam*, the possible long-term effects of eating such biochemically adulterated lean meat remain practically uninvestigated.

It's not that I would advocate that we all go out of our way to eat more lard and beef dripping. It's just that when it comes to society's problems with fat, the raw meat you take home for cooking simply isn't the main culprit. For those who have a genuine problem with high cholesterol or excess body fat, it is not grilled steaks, roast leg of lamb or even a penchant for pork chops that are likely to be the cause. Highly processed, fat-laden snacks and sweets, deep-fried foods and perhaps an overindulgence in dairy products do most of the damage. And when meat fat is a factor, it is the highly processed sausages, burgers and pies – where all the unwanted fat and unsellable 'meat' (often mechanically recovered) from intensive systems ends up – that do the damage.

Personally, I reckon I probably should (and I vaguely intend to) cut down on fats. But I know with absolute certainty that it is my penchant for butter, cheese and cream (especially ice-cream) that could be most effectively targeted. When it comes to the fat I eat with and in my meat, I am very relaxed. And this brings me to an almost insultingly obvious point about fat. The fat on the outside of meat – around the joint, along the edge of the chop, beneath the skin of the chicken – is highly visible and easily removable. Once the meat is cooked, it has done its job. If you're worried about your fat consumption, you don't have to eat it. *You can leave it on the side of your plate!*

The fat on the inside of the meat, the now-invisible marbling, is, in terms of quantity, almost negligible. It'll do you no harm whatever. But in terms of your enjoyment, rest assured that it's doing a grand job. So grand that you wouldn't want to remove it, even if you could.

So, please, don't be afraid of naturally occurring fat, either outside or inside your meat. And if, as you change your meat-shopping habits from the supermarket to a more direct source, you begin to encounter more of it, don't worry. It's just a sign that the farmer and the butcher are doing their jobs properly. And if you do yours, you should be in for a treat.

Hanging meat

There is no doubt whatever that hanging is vitally important to the quality of meat. So what is hanging, and why does it matter so much? And why is it something that the industrial food sector can no longer be bothered with?

Hanging is the process of ageing or maturing the meat by hanging the carcass, or a part of it, from a meat hook. It needs to be done in a controlled, ideally cool, temperature, with a reasonable movement of air, ideally away from the danger of contamination by flies. Traditionally it is done in a walk-in cold room, either at the abattoir or at the butcher's.

What happens to the meat during hanging is that natural enzymes begin to act on the fibres of the muscle meat, making them softer and more elastic, so that the meat becomes more relaxed and tender. Effectively this is the onset of the beginning of decay – but it's nothing to be alarmed about. Under carefully controlled conditions, actual putrefaction, of the kind that will taint the flavour of the meat, need not occur for weeks, or even months.

The meat will also begin to lose moisture as it hangs. Paradoxically, this is a good thing when it comes to cooking. Wet, fresh, under-hung meat carries too much water, which expands as the temperature rises during cooking, stretching the fibres of the meat and leaching out between them – especially when the meat contracts again after cooking and during carving. This means that wet meat actually ends up drier after cooking and vice versa.

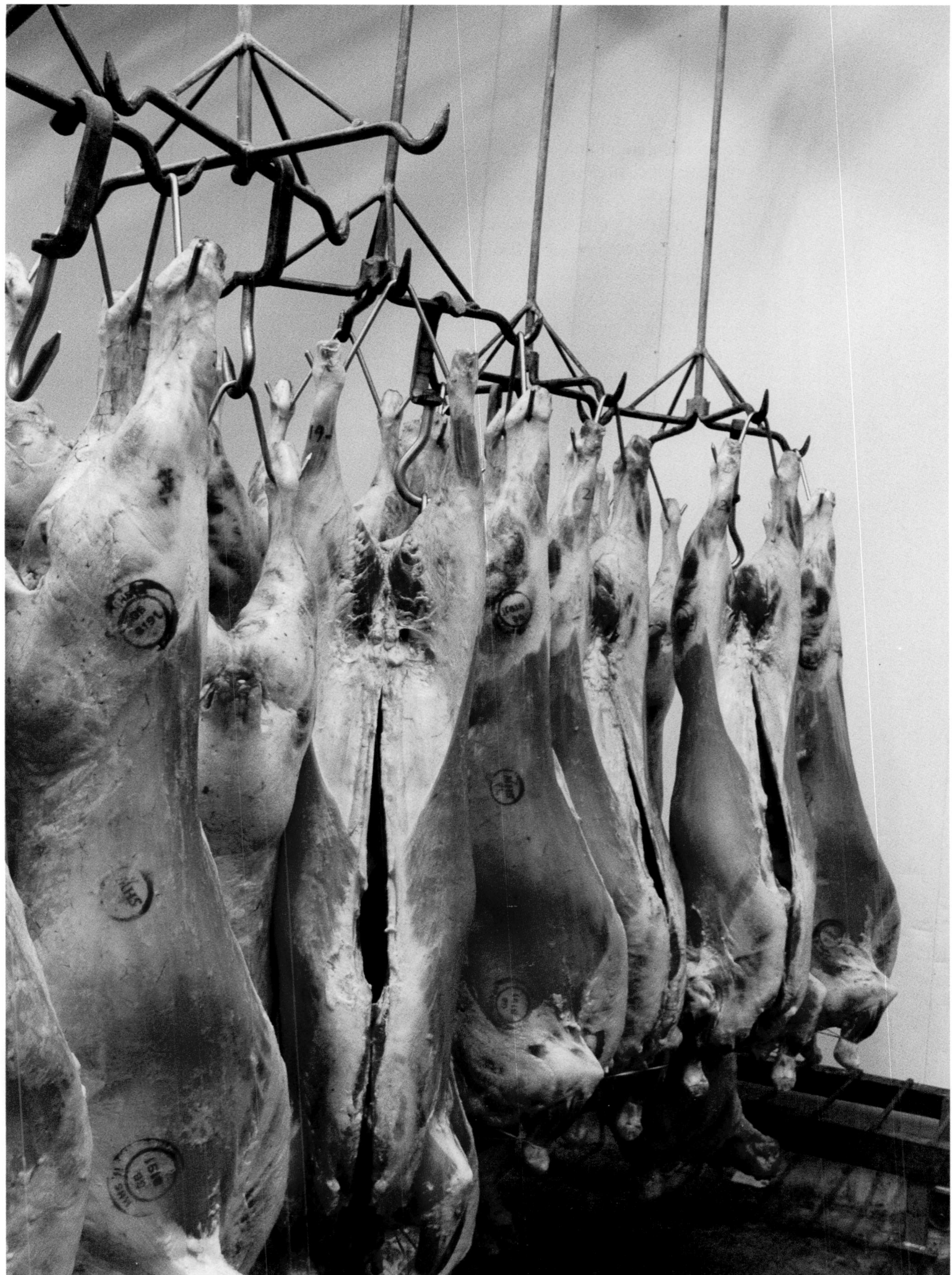

The beneficial effect of hanging meat, in terms of both flavour and texture when it is cooked, is beyond question. Well-hung meat is, quite simply, tastier and more tender than unhung or under-hung meat.

There are, of course, limits to the benefits of hanging – fairly obviously, given that the process permits the beginnings of the onset of decay. All meat will benefit from a few days' refrigerated hanging to settle and relax the muscle meat and solidify the fat (which is almost liquid when the animal is alive). However, immature meats, such as pork, young (spring) lamb and veal, do not stand up to lengthy hanging, as they are unlikely to have the fat covering or the marbling to protect them from deterioration as they hang. In the case of pork, there are usually some bacteria present that make the meat more susceptible to rapid tainting. Nonetheless, about five to seven days' hanging is suitable, and desirable, for all these meats (though if destined for the supermarket, they'll probably get only a couple of days).

In terms of properly developing the flavour of meat, lengthy hanging of ten days or more is suitable for mature beef and mutton and, with some provisos, certain game birds and animals. I'll discuss specific hanging times for these in their relevant chapters below.

In general, another great, but rarely discussed, benefit of proper hanging, which is vitally important for those of us who raise some meat of our own, is that well-hung meat will emerge from a spell in the freezer with far greater credit than immature, wet meat. Again, moisture is a key issue. Water expands as it freezes, so that ice crystals will tear and push apart the fibres of the meat. Not only will a well-hung joint contain less of the damaging moisture but the more elastic fibres will cope better with the expanding ice crystals. So as the joint defrosts, and again as it cooks, there will be less of a tendency for the water to leach out.

At home we eat, and serve to our guests, a lot of beef and mutton that has been frozen, all of which has previously been hung for three or more weeks. We are confident, and the compliments confirm, that it makes for far better eating than fresh meat that has not been properly hung. It's further confirmation of the paradox that 'dry' meat is 'moister' than 'wet' meat.

Throughout this book I will have plenty to say about the shortcomings of the supermarkets' dealings with meat. But aside from issues of welfare and provenance, the single biggest reason that supermarket meat is so disappointing is their abject failure even to begin to hang it properly. There is a sad and cynical reason at the heart of it, and of course it's to do with money. As I have explained, traditional maturation of meat by hanging, sometimes called 'dry ageing', leads to significant moisture loss and therefore weight loss. A well-hung side of beef, aged for a full three weeks, will have lost anything up to 20 per cent of its 'warm and wet' weight. Weight (rather than quality) is, of course, money in the obscenely competitive world of the supermarkets, and a weight loss of 20 per cent, or even 5 per cent, is just far too alarming to contemplate. Industry insiders tell me that the avoidance of weight loss is such a paramount issue for the supermarkets that the huge abattoirs supplying them are often instructed to hose down the carcasses regularly with warm water.

If weight is money, so are time and space. They can't leave these warm, wet carcasses hanging around for anything like the time it would take to tenderise the meat. And anyway, they take the view that only the prime roasting and steak cuts need any kind of maturation. The result is that supermarkets have invented their own unique way of 'ageing' meat, without losing any moisture. They vacuum pack it! Whole rumps and loins of beef are sucked into giant vac-packs and left to marinate in their own blood, sometimes for several weeks, safe in the knowledge that not a precious gram of weight will be lost.

Pressed on quite what they achieve by this (apart from the obvious financial savings), they insist that, under these conditions, 'tenderisation of the meat fibres does take place'. In a limited sense, this may be true. But you will realise from the wet-meat-becomes-dry-meat paradox explained above that, from an eating point of view, this is the worst possible thing they could do to the meat. Of course, it does allow them to claim in their literature that their prime cuts of beef (for example) are 'aged for up to twenty-one days'.

By way of apology, perhaps, for this meat abuse on a massive scale, most supermarkets now offer a 'premium' meat range, particularly of beef and lamb. These are prime cuts, sometimes from named breeds, that have been 'traditionally matured' or 'dry aged' (supermarkets can't bear to use the word 'hung'). You'll pay a lot extra on top of that missing 20 per cent for them, too. It's insane really – tantamount to admitting that the rest of their range is second-rate meat inadequately prepared for sale.

Of course, their presentational trick is to turn what ought to be standard practice into a gourmet speciality. Apparently Sainsbury's spent millions of pounds developing its Jamie Oliver range of 'dry-aged' beef. I've no doubt that Jamie insists on quality, and to that extent he has done Sainsbury's customers a big favour. But in the end this costly technology revamp, and hefty price mark-up, is all in aid of bringing you something that any enlightened butcher or conscientious small producer would offer you as standard. Hanging meat properly is the first and most important stage of good butchery. From this point on, each stage in the care of the meat, from storage and cutting to preparing and packing, is a skill that can be practised well or badly. The way in which these tasks are carried out affects the final quality of the meat – and varies according to who is selling it and what their priorities are.

Cutting meat

Cutting up a carcass is a considerable skill, and one in which my personal learning curve is still steep. I could just about butcher a lamb for the freezer but would struggle with a pig, and still be totally at sea with a beef carcass.

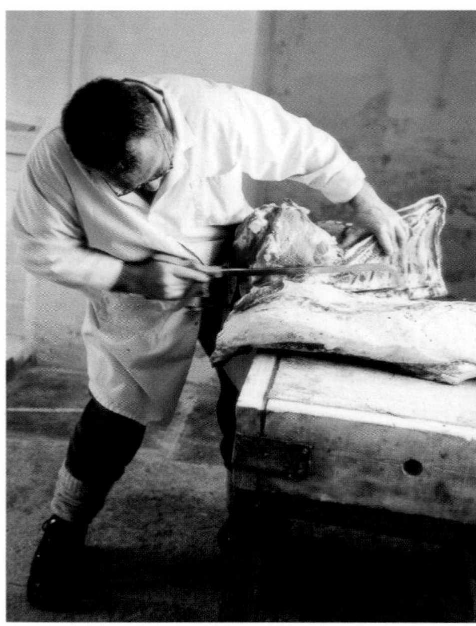
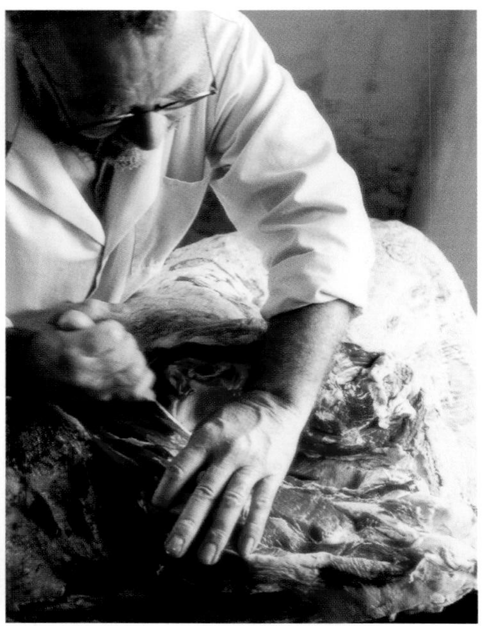

The art of good butchery is essentially twofold: firstly, for the benefit of the customer, to produce manageable joints and cuts that are suitable for a certain type of cooking and recognised as such by the cook; and secondly, for the benefit of the butcher or retailer, to minimise waste so that the best financial return is gained on the carcass. The combination of these two motives defines the holistic tradition of meat consumption – the thrifty, nose-to-tail philosophy of meat use that has given rise to ingenuity in the kitchen – and thousands of fabulous recipes.

Unfortunately, the industrial production of meat, and the sale of it in supermarkets, militates against these traditional values. From a cost point of view, speed becomes more important than thrift. The attitude is, 'These raw materials are cheap, so let's just bash out the main cuts and not waste time worrying about the fiddly bits.' Waste at the cutting stage is acceptable because, in the end, it can all be efficiently recovered by industrial technology. 'Mechanically recovered meat', or MRM as it's known in the trade, has changed the economics of meat production. This grisly process involves blasting any remaining meat off a carcass with a high-pressure hose. The remaining slurry is industrially sieved to separate the liquids from the solids, which are then minced into a fine paste. This can be used in sausages, burgers, meat pies and cheap pâtés. It may be cheap but it's produced, and used, in such quantities that it easily balances the books in favour of this industrial, high-tech approach.

So the battle to preserve and revive the production of quality meat is in part a battle to preserve and revive the art of butchery. It's why, in Chapters 4-9, I've included a full description, and diagrams, of all the traditional butcher's cuts and, in the recipe sections, plenty of suggestions for what to do with them.

Meat packaging

After cutting comes packaging – not the most exciting subject for discussion but it is important. I'll try and be brief. Basically, meat likes to breathe. The natural circulation of air around it carries away excess moisture. In contrast, meat that sits in a pool of blood or, worse still, marinates in a coating of it (which is what happens when meat is tightly wrapped in plastic, or vac-packed) takes on a curious metallic tang, as well as a nasty grey-brown colour, from the oxidised blood that leaches out of it, then soaks back into it.

This is why a good butcher won't pre-pack any of his meat. He'll cut it, or at least bag it up, to order. And if he's a good sort, he'll advise you to unpack it when you get home. If you're going to keep fresh meat at home for any length of time, then wipe off any wetness, put it on a plate, cover it with a tea towel and leave it in a cool larder, or the fridge if the weather is warm.

The worst kind of packaging for meat, as I've explained in the section on hanging meat above, is the vacuum pack. Yet I understand completely why so many small producers vacuum pack their butchered meat cuts for retail. It's by far the easiest way to satisfy the rigorous health and hygiene requirements when they are cutting their own meat and selling it in farm shops and farmers' markets. Vac-packed cuts are leakproof and 'clean'. They can be slung in a cool box, bounced around down the farm track, unloaded at the other end, and they're still clean. But the inevitable blood marinade does the meat no good at all. And the longer the meat stays in the vac-pack, the greater the damage done.

The old-fashioned polystyrene or cardboard tray, much favoured by the supermarkets until recently, on which a cut of meat sits with a clingfilm wrap stretched over it, at least keeps the meat relatively dry, if not exactly breathing hard. I know some small producers who are using this, and it certainly presents the meat in better condition. They reckon the customer, who so often shops by eye, prefers it as well.

The latest technology used by the supermarkets is the moulded polythene tray with a sealed film lid stretched tight across the top. It's called 'Controlled Atmosphere Packaging' (CAP), because it's not air inside the pack but inert gases that further slow any process of decay, earning the meat a couple of extra days on the shelf. It's hard to imagine the meat in such packs is in any sense 'breathing' but at least it's not getting the blood marinade.

In the end, provenance counts for more than packaging. On balance, I'd rather have a piece of well-hung, quality meat from a local small producer, even if it has been in a vac-pack for a day or two, than a lump of the unknown from a supermarket. And I'd take it out and wipe it off and let it breathe as soon as possible. However, I'd sooner try and persuade the producer to give up his or her vac-packing ways – or at least to make an exception in my case.

Recognising Good Meat

I hope the respective profiles of good and bad meat are becoming clear. On the one hand, extensively farmed, slow-grown animals, slaughtered locally perhaps, nicely fatted, properly hung, carefully butchered and sensibly packaged (or unpackaged). On the other hand, intensively reared stock, rapidly grown to slaughter weight on a distorted diet, driven long distances to slaughter, barely hung, lean and bloody, cut and packaged within a few days of slaughter.

It's hardly surprising that such big differences in production are reflected in big differences in the final character of the meat. In each case the meat from one system has a different colour, texture, smell and taste from the meat produced by the other system. I'll get to some more specifics in later chapters when I discuss each of the main farmed meats in turn. But in terms of general cooking and eating quality, I'll have a go at describing the differences as I see them – and taste them.

Intensively farmed meat is usually paler in colour, often looking wet and weepy compared to slow-grown, extensively reared meat, which should be shiny but not sweaty. To handle, poorer-quality meat is often wet and slippery, almost fish-like, rather than lightly tacky. When you come to cook it, it tends to shrink a lot, and may leach watery juices into the pan. In a frying pan, for example, this can make it harder to brown the surface of the meat.

Despite the wetness, when you come to eat it, the mouth feel of intensively farmed meat is usually dry and the texture is often soft and pâté-like, as if the meat has already been processed in some way. The flavour often seems to be on the outside rather than the inside of the meat. This means the taste experience has no 'length', as a wine buff would say. With good meat, the flavour will increase and develop with chewing; with poor meat, it will diminish and dissipate rapidly.

A few good chews of the best meat and it slips easily and pleasingly down the gullet. With inferior meat, you're all too often generally left with a pith ball of dry, tasteless pap in your mouth, like squeezed-out cotton wool.

Incidentally, it is no great matter of expertise to make these observations. I'm confident that if I served you a steak from one of my cows alongside the cheapest equivalent off the supermarket shelf, you would easily discern a marked difference. And I'd take a pretty large bet as to which you'd prefer.

I'm not sure my money would be entirely safe, though. Very often people grow to like what is familiar to them. At the same time, there are many ingenious technologies now available to 'enhance' the eating qualities of intensively farmed meat. The addition of beef extracts and other meat proteins to chicken, for example, is routine.

The ultimate achievement of industrial meat farming, and supermarket retailing, would, I suppose, be to influence a whole generation to prefer their 'modern' product to what has, for centuries, been regarded as good meat. Injecting meat with additives and extracts is the current means to this end. The genetic modification of livestock – for example, flavouring the chicken with beef while it is still alive – may well be the next tool in the box.

I take the optimistic view that such endeavours will fail – because the gulf in eating quality between what I am inclined to call 'real' and 'artificial' meat seems to me to be widening all the time. Now that I have the regular pleasure of eating meat from animals that I have raised and taken to slaughter myself, I am completely convinced that nothing produced through intensive farming comes anywhere close.

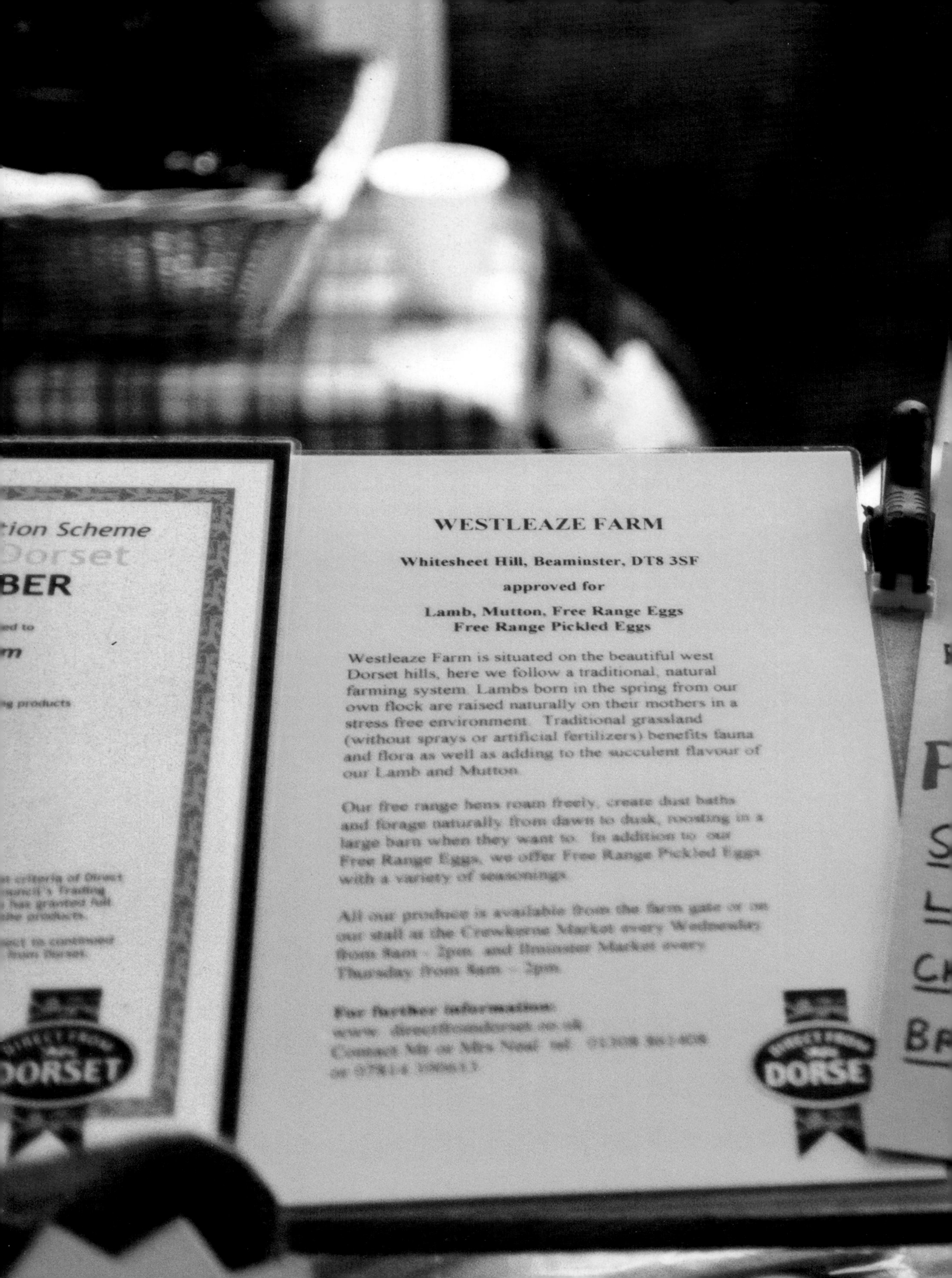
WESTLEAZE FARM
Whitesheet Hill, Beaminster, DT8 3SF
approved for
Lamb, Mutton, Free Range Eggs
Free Range Pickled Eggs
Westleaze Farm is situated on the beautiful west Dorset hills, here we follow a traditional, natural farming system. Lambs born in the spring from our own flock are raised naturally on their mothers in a stress free environment. Traditional grassland (without sprays or artificial fertilizers) benefits fauna and flora as well as adding to the succulent flavour of our Lamb and Mutton.
Our free range hens roam freely, create dust baths and forage naturally from dawn to dusk, roosting in a large barn when they want to. In addition to our Free Range Eggs, we offer Free Range Pickled Eggs with a variety of seasonings.
For further information:

3. BUYING MEAT

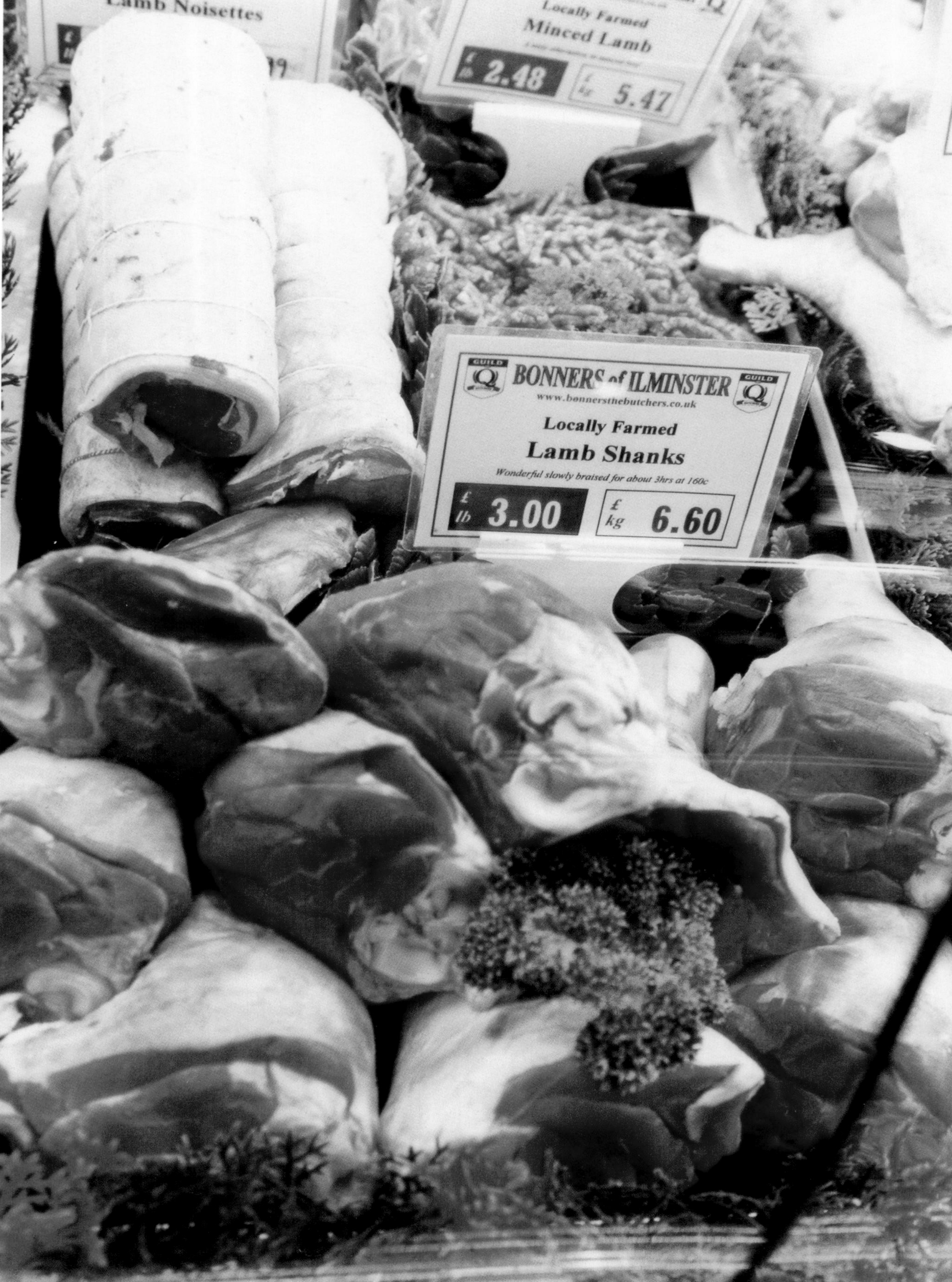

Lamb Noisettes
Locally Farmed
Minced Lamb
£ lb 2.48
£ kg 5.47
BONNERS of ILMINSTER
www.bonnersthebutchers.co.uk
Locally Farmed
Lamb Shanks
Wonderful slowly braised for about 3hrs at 160c
£ lb 3.00
£ kg 6.60

3. BUYING MEAT

None of the information about good and bad meat counts for much if you can't find the good stuff and avoid the bad. There are various ways to buy meat, and the most obvious are from the local butcher's and the local supermarket. The supermarkets now account for over 70 per cent of all fresh meat sales in the UK. That means that the vast majority of meat is bought through a veil of cellophane, its origins obscured by a label that withholds far more information than it discloses. And it is bought without any personal contact with an expert who might illuminate us further. I don't like to buy any food like that, and I particularly don't want to buy my meat like that.

I really don't like shopping in supermarkets. That isn't just a food politics stance, I actually don't enjoy it. Of course, a lot of people don't expect to enjoy their food shopping. It is simply a chore. But I don't think shopping for food should be tedious, any more than cooking or eating it should be. I expect to enjoy all my contact with food, from beginning to end.

Shopping for meat can be particularly good fun. A really good butcher's shop, like a really good fishmonger's, is an exciting place to be, full of potential and interest. A farm shop, selling meat produced on site, is an adventure and an education, presenting as it does an opportunity to see the animals from which the meat comes. And a genuine farmers' market, which is likely to be particularly well represented for meat sales, has the added *frisson* of competition: local meat producers vying to persuade you that their sausages, beef or bacon are the best in town. The smart ones will try and make the point by frying up a few samples for you, so you can breakfast before you buy. You don't get that sort of service, or that sort of pleasure, when shopping in a supermarket.

I constantly hear from people that they'd love to shop like that but they just *don't have the time!* And the supermarket is *so much more convenient.* But how true is that really? If anyone who lives near here tries that line on me, I know I've got them bang to rights. I'm lucky enough to live near a village (Beaminster) that has two good bakeries, two good butcher's, an excellent greengrocer's selling local fruit and vegetables, and a pretty good general store as well. The furthest distance between any of these delightful shops is probably about half that between the wine aisle and the fresh fruit in the massive Safeway superstore five miles away, and about one-tenth of the distance of its car park, measured corner to corner. How inconvenient is that?

I know we're spoiled for local food here in Dorset – there's also a great farm shop, Washingpool, not four miles from Beaminster, and a pick-your-own fruit farm, Elwell, roughly half way between the two – but my point is that if you support your local food producers they will support you. There is really nothing inevitable about supermarket domination. The choice is yours. And when it comes to meat, your decision is critical. It will determine the future of meat quality and farm animal welfare in the UK for years to come.

What follows is my assessment of the benefits and pleasures, caveats and pitfalls, of the current retail choices for the meat consumer.

A Good Butcher's

Retailing meat is a skill in itself, because it involves such vital decisions as how long the meat will be hung, how cut up and how packaged. Traditionally, the person who does the job best – because doing it well is the be all and end all of his job – is the butcher. And if you can find a good one – a really good one – then the problem of finding good meat may be solved at a stroke.

Most housewives of my grandmother's generation would have had a local butcher whom they knew by name and visited weekly at the very least. He in turn (it certainly would have been, and probably still is, a 'he') would have known them, remembered what they liked and, more crucially, what they didn't like. For they would have made no bones about telling him if a joint of beef had been tough, a chicken on the skinny side or a piece of lamb's liver less than perfectly fresh. Equally, they would have taken the trouble to thank and congratulate him when his meticulously prepared crown roast of lamb had gone down a treat with their dinner guests.

That tradition of customer feedback, and the knowledge that there was always a competitor no more than a few miles away, was what kept standards of butchery high. The tradition is not quite dead, but right now it doesn't look too perky. Some high-street butcher's shops, which may be part of a chain, respond to competition from the supermarkets by trying to keep costs low – cutting staff and cutting corners. The sharp practices of the worst culprits go way beyond the traditional sin of putting too much bread in their sausages. They sell defrosted meat as fresh, label imported meat as British, and prolong the life of ropy meat with lurid pink preservatives unconvincingly called 'Chinese-style' marinades.

Even those who would never countenance such dishonesty may nevertheless have more or less given up butchery in the true sense – buying most of their meat pre-packed and doing very little cutting on site. In such shops it's barely any easier to find out about the provenance of the meat than it is in the supermarket.

Yet the independent, local butcher offering a personal service and the very best local meat, does still exist and, in some places, thrives more than ever. The best are those who realise that an assured future rests not in competing in price and convenience with the supermarkets but in offering a level of skill, service and expertise, and, above all, solid reassurance on the provenance and quality of their product, that no supermarket can ever hope to match.

If you are lucky enough to have such a butcher within striking distance, you should use him. As a regular customer, you may find the experience of shopping there is itself an education about meat.

So how do you recognise a good butcher's when you see one? A superficial assessment can be made with a quick glance around the shop. How is the meat presented? Sloppily, with lamb chops thrown in a pile, and lumps of liver sitting in a pool of blood, or neatly, in a well-ordered display that allows you to find easily what you are looking for? How clearly is the meat labelled? Are there custom-made tags giving information about the origin and character of the meat, whether it's local, free range, organic etc? Or are there simply the standard-issue plastic spikes saying Welsh Lamb, Scotch Beef and no more? Is the shop well staffed, with assistants busily preparing meat to the specifications of waiting customers? Or is there one grumpy man in a grubby apron, with a look that says, 'I hope you're not about to ask me to *do* something.'

Beyond what is plain to see, I'd say the two essential factors in a really good old-fashioned craft butcher's would be KNOWLEDGE and SERVICE. My top ten key indicators, ascending from the essentials of good butchery to indicators of exceptional skill and service, would be:

1. He knows where his meat comes from (and is never shifty about telling you).
2. He knows how long it's been hung (and will hang it longer for you, if you ask).
3. He can advise you on the right cuts for particular dishes.
4. He will order special things, with a bit of notice (game in season, an ox tongue, a goose, pig's trotters, organic meat, if he doesn't already stock it).
5. He'll prepare cuts of meat to your requirements, and mince meat to order.

6. He won't grumble when you ask for (4) or (5), but will actually be pleased at your knowledge, and your level of interest.
7. He makes a variety of his own sausages.
8. He makes some or all of the following (or stocks examples made by local artisan producers): bacon, black pudding, faggots, pork pies and pasties, pâtés.
9. He has his own brine tub for pickling salt beef, ox tongues etc.
10. He chalks up on a board a profile of his best meat – for example, 'beef steer of the week', naming the farm, breed of cattle and how long it has been hung.

This last item may seem oddly specific but I have seen it done in several good butcher's shops recently and I think it's a brilliant idea. Just the kind of information and reassurance we discerning punters are looking for.

Finding a good butcher – one who scores at least eight out of ten on my checklist – is not quite the end of your meat mission. The way to ensure you get the best of the best is to persuade him that you are going to be his most discerning – and demanding – customer. Not by being a pain in the neck, I hasten to add (unless some lapse in standards means that approach is genuinely called for), but by showing your interest in his craft, in the provenance of his meat, and by demonstrating that you at least are prepared to revive that invaluable tradition of customer feedback. Be in no doubt that if he is the genuine article, he will thank you for it – with a bit of luck by slipping a few extra sausages, or a couple of lamb's kidneys or pig's trotters, in your shopping bag once in a while.

I should point out that there is a curious anomaly among the ranks of butchers, good and bad, who is hard to place on the scale: the man who undoubtedly knows his craft, who gives a personal service, and can dress any piece of meat just the way you want it, but who nonetheless resolutely refuses to consider issues of welfare or provenance as remotely relevant to his trade. This is the butcher who can't see the point of free-range chickens, and thinks organic meat is a con, if not the product of a hippy conspiracy. In short, his service is better than his meat.

In the end, the acid test is to ask him if he can procure something specially for you, even if he doesn't normally stock it – an organic chicken, for example, or some rare-breed pork, rosé veal, or mutton (that might just perk him up). If he refuses, then I should go elsewhere for your meat. Maybe just sneak back once in a while when you want him to tie up that beautiful crown roast of lamb.

Incidentally, if you want to see what a great butcher's shop looks like (one who I'm pretty sure gets ten out of ten on my checklist above), and you happen to be down in the West Country, then pay a visit to Bonner's, in Ilminster, South Somerset. They'll set a benchmark you may find useful. I have noticed that they are, like some (but by no means all) of the good butchers I know, members of the Guild of Q Butchers. This is a trade organisation that aims to maintain traditional standards of butchery and customer service, and to help butchers develop their range of skills. I would hesitate to say that Guild membership is a cast-iron guarantee of quality or exceptional welfare, as I have not had first-hand experience of more than a few of its members. But it is certainly a fine place to start looking for a good butcher, not least because they have a very useful website, *www.guildofqbutchers.co.uk.*

Meat in the Supermarket

As I have said, over 70 per cent of fresh meat retailed in the UK is now sold in supermarkets. I have a take on that statistic that I find makes it a lot less depressing. I dare to assume that, in terms of driving high-street butchers out of business and luring shoppers to their megastores, supermarkets have pretty much done their worst. If 30 per cent of us are prepared to look elsewhere for the really good stuff, I think there's a fair chance we'll stick to our guns. We are the core consumers protecting the craft of butchery, and/or helping small producers develop their direct-sales strategies. In time, as more and more people discover just how good meat can be, our numbers will swell, and the real-meat renaissance, something I believe is already under way, will gather pace.

Meanwhile, the supermarkets are where most of our intensively farmed meat is ending up. If a genuine lack of local alternatives means that that is where you have to buy your meat, then I would suggest that the very least you can do is eliminate the intensively farmed product from your trolley. If only every pack or product bore a dayglo orange label saying 'Warning, contains intensively farmed meat', the mission would be so much easier. Yet often it seems that the systems for labelling meat in the supermarket are designed not to inform the consumer but to protect the industrial chain of supply by obscuring the origins of its products. I'll deal further with this knotty problem in my discussion of the specific meats below. But as a general rule you should assume that supermarket meat is guilty of being intensively farmed, and poor quality, until proven otherwise.

That may seem harsh. The point is simply that the onus to prove quality and high welfare is on the supermarket. This is something of which the supermarkets are increasingly aware, and if basic farming practices haven't changed much in the last few years, the supermarkets' ability to peddle euphemism to the consumer has come on in leaps and bounds. Of course, marketing is an art form, and the impression the supermarkets would like to give you is not merely that all the animals from which their meat derives live in a state of Arcadian bliss, but that this state of affairs is rigorously maintained by constant inspection. Hence, whilst the meaning of the on-pack labels remains obscure, most of the supermarkets now produce glossy brochures or leaflets with pictures of happy animals in sunny fields, in which they present an 'explanation' of the various assurance schemes that authorise the labels.

You might think this is progress. The problem is that none of the schemes, and explanations thereof, stand up to much scrutiny. Instead of telling you what you want to know about the welfare of the animals, they offer meaningless generalisations and entirely circular references to the schemes they are purporting to describe. Here are some examples from various supermarket brochures:

- 'Housing and feeding facilities must meet the space requirements of the relevant assurance schemes' – circular or what?
- 'Each farm must have access to veterinary advice on the use of medical products' – surely ANY farm with the luxury of a telephone has access to such advice.
- 'All persons involved in care of cattle must be competent in the tasks they are required to carry out' – easy to say, impossible to enforce.
- 'We support regular inspection of our suppliers to ensure consistent compliance with the requirements of the relevant independent quality systems' – if this means anything at all, I have yet to work it out.

In the end, most of the many assurance schemes accepted and promoted by the supermarkets do little more than offer an independent rubber stamp indicating that minimum legal requirements of husbandry and welfare have been met. With the exception of organic labels (see page 57), they should certainly not be taken as any indication that meat has been farmed extensively. However, two frequently occurring labels, which do purport to offer specific welfare assurances, are worthy of brief discussion here. I have mixed feelings about them. On the one hand, as baseline indicators of compliance with minimum standards, and therefore a way of avoiding the horrors, known and unknown, of unregulated and imported meat, they are useful. On the other hand, as indicators of true quality and genuinely rigorous welfare standards, they largely fail.

Little Red Tractor

The Little Red Tractor logo indicates that the producer of the meat in question is a member of the British Farm Standard assurance scheme. Go to its website, and you will see that much is made of the scheme's commitment to ensuring that participating farms uphold the so-called Five Freedoms, described as:

- Freedom from hunger and thirst
- Freedom from discomfort
- Freedom from pain, injury or disease
- Freedom to perform normal patterns of behaviour
- Freedom from fear or distress

As welfare standards go, this is a pretty admirable selection of criteria. It looks good on paper, and it's no surprise that the supermarkets make much of their support for schemes that claim to uphold it. But read further on the website and it becomes clear that the scheme is really just a system of endorsement for Defra's Codes of Recommendation for Welfare, all of which also claim to uphold the Five

Freedoms. They do so on the basis that the five issues highlighted above are at least addressed in the Codes. Whether they go anything like far enough is an entirely different matter.

In the case of pigs, for example, they certainly don't insist on any period of outdoor rearing. And when it comes to the space allocated for their indoor housing, it's based on the notion that they 'are all able to lie down at the same time' – but presumably only just! The scheme also allows for tail docking of piglets – the measure that prevents aggressive pigs from chewing their fellows' tails off. Of course, strictly this is a measure to prevent pigs performing an 'abnormal' behaviour, but it's hard to see how it's compatible with the 'freedom to perform normal patterns of behaviour'.

I'm not saying that the mark is meaningless. It at least indicates a degree of openness on the part of the farmer and a willingness to be subjected to inspection. But you should not read it as an indication of extensive, as opposed to intensive, farming practice, or of any exceptional welfare standards. In fact, the scheme was developed (in the late Nineties) largely with a view to regaining the public's trust in the intensive end of the meat industry following the BSE crisis. Whilst meat with the Little Red Tractor label is preferable to unregulated intensively farmed imports, the real meat lover could do a lot better.

RSPCA Freedom Food

This is an assurance scheme set up and monitored by the charity, RSPCA, whose brief, expressed clearly enough in its acronym, is the prevention of cruelty to animals. Begun almost a decade ago, it has been successful in signing up a large number of meat producers and is particularly popular with the supermarkets – no doubt because the involvement of an institution as well known and respected as the RSPCA would seem to remove consumer anxieties about welfare at a single stroke. If only that sentiment were justified.

The first point to note is that the Freedom Food label should not be taken as any kind of indication that the meat thus certified is either extensively farmed or in any sense free range. Most of the animals to which it is applied are reared under fairly intensive conventional systems. In fact, pretty much the stated aim of the scheme is to give intensively farmed animals a better deal.

I want to be clear that I certainly don't think that's not a worthwhile aim. Even a marginal improvement in the lives of factory-farmed livestock is worth implementing, not least because we are talking about millions of animals in the UK alone. Freedom Food, for example, insists on straw bedding and a little bit more space 'per kilo' for indoor-reared pigs, and I'm sure those improvements are significant – genuinely meaningful to the pigs concerned.

However, I have a problem, a big problem, with the scheme's use of the word Freedom, which I consider cavalier to say the least. Let's face it, freedom is a pretty big word. Its use in the context of animal welfare is not to be taken lightly.

I would expect, and I'm afraid I think most consumers assume, that a Freedom Food label, awarded by the RSPCA no less, would indicate a very high degree of animal welfare indeed. I would expect pork thus labelled to come from outdoor-reared pigs, beef from genuinely extensive suckler herds, and chickens to have a genuinely free range. But they do not.

In fact there are free-range meats available within the Freedom Foods range. The standards set for them are pretty rigorous, and generally to be commended (they insist, for example, on systems where free-range chickens are genuinely encouraged to find and make use of their allotted outdoor space, where they can scratch for grain). I think it is a great pity that the RSPCA chose not to reserve their Freedom label exclusively for products making such genuine advances in welfare standards, and away from intensive farming practices.

Foreign Meat in Supermarkets

One thing to be said in favour of both the Little Red Tractor and the RSPCA Freedom Food label is that they indicate, for the time being at least, that meat is from British-born, British-raised, British-slaughtered stock. And one thing to be said in favour of that is that British meat farming, for all its faults, is more rigorously monitored, and less flagrantly abusive, than anywhere else in the world.

All the supermarkets love to shout about their commitment to supporting British farmers. Yet almost all of them will happily buy foreign meat when it suits them. They'll say they only do it when it is the only way left to 'satisfy customer demand'. What that really means is that they'll do it whenever the financial stakes are high enough to justify the risk of angering British meat producers and the farming press and losing a few patriotic customers.

I see no reason for the conscientious consumer ever to buy foreign meat. It only adds to the pressure on British farmers to cut costs and corners, which compounds the problem of declining quality. I remain convinced that the best British meat is the best in the world – and that's what you should be after. But in the supermarket, even bog-standard British is preferable to most foreign meat, whose provenance and welfare standards are usually complete unknowns.

One of the worst scandals of meat retailing is that it remains quite legal to lie on labels about the true country of origin, since meat is deemed to become 'British' if the animals have spent a matter of mere weeks in this country prior to slaughter. And processed meats and meat recipe dishes may be described as British provided they are manufactured and packed here – wherever the meat comes from. This disgraceful scam needs legislative correction, but until that happens the Little Red Tractor and RSPCA labels look pretty virtuous by comparison.

Premium Labels

Most of the leading supermarkets offer what they generally refer to as their 'premium' meat labels. These tend to use words like 'traditionally reared', 'heritage' and 'finest'. They are more expensive, usually by about 20-40 per cent. The clear implication is that this is something special, the good stuff. But look closely and only a few of them (usually pork, specifying 'outdoor reared') offer any assurances about lifestyle and welfare. What most of them indicate is that a little more care has been taken over the butchery and a little more time over the hanging (you'll see phrases like 'extra-aged', 'dry-aged' and 'matured a little longer').

I have discussed the supermarkets' appalling meat-ageing practices in the last chapter. As I concluded there, in the end all these labels say is, 'Here is some meat that we've bothered to prepare properly' – pretty much what you would expect from any half-decent butcher. It compares to that irritating label on a pack of tomatoes, 'grown specially for flavour' – a tacit admission, in effect, that the rest are rubbish.

Were my choice of meat retailers restricted, by some vile edict, to the supermarkets, I would certainly be inclined to choose among these premium labels, along with any organic options (see below), in search of the best – but not without grievous resentment that they were claiming credit, and charging extra, for doing what they should be doing anyway.

Incidentally, in researching this book I contacted all the leading supermarkets directly, in the hope of getting beyond those glossy PR leaflets and uncovering some more enlightened meat production policies, or a genuine commitment to improving farming practices significantly beyond the basic legal requirements of husbandry and welfare. It was an uphill struggle, which generally involved a long wait for any reply at all – and then contending with a lot of waffle that pretty much regurgitated what I had heard already. The exception, I would say, is Waitrose, who took considerable trouble to answer my questions accurately, in detail, and with impressive promptness. I am not yet entirely persuaded that it has the welfare or quality initiatives to put it significantly ahead of the competition. But I can certainly state that it has an openness and a willingness to engage with both the media and its customers over welfare issues that put the other supermarkets to shame.

I would say that it has its foot on the bottom rung of a ladder that would allow it to climb out of reach of the other supermarkets, in terms of transparency, provenance and welfare. But it has to have the commitment to take the next few steps. If it does, I honestly think its customers will respond to the challenge.

Organic Labelling

I have long been a supporter of organic farming. We have been in organic conversion since we bought our little forty-acre farm two years ago, and should achieve certification later this year for the meat it produces. Apart from the environmental benefits of non-chemical farming, the principal assurances you get from an organic label, particularly the one certified by the Soil Association, are in the three key areas where other assurance schemes consistently fail to deliver: welfare, extensiveness and the content of feeds.

The first two are closely related. From conditions for livestock birthing, compulsory outdoor allowances, through indoor/winter housing and transport times and rest stops to slaughter, the welfare standards under SA certification far exceed those for conventional farming practice.

To give you a couple of simple examples, an organically farmed pig will spend a maximum of one-fifth of its lifetime indoors. Outdoor stocking densities depend on the type of farmland but average about eight sows to the hectare, compared to twenty-five under conventional farming. When an organic pig does come inside, it is allocated at least twice as much space, by regulation, as an intensively farmed one – and, by voluntary practice, usually much more.

Similarly, an organic broiler chicken (i.e. reared for meat rather than eggs) raised to Soil Association standards will be guaranteed forty times more space, including a compulsory outdoor allowance, than the Defra minimum that is followed by the majority of conventional, intensive poultry farms.

Given these strictly enforced parameters on stocking density, it is safe to say that there is no such thing as intensive organic meat farming, at least where SA certification is in place. Add to this the ban on growth promoters, antibiotics and GM material in feeds, and you have a fine collection of reasons to buy organic meat.

However, it would be rash to suggest that an organic label is an unassailable guarantee of meat quality. Welfare is one thing, taste another. I know from personal experience, not least as a judge of the annual Organic Food Awards, that the eating quality of organic meat is very variable. At its best, it's unbeatable, but at its worst, it's no better than average. Although lifestyle and the right feed count for a great deal in making the best meat, they are not, as we have seen, everything. The Soil Association is beginning to respond to this problem by helping small organic meat producers develop their meat-ageing and preparation skills – so that the organic label on meat becomes not only an indicator of the highest welfare standards and environmentally responsible farming practice but also an unsurpassable benchmark of excellence for the discerning cook.

Buying Meat Direct

Given the many iniquities of the meat industry, the bottom line, for me at any rate, is traceability and transparency. Of course, the supermarkets now (since BSE and foot and mouth) claim to be able to trace any piece of meat back to the farm from which it came – and so they damn well should. But it's not as if they're offering any of this information, unsolicited, to the consumer.

What I want to know, up front, is as much detail as possible about the origins of the meat, including the lifestyle and diet of the animals it came from, and the processes to which it has been subjected after their death. And the people who are in the best position to give me that are those who have produced the meat.

If you are beginning to share this sense of priorities in choosing meat, then you may wish to start buying it direct – from people who produce it the way they should, with integrity. Effectively that means farmers' markets, farm gate sales, mail order or direct delivery.

Farmers' Markets

Your nearest farmers' market is a great place to start, as small, local meat producers should be very well represented there. It is a stipulation for all markets registered with the National Farmers' Retail and Markets Association that the stalls must be staffed by family members or employees of the farm producing the meat. They are therefore in an excellent position to give you chapter and verse on the meat – breeds, feeds, living conditions, age at slaughter, length of hanging etc. They might even be able to tell you its name – or more likely its mother's name if, like me, they reserve such intimacies for their breeding stock.

Bear in mind that, by definition, producers at farmers' markets are also busy farmers. Many are quite new to the business of meat retailing. Adding such skills to an already overstretched small-farming commitment is a tall order. As I have mentioned, you will only rarely get the same level of skill and service you'd expect from a good butcher. Particular niggles are likely to be shorter hanging times than you might ideally like (though they'll probably be much better than supermarkets on this), and an unfortunate tendency to vac-pack every cut of meat.

There is no point in moaning about such shortcomings on your first encounter with a stallholder. But if you can establish the quality of the provenance of the meat, then you may be able gently to influence the taking of it to its full potential. If you show every sign of becoming a loyal customer, there is no reason why you can't enquire about the possibility of having a joint or two hung for a little longer, or an advance order wrapped up for you without the vac-pack.

Farm Shops

I am aware of at least four farm shops that have opened within a thirty-mile radius of me here in Dorset in the last twelve months. All of them sell locally produced meat, and much of it is excellent. A good many farm shops are selling their own meat – in which case a visit to the shop is a visit to the farm on which the meat is produced. In this instance you can see for yourself how the animals live.

Where they're selling the meat of another local farmer, there will still be a personal point of contact with the source. And if you want to take it further (with a view, perhaps, to buying direct for your freezer – see below), in most cases the farm shop will be only too happy to pass on a name and number.

Farm Gate Sales

This is a less formal version of the farm shop. The farmer is generally selling only his or her own meat or produce. There may not be a staffed shop, as such. You can take a chance by dropping in. Or, if such spontaneity is not your bag, you can generally place an order by phone and pick up the meat by prior arrangement.

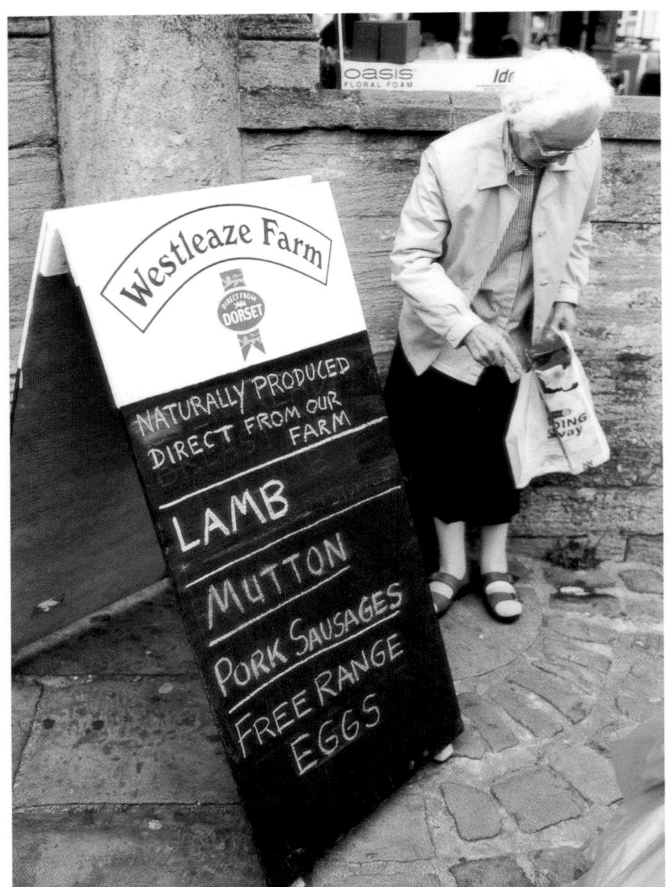
oasis
FLORAL FOAM
Westleaze Farm
DIRECT FROM DORSET
NATURALLY PRODUCED
DIRECT FROM OUR
FARM
LAMB
MUTTON
PORK SAUSAGES
FREE RANGE
EGGS

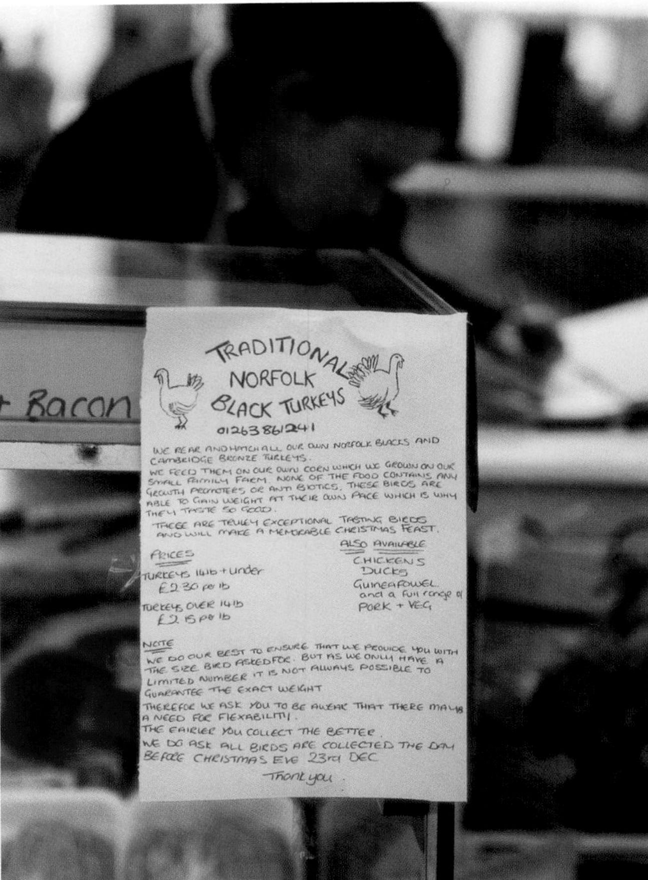
Bacon
TRADITIONAL
NORFOLK
BLACK TURKEYS
01263 861241
WE REAR AND HATCH ALL OUR OWN NORFOLK BLACKS AND CAMBRIDGE BRONZE TURKEYS.
WE FEED THEM ON OUR OWN CORN WHICH WE GROWN ON OUR SMALL FAMILY FARM. NONE OF THE FOOD CONTAINS ANY GROWTH PROMOTERS OR ANTI BIOTICS, THESE BIRDS ARE ABLE TO GAIN WEIGHT AT THEIR OWN PACE WHICH IS WHY THEY TASTE SO GOOD.
THESE ARE TRULEY EXCEPTIONAL TASTING BIRDS AND WILL MAKE A MEMORABLE CHRISTMAS FEAST.
PRICES
TURKEYS 14lb + under
£2 30 per lb
TURKEYS OVER 14lb
£2 15 per lb
ALSO AVAILABLE
CHICKENS
DUCKS
GUINEAFOWEL
and a full range of
PORK + VEG
NOTE
WE DO OUR BEST TO ENSURE THAT WE PROVIDE YOU WITH THE SIZE BIRD ASKED FOR. BUT AS WE ONLY HAVE A LIMITED NUMBER IT IS NOT ALWAYS POSSIBLE TO GUARANTEE THE EXACT WEIGHT
THEREFOR WE ASK YOU TO BE AWEAR THAT THERE MAY B A NEED FOR FLEXABILITY.
THE EARLIER YOU COLLECT THE BETTER.
WE DO ASK ALL BIRDS ARE COLLECTED THE DAY BEFORE CHRISTMAS EVE 23rd DEC
Thank you.

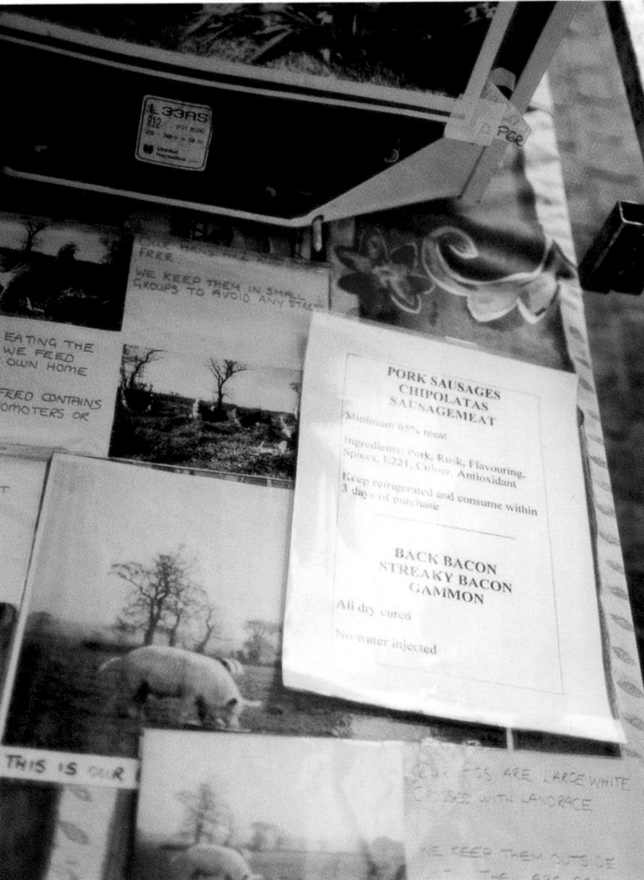
WE KEEP THEM IN SMALL
GROUPS TO AVOID ANY STRE
EATING THE
WE FEED
OWN HOME
FEED CONTAINS
PROMOTERS OR
PORK SAUSAGES
CHIPOLATAS
SAUSAGEMEAT
Minimum 65% meat
Ingredients: Pork, Rusk, Flavouring, Spices, E221, Colour, Antioxidant
Keep refrigerated and consume within 3 days of purchase
BACK BACON
STREAKY BACON
GAMMON
All dry cured
No water injected
THIS IS OUR
PIGS ARE LARGE WHITE
CROSSED WITH LANDRACE
WE KEEP THEM OUTSIDE

Incidentally, my pig mentor, Peggy Darvill, now sells almost all her pork direct to locals who just call by. I understand the hours of the morning and afternoon school runs can be particularly busy.

Buying Meat for the Freezer

Despite what some may tell you, freezing meat does not necessarily have dire consequences for its eating qualities – particularly, and this is very important, if it has been properly hung. It also helps if it has been well butchered into sensible joints and portions.

So, if you have sourced a ready supply of top-quality meat but its location, or your lifestyle, makes regular purchases difficult, then you should certainly consider buying in bulk for the freezer. You can buy a whole or half sheep (well-hung mutton and hogget freeze particularly well), half a pig, or a quarter steer or 'beef pack' – in each case comprising a useful mix of roasting joints, chops or steaks, and meat for slow cooking or mincing.

Most offal doesn't freeze well for thawing out to use 'as fresh' (unless it's going to be cooked long and slow). But for pâtés and terrines, offal frozen when fresh is preferable to offal that hasn't been frozen but is less than fresh.

Using the Internet to Find Good Meat

You can use the Internet to find good meat in all kinds of ways. Firstly, you can check when and where the next and nearest farmers' markets are taking place (*www.farmersmarkets.net*). You can go on-line to search for good butcher's shops at *www.guildofqbutchers.co.uk*. You can track down local meat producers who sell at the farm gate, or by mail order, on websites such as *www.bigbarn.co.uk*, and you can obtain a list of organic meat producers by contacting the Soil Association on *www.soilassociation.org*. And there is now a special section of my own website, *www.rivercottage.net*, developed to coincide with the publication of this book, to help you track down the best meat in your area.

Time for a Change

I'd like to end this chapter with a simple plea. If the discussion above persuades you that the meat you're currently buying could be better, both ethically and on the plate, then why not change the way you buy it?

Once you are fully confident of your source, and the quality of your raw materials, the way you cook meat will enter a new phase. You may find, almost without effort, that a spirit of excitement and adventure begins to enter your kitchen. That's when you will want to understand and explore the full range of possibilities, with the many different cuts, from the various domesticated and wild animals we use for meat.

And that's where I'm heading in the next chapter.

4. BEEF AND VEAL

4. BEEF AND VEAL

For many an Englishman and, with a bit of luck, the odd Scotsman, Welshman and Irishman too, beef at its best is almost the definition of good meat – so much so that for centuries now it has been a symbol of the national character in general and a staunch resistance to the influence of foreign cultures in particular (it is telling that the French have long acknowledged our defiance in such matters by calling us *les rosbifs*). The cultural and historical reasons for this are explored in depth in Ben Rogers' fascinating book, *Beef and Liberty* (Chatto & Windus, 2003), which I highly recommend.

The reasons for beef's supremacy in British cooking and society may be complex but I believe there's something pretty simple at the heart of it: we are extremely good at producing beef. The British climate and pastures are perfect for it. Our ability to develop well-adapted local cattle breeds for meat has been second to none for centuries. The result is that, as a nation, we have enjoyed levels of connoisseurship in the product that, throughout the eighteenth and nineteenth centuries and probably the first half of the twentieth, more or less transcended class and wealth. During this time, just about everyone, from the king's court down, would have recognised and appreciated what good beef was, whether it was a daily or an annual treat. If the French were born with a nose for good wine, we came into the world with an eye and a palate for the finest beef.

Alas, we are in danger of squandering this outstanding heritage. A new generation – my generation, I'm sorry to say – has grown up without this instinctive understanding. It's hard to be sure precisely how the legacy was lost. Undoubtedly the subsidised industrialisation of farming in the post-War years, coupled with the canteen culture of the Sixties and Seventies, has taken its toll. The rise and rise of the hamburger must be a factor, too. The result of all these trends has been an overwhelming determination to cut costs, increase productivity, and make beef *cheap*.

What residual pride there might have been in the dwindling percentage of British beef that could still be recognised as superb was dealt a near-fatal blow by the BSE crisis. It allowed our European competitors in beef production – the French in particular – to leapfrog us in an instant. Having found it impossible to convince even their own people that British beef was inferior, the French government now had the ultimate stick with which to beat us – British beef might actually be lethal. And even after we'd put our house in order, they extended their advantage with an illegal ban. The resulting shame and anger among British beef producers is only just beginning to subside.

Yet the legacy of the BSE crisis is not entirely ignominious. A recognition that small, closed herds of traditional grass-fed beef breeds, along with organic beef farms, were scarcely troubled by BSE has led to a resurgence in small-scale, quality beef farming, often marketed directly to customers at the local level. Factor in the post-BSE legislation – for example, we are now the only country in the world to ban the use of animal derivatives in cattle feed across the board – and there is also a credible argument that British beef is currently the safest in the world. Add to that, recent incentives to maintain or restore the kind of environmentally friendly land management that is compatible with traditional extensive beef grazing, and it seems that the stage may well be set for a revival of quality British beef, first domestically, then internationally.

Beef Production Systems

The first thing you should know about beef is that these days a lot of it comes from cows that are literally only half good for beef in the first place. This is because they are genetically half dairy cow. The Holstein Friesian, the most popular and productive dairy cow, is that unmistakable black- and white-patched, long-legged, rangy creature with a massive pink udder swinging down below. It has been bred over centuries to produce up to forty litres of milk a day. That's enough to keep a large family in tea, coffee and breakfast cereals for a month. Because all its energy is directed into milk production, it puts on very little in the way of muscle or fat, and therefore meat. It has, to put it bluntly, a distinctly bony behind.

In order to keep them productive, dairy cows must take a break from milk producing, and have a new calf every year. As you can imagine, the number of calves born to all the dairy cows in the country is staggering – far more than is necessary to provide replacements for retiring dairy cows, who may be productive for as long as six or seven years. And of course, what's going to happen to all those boy calves, who couldn't replace a dairy cow even if you wanted them to?

The answer is that calves unwanted for, or unsuited (by sex) to, milk production may be fattened for meat production. But putting valuable grass, hay and other feedstuffs into pure-bred dairy calves is a pretty pointless exercise. Such is the tendency and character of the breed that you still won't get much decent meat. If, however, you mate your dairy cow with the bull of a prime beef-producing variety, the resulting offspring will be much better disposed towards fattening for meat. This, then, is what almost all dairy farmers do.

These 'dairy-cross' calves, as they are known, are separated from their mothers as soon as possible – often at birth – so the cow can get back to the important business of producing milk for the farmer. The calves will then be reared indoors and bucket-fed milk until they are old enough to eat solid food – usually in the form of pelleted cereals and protein known as 'cake', or 'concentrates'. Some dairy farmers have a sideline in fattening their dairy-cross calves for market themselves. Others sell them as soon as they can, as 'store cattle', to those who make a business out of preparing such animals for slaughter for the beef trade. In either case, they may or may not spend some part of their lives grazing out of doors, depending on the production system favoured by the farmer.

Incidentally, you may be wondering how the dairy farmer goes about replacing retired milking cows without ending up with a second generation of half-bred, less productive milkers. The answer is that he or she chooses the best (most milk-productive) cows and mates enough of them, often enough, with a prime dairy bull to provide replacement pure-bred dairy cows. The bull himself will rarely visit. His role is taken by a man with green overalls and a suitcase full of frozen sperm.

Have you spotted the unanswered question yet? What happens to the 50 per cent or so of pure-bred replacement calves that turn out to be male? Once the answer was that they would probably be milk-fed for four to six months or so and sold as veal. More about this controversial meat, and why personally I'd like to see more of it, later. For now I'll just say that the British veal industry is in such steep decline that the majority of pure-bred male dairy calves are shot within a few hours of birth, and either incinerated or fed to local foxhounds.

It is, in large part, an awareness of this practice, and the fact that, to a very large extent, the dairy industry and the beef industry are one and the same thing, that makes some vegetarians into vegans. Personally I can only admire such moral consistency – there's so little of it around.

At its best, dairy-cross beef is produced through a system that will combine extensive spring and summer grazing with indoor 'finishing'. These animals are hard to fatten on extensive systems, and it takes a period of concentrated feeding indoors to bring them to reasonable market weight. But it's fair to say that dairy-cross beef, finished by a skilful practitioner, can be of good quality, and the animals may enjoy a reasonable standard of welfare.

Unfortunately, it's equally fair to say that it is in the finishing of dairy-cross store cattle that the beef industry inevitably becomes more intensive. Once the animals are taking up indoor space, and being given feeds that must either be grown and processed on site or bought in, there will always be a financial incentive, and a big temptation, to get the job done as quickly as possible, and on the cheap. Antibiotic growth promoters are frequently used to speed up the process. The quality of bought-in feeds is often poor, and attention to the cattle's welfare may start to slide.

The fact is, hungry cows, kept indoors without grazing, will eat just about anything you give them. For several decades, the cheapest cattle feeds of all were the ones that contained a lot of animal protein from reprocessed abattoir waste and recycled 'fallen stock' – the euphemism for animals that die prematurely on a farm from disease, stress, accidents or abuse. That the unnatural casualties of one intensive livestock system had become the bargain feed of another was for many years the shameful secret of factory farming, only revealed to an appalled public when it suddenly became clear that it was also the reason BSE came into the world.

Thank goodness such feeds have now been banned. These days, the cheapest cattle feeds on the market are those made from genetically modified soya. And you can be assured that if this GM technology can allow feed firms to make animal feeds any cheaper, they'll be doing it. Only time will tell if the new experiment in unnatural biology can produce a monstrosity as horrendous as the old one, but I'd sooner not be one of the guinea pigs.

Suckler Herds

The alternative to dairy-cross beef is beef from herds that are never milked but exclusively managed for beef production. Traditionally, the best of these are pedigree herds of cattle bred over the years specifically for the quality of their beef, and their adaptability to local environmental conditions. Throughout the UK, and indeed across the Continent, this practice has given rise to numerous beef breeds. Undoubtedly the best-known British breed is the Aberdeen Angus. Its reputation for quality still packs a punch with many consumers today.

The next best known is the Hereford. Other pedigree or 'rare' breeds, much beloved of their supporters, include the Belted Galloway, Short Horn, Long Horn, White Park, Dexter, North Devon, South Devon, Welsh Black and Highland. There are dozens more (and used to be hundreds), some of which are now officially designated as Rare Breeds. Amongst these breeds you will find subtle differences in taste, muscle size and shape, and tendency to produce marbling, but what they all have in common is the ability to thrive outdoors in harsh and changeable weather, grow fat (though not quickly) on good grazing and hay and not much else, and produce superb meat at the end of it.

So-called Continental beef breeds are less hardy (they need to be overwintered indoors) but tend to grow bigger, faster and leaner, with a greater weight of muscle meat. They include the Limousin, Simmental, Belgian Blue and Charolais. They are often used by British beef farmers (those who are not pursuing a pedigree path) for 'improving' their stock. Improvements, though, tend to be measured in overall size and speed of weight gain. My view, and that of many beef enthusiasts, is that the more open-grained flesh of their larger muscles makes the meat just a little tougher, and the flavour a little less intense.

Herds of cattle raised solely for beef are called suckler herds, because the calves are allowed to suckle their mothers, usually in an extensive grazing environment, for the first six to nine months of life. After weaning, they usually remain in family groups, grazing extensively throughout their lives (though some farmers will sell some of their weaned calves at about nine to twelve months as store cattle, to be finished on a more intensive system). Depending on the quality of pasture, the breed in question, and the time of year they are sent to slaughter, suckler beef cattle may be finished exclusively on grass or with a supplementary feed of cereals and/or legumes (peas and beans), either indoors or out.

The best suckler-herd beef cattle are traditionally fully matured animals of two to four years old. Since BSE, the legal maximum age for beef cattle has been thirty months (i.e. two and a half years), and the most conscientious beef breeders will take their steers as close to this as possible. In contrast, intensively reared dairy-cross cattle are often slaughtered aged twelve to eighteen months – time and space are both money for the intensive beef finisher, so the carcass is cashed in as soon as it reaches marketable weight.

Incidentally, my own little suckler herd of seven cows, their various calves, and a bull consists of North Devon cattle, also known as Devon Ruby. You can see them on the back cover of this book, and again on pages 62-3 and 71. They have an excellent, mild temperament and are extremely well adapted to the unfertilised rough grazing of our forty-acre holding. And they produce the best beef I've ever tasted – though, of course, I am biased.

Most British beef varieties will tend to do well even on poor grazing. Bred to withstand harsh winters, they grow more slowly, and have a natural ability to put on fat reserves, both under the skin and also within the muscle. It is this natural growth pace, natural diet, and natural tendency to run to fat that make for the close-grained, well-marbled meat that is British beef at its best.

There are some who will try to persuade you otherwise, but to my mind the best beef you can buy, not only in terms of eating quality but also as far as general welfare standards and traceability are concerned, will always be from a good suckler herd of a British beef breed. It's hardly surprising when you consider that for centuries this has been precisely the intention of the enterprise.

Unfortunately though, by the time it gets to the supermarket (where over 70 per cent of British beef is now sold) it's extremely hard to tell whether any given piece of beef is from a suckler herd or not. This is largely so the supermarkets can exercise careful control over the way they market their meat: they don't want their customers to become any more discerning, except on their own carefully dictated terms. They don't want to start telling you that suckler-herd beef is best, because they never know when it might suddenly suit them to change their minds.

The beef industry is in a state of flux, with trends in production and the requirements of the wholesale buyer constantly changing. For example, most agents and middlemen will pay a premium for beef carcasses from suckler herds. By contrast, other buyers, including some of the supermarkets, prefer to do business exclusively with large-scale finishers who specialise in dairy-cross beef. They argue that 'quality' is more 'consistent'. What they really mean is that the meat is reliably lean, which is what they think their customers want (perhaps because they have spent the last three decades telling them that that's what they ought to have). Talk to beef farmers, and you'll find that some are predicting the death of the suckler herd, while others declare with equal confidence that it is 'the future of the industry'.

The contrasting pictures I am painting, then, are of beef from intensively raised dairy-cross cattle, fed on high-protein compound feed largely based on soya; and beef from extensively grazed suckler herds of fully fledged British beef breeds, fed principally, or even exclusively, on grass and natural forage. It's easy to make the one sound more attractive than the other. But it's reassuring that the stark contrast between them is discernible not merely in the mind of the beef enthusiast and connoisseur but also in the laboratory of the impartial scientist. A recent study at Bristol University examined the differences between samples of each kind of beef, both in terms of nutritional value and physical character. The results demonstrated that cattle fed on grass-based diets (grazing in summer and hay or silage in winter) have a different fatty acid profile in the meat compared with those fed a predominantly concentrate-based diet. The desirable omega-3 fatty acids are higher in grass-fed animals and the less desirable omega-6 fatty acids are higher in concentrate-fed ones. Grass-fed beef is also higher in vitamin E, which has various beneficial effects, including preserving the fatty acids during hanging.

The research has also conclusively shown that the two systems produce a discernible difference in taste. A 'trained taste panel' of ten people was asked to give scores for various flavour characteristics, including 'beef flavour' and 'abnormal flavour'. For the grass-fed beef, the scores for beef flavour were generally higher than for those fed concentrates and abnormal flavour scores were generally lower. (Incidentally, in similar experiments for lamb, the scores were even more dramatically in favour of the grass-fed product.)

In layman's terms, what this means is that grass-fed beef (and lamb) not only has a better taste and texture, it's better for you as well.

Hanging Beef

As discussed in Chapter 2, What is Good Meat?, hanging meat is far more than just a quaint tradition. And in the case of beef, it is critical. There is no doubt that the practice radically alters both the taste and texture – the whole eating experience – of the meat. Well-hung beef, cooked with skill, will be more tender and juicy, more rounded and full in flavour, and altogether much more exciting to eat, than beef that has been inadequately hung or inappropriately aged (for example, in the dreaded vac-pack favoured by the supermarkets). So important is hanging to the final quality that it will bring the best out of even only average beef. By the same token, failure to hang well will prevent even the finest meat reaching its full potential.

So how long should beef be hung? It's a question that aficionados squabble over endlessly. The truth is, there are many variables that will affect the speed at which the desired results are reached – principally temperature, humidity and air flow. But since most beef will be hung in a fan-cooled cold store at a temperature of 2-6°C, one can come up with a rough prescription. Mine would be a minimum of two weeks to get the beef to the 'interesting' stage and closer to a month to achieve perfection. Even longer than a month is nothing to fear.

With my own home-produced beef, I have been able to experiment with the length of hanging time to a point that no butcher, let alone a supermarket, would risk. My conclusion, however, is that there really isn't much risk involved. My longest hanging time is almost nine weeks. I killed one of my Devon Ruby steers in the last week of October. It hung in the abattoir cold room for a month, at which

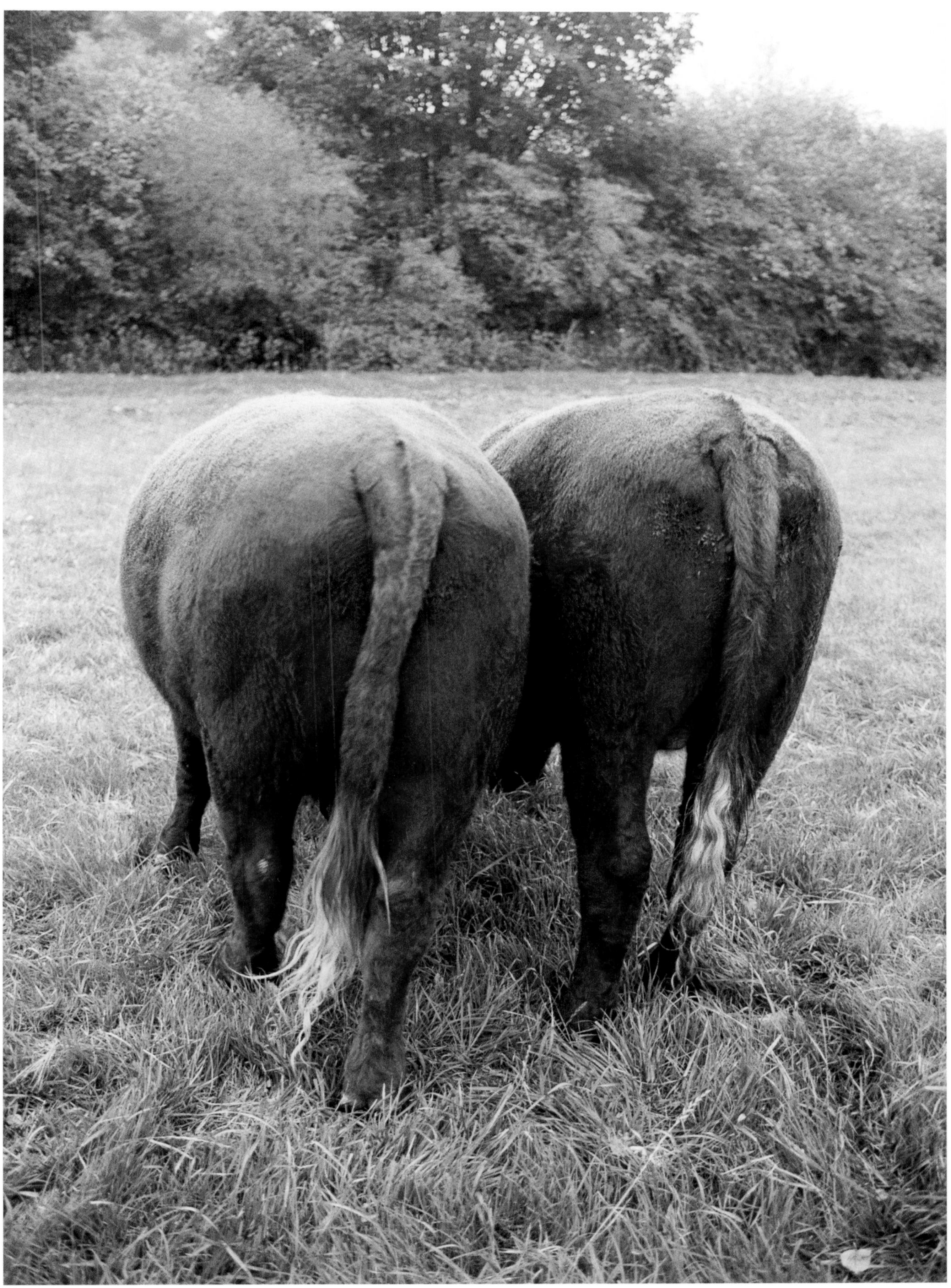

point my butcher friend Ray and I cut it up. Most of it went to a chef friend in Bristol, who was kind enough to say it was the best he'd ever had in the restaurant. But I retained a large forerib joint on the bone, much like the one on the cover of this book. I wrapped it in muslin and hung it from a hook in the porch. The plan was to whip it into the fridge if the weather got too warm but, as luck would have it, it stayed cool and breezy right up until Christmas. The nights were close to freezing, and I don't suppose the daytime temperature went much above 8-9°C.

I unwrapped the beef on Boxing Day to find an impressive bloom of white mould under the muslin on the two cut sides of the meat. I trimmed this off, discarding perhaps the outer 3-4mm on either side of the joint, and I could see straight away that the meat underneath was in great condition. We had an unforgettable Boxing Day feast – much as described in Roast Beef – The Full Monty on page 232. There was no question of any taint or gaminess in the taste, just superbly tender, deeply flavoured beef.

I am often asked if it is possible to improve the quality of under-hung beef by hanging it yourself at home. As the above story indicates, the answer is yes – but only up to a point. Basically it depends on the size and shape of the cut. It goes without saying that you can't hang a burger (!), and once it's sliced, there's not much you can do for a steak. It'll simply dehydrate rather than mature. You can't do much with any joint that has been boned, rolled and tied by the butcher. The meat, under pressure from the butcher's string, simply won't relax.

But a good joint of forerib or sirloin, ideally on the bone, can certainly be further matured at home, just as I described above. Pick a cool, airy place such as a larder, or a cellar if it is not too damp. Or, in cool weather, simply hang the meat outside, under cover. Wrap it in muslin or a cotton cloth to discourage not only flies but also garden birds that might have a peck at the fat. If squirrels are a problem, hang it in a wire-mesh cage. Give it an occasional sniff to check there is no taint that should concern you (a mild mustiness is no problem, but the whiff of the start of putrefaction should be quite unmistakable).

It is in the eating of roast beef joints and fried or grilled steaks that the appreciation of fully matured beef reaches its zenith. In slow-cooked dishes such as stews, well-hung beef will still be preferable to wet beef but the differences will not be as dramatic.

In the interests of fairness, I should also point out that quite a few of the small producers who sell beef from their own suckler herds direct at farmers' markets or locally at farm shops are also somewhat reticent in their hanging policy. Though most are happy to give their meat a week or ten days (which is certainly a start), few seem prepared to embrace the full three to four weeks that could give their product such marked character and superiority over the supermarket competition. I think it's probably a question of confidence, and perhaps the terror of falling foul of the local health and hygiene inspector, who is more than likely urging them to err on the side of caution.

If you are developing a relationship with such a producer (which is a fine idea), then tell them that in your case, he or she should throw caution to the wind and hang you a nice forerib for a good three weeks. And when it comes to packing it for collection or delivery, beg them not to vac-pack it either.

(Incidentally, the home-hanging option described above is not a bad salvage procedure for a large joint of beef, particularly a forerib or sirloin, that has been a little under-hung, and vac-packed to boot. But always wipe the meat as dry as possible before wrapping and hanging it.)

What Good Beef Looks Like

However you buy your beef, and however confident you are in your source and supply line, it certainly never hurts to know what good beef looks and feels like. Essentially, you are looking for clues that the animal has lived well and matured slowly, and that the carcass has been well hung.

Once you become familiar with it, and have cooked with it a few times, you'll quickly begin to recognise good beef when you see it. The colour should be a pleasing deep red, almost purplish, not pink or bright crimson. It should look dry but shiny, rather than wet or sweating, and be pleasantly tacky to touch. If you are allowed to touch it, so much the better – prod it with a finger and it should be nicely yielding, not too firm or resistant (the opposite of fresh fish, in fact). A dent made with the thumb should remain, rather than bounce back.

Look closely at the grain of the meat for the all-important marbling. Marbling (see page 36) is the term used to describe the fine threads of fat that run through the muscle meat. If you've always lacked confidence in assessing marbling, or think you may not have seen much of it, then the photograph on page 74 gives a pretty clear indication of what to look for. Those internal threads of fat, which you can see so clearly in the eye-steak of that forerib, are the holy grail of good beef, providing lubrication of the meat while it cooks, and brokering the beefy flavour of the meat on your palate even as you chew it.

On the subject of fat, I would say that a good outer layer of fat is also an excellent sign, providing the marbling is present, too. It indicates the likelihood that the animal was in rude health at the time of slaughter, and also that it was a suitable carcass for lengthy hanging (a good covering of fat protects a carcass from contamination while it matures). Add to this the natural basting properties you'll get as the joint roasts and it's clear that fat on beef, pretty much wherever you find it, is a Good Thing. You want it there in the meat and there in the cooking – but, of course, that doesn't mean you have to eat it.

The beef in the pictures throughout this chapter is from one of my own cows, slaughtered at the end of the summer at the legal maximum age of thirty months, and hung for nearly a month. If you'll forgive the lack of modesty, it doesn't get much better than this. I hope the pictures will help you to know, in the future, what you should be looking for.

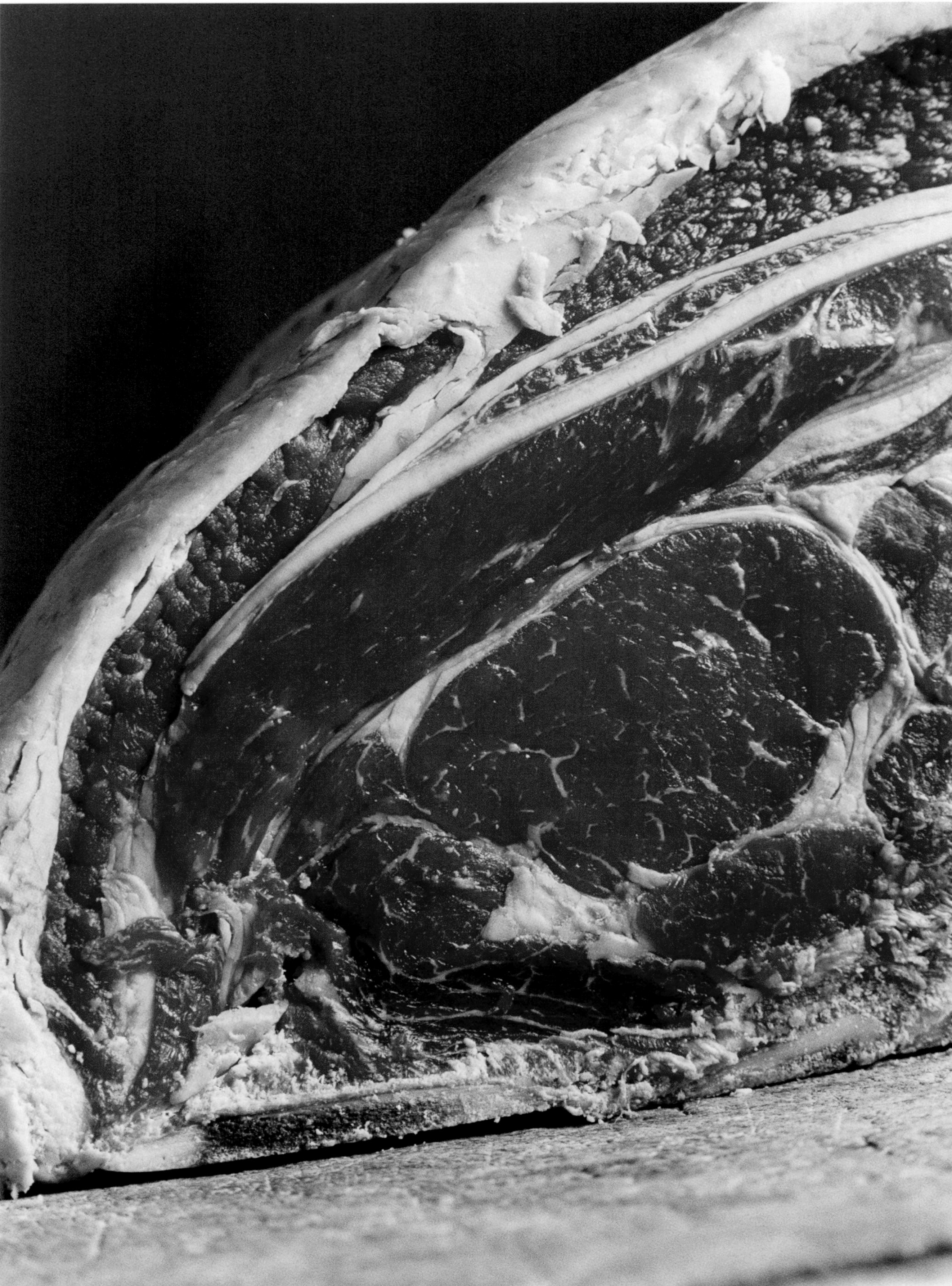

Organic Beef

Most organic beef you encounter will be from suckler herds for the simple reason that the extensiveness of the system and a pasture growth unforced by chemical fertilisers suits a suckler beef herd just fine, whereas dairy-cross cattle will struggle to keep condition. And certainly the intensive end of the dairy-cross finishing business is not permitted under organic certification.

The good news is that many entrepreneurial farmers, especially here in the West Country, are beginning to demonstrate that even relatively small farms (a hundred acres or less), of the kind that are no longer viable for dairy production (organic or conventional), can make a tidy business producing organic meat, provided they can sell it direct – for example, through farmers' markets or home delivery. Beef is usually the mainstay of such operations, and there is no doubt that meat from an organic suckler herd of a good British beef breed has the potential to be among the best you'll find.

The problem is what happens to the meat after slaughter. It's a problem that applies not only to organic producers but to all producers who choose to sell direct, so I'll discuss it in the Buying Beef Direct section on page 77.

Beef at the Butcher's

The proverbial good butcher, a rare breed himself, but happily not yet extinct, will always be one of the best people from whom to buy reliably good beef. This is largely because every butcher worth his salt understands that beef must be properly hung, and also knows what it looks like at its best. The very finest butchers also care passionately about the provenance of their beef – they should be able to tell you the breed, and even the sex and age at slaughter. And they should certainly know whether their beef is from a suckler herd or is dairy cross. In short, top butchers deal not merely with a commodity called beef but an individual herd, and even an individual animal. They'll also be dealing with an individual customer – perhaps you. And they should be ready to give you exactly what you want – a forerib roast, trimmed, chined and oven ready; a topside roast, rolled and tied; or a rump steak, cut exactly as thick as you want it.

In the end, though, I would say that provenance counts for more than service. A butcher who is obliging in preparing a joint of beef but who can't tell you where it comes from has his priorities back to front.

Beef in the Supermarkets

Undoubtedly the biggest drawback in buying beef, as with any other meat, from the supermarkets is the lack of available information. With very few exceptions, it is simply impossible from looking at a supermarket label to answer any of the key questions: is it from a suckler or dairy-cross herd, what kind of welfare status did the cattle have, and what were they fed on? At what age were the animals slaughtered, and how long has the meat been hung?

Sadly, even those prepared to take the trouble of contacting the supermarkets directly will find much of this information extremely hard to come by – as I have discovered in researching this book. I asked Jane Middleton, my researcher and recipe tester, to contact all the major supermarkets to ask about the provenance of their beef. I didn't want her to say, at least initially, that she was working for me, or for a book. Approaching them as a regular (but concerned) supermarket shopper, she asked for details on all of the above key points.

In most cases, the response was pitifully poor. It took weeks, for example, for most of them to respond to either phone calls or e-mails (after three months of regular calls from Jane, Tesco still hasn't replied at all!). The question of suckler versus dairy was usually fudged, by saying that they 'preferred' to source from suckler herds but that this wasn't always possible. Only Marks & Spencer said that all its beef was from suckler herds, and Safeway that its was from suckler herds 'at the moment'.

The hanging question was equally hard to get to the bottom of. Several of the supermarkets claimed that all their prime cuts of beef (sirloins, foreribs and rumps) are aged for 'up to twenty-one days'. Apart from the severe ambiguity of the phrase 'up to', making it impossible to get a genuinely meaningful figure, it turned out that by 'ageing' they don't mean hanging at all. They call it 'ageing in the bag' – which means storing the meat in vacuum packs and keeping it in a fridge for a couple of weeks. As I have explained (see page 41), this is really not something that should ever happen to good beef – but it saves the supermarkets a great deal of money!

Their total lack of comprehension of the art of hanging (or at least total reluctance to engage in it) completely undermines the supermarkets' credibility when it comes to selling beef. There is no question that some of them are taking in some pretty decent beef animals at the abattoir. Yet few are taking the trouble to mature it to anything like the quality it should have.

Until recently I had assumed that at the very least, the premium beef lines of the individual supermarkets (the ones whose labels boast of 'heritage', 'tradition' and 'extra ageing') would all be exclusively from suckler herds, and would have at least some extra welfare points. It turns out not to be the case. Even when the great names of Aberdeen Angus and Hereford are being splashed on labels and marketing leaflets, it would be a mistake to infer that we're talking about pedigree beef. Labelling laws, once rigid, have now been relaxed, so that these days you can call beef Angus or Hereford even if it's dairy cross, *provided the sire in question is a registered pedigree bull.* Since the sire will be represented by a man in green overalls travelling the country with a suitcase full of frozen bull sperm, this requirement is easily fulfilled, even at the intensive end of the industry.

In the end, the premium ranges seem little more than a marketing ruse. Read between the lines, and they are a tacit admission that the rest of the supermarket's meat range falls well below any reasonable benchmark of quality. For example, some premium lines may indicate that the beef in question has at least been properly hung, rather than aged in the bag, prior to butchering and packing. Hanging is better than not hanging – but it does seems outrageous that we should be asked to pay more for beef just because it has been hung adequately. My view is that ALL supermarket beef should be brought into line with their premium ranges, and then improvements made from there. Grass-fed pedigree suckler-herd beef cattle might fly.

Buying Beef Direct

If it's a guarantee of suckler-herd origin or extra-high standards of welfare you're after, or indeed the knowledge that the beef you're about to buy is from cows that have lived outside for at least part of their lives; if you're looking for the marbling that implies slow growth, suggests superior welfare and promises the best flavour, then I would suggest you try to buy your beef direct from someone who can answer all these points.

Small producers of suckler-herd beef, often organically reared, are increasingly moving into direct marketing to get the best price for what is genuinely a premium product. Farmers' markets, local farm shops, the Internet – and my own Directory at the back of this book – should help you make contact with such suppliers. Try as many as offer you a convenient opportunity to buy regularly. Compare and contrast. Then, with a bit of luck, you can develop a loyal and lasting relationship with the one that comes up trumps.

I offer one important caveat – to both buyers and sellers. Not all beef sold in this way is as well hung, or well butchered, as it could and should be. I know it's a lot to ask of busy farmers that, besides delivering fine beef cattle to the slaughterhouse, they also learn the art of hanging meat and the craft of butchery. But if organic beef from small producers, sold direct, is going to claim its rightful place at the pinnacle of beef quality, it is something they will have to address, either individually or perhaps collectively. The latter approach has tremendous possibilities, and is already proving a success here in Dorset. By banding together to share resources – such as a cold store, a cutting room and the skills of a freelance butcher – small producers can reduce their costs and greatly improve the quality of their end product. But the cardinal do, and the cardinal don't, of small-producer beef processing would be DO hang your beef for at least a full three weeks and DON'T vac-pack it – especially not the prime roasting cuts and steaks.

There is no reason why you can't make these two provisos conditions of your custom. The great thing about buying direct is that you are in a position to communicate with, and even influence, your supplier. Once you've found a supply, nurture and treasure it. It may serve you well for years. One thing you might seriously wish to consider is buying a quarter of a well-hung cow for the freezer. You can then begin to explore the extraordinary variety of wonderful dishes that can be compiled from its various muscles and body parts.

The Cuts

I would concede that you don't *have* to understand the anatomy of a cow, and how it is butchered, to be a good and adventurous beef cook – but it certainly helps. And there is always a chance that you may find the subject intrinsically interesting.

THE HINDQUARTER CUTS

RECIPES
Pot-au-feu (p.284); Potted Hough (p.456); Spaghetti Bolognese (p.497)

Leg of Beef (A): A cut from the top of the back leg. It is tough but lean, and can yield plenty of meat for long, slow cooking. I prefer to cook it in the piece and on the bone, with vegetables, as a kind of pot-au-feu, or to bone it out and salt it. Trimmed and cut up, the meat can be used, along with shin, for well-flavoured stews. The leg is also known as the hock, or, in Scotland, the HOUGH (potted hough is a classic Scottish spiced beef paste). Leg is also good for making your own mince, not for burgers but for bolognese.

Pot-au-feu (p.284); Potted Hough (p.456)

Marrow Bone: The classic marrow bone is the bone of the shin, including the ball (as in 'ball and socket joint') at either end. The bone from the hindquarter leg can also be used as a marrow bone. In order to fit in even a large stockpot, a marrow bone will have to be sawn at least in half, if not into smaller sections.

Principally, marrow bones are used for making beef stock, but after simmering for an hour or so the soft, jelly-like marrow can be removed and eaten on toast, as a chef's perk. A whole roast marrow bone, split and then served sprinkled with coarse salt and parsley, is an old Smithfield treat, recently revived with great success by the chef Fergus Henderson at St John restaurant in London.

Top Rump aka Thick Flank (B): The cut immediately above the leg, which yields a greater amount of similarly tough meat. The leaner parts can be trimmed into strips for marinating and flash-frying or stir-frying, or minced for burgers. Larger pieces are good for slow-cooked daubes and casseroles. Boned, a whole large piece can be brined to make excellent salt beef.

Beefburgers (p.398); Bresaola (p.436)

Silverside (C): A classic cut from the back of the thigh, which gets its name from the silvery sheen of the membrane covering its internal surface. Silverside comprises a pair of overlapping muscles, whose wide-grained texture is a testament to the hard work they do in propelling their owner from one place to another; it is tough – tougher even than topside. In some butcher's, it is tied up with fat and sold as a cheap roasting joint. Conventional fast roasting with a view to serving it rare is, in my view, a complete waste of time, though a slow pot roast with plenty of added fat and aromatics will turn out well. I use it for stews, and also, like top rump, for marinating for the frying pan or barbecue, and for burgers.

The two muscles of the silverside can be divided along the natural seam. The larger is perfect for dry-curing as bresaola, or brining and boiling as spiced beef. The smaller, traditionally known as POPE'S EYE, makes a good little pot roast.

Cold Roast Beef Open Sandwich (p.236); Stir-fried Indonesian Beef (p.346); Seared Spicy Beef in a Wrap (p.348); Bresaola (p.436)

Topside (D): This is the long, inner muscle of the cow's massive thigh. It is a little more tender than silverside, and in a top-quality animal, where the meat has been well hung and properly butchered (parcelled up and tied with a good covering of beaten-out beef fat), it certainly cuts it as a roasting joint, and can be served just pink. It should not be roasted fast, however, like a forerib or sirloin, but more slowly (at about 150°C/Gas Mark 2), with a little stock or water in the tin. Braising, on a bed of vegetables moistened with stock, is also appropriate. Roasted or braised, a good piece is excellent served cold – ideally uncut until completely cool (see page 236).

The topside from one whole hindquarter gives you two large or three medium joints – with my own beef I don't consider it extravagant to use one of them for bresaola, which will be even better than if made with silverside.

Thickly sliced and cut into strips, topside is perfect for quick marinating and flash-frying.

Oxtail with Rich Red Wine Sauce (p.282); Pot-au-feu (p.284)

Oxtail (E): The most anatomically unmistakable cut, perhaps, along with the tongue. The whole tail, skinned, is conventionally divided into short lengths by cutting between the articulated tail bones. Oxtail requires a minimum of three hours' slow simmering, but rewards the effort with an extremely well-flavoured liquor and gelatinous meat and sinew that falls meltingly off the bone. (See also Chapter 9, Offal.)

Seared Spicy Beef in a Wrap (p.348); Carpaccio of Beef with Shaved Beetroot (p.349); Steak and Chips (p.352); Beefburgers (p.398); Steak Tartare (p.442)

Rump (F): Considerably cheaper than fillet, RUMP STEAK (not to be confused with top rump) is also tastier and chewier, though if it is not properly matured it can be less than tasty and far too chewy. It is suitable for frying, grilling and barbecuing, in thickish slices. The steaks in the pictures on pages 327 and 353 are rump steaks. And very delicious they were too.

When you are really sure of the quality and maturity of a piece of rump, and if it has particularly good marbling, then a large piece of the 'eye' (a muscle that can be separated from the rest of the rump) makes a fabulous roast, which can be cooked fast and served rare. The meat from the lower muscle of the rump is rather tougher. It should be separated from the piece from which you cut your rump steak and used as silverside. Good, well-hung rump steak makes the best steak tartare, but you must scrupulously remove any sinews (see page 442).

Roast Beef – The Full Monty (p.232); Carpaccio of Beef with Shaved Beetroot (p.349); Steak and Chips (p.352); Steak Tartare (p.442)

Sirloin (G): There is some confusion as to what the sirloin is these days: the term is often used to refer to a small part of the whole sirloin, i.e. a trimmed, boneless piece of meat from which SIRLOIN STEAKS or entrecôtes are sliced to order by the butcher. In fact, a whole sirloin is a large piece taken from the lower middle of an animal's back, which includes the much-prized FILLET (see below). The sirloin on the hindquarter joins on to the foreribs on the forequarter. The muscle that is the fillet is attached to the underside of the sirloin (it is the 'undercut' of the

E. OXTAIL

RUMP STEAK

F. RUMP

FILLET STEAK

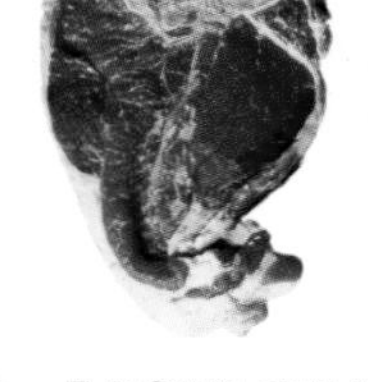

T-BONE STEAK

FILLET aka UNDERCUT

D. TOPSIDE ROAST

B+C+D. TOP BIT

POPE'S EYE

C. SILVERSIDE

B. TOP RUMP aka THICK FLANK

BRAISING STEAK

A. LEG OF BEEF (SLICE)

H. HINDQUARTER FLANK

MARROW BONE

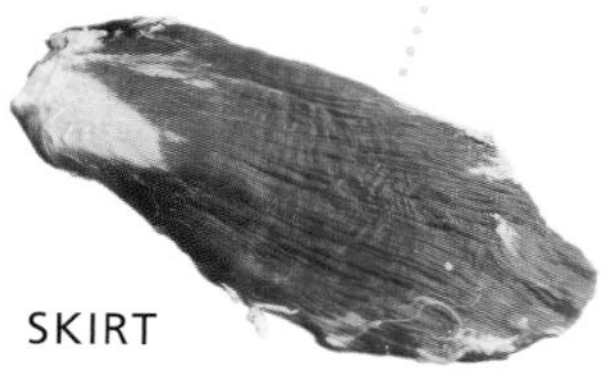

SKIRT

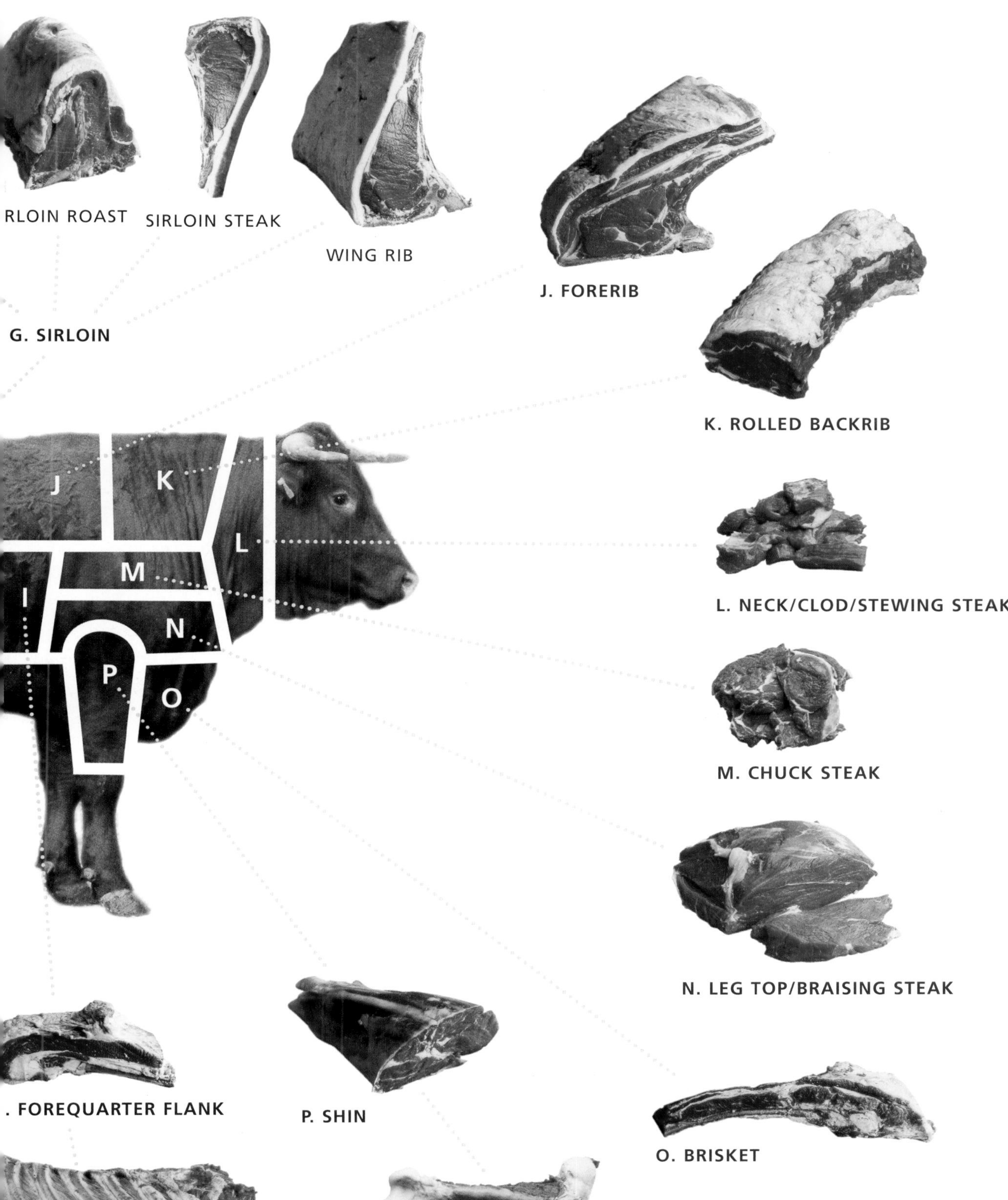

RLOIN ROAST
SIRLOIN STEAK
WING RIB
J. FORERIB
G. SIRLOIN
K. ROLLED BACKRIB
J
K
L
M
I
N
P
O
L. NECK/CLOD/STEWING STEAK
M. CHUCK STEAK
N. LEG TOP/BRAISING STEAK
. FOREQUARTER FLANK
P. SHIN
O. BRISKET
MARROW BONE
SHORT RIBS

sirloin), and in fact whole sirloins are usually hung with the fillet still attached. A T-BONE STEAK is a cross-section of the unfilleted sirloin. On one side of the T-bone is a piece of fillet, on the other the meat which, when taken off the bone, is the entrecôte or 'sirloin steak' of common butcher's-shop parlance.

The whole sirloin can be divided into joints, small or large, on the bone, that are among the finest roasting joints. A joint from the hindquarter end, i.e. potential T-bone steaks as yet uncut, is the SIRLOIN ROAST, and will have the fillet on one side and the contre-filet on the other. The joy of this cut is that it retains and absorbs flavour from the bone, and you can offer your guests a choice of incredibly tender fillet and especially tasty contre-filet. The joint comprising the last three ribs at the other end, i.e. that which would attach to the foreribs on the forequarter, is called the WING RIB. It is a little less well endowed, since it lacks the fillet, but is a wonderfully elegant joint that cooks beautifully.

When the entrecôte side of the sirloin is removed from the bone, trimmed of all gristle and excess (but, please, not all) fat, and neatly parcelled up, it is a fine boneless joint for posh roasting. This is the eye of the sirloin, what the French call contre-filet (because it is on the opposite side of the bone from the fillet). A little cheaper and a little tastier than the fillet, it is almost as tender, and should be roasted fast and served pink.

Finally, and just for the record, a 'chop' cut from the wing rib end of the sirloin, or the tail end of the foreribs, is traditionally known (especially in America) as a PORTERHOUSE STEAK. I have no idea how it got this name but it seems wonderfully appropriate for this gargantuan portion of meat.

Fillet aka Undercut (G): In a 300-350kg beef carcass, there is a scant 2-2.5kg of fillet, which is the least exercised muscle of the animal – no wonder it is so expensive. In fact, one of the reasons beef bullocks are castrated is that, as you might imagine, it makes them less inclined to mate, or even practise mating, and so prevents a rigorous form of exercise that would strengthen (and toughen) a great number of muscles, the fillet in particular. Fillet is therefore supremely tender, especially from a well-hung carcass, and consequently much prized by chefs. But it has less flavour than other cuts – and an overcooked fillet has practically no taste at all. Frying, grilling and quick roasting (of a whole or large piece) are all appropriate cooking methods. I try to avoid freezing a fillet, so when I bring a beef carcass back from the abattoir it's one of the treats I get to grips with within a day or two. I like to roast it whole in a very hot oven and serve it very bloody and rare – almost fridge cold in the middle.

Pot-au-feu (p.284); Salt Beef (p.438)

Hindquarter Flank (H): This is the chunk immediately below the sirloin and before the ribs begin. In other words, the belly. It is boneless, cheap, very fatty, but quite delicious if cooked slowly in casseroles or a pot-au-feu. It makes a fatty but extremely tasty cut of salt beef.

A Provençal Daube (p.280); Steak and Kidney Pie (p.286); Beefburgers (p.398)

Skirt (H): The term skirt refers to a group of several very distinctive lean muscles from the inside of the animal, so called because of its wide, open-grained fibres, which give it a curiously pleated texture. The biggest piece of skirt, sometimes called goose skirt, comes from the inside of the flank. Another piece comes from just under the skin of the inner thigh. Skirt is tough, but very lean and tasty, and so generally requires long, slow cooking. One of its classic uses is in steak and kidney pies and puddings. In complete contrast, thoroughly trimmed and finely minced to break down the fibres, it can also be used to make delicious lean burgers, which can be served very pink.

THE FOREQUARTER CUTS

Pot-au-feu (p.284); Salt Beef (p.438)

Forequarter Flank (I): This is a similar cut to the hindquarter flank, with the principal difference being that it has ribs in it. Some may see this as a snag, but when it comes to flavouring the liquor of your pot-au-feu (for example), those ribs are definitely an asset. A small 'rack' of ribs from the flank is sometimes referred to as SHORT RIBS (especially in America). They are quite a cheffy thing at the moment, especially cooked long and slow and served, rather like oxtail, in an intense, winey reduction of their own stock. They can also be salted like brisket. The ribs slip out easily after long, slow simmering.

Roast Beef – The Full Monty (p.232)

Forerib (J): The bovine equivalent of a rack of lamb is roast forerib of beef. There is plenty of lean meat in the eye of these 'chops', and a single rib 'cutlet' makes a good two-person portion. A three- or four-rib piece from a well-hung, quality animal makes, to my mind, the ultimate roasting joint. It has the fat to keep it lubricated, the bone to keep in moisture and flavour, and, in a slow-grown, grass-fed animal, excellent marbling in the eye of the meat. The miniature rib roasts from my own cattle have been some of the best beef I have ever had, even after freezing. The trimmed fillet, or eye, of the forerib gives a cut that is particularly popular in America – the RIB-EYE STEAK.

Backrib (K): Like the forerib, only less so. In other words there is less lean meat and what there is will be a little tougher. A fine-quality joint of backrib that has been well hung can, however, certainly still be roasted. A boned and rolled backrib is a lovely easy carving joint, which I like to serve not too rare and bloody but definitely a bit pink in the middle.

Neck/Clod (L): What's left of the carcass meat – mainly from around the neck and shoulder – used to be called neck and clod but these days will probably find its way into a butcher's tray or supermarket pack labelled STEWING STEAK. However, without knowing exactly where it comes from, I would hesitate to use it for that. You might want to consider it for mincing though; not for burgers, but for slow cooking, as in bolognese, chilli con carne and the like.

Steak and Kidney Pie (p.286); Beef in Stout (p.288); Beefburgers (p.398); Spaghetti Bolognese (p.497)

Chuck Steak (M): This is the meat taken from around the blade bone in the animal's shoulder. In the butcher's, it is sold, usually ready-cut, for stews and casseroles. Larger pieces of chuck steak (often sold as braising steak) are good for daubes and stews. Or it can be minced and used for bolognese. At its best it is borderline burger meat – but should be well trimmed of tough membranes.

A Provençal Daube (p.280); Steak and Kidney Pie (p.286); Beef in Stout (p.288)

Leg Top/Braising Steak (N): Good-looking slices of meat can be taken from the leg top, but they are too tough for fast cooking and are usually sold as 'braising' steak. Braising usually refers to slow cooking larger pieces of meat in a limited amount of flavoured liquid – i.e. somewhere between pot roasting and stewing. My view is that where lean beef cuts are concerned it is never quite as satisfactory as either, so I would tend to use leg top, in large cubes, for a stew.

Pot-au-feu (p.284); Bollito Misto (p.304); Salt Beef (p.438)

Brisket (O): A cut from further up the ribcage, often with the breastbone attached, brisket is marginally leaner than flank but still pretty fatty. It is the ultimate cut for salting, but it also goes wonderfully well in a pot-au-feu.

Main-course Borscht (p.279); Beef in Stout (p.288); A Provençal Daube (p.280); Pot-au-feu (p.284); Bollito Misto (p.304); Potted Hough (p.456)

Shin (P): The top of the foreleg of an animal, this is a bargain cut that is quite delicious if cooked very slowly in a flavoursome liquor. On the bone, it can be braised with wine and vegetables; off the bone it makes excellent stew, and can be mixed with leg of beef (see page 78). Do not, however, mix it with chuck steak, as this does not take as long to cook. Cross-sections of the shin, sawn through the bone about 2 cm thick, can be prepared 'osso buco' style – see Veal below – cooked very slowly with wine, herbs and tomatoes, until the meat is completely tender. The little morsel of marrow in the bone is a particular delicacy.

Pasticcio (p.491); Picadillo (p.494); Chilli con Carne (p.495); Spaghetti Bolognese (p.497)

Minced Beef: I find that commercial minced beef in the butcher's and supermarket is usually too finely ground and so lacks texture when cooked. I would rather make my own mince at home on a coarser setting. For burgers, I tend to use topside or silverside or, for a lean *steak-haché* burger, skirt with the sinews trimmed out. For bolognese, lasagne, chilli and other slow-cooked mince dishes, I will happily use any of the cheaper stewing cuts, untrimmed, as the long cooking times will tenderise everything. If making your own mince seems onerous, you can certainly get your butcher to do it for you on the spot. Just choose the cuts you want and ask for them to be minced on the coarse setting.

Veal

Veal is the name for the meat of calves and young cows, and its production and consumption are controversial to say the least. Now widely rejected by the British consumer for the much-publicised cruelty of the crate production system, veal is also a meat that is much misunderstood.

Let me say straight away that I believe the crate system is indefensible. The calves are so confined that they literally can't turn round. All they can do is stand up, lie down, and eat their daily dosage of powdered-milk-based liquid feed. Denied any grazing or cereal food (which they would normally begin eating alongside their mother's milk within a few weeks of birth), the calves' stomachs fail to develop properly. The objective of this system is, above all, to keep the meat of the animal as pale as possible – in the end, sheer whiteness, rather than flavour or tenderness, has become the principal marker of 'quality' in Dutch crate-reared veal. As a symbol of human indifference to the suffering of animals, that takes some beating.

But that isn't the whole story. Because what few consumers realise is that to banish veal forever from our shopping list and our menu is to condemn potential veal calves to a fairly heinous alternative to being reared for meat. If there is no market for veal, then the thousands of pure-bred dairy calves (see page 67) born each year that are neither suitable for beef production nor needed for replacing the dairy herd will be shot within a few hours of birth.

The fact is that the production of veal is not intrinsically cruel, any more than the production of pork, beef or lamb is. Crucially, the age of the animal at slaughter really isn't, or shouldn't be, the issue. Veal calves are generally slaughtered at five or six months – precisely the same age range as pigs for pork and sheep for lamb. You may think that's too tender an age to be slaughtering any animal for meat, in which case you should stick to mutton and beef, and try to find someone who keeps pigs to bacon age. But to make one rule for pigs and sheep and another for cows just doesn't make sense. I don't want to get into a debate about whether a short life of misery is ethically any more acceptable than no life at all (I happen to think it isn't). But fortunately I don't have to. Because the cruelty of confinement or the shame of execution at birth are not the only alternatives for these animals. There is a system of veal calf rearing that is far more extensive than the classic Dutch crate. The resulting product, from free-range calves who have lived unconfined, used to be known as bobby veal but is now being marketed as rosé veal, in acknowledgment of the pink tinge of its meat – an indication that as well as enjoying freedom of movement it is also able to ruminate on a diet that includes some roughage.

Calves for rosé veal are now being reared under both conventional and organic systems. In the former, calves are weaned from their mothers shortly after birth (the fate of almost all dairy calves, since the cows are returned as soon as possible to milking). They are then reared in loose stalls, in large barns open at either end to let in daylight, in small groups, with straw bedding and an 'ad lib' diet (accessible at all times) of both milk and cereal-based feed. They can also graze freely on their bedding. It's an indoor system, without the obvious and desirable benefits of grass underfoot and sunlight overhead. The standard of welfare depends, in the end, on the conscientiousness of the practitioner. But well-maintained indoor housing, with plenty of space, is at least an environment in which a group of calves can thrive and grow, and should not suffer unduly. The RSPCA has already begun monitoring a number of pilot rosé veal-production schemes, and awarding them its Freedom Food label (see page 55).

The organic system of rosé veal production, currently being pioneered at Eastbrook Farm in Wiltshire (see page 526), is also based on a loose housing system, supplemented by free access to outdoor grazing on organic pastures during the spring and summer months. It also has the unique welfare feature that the calves are actually reared with, or rather by, surrogate mothers, or 'nurse cows', who continue to suckle them throughout their five-to-six-month lives. Both mother's milk and the supplementary cereal-based feeds to which they have unrestricted access are, of course, certified organic.

I have tried Eastbrook Farm's organic veal and I think it is excellent. The meat is delicately flavoured compared to beef but it is still robust and tasty. The veal chop that I had grilled with garlic and rosemary was far more interesting to eat than any white veal I have ever tried. And the osso buco, prepared as on page 289, was superb. I think the entire venture is commendable, offering as it does not just a very worthwhile addition to the meat marketplace but one of the most constructive and humane solutions to the particularly challenging ethical problem of redundant dairy calves.

I can only hope that other organic meat producers will follow suit, and that you, the consumer, will stimulate the market with your custom so that the high-welfare organic product puts British veal back on the map.

The Veal Cuts

Pot-au-feu (p.284); Osso Buco alla Milanese (p.289); Veal with Lemon and Capers (p.342); Wiener Schnitzel (p.354)

Generally speaking, the veal cuts are described as for lamb (see pages 100-101). The exceptions are the various cuts from the leg, which use beef terminology. Hence you have SILVERSIDE, THICK FLANK and TOPSIDE, which is the favoured roasting joint. When rolled and tied into a neat parcel, the topside is called a CUSHION OF VEAL, an excellent joint for slow roasting or pot roasting. Silverside and thick flank are not much good for roasting, and are usually sliced for ESCALOPES. This can be done well or badly. The lazy way is to slice across the connected muscles, leaving a 'steak' of several pieces, which is held together by threads of connective tissue. The slice is then beaten flat with a mallet to disguise the joins. But the resulting escalope will buckle and curl when fried. The correct procedure is to separate out the larger muscles, and slice them at a slight diagonal across the grain. These true escalopes shouldn't need beating at all, but may be slightly flattened by the flat blade of a large knife, pressed with the base of the hand. Unless you have a butcher who is particularly well versed in veal, you're probably better off buying veal in a piece and slicing it yourself.

There will be leftover trimmings and wastage from the proper preparation of veal escalopes, but this can always be minced. Combined with pork, and/or beef,

Right: Shin of veal.
Far right: Veal chops.

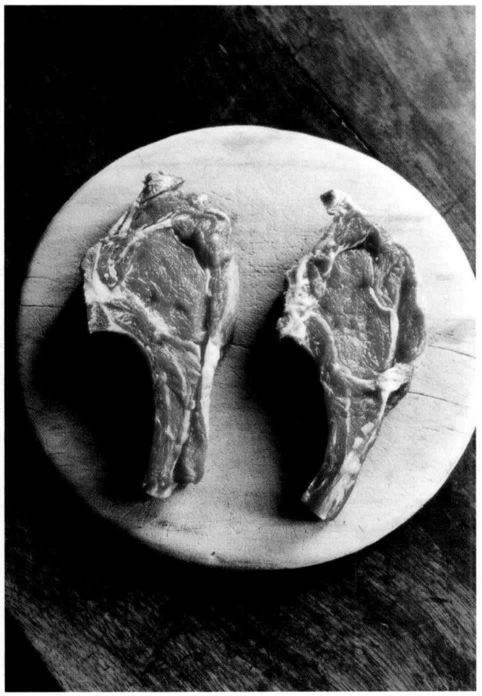

veal mince makes excellent meatballs – perfect for a Pasticcio (page 491). Like minced pork, it also makes a good addition to many pâtés, terrines and stuffings.

As with lamb, there are three more potential roasting joints – the BEST END, the LOIN and the CHUMP END (sometimes called the FILLET ROAST). These can be roasted on the bone, as racks, or boned out, stuffed, rolled and tied. Pot roasted with a little wine, herbs and lemon zest, and regularly basted while they cook, they make very special joints. These cuts can also be divided into VEAL CHOPS, for grilling, baking, barbecuing or pan-frying. As with pork, some loin chops used to have a slice of the kidney attached, but EC slaughter and butchery guidelines now make this practically impossible.

The other prime roasting joint of veal is the SHOULDER, which is usually boned and rolled, and may be stuffed. The BREAST, which is sometimes further subdivided into FLANK and RIBS, requires long, slow cooking. It is traditionally boned, stuffed and rolled for either poaching or pot roasting, or sliced to make the classic blanquette – a slow-cooked stew whose liquor is finished as a sauce by thickening with cream and egg yolks.

The remaining classic cut is SHIN OF VEAL, often known by the name of the classic Italian dish that uses it, osso buco. Cut in 2-3cm slices across the bone, each piece contains a cross-section of veal bone, whose tender marrow is one of the treats of the dish.

The remaining meat from the NECK can be tied as a cheap pot-roasting joint, but is usually cut up for stewing or mincing, along with the SCRAG END.

5. LAMB AND MUTTON

5. LAMB AND MUTTON

Thanks to the sheep's ability to thrive on fairly marginal land, British sheep have not, generally speaking, been subjected to the horrors of intensive farming – confined housing, unnatural feeds, growth promoters – that have so threatened the quality of our beef and pork. Good lamb really isn't that hard to find. It is by nature a distinctive and flavourful meat. There are also some interesting regional variations in taste and texture – the result of different breeds of stock and the variable quality and character of the land on which they graze. And who would have it any other way? Life would be very dull if a sheep that grazed on the coarse grasses and wild plants of the Welsh hills tasted exactly the same as a West Country animal that spent its days on the rich pasture of the Dorset downs. In fact, wherever you live in the UK, I think it's fair to say that lamb is a relatively dependable meat – certainly in comparison to beef and pork.

However, although the quality of British lamb is, in general, something to be proud of, it would be misleading to imply that a second-rate British product does not exist. It certainly does. Such meat is often the product of farms where sheep are not a priority but an adjunct to intensive arable farming. Lambs are grown fast, either indoors or on impoverished arable land, and fed up on cheap bought-in feeds or arable by-products.

There is also the semi-intensive rearing of 'new season's' lamb, for the ever-reliable Easter market. You shouldn't have to stop and think for long to realise how out of kilter this annual lamb-marketing bonanza is with the natural life cycle of the sheep. Most breeds would naturally be lambing at Easter time. So where does all this spring lamb come from? Are we eating newborns, or animals just a few weeks old? Of course not; it comes from lambs born the previous November and December, from flocks specially managed for autumn lambing.

This is not an entirely artificial practice. Some breeds, the Polled Dorset and Dorset Horn in particular, are naturally inclined to autumn lambing. The breed's tendency to put on and store fat, and the relatively mild winter climate of its southern coastal habitat, mean that Dorsets can feed their lambs successfully throughout the winter, so they are ready to take advantage of the first surge of early spring growth in the pasture – which may be as early as late February in the south.

However, left to their own devices, even these ewes wouldn't produce lambs fit for slaughter as early as Easter (though they'd be pretty fine by May/June). So they are fed up on concentrated feeds throughout the winter months to keep their milk production high. (Some years ago these feeds would often have included recycled animal proteins, but since BSE, this practice at least has been banned. Now the preference is for high-protein cereal pellets.) The resulting 'suck' lambs, as they are called, feed almost exclusively on milk. They may be reared indoors, or may be turned out with their mothers in mild weather. Either way they do not, in my view, make for the best eating. They grow too fast and ruminate hardly at all, so the resulting meat is pale and 'vealy', without the full, grassy, *lamby* flavour that makes good lamb so distinctive. It doesn't hang well and tends to be tough when served pink – and rather dry and tasteless when overdone to compensate.

It's fair to conclude that March and April, contrary to everything the supermarkets and, I'm afraid, most butchers, would have you believe, are not really the best times for buying lamb. You're better off waiting until early and mid-summer, by which time almost all lambs will be grazing out of doors, as no farmer in their right mind would go to the expense of feeding concentrates and investing man-hours in indoor management when there is so much free grazing out there. Genuine spring lambs (i.e. lambs born, not killed, in the spring) will often continue to suckle their mothers, as well as thriving on the best grazing, throughout the summer, so that come late summer and autumn you have the very best, sweetest lamb, perfect for roasting fast and serving pink.

These later lambs will also be better endowed with the aforementioned fat. This is a boon not just in the oven as your leg of lamb roasts but before that, at the hanging stage. A reasonable covering of fat is necessary if meat is to be hung for any length of time at all. So, while an indoor-reared 'spring lamb' sold at Easter will barely stand a week's hanging, a late-summer or autumn lamb, nicely but not excessively fatted, can be hung for a good ten days. The resulting meat will have just the right balance of 'youth and experience' for fine eating.

Incidentally, a whole leg or shoulder of well-fatted, late-summer or autumn lamb is another good example of the sort of joint you can hang yourself at home, though you must have the necessary cool space to do this properly. A leg of lamb should be hung, preferably covered in muslin or a clean cotton cloth, from a butcher's hook, hip-down, knuckle-up, in a well-aired place where the temperature is reliably less than 10°C. In autumn and winter a cold stone outhouse should just about fit the bill. In the summer months only a very cool cellar is likely to fulfil these requirements – unless you can make enough space to hang it in your fridge. Since the temperature at home is likely to be unreliable, it would be unwise to hang a leg of lamb for much more than a week.

New Zealand Lamb

Everybody knows that we import huge amounts of New Zealand lamb. Principally this serves the big meat retailers as a competitively priced seasonal stopgap. It keeps butcher's and supermarkets well, and more importantly cheaply, supplied during the late-winter and early-spring months when British lamb is in short supply, and therefore more expensive. Almost all of it used to arrive frozen but these days a significant proportion is air-freighted for sale fresh.

I have nothing against New Zealand meat producers and I'm sure that, like us, they're capable of producing lamb that is good, bad and indifferent. The problem, of course, is that the British consumer, sizing up the New Zealand imported

product, really has no way of telling which of these three any given piece of NZ lamb is going to turn out to be. And there is precious little information to be had about welfare and provenance either.

In fact, we produce more than enough lamb in the UK to meet our domestic consumption – we export plenty of lamb ourselves. Once you've hooked into a reliable supply of the very best UK-produced lamb, there's really no need to step outside of it. The best way to have a ready supply of British lamb (or hogget, or mutton – see page 94) throughout the marginal months is to buy top-quality, well-hung British meat in the autumn – maybe half an animal, jointed up – and keep it in the freezer.

Lamb at the Butcher's

Spotting poor-quality lamb at the butcher's is not always easy. Blood spots and wet-looking meat are signs of immaturity and/or under-hanging, but these are only likely to come to light with close scrutiny. As ever, a good dialogue with the butcher is the best assurance. Butchers who have proved their worth in other areas are unlikely to fail you when it comes to providing a good piece of lamb, and even butchers whose beef and pork are not always excellent may have access to local lamb that is less disappointing. Good lamb is available locally almost all over the country, and there is little reason for a butcher to source it from outside the region – unless he's being offered a knockdown wholesale price on meat that may be less than special.

Don't necessarily expect your butcher to know about the breed of sheep or the age at slaughter – but be impressed if he does. And it's definitely worth asking about the hanging time. Many of his customers may not consider this an issue with lamb, and he may be inclined to go along with that. But he ought to be ready to discuss it, and there's no reason why he can't make an exception for you. If the worst comes to the worst, just point to the leg you like the look of and tell him you'll come back for it in a week!

Lamb at the Supermarket

British lamb at the supermarket is a little less problematic than British beef, in the sense that, with the exception of the aforementioned 'spring lamb', you should get meat from reasonably extensively farmed animals for most of the year. But don't expect it to be properly hung.

Again, some of the supermarkets have 'premium' labels for lamb, boasting 'traditionally reared', 'extra matured', 'heritage' or whatever. And again, this begs the question, why can't they source all their meat well and look after it properly – and why should we pay extra for what, in a good butcher's, would be nothing more than standard service?

But, if the supermarket is really your only option, and you want to go home with the best lamb in the store, then you should be ready to pay the extra.

Buying Lamb Direct

Buying lamb direct, through farmers' markets, farm shops or the Internet, or by special arrangement with a local farmer, is an excellent idea, particularly if you are willing to buy a whole or half animal for the freezer. As with the butcher, a good dialogue is the key to success – you can even specify what sort of animal you are after – i.e. how old and how well hung you would like it.

I now produce enough lamb to sell a couple of dozen carcasses each year direct to a few friends and neighbours here in Dorset. Because I lamb outdoors, generally from mid-March through April, I won't take anything to slaughter much before September, and even then only the fattest and fittest of the stock. These I will hang for ten days, or two weeks if the carcasses are showing particularly good fat. The rest of my lambs will be kept at least until their second spring, when of course they will no longer be lambs at all.

This mature sheep meat is a great passion of mine, and of a growing band of aficionados, and I believe it offers great potential, both for cooks looking for something of real character and quality and for small producers who are ready to explore new markets. You will find it referred to often in the recipes in this book. Traditionally – and, I hope, in the future – it goes by the name of . . .

Mutton (and Hogget)

With the exception of a few early spring-born lambs that are slaughtered in late autumn and winter, very few animals go beyond their sixth month, and most are killed at around their fourth or fifth. Yet without doubt the best sheep meat I have ever eaten has come from animals over a year old. In old-fashioned parlance, a lamb in its second spring and summer (i.e. one year old plus) becomes a hogget, and from its third onwards, the meat from it is known as mutton.

Today, mutton barely exists in the mainstream meat market, and consequently barely registers at all on the average meat consumer's radar. If they know or use the word at all, it is probably in the context of 'mutton dressed as lamb'. If they have even a vague sense of what the meat mutton is all about, they probably think of it as coming from some clapped-out old ewe that is no longer productive, or a knackered ram that is being retired.

This is a grievous misunderstanding. Mutton 'wethers' (castrated male sheep) are usually slaughtered (by those in the know) in their second or third year after fattening on spring and summer grass, when they will be physically mature but still young animals in the prime of life. Their meat is quite superb, and far from requiring marinating or slow cooking, it can be roasted and served pink, like the best cuts of prime beef.

In fact, it is in comparison to beef that mutton may be best understood, and perhaps best marketed to a public who will obviously need some converting to appreciate its special qualities. The truth is (and this was once well understood by the British meat consumer), mutton is to lamb what beef is to veal. A good case can be made that mutton ought to be the main thing, while lamb is a seasonal speciality – for this is precisely how it used to be. The key, of course, is that to reach its full potential, mutton does need to be properly hung – like the best beef, for at least two weeks, ideally three.

All this is too much to deal with for most farmers, most butchers, and certainly the supermarkets. But with a bit of detective work, top-quality mutton of this kind can be found. As so often in the quest for good meat, the answer lies in direct contact with producers who are butchering and retailing their own meat. As discussed in Chapter 3, Buying Meat, you may find them at farmers' markets, through the Internet, or by consulting my Directory on page 525. Some of them will be organic and some won't. Some of them may require you to take possession of half an animal. But they will portion it up for you, ready for the freezer, and probably deliver it too. These are the people to talk to about mutton and hogget, and when you mention the 'm' word, the chances are you will get an appreciative, knowing response. It's probably what they prefer to eat themselves.

For those of us who produce hogget and mutton, there is another source of satisfaction beyond the question of taste. Being able to take a significant proportion of our stock into its second or even third year, rather than killing all but one's breeding ewes at six months old, feels like a distinct gain in terms of welfare.

The word about mutton is starting to get around. Smart chefs are already putting it on their menus. And a few enlightened butchers are beginning to market it as something rather special. The winning 'lamb' entries in the organic meat awards organised by the Soil Association have, for the last three years, all been from animals over one year old! These awards are strictly based on blind tastings, so it's sheer quality talking, not a bunch of in-the-know foodies trying to give mutton a better name.

Having said that, putting mutton back on the British culinary map is certainly an unashamed mission of mine. So if you have a good butcher, badger him till he comes up with the goods. If you're buying lamb direct, ask the producer to grow on a hogget for you, for the freezer. If you can't manage a whole one, find a friend to split it with. And once you do get hold of some, and decide that you like it (as I'm sure you will), please help spread the word.

The Cuts

The butchery of lamb and mutton is relatively straightforward. It's the easiest carcass for a good butcher to negotiate. My butcher friend, Ray, can have a whole animal butchered and bagged for the freezer in less than an hour – and that includes cutting up chops and boning and rolling the shoulder.

It's also the animal for which the cook can most easily become familiar with all the available cuts. As an educational exercise, and a big step on the way to a truly holistic relationship with meat, why not buy a whole half animal (or a whole whole one), and use this book to help you cook your way through all the different cuts.

RECIPES
Roast Lamb (p.239); Souvlaki (p.401); Indian-spiced Lamb Skewers (p.402); Barbecued Rosemary Lamb with Salsa Verde (p.404); Kibbeh Naye (p.443)

Leg (A): Every cook knows what a leg of lamb looks like and knows, more or less, how to cook it. There is no doubt that a good leg of lamb makes a fabulous roast (and a good leg of mutton an even better one). There are two classic approaches to the dish – you either roast it fast and serve it pink, or bake it slow and serve it falling off the bone. Both can be excellent. For the latter, a fatty leg of well-marbled mutton is far preferable to a lean leg of lamb, which may end up very dry.

The leg can also be divided into two, producing smaller versions of these classic roasts, based on 'half-legs' (either the chump end, or the knuckle or shank end). However, they are never quite as satisfactory, and my own preference is to roast a whole leg and really go to town with the leftovers.

You shouldn't feel constrained to keep a leg whole and on the bone. It can be boned and stuffed for an 'easy carving' joint (though I prefer a shoulder for this treatment). It can be sliced as LEG STEAKS, for frying, grilling or barbecuing. Or the boned meat can be divided into its constituent muscles and subdivided into lean portions, which are then 'butterflied'. This, along with jointing poultry and game birds, is one of the very few butchery skills that I think it's worthwhile for the amateur cook to learn.

It isn't at all hard to do, though it's a bit tricky to explain. Check the step-by-step pictures on the opposite page and you'll soon get the hang of it. Basically, start with a boned-out leg (ask the butcher to bone it for you, or do a hatchet job yourself – it's quite easy to improvise). Remove most, but not all, of the fat from around the muscle meat. Trim off the very sinewy parts from the shank end. Then divide the meat into six or seven roughly equal, roughly fist-sized portions, where possible following the natural contours of the muscles. Take each chunk of the muscle meat and, with a sharp knife, cut it along, not across, the grain, *almost* in half. Then turn it over and cut each of the two halves almost in half again. You are effectively creating a series of slashes through the meat so that it opens up like a concertina. Spread the meat out with your fingers, and feel free to make a few extra, smaller slashes where this helps to open it out.

These butterflied portions have several advantages over straight-cut leg steaks: firstly they go with the grain of the meat, and do not cut across different muscle sections, so they won't shrink or buckle when cooked. Secondly, the concertina effect considerably increases the surface area of the meat. This allows it to take on more of any marinade. And it makes them perfect for barbecuing, as more of the meat is exposed to the char-flavoured heat of the grill.

Incidentally, if you're using this section as a 'teach-yourself-butterflying' course (and I hope you will), then don't get too downhearted if there are a few botched portions along the way. Just cut them up into smaller pieces, marinate them along with the more successful pieces, and mount them on a skewer for cooking. Or mince them up and make my Souvlaki Lamburgers (page 401).

Steaks of mutton, either straight cut or butterflied, are also very viable. This meat is far more versatile than most people think.

1
2
3
4
5
6
7

Citrus-braised Lamb Shanks (p.300)

Shank (B): The shank is the knobbly, knuckly bit at the end of a leg of lamb, which is traditionally left on the leg, after being cut through by the butcher and folded over, with a section of tough sinew and skin acting as a hinge. After roasting, it is usually distinctly on the overcooked side, if not blackened to oblivion – though, as a perk to gnaw on, it has its enthusiasts (including me). But as a cut in its own right, rich in gelatinous sinew, a shank can also be transformed fabulously by slow cooking. To work like this, it needs to be cut more generously, including a little more meat from further up the leg. For this reason, many butchers are reluctant to sell you shanks on their own, as most of their customers still expect to find them on the legs they buy for roasting. However, as lamb shanks are catching on in restaurants, cookbooks and colour supplements, so some butchers are catching on, too – dividing some of their legs into shanks for slow cooking and two neat half-leg joints for roasting.

In the absence of such enlightened cooperation, one solution is to accumulate shanks over time – whenever you buy a leg of lamb. Saw them off (or ask the butcher to do this) and pop them in the freezer until you have four or more. Whenever I butcher my own sheep, I usually remove and freeze the shanks, along with the shins (see page 103). Both are perfect for long, slow cooking with wine, stock vegetables and some strong flavourings. You end up with a muttony equivalent of an oxtail stew, meltingly tender meat falling off the bone – and into an intense, winey gravy. My own shank recipe, with citrus zest, is one I developed especially for this book, and I am very proud of it.

Mrs Wheeler's Irish Stew (p.292); Lamb with Garlic and Anchovies (p.342); Kibbeh Naye (p.443)

Chump (C): This is the equivalent of the rump of beef, and comes from the point at which the leg meets the loin. In fact, a leg of lamb can be cut extra long to include the chump, and a whole chump, or 'chump end', makes a nice small roasting joint, either on or off the bone. There is a trend among chefs for serving a whole, lean, trimmed 'chump' as a fancy two-person roast, usually very pink. And with good, well-hung meat, skilful cooking, and resting, it can work very well.

In the butcher's and supermarket the chump is most often encountered in the form of lean, generous CHUMP CHOPS (these would turn into leg steaks as the butcher slices further down the leg). They are slightly more expensive than loin chops or neck cutlets.

Loin of Lamb Stuffed with Apricots and Pine Nuts (p.242); Lamb with Garlic and Anchovies (p.342)

Loin (D): A loin is the ovine equivalent of the sirloin of beef: it is where LOIN CHOPS are taken from but it is also, in its entirety, a good roasting cut. I often roast a loin whole, with the ribs still in, and untrimmed, so that it remains well lubricated by all available fat. There may well be more fat clinging to the joint than you would wish to eat – but it will have done a good job, and you don't have to eat it.

However, I'm equally happy to use a boned-out loin. It certainly makes a very smart joint for stuffing, rolling and tying, with a lovely eye of meat that will end up bound tight to the stuffing.

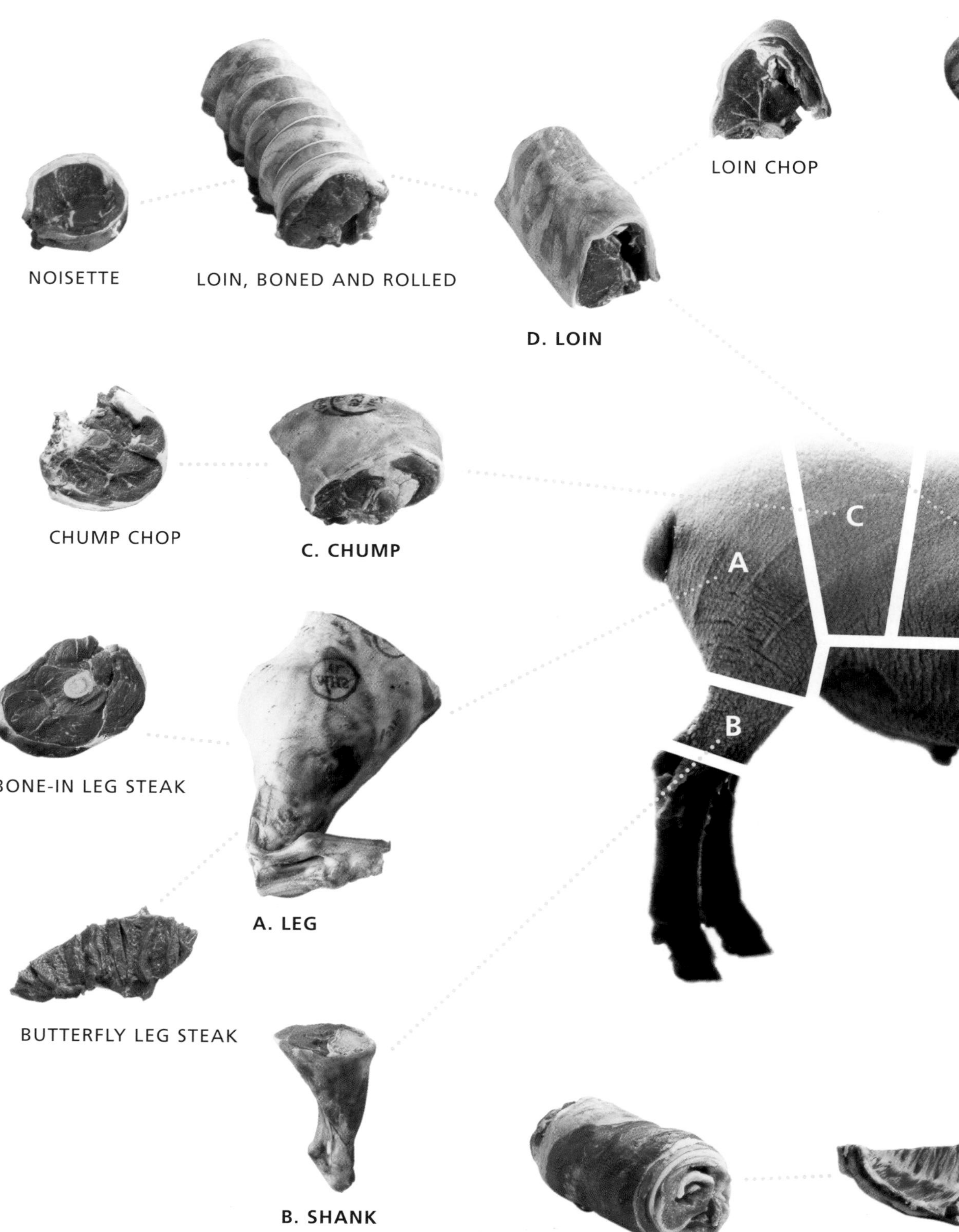

NOISETTE
LOIN, BONED AND ROLLED
D. LOIN
LOIN CHOP
CHUMP CHOP
C. CHUMP
C
A
B
BONE-IN LEG STEAK
A. LEG
BUTTERFLY LEG STEAK
B. SHANK
BREAST, ROLLED
F. BREAST

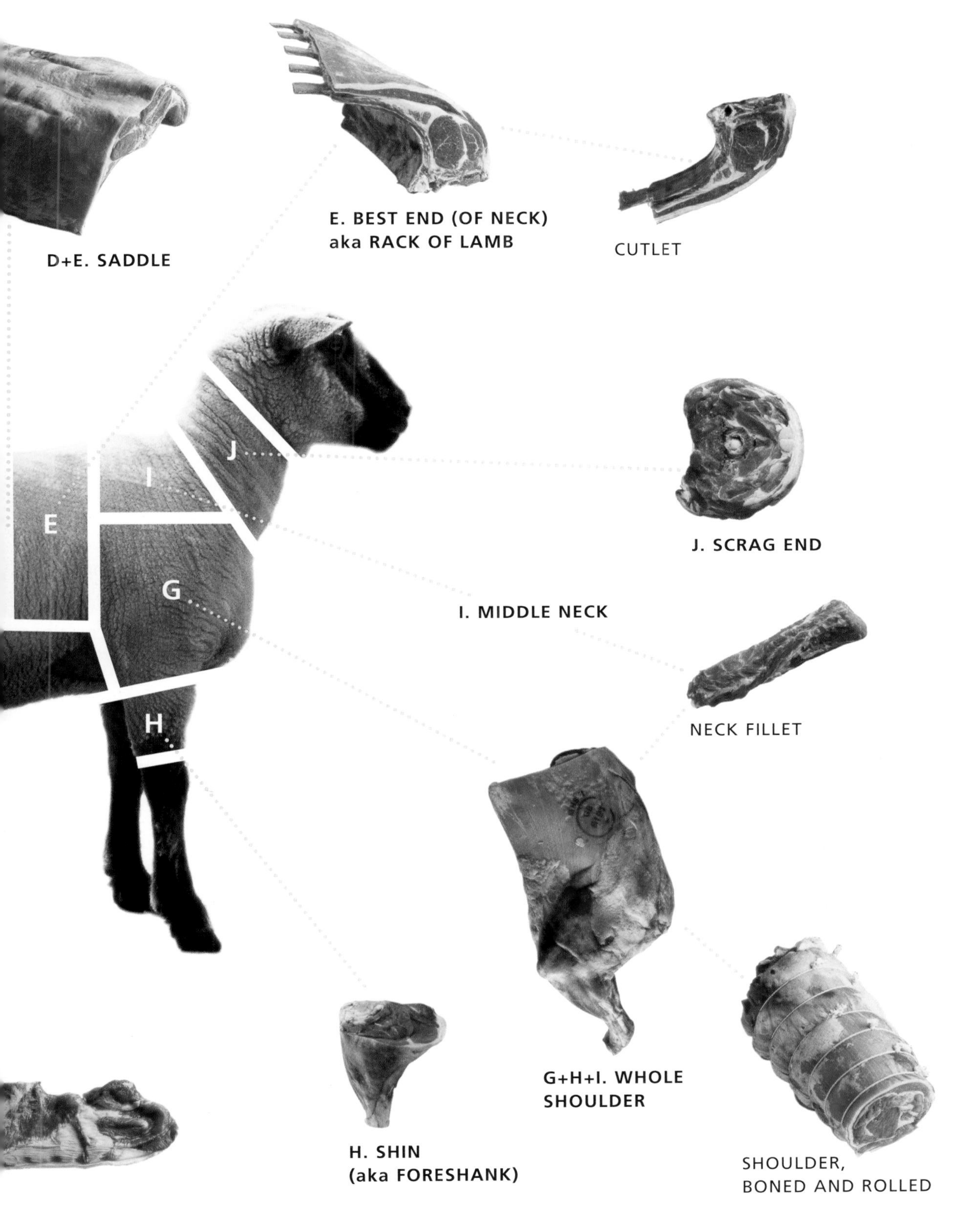
D+E. SADDLE
E. BEST END (OF NECK)
aka RACK OF LAMB
CUTLET
J
I
E
G
H
J. SCRAG END
I. MIDDLE NECK
NECK FILLET
G+H+I. WHOLE
SHOULDER
H. SHIN
(aka FORESHANK)
SHOULDER,
BONED AND ROLLED

The eye of the loin can also be trimmed of all fat and sliced into miniature fillet steaks, called NOISETTES of lamb. These, the leanest and most delicate lamb cut of all, are traditionally fried, but they are easily rendered pointless by overcooking. By contrast, mutton noisettes – hardly a conventional cut, but one I have experimented with from my own animals – are a revelation. These lightly marbled nuggets of lean meat, fried for just a few minutes and served pink, are the sheepy equivalent of the perfect, well-aged sirloin steak – another reason I am trying so hard to champion this wonderful meat.

Saddle (D+E): Two loins, from either side of the animal, still joined together, are called a saddle. It makes a spectacular roasting joint. With more lean meat than a single leg or shoulder, a whole roast saddle of a good-sized hogget or mutton wether should happily serve twelve people. For serious feasting, and with the cooperation of a good butcher, the concept of the saddle can be extended to include best end of neck (see below) – provided your oven is large enough to accommodate it.

Roast Rack of Mutton Chops (p.239); Lancashire Hot Pot (p.290); Lamb with Garlic and Anchovies (p.342)

Best End (of Neck) aka Rack of Lamb (E): The best end of neck is the next joint along from the loin, comprising the first eight ribs and the lean meat between them and the chine (the split backbone). A versatile cut, it can be trimmed and subdivided in various ways. It can be cut into tidy little chops which, when trimmed of excess fat and the chine bone to which they were attached, are known as CUTLETS. When the little nugget of meat from a single cutlet is removed and further trimmed, you once again have a noisette – an even smaller one than you'd get from a loin. If all eight trimmed cutlets on a best-end joint remain attached you have a roasting joint called a rack of lamb. Those miniature paper chef's hats to go on the end of each chop are traditional but, I'd like to think, optional!

As with the saddle, two racks of lamb, one from either side of the carcass, may be left joined together. Deftly cut by the butcher to form a circle, then trimmed up, you have that great party piece known as the CROWN ROAST. An elaborate stuffing can be piled into the centre (which practically forms a cake tin) and the number of chef's hats required naturally doubles ...

Breast of Lamb Ste Menehould (p.295)

Breast (F): An underused and underrated cut, the breast (which includes part of the belly) is admittedly not ideally suited to the Jack Sprats of this world, being undeniably fatty. But rolled up round a dry stuffing (say, of breadcrumbs, garlic and herbs) to absorb the fat, it makes an economical cut for long, slow pot roasting. Pour off the excess fat as it cooks (as you might for a duck or goose), then finish the roast at a high heat to crisp up the outside.

A more time-consuming, but ultimately very rewarding treatment is the French method known as Ste Menehould. There is a full description of the process, and some tempting pictures, on pages 294-5.

Roast Lamb (p.239); Rolled Shoulder of Lamb or Hogget with Capers and Anchovies (p.240); Baker's Oven Shoulder of Mutton (p.241); Lamb Braised with Stuffed Vine Leaves (p.291); Ndole (p.296); Curry Goat (p.297); Tunisian Lamb with Aubergine (p.299); Cassoulet (p.302); Souvlaki (p.401); Indian-spiced Lamb Skewers (p.402)

Shoulder (G+H+I): Wrongly thought of as the poor man's leg, the shoulder offers plenty of tender meat, albeit in a form that is not as easy to carve. One way round this problem is to bone and roll it – it roasts particularly well in this shape, as some of the plentiful fat on the shoulder is rolled into the inside of the joint and bastes it from within. And if you're going to roll it, you may as well stuff it. Not necessarily with something substantial or stodgy, but rather with some punchy herbs and piquant flavourings, so the meat sort of marinates from the inside as it cooks. Garlic, anchovies and capers are always good additions that will help cut the fat of the meat.

Whether on or off the bone, the secret of success is a slightly longer, slower roast than you would give the leg, aiming for meat that may still be pink close to the bone – but only just. A shoulder of mutton is the perfect joint for even longer, slower cooking, in the method known as *à la cuiller*, because the meat is so tender it can be eaten with a spoon.

Shin (aka Foreshank) (H): This is the equivalent of the shank but on the front leg – you will encounter it on a roast shoulder as the thin, tapering bit that becomes very crisp. It is barely recognised as a cut in its own right. However you cut it, it will be even more frugal, and less meaty, than the shank, but it is worth including when you cook some shanks, for the extra body and the modest amount of extra meat it will provide.

Lancashire Hot Pot (p.290); Mrs Wheeler's Irish Stew (p.292); Ndole (p.296); Curry Goat (p.297); Tunisian Lamb with Aubergine (p.299)

Middle Neck (I) and Scrag End (J): As the neck continues towards the head from the best end (E), and the muscles therein expend their energy lifting the sheep's head up and down from the pasture on which it is grazing, the meat becomes tougher and a little more sparse, but no less tasty. Filleted neck and scrag make great stewing meat, but I think they are even better if cooked on the bone. Middle neck chops, and cross-sections of scrag with the neck bone still in (a bit like thinner sections of oxtail), are perfect for long, slow cooking. Irish stew and Lancashire hot pot are two classic dishes that use these cuts admirably. Cooked long and slow, even the bones will be tender enough for those so inclined to chew them up with everything else.

Souvlaki Lamburgers (p.401); Indian-spiced Lamburgers (p.402); Moussaka (p.503); Shepherd's Pie (p.504)

Minced Lamb: Middle neck, scrag end and the leaner parts of the belly can all be minced up to make good mince for moussaka and shepherd's pie. The adventurous can also use this fresh, lean mince to try their hand at making merguez, highly spiced North African sausages. I am a big fan of the spicy lamburger (see Souvlaki Lamburgers on page 401) – and for that I am ready to sacrifice the occasional leg or shoulder to produce a leaner mince that will respond well to fast barbecuing or griddling, and may be served, to those who like it so, a little pink in the middle.

Of course, leftover cooked lamb also makes a very versatile mince for shepherd's pie, moussaka or some kind of improvised hash (see page 477).

6. PORK AND BACON

6. PORK AND BACON

It would be nice to begin this chapter, like the last two, with a fairly upbeat discussion of just how good this meat can be at its best. I'm afraid in the case of pork that would be disingenuous. Its production is a travesty on such a huge scale that I feel the gloom must come first.

The pig is, both at home and abroad, the most abused of all our farm animals. We can say this partly because of all of them it is certainly the most intelligent and gregarious. Pigs can form strong bonds with other animals, especially humans. They can, like dogs, be trained to perform complex tasks – including hunting truffles and even retrieving game. They can be fully housetrained and kept as very responsive and rewarding – and surprisingly clean – domestic pets.

Pigs, even more than cows and sheep, have a complex set of behavioural instincts – one could justifiably call them needs and desires. They thrive on the company of their peers, provided they are not overcrowded. They are highly responsive to changes in the seasons and the weather, in that they will deliberately create mudwallows for cooling off, and nests or layers in thick cover for sheltering from the worst winds. And they have an almost unstoppable drive to root – that is, to turn over the ground with their powerful jaws and snouts, in search of roots and buried nuts to eat.

Yet despite these characteristics, which mark out the pig as particularly in need of extensive husbandry, this animal has become the most intensively farmed of our domesticated mammals – its movements highly restricted, its powerful instincts denied any opportunity of expression by the featureless concrete environment in which it is kept. Worse than that, pigs are reared in such crowded conditions that their one potential solace, the company of their fellows, becomes their worst torment. Pigs, like people, need 'personal space'. Yet the space allowance per animal means that, in most conventional systems, they are literally shoulder to shoulder. Even to turn around or lie down, they require the cooperation of their peers. Injuries from fighting are ubiquitous. Ears in particular are often torn (the intensive pig has been bred over time to have smaller and smaller ears). The tail is so vulnerable to attack that it is routinely amputated shortly after birth.

Injured animals in such close confinement are obviously at risk of infection. The solution is to dose them routinely with antibiotics, with which their feed is laced. The drug cocktail of factory-farm pig feeds often includes growth-promoting antibiotics as well, which artificially speed up muscle meat development.

Such is the demand for pork – particularly in its cured form, as bacon – that producing it has become a sheer numbers game. A veritable industry is at full throttle, inputting cheap feed and outputting cheap pork so efficiently that the central provider is barely recognised as sentient, let alone complex. The term factory farming – emotive and perhaps sometimes a little unfairly loaded –

certainly comes into its own when describing an intensive pig unit. It's hard to understand, and a little shameful to contemplate, how we have managed to get so angry about Dutch veal production (to the extent that veal is now almost completely taboo in the UK) while barely raising any audible opposition to our own (and indeed Dutch and Danish) intensive pig systems.

The bitter irony is that the system produces a meat so bland, flabby and tasteless that only an artificial cure, laced with chemical preservatives and flavouring E-numbers, can produce a taste that the consumer will recognise as the beloved bacon. Un-'cured', the pork is so dull as to be almost unrecognisable as meat. It is simply an insipid sponge – perfect for soaking up a whole new set of flavours, many also artificial, in the staggering range of bottled condiments, cook-in sauces and fancy marinades now available. It's a double whammy for the supermarkets: their pork may be cheap but it is so boring that you have to load your trolley with expensive, value-added products to compensate.

The final irony: to produce a substance that does this job, you don't really need animals at all. You could create 'artificial' meat of comparable or superior character without so much as troubling a pig. In fact, it has already been created, from the very vegetable that provides most of the calorific intake of the poor factory-farmed porker – soya beans. Personally I'd rather eat tofu than factory-farmed pork any day (and believe me, that's saying something).

My point is that factory-farmed pork is not just a moral outrage of crate-veal proportions, it's a waste of time in the kitchen as well. Don't bother with it. In fact, don't buy any pork, bacon or sausages at all unless you can be sure it comes from animals that have felt the sun on their backs and got their snouts stuck into a bit of good British soil. As far as I'm concerned, outdoor-reared is an absolute minimum for welfare, and the first step on the road to decent-tasting pork.

The Search for Flavour

Rearing my own pork has been a revelation. The stock I have chosen are true outdoor pigs – so called 'rare breeds' or 'coloured' pigs, such as the Gloucester Old Spot, Saddleback and Tamworth, and crosses thereof. I buy them as 'weaners', at about eight weeks old (when they are the size of plump Jack Russell terriers) and they grow on at their natural rate. I feed them a baseline diet of organic cereal pellets, which is supplemented by the natural forage of their run, including grass, wild plants and roots, along with plenty of fresh vegetables (the pods, outer leaves, peelings and leftovers of our own garden produce) and even, in the late summer and autumn, windfall apples and plums.

I generally keep them twice as long as commercial pigs – nine to ten months, instead of about five, by which time they are pretty enormous (like small hippos). This is the age and size of the traditional 'baconer' (as opposed to porker), yet as well as making fine hams and bacon, I find the fresh pork cuts – the loins, thick ends and spare rib roast – are perfectly tender and roastable.

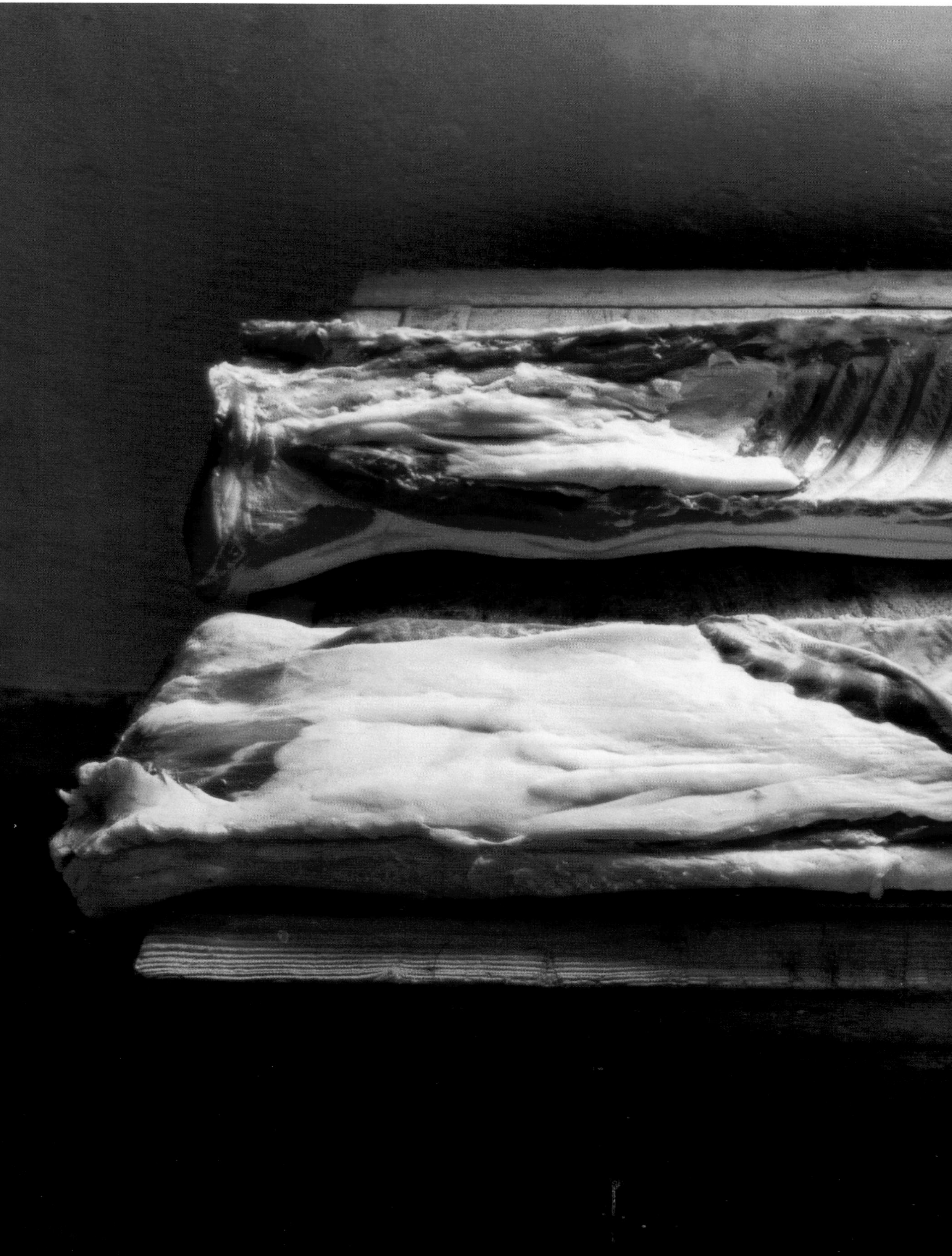

Their meat is superb. In the raw, it is not white or grey but pleasingly pink and firm, with fine threads of marbling in the rump of the leg and the eye of the loin (more visible when cured than in the raw). In the smaller, tighter muscles, usually those closer to the bones, the meat becomes darker – a distinctive, pinky brown. The flavour is outstanding – deeply porky and robust, rich and savoury, but never too strong or gamy.

I didn't know just how good pork could be until I raised my own pigs. Now I sometimes imagine a global band of smallholders and subsistence farmers, from the forests and lakes of Savoie or the Auvergne to the sweaty jungles of Vietnam or Korea, from the mountains of Corsica to the foothills of the Chilean Andes, whose pigs all root and forage freely and are fattened up on whatever surplus scraps of cereals or roots, fruits or vegetables come to hand. We all have one thing in common: we know what pork is meant to taste like.

I'm sorry if that sounds over-romantic – not to mention smug. The sad truth is that pork of this kind is very hard to produce commercially, and therefore very hard to buy. Even most organic, outdoor-reared pork is from pigs fed day in day out on the same kind of pellet, and even when this pellet is well balanced, healthy and made of good organic ingredients, you will not get pork of the quality and depth of flavour that a truly varied diet can produce. It will still, however, be in an entirely different league from the factory-farmed meat.

With pork, lifestyle is everything. For the pork enthusiast who wants to discover the true taste of the meat, the mission becomes hunt the happy pig – and, in a perfect world, the happy gourmet pig. The best pork you can buy in the UK comes from small producers who understand this, and who not only give their stock space but also take the trouble to feed it with a varied diet. In ideal circumstances, the pigs will have sufficient outdoor space for the grass beneath their feet to contribute significantly to their diet. Grass silage and pea silage are excellent supplementary fodder for pigs, as are root crops such as turnips and beet, and leaf crops such as kale (pigs *love* green fodder). Some pig farmers grow these crops especially for their pigs, others may buy them in. Still others mix up their own balanced feeds, using rolled oats or barley, maize and dried beets, dried peas or other legumes. The result of such a commitment to excellence is, quite literally, a different animal. And the difference is apparent in the colour, texture and taste of the meat it produces.

You may end up paying twice as much, or even more, for pork raised in this leisurely, extensive manner. But given that the end product will be *infinitely* better eating, I would call that a bargain.

Rare Breeds

The commercial indoor porker – the classic pink pig – has been bred for thousands of generations to gain weight fast, to be long in the body, lean in the flesh and, to a limited extent (from which one should derive no great comfort), to tolerate intense crowding. By contrast, the traditional breeds of pig, some of which are officially designated as 'rare breeds', have a different character altogether, and so does their meat. Breeds such as the Gloucester Old Spot, Berkshire, Saddleback, Tamworth, Middle White, Large White, Large Black, and Oxford Sandy and Black are classic regional pigs. Hardy and well suited to outdoor living, they were bred to inhabit orchards, farmyards, scrubby woodland and open grassland.

The bottom line is that these types of pig simply won't stand intensive farming. Nor are they easily forced into rapid weight gain. Given the opportunity, they will happily graze on grass. Their slow-grown meat is much more inclined to show marbling, and they will tend to put on a copious outer layer of fat. All these qualities naturally make for better, as in *tastier*, pork. (For a long time the equation of quality with leanness has been forced on the mainstream pork consumer by both butchers and supermarkets. How wrong that is.)

It might be pushing it a bit to insist that rare-breed provenance is a cast-iron guarantee of pork quality. But pigs with character farmed by people with character will tend to produce pork with character. And it is certainly true to say that rare-breed stock is the natural choice of enthusiasts aiming for quality, rather than agribusinessmen aiming for profit. In the search for flavour combined with high welfare standards, that's a very good start.

Organic Pork

I have said that I don't regard organic status as the be all and end all in the search for quality meat. But there is no doubt that if you're after good pork from a high welfare system, then the organic label, particularly when certified by the Soil Association, is a very useful one indeed. On the welfare side, it guarantees an outdoor lifestyle – the basic freedom to roam that is essential to porcine contentment. On the feed side, it guarantees that feeds are free from chemical preservatives, routine medical prophylactics (including antibiotics) and all GM materials. And on the slaughter side, it specifies more humane transport conditions and places a limit on waiting times at the abattoir – particularly significant when dealing with creatures as attuned and intelligent as pigs.

Another thing to factor in is that many organic pig farmers, particularly those operating on a relatively small scale, tend to favour the rare breeds. This is partly because they naturally fit in with the more extensive style of organic pig farming. But it's also because, since the farmer is going to have to charge a considerable premium to meet the extra expense of organic practice, it makes sense to choose stock that will itself add further character and distinction to the end product. In other words, in pursuit of excellence, they might as well go the whole hog (sorry!).

So, to summarise, if you can lay your hands on pork that is both organically certified and of rare-breed provenance then, short of being in direct contact with a producer who can give you chapter and verse on every aspect of his or her pig production, you are probably doing the best you can.

Pork at the Butcher's

I mentioned that even a so-so butcher can often turn out pretty good lamb. The flip side of this, I'm afraid, is that even butchers who excel in other areas may sorely disappoint with their pork. Unlike lamb and even beef, top-quality pork doesn't just turn up in your shop by accident. You have to go looking for it.

Many butchers know less about the provenance of their pork than any other meat they stock. It's a depressing sign that, with such a uniformly characterless product, so widely available from such a huge marketplace, provenance is almost an irrelevance.

The silver lining here is that a butcher who is able to provide any salient information at all about his pork, for example that it's outdoor-reared on a nearby farm, is probably offering something above and beyond the rank and file. If he takes the trouble to source organic pork, you're definitely on to a good thing. And a butcher who stocks pork from local rare breeds and names them on his labels is a rarity to be treasured – and his pork will be, too.

Pork at the Supermarket

The supermarkets are where almost all of our intensively farmed pork ends up. In fact, cheap bacon and ham – what you might call 'embalmed' pork products – so dominate the chill cabinets that I sometimes think of them as strip-lit morgues for millions of miserable pigs. I'll discuss these hugely popular cured pork products in more depth shortly, but when it comes to finding fresh pork with some semblance of flavour, from pigs with some modicum of dignity in their lives, the supermarket is not a great place to look.

Forced to buy pork in the supermarket (which I would truly hate to be), I'd look straight away for an organic label, preferably sporting the Soil Association logo, as they have the most rigorous welfare standards of the various certification bodies. Organic pork that finds its way into the supermarket is likely to have been produced on a large scale, so you probably won't get the flavour benefits of tailor-made, seasonally varied feeds, or a significant proportion of natural forage in the pig's diet. But you will get pork from animals that have lived outdoors, eaten a healthy and unadulterated feed pellet, and not suffered the pain and indignity of tail docking. The bottom line is that, under SA certification at least, there is no such thing as intensively farmed organic pork – and that counts for a lot.

The other label to consider is the supermarket's own premium label – the one that says 'traditional', 'heritage' or 'finest', and that costs half as much again as the bog-standard pork in the next-door chill cabinet. But I'd look hard for proof that this premium reflects a genuine improvement in the quality of the meat and the lifestyle of the animals from which it comes. In the case of pork, this should guarantee at the very least an outdoor lifestyle. Ask in-store for the leaflet that explains the scheme in detail, and unless it gives unambiguous assurance on these points, then don't bother with it. Buy some lamb instead.

The big problem with organic and premium-label pork in the supermarkets is the simple one of availability. They tend to be sold in only a 'select' few stores – usually the ones serving a catchment area of particularly high-spending consumers. This reflects the depressingly cynical view that an interest in exceptional welfare and quality of meat is confined to the monied classes. I know from the success of meat producers at my local farmers' markets in attracting new customers from across the social spectrum that this is simply not the case.

Buying Pork Direct

The mission to hunt down the happy pig is likely to lead you in the end to one of a select few small producers of slow-grown, rare-breed pork, which may or may not be organically certified. They may have their own farm shops, you may find them at a farmers' market, or perhaps you'll track them down through the Directory at the end of this book, or my website, *www.rivercottage.net*.

My bet is that when you taste the meat they sell, you'll vow never to backslide to the mainstream, factory-farmed product again. If you are lucky, you will develop a personal relationship with the producer, so that your supply of top-quality pork is dependable for years to come. And if you are very lucky, you may even enjoy levels of personal service that most consumers couldn't contemplate. With the right supplier, you can buy a whole or half pig, butchered the way you like it, for the freezer; you can get cuts prepared for special occasions; you can buy a suckling pig for Christmas, or a whole porker dressed and ready for a spit-roast. Or you can ask the farmer to keep on a pig for a few extra months, so you have yourself a real baconer, ready for a weekend of home-processing into hams, bacons, sausages, pâtés and salami (see *The River Cottage Cookbook* for all you need to know).

Here in Dorset, this way of doing business is becoming commonplace. I've even known punters, buying direct from a small farm, who get to choose their own piglet and drop in occasionally to check on progress. They bring 'treats', such as a sack of turnips or windfall apples, or a bag of overgrown runner beans from their garden, that will enhance the life of their porky protégé, and hence the taste of its flesh.

Short of rearing a pair of pigs yourself (not necessarily such a far-fetched option, if you have even a small patch of land), this is the ultimate way to buy pork. It may not be practical for all of us, but in terms of quality of meat and welfare of stock, and above all in its nurturing of a full appreciation of the provenance of good meat, and the skill and dedication that go to producing it, it sets a benchmark of excellence to which we can all aspire.

Buying Bacon, Ham and Sausages

Huge amounts of the pork that we eat will have been either cured by salting, and/or smoking, and/or the injection of large amounts of preservatives, or processed by mincing and the addition of various flavourings, both natural and artificial. The resulting products, which we know as bacon, ham or gammon, and sausages, are even more variable in quality than the raw pork from which they are derived. This is pretty logical, if you think about it. Combine good and bad pork with good and bad curing practices, or inspired and devious sausage-making practices, and you will get some very fine, craft-made products from the finest slow-grown pork, and some very bad, chemical-laced cured products made from the worst and most watery factory-farmed pork.

You'll also get everything in between, including some paradoxical and problematic cured pork products, such as poor to average pork that has been cured with great love and skill, resulting in an undeniably palatable end product and, very occasionally, its frustrating (but thankfully rare) counterpoint – the finest pork rendered all but inedible by clumsy and ignorant curing. And you'll get sausages that range from the seriously sublime to the criminally awful.

How you pick and choose from along these sometimes conflicting continua of quality and ethics is up to you, but you shouldn't forget that the choices you make when you buy bacon, ham and sausages will impact just as much on the means of production – the shifting tenets of pig husbandry – as the fresh pork you choose.

This seems obvious enough, but I make the point because of a curious phenomenon that I have observed whereby otherwise ethical meat shoppers have a mysterious tendency to let themselves down when it comes to shopping for cured pork generally, and their beloved bacon and sausages in particular. You could call it temporary welfare blindness – the ability selectively to overlook the issues that usually influence ethical shopping practice in the case of certain goods. And for some reason bacon and sausages are among the worst offenders.

It's hard to explain, but I think there are at least two factors at play here. One is to do with what you might call the 'distance travelled' of the products. The further meat gets in appearance, texture and taste from raw flesh, or a live animal, the less we are inclined to consider issues – particularly ethical issues – concerning its production. It's the reason many vegetarians remain blind to the hypocrisy of wearing leather. And before we 'caring carnivores' get too smug, it's the reason few of us stop to consider whether our own leather goods derive from intensively farmed animals rather than the more extensively reared alternatives whose meat we seek to champion (where are those organic biker jackets, goddammit?).

The fact is that a rasher of bacon looks a lot less pig like, or even flesh like, than a pork chop, and the same can be said of the sausage. It makes it that much easier to push questions of provenance and ethics to the back of one's mind.

Another more subtle, and related, factor that I think is at play is to do with the intrinsic nature of these incredibly distinctive products, which results in a kind of torpor of conservatism, or complacency of historical continuity. The fact that the sausage and the bacon rasher are so firmly embedded at the very heart of British food culture has made them, in the subconscious of the consumer herd, almost impervious to moral reassessment. They are what they are, and have been for centuries, and who are we to question that?

But in the case of bacon and sausages the torpor is particularly shameful, and the complacency particularly ill-founded, not least because there has in fact been much change in the means of production. The problem is that it has largely been invisible to the consumer. In the last fifty years the efficiency of factory-farming pork, the artifice of flavouring it and preserving it to resemble bacon, and the science of recovering every scrap of it for processing into sausages have come on by leaps and bounds. And while the welfare of the pigs has declined in inverse proportion to the scale of the operation, the manufacturers' increasing ability to hide the whole process from public scrutiny has more than compensated.

A third ingredient in the curious cocktail that leads to welfare blindness concerns the ambiguity of quality I mentioned at the beginning of this section. There's no denying that mass-produced pork can be made tempting by a skilful sausage maker. And even I would admit that the worst kind of bacon, injected with water and riddled with E-numbers, can – provided it is fried until crisp, smeared with ketchup and folded in a comforting wrap of similarly overprocessed white sliced bread – make a breakfast that is on certain occasions (for example, early-start filming days when you are ravenously hungry and nothing else is on offer) strangely gratifying. Cheap bacon and sausages from intensively farmed pigs are somehow not quite as unambiguously awful as raw pork from the same animals. Which makes the way they are produced just a little bit easier to overlook.

In the end, though, the potency of these products in the marketplace is based on an illusion. Cheap bacon and sausages may sometimes seem tempting and moreish, not because of any real qualities they possess but because of the combination of the comfort of familiarity and the deceptive, almost hallucinatory effect on the taste buds of artificial flavours and preservatives, such as monosodium glutamate, dextrose and a whole raft of E-numbers. As with bad Chinese food and cheese and onion crisps, there is a shallow, pharmaceutical gratification of the taste buds but little, if any, lasting pleasure or satisfaction. The moment you turn to comparable products of worthy provenance and true quality, you realise what a cheap trick (literally) it's been.

Take slow-grown, rare-breed pigs, make dry-cured streaky bacon from their backs and bellies, and sausages of coarsely ground pork from their neck and shoulders. Flavour the former with nothing more than salt, brown sugar and a little black pepper, the latter with a pinch of mace and a dash of white pepper, and you have all the robust flavour, deep savouriness and lasting pleasure that you could ever wish for from a rasher or a banger. You have a butty or a breakfast that will never fail you. And you have it with a clean conscience.

That's the benchmark to aspire to. Along the way, there will be some undeniably tempting offerings of dubious ethical background: butcher's bangers cunningly seasoned with a lifetime's skill and know-how – but from pork that cannot even muster an outdoor-reared label; dry-cured bacon that looks wonderfully authentic – but whose origin, on enquiry, turns out to be quite untraceable.

In the end, the fact that something is well made or tastes good is not a valid reason for lowering one's ethical guard. There is no reason why you can't have your ethical cake and eat it, even when it comes to bacon and sausages. The organic label may again provide useful steerage. Or, better still, with a bit of luck, the same small producer who solves your fresh pork problem will give you fine bacon, ham and sausages, too. If they don't yet cure their own pork, encourage them to give it a go – give them a copy of *The River Cottage Cookbook*!

Or have a go yourself. An afternoon spent salting bellies can, if you have a freezer, give you enough bacon for a year. A weekend of pig processing can provide the annual supply of sausages, hams and salami, too.

I have no doubt that tracing truly fine pork is the single biggest challenge facing the modern meat consumer. I am equally sure that facing that challenge, and cracking the problem, is one of the meat lover's ultimate rewards.

The Cuts

RECIPES
Brawn (p.486)

Head (A): It certainly takes some courage to go home with a pig's head in your shopping, and it may not be something you want to rush out and do tomorrow. But as your confidence and curiosity develop, and particularly if you get a taste for making terrines and charcuterie, I hope there will come a time when you want to try making a brawn. If so, ask the butcher to quarter the head for you – this should be done with a saw, not a cleaver, to avoid splinters of bone ending up in your brawn (you can also ask the butcher to salvage the brains and put them in a bag – see Offal, page 187).

Chaps (A): The chaps are the cheeks from the pig's head. Traditionally they were lightly brined for slow simmering to melting tenderness. They were then eaten hot or cold. They are very hard to come by these days, but if you have a good butcher of the old school, he might just be delighted to prepare some for you.

Ear (A): Can be removed from the head and treated separately – see Offal, page 185.

Cassoulet (p.302); Cotechino with Lentils and Salsa Verde (p.441); A Raised Pork Pie (p.444); Mexican-style Chorizo (p.446); Pork Rillettes (p.447); Feijoada (p.487); Chinese-style Spare Ribs and Pig's Trotters (p.490); Chilli con Carne (p.495)

Spare Rib Roast (B): Not to be confused with racks of spare ribs for marinating and barbecuing, this is a large joint from the shoulder of the pig, with a piece of the neck end of the chine (the split backbone) included, plus a few centimetres' length of the first ribs that are attached to it. Whether on the bone, or boned out, rolled up and tied, the spare rib is one of the prime roasting joints of pork. It has plenty of lean meat, but is also interlaced with fatty connective tissue that helps keep it well lubricated as it roasts. The same boneless joint can also be cured as COLLAR BACON, then boiled and/or baked and glazed.

Traditionally, the spare rib roast was subdivided into two smaller joints, the SPARE RIB and the BLADE. Few butchers make this distinction today, though some may remove the blade.

Hand (C): A small, parsimonious, bone-in joint on a porker, hand of pork actually becomes quite an impressive-sized piece on a large baconer. Cured on the bone, then boiled, it makes what butchers call the PICNIC HAM, and off the bone what the French call *jambonneau*. Uncured, the bone-in joint also works well for long, slow cooking – either slow roasting or, better still, a long, slow simmer with highly flavoured ingredients. In both cases, it should end up falling-off-the-bone tender.

Aromatic Shoulder of Pork 'Donnie Brasco' (p.231); Stir-fried Indonesian Pork (p.346); Cotechino with Lentils and Salsa Verde (p.441); A Raised Pork Pie (p.444); Mexican-style Chorizo (p.446); Pork Rillettes (p.447); Feijoada (p.487); Chilli con Carne (p.495)

Shoulder (B+C): The whole shoulder, comprising the spare rib, blade and hand, all undivided, makes for a massive on-the-bone roasting joint that will feed twenty plus. It is excellent for slow roasting – better even than a leg which, because it is so lean, may have a tendency to dryness. In particular, it is uniquely suited among pork joints for overnight cooking in a very low oven, a technique that results in supremely tender, almost 'spoonable' pork, comparable to a spit roast. However, a whole shoulder is not really a regular joint, so you may have to ask for it in advance from your butcher or small producer.

Cubed pork, either for slow cooking or stir-frying, is usually taken from the shoulder, and is sometimes labelled as 'cubed shoulder'. It's also good, lean meat for salami making, pork pies, cotechino etc.

Cotechino with Lentils and Salsa Verde (p.441)

Back Fat (B+C): Not exactly a cut of meat, but a useful porcine commodity even so. The layer of hard, subcutaneous fat may be as much as 3-4cm thick in a well-fattened pig. It doesn't come only from the back but also from the hams, shoulders and flanks. In the cuts that are jointed up for roasting with the skin (which will become the crackling) still attached, the fat obviously stays on the joint – between the meat and the crackling. But where a joint, often a shoulder/spare rib, is boned out and plundered for lean meat for stewing or mincing, the covering of fat may also be trimmed out. It can, of course, be rendered for lard (place in an ovenproof dish in a moderate oven, pouring off the liquid every twenty minutes or so, until all the fat has been rendered). But it can also be finely diced and included in dishes where you want it to retain some shape and texture rather than just melt into liquid. Its two classic uses are in black pudding and salami.

Barbecued Glazed Spare Ribs (p.397)

Hock (D): The first joint of the front leg, the bony part of the hand, can be removed, when it is called the hock. Mostly skin and bone, with a little tough meat and lots of connective tissue, it renders up plenty of gelatine and flavour – think of it either as a poor man's hand or a rich man's trotter. Like either, it can be used to make pork stock or added to stews to give body. A cured hock is known as a KNUCKLE of bacon – good for boiling with lentils, dried peas and other pulses. In both cases the gelatinous meat and skin can be chopped up and added back to whatever soup, stew or braise the hock is being used to flavour.

When the hock and picnic ham are removed from the hand, there's a funny bit left over called the STICKING. It's great for marinating and barbecuing.

ROLLED SPARE RIB ROAST

B+C. SHOULDER

B+C. BACK FAT

B. SPARE RIB ROAST

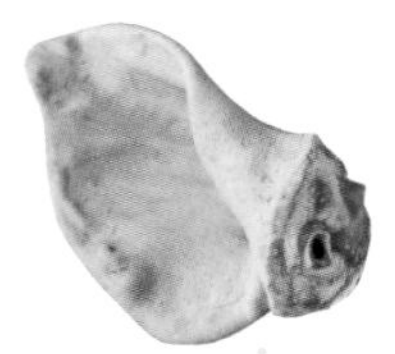

EAR

CHAPS (CHEEKS)

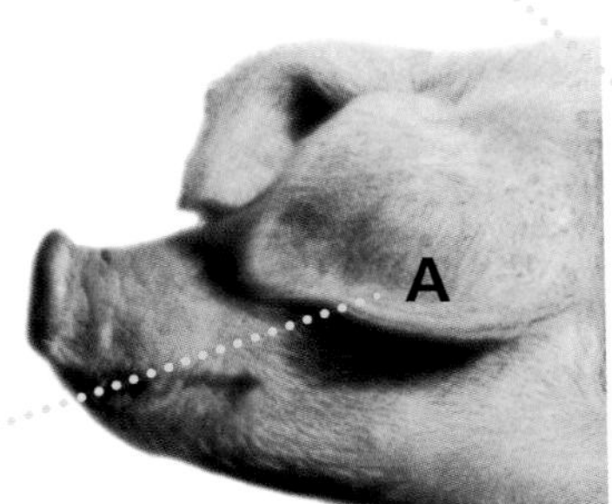

A. HEAD

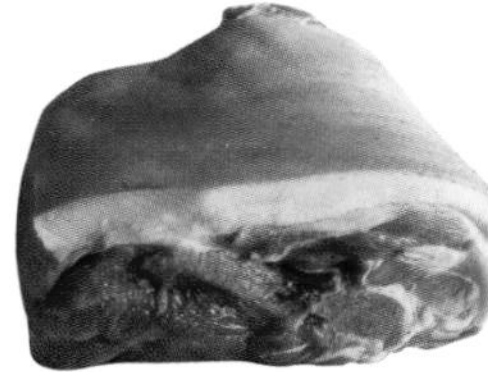

PICNIC HAM

STICKING

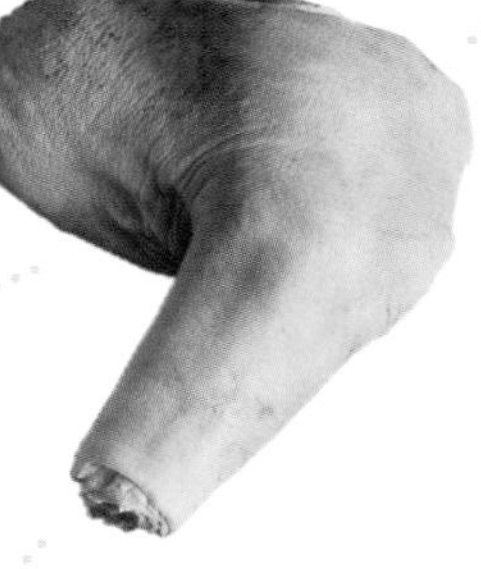

C+D. HAND & HOCK

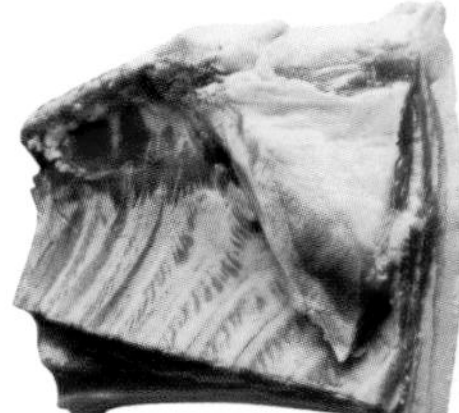

THICK END

D. HOCK

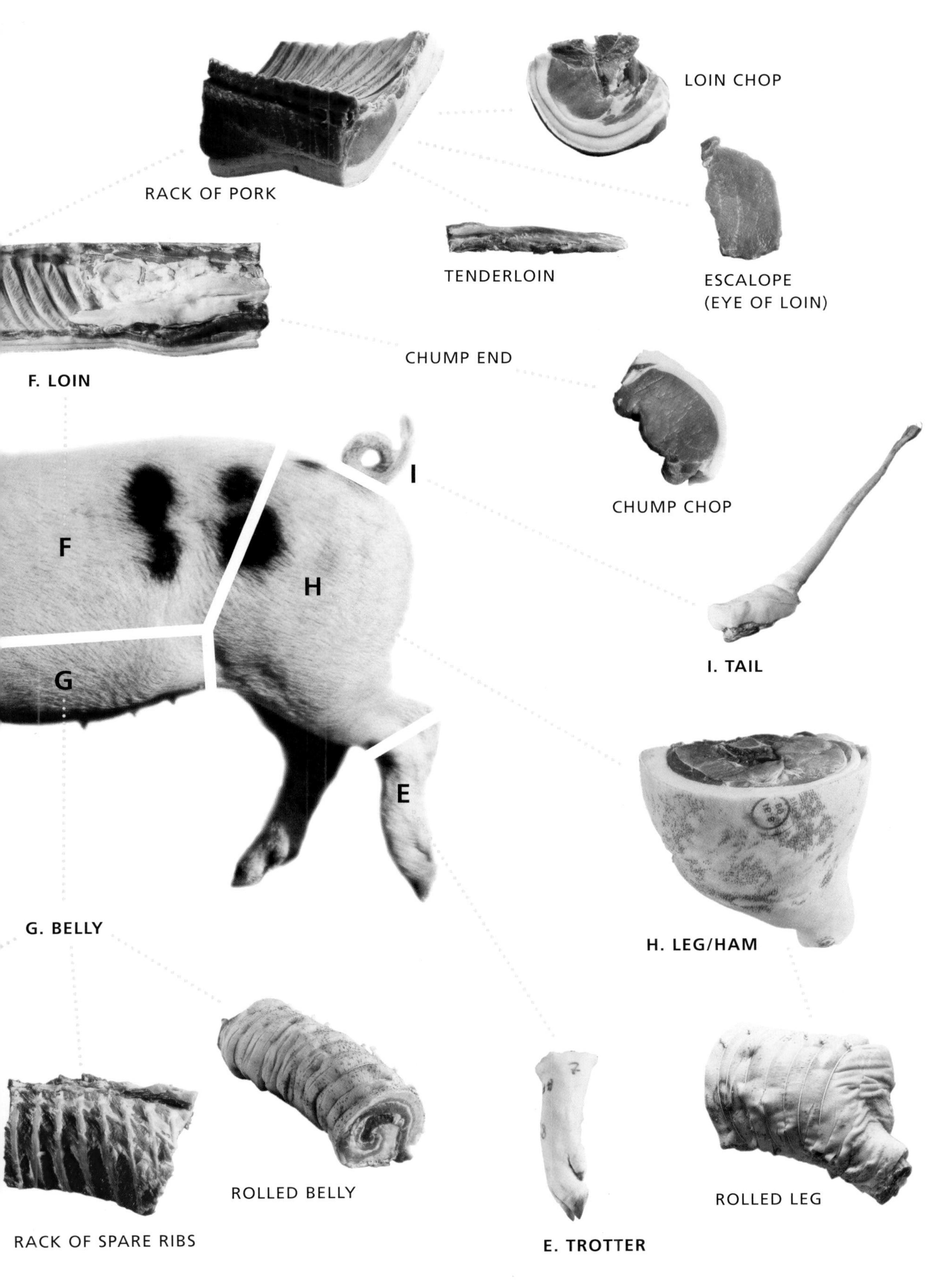

RACK OF PORK
LOIN CHOP
ESCALOPE
(EYE OF LOIN)
TENDERLOIN
F. LOIN
CHUMP END
CHUMP CHOP
I
F
H
I. TAIL
G
E
G. BELLY
H. LEG/HAM
RACK OF SPARE RIBS
ROLLED BELLY
E. TROTTER
ROLLED LEG

Pig's Trotters Ste Menehould (p.295); Brawn (p.486); Feijoada (p.487); Chinese-style Spare Ribs and Pig's Trotters (p.490)

Trotters (E): These, of course, are the feet of the pig, the ones from the front legs usually being cut longer than the ones from the back legs. The amount of meat on them is marginal, but what they offer the adventurous cook is something very precious – rich, gelatinous sinews, flavoursome, body-giving bone and a tough skin that can be simmered, over hours, to melting tenderness. The result is that they have a unique and almost revered place in many cooking cultures, although they are all too often overlooked by British cooks. For a more detailed appraisal of their merits, see Offal, page 190.

Rice Pudding Pork (p.278); Pan-to-oven Pork Chops with Garlic (p.342); Salt and Pepper Pork 'Squidlets' (p.345)

Loin (F): Loins are very long on a pig, and an undivided whole loin on the bone would produce a wonderful, lean roasting joint – though too big for most ovens. The classic roasting joint of bone-in loin, sometimes called a RACK OF PORK (*carré de porc* in French), comprises the first eight to ten ribs from the head end. Or the loin can be divided into three smaller roasting joints – FORELOIN, MIDDLE LOIN and CHUMP END (though not all butchers still make this distinction). Each of these joints can be subdivided into CHOPS. Chops from the foreloin are sometimes called pork cutlets. Middle loin chops would traditionally include a slice of kidney – sadly, that's now a rarity. And the chump chops are the most generous, being boneless, wider and leaner, as they run into the top of the leg.

Any loin joint can be boned out to give an excellent joint for stuffing, rolling and tying. The eye of the loin can be trimmed out and sliced to give pork ESCALOPES for sautéing. Cured, the loin will give you what is called BACK BACON or, if kept on the bone, old-fashioned bacon chops (sadly, very hard to find these days). A whole loin and belly cured together is a side of bacon, and the combined double rashers sliced from it are called middle bacon.

Mincemeat-stuffed Pork Tenderloins (p.229); Salt and Pepper Pork 'Squidlets' (p.345)

Tenderloin (F): This is the fillet of delicate lean meat that runs along the other side of the loin from the ribs (the pork equivalent of fillet steak). It is extra tender but dries out very easily if overcooked. This is why a tenderloin, or better still a pair, is often rolled up and tied with a nice, moist stuffing inside. There's also a good case for wrapping the parcel in well-greased foil or paper.

Roast Belly of Pork with Apple Sauce (p.226); Aromatic Pork Belly Hot Pot (p.277); Main-course Borscht (p.279); Beef in Stout (p.288); Cassoulet (p.302); Home-cured Bacon (p.429); Petit Salé (p.430); Cotechino with Lentils and Salsa Verde (p.441);

Belly (G): As you can see from the diagram on pages 118-19, the belly is about the same length as the loin, taken from the underside of the pig. Principally, belly is cured to make STREAKY BACON or pancetta but actually it is a far more versatile cut than it is often given credit for. For a start, the first third of the belly from the head end, known as the THICK END, makes a fabulous and forgiving roast – so richly fatted that it is almost impossible to overcook. It also produces outstanding crackling. Chunky cubes of pork belly can be slow roasted in their own fat with garlic and thyme, like a confit, to produce *rillons*. And they can also be slow braised, particularly with oriental flavours, to give meltingly tender meat and a pleasingly sticky skin in a highly aromatic dish to serve with noodles.

A Raised Pork Pie (p.444);
Mexican-style Chorizo (p.446);
Pork Rillettes (p.447);
Boston Baked Beans (p.484);
Feijoada (p.487);
Spaghetti Bolognese (p.497)

It is well worth buying bellies to try your hand at home-made bacon, and to draw attention to your prowess you can make a fine *petit salé* – a piece of boiled cured pork belly. Chunks of belly, uncured, plain cured, or cured and smoked, can be added to all sorts of stews and casseroles, particularly ones made with beef, venison and game, to help lubricate the meat while it cooks. And lastly, belly can be added to leaner meat from the blade and elsewhere for mincing, to give well-balanced, nicely fatted sausage meat.

Barbecued Glazed Spare Ribs (p.397);
Feijoada (p.487)

Spare Ribs (G): The spare ribs are those trimmed from inside the belly, especially the thick end. They'll always have a reasonable amount of meat attached, and between the ribs is a particularly promising blend of lean meat, fat and sinew, offering much finger-licking delight when properly prepared. Spare ribs generally come as a rack of five or six ribs, sometimes still attached to the breastbone if from the thick end, or just joined together by the meat and tissues between them. Some butchers cut them into pairs of ribs. The classic preparation, which can hardly be bettered when done well, is to marinate them, usually in a sweet and sour glaze, then barbecue or bake them, basting with the glaze so they become well coated.

A Cider-cured Ham (p.432);
Glazed Baked Ham California (p.433);
Ham in Hay (p.435)

Leg/Ham (H): Most legs of pork go for curing, to make hams. A whole leg produces a massive ham on the bone, of the kind you might glaze and bake for Christmas, serve hot once, then keep carving cold for friends and family well into the New Year. Since few households will want to embrace such a mammoth cut more than once or twice a year, most legs are now divided into two or three smaller hams: CORNER GAMMON, FILLET END and KNUCKLE END. The corner gammon is a boneless piece, while the fillet end and knuckle may be on or off the bone.

Not all legs are cured for ham, and the same cuts may be dressed as fresh pork. The corner fillet, effectively a continuation of the chump end of the loin, will usually be sliced and sold as PORK LEG STEAKS. The fillet end and knuckle are sold as roasting joints, either on the bone or boned, rolled and tied. The leg is very lean, so you need the best possible pork for a roast that won't dry out – a good layer of fat to protect it, plus as much marbling as possible. Slow roasting will keep the meat tender, with just a blast of heat at the end to crackle the crackling.

Tail (I): See Offal, page 188.

A Raised Pork Pie (p.444);
Rich Liver Pâté (p.452);
Pasticcio (p.491);
Picadillo (p.494);
Chilli con Carne (p.495);
Thai Pork Dumplings (p.508)

Minced Pork/Sausage Meat: A butcher (or supermarket) will put all kinds of odd bits of pork through the mincer for sausage meat, and usually mince it very finely so it's almost a paste. If the pork is of good quality, then this kind of sausage meat is useful enough for pâtés, stuffings, meatballs etc. But for home-made sausages, I prefer a more considered, roughly 50:50 combination of lean meat from the shoulder and fattier belly, minced on a coarser setting. A good butcher should be happy to mince your chosen cuts of pork (or any other meat) to your specification.

7. POULTRY

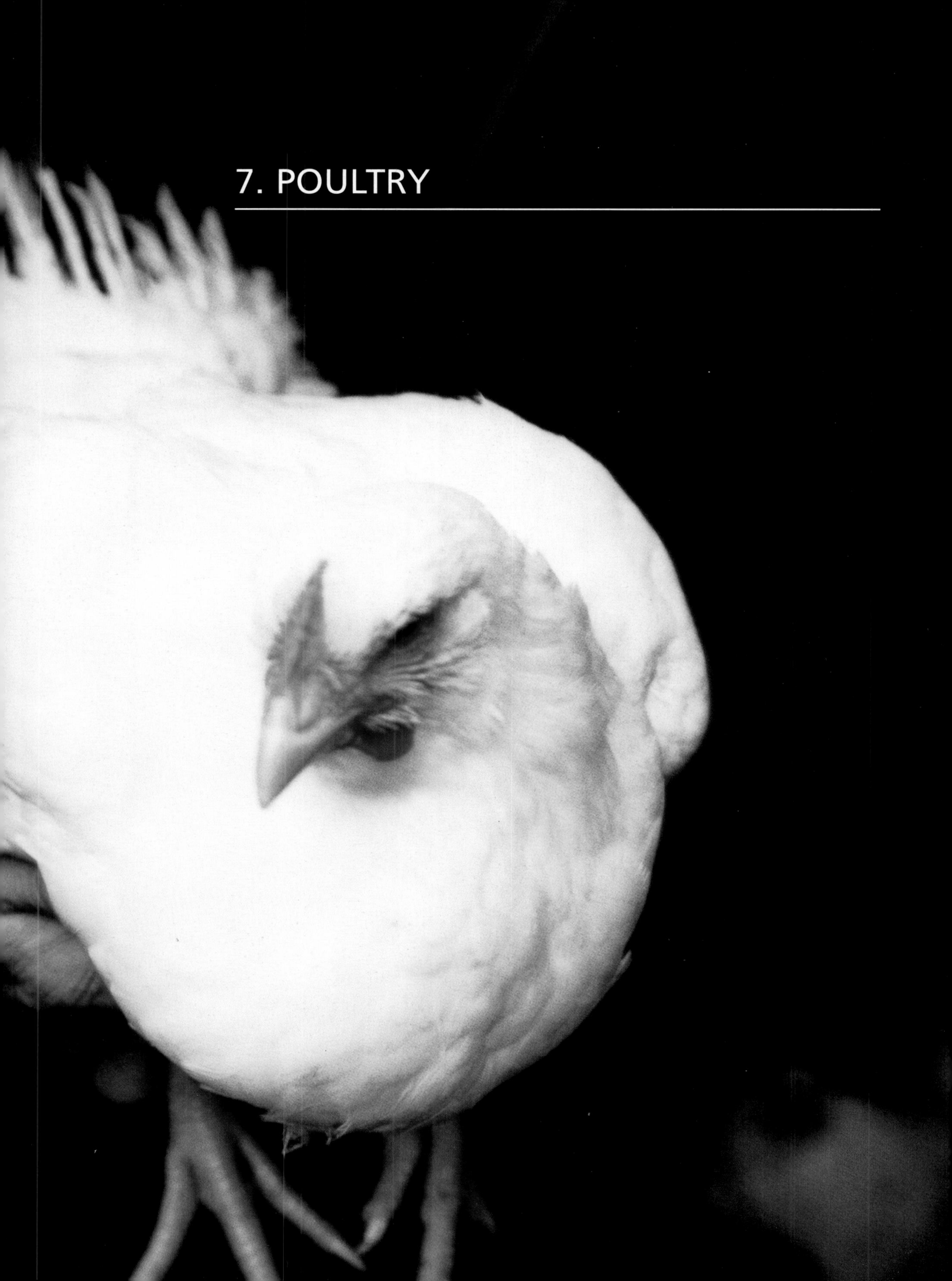

7. POULTRY

Roast chicken is an iconic dish in British culture. It probably ranks close to the top of most people's list of favourite foods – right up there with roast beef, fish and chips, and ... well, chicken tikka masala.

Roast chicken has put down deep roots in our food culture. It thrives as something loved not only for what it is but for what it represents. It may be affordable for the masses but it is also fit for a king. A whole bird, slaughtered for the nourishment and pleasure of the entire family, is a conspicuous display – if not of serious wealth, then at least of comfort and contentment.

These days it is also one of the few family meals that demands to be eaten at the table rather than in front of the telly. And, more importantly perhaps, it is one of the few dishes that is actually capable of getting disparate family members around that table without protest. The brooding teenager, the disapproving granny, the flown-the-nest careerist ... all can be lured back into the mother kitchen with the promise of the sizzle of a roasting bird – and roast potatoes, of course.

This is pretty remarkable. We live in a world where convenience, portability and branding dominate our daily food choices and threaten to overwhelm all sense of tradition, self-reliance and shared values. Like it or not, we are a fast-food nation. Against this background, the roast chicken is almost unique among old-fashioned, home-cooked dishes in its ability to withstand the culture of instant gratification, and to continue to command the respect and attention of all.

This is not a mass romantic illusion. A good roast chicken has real culinary merit: crisp skinned yet succulent, savoury but delicate, robust but digestible – these are the qualities of the bird that ensure it will always remain special, however familiar it is. No wonder the chef and food writer Simon Hopkinson (whose gift, besides good writing and good cooking, is impeccably good judgement about food) gave it the lead in his brilliant book, *Roast Chicken and Other Stories* (Ebury Press, 1994). His procedure for roasting a bird outlined in that book is exemplary, and the basis for my own roast chicken in this book.

That's chicken at its best. But, as we all know, there is a flip side. And it's a dark side. The bad, sad story of chicken at its worst is perhaps the baddest, saddest story in the whole sorry business of modern meat production. It's a story of corporate greed, systematically cruel farming practices and, in some cases, outright criminality. It's a story of the unstoppable force of globally branded advertising, aimed at brainwashing the young and the financially vulnerable; of the shameful secrecy of farming behind barbed wire, intended not to keep animals in but inquisitive humans out; and of the adulteration, disguise and illegal distribution of a food that is barely fit for human consumption. It's the story of nuggets, bargain buckets, breaded drumsticks and 'turkey ham' (whatever the hell that is), along with dirt-cheap poultry meat from all over the world that is frozen, defrosted, injected with a cocktail of watery proteins and preservatives, then refrozen before being packed off to a takeaway, school canteen or supermarket near you. For the very same bird that graces the family table to spread such warmth and provoke such relish is also the prime ingredient in the junk food culture that threatens to undermine that family table forever.

I have neither the time nor the space here to lay out in full detail the specific cases against the companies and individuals who perpetrate this sorry state of affairs. But it's hardly a secret who the culprits are: the big fast-food chains; all the major players in the factory farming of poultry; the big four supermarkets who pressurise farmers constantly to deliver cheaper and cheaper meat; and the companies (mostly Continental) who use dubious, and in some cases banned, technologies and substances to bulk up and process poultry meat. Plus, at the truly criminal end of the business, a few nameless, faceless gangs who complete the dirty work, as it were, by recycling condemned poultry meat illegally back into the food chain.

All these businesses are almost entirely dependent for their supplies of chicken meat on the broiler industry (broiler is the industry name for a chicken reared for meat, rather than for egg laying). The UK broiler industry rears and slaughters between 750 and 800 million chickens each year (that's almost fifteen chickens a year for each of us). A staggering 98 per cent of all these broiler chickens are reared in intensive indoor systems. Less than 2 per cent are free range or organic. What this means, of course, is that almost any chicken meat you encounter anywhere – in supermarkets and fast-food takeaways, as well as schools, hospitals and most pubs and restaurants – is, unless it is clearly and boldly stated otherwise, from intensively farmed birds. (I think we can assume that anybody selling or serving the remaining 2 per cent of free-range or organic birds will be sure to let us know of the superior provenance of their product.)

I've already described in Chapter 2 some of the physical horrors of intensive poultry farming – for example, the cruel practice of de-beaking and the phenomenon of smothers (page 33). But let me fill in a few more details. Broilers live in one large shed, usually housing between 10,000 and 40,000 birds. The typical stocking density is around 36-38 kg per square metre. In their last week of life, this is equivalent to each bird having a living space just a little smaller than this page. The recommended maximum in the guidelines issued by the Department of Environment, Food and Rural Affairs (Defra) is actually 34 kg per square metre. But this is not legally enforceable, and most producers argue that they cannot deliver chicken at the price demanded by the supermarkets without exceeding this density. The birds are generally reared on an eight-week cycle, known as a 'crop'. It takes just six weeks (forty-one to forty-three days) to rear the chicks to slaughter weight. (At home, outdoors, on grass, the old-fashioned roasting breeds that I rear for the pot take at least three times that – twenty weeks or more). The business of the remaining two weeks is to clear, clean, and disinfect the sheds in preparation for the next crop. (The floor, which is covered with a litter of woodshavings, is not cleaned at all during the six-week period.)

The average premature mortality rate is about 6 per cent (though in some crops, due to the occurrence of suicidal 'smothers', the loss may be anything up to 30 per cent). This means that each year in the UK, over 50 million chickens die before they reach their slaughter weight. In theory, these birds are banned from the human food chain, and go to make pet food, fertiliser, or maggots for anglers. But it is far from rare for this meat to be illegally recycled for human consumption.

The life cycle of the broiler chicken is somewhat different from its parent and grandparent birds, which are specially selected not for meat but for breeding. The genetic stock for intensive farming has been, for many years, systematically selected for its ability to put on weight rapidly with minimal energy input (i.e. feed). This means that the most popular broiler breed, the Ross Cobb, bred especially for fast growth within an intensive system, has both an unnatural appetite and an unnatural ability to convert feed to meat. Effectively the stock is now genetically obese. This of course, in conjunction with special high-protein feeds that routinely contain growth-promoting antibiotics, is how a slaughter weight of 1.5-2kg is achieved in such a short space of time.

Birds raised on this regime would never be able to breed. Their obesity would inhibit the development of their sexual organs – and almost certainly kill them before they reached sexual maturity anyway. So birds selected for breeding must be placed on a very restrictive feed regime. In the end, it takes them eighteen weeks to reach sexual maturity and the same 2kg slaughter weight as their siblings reared for meat would achieve in just six. But though breeding stock have a longer life, it is not a cushier one. They are in a near-permanent state of hunger, a symptom of which is that they drink water incessantly.

Broiler chicks will never see their mothers and consequently lack the gut micro-flora of their parents that would naturally be passed on if their feeding space was shared. In health terms, this constitutes a severe handicap from the start. It makes them highly susceptible to air- and food-borne pathogens – which in turn cause the diseases that help to create those premature mortality statistics. And it's the principal reason they are heavily dosed with antibiotics and other prophylactic drugs, most of which are routinely delivered in their feeds.

As you can imagine, there are many health problems associated with these gulag-like conditions and abnormal growth rates. But in terms of the welfare of the birds, there is one particular health statistic that makes chilling reading, and little is being done to relieve it. Rapid weight gain combined with severely restricted movement means that skeletal and muscular development in the legs of the birds is highly compromised. Severe abnormalities of bone development are common. A report published by the University of Bristol found that almost 90 per cent of broiler chickens have leg problems. Over one in four birds suffered 'an abnormality of sufficient severity that their welfare was compromised'.

As a result of these problems, large numbers of the birds spend their last days or even weeks literally on their knees. It's led to an industry phenomenon known as 'hock burns' – areas of dark discoloration around the knee joints. For a time it was thought that these were a form of friction sore – caused by rubbing. It's now known that in fact these injuries are ammonia burns, caused by the high levels of this chemical saturating the litter from the birds' faeces.

Hock burns, even severe ones, will not disqualify a bird from entering the human food chain. The result is that these are among the very few of an intensively reared broiler's many potential health problems that are clearly visible to the consumer (in a clingwrapped, whole, oven-ready bird, you can see them through the packaging, around the knee joints). In a national survey conducted by Compassion in World Farming (CIWF) in 1996, it was found that all the major supermarkets were stocking chickens with hock burns. None of the supermarkets I spoke to in researching this book could claim to have eliminated the problem.

It's clear that the freakish genetic disposition of these birds means that decent welfare standards are almost impossible to achieve, as susceptibility to painful malformation and disease is now 'hard-wired' into the stock. It is this abominable fact that in 2003 led CIWF to take Defra and the government to the High Court. The legal essence for its case is to be found in the EU's 1998 General Farm Animals Directive. Paragraph 21 of the Directive's Annex provides that 'no animal shall be kept for farming purposes unless it can reasonably be expected, on the basis of its genotype ... that it can be kept without detrimental effect on its health or welfare'. You would have thought in the face of such clear-cut legislation, the broiler industry and Defra, whose welfare regulations uphold the disputed practices, haven't got a malformed chicken leg to stand on. Furthermore, Paragraph 14 of the Annex stipulates that animals must be given a sufficient quantity of food to maintain them in good health and satisfy their nutritional needs. The systematic starving of parent and grandparent birds as part of the breeding cycle would seem to be in clear breach of this article too.

Yet, predictably perhaps, the outcome of this legal action went in favour of big business and the government. Their vested interests were simply too huge, and their lawyers too well-resourced, for good sense, and arguably good law, to prevail.

In conclusion of our whirlwind tour (believe me, I have spared you much gory detail – about transport and slaughter, for example) of the lifestyle of the intensively farmed broiler, let's save a final word for the supermarkets, most of which are falling over themselves to cite the Five Freedoms as the basis of their farm animal welfare practice. Freedom from hunger and thirst. Freedom from discomfort. Freedom from pain, injury and disease. Freedom to express normal behaviour. Freedom from fear and distress. Yet there is no question that the intensive broiler industry – which, remember, rears 98 per cent of all meat chickens in this country – is failing dismally on all five counts. Or, to put it another way, it is wilfully inflicting on its animals what we may re-term the Five Miseries: Hunger and thirst.

Discomfort. Pain, injury and disease. Abnormal behaviour. Fear and distress. Stick that on the label of a supermarket chicken and see how it sells.

I hope you hardly need further reasons to boycott intensively farmed poultry. But if you really want them, they can be found in the bland, white, tasteless pap that is the meat of these birds. The lack of flavour is not in the mind of the spoiled gourmet. It is such a serious problem for the fast-food industry that beef extract is routinely injected into factory-farmed chicken meat to compensate.

Shopping for Poultry

So far I've referred mainly to chicken, but I want to emphasise that it would be a mistake to imagine that the other birds farmed for meat escape the horrors of intensive production. Turkeys, ducks, geese and even guinea fowl and quail (all of which I will discuss individually below) have been subjected to the intense pressures of production systems based on accelerated growth and mass crowding. In every case the mission is to push these creatures to the limits of their physical tolerance, or more often, a little beyond them. The grisly attitude of this hard-nosed industry is that if you're not losing at least a small percentage of your stock, then you're guilty of inefficiency – it must be possible to cram a few more birds in and push the system just a little bit harder.

If I've tried not to hector and preach too much in the preceding chapters (you hadn't noticed?), perhaps it's because I've been saving the full-on pleading until now. I'm going to cut to the chase and make a very straightforward proposal. In your approach to buying poultry meat, of all kinds, I'd like you to make a fresh start. Draw a line in the sand (or the butcher's sawdust, or even the tiled floor of the supermarket aisle). From now on, don't even consider factory-farmed poultry meat as an option. Wipe it off your mental food radar. Shun it and refuse it wherever you find it: in a sandwich, a chill cabinet, a soup tin or a restaurant.

Yes, I realise that, taking into account the statistics I've presented above, I'm asking you to reject a full 98 per cent of the entire UK production of broiler chickens (and probably something close to that for turkeys and ducks as well). I'm asking you to agree that of the 750 million chickens produced for meat each year, over 735 million are not even worthy of your attention. Why? Because they are barely edible rubbish produced by ignorance, greed and cruelty. And why, honestly, would you want any part of that?

Free-range Poultry

This means you have a new starting point (from which, as I will explain shortly, there is still considerable room for improvement). From now on only free-range poultry is admissible in your enlightened spectrum of the shopping and eating of poultry (and, of course, eggs). You're interested only in that remarkable, elitist 2 per cent of happy, carefree, cosseted birds. I'm asking you to be a born-again poultry snob. Or am I?

If my evangelical fervour seems extravagant or excessive, just consider for a moment what is implied by the term, free range. It means, or ought to mean, that the movement of birds is unrestricted. That they can roam where they please. Does this strike you as an unusually luxurious lifestyle allowance for a bird? Are we talking about unnecessary pampering? Hardly.

The problem is that the food industry is addicted to a kind of Orwellian doublespeak, where it tells us only what it thinks we want to hear. In the surreal world of food labelling terminology, the Ministry of Truth really is the Ministry of Lies. Because if labelling was in any way fair, true or genuinely descriptive, there would be a legal obligation to label non-free-range chickens with a similarly meaningful epithet – and we would all be familiar with the concept of 'confined-space' chickens, perhaps, or 'cage-bound' poultry. When you think about it like this, it is entirely clear and logical that free range should be the norm. The idea that it represents some unusual degree of freedom for a chicken is absurd. It is, at best (and even this turns out to be debatable, as we shall see), a baseline standard of decency in poultry husbandry. The appalling truth is that it just so happens that 98 per cent of the entire industry fall below this standard.

There is one obvious and unavoidable objection to my plea for a fresh start – that free-range poultry is so much more expensive. And as for organic birds – well, you'd better take out a second mortgage to get one of those. It's hard to know what to say to that, especially as I'm arguing from the relatively comfortable position of someone who doesn't have to worry unduly about the price of poultry.

The tricky situation we are in is that in general terms, the shopping population of Britain thinks that a little over £3 is about the right price for a 1.5-2 kg chicken. If you start asking a fiver for it, they'll think that's a rip-off. And if you tell them they should be ready to pay around £10 for a slow-grown, organic, corn-fed bird, then you should probably expect their language to get a touch colourful.

Well, I guess I'd better prepare myself for some strong verbals, because I'm afraid that really is precisely what I want to argue. The simple truth is that the horrible, artificial means of production mean that poultry prices are horribly, artificially low. Last week I heard a supermarket was bashing out discounted chickens at £1.59 each. A couple of aisles over they were selling 2 kg bags of potatoes for £1.99.

We should and must be ready to pay more, to encourage the industry to move away from an intensive system that is intrinsically abusive. It's time to acknowledge that what lies at the heart of the system of production for the commodity known as chicken is not a mechanical, electronic or chemical process but a living, breathing, feeling animal – also, as it happens, called a chicken. And whilst I would never presume to dictate how a family genuinely struggling to balance its food budget should choose to spend its money, I'm sure that those of us for whom a few extra quid on the price of a bird would scarcely sting at all number not in the thousands, or even hundred thousands, but in the millions. And that's enough to make a huge difference.

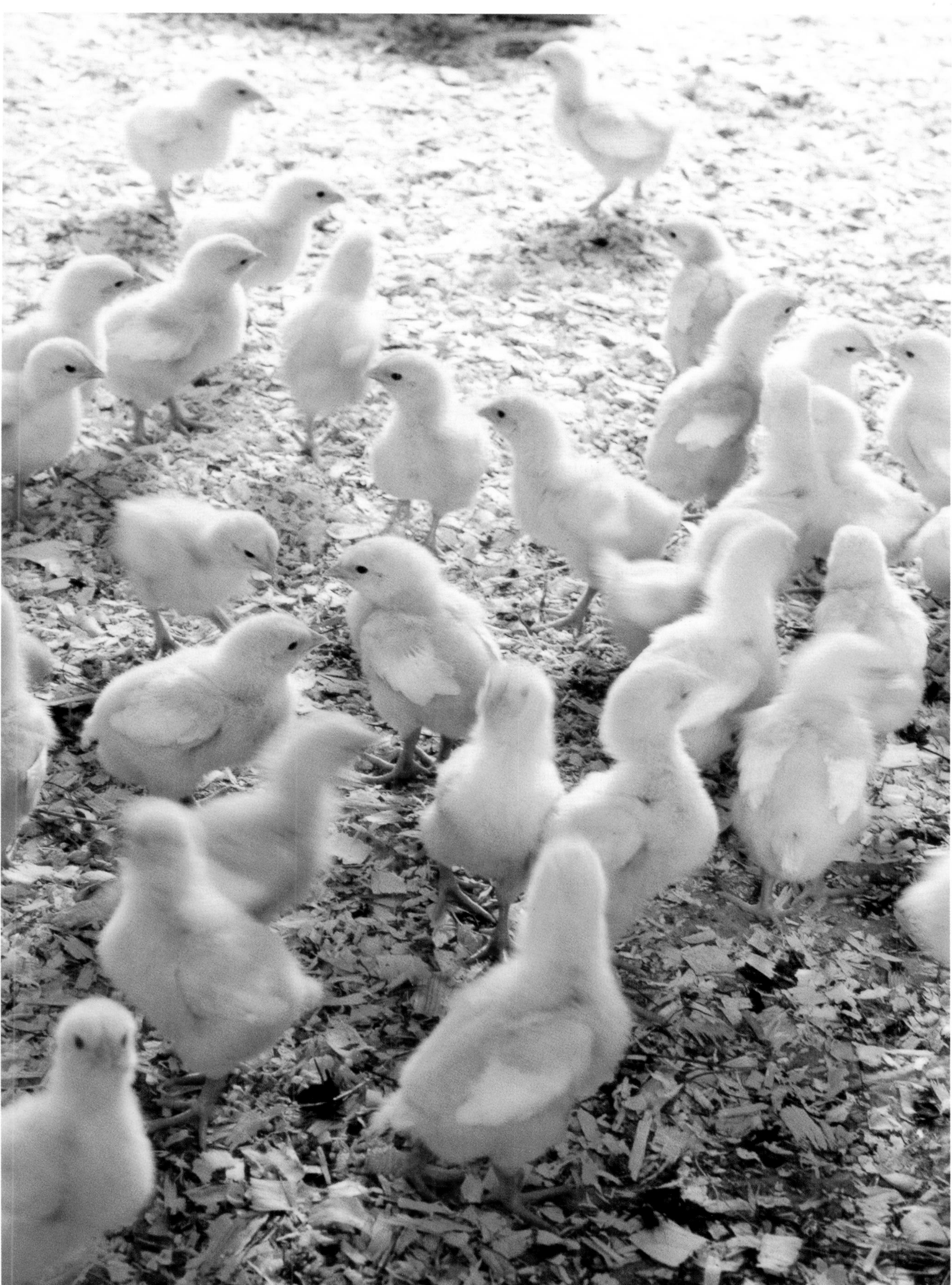

How free is free range?

Although I genuinely believe that the concept of 'free range', and the spirit of that phrase, is the correct starting point for the appropriate husbandry of farmed poultry, there is no doubt that it is being applied, in practice, with alarming flexibility. Just as some of the inhabitants of Orwell's *Animal Farm* turned out to be more equal than others, so some free-range birds are a lot freer than others.

As you would expect, any poultry product calling itself free range must conform to regulations regarding indoor stocking densities and access to an outdoor run. However, other welfare factors – for example, transport conditions to slaughter, as well as heating, lighting, ventilation and feeding regimes – remain more or less the same as for broiler chickens. Incidentally, the current legal indoor stocking density for free-range chickens is 27.5 kg of birds per square metre (a small but significant improvement on the intensive houses' recommended maximum of 34 kg per square metre). The real supposed freedom comes, of course, in the compulsory allowance of outdoor space (a reasonably generous square metre for every bird). These birds also reach a minimum slaughter age of fifty-one days (as opposed to forty-one to forty-three). This reflects the extra time needed to get them to slaughter weight, given that exercise, and lower average temperatures from time spent outdoors, affects their ability to convert food into meat.

The problem is what is referred to as 'minimal compliance'. The phrase alludes to farms whose basic objective is to observe only the letter of the regulations, so they can continue to produce poultry as cheaply as possible under the scheme and create the greatest possible margin between their production costs and the marked-up price they can expect to ask for poultry carrying the free-range label.

So, even at 27.5 kg per square metre, free-range poultry is often still so overcrowded that the normal behaviour patterns – essential if the birds are to seek and use their allowance of outdoor space – are compromised. In other words, although technically the birds have the choice to be free range, in practice they remain too stressed and confused to make that choice. The so-called 'popholes' that give them access to their outdoor range may be too small or too far apart (or both) for all but a few of the birds to find, let alone use. So, without good husbandry – effectively, adequate encouragement to roam in the form of wide exits and entrances and outdoor feeding stations – a bird may be free range in label but scarcely in life.

At the same time, whilst free-range stocking densities are regulated and monitored, the breed selected for them is, in most free-range systems, the very same genetically obese Ross Cobb used in the intensive broiler house. The ad-lib feeding regimes are similar, too. The result is that problems associated with poor leg development, whilst significantly reduced on account of the birds' increased ability to exercise, are by no means eliminated.

So, how do you tell genuine free-range poultry from the products of cynical, minimal-compliance practice? Well, under EC regulations there are two further subcategories of free range that offer improved welfare beyond the norm. The term 'traditional free range' has been defined in order to encourage the use of 'mobile home' free-range systems, in which smaller houses on wheels can be moved from tired to fresh pasture – thereby increasing the quality of natural forage. It also requires a further-improved indoor stocking density of 25kg per square metre. This is important in that this is the density at which major improvements in problems associated with skeletal development begin to be seen. Outdoor allowances are doubled: to 2 square metres per bird. The standards also stipulate a minimum slaughter age of eighty-one days, effectively requiring farmers to use slower-growing breeds with which it is much easier to maintain welfare.

A further-improved version of this is the label using the phrase 'free range – total freedom'. The regulations are broadly the same, except that the open-air runs are of 'unlimited area' (which actually means more than 5 square metres per bird) and access must be continual during daylight hours.

In both cases I'm inclined to say, 'Now you're talking.' Unfortunately, the uptake of these systems is pitifully small in the UK (a few exceptions are discussed below). In France, by contrast, the equivalent standard of free range (which they call Label Rouge) now accounts for 30 per cent of all chickens sold whole for the table.

It is also worth remembering, as I mentioned in Chapter 3, Buying Meat, that the RSPCA Freedom Food label on a roasting chicken does not imply that the bird is free range. However, the scheme does have an improved stocking density for broiler houses compared to the industry norm – a maximum of 30kg per square metre. The scheme has separate standards for free range, and these are also marginally more rigorous than the legal minimum. So, whilst not all birds sporting the RSPCA Freedom Food label are genuinely free range, those that also carry a free-range label are perhaps a little better than 'minimal-compliance' free-range birds. It's confusing, I know, but worth getting to grips with.

On the other hand, I'm afraid that Little Red Tractor is no help at all. You'll see it proudly sported on many a clingwrapped roasting bird but there is nothing exceptional about its welfare standards, and the vast majority of birds bearing the mark are from bog-standard intensive broiler houses.

Another poultry label that is often misinterpreted is the one that tells you a chicken has been 'corn fed'. Feeding corn, or maize, to chickens is, in general, a good idea. It improves the flavour of the bird – especially compared to those whose feed is based on fishmeal and/or soya. The fact that corn-fed birds are more expensive, and are often marketed in the supermarket as somehow being the 'gourmet choice', leads many shoppers to *assume* there are also some welfare improvements involved in the production of these birds. This is emphatically not the case. Unless they also carry an unequivocal free-range label, 'corn-fed' birds come from the same kind of intensive broiler houses as the bog-standard birds. And most corn-fed birds are *not* labelled free range.

The future of free range

Evidently what is urgently required is the development of genuine free-range systems that are not dependent on the genetically obese Ross Cobb for their stock. Unfortunately very few of the big free-range producers are taking the trouble to experiment with what you might call more 'welfare friendly' breeds. One exception is a company called Lloyd Maunder, which happens to be based here in the West Country. I contacted it by way of research for this book, and when the boss, David Lanning, offered to take me on a tour of some of its free-range and organic farms I leapt at the chance. But I insisted on seeing one of its intensive broiler houses first. It confirmed my worst fears – and informed much of what I have already written in this chapter. The sight of 40,000 birds in a hot, stinking, strip-lit shed immediately provoked two overriding thoughts which I would expect anyone who ever enters such a place to have: 'This is not right', and 'I don't want to eat one of these'.

However, I am grateful to David Lanning for his time, his honesty and openness, and for one telling comment in particular. He explained that he and his farmers would love to be able to lower the stocking densities in the sheds and improve the welfare conditions of the birds. But without the support of the supermarkets that he supplies, such a move would be commercial suicide. It would push the cost of his birds up to a price the supermarket buyers would simply not be prepared to pay. It is nothing more nor less than competition on price that has driven the industry to its current intensive practices.

Lloyd Maunder is a big player in this industry – packaging over 350,000 chickens a week, mainly for the supermarkets – and it deals with a large number of farms in the West Country, providing chickens for all sectors of the market. Most of its business is still in intensive broiler birds, of the kind I would passionately urge you to avoid. But some of its recent initiatives show that it is open to the idea of change – and particularly improved welfare. To this extent, it could be said to represent a glimmer of hope for the future of the industry.

Partly as a result of dialogue with CIWF, it has introduced into many of its free-range systems a slower-growing breed of chicken called the Hubbard ISA. Production to slaughter weight takes around eighty-five to ninety days – around double that of the Cobb. Stocking densities are well within free-range limits. Nor do the parent and grandparent breeding stock require the starvation rations of the Cobb-based systems, and their feeding is adapted to a far more normal pattern.

I went to visit just such a free-range farm with David. Although it was raining, I found around half of the 2,000 birds from each shed were outside, scratching among trees that had been specially planted to give them cover and environmental stimulus. Those who chose to remain inside had bales of straw to perch on, which many made use of. The demeanour of these birds was entirely different from the cowering, stumbling gait of the intensively farmed Cobbs in the broiler house. I wouldn't want to use the word 'happy', and maybe I'd hesitate over 'contented', but I'd at least say that they were not unduly stressed – chickens allowed to do, for the most part, what chickens are inclined to do. It struck me that if a video of this 'lifestyle' were playing on a monitor above the chill cabinet of the supermarket where such birds were being sold, alongside similar footage of the intensively farmed birds, the intensive industry would be on its knees in a matter of weeks. I'm convinced that hardly anyone faced with such explicit illustration at the point of purchase could choose the factory-farmed bird over the free range, whatever the price differential.

David also told me about a pilot scheme he is backing to develop a more humane (i.e. less intensive) broiler house system – not free range (because they will have no outdoor access) but nevertheless based on these slower-growing birds reared at significantly lower stocking densities. Effectively he is aiming to create a welfare middle way between the intensive and the free-range birds, and an in-between price to match. He is hoping to persuade RSPCA Freedom Foods to back the scheme, and one of his supermarket customers to guarantee to take the birds.

I have mixed feelings about this kind of enterprise. Whilst my own preference would be to see companies like this going all out to embrace and promote free-range, slower-growing systems across the board, I suppose we must accept that change will only ever be incremental. All improvements should be welcomed, so that as many consumers as possible can 'upgrade' to an improved-welfare chicken at a price with which they feel comfortable.

David also reminded me that initiatives of his, even when supported by the supermarkets, ultimately depend on the support of the consumer for their momentum and success. We can, he told me, bring a spectacular end to the intensive broiler industry any time we like, by simply refusing to buy the intensively farmed product. He's right, of course. I say, let's get on with it.

Organic Poultry

The last farm I went to visit with David was an organic one. And for the first time I found myself looking at a chicken I was actually quite interested in eating. The birds were housed in small mobile sheds that could be towed around the farm, giving the chickens almost unlimited access to open pasture. The farmer explained that, along with an organic, GM-free pellet, grass, weeds, grubs and bugs played an important part in the birds' diet.

I remain convinced that, for the time being at least, probably the only label on poultry that is categorically able to remove doubts about welfare and feed quality is the organic one – and the most rigorous is the one awarded by the Soil Association. It has a set of welfare regulations that go beyond conventional free range. Yes, there are organic poultry producers who will push stocking densities to the maximum allowable (25 kg per square metre) and bring the production period to the minimum allowable. And many organic farmers continue to favour the Ross Cobb, not least because there are so few alternatives available. However, the good news is that, where Soil Association rules are applied, even such minimal compliance assures a reasonable standard of welfare, a good quality of feed (free of antibiotics and GM ingredients), and systems of outdoor access that genuinely encourage birds to get outside and graze and forage with the sun on their backs. So, even though there are degrees of organic compliance, what we can safely say is that there is no such thing as an intensively farmed organic chicken.

However, I'd like to think we can do even better than that. We should be concerned not just about welfare assurances but also about excellence in taste. What is of most interest to those seeking a really worthwhile bird for the table is a poultry farm where the objective is not profit through minimal compliance and maximum mark-up but through sheer quality. I'm talking about organic producers who select traditional slower-growing meat breeds, give them a feed based not on soya but on whole organic grains, use mobile housing to ensure their stock always have plenty of natural forage on fresh pasture, and take them to slaughter not when they hit a certain date in the diary but when a proper examination indicates that they are ready. They then dry-pluck them and hang them properly to ensure a fully developed flavour.

There are not many such producers in this country. But there is undoubtedly room in the market for many more. Those I know who have decided to take this approach have found that the response has been phenomenal. My friends, Pammy and Ritchie Riggs, at Providence Farm in Devon have won awards for their slow-grown organic chickens. Sometimes they have to ration their loyal and regular customers to a bird or two a month just to keep up with demand. Take steps to acquire such a bird for yourself (using the Directory at the back of this book) and you'll soon see what all the fuss is about. There is really no better incentive for giving up intensively farmed poultry than tasting a bird that has roamed free and foraged naturally.

Poultry at the Butcher's

Obviously, given all that I have said above, I want you to find a butcher who stocks poultry that is at least free range – preferably organic. Beyond that, the more extra information your butcher can give you about the provenance of the birds – for example, that they are GM free and corn fed – the more you can be assured that they have been sourced wisely and well.

Unfortunately, some butchers have also begun to grasp the rudiments of poultry doublespeak. 'They're not free range but they are local' is a response you may encounter from time to time. It is, of course, wholly inadequate. Just because the gulag is only a few miles down the road, it doesn't mean the inmates are any happier (or tastier!) than those on the other side of the country.

If your butcher is reluctant to take the trouble to source something better for you, then whatever you think about the rest of his meat range, for your poultry at least, go elsewhere.

Poultry in the Supermarket

Supermarkets are aware that feelings about poultry husbandry have already pricked the surface of public consciousness. In the last twenty years, sales of free-range eggs have risen from almost nowhere to account for roughly 35 per cent of all supermarket egg sales. Yet when it comes to meat birds rather than layers, the ethical market has been far slower to make inroads into the conventional one. Clearly the life of an intensively farmed broiler chicken is at least as miserable as that of a battery-caged layer. It's only a matter of time before this begins to percolate through to the shopper's conscience (and the sooner the better).

Despite the still underwhelming demand, all the supermarkets now stock at least a few free-range chickens in most of their stores. And most of them carry organic poultry in their larger branches. What this tells us is that they are already poised to respond to public demand for more ethically produced poultry meat – just as they did for eggs a few years back. If free-range birds start moving a little quicker, at the expense of conventional broilers, which then begin to linger beyond their sell-by date a little more often, be assured that the pattern will have rapid repercussions throughout the industry. The big supermarkets will soon be in discussion with their free-range suppliers, asking if they can increase production – or with their conventional suppliers, discussing the possibility of them moving over to free range. This, of course, is precisely what we want to happen.

I have a simple fantasy about this chain of events. That one day the space in the supermarket chill cabinet devoted to free-range and organic birds will actually be bigger than the space devoted to bog-standard factory-farmed ones. So that those who choose from the latter will no longer have the luxury of thinking they are the 'normal' consumers (as opposed to the flash big spenders who plump for the 'posh' birds). They will have little choice but to accept that they are part of a callous, uncaring minority who would rather save money than shop ethically. And, of course, once the truly free-range bird has become the norm, then there is an opportunity to create an even better premium bird a step or two closer to the farmyard chicken that would be the tastiest of all. We may even get a supermarket bird that's been hung for a couple of days with the guts in, and then we'll discover what a good roast chicken tasted like to our grandparents.

With this desirable future scenario in mind, I am perhaps a little less inclined to urge a supermarket boycott of chickens than I am with other meats. Whilst I believe it is within most people's orbit to buy beef, lamb and pork direct from small producers, this kind of alternative market barely exists for chickens. So, though personally I'd rather give my custom to those who sell free-range and organic poultry direct, or supply to local butcher's and farm shops, I can see that, at least where chickens are concerned, a kind of positive discrimination within the supermarket, again in favour of free range and organic, is probably the most proactive choice for change that a concerned consumer can currently make. And it is certainly better than buying intensively farmed poultry from a butcher!

Incidentally, my current pick of the supermarket birds both come from Waitrose. Their 'Poulet d'Or' is a corn-fed traditional free-range bird from a slow-growing French breed. Reared on a cereal-based, GM-free diet, it has an indoor stocking density of 24 kg per square metre and is killed at a minimum of eighty-one days. Selected branches of Waitrose also stock Soil Association-certified organic chickens from Sheepdrove Farm in Berkshire (see Directory, page 527).

Buying Poultry Direct

If you want to move on from the ranks of the merely ethically acceptable to embrace the truly free, naturally fed and uniquely delicious, then you will want to buy your poultry direct – from one of a very few select organic suppliers, whose annual production is often still measured in the hundreds rather than the tens or hundreds of thousands. I have warned that this may not be easy, but if you succeed it will be very satisfying. For chickens in particular, you'll have to be a bit of a detective – use word of mouth at farmers' markets, or the power of technology by getting on the Internet.

Such is the cost of conscientious husbandry, and a genuinely wholesome grain-based feed, that these small poultry producers need to sell direct to make a reasonable profit. And at current prices you might expect to pay £10-15 for a chicken, around £20 for a duck, and perhaps twice that for a goose or turkey.

In the light of rock-bottom prices at the other end of the poultry market, this seems extravagant. But if the comparison is made not with their miserably abused relatives but with average market prices for red meat, then they hardly seem so outrageous. Even at £6 a kilo, an organic chicken is still considerably cheaper than supermarket sirloin steak (currently about £12 a kilo) – and I know which one I'd rather eat. (Don't forget you'll be getting two or three meals from the chicken, and just one from the steak – see pages 475-6.)

A Farmyard Chicken for the Table

I rear my own chickens for the table – an option that is perhaps not as impractical as you might think. I discussed it at some length in *The River Cottage Cookbook*, so I won't repeat myself here. I will say, however, that rearing a few chickens for the pot is hardly more demanding than rearing hens as egg layers – and there are already hundreds of thousands of you doing that. My own practice is simply to raise any cockerels that I hatch in a separate run from the hens. And sometimes I take donations from friends and neighbours – those who I can't persuade to fatten the birds themselves. Spring and early-summer chicks are fed up through the summer and early autumn on organic pellets and maize, along with green garden scraps and the grass they graze, then killed from about twenty to twenty-five weeks, whenever they look ready – or when I simply can't wait any longer.

Most of the popular traditional breeds are anyway 'dual purpose' – i.e. good for meat as well as for eggs. You'll struggle to get them as fat in the breast as the poor

Ross Cobb – and so you should. Don't be downhearted if they look a bit scrawny when plucked. The sublime flavour will more than compensate.

I also take a few birds through the winter, into their second spring. Once they have regained their condition on spring grass and longer days, at around one year old, they are the perfect birds for a Coq au Vin (see page 311) or a Bollito Misto (see page 304), or any slow-cooked casserole you might care to improvise.

But thanks to the ubiquitous Cobb, the tradition of rearing such flavourful mature birds for market, and therefore the true character of the dishes they go to make, is all but extinct. With your help as consumers, it could just about be revived – but only by bringing an insanely reckless sector of farming to its senses and restoring a long-dormant interest in quality and flavour.

Imported Poultry

The cheapest chicken comes from Third World poultry producers – chiefly in Brazil and the Far East – where conditions are even more intensive, unpleasant and less regulated than our own. They supply vast quantities of meat – often frozen, defrosted, adulterated with alien and sometimes illegal meat proteins, and then refrozen – to the fast-food industry (including, I'm afraid, those oh-so-handy sandwich bars) and institutional kitchens, and for ready-made meals (including many sold in supermarkets). And, when needs must, the supermarkets will buy from them too. Almost all imported poultry meat should be strenuously avoided.

The exception is a very few 'connoisseur' poultry lines, such as some free-range chickens and guinea fowl, of which the most familiar in the UK are probably those imported from France (including Tesco's corn-fed free-range birds). Look out also for birds bearing the Label Rouge logo. These can be excellent eating. Otherwise standards of welfare and quality in imported poultry are, almost universally, even lower than ours across the board. But let's not be complacent. Rather, let's use our consumer power to get our own house in order and create an enviable British product that puts down a marker for excellence.

Cooking Poultry

Cooking poultry is easy. Acquiring a welfare-friendly, truly delicious bird is well over half the battle. Almost everything I do with poultry involves keeping the bird whole and roasting it in some manner or other. I have but a trio of favourite treatments for a good young roasting chicken: the one in this book (page 244) and the two in *The River Cottage Cookbook*. Only rarely do I dismember a bird for any recipe, the notable examples being perhaps a cockerel for a Coq au Vin (page 311) or my favourite North African chicken dish (page 313), a duck or goose to make a confit of its legs (page 451) and roast the rest, and ageing pheasants for a Mexican Mole (page 314) or perhaps some other casserole. But since I hope you will at some point want to try all of these recipes yourself, I think some simple instructions for jointing a bird are in order here.

Jointing a Chicken (and Other Birds)

RECIPES
Herb Roast Chicken (p.244); Bollito Misto (p.304); Coq au Vin (p.311); Chicken with Preserved Lemons and Olives (p.313); Mole (p.314); Stir-fried Indonesian Chicken (p.346); Murgh Makhani (p.355); Chicken Kiev (p.356); Lucy's Jerk Chicken (p.405); Fried Chicken with Potatoes and Anchovies (p.506); Coronation Chicken (p.506); Valencian Paella (p.509)

You should think in terms of four large but unequal portions, or six roughly equal ones, or eight smaller ones (effectively the first four divided in half). They are all versions of the same procedure. In each case you'll also be left with the back piece of the bird, which doesn't have a lot of meat on it but should always be included in your casserole. The bones and skin will give valuable extra flavour, while the meat on them provides very pickable seconds for the hungry and greedy.

You'll need a heavy, robust cook's knife with a good, sharp edge.

1. *Remove the legs.* Place the chicken, breast up, on a good solid chopping board. Pull the first leg gently apart from the body and slice through the skin between the body and the thigh. (See pic 2.)

Now push the whole leg firmly downwards and outwards until the ball of the thigh bone tears free of the socket. Cut through the attaching sinews and the leg will come cleanly away. (See pic 3.) Repeat with the second leg.

2. *Separate the breast from the back.* Turn the bird breast down on the board. Place the knife across the cavities where the two legs have been removed and slice between the ribcage and the shoulder joints, cutting below the wings so that they stay attached to the breast. (See pic 4.) Slice right through the ribcage on both sides of the bird. The breast and back of the bird are now attached only at the rear end, beneath the wings. Press on the breast section with one hand and firmly pull the back section up with the other, tearing it away from, and exposing, the shoulder bones. Now cut down between these bones, trimming through any sinews, to separate the two sections. (See pic 5.)

3. *Splitting the breast.* You now split the breast section in half, leaving a wing attached to each half. Place the breast skin-side down. Slice through the breast meat slightly to one side of the centre of the breastbone, pushing firmly and strongly to cut through the flat part of the bone. (See pic 6.) You now have four 'good' portions – two whole legs and two breast-and-wing portions (the latter being a bit more generous than the former), plus the back section. (See pic 7.)

4. *Halving each breast portion.* To achieve six, more equal, portions, you can now divide the breast and wing portions by cutting at an angle across the breast, so you have one portion comprising about two thirds of the breast, and another comprising the wing and the remaining third of the breast.

5. *Dividing the leg into thigh and drumstick.* Cut through the flesh around the joint, then bend and break the joint to tear and expose the ball and socket. Slice through any exposed sinews to separate thigh and drumstick. You now have eight portions. (See pic 8.)

1
2
3
4
5
6
7
8

All the above procedures for jointing apply to all types of poultry – and to game birds, too. Just how far you go in each case depends on how big the birds are and what kind of dish you are cooking. For a pheasant, for example, I'll usually stick with the original four pieces. For a coq au vin using a large, mature cockerel, I'll go for the eight (actually ten, when you include the back section, cut straight across the middle to give two more pieces).

There are very few dishes where I want to use boneless chicken meat (the only ones in this book are Murgh Makhani on page 355 and Chicken Kiev on page 356). When I do, I would always rather start with a whole bird. Joint as above and then trim out the lean meat from each joint. Roast the bones and make a stock (see pages 470-72), then proceed to your recipe with the lean meat.

The Other Poultry Meats

Since it is the nation's single most popular meat, I think it is only right that chicken has been the principal focus of this chapter so far. Though the story of the other main poultry varieties is hardly suffused with joy, I'll now go on to say what I think is appropriate in each case to help steer you away from the irredeemably wretched and towards the genuinely worthwhile.

Turkeys

In its mainstream intensive production, the turkey is a bird every bit as abused as the chicken – if not more so. In life they, too, are subjected to appallingly cramped conditions and dubious additive-laced, high-protein feeds. And in death they suffer the indignity of being squeezed, extruded and processed into all kinds of 'value added' (taken away, more like) convenience foods. Among the more disturbing products derived from their near-tasteless flabby white breast meat is a range of low-fat alternatives to traditional cured pork products. So you now have 'turkey ham' and 'turkey rashers' that boast of being '98 per cent fat free' – as if that was any kind of recommendation. Medium Density Fibreboard could probably claim a similar fat composition – and slightly fewer artificial additives.

Once again, the fast track away from iniquitous stocking densities and unnatural growth rates and towards true turkey texture and flavour is to go the free-range and organic route. Luckily, perhaps because of the long association with seasonal celebration, a really special turkey is actually an easier thing to lay your hands on than a really special chicken. Free-range birds account for about 4 per cent of the turkey market – still a pretty feeble figure but an improvement at least on the chicken's 2 per cent.

A good month before Christmas, the best butchers start taking early orders for what you might call their 'limited-edition' birds. Look out for slower-growing breeds such as Kelly's Bronze and Norfolk Black. Aim to get chapter and verse on the provenance of these – you want outdoor-reared birds that have been hung 'long-legged' (butcher's parlance for 'with the guts in') for at least a week.

Supermarkets want to sell a lot of turkeys at Christmas. And so their stock will run the full gamut of welfare and quality, from the bargain-basement frozen butterball monster, which is sure to have lived and died in abject misery, to the organic, premium-line bird, which may even have been properly hung. For reasons of good taste and good conscience, these latter are the only birds even worth considering in the supermarket, even at three or four times the price.

Increasingly it is possible, and therefore naturally desirable, to source good free-range and organic turkeys direct from small producers. To tap into this market, start asking around your local farmers' market and/or farm shop a good couple of months before Christmas. Or get on the Internet. Try to speak to the producer in person, so you can get the full story of how the birds are raised. Some of these operations may be very small scale – a seasonal sideline for an enthusiastic small producer of perhaps fifty to a hundred birds. And if you can get your name on one of those, you're likely to be in for an unusually delicious festive feast. The best way to roast such a fine bird is unstuffed, and without its legs (which should be cooked like Coq au Vin – see page 311). That way you can cook the bird fast (in under two and a half hours) without drying out the breast.

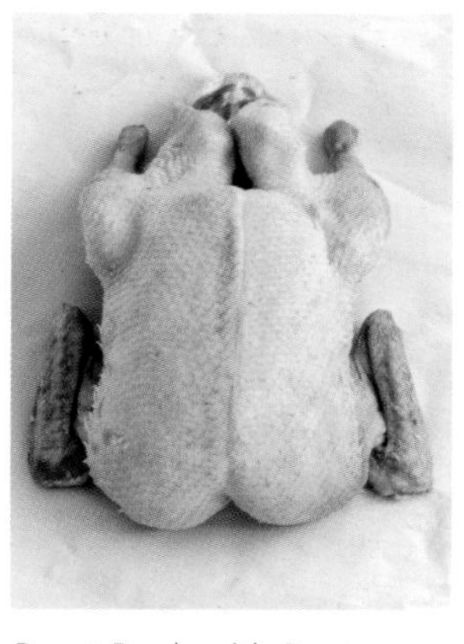

Roast Duck with Beetroot (p.246); Cassoulet (p.302); Duck Breasts with Pineapple, Chilli and Soy (p.366); Duck Rillettes (p.447); Preserved Duck Legs (p.451)

Ducks

Compared to chickens, the market for farmed ducks may seem small but, at twenty million birds reared per year in the UK, it is still quite large enough to have encouraged the development of highly intensive production units. Needless to say, they have driven the birds' quality of life, and in turn the eating quality of their meat, to a pitifully low standard. Most ducks can't even dream about swimming on a pond, because they'll never get to see one in their short and sorry lives.

More even than chicken, the taste and texture of duck reflect the quality of the bird's diet. The use of cheap, soya-based feeds tends to produce flabby and insipid meat, while feeds bulked with fishmeal (as many are) will pass on a distinctly unsavoury fishiness to the flesh. In contrast, a bird fed on a good grain-based diet, with access to natural forage, will shine through in terms of flavour.

People tend to buy a duck 'for a change', in the expectation that it will be a bit of a treat. There is really no point in buying one unless it is going to fulfil this promise. So, as a minimum, you are looking for a free-range bird that has been grain fed until nice and plump, creating a layer of fat that keeps the meat beneath succulent and helps the skin above roast to a fabulous crispness. You are more likely to find a bird like this at a good butcher's than a supermarket.

A better bet still would be a farmers' market or farm shop selling birds that are the speciality product of a devoted small producer. This is an enthusiast's game – and you will taste the enthusiasm in every mouthful. And you should find out what breed of duck they are using, too. Good-quality eating breeds include the classic Aylesbury and Gressinghams and the smallholder's favourite, the Muscovy.

See also Wild Duck (pages 165-6).

Goose Breasts with Pineapple, Chilli and Soy (p.366); Goose Rillettes (p.447); Preserved Goose Legs (p.451)

Goose

I love goose. It's about as meaty as farmed poultry gets, with a rich savour that is a touch beefy (they graze on grass after all) and, when properly free range, a touch gamy too. The skin is so robust you can practically get crackling out of it, and the fat on a good bird is so copious that not only is it almost impossible to dry out the bird's meat but you have enough surplus to roast a massive tray of potatoes and other winter vegetables.

Goose remains a bit of a speciality bird, with overall UK production at just 300,000 birds a year. In terms of welfare and lifestyle, this can only be good news. Geese like to graze on grass, and more or less demand to be raised out of doors. As yet they have resisted attempts to intensify their production, and so pretty much all UK geese are technically free range – though inevitably, in the Orwellian sense, some are more free range than others. Supermarkets hardly sell them at all (another reason they've avoided intensification). But a good butcher will find one for you.

Goose is relatively popular down here in the West Country, and there are many small producers raising, say, 50-500 birds especially for the Christmas market. These are often hand reared on grain, with the run of the farmyard and a decent bit of pasture to graze on. As you can imagine, at their best they are among the finest farmed poultry you can buy. You've got to book your bird, though – some of these small producers have all their birds pre-sold by Guy Fawkes Night.

I like to get my hands on several geese during the course of a winter, and I have two favourite local suppliers. One of them, Goose Slade Farm, just outside Yeovil, is on the larger side of small-producing. This year, Phil Dunning and his wife Liz are raising 2,000 geese. They expect to sell slightly more than half of them direct to local customers, while the rest will supply local butchers. Despite the size of the operation, the geese are entirely free range, grazing on grass supplemented by a GM-free and additive-free cereal-based compound feed, and finished with wheat grown on the farm by Phil. The birds are dry-plucked (essential for that crispy skin) and hung for seven to ten days before eviscerating, so the flavour and tenderness of the meat is fully developed. Phil's operation is a perfect example of how a well-run medium-sized poultry business can deliver a quality product to an all too eager local market.

My other supplier, fifty-odd miles to the west of me, sells some very special geese indeed. Pammy and Ritchie Riggs run an organic smallholding called Providence Farm, near Holsworthy in Devon, which over the last four years has been showered with Soil Association Organic Food Awards for its pork, beef, guinea fowl and chickens. I've no doubt whatever that they would win for their geese as well, except that they won't enter them because they only do sixty geese a year and they're in such demand that they'd hate to let down any of their local customers. The two geese they would have to sacrifice to enter the competition would mean two very disappointed Devon families at Christmas.

I wish you luck in finding your own equivalent of Phil and Liz or Pammy and Ritchie. And when you do, may I respectfully suggest that you have a look at my ultimate goose feast recipes in the December chapter of *The River Cottage Year.*

Guinea Fowl

Salmi of Guinea Fowl with Roast Chestnuts (p.249); Valencian Paella (p.509)

Like the pheasant, the guinea fowl is a non-native breed of game fowl with its origins in the jungle. Unlike the pheasant, it has not been reared for sport but as a decorative, exotic and occasional eating bird. It also makes a good alarm bird. It seems to be a light sleeper, and even in the middle of the night will awake on its roosting perch to warn of foxes and even human intruders with its loud cackle.

As a food bird, it's far more popular on the Continent, particularly in France, than it is in the UK. At its best – reared free range and well fed on corn to get a nice subcutaneous layer of yellowy fat – it's delicious, deeply savoury and satisfying without being quite gamy. However, birds raised intensively on cheap, soya-based feed are barely more interesting than a factory-farmed chicken.

It's very hard to get to grips with the provenance of guinea fowl. Something like 40 per cent of ones sold in the UK are imported, and of these, many are intensively reared. Some supermarkets dishonestly label them as 'game', even when they are the product of a broiler house. However, it's worth looking out for the French Label Rouge birds, which are free range and, usually, corn fed. Waitrose is currently working on an own-label free-range bird.

As far as I can tell, most guinea fowl reared in the UK are intensively farmed, with just a very few small producers raising them in a properly free-range manner. Providence Farm (see Goose, above, and the Directory, page 527) won an award for its superb organic guinea fowl. I know how good it was because I was one of the judges – and it's their birds that we photographed here and used for the salmi on page 249. You can buy direct from them, though the market is strictly seasonal, as they raise only two or three batches of thirty to fifty birds a year. There are a few other small producers like them operating at a very local, and therefore word-of-mouth, level. A couple are listed in the Directory, but if you encounter any others, perhaps you could e-mail me at the River Cottage website, *www.rivercottage.net.*

Quail

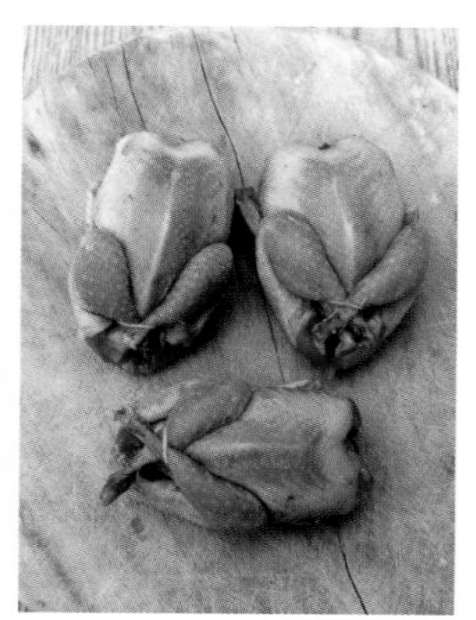

The quail is a surprisingly, and increasingly, popular meat bird. Chefs love it, because it is readily available, a handy one-person portion size and has an exotic 'gamy' ring about it. And supermarkets are starting to push it for similar reasons – it's cheffy, therefore posh and 'aspirational'.

Inevitably, these factors have conspired to make the poor quail factory farming's smallest victim. There are now, in Britain, battery-laying quails and intensive broiler quails in their hundreds of thousands. The reality of this bird's existence is a far cry from its trendy and wholesome image. For the most part, these birds are every bit as abused and miserable as the average broiler-house chicken – arguably more so, as their shy and sensitive temperament, and strong instinct to get airborne, means they are even less suited to this kind of overcrowded confinement. Again, some supermarkets are dishonestly labelling quail as 'fresh game' – a description that is so wilfully misleading of its lifestyle as to be, I would argue, an offence under the Trade Descriptions Act. In fact, one of the biggest producers of quail in the country (supplying most of the supermarkets) actually calls itself Fayre Game – a double disingenuity since its product is not what I would call game and its methods are not what I would call fair, since its birds do not even qualify as free range. Waitrose has recently started rearing laying quails in large and airy aviaries (tall enough for a person to stand up in) so the birds can follow their instinct to fly upwards, and is looking at ways of developing the system for table birds.

In fact, I've only been able to track one producer of free-range quail (see the Directory, page 527) and, sadly, none at all raised to organic standards. Meanwhile, a large proportion are imported – and none of these are free range either. So, unless you find a small producer who can give credible reassurance of genuine free-range husbandry, I'd leave quails well alone.

8. GAME

8. GAME

The ethical issues of pursuing and consuming game may be knotty, and I'll come to them in a moment, but there is no question that the meats from the many different animals covered by that term open up the carnivore's repertoire to a whole range of exciting tastes and textures.

Given that the term game covers so many species of both mammals and birds, there is no reason to assume that they will have a great deal in common in terms of what they taste like. Yet, curiously, they often do. Something about the relative wildness of their lifestyle seems to bring a common flavour note to all of them – the flavour we like to call 'gamy'.

At a barbecue I went to recently, a friend was serving kebabs made of venison and Canada goose. We all decided it was very hard to tell the two apart – though there was no doubt at all that both were 'gamy' (interesting to note, perhaps, that both are predominantly grass grazers). Of course, there are huge individual differences, too. A rabbit doesn't taste much like a woodcock, which is easily discernible from, say, a partridge. Partridge, on the other hand, is curiously similar to squirrel ...

There are probably two principal factors that determine a meat's tendency to taste gamy. Diet is one, and a mixed, foraged diet of wild grains, grasses, grubs, insects and berries will always make for a more developed flavour in the resulting meat than a monotonous diet of just grain or grass. Many of these wild foods are themselves strongly flavoured, and there is every reason to suppose that this will affect the taste of their consumers' flesh. (In the same way, pigs fed on garlic will produce garlic-flavoured pork, and ham from pigs that eat acorns and beech mast tastes uniquely nutty and delicious.)

Exercise is the other critical influence, and the fact that wild birds and animals must, in pursuit of food and avoidance of predators, expend considerably more energy than their domesticated relatives will help to keep their muscles highly toned. This makes for a leaner, denser muscle (especially in the breast, which powers the wings), which tends to concentrate the character of the meat.

It's no great surprise that the game bird whose lifestyle and diet most resemble that of the domestic chicken is also the one that tastes the least gamy – I'm talking about the pheasant. Reciprocally, a chicken that is allowed to range freely – such as a true farmyard bird – and get a few grubs, insects and berries in its diet will taste more like a pheasant and less like a factory-farmed Ross Cobb (which is to say, less like nothing at all).

What is Game?

The word game refers to birds and mammals that are hunted, usually by shooting with a gun, for sport and for the table. Only a very small proportion of game is truly wild. Much of it – in particular the two most popular game birds, the pheasant and the partridge – is bred and raised for the first few weeks in what are effectively fairly intensive poultry-rearing systems. The birds are then gradually released into open countryside to develop a more natural lifestyle and a 'wilder' set of behaviours – including, most crucially from the point of view of sport, the ability to fly.

On many farms these days, a managed shoot, where shooting days are hired out to syndicates, individuals or corporate clients, is a significant or even principal source of income for the farmer. Reared pheasants and partridges are the mainstay of such businesses but ducks, particularly mallard, are also raised on lakes and ponds (often man-made) specifically for sport. Other popular game species, such as grouse, woodcock and snipe, and other species of wild duck and goose, have proved all but impossible to raise and release. Yet their populations are still carefully managed in order to maintain healthy numbers for sport. It's done not by captive breeding but by careful maintenance and improvement of their habitat, and sometimes the ruthless removal of the predators that threaten them.

For example, in the north of England and throughout Scotland, many of the heather moors are fairly intensively managed for the benefit of the grouse – and therefore for those who like to shoot them. Patches of old heather are burned to encourage new young growth, which is the grouse's principal food. Predators, such as foxes, stoats and weasels, are controlled by trapping and shooting, and in some areas mountain hares, which carry a tick that may be the host of a parasite that can infect and kill grouse chicks, are also shot in large numbers by gamekeepers. Ironically perhaps, across much of our countryside, the only truly wild food animals are those that are regarded by many shooting aficionados not as game but as vermin: pigeons and rooks, rabbits and roe deer. It's a mystery why such species have not traditionally been considered good sport – at least for a 'gentleman' – but it's certainly no reflection on their worth in the kitchen. All can be delicious.

The economics of game are evolving all the time, but it is safe to say they are the economics of a leisure pursuit, and not of food production. On many small farms a lightly managed shoot is, at best, a break-even affair. But on an increasing number of large estates, shooting, in particular of pheasants, partridges and grouse, is big business. People will pay a lot of money, sometimes thousands of pounds, for a day of 'quality' sport. This is defined usually by the number of birds shot and, to a lesser extent, the challenge involved – measured loosely by the speed and height at which the birds fly (hilly ground can generally be managed more profitably for shooting than flat ground).

Now that sport as business enterprise is at the heart of land management for game (or 'game farming', as perhaps it should be called), the question of the food value of the birds and animals that are shot has become, if not quite irrelevant, certainly secondary. A well-managed shoot is likely to have far more dead birds on its hands than its paying guests will want to take home for their own use.

Traditionally the excess will be sold to a game dealer, who may pluck and prepare the game for selling on to butcher's shops and even supermarkets. In recent years, however, the economics of this system have not always stacked up. In order to get the maximum return from their (often staggeringly wealthy) clients, who want to see and shoot as many birds as possible, some shoots have raised huge numbers of birds – sometimes tens of thousands for a single season of sport on an estate of perhaps a couple of thousand acres.

The resulting massacres have, in recent years, flooded the local market with far more game than it is used to handling. In some well-publicised cases, sporting estates have found it easier and cheaper simply to throw away their excess birds – usually bulldozing them into the ground – than actively to pursue wider markets.

Since this appallingly wasteful practice was first reported a few years ago, it has been widely condemned from both outside and within the sport of shooting (both The Game Conservancy Trust and the British Association for Shooting and Conservation have spoken out against it). Some of the guilty parties have mended their ways, usually by taking the trouble to find markets for the birds, even if the distribution process actually loses the shoot money. Others, disgracefully, have carried on regardless. In my view, the practice of bird-dumping by shoots should not merely be severely frowned upon. It should be illegal.

The Ethics of Game as Meat

It is against this background of commercialisation that an ethical assessment of game as meat must be made. There are two main questions the consumer needs to ask of him or herself. Firstly, do I want to take part personally in the sport known as shooting – and if so, at what level? Secondly, if I don't, then do I want to condone and support the whole business by buying its end product and using it in my kitchen?

Since I myself shoot, and eat game with much pleasure, the most and least I can do is to offer my personal perspective on these questions. As I have argued earlier, I do not believe that the moral authority to kill animals for food is either inalienable or God given. It is based on a balanced pragmatism, and a kind of symbiotic contract. In the case of domesticated livestock, the foundation of this contract is good husbandry. Though our contact with the wild, or semi-wild, birds and animals that we shoot is less direct, our lives are sufficiently intertwined with theirs for the symbiotic contract model, and the concept of husbandry, to remain apt. This is because, rightly or wrongly, we effectively manage their habitats. There is no getting away from this. There is barely a square metre of Britain left – and not much of the whole world, come to that – that is not made the way it is by our interference, or at the very least allowed to remain the way it is by our concerted effort not to interfere.

So, when it comes to management of the landscape and its natural habitats for the benefit (or otherwise) of game species, we are still farming. (It is of course on farmland, and alongside domesticated livestock and arable cultivation, that most game lives – and dies.) The preservation, or stewardship, of certain rural features, such as woodlands and hedgerows, wetlands and rough pasture, is often solely or largely undertaken for the benefit of game species. Of course, a wealth of other species – songbirds, insects and small mammals, as well as diverse wild and semi-wild flora – benefit by association.

It seems to me reasonable that this environmental husbandry should be a factor in the ethical assessment of game as meat. Not a clincher, perhaps, but a definite plus point. (The vegetarian environment, in contrast, would not have an intrinsic need for such a diverse and wooded landscape. Of course, it may insist on one, by edict, but it is not symbiotically bound into the deal.)

The level and nature of our direct contact with the game birds and mammals themselves – the physical husbandry that impacts on what we call welfare – vary from species to species. In the truly wild species, for example a wood pigeon or wild mallard, you have the ultimate welfare pledge – total freedom. And that, of course, is a state of being, not a supermarket label. They live a life, however short (though usually longer than their domesticated counterparts), as nature intended, free of the many stresses that give so much cause for concern about the welfare of our farm animals. They are born free, and live free and unmolested – until the moment a blast from a shotgun brings them crashing to the ground. It's a lifestyle that carries with it a unique guarantee of quality, as well as welfare, not least because of their diet: this, too, is natural, as the wild birds or mammals forage and graze freely, on wild plants unadulterated with chemicals. The combination of total freedom of movement and diet makes for the healthiest and tastiest of meats.

So, for me at least, truly wild animals, dispatched efficiently by a good shot, provide us with meat that is perhaps the least ethically problematic of all. If a wild animal has lived well and been killed without suffering, it is, in a true sense, fair game. And I'd stand by that for all non-endangered wild animals, from pigeons to elephants (that's a can of worms, I know, but I certainly believe that in areas where large numbers of elephants are culled to keep the population in check, they should, just like roe deer or rabbits, be put to good use – as food).

Unfortunately, it is necessary to muddy the moral waters, because for most of the so-called game you're likely to encounter, particularly in butcher's shops and supermarkets in this country, the story of its life and death isn't so simple. Let's take the most familiar game bird, and therefore the most relevant one. Most pheasants, as I have explained, are only half wild. They are hatched in incubators, then the chicks are raised for the first few weeks much like factory-farmed chicks – in huge crowds that often require health management by routine dosing with antibiotics. The next phase is a couple of months of relatively free-range status (as poults, in large pens in woodland, where they are fed on a grain-based diet). Finally, about six to eight weeks before the shooting season begins, they are given more or less total freedom of movement and flight, albeit that as adults they will

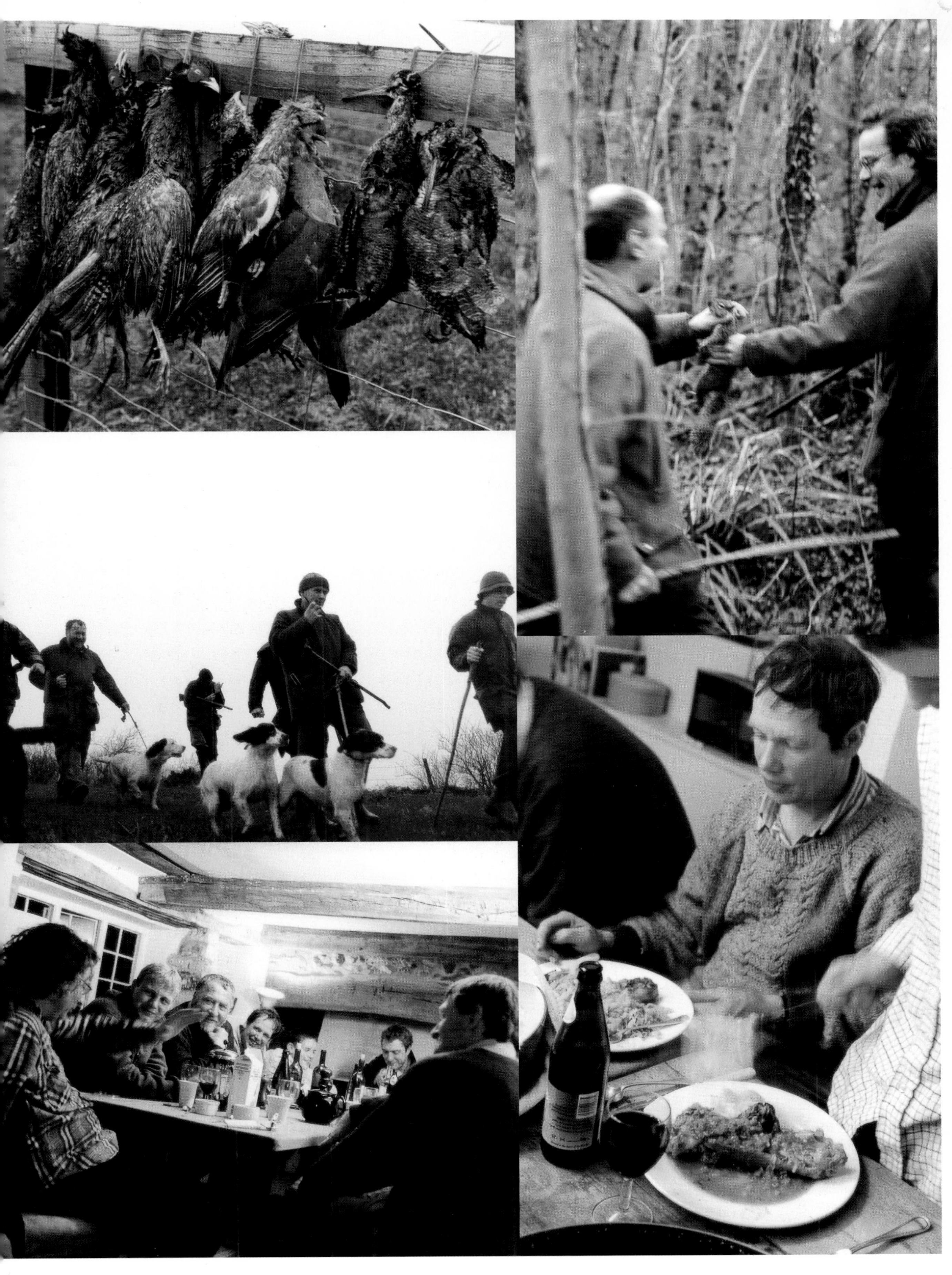

continue to get most of their feed from grain dispensers dotted about their habitat. (Currently no pheasant could reasonably be described as, or would ever be certified as, organic.) They may be shot any time from early October to the end of January – and a few lucky ones (maybe 10-20 per cent) will survive a whole year until the next season.

The life cycle of the pheasant perfectly illustrates the continuity between good husbandry of domesticated livestock and the 'husbandry-lite' of game management. From a welfare point of view, it's a half-and-half status that could take the ethical argument in either direction. You could argue that pheasants are never really free. That these birds are effectively factory farmed, given the illusion of a brief freedom, only to be dispatched by inefficient slaughter for the gratification of bloodthirsty toffs.

Or you could argue that the pheasant has the best of both worlds. Efficient, monitored breeding programmes with a high survival rate. Protection from predators and disease. Then a gradual release into a semi-wild environment in which it can express the full range of pheasanty behaviour. Compared to the life of a factory-farmed chicken, or just about any chicken, it sounds pretty good.

I find the second position more persuasive. But then I enjoy shooting. And here's the crunch. Questions of morality where game animals are concerned arise not, on the whole, from the way we impinge on their life but from the manner in which we bring about their death – with guns, as part of a sport we actively enjoy. I know that, for some, this is never likely to be acceptable. It's almost impossible to explain to an 'anti' that enjoying shooting does not make you a sadist. But that doesn't mean it's not worth a try.

For me, the pleasure of shooting, and indeed fishing, lies in the exercise of a certain skill, in a special place, in the pursuit of an edible quarry. I enjoy shooting, even when I don't kill or catch anything, because I enjoy the interaction with the rural landscape (the wilder the better) and the many incidental, unexpected encounters with the animals (and plants) I am not intending to shoot or catch. But I admit that I enjoy it even more when I am successful. As I pull the trigger and the bird falls, or the beast tumbles, I feel the gap between me and the quarry, which a moment ago seemed unreachable, closed in an instant. A successful kill is undoubtedly a buzz – much as I imagine it is for the Amazonian Indian with his blowpipe or the Inuit whale-hunter with his harpoon. The fact of the creature's death produces mixed and, I accept, morally ambiguous feelings – of power and possession, tempered by respect and regret. But desire for, or pleasure in, the creature's pain is certainly not among them. A clean kill is always a more clear-cut pleasure than the need to knock an animal on the head to finish it off.

And I particularly enjoy taking the dead bird, mammal or fish home to the kitchen to prepare what is always a very special meal – one that stirs the emotions and brings a sense of holistic achievement to the cooking. It's a similar feeling, actually, to the one I have when I'm eating home-grown vegetables or home-reared meat. It combines the sense of personal achievement with the near-certain knowledge that what you're eating could not be improved upon.

In trying to describe as honestly as possible the pleasure I get from shooting, I'm aware that I've hit on the second morally murky area – and what is, to my mind, the biggest ethical problem with wild meat. It is to do not with the pleasure we take in shooting (a utilitarian would argue that anything that brings about pleasure is a moral plus point) but its relative inefficiency as a means of killing. In particular there is the issue of wounding, and the pain and suffering of birds and animals that are injured by shooting, rather than killed outright.

Whatever you imagine goes on at an abattoir (see pages 19-22), one thing in its favour is that death, when it comes, is rapid and relatively painless. This is also true of most birds and mammals that are shot for sport – but is 'most' good enough? Even the best shots will sometimes miss, and sometimes wound the birds and mammals they are trying to kill. And the worst shots will do so frequently.

Even if you believe, as many who defend the sport will argue, that it is a very small percentage of game birds or mammals that are not either killed outright or retrieved by dogs and dispatched within a few minutes of being shot, it is a troubling percentage nonetheless. These are creatures that will die of their injuries hours or even days after being shot. And there is no kidding ourselves that those hours or days will not be spent in some pain. Personally, I would feel better about the sport I enjoy if this statistic of suffering could be eliminated. But it is in the nature of shooting, shotgun shooting in particular, that it can't.

One option for those seeking moral absolution is to fall back on the argument that an element of inefficiency and, let's face it, occasional cruelty, in the method of slaughter is offset by the (almost) complete freedom of the creatures during their lifetime. You trade a happier life for a less clinically efficient death.

To me, that doesn't quite wash the slate clean. I'd rather own up to the moral shortcomings of this aspect of my sport, admit they can't be eliminated, but determine that they can at least be minimised. Some kinds of shooting produce more injured birds than others. Small shoots with fewer guns, plenty of dogs and beaters, aiming for a bag of just a few dozen birds in a day, will be able to mark and pick up almost every injured bird. As the numbers mount – not merely of birds but of money changing hands – this priority starts to slip. Personally I feel increasingly uneasy about the kind of gin-and-tonic-fuelled, fee-paying pheasant slaughter, where several hundred birds are killed in a day, by several thousand cartridges, which may also leave several dozen birds injured and unretrieved. These are the same kinds of shoots that struggle to find a ready market for their excess, and have ended up burying hundreds of birds in the ground.

For me any argument in defence of shooting is *inextricably* linked with the food value of the creatures shot. And the moment we start wounding indiscriminately, and bulldozing birds into the ground, it suddenly and dramatically collapses.

The shooting I enjoy most is the kind that feels like an adventurous food-gathering exercise, not a grand social occasion or a corporate jolly. It may be a solitary pursuit: me, a dog and a gun, walking up the hedge in the hope of a pheasant, pigeon or woodcock breaking cover. Or a so-called 'rough shoot', like the one near me organised by a couple of local farmers. I take a day or two each winter to amuse, thank and feed a few like-minded friends. The experience is very different from that for which syndicates and corporate clients pay such big money. For a start, we'd be lucky to fire a dozen shots each, in a day of hard walking across marshes, up hedges, and through woods. We've never shot more than twenty pheasants, there's usually a few pigeons too, and with a bit of luck the occasional woodcock and snipe. The bag is divided up between the guns in the certain knowledge that every bird, and even the odd squirrel, will be cooked with pleasure and eaten with relish – or perhaps with game chips and bread sauce. On which note, back to the subject of eating game, and how to enjoy it at its best.

Hanging Game

The other thing to say about gaminess, besides, perhaps, that not everyone likes it, is that its level, or intensity, is not a given. It can be encouraged or discouraged, according to the length of time for which the creature is hung.

There is much discussion among game aficionados as to how long game birds should be hung. Those who tell you they should be hung until the body finally parts company from the head are not only spouting bravado, they are likely to be left waiting a very long time. I once forgot about a brace of pheasants that hung for over a month. They smelled none too pleasant when I was reacquainted with them and I would not have dreamed of eating them, but they were still firmly in touch with their heads.

Nevertheless, there is no doubt that hanging game makes a considerable difference to its eating quality. As with beef and lamb, a period of hanging relaxes the meat so that it will be more tender. But in game birds and small mammals that are traditionally hung whole – in the fur and feather, with the guts still in – the effect on flavour is even more pronounced. The strong, gamy flavours that originate in the gut and intestines begin to spread subtly but discernibly through the muscle meat. It's a continuous process of decomposition that leads eventually to the meat tasting extremely 'high', almost rotten.

Some, as I have said, profess to like their game very high, and for a while I used to embrace this hard-core approach to game cookery. Then I realised that it was, in my case at least, a kind of macho culinary posturing; that I was really just tolerating this overpowering flavour rather than enjoying it. I also began to suspect that it tended to make all game birds taste the same. These days I much prefer the subtle hint of gaminess that complements, rather than overpowers, the natural character of the beast or bird. So I try to hang my game long enough to bring this taste into play but not so long as to make it dominant.

Unfortunately it's hard to be accurately prescriptive of hanging times, as many other variables affect the speed at which the desirable – and undesirable – flavours develop in the meat. Temperature, as you might expect, is critical. On chilly winter days when the temperature is just a few degrees above freezing, a pheasant could hang for a fortnight to reach what I would consider optimal gaminess. But in a warm November, where the temperature may be upwards of, say, 12°C, and not dropping much at night either, the same bird would spoil well within a week. Four to five days would be about right for me.

It's obvious, then, that the best place to hang game is somewhere the temperature tends not to fluctuate – for example, in a cool larder, outhouse or cellar. A shady porch would also just about do, but direct sunlight should be avoided. And if you see flies buzzing around your birds, get them down and plucked as soon as possible.

The other factors that come into play are the size of the creature – generally smaller birds and animals need less hanging – and the extent to which it has been damaged by shooting. A badly damaged bird, particularly one whose breast skin is torn or whose gut is penetrated, will spoil much more quickly than one that remains whole and intact.

The effects of hanging also differ according to the species. For example, pigeons seem to go off much quicker than other birds, while waterfowl, such as ducks and geese, are not usually hung too long as the different set of bacteria in their guts can make for a rather fishy flavour.

In each of the species-specific entries on pages 163-77, I have given a rough hanging guide, in days, which aims to give a distinct, but not overwhelming, gamy flavour. Add to or subtract from it according to your personal taste. These recommended times assume that the air temperature in which the birds are hung is reliably cool, but not absolutely frigid (between, say, 6 and 10°C), and that the animal in question is not too badly damaged.

All hanging game should be checked daily, with an inquisitive sniff, and taken down for plucking and drawing (that's butcher's speak for gutting game and poultry) at the first whiff of decay.

Buying Game

In terms of both welfare and quality, and compared to the meat of our domesticated livestock, the various retail options for game are on a relatively level playing field – it is in the nature of the beasts. Though the choice of game in supermarkets is usually limited to pheasants, and only occasionally partridges, pigeons and rabbits, you can at least be confident that when you do encounter it it has not been farmed by Bernard Matthews (though it's just possible he may have shot it – he does a lot of that, apparently). Unfortunately no supermarket label, and few butchers come to that, will tell you what size or kind of shoot a bird has come from – and certainly not the ethical outlook of the person who pulled the trigger.

The advantages of buying your game in the butcher's, fishmonger's or directly from a game dealer are choice and personal service. For example, you may, with a bit of luck, get to specify how long you'd like your game hung. An oven-ready pheasant in the supermarket is, in the interests of caution, likely to be scarcely hung at all. You may be able to choose between an older bird (more suitable for casseroling) or a younger bird (which will make a better roaster).

Generally, you will probably want to buy your game plucked (or skinned) and drawn – more or less oven ready. But if you are not averse to these visceral but, I think, rather satisfying tasks, and you're prepared to take whole birds in reasonable numbers, then you should expect to pay less at your butcher's, or better still get a bargain price from a local shoot or gamekeeper.

If you are regularly on the receiving end of game that is unplucked and undrawn, either because you shoot yourself or because you like to buy it that way, then it is handy to be able to distinguish old birds from young. Young pheasants, partridges and pigeons all tend to have a pliable beak and short, blunt spurs (the talons on its feet); both beak and spurs are harder, longer and sharper in birds of more than a year old. Even if they are large, young birds are likely to be rather more streamlined in shape than birds of the previous season. A particularly fat hen, or large cock, with a really magnificent tail, is bound to be an older bird.

If you become a real enthusiast for game, then a good butcher or game dealer who is prepared to go looking for what you want is a tremendous asset. With a bit of notice, they can, over the course of a season, track down mallard, snipe, woodcock, grouse, hares, rabbits and venison – any of the game meats listed below, in fact.

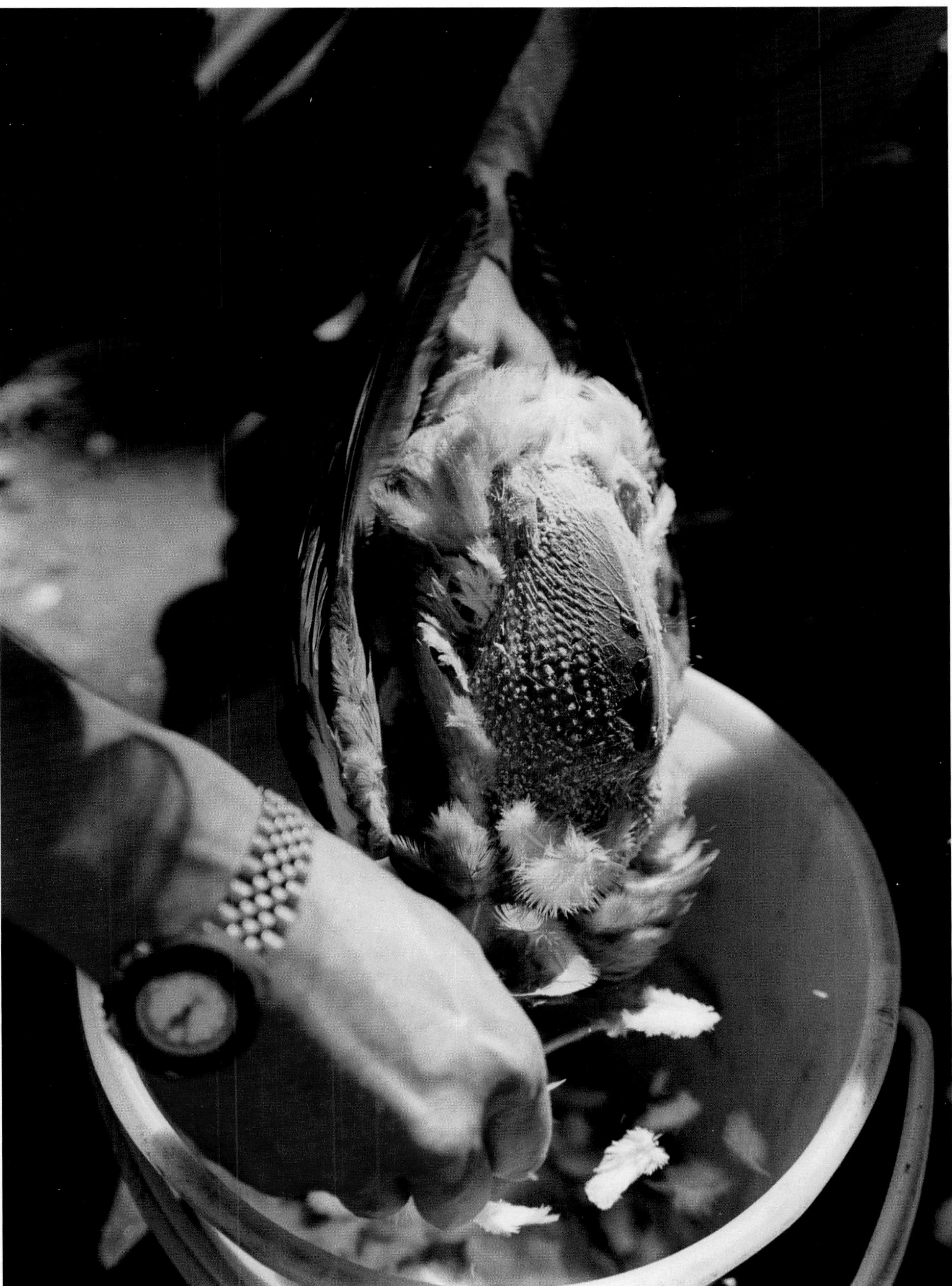

Plucking and Drawing Game Birds

Some game birds are easier to pluck than others (pigeons and grouse always seem to be a doddle, pheasants and mallard a bit tougher) but the procedure is more or less the same in all cases.

To pluck, just take up a whole bird and, using your thumb and forefinger, pull out a few feathers at a time (if you grab too many at once, you may tear the skin). Work over the breast and back, the tail, then the legs and wings (see previous page). Don't worry about the wing tips, or the head and neck of the bird. Once you've denuded the rest of the bird, these extremities should be cut off, along with the feet – a strong pair of kitchen scissors or poultry shears is best for this. A little care is needed when removing the head: below the neck and above the breast is the crop. This is likely to be full – of corn, clover, peas or whatever the bird has been feeding on. I like to remove the head and neck by cutting right through at the base of the crop, about a centimetre above the breast. It means that some of the contents of the crop may be spilled, or left sticking to the carcass, but they are easily wiped off. The reason I don't cut closer to the breast is that a bird I am plucking is going to be cooked whole (otherwise I would just take the breast off), and I want the breast to be fully covered by its skin.

Once plucked, the bird should be drawn – i.e. gutted. This is a bit messy but unless the bird is very high it shouldn't be too smelly. With the tip of a sharp knife, make a small slit in the skin between the tail of the bird and the point of the breastbone. Push two fingers through this opening back into the cavity of the bird and pull out all the soft offal inside. It comes out quite easily. If you can identify the heart and liver, these can be kept and used, but the rest should be thrown away (except in the case of woodcock and snipe). If you really don't like this kind of thing, you could wear rubber gloves.

Freezing Game

If you shoot regularly, or buy game wholesale directly from those who do, you will inevitably want to freeze some, or even most, of what you bring home. Hang it first, though, to the point where it is just as you like it, then pluck and draw it, and wrap and freeze without delay. That way it will be ready to go as soon as it is defrosted. A bird that still needs plucking, or a beast that still needs skinning, is liable to stay in the freezer a long time.

No meat is entirely unaffected by freezing, but it is safe to say that game survives the ordeal reasonably well. This is because the muscle meat of wild birds and animals is, by virtue of its hard work, dense and close textured. I have roasted young pheasants, partridges, mallard and grouse after defrosting and found them to be almost as good as fresh (though perhaps a shade drier), even when served a bit pink (see page 212 for suggested roasting times). Any older birds, or perhaps those that have lingered so long in the freezer that the next season is almost upon you, can be casseroled or braised or, of course, made into a fabulous game pie.

The Birds and the Beasts

Pheasant

Coq au Vin (p.311); Mole (p.314); Murgh Makhani (p.355); Flying Toad in the Hole (p.492); Game Soup (p.507); Valencian Paella (p.509)

The huge increase in the number of pheasants reared for shooting in the past few years means that supply considerably outstrips demand and for a while now, pheasant has been something of a bargain buy, especially in country butcher's shops. And there is probably still room for an increase in demand without provoking a corresponding increase in price. A brace (pair) of pheasants will certainly cost you less than a whole organic chicken, and will feed a similar number of mouths.

In the winter months, when pheasant is in season, there's a lot to be said for considering it less as an exotic game bird, and therefore an occasional treat, and more as a practical and tasty alternative to chicken, and therefore a more regular item on the seasonal shopping list. It's infinitely preferable, ethically and gastronomically, to broiler-house chicken, and pretty much as versatile. You don't have to have a well-hung, gamy bird if that is not to your taste.

Bear in mind, however, that unlike chickens, not all pheasants you encounter will be young birds. And you'll want a young bird if you're going to serve it roasted. A young pheasant quickly roasted and well basted, or lubricated during cooking by barding with strips of streaky bacon, will retain its juices and can be served just a fraction on the pink side.

Older birds (i.e. of more than one year) given the same treatment are likely to be tough and chewy if you try to serve them pink, but dry and bland if you roast them for too long. You will get a much better result if you braise or casserole them long and slow. Think not only in terms of classic casseroles, such as coq au vin, but also the more exotic repertoire. Pheasant makes good curry, for example, and excellent Mexican Mole (see page 314).

If you are dealing with birds in the feather, the easiest way to age them is to look at their beak and claws. In younger birds, these will still be soft and pliable. In older birds, both beak and claws will be thicker and harder, and the claws may be a little ragged after a year of learning to scratch around for food beyond the feeder bins.

If you are buying an oven-ready bird from the butcher rather than ordering your game in advance, it is not at all easy to age it, though if it is unusually large (getting on for small-chicken size) it is probably a cock bird of over a year. Apart from this rather unreliable guide, you can only ask your butcher if he knows, and hope he is honest (you probably have some idea about that already).

According to purists, a cock pheasant will require about two more days' hanging than a hen. This makes sense in principle – the cock is larger and generally tougher than a hen – but it is often impractical to follow this advice, as you may well want to cook a brace together. You can always serve the hen to guests who like gamier meat.

Classic Roast Partridge (p.251); Game Soup (p.507)

Partridge

Most of what I have just said about the pheasant applies to the partridge, with allowances made for the fact that the average weight is about half that of a pheasant. In other words, it shouldn't be hung, or cooked, quite as long.

For some reason, partridges seem to have the gastronomic edge over pheasants. I would speculate – and gamekeepers I have spoken to tend to confirm this – that there is a tendency among reared partridges to roam further from base and forage more extensively on wild food than reared pheasants.

Of the two species, the red-legged, or French, partridge is by far the most common now, because it is the preferred bird for rearing. The native English partridge is becoming increasingly scarce. The English bird is better eating, probably because it is more inclined to lead a truly wild life.

Generally the same rule of young 'uns for roasting and oldies for the pot is sound, and when it comes to telling one from the other, the same beak and claw test applies to birds in the feather. With plucked, oven-ready birds, a hard and slightly protuberant breastbone indicates an older bird.

For those who like game but don't like it *too* gamy, a young, plump partridge, hung for five to seven days and roasted for a scant half hour, may be the perfect treat. A devotee can usually manage a whole one.

Salad of Seared Pigeon Breast with Pan Juice Vinaigrette (p.369); Pigeon Pâté (p.458); Flying Toad in the Hole (p.492); Game Soup (p.507)

Pigeon

Pigeons are on a constant mission to find food, which makes them the sworn enemy of the arable farmer, whose wheat, barley, maize, peas and kale will all do very nicely thank you. Often flying dozens of miles a day, the wild pigeon is a little powerhouse of a bird, perhaps the hardest-exercising of all birds that are commonly killed for food. This means its breast muscles are firm and close-textured but inclined to be on the tough side. It is worth getting to grips with this problem, because pigeons are cheap, readily available throughout the year, and very delicious.

Young pigeons, especially plump birds nearing the end of their first summer, can certainly be roasted. It is not easy to be sure of a pigeon's age, and therefore suitability for roasting, unless you encounter the bird before it is plucked and drawn. In this state you should, as ever, look for a flexible beak and soft claws – but also a thick, short neck and supple, pliable breastbone. You may also perceive the 'flush of youth' in the fine colour of its feathers.

If the bird is 'oven ready', you still have a bit to go on: press gently to see if the breastbone is supple. Does the skin look slightly rosy, as if it is stretched from beneath by a plump and youthful breast? Or is it whiteish-grey, slightly wrinkled, contracting over a hard, prominent breastbone and tough, dark meat? Experience will sharpen your response to these factors, and in time you may be able to tell a youngster even through the clinging cellophane of a supermarket wrapping.

A good butcher should be able to get pigeons for you, but it can be a bit of a blind spot for some. If you want a regular supply of pigeons and your butcher is not forthcoming, you may be able to buy direct from a gamekeeper or farmer, if you are in touch with one who shoots them regularly. Otherwise, buy from a game dealer.

If you have shot some pigeons, or acquired freshly killed birds from a keeper or dealer, they can be cooked straight away, and should certainly not be hung for more than four days. If it's hot, don't hang them at all. Either pluck and draw them, put them in the fridge and use within two days, or just cut out the breasts.

This is certainly one of the easiest ways to deal with pigeons, but should be done with care so as not to waste meat. Pluck away a few feathers on the breastbone then, using a very sharp knife, slit the skin along the breastbone. Slip your fingers between the skin and the breast muscle and pull back the skin and attached feathers to expose the raw meat. Cut the breasts as close as possible to the breastbone, by slicing the meat away from the bone with the tip of the knife; cut right back behind the wing, so as to include as much meat as possible. The breasts can then be wrapped in clingfilm (or, if you suspect they are old birds, placed in a simple marinade of olive oil and sliced onions) and kept in the fridge until needed, but not for more than a couple of days.

If you plan to sear pigeon breasts (or, indeed, goose, duck or chicken breasts) over a high heat, they will cook much more evenly – and much quicker – if you 'butterfly' them first. Place the breast skin-side down on a board and score down the length of it in the centre, cutting only half way through the meat. Then open the cut slightly with your fingers and make two parallel cuts, one on each side, slicing into the cut surface of the meat and again being careful not to go all the way through to the skin. Cover with a sheet of greaseproof paper and tap with a meat mallet or rolling pin to flatten the meat slightly.

It is a shame to waste the carcasses of de-breasted birds, as they make excellent stock (see page 472).

Citrus-braised Mallard (p.300); Valencian Paella (p.509)

Wild Duck (chiefly Mallard and Teal)

Wild mallard can be delicious but they can also be a bit dodgy – very tough and with a slightly fishy tang – depending on how old the birds are and where and on what they have been feeding. There will be a particularly marked difference between truly wild birds and those raised for shooting, which are likely to have been generously fed on grain to keep them close to the pond on which they were reared, and above which they will be shot.

These half-wild birds are dependably good eating – they tend to have slightly more meat on the breast and a little extra fat, due to their relatively sedate lifestyle.

There are also, of course, a lot of 'townie' ducks, whose opportunistic diet may include anything from cheese and onion crisps and Mother's Pride to a Mr Whippy ice-cream dropped by a child (I swear I've seen hard-case ducks at the Round Pond in Kensington Gardens actually hassling kids to this end). Inevitably a few of these townies will occasionally stray over a line of guns and pay the penalty. They may account for at least part of the phenomenon of the dodgy duck.

When you buy mallard, there is always an element of pot luck involved, dependent on the age and largely unknown lifestyle of the bird you happen to procure. A butcher or game dealer may be able to tell you precisely where it has come from, so you can ascertain whether it is in the 'half wild' or 'totally wild' camp. In the unlikely event that you encounter one in the supermarket, you won't have much to go on – but you may feel inclined to reward them for adventurous stocking by buying it anyway.

When it comes to hanging, three to four days is normal, a week an absolute maximum. (A duck, being semi-aquatic and at home in cold waters, contains some bacteria that thrive at low temperatures. It will therefore decompose at a marginally faster rate than other game birds.)

Besides the mallard, two other wild duck species fall fairly regularly to the gun – widgeon and teal. Being much shyer than mallard, both are almost certain to be truly wild – and truly delicious. It's interesting to note that the gamier of the two, the teal, feeds principally on seeds and small invertebrates, whereas the milder, sweeter-fleshed widgeon is a grass grazer. The mallard, meanwhile, is an opportunistic omnivore – hence the lottery element in the character of the meat.

The meat on a wild mallard is often scant, and if it is the main feature of a meal, I would reckon on half a bird per person. Widgeon and teal are smaller, and hearty appetites could manage a whole one.

Again, plumper, younger birds are the ones for roasting. Ageing wild duck in the feather is not easy – except that in the early part of the season very young male birds may not yet have acquired the sharply defined green head and chestnut breast of the adult plumage. Without this clue, it's best to let general condition and plumpness determine your cooking procedure – the obvious choice being between a fast roast with a view to serving just pink, and a scant gravy scratched up from the roasting tin, and a slower pot roast or braise with a view to serving well done, with plenty of well-flavoured juice from the pot.

See page 212 for roasting times for mallard, teal and widgeon. For a good braising recipe, see my variation on the Citrus-braised Lamb Shanks on page 300.

Goose

As well as the duck, various of our native species of goose are also shot as game, in the sport traditionally known as wildfowling. Because these species – including Greylag and Barnacle geese – are migratory, and because the wetlands and coastal marshes on which they generally spend their stopover stays in Britain are in many cases threatened habitats, there are strict controls limiting the season for shooting them and the numbers in which they may be taken. While some argue that these species are under such environmental pressure that the shooting of them should be banned altogether, the wildfowlers counter that it is they more than any other group who are active in protecting the habitats and securing a sustainable future for these birds.

Goose Breasts with Pineapple, Chilli and Soy (p.366)

Of the relatively small numbers of wild geese shot by wildfowlers every year, few make it to market with game dealers or butchers. Yet all are potentially delicious, and one can only hope they are made good use of in somebody's kitchen. If you live in an area where wildfowling is practised (such as East Anglia or the Bristol Channel), and you're keen to get a wild goose for the table, you could probably track one down with a bit of detective work. For starters, you might try a local game dealer, a local wildfowling club, or the nearest branch of The Game Conservancy Trust (see Directory, page 530).

Of greater interest to me than traditional wildfowling is the control of one species of goose that has become something of a problem creature, bordering on vermin. Britain's large and growing population of Canada geese is almost entirely descended from domesticated or 'ornamental' stock. The Canada goose was a popular 'decorative' creature for parks and estates with large ponds and lakes, largely because of the ease with which its migratory instincts were bred out to create a resident population that would stay on a given piece of ground, year in, year out. Inevitably they increased in number beyond their capacity to charm.

The legacy of this fashion is that many parts of Britain have roving populations of Canada geese that are no longer under the control of any particular landowner. Flocks, sometimes in the hundreds, will settle on farmland near water, grazing their fill until such time as bird scarers or twelve-bores persuade them to move on. They are greedy birds. It takes only three or four adult geese to compete with a growing lamb in terms of grazing, so farmers rightly regard them as unwanted competition for their livestock. They are messy, too. In a residency of just a couple of weeks, a flock of a few dozen birds can cover an acre of land with an even scattering of their droppings, so you can't put a foot down without treading on it.

These are all excellent reasons, I would say, for controlling the population by shooting and eating them. One of the saving graces for the birds, however, is that they have a widespread reputation for being pretty poor eating. In fact, this is wholly undeserved – and, as you would expect from enthusiastic grass grazers, their meat is excellent. I suspect the malicious and unfounded gossip regarding its gastronomic qualities is tied up with the fact that it is regarded as vermin rather than game – i.e. it's snobbery – combined with the fact that the meat is unusually dark (a rich chocolate brown, in fact) and, like all wild geese and ducks, prone to dryness if overcooked.

But take it from me, this bird is very good eating. So, if you know anyone who has a Canada goose problem, may I strongly suggest that you volunteer to help them solve it – at the very least by offering to take culled birds into the kitchen and do them justice. This you can do by roasting them (see page 212) or removing the breasts and either following recipes like the one on page 366 or using the lean meat, after marinating for an hour or two, in kebabs. Incidentally, the meat from older, tougher birds (the indicators for which are dry, scaly feet and a hard, pronounced breastbone) makes excellent sausages and salami.

Classic Roast Grouse (p.250); Game Soup (p.507)

Grouse

A close contender, along with woodcock, for my favourite eating game bird of all, grouse gets its unmistakable herby tang from the young heather on which it feeds almost exclusively. It's not to everybody's taste (there is a bitter note, almost like Campari, present in the meat) but those who like it generally love it. Unfortunately grouse are often madly expensive, particularly at the beginning of the season in August and September (up to £25 a brace as I write, in late September), but they will get cheaper as the novelty of the new season wears off. It's worth waiting until mid-October, then shopping around – though grouse will never be cheap.

The usual distinction between young and old birds is particularly important with grouse. Any attempt to do battle with an old bird that has been roasted is likely to be a grave disappointment – whereas a pot roast, casserole or braise will be a delight. Fortunately, they are among the easiest game birds to age, not only in the feather but even when plucked. The outermost flight feathers on young grouse have pointed tips, whereas by their second summer, these have become rounded. Like partridges, the young birds have pliable beaks, which harden distinctly with age, and delicate, soft legs, which become coarser and scaly in their second year. Their skulls, when pressed firmly with the thumb, will give way – gruesome but telling. For plucked, oven-ready birds, the breastbone is the telltale sign – soft and pliable in a young bird, hard and protruding in an older one. Most retailers who regularly stock grouse should be switched on enough to be able to offer you a choice between young and old birds.

However, there's no doubt that acquiring grouse may prove something of a challenge, particularly in the south. Many butchers may throw up their hands at the suggestion that they try and get some for you – but the best of them will rise to the challenge and start ringing around game dealers until they score a hit. Of course, if you have the time, you can conduct the investigation yourself. Certainly if you want more than a couple of brace, you should buy direct from a game dealer – any more than a couple and expect to get a trade price. See the Directory (page 525) for suggested starting points.

A grouse can be hung for anything from two to ten days, depending on the weather (balmy August versus icy December), but there is no doubt in my mind that they are far better if not served very high and gamy (some aficionados would disagree fervently – perhaps violently). On the other hand, fail to hang them at all and you will certainly be missing the point. Those grouse traditionally parachuted into top restaurants and hotels on the Glorious Twelfth, straight from the moors, are not only the most expensive game birds you could ever eat, they are also among the least interesting. The last grouse I had were shot by my father, hung for three days in a coolish Scottish game larder in a hot September, travelled south in a cold box for the best part of a day, hung one more day in a coolish outbuilding of mine and eaten the next. Dare I say they were absolutely perfect – another day would have tipped them over for my taste.

Sitting down to eat grouse is a special event in anybody's culinary calendar. I would always allow a whole bird per person, and if any modest or sceptical appetites cannot manage that, there will be enthusiasts who can manage another half. Be sure to save every scrap of carcass for the best of all game soups.

Classic Roast Woodcock (and Snipe) (p.252)

Woodcock and Snipe

Highly prized game birds, held to be the most difficult to shoot, woodcock and snipe are marsh-loving birds, though woodcock, as the name implies, will tend to roost and rest up in wooded areas. Their long beaks will probe for seeds and berries as well as grubs and insects. Both are delicious, though woodcock is generally held to be the finer of the two.

They scarcely seem available on the open market – you'll almost never see them hanging in a butcher's shop. But if you're ready to do some detective work, they can be found. See if your butcher will get on the case for you. If he will, you may want him to get back to you with a price – they might turn out shockingly expensive, or a surprising bargain. Otherwise do your own detective work. Use the Directory on page 526 and you'll soon track them down. December and January are usually the best months when, particularly here in the West Country, and especially in Cornwall, woodcock are shot in surprisingly large numbers.

In my view, neither bird should be hung for more than a week. The old bird/young bird distinction is not traditionally made – and I certainly haven't encountered either a snipe or a woodcock that turned out too tough and old for roasting. Neither have I ever been so flush with them that I've experimented much beyond the classic preparation: that is, roasting the birds with the intestines inside and the head still on.

One woodcock per person makes a main-course portion – though I'd happily share another one for seconds! One snipe makes a nice starter, though a hearty appetite could probably dispatch three or four as a main course. Either bird should be honoured with your best claret.

Rabbit

The rabbit is the most populous edible mammal in Britain – so it is a little odd that it's regarded as something testing and exotic, or even quite beyond the pale, by most of the food-shopping public. It's not a strong-tasting meat, and it is not entirely unfair to use that ubiquitous phrase that damns so much unfamiliar fare with faint praise, and say that it tastes 'a bit like chicken'. Happily the chicken that it is most like would be a contented, free-ranging farmyard bird, with a bit of depth of flavour and just the subtlest hint of gaminess. Rabbit is hugely underrated, and has the potential to play a far bigger role in the national diet.

Its main problem, from a marketing point of view, is undoubtedly its small size and irrefutable four-leggedness, so that a rabbit ready for sale, skinned and gutted but entire, is not only unambiguously recognisable as a creature, but also bears an

Rabbit Stew (p.316); Stir-fried Indonesian Rabbit (p.346); Rabbit Rillettes (p.447); Valencian Paella (p.509)

undeniable resemblance to a small primate, or even a miniature human. Compared to poultry, or game birds, and certainly compared to butchered and packaged red meat, it lacks otherness. I guess most people just can't get beyond that uncomfortable reminder of shared DNA.

From a cook's point of view, its main problem is a tendency to dryness. Its natural fat reserves, both in and around the meat, are negligible. Although a tender young rabbit can be delicious roasted or sautéed, it needs handling with some skill to present it at its best. On the other hand, a mature animal is easy to make into a fabulous stew or fricassée, provided some generous extraneous fat, from pork belly or bacon for example, is added to the concoction.

One way to make rabbit palatable to almost anyone, I have discovered, is to mince its meat, combine it with about 20 per cent minced pork belly, season it well, press it into patties, and toss on a griddle. Whenever I have sold 'bunny burgers' at farmers' markets they have shifted like hot cakes. Once you have disguised the physical origins of the meat, a jovial reference to a cute cartoon rabbit, far from offending the public, seems to be a definite marketing winner.

Although hugely under-exploited (they eat more of Britain's grass than sheep do), rabbits are at least available. Many butchers sell them, and any butcher could get one or two if you asked. Even some supermarkets sell them. What this means is that the way to increase supply is relatively straightforward – consume more, and thereby increase demand. Just ask, and rabbit shall be given unto you. (One of the few ways in which I would contemplate 'getting into bed with' a supermarket would be to help bring wild rabbit meat to the attention of a wider public.)

That's wild rabbits. But there are also farmed rabbits to contend with. And they are, in my view, an unhealthy and irritating distraction from the pleasures and possibilities of their wild relatives. There is a notable difference in flavour and texture between the two. As you might expect, farmed rabbits are bred for size rather than flavour. They can weigh as much as 3 kg (as opposed to a top weight of about half that for a plump wild rabbit). There is plenty of meat on them, which is pale, almost white, and could most politely be described as 'delicate'. I think it is terribly bland, no less dry than wild meat, and generally far less interesting than a well-chosen chicken. And if that isn't enough to put you off, be aware that farmed rabbits are often every bit as intensively reared as cheap poultry. They'll never leave a hutch to graze on grass, but will be rapidly stuffed to market weight with cheap, drug-laced, high-protein feeds. Forget about them.

So do check with your butcher that his rabbits are wild and not farmed. (Though it's easy enough to tell by looking – the colour difference being like that between good and bad pork: pale pinky brown = good; flabby grey-white = bad).

The commonest way to buy a rabbit is headless and skinned, but whole – though the butcher should be happy to joint it for you. All too often the rabbit's liver is not available, having been thrown away when the animal was skinned. This is a great shame, as the liver is quite delicious. If you are ordering rabbits in advance it is well worth requesting that it be kept for you – and the heart and kidneys, come to that. This little trio of rabbit offal makes a fine warm salad, quickly fried up with chopped streaky bacon or pancetta and scattered over a mixture of bitter and sweet leaves (e.g. frisée or chicory and good lettuce). It is also worth asking for the (skinned) head. Along with the forelegs (on which there is very little meat), the neck and the skinny little flaps that can be trimmed from the lower ends of the rib section, it can be used to make a stock. This can then become the medium for your casserole, or a baste, if you are roasting the animal, which will become a fine gravy.

In the supermarket, rabbit is sometimes available whole but more often cut into portions; it should be labelled as either wild or farmed. If it isn't, and the label contains no warning that 'this produce may contain lead shot', then assume that it is farmed, and avoid.

Buy direct from a game dealer, or even a local gamekeeper, and you can obtain a quantity of rabbits for very little money – though you may have to take them unskinned. The advantage of buying an unskinned rabbit is that you can tell its age. This is important if you are planning to roast it, which requires a young animal. Ragged, blunt claws, worn and broken teeth and tough, leathery ears are signs of an old rabbit, fit only for a long, slow simmer. Smooth, sharp claws, and soft ears that tear easily, are the surest indicators of youth and roastability.

Rabbits are best for eating when they are not breeding or feeding their young: this means from August to February.

Skinning a rabbit

Almost all rabbits you buy will have been gutted, but they won't always have been skinned. So you'll have to skin it yourself. Luckily it's very easy. Take a pair of pruning shears or strong kitchen scissors and cut off all four feet above the 'knees'. Lay the rabbit on the table on its back, tail end towards you. With a very sharp knife, make a crosswise slit, at right angles to and a couple of centimetres or so below the cavity slit, across the belly and the tops of the thighs. Take the skin that is released, pull it down off the thighs and turn the back legs out of the skin, pulling it inside out like a pair of socks, and down over the tail (hard to describe but really quite easy to do). Then turn the body over so the head is towards you, get a good grip of the skin and pull down towards the head as far as it will go. Ease out the front legs, one by one. You can either cut through the neck and discard the head with the skin or, to keep the carcass whole and the head on, use the point of the knife to loosen the skin around the head until it can be pulled right off.

If you shoot a rabbit for the pot yourself, or are given a freshly killed specimen, it should be gutted (or 'paunched') as soon as possible after killing – ideally then and there in the field. This is also very easy. With a very sharp knife, make an incision no deeper than is necessary to pierce the skin (you want to avoid piercing the intestine if possible), starting at the urinary tract between its legs and working up to the beginning of the breastbone. Pull out the stomach and intestines, carefully separating the membrane that attaches the stomach to the kidneys, so the two kidneys remain attached to the carcass. Leave the liver and heart attached to the lungs inside the chest cavity. At the first opportunity, remove the offal, discard the lungs, but keep the liver, heart and kidneys (wrap them in clingfilm and store in the fridge), and rinse out the inside of the beast. In this state the rabbit can be hung for three or four days before skinning and using – though twenty-four hours is enough in warm weather.

Jointing a rabbit

You can roast a rabbit whole, even with the head on, but almost all other recipes require it to be jointed. Another doddle.

First cut off the legs: use a sharp knife to cut between the muscles that join the legs to the hips and shoulders, then cut through the bone with a heavy knife or cleaver. Cut away the thin flaps of meat that joined the ribs to the belly. These look almost useless, but don't discard them: they contract when cooked and make very tasty little boneless portions. Cut off the neck and head (which can be used for stock, or included in your casserole then discarded). The remaining back, or 'saddle', should be cut into three or four equal pieces with a cleaver.

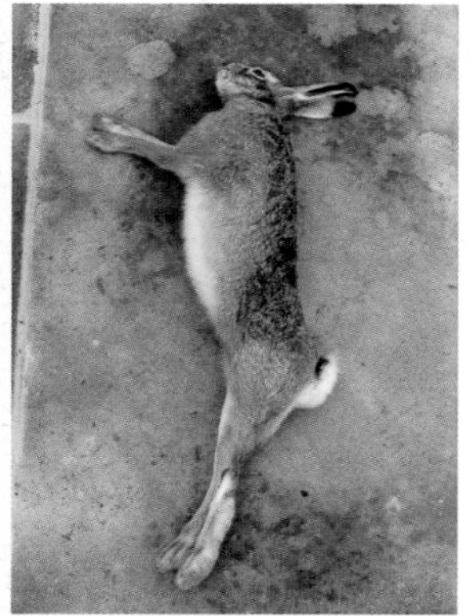

Jugged Hare (p.317); Game Soup (p.507)

Hare

There are two kinds of hare to be found in the British Isles. The brown hare, the larger of the two, is widespread throughout the country. The blue or mountain hare is common only in Scotland, where it greatly outnumbers the brown hare. The blue hare is a leaner, meaner creature, and though it is good eating it is not in the same league as the brown hare. But then the brown hare is, I happen to think, quite one of the most delicious wild creatures you could ever hope to eat. Most butchers and game dealers in the south deal only in brown hares, though in Scotland and the north of England you might occasionally be offered a choice.

The price of hare can vary considerably according to local availability but they are rarely expensive. At the time of writing, you might pay a tenner for one at a local butcher's in an area where hares are shot in numbers, or double that if you have to order it from a posh butcher in London. Even the higher price may not seem entirely excessive if you consider that a good-sized specimen will happily feed six to eight people.

Cooking a hare is a special occasion, and it is worth going to some trouble to get a decent specimen. You'll need to ask a good butcher to get you one, or go direct to a game dealer (I don't believe any of the supermarkets ever sell hare – but I'd love to be told I'm wrong on that). Order it well in advance; be clear that, ideally, you want a fresh animal, not a frozen one. (Since demand is, at best, sporadic, many butchers keep hare in the freezer. Like most game, whose meat is always close-textured, it freezes reasonably well, and a defrosted hare would make

Freshly ground

an okay casserole if very slowly cooked. But fresh is preferable, and essential if you are roasting it.)

Request that it should have been properly hung, undrawn, for seven to ten days. A reasonable hanging time is essential for hare, serving both to tenderise the meat and to develop its unique, gamy flavour. It should be drawn and skinned on the day you collect it; ask for any blood from the hare to be saved and given to you along with its liver, which can be gainfully included in the sauce or gravy.

If you shoot a hare or are given one just shot, you should hang it head downwards with a plastic bag over its head, secured around the neck with a rubber band or string, to collect the blood that drips while it is hanging (the blood is used either to enrich the gravy, if you are roasting a hare, or to thicken the liquor in that most brilliant of English dishes, jugged hare). The hare should then be skinned and drawn the day before you want to cook it. Skinning it is easy (see Rabbit, above) but drawing a hare is a messy and smelly business, not for the fainthearted – the first time you tackle this you may want to enlist the help of a butcher or gamekeeper.

Incidentally, hare is jointed in the same way as a rabbit (see above) except that you will get five or six good pieces from the saddle instead of three or four, and the forelegs have enough meat on them to be worthwhile including in your stew.

A young hare, suitable for roasting, is identified by its soft fur and ears, and its white (as opposed to yellow) teeth. It is usual to roast only the saddle, as the legs, even of a younger animal, are inclined to come up a little dry and tough, however much you bard and baste them. A single saddle will only serve two generously, but if you are entertaining, and looking to serve up a bit of a hare feast, a good strategy is to acquire a pair of young hares, trim the saddles for roasting, and use the legs, fore and aft, along with the neck, for a jug or some other stew. You can then serve two courses of hare: a taster portion of roast saddle for, say, eight diners, could be followed by jugged hare – or my favourite variation, lepre con pappardelle – see *The River Cottage Cookbook*.

Make the stew first, then steal some of the stock to baste and glaze the saddle as it roasts – it'll take about ten minutes at 220°C/Gas Mark 7, another ten at 160°C/Gas Mark 3, followed by a ten-minute rest while you rustle up a sauce with the pan juices, a splash of wine, a smidgen of redcurrant jelly and perhaps a little blob of cream. To carve, slice straight through the saddle between every second rib.

There are endless variations on the jugged hare/hare stew/civet of hare theme, and you'll probably find that many such recipes call for the hare to be marinated for anything up to twenty-four hours. I have come to the conclusion that this tradition does more harm than good, especially when the marinade has a high proportion of alcohol (it usually does). Alcohol tends to pickle meat, and meat as lean and fatless as hare does not need pickling in advance of cooking – it will only exacerbate the problem of dryness. My adaptations of these recipes usually involve dispensing with the marinating phase and including the marinade ingredients at

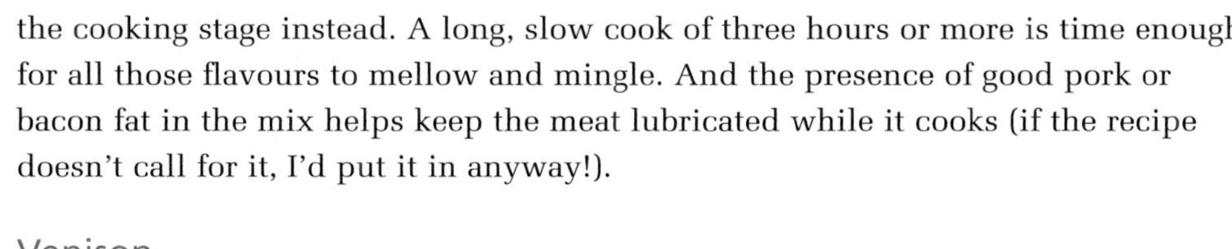
the cooking stage instead. A long, slow cook of three hours or more is time enough for all those flavours to mellow and mingle. And the presence of good pork or bacon fat in the mix helps keep the meat lubricated while it cooks (if the recipe doesn't call for it, I'd put it in anyway!).

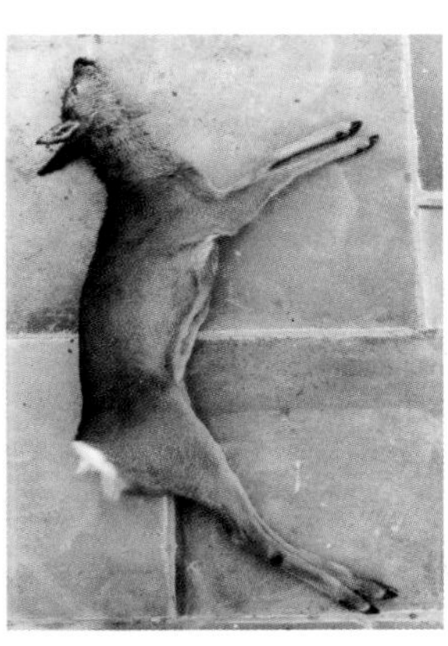

Venison Steak au Poivre (p.357); Venison Bresaola and Venison Jerky (p.436)

Venison

In the UK, venison is a generic term for meat that comes from any of our native or adopted deer species. Until the early Eighties, the supply was limited and seasonal, and venison was pretty certain to come from the annual cull of red deer on Britain's sporting estates, mainly in Scotland. It was expensive and in short supply. Now that venison is widely farmed, it is both more affordable and more available. This is good news, as it is an excellent meat that deserves your attention.

In fact, much of the venison sold in this country is still from wild animals, shot as part of a cull. There has been something of a boom in the Scottish deer population in recent years, and the channels that have opened up for the processing and distribution of farmed venison have helped facilitate the marketing of wild deer, too. The result is that you may not always know whether your venison is farmed or wild – though if you buy it at the supermarket it is almost sure to be farmed.

In the south of England there has been a similar boom in the population of the other, smaller deer species, particularly roe. As a boy growing up in Gloucestershire, I never once saw a roe deer, despite spending day after day of my holidays in the fields and woods. Now my parents, who still live there, have roe coming into the garden to nibble the young trees and vegetables.

Here in Dorset, roe deer are rife – I probably see a dozen a week in the fields and on the roads. And there are plenty of fallow, too, along with sika, an introduced variety that has escaped from parks and done well. East Dorset also has a fair number of muntjak, another escapee made good. I've never eaten one but those who have tell me it's the best of the lot.

Wherever they proliferate, all these species are now shot in reasonable numbers more or less throughout the year (March is the only month when neither bucks nor does are in season). All are good eating – and, as far as I can tell, very little of their meat is ever wasted.

The result is that venison must be one of the very few game meats that actually seem to be gaining in availability and popularity. The best butchers here in Dorset regularly have roe venison in stock – and there are numerous local stalkers who can arrange to drop off some meat, too. Supermarkets are also getting in on the act, promoting venison as a lean, low-fat and therefore healthy alternative to the main farmed meats.

As with rabbit, to make venison more and more widely available you just need to keep asking for it where you don't see it, and keep using it where you do. You needn't see it as either exotic or an extravagance.

The difference in eating quality between farmed and wild venison is discernible but not huge: both farmed and wild deer graze naturally, and though farmed deer may get supplementary feeds they are not, to my knowledge, being reared at a forced pace. In general welfare terms, in fact, farmed deer do pretty well. Such is their natural resistance to full domestication that any intensive approach is impractical, if not impossible. Like wild deer, they are not taken to slaughter but shot with rifles. But unlike wild deer, because this is slaughter, not sport, the range is point blank, and in almost all cases the animals will be grazing one moment, dead the next.

As farmed deer lead less active lives and are slaughtered at a relatively young age (rarely more than eighteen months), their meat is likely to be slightly more fatted, less dense, and therefore more tender. Wild deer, on the other hand, range more widely and enjoy a mixed diet, so they have closer-grained meat and will perhaps have the edge in flavour.

In both cases, proper hanging is important. Most venison farms who retail independently (through their own farm shops, for example) understand the importance of this, and those I have spoken to routinely hang their carcasses for ten to fourteen days. It's very hard to get information about how long supermarket venison has been hung – just the kind of question no one can seem to find the answer to. If you are buying wild venison from a butcher or game dealer, and especially if you are ordering it in advance, look (or ask) for a hanging time of around two weeks (though a fit young stag or hind with a good covering of fat could happily hang, like beef, for a good three weeks).

The prime roasting cuts of venison are the leg (often referred to as the haunch) and the saddle, which on smaller species is traditionally kept whole (i.e. taken from both sides of the animal). The shoulder is tougher and more sinewy – suitable for pot roasting and braising. Or it can be boned out and cubed for stewing, or minced for sausages or venison burgers (which, mixed with a little fatty minced pork, can be outstanding).

The breast (or flank, as it is sometimes called) and neck are also firmly in stewing and/or mincing territory. It's worth bearing in mind that venison mince has a versatility beyond sausages and burgers. I have a friend who delights in serving up what he calls Bambi bolognese and Bambi lasagne. He may be a mite unsubtle in marketing his creations to his guests, but he's a good cook. Mixed with about 20 per cent coarsely minced pork belly, his venison meat sauce, and these two dishes that he makes from it, are excellent.

On the larger red deer, the saddle is usually split, and subdivided as per a lamb – i.e. a rack of chops for roasting and a loin that can be roasted on the bone or boned, stuffed and rolled. Venison chops can also be trimmed from it, and braised, baked, grilled or barbecued.

The fillet can also be separated from a loin or a saddle, on any of the deer species. It is quite substantial from a red deer and can be cooked in steaks or roasted whole. It's small but delicious on a roe. A whole roe fillet can be fried to brown the outside, then finished in a hot oven in about eight minutes for a perfectly pink two-person roast. The boned-out loin also makes a superb roasting joint, varying in size, of course, according to the species. Slices of boned loin, the equivalent of sirloin steaks, are the ultimate fast-cooking cuts. See page 357 for my favourite recipe.

The great challenge when cooking venison is to keep the meat tender and moist. Long soaking in a wine-based marinade prior to roasting, often prescribed as the solution to this problem, is counterproductive. The alcohol actually draws moisture out of the meat and it will cook up drier. More constructive, particularly when roasting a haunch of roe, is to stud the joint liberally with slivers of bacon fat or back fat, pushed into slits made with the point of a knife. Then you can roast it hot and fast, with a view to serving it as pink as you dare. Longer roasts aiming for well-done meat tend to be disappointing – there just isn't the internal marbling fat in the meat to get that falling-off-the-bone, leg-of-mutton-style tenderness you might hope for, and the meat will end up dusty and dry.

For all the coarser cuts, there's no end of variations on the stew/casserole theme. My tips are always to use decent-sized chunks of meat (small cubes will tend to break up into fibrous nothingness) and to include plenty of fat bacon or pork belly – even if the recipe doesn't call for it!

Incidentally, venison liver, particularly from young roe, fallow and sika, is an absolute delight. But more of that in the next chapter …

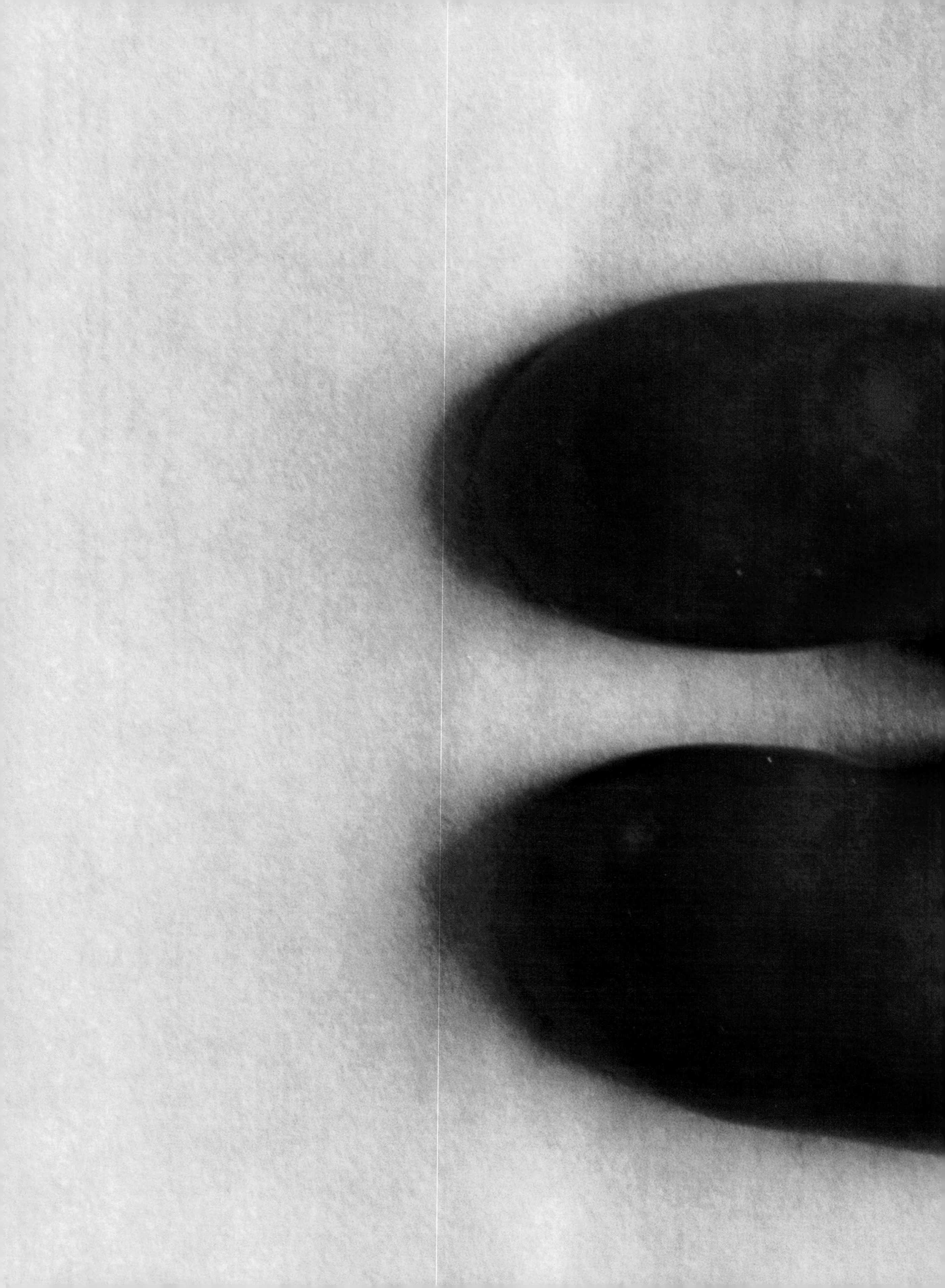

9. OFFAL

9. OFFAL

Offal is a loaded word that seems to divide people into two passionate camps. It's not just 'for' and 'against', but 'yuk, never in a million years' versus 'this, truly, is the food of the gods'. There's no getting away from the fact that we are talking body parts here – organs and glands, no less – and that this is where meat becomes unapologetically anatomical. While some simply can't stomach this (no pun intended), others positively revel in the goriness of it all. Like those who profess a love for well-hung (or over-hung) game, offal lovers often can't resist allowing their passion to slide into a kind of competitive macho posturing, as in, 'What's the weirdest bit of an animal *you've* ever eaten?' I can say this with confidence, because I definitely served a bit of time in that camp.

I enjoy almost every kind of offal, and some of my very favourite dishes of all are made with offal cuts. But I try to be less stridently and provocatively pro-offal than I used to be, because when it comes to making converts it often seems to be counterproductive. Instead of being won over, recipients of over-enthusiastic offal evangelism may be further alienated or antagonised. What we offal enthusiasts have to remember is that the very good reasons to explore offal cookery are not because it's big, or clever, or makes us tough. It's because it offers a whole extra range of unusual and exciting tastes and textures, which are quite unlike those of muscle meat, or any other food you could lay your hands on. It is, literally, incomparable and inimitable.

Some feel that the word itself could perhaps do with improving. The fact that it sounds a bit like 'awful' has led not merely to some very poor puns among food writers (I myself once wrote a proposal for a book called 'Simply Offal') but also to a subliminal connection between the two words in the collective subconscious of the food culture, so that many people think offal really is awful, without ever having given it a chance. For such knee-jerk offal gainsayers, it's guilty until proven innocent.

The American euphemism for offal is 'variety meats', which certainly has the merits of expressing the sheer diversity of the offal eating experience. It makes something of the simple observation that the difference between a fillet steak and a lamb chop in terms of flavour and texture, while considerable, counts for little compared with the difference between sheep's brains and oxtail, or calf's tongue and pig's liver. But I don't wish to champion a move to adopt the transatlantic term. The problem is, the phrase 'variety meats' just makes me laugh. I can't say it or read it without giving it a phony American accent – and without involuntarily forming a mental picture of an all-singing, all-dancing troupe of pig's trotters, calf's tongues, sheep's sweetbreads and oxtails ...

So we're stuck with offal, a word whose etymology is uncompromisingly straightforward. Literally, it is off-fall, or fall-off, as it principally comprises the internal organs that fall to the floor when a hanging carcass is disembowelled. Perhaps for many this crude image is also encapsulated, unconsciously, in the sound of the word. Far more than the word meat, which has somehow been sanitised over the centuries, the word offal serves as an unwelcome reminder that sentient beings – usually mammals, no less – must be killed, eviscerated and cut up before the feasting can begin.

However, I believe we can and should turn these negative connotations on their head. Just why should a reminder of the animal origins of our meat be so unwelcome? Offal offers us a chance to pay our respects, in a full and holistic manner, to the animals we've raised for meat. The nose-to-tail approach to using the animals we kill for food must, as I argue in the introduction to this book, be a central tenet of the contract of domestication and good husbandry. Waste is not acceptable. It's all or nothing. These are sentiments that have long been readily embraced by cultures more in tune with their environments, and more fully and mutually engaged with their livestock, than ours. Sacrifice and libation at the time of slaughter, of an animal's heart, say, or a little of its spilled blood, are not only about thanking your god, they are about thanking an individual animal, by ritually acknowledging the passing of its life.

Even the word association game can be flipped over. There's positive assonance in the word offal as well as negative, if you'll only allow it in. In fact, you may already have picked up on it. Offer-full, or offer-all, makes a satisfying counterbalance to off-fall and awful. We are *offered* a *full* and eclectic range of foods from a single animal. It's a notion that can, if we let it, take us a long way away from the awful and the ugly, and into the realms of the tempting, and even the sublime.

I don't want to force offal down people's throats. I accept that there are strong flavours and challenging textures here that may not be everyone's idea of good eating. And of course, the risk of aversions is hugely increased when offal is of poor quality, stale or simply badly cooked. We all know people who have vowed never to revisit liver or kidneys after traumatic encounters with them in school dinners. I once made that vow myself. The coarse slabs of ox liver I was served up at school were braised to the texture of a giant pencil rubber, with hideous veins like bicycle inner tubes. And they tasted as if they'd been marinated in the school urinal. I couldn't get a morsel past my lips without gagging. In the end I persuaded my mother to give me a note containing that magic word, 'allergic'. And I didn't go near a piece of liver for another fifteen years.

However, when I went to work at the River Café, in London, everything changed. Rose Gray wouldn't hear of my alleged aversion. She fried me up little morsels of the best calf's liver, dusted with seasoned flour and fresh sage and served tender and just a mite pink in the middle. There was no not liking it. It was *delicious.* It didn't even remind me of my former trauma. Now I rank liver as among my favourite foods. It's my special treat, achingly fresh from the abattoir, whenever I take one of my own animals to slaughter. Pig's liver, lamb's liver, steer's liver – all different, all delicious.

It was also at the River Café, after graduating in liver appreciation, that I went on to discover the pleasures of sweetbreads, tongues and brains. All of these had been firmly on my 'not right now, thanks (and probably never)' list. I now consider them to be great treats – fun to prepare, exciting to cook and an absolute delight to eat. What I learned was that, far from being at the crude end of the meat spectrum, all coarse textures and intense, visceral tastes, offal includes some of the subtlest tastes and most delightful textures that we can find in the vast food firmament.

So it is as a direct result of my personal offal history that I am not only inclined to insist on the 'don't knock it till you've tried it' maxim but also determined to extend it to suggest that being once bitten shouldn't make you offal-shy forever. And, this next bit may sound a little over the top, but I genuinely believe that overcoming a food aversion, and learning truly to relish and appreciate a taste and a texture that you once loathed with a passion, is not only a satisfying triumph in the kitchen it's a little victory in life, as well.

Offal Provenance

To my mind, the issue of provenance, vital at the best of times, becomes particularly acute where the 'soft offals' – i.e. the various glands and vital organs that we use for food – are concerned. This is because these are the parts of the body where stress, inappropriate feeds and unnecessary chemical and medical dosing are most likely to make an impact. They are far more vulnerable than muscle meat to the build-up of toxins and the occurrence of cysts, tumours and other stress- and disease-related damage. Indeed, it is invariably as a result of the inspection of offal – liver and kidneys in particular – by an abattoir's veterinary officer that meat may be condemned as unfit for human consumption.

This means that when choosing offal, there is a particularly strong case for sourcing from small producers in general and organic small producers in particular, since these are the people whose animals are reliably the most stress free, additive free and naturally fed.

Shopping for Offal

Almost without exception, the golden rule when choosing offal is the fresher the better. Whilst oxtail and tongues will make some gain in depth of flavour and tenderness if hung for a week or two, cooking them fresh is hardly a crime – the long, slow cooking that both require will render them tender as anything whether you hang them or not.

As for the other offal cuts, freshness is essential. They should not be hung on or with the carcass, but should find their way as quickly as possible from the abattoir to the kitchen. The 'soft offals' are all organs or glands of one kind or another and, due to a combination of their fragile cell structure and the special sets of bacteria they harbour, they will deteriorate far faster than muscle meat. (With this in mind, the habit of leaving kidneys on the carcass, so a slice may appear on the chop, is suitable only for pigs, which should not anyway be hung for more than a few days before butchering.)

Buying offal is therefore a bit like buying fresh fish. In a perfect world, you would want to be able to poke and prod and sniff a bit. This is not generally encouraged in butcher's shops, and impossible in the supermarket, but a decent butcher should at least be prepared to hold out a slice of liver or a tray of kidneys for you to have a good look at. Generally speaking, fresh offal should never be dry, wrinkled or crusty, but should look firm, glossy and wet. And it should have no strong smell.

The best place to buy offal is, of course, the place that sells it freshest. In the case of butcher's shops, that'll generally be the ones who do a brisk trade in offal, so that they are taking delivery several times a week. The range and freshness of the offal on offer should be one of the most exciting things about going to a really good butcher's, and even then it's worth making sure the proprietor has you marked down as a real offal enthusiast. He will be delighted to see you spending your money on cuts that some of his other customers do not fully appreciate. And you, in turn, should reap the benefit, always being steered towards the best and freshest. If you think that's not happening, gently but firmly make your feelings known. If you ask nicely, for example, he may be ready to fetch you from the back of the shop a slice of the liver that came in that morning, even before he's finished one in the tray in the chill counter that's been there for a few days. (However unfair it may seem, my advice would be never to say no to a bit of special treatment from your butcher!)

Many aficionados already know that a particularly good place to source fresh offal is any butcher's that specialises in servicing one of the ethnic communities – particularly in our larger cities. At the risk of generalising, I think it's fair to say that Portuguese butchers are particularly good on pork offal, Caribbean on beef, and Turkish and Arabic butchers (often halal) will usually be able to sell you just about any part of a sheep.

The range of offal stocked by most supermarkets is very limited – liver and kidneys is about it in most of them (maybe a bit of tripe in some). About the only thing I can think of to say about supermarket offal is that you do at least have one extra clue to freshness that you won't necessarily find at the butcher's – a use-by date. As with fish, it may well be worth scrabbling around at the back of the chill cabinet for the pack that has a few extra days on the label. And talking of labels, bear in mind the extra importance of provenance and look for organic, or at the very least free range. But don't hold out too much hope of finding either.

If you're getting in the habit of buying meat directly from local small producers (and I hope you are), then you may be in a position to enjoy the best and freshest offal of all. Once you have a dialogue with such a supplier, you may easily be able to find out when they are taking animals to slaughter. That's the time to put in your special request for some outrageously fresh offal – which they'll probably go out of their way to try and accommodate.

What follows is a brief guide to offal shopping, starting from the outside, and the head end, then working tailwards and inside the animal! The list is categorised not according to the different species of animal but according to their common anatomy – in other words, by body part. Differences in character and use between similar body parts of different animals are explained as we go along. For the benefit of the relatively uninitiated, I've included a few simple preparation and cooking suggestions to help build your confidence.

Brawn (p.486)

Head

Any good butcher will sell you a whole pig's head, from which you can make brawn or which can be further subdivided to give the derivative offals described below. Currently, however, the pig is the only one of our domesticated mammal livestock whose head is allowed into the human food chain. Since the BSE crisis, the heads of all cows, sheep and goats have been condemned – the only part allowed out of the abattoir for sale is their tongues.

The good news is that it seems sheep's heads, or lamb's heads at least, will soon be legally saleable again. The legislation is due to be reworked, allowing the head to be sold on with the rest of the carcass. So by the time this book is published, lamb's heads, and therefore, more excitingly, lamb's brains (see below), may be back on the menu. I can only hope that those few butchers who ever sold them in the first place (often those serving the Middle Eastern community) will take up the mantle again. If it happens, and you want to know what to do with a whole sheep's head, check out the Turkish restaurants in Stoke Newington, London.

Pig's Trotters and Ears Ste Menehould (p.295); Feijoada (p.487)

Ear

Pig's ears, like trotters, used to be something that a friendly butcher would give you for next to nothing, or throw in for free with the rest of your shopping. Perhaps you can persuade your own butcher to revive such a civilised tradition. Of course, if you buy a whole pig's head you can reasonably expect to get a pair of them – provided the pig in question hasn't been genetically modified.

They need long, slow cooking – two or three hours with plenty of stock vegetables – to make them properly tender. When I'm doing a pig at home, I usually cook the ears along with the rest of the head for my brawn. Although the ears can be chopped up and mixed with the rest of the brawn, I like to put them on one side for special treatment. I am rather partial to the classic French brasserie dish in which the tender, boiled ear is patted dry, then finished by turning for a few minutes on an extremely hot griddle, until crisp. I usually have a cooked ear or two in the freezer, and this treatment is the perfect way to revive them after defrosting. (The full recipe for this brasserie classic is in *The River Cottage Cookbook*.)

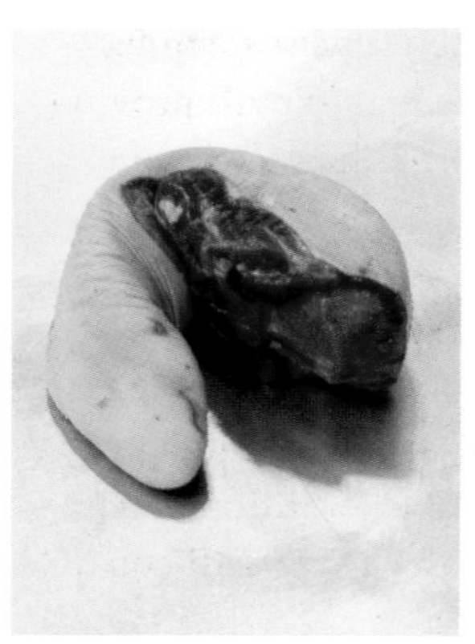

Tail and Tongue with Rich Red Wine Sauce (p.282); Pot-au-feu (p.284); Bollito Misto (p.304); Paprikash of Hearts, Livers and Tongues (p.308); Fritto Misto of Offal with Sage and Capers (p.362); Salt Beef (and Pickled Tongue) (p.438); Cold Tongue with Lentils and Green Dressing (p.438)

Tongue

The tongue is not a gland or an organ but a muscle, so strictly speaking it need not be classed separately from other meat cuts. It always is, however, and for many people it remains the source of great gastronomic squeamishness. I guess there is something a little weird about eating a muscle that is, on our own bodies, so orally familiar – given that all of us have a tongue in our mouth all the time. A whole tongue in the raw has an alarming familiarity about it. However, once it has been cooked to melting tenderness, we are into an entirely different realm of texture – for my money, one of the most interesting and enjoyable of any cooked meat.

The tongues you are most likely to encounter in the butcher's will be those of either calves or beef cattle (known as ox tongue). Calf's tongues are delicious, but to find one that has not come from a Continental veal calf you will, unless you have a scrupulously honest and resourceful butcher, have to go direct to a producer of free-range British rosé veal (see Directory, page 525). Ox tongue is anyway undoubtedly better value than calf's – but a whole one can weigh over 2 kg, so if you are buying one you must either be sure you are feeding an enthusiastic bunch of tongue lovers, or be a big tongue sandwich fan yourself (I am).

Sheep's tongues crop up from time to time, and are very tasty and easy to cook (poach in a well-flavoured stock until tender – about an hour and a half – then skin and sauté or quick-braise). They are becoming 'trendy' in a number of restaurants, which perhaps explains why they are not always as cheap as they should be.

There is nothing wrong with pig's tongue – you will find plenty of it in every good brawn – but it is rarely encountered as a separate item in the offal trays. This is almost certainly because most pig's heads can be sold whole, either to pork processing plants for sausages, pork pies and the like or to the occasional discerning cook who wants to make their own brawn (see page 486).

Neither calf's nor ox tongues have to be salted but both benefit from it, in my view, as the texture becomes more yielding and the flavour is enhanced. You can buy whole tongues 'ready-salted' by the butcher, or it can easily be done at home (see page 438).

Cheek

Cheek, the muscle that works the mouth and face, is really just another cut of meat, but because it comes from the head it has become classified as offal. It is a rich but tough and fibrous meat, which is extremely rewarding when cooked slowly. The scant meat on a sheep's cheek does not amount to a cut that is ever separated from the rest of the head, but on both pigs and beef cattle the cheeks were traditionally removed and sold separately.

Pig's cheeks were often brined and sold as 'Bath chaps' – poached long and slow until very tender, then eaten either hot with a piquant sauce, such as tartare, or cold with a dressing or pickles. The tradition has all but died out, but there are a few diehard, old-school butchers who might be persuaded to prepare some for you (or see Directory, page 526). If you're making a brawn, the cheeks will provide some of the most delicious, tender meat. And on a spit-roast pig, the cheeks are one of the delicacies to fight over.

Ox cheek, as the beef version of the cut is known, has been completely unavailable for several years now. Since BSE-related legislation took force, the tongue is the only part of the cow's head allowed out of the abattoir. It's a pity, as cheek is a very versatile meat which, after long, slow cooking, has a delicious, melting texture somewhere between tongue and oxtail. It's a great addition to a pot-au-feu, and the chef Alastair Little once told me it makes the best chilli con carne. If it ever comes back on the market, expect to see me furiously trying to publish recipes for it in the hope of stimulating a revival.

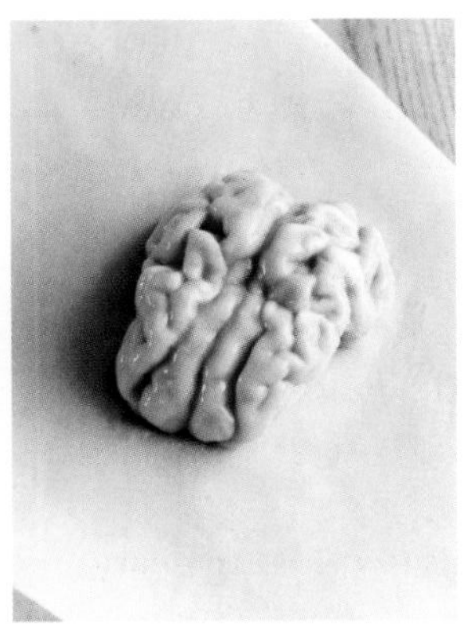

Fritto Misto of Offal with Sage and Capers (p.362); Brains on Toast (p.362)

Brains

Brains are perhaps the most stigmatised of all offal cuts – no doubt because of the mystery surrounding this organ generally. People who have never tried brains somehow imagine that they must taste disgusting. Someone once told me that they thought brains would taste 'like the inside of a burnt-out fuse box because of all those synapses firing and stuff'. Other charming speculations I have canvassed (none of which is based on experience) include 'rotten scrambled eggs', 'acrid jelly' and 'fishy haggis'. In fact, brains are quite delicious, tasting mild and very slightly sweet, with a rich, creamy texture that bears some comparison with soft herring roes – but very much without the fishiness. Coated in flour, then fried until crisp on the outside, with a sprinkling of sage leaves and capers thrown into the pan, they really are one of my very favourite foods. Few who try this dish fail to be instantly converted.

The brains of calves, sheep and pigs – and indeed probably almost every other animal – can all be eaten. In my experience, the different types of brains are practically indistinguishable in flavour. The problem, for the time being at least, is acquiring any type of brain at all. Under current legislation, only pig's heads have remained viable for sale, and no butcher that I know is prepared to take the trouble of removing the brain from the skull. Fair enough. It's more or less surgery – a job normally done at specialist abattoirs with a special kind of powered saw. To get the picture of an undamaged pig's brain on this page – from one of my own pigs – poor Ray had to chip away for the best part of an hour. It was worth it, though – not just for the picture but for a lovely dish of Brains on Toast (see page 362).

When they do become available again (see Head, above) I hope some of you will be among those adventurous enough to seek out brains, and so stimulate the market and keep alive the tradition of putting this very special and rewarding offal to good use. If you're interested in trying brains for the first time, but shy of actually cooking them, then my tip is that London's Lebanese restaurants will no doubt be among the first to put them back on the menu. Keep your eyes peeled(!).

The preparation of brains is simple, but takes a little time. They should first be picked over and any little flakes of skull or large clots of blood removed. Then soak the brains in a bowl of cold water for four or five hours to leach out the rest of the blood. You should either change the water frequently or, better still, stand the bowl under a trickling cold tap in the sink, allowing it to overflow gently. If you want to be a perfectionist, you should then pick off the membrane that covers the outside of the brains and, holding the brains directly under a trickling cold tap, remove the last traces of blood by running a finger through the crevices. This is not strictly necessary, but it is a task I find strangely therapeutic.

The brains should then be gently poached for about five minutes in water acidulated with half a cup of wine vinegar per litre of water and flavoured with half a small onion, or one garlic clove, and a few black peppercorns. Drain the brains – or they can be left in the cooled bouillon in the fridge for twenty-four hours. They can then be dressed in a vinaigrette to eat cold in a salad, or rolled in seasoned flour and fried in hot butter, olive oil or bacon fat until golden brown.

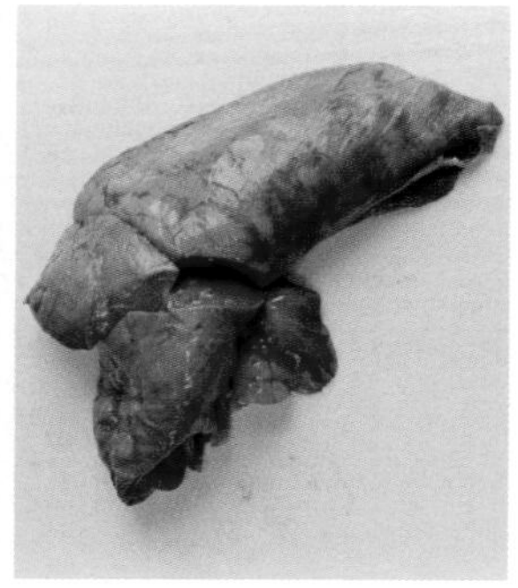

Lights

Lights is the butcher's euphemism for lungs, which, if you've never seen them, are bright pink- and red-speckled spongy lobes (at least, they are in non-smoking livestock). Sometimes the term pluck is used, although technically this refers collectively to the liver, heart and lungs, which traditionally arrived from the abattoir attached together at the aorta.

Outside of ethnic communities, raw fresh lights barely feature in the modern butcher's shop – except that they will be a principal ingredient in that rather charming product known as the 'pet stick'. It's a kind of giant sausage of minced discarded offcuts sold, usually frozen, for dogs and cats (and, in rural areas, very popular for ferrets, too). I must admit, I make my own version of the pet stick from time to time, and the lights from my own animals always go into that.

Aside from this, sheep's lights are a key ingredient, along with the rest of the pluck, in a classic haggis, and this is the only way I have used them myself. There are some other traditional recipes for lights – in Mrs Beeton, for example – but I must admit I haven't experimented with them.

Tails

Oxtail, or Tail and Tongue, with Rich Red Wine Sauce (p.282); Pot-au-feu (p.284); Feijoada (p.487)

For lovers of full-bodied stews and tender but gelatinous textures, oxtail is perhaps the ultimate treat. It has plenty of meat, plenty of bone and plenty of gelatine.

Even good butchers can be a bit intermittent about stocking oxtail, so to be sure you're going to get a fresh one, it may be worth ordering a day or two in advance. On the other hand, given the treatment it's going to get, it doesn't matter unduly if it has been frozen. Most butchers sell it all ready and cut up, the portions bound together with string. It is not sensible to buy it in a piece unless you have a butcher's block and a heavy meat cleaver.

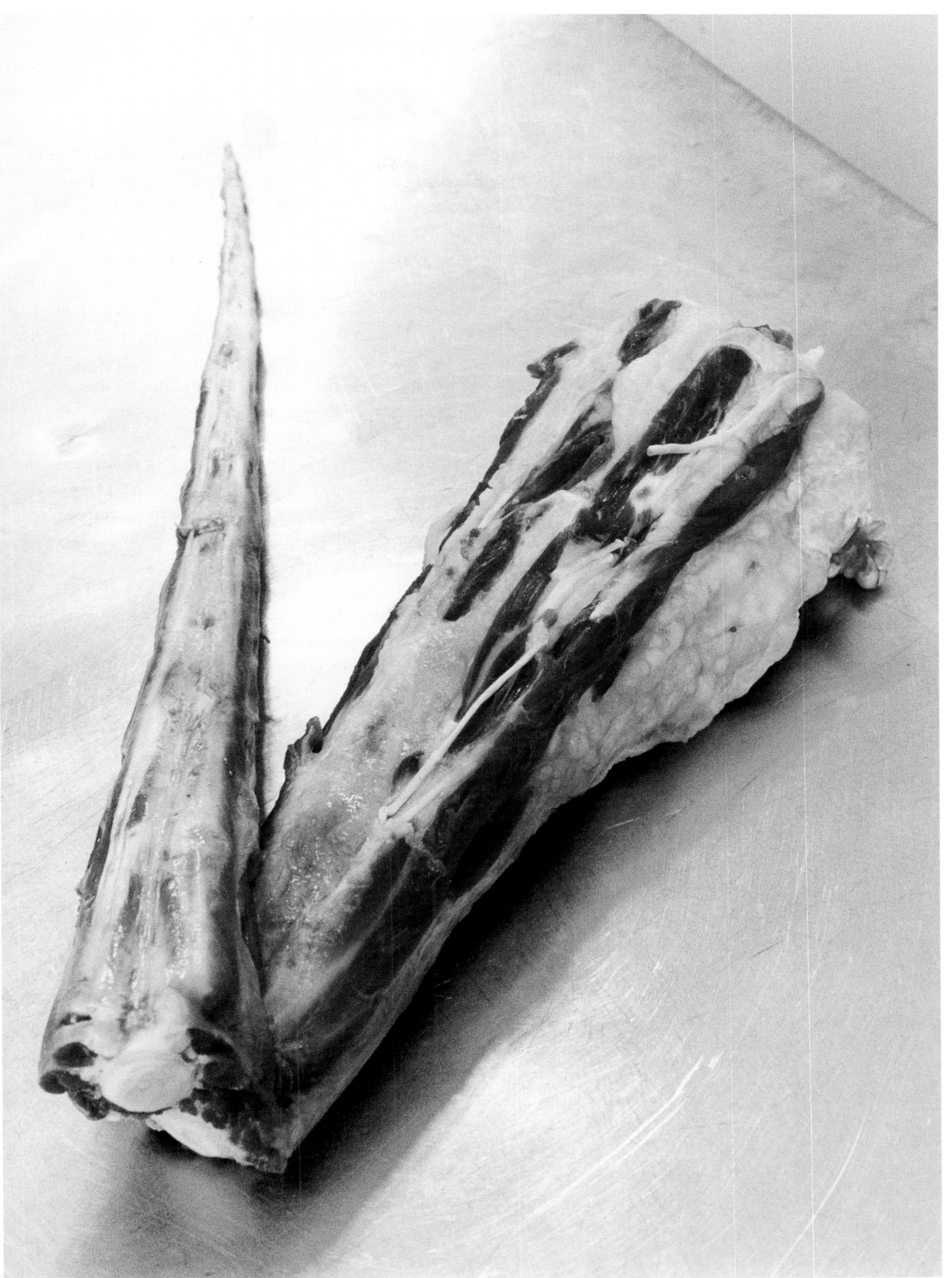

Supermarkets do sometimes carry oxtail, but not as regularly or reliably as they should. In the spirit of encouraging initiative, you might want to snap it up when you see it. Small producers selling direct will probably offer you oxtail in a vac-pack, which is okay if you follow the pre-preparation procedure below.

A medium-sized oxtail weighs around 1-1.5 kg, and will make a hearty stew to feed four. All recipes for oxtail benefit from the same basic pre-preparation, and if this is not specified in your recipe it should ideally be done anyway. Untie the bundle and soak the oxtail in plenty of well-salted cold water for an hour or two. Place in a pot of fresh cold water and bring slowly to the boil, skimming regularly as the scum rises to the surface. Simmer gently, continuing to skim, for about ten minutes. Drain, cool and wipe dry with a clean cloth. This blanching and skimming process will prevent your soup or stew from being scummy-brown in appearance and tainted in flavour. A short cut for this procedure is simply to make sure you thoroughly skim your stew for the first ten to twenty minutes of its cooking time, until the rising scum is a clean white colour, rather than a dirty grey-brown. In other words, you don't have to remove the oxtail and start again from scratch – but you do have to be particularly vigilant and keep skimming until the froth is clean and white.

The tail of the pig deserves a quick mention: it can be salted, for inclusion in a feijoada, or cooked in the same way as the ear (see page 185) and crisped up on a griddle before serving.

Trotters (and Other Feet)

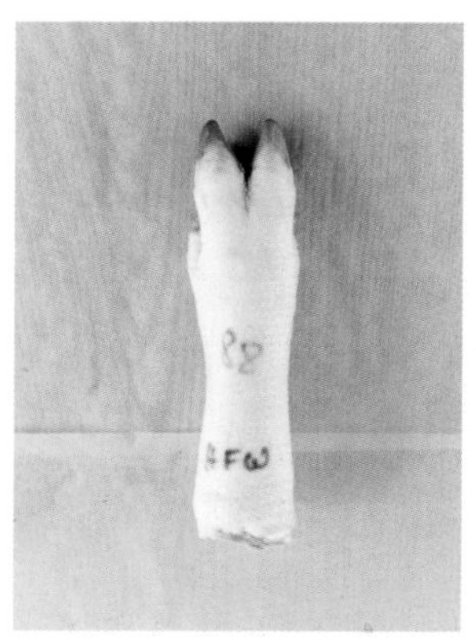

Pig's Trotters and Ears Ste Menehould (p.295); A Raised Pork Pie (p.444); Brawn (p.486); Feijoada (p.487); Chinese-style Spare Ribs and Pig's Trotters (p.490)

Trotters, and feet generally, may seem like just about the least promising part of any edible animal's anatomy, being all skin and bone and hardly any meat. But these apparent shortcomings are also their strength. Sometimes a tidy, intense package of skin and bones is just what you're after. These attributes mean that trotters have plenty of flavour, gelatinous body, and the ability to cook down to a unique glutinous stickiness that cannot be achieved with any other meat or offal cut (though tails and ears are roughly in the same ball park). This kind of very textural food is admittedly out on a limb (geddit!) – not everybody will like it. But those who do will often love it.

Pig's trotters, always a highly respected ingredient in French cooking, enjoyed a great gastronomic revival in the Eighties, becoming the signature dish of one of London's greatest chefs, Pierre Koffman. Many disciples followed suit. But it is not necessary to stuff a pig's trotter with expensive wild mushrooms and luxurious truffled forcemeats to make it palatable. A very simple Chinese recipe makes a lip-sticking sweet and sour treat out of them that should tempt many out of scepticism (see page 490).

Even if you're struggling to be persuaded of the merits of trotters presented as a dish in themselves, you may still find good use for them in the kitchen. They can happily be added to almost any stock, and will enrich the flavour, adding valuable gelatinous body. It is particularly sensible to do this if you want to make sure your stock, or the liquor in a terrine or pie, will set into a jelly when cold. The inclusion of a trotter is pretty much a cast-iron guarantee of jellification.

Not all butchers put trotters out front in their display – perhaps because they think they will put off more punters than they attract. But every butcher could get trotters if you asked for them. In fact, many butchers are throwing away pig's trotters every week, so they should be only too happy to sell them to you for, say, fifty pence each at most. If you're a regular, you may find you can get them for nothing. And if you begin to buy your pork direct from a small producer, as I hope you will consider doing, you will almost certainly find that they, too, have trotters to spare at knockdown prices. As for the supermarkets, I am not aware of any that offer trotters for sale, though I invite them to disillusion me.

Calf's feet are almost unheard of these days, though they do crop up in ethnic butcher's shops in some of the big cities. If you do use a calf's foot in a stock, and cook it for long enough to make the foot tender, then the meat that you can pick from it is delicious eaten cold, with creamed horseradish or a vinaigrette made piquant with the addition of chopped capers and gherkins.

Sheep's trotters have so little to offer besides skin and bones that they are barely viable for the home cook, though Mrs Beeton, the grand mistress of good kitchen economy, has some recipes for them.

Fries

Fries are the euphemistic, and prevailing, culinary term for the testicles of cows, pigs and sheep. On the Continent all are used (in Spain, bull's testicles are considered a great delicacy and an enhancer of masculinity). In this country you're only likely to find lamb's fries, and they are pretty hard to come by – not least because most male lambs are castrated shortly after birth. A good butcher might be able to track some down, but your best bet would be to visit a butcher serving the Arabic community.

They do not appear very appetising in the raw – they look like what they are. But once prepared, they lose their fearsome aspect and, like brains, I think most people would find them quite palatable if they didn't know what they were.
If you're ready to take the plunge, here's how I suggest you deal with them. Before cooking, they should be blanched in boiling water for about two minutes, refreshed under cold water and skinned immediately. Then marinate the blanched, skinned fries in a couple of tablespoons each of olive oil and vinegar, a sliced onion and a few sprigs of thyme and parsley. Change this marinade after an hour, and leave them in the fresh marinade, supplemented with the juice of a lemon, for a further two hours. They are then ready to cook.

Slice them into three or four pieces, toss in well-seasoned flour and fry in hot butter or oil until golden brown (about six minutes). Serve with a lemony vinaigrette into which you have stirred finely chopped parsley and shallots.

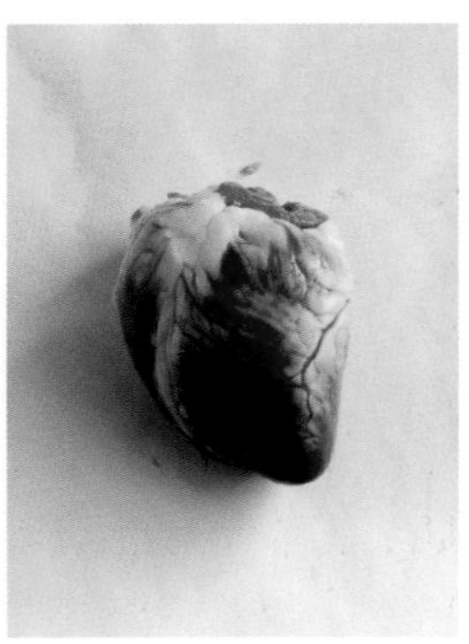

Paprikash of Hearts, Livers and Tongues (p.308); Faggots with Onion Gravy (p.459)

Heart

The hearts of pigs, sheep and cows all make good eating. Once again it is probably the ethnic butchers in the cities that now account for most sales. But good butchers everywhere still stock them – and can probably count a few enthusiasts, perhaps among their older customers. It will be a great pity if the British tradition of eating hearts dies out with our grandparents' generation. They can be delicious, and it is not at all difficult to make them so.

Sheep's and pig's hearts are the easiest to come by and to deal with. Ox hearts can be found easily enough, but they are pretty huge, and tough, so they really need to be trimmed of tough membranes and ventricles before cooking. I wouldn't want to discourage you from trying, but first-timers are certainly better off with pig's and sheep's hearts. They are roughly the same size, weighing 300-400g each and so make a generous portion for one.

To prepare a heart, cut away all veins and arteries back to the muscle itself, but leave the fat, as this helps to lubricate and moisten the meat as it cooks. A long, slow braise is the best approach to this densely textured and naturally tough meat – up to three hours in a little stock and wine, with finely chopped stock vegetables and a few fresh herbs. Traditionally this cooking liquor is reduced at the end to a rich, well-flavoured gravy, though there is really no need to thicken it with flour, as many old recipes recommend.

The heart's natural cavity lends itself to stuffing, and a good stuffing can help to baste the heart from the inside. Sage and onion is a classic, but make sure yours is a moist version, incorporating some butter or fat. More simply, a couple of prunes wrapped in good fat bacon will do the trick.

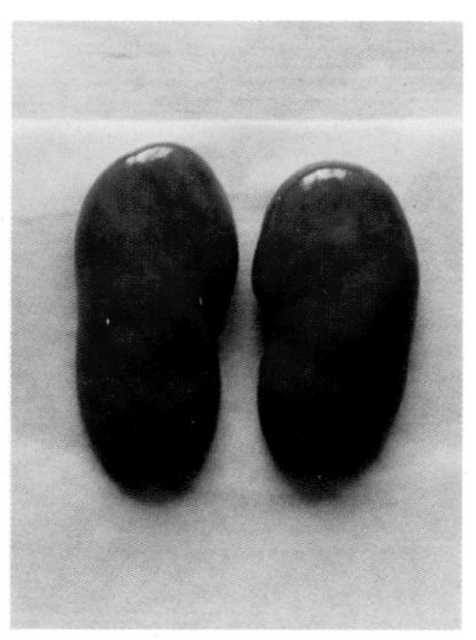

Steak and Kidney Pie (p.286); Lancashire Hot Pot (p.290); Devilled Kidneys (p.361)

Kidneys

If you've already decided that you don't like kidneys, I wonder what I can say to change your mind. Get some really fresh lamb's or calf's kidneys and try the recipe for Devilled Kidneys on page 361. It worked on a friend of mine just a few weeks ago. I made them at home on the day I took a sheep to slaughter. A polite tasting of a tiny morsel, intended to confirm her aversion, became a proper sampling, then a small helping, and then seconds.

Freshness is all. As the function of the kidney is to filter the animal's urine, you can imagine that there are things in it that will make the best possible use of time spent hanging around waiting to be bought – and render the flavour less than delicate for the unlucky late buyer.

Calf's kidneys are excellent, but expensive. And they will usually be from Continental veal calves – with all the ethical anxieties that that implies. Once you've found a source of UK-produced rosé veal (see page 526) – organic, perhaps – you have, with a bit of luck, found a dependable source of cruelty-free kidneys as well.

Otherwise go for lamb's kidneys. Provided they are extremely fresh, they will be very nearly as good. Pig's are good, too, but only when you are very sure of their provenance and scrupulous freshness. Because of the pig's omnivorous tendencies, they harbour a different set of bacteria – they turn that much quicker, taking on a bitter and rather tainted flavour. Having said that, the kidneys of my own home-reared pigs, eaten on the day of slaughter, are one of my favourite of all offally treats. They give me fortitude for the up-coming session of black-pudding making, which often lasts long into the night.

The kidneys of mature beef cattle, known as ox kidneys, inevitably tend towards toughness. But when fresh, they are very good cooked slowly until tender (as in the best steak and kidney pies and puddings).

Uncut, whole kidneys are likely to be in better condition than ones that have been chopped up and left in a pool of their own blood in a butcher's tray. This is why the best butchers keep kidneys in their natural surrounding of fat for as long as possible, breaking it open and preparing the kidney for customers on request. It used to be traditional (and extremely delicious) to cook a whole calf's kidney by roasting it still sealed in this natural casing of suet. However, this is no longer possible, since EC regulations declared that the kidney fat must be at least partially broken open (so that the condition of the kidney can be checked) before the product can be passed on to the consumer.

There are various ways to prepare kidneys for cooking, and they're all pretty simple. If you buy whole kidneys, they must be 'skinned' by removing the outer membrane with a sharp knife, then sliced to the size you require, trimming off the gristly central core (a small, sharp vegetable knife is useful for this task). Kidneys are very often chopped into bite-sized pieces, which is perfectly sensible if you are making a stew, ragout or pie in which they are to be combined with mushrooms, vegetables or other meats. But if you are braising, grilling or frying kidneys more or less on their own, cutting them up small will merely allow all the natural juices to run out, and the resulting morsels will lose both succulence and flavour. Lamb's kidneys can be cooked whole, or else cut straight across their width into three or four thick slices.

The appropriate 'doneness' of kidneys is a matter for debate – and, of course, personal taste. My view is that they should ideally be presented in one of two ways. If cooked fast (fried, grilled or sautéed), they should be still just pink in the middle (or, if not pink, then only just not pink) – six to eight minutes is usually enough. If cooked more slowly (i.e. braised or stewed), then you should ensure that they are thoroughly cooked and quite tender before serving – this is likely to take a good half an hour of slow braising, or more like an hour in the case of ox kidney. In a classic steak and kidney pie or pudding, the final cooking time for the ox kidneys is likely to be upwards of two hours – and they will be meltingly tender and delicious as a result.

I always think kidneys are best served with a sauce that is slightly sweet or spicy: devilled kidneys are a classic. My other favourite recipe is with chilli and lentils (see *The River Cottage Cookbook*).

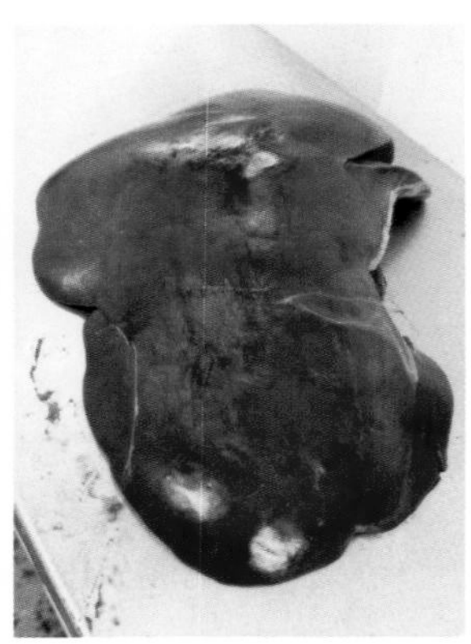

Paprikash of Hearts, Livers and Tongues (p.308); Calf's Liver with Little Onions, Sage and Aged Vinegar (p.358); Fritto Misto of Offal with Sage and Capers (p.362); Spiced Hot-smoked Liver (p.408); Rich Liver Pâté (p.452); Faggots with Onion Gravy (p.459)

Liver

The denigration of liver has become almost proverbial. It's the meat that the British, particularly the younger generation, love to hate. Just say the word 'liver' to a school-age kid and watch their face pucker up in revulsion.

Among professed adult foodies, on the other hand, it's been steadily gaining in popularity. Calf's liver became immensely popular on restaurant menus of the Eighties, and we all tried to have it pinker than the next person. The enthusiasm shows no signs of abating.

However, I suspect that many non-veal-eating liver enthusiasts are not aware that almost all calf's liver in this country comes from Dutch veal calves. The conscientious should take the trouble to look for English calf's liver, from UK-reared rosé veal calves (ideally organic). I don't promise it will be that easy to find, but my Directory, on page 526, should point you in the right direction.

So, on the one hand I'm encouraging liver-shirkers to give it a go. On the other hand I'm calling for a boycott of Dutch calf's liver. Sorry if it seems there's no pleasing me, but one definite way forward is to increase your acquaintance with lamb's liver. It is certainly a little less tender and a shade stronger in flavour than calf's liver. But if it's fresh and you don't overcook it, it can still convert the sceptic – and bring a beaming smile to a liver lover's face. The best lamb's liver deserves respectful treatment: like calf's liver, it can be sliced thinly, flash-fried or grilled, and served pink to those who like it so. Five minutes in all, turning once, is usually enough to cook a piece of liver 1cm thick. If your bacon, mash and fried onions are also cooked with care, then you have a traditional liver platter on which it is hard to improve.

Pig's liver is a tougher prospect, both literally and figuratively. The liver of my own home-reared pigs, eaten within a day or two of slaughter, has always been delicious. It stands up to reverential calf's liver-style presentation – i.e. sliced thin and served pink – as well as making fabulous pâté. So if you can acquire liver this fresh, direct from a small producer of top-quality pork, then you are in for a similar treat.

But pig's liver of questionable provenance will be much harder to serve palatably. The extremely intensive way in which most pigs are raised undoubtedly takes a heavy toll on their livers, which, along with the kidneys, play a key role in the assimilation and dispersal of toxins in the diet. It just doesn't seem like anything I would actually want to eat.

Chicken livers are scary for similar reasons. Given the vast number of chicken livers that are available from the intensive poultry industry, it's no surprise that chicken liver pâté has become popular in recent years, and every supermarket deli counter has its version. Personally I shudder at the thought of it. It seems to me that all the worst chemical additions of factory farming must inevitably collect on this organ. Whole chicken livers of similar intensive provenance are available, usually frozen, in almost all butcher's and supermarkets. Again, I just don't fancy them.

Only when you've taken the trouble to source top-quality free-range chickens, ideally organic, should you start thinking about cooking their livers. Once you have found a butcher or small producer who deals in such birds, you could ask them, with a couple of days' warning, to put the fresh livers of half a dozen birds on one side for you. Then you can make a chicken liver pâté worthy of the name. (Or, better still, you can sauté the livers in hot oil for just two or three minutes, adding a couple of very finely chopped garlic cloves and a tablespoon of finely chopped parsley for the last minute of cooking. Serve up on a bed of green salad leaves with a good olive oil vinaigrette.)

Ox liver, taken from mature beef cattle, is, pound for pound, the cheapest of the lot. Stale, from a factory-farmed beast, and perhaps defrosted from frozen to boot, it certainly offers school, hospital (and no doubt prison) caterers ample opportunity to spread untold misery among their charges. But when it is fresh, and taken from a top-quality grass-fed beef animal, it may just surprise you. It can be almost as sweet and delicately flavoured as calf's liver and, after a long, slow braise, it needn't be tough either.

The most controversial liver, outside of the school canteen, is that of the goose and duck. Foie gras (literally, 'fat liver') is a rich man's playfood. It is created by force-feeding either geese or ducks, whose natural ability to store fat in their livers has evolved to provide fuel for lengthy migrations. In farmed birds, bred to be more passive and denied the opportunity to fly, let alone migrate, this physiological phenomenon causes the liver to swell to almost half a kilo, and about 80 per cent fat, so that it is rich, creamy and sweet. It is not true, as many opponents of foie gras argue, that the fattened liver is diseased. But nor could one say with any certainty that a bird with such a liver is not in pain, or under stress.

I must admit I find foie gras delicious. But I also find it impossible to ignore the ethical dilemma posed by the means of production. However, since visiting a small producer of foie gras near my parents-in-law in France, I have a slightly altered perspective. After observing it first hand, I don't think the force-feeding of ducks and geese, when it is done by a skilled hand (in this case the farmer's wife) is excessively cruel. It looks a bit bizarre, as the specially prepared maize porridge is pushed into the bird's mouth through a funnel, then massaged down its throat with a firm hand. But it really doesn't seem as if the birds are in any way terrorised by the process. They actually queue up for their turn and, when it's over, waddle off no more than a little ruffled by the experience.

The farm I visited raises only 200-300 birds a year. The foie gras it produces is processed on site, the rest of the slaughtered birds are made into delicious *confit*, and all these home-made products are sold at the local market. Given the horrors of the factory end of poultry farming, I feel it would be most unfair to single out such producers for moral condemnation. The real ethical problem with foie gras, in my view, is not in the traditional force-feeding of birds by hand but, as ever, in the inevitable industrialisation of the process. These days, sadly, most foie gras comes not from hand-reared birds on small farms but from industrial units, in which birds are raised initially in intensive broiler-house conditions, then transferred to small individual cages, where they remain for the five or six weeks it takes to force-feed them (by machine) until their livers are of marketable weight. I haven't seen it done, but a report on Radio 4's 'Food Programme' gave an uncompromising account of the miserable confinement of the ducks in question and their obvious distress at feeding time. This is not a product I could buy with a clear conscience.

Foie gras is not produced at all in the UK but we clearly have a growing taste for it. Factory-farmed foie gras, I'm sorry to say, currently accounts for about 90 per cent of UK imports. It comes not only from France but also Spain and Eastern Europe. Unfortunately, I'm afraid most of the foie gras you encounter, even in the very best restaurants, is of this industrial provenance. You are well within your rights to enquire of a waiter, or even ask when you book a table, whether the foie gras is from a small craft producer using free-range birds (the French expression is *fermier*), or an intensive source, though I can't guarantee you'll get an honest answer.

Incidentally, the liver of regular free-range or organic geese or ducks raised in this country will never be foie gras but it will still be delicious. You should receive it with the rest of the giblets and you certainly shouldn't waste it. If you're not going to include it in some kind of giblet pâté, then fry it gently in a pan for a few minutes, seasoning well with salt and pepper and, intermittently, with a few drops of port. Then serve hot, on toast. This is 'chef's perks' of the highest order. The kind you want to avoid sharing if at all possible.

Finally, a few words on venison liver: it is quite delicious – particularly from roe, sika and fallow deer. Talk to someone who stalks, and ask them (beg them) to save you the liver from a freshly killed beast. Or contact a venison farm and discuss picking up a liver a day or two after slaughter. Slice thinly and serve pink, as for calf's liver. Or try the extraordinary but very wonderful Scandinavian procedure described on page 408.

Sweetbreads

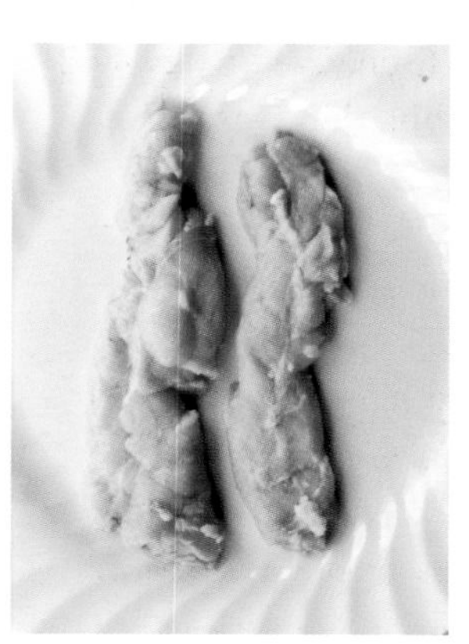

Sweetbreads, or sweatbeards as a dyslexic chef I know used to write on his menu, are one of the most highly prized of offal cuts, and rightly so. Tender and creamy, with a delicate flavour, they have long been popular with restaurant chefs, less so with home cooks. This is partly because of the elaborate, but necessary, preparation to which they must be subjected before they are ready to be transformed into a finished dish. But if this procedure is a little time consuming, it is certainly not in the least difficult.

I don't know who first applied the term sweetbread but it was undoubtedly a good marketing move: neither pancreas nor thymus gland – the heart sweetbread and throat sweetbread respectively – has quite the same appeal. No particular

Fritto Misto of Offal with Sage and Capers (p.362); Sauté of Sweetbreads with Peas and Beans (p.364); Terrine of Sweetbreads with a Broad Bean Purée (p.455)

distinction is made between these two different kinds of sweetbread, and both are prepared in exactly the same way. For the record, the rounder and slightly larger ones are likely to be heart sweetbreads (pancreas).

Both calf's and lamb's sweetbreads are available, although you'll probably have to order them in advance from all but the most comprehensively stocked cosmopolitan butcher. With calf's 'breads, the usual caveat applies: they've probably come from Continental veal calves. Tastewise, lamb's 'breads are every bit as good – and cheaper, too.

The basic preparation of sweetbreads is as follows: ideally, soak for three hours in several changes of cold water – but you can omit this step if you're in a hurry. Then, in unsalted fresh water, or a light vegetable court-bouillon, bring the sweetbreads to the boil and simmer gently for just five minutes. Drain and leave to cool. When cold, or at least cool enough to handle, take each sweetbread in your hand and pick over it, teasing out the fatty, gristly, sinewy or horny bits and discarding them as you go. Use a sharp knife where necessary. The trick, which is quickly learned, is to do this without peeling off the thin membrane that holds the smaller parts of each sweetbread together. If you do not always succeed in this, it is not the end of the world; you will simply be dealing with bits of sweetbread that are slightly smaller than might be ideal.

Your sweetbreads are now ready for whatever recipe you have chosen. Many Italian and French chefs like to serve them in rich, creamy sauces – something I have always found a cloying disappointment. The tender interior is itself almost creamy, and is best enjoyed with some sort of crust on the outside. For this reason I recommend the same treatment as for brains, i.e. coat in seasoned flour, then fry in hot oil until crisp and golden. For a classic fritto misto of lamb's offal, serve with identically treated lamb's brains and small slices of liver, with sage leaves and capers. Two irresistible companions for sweetbreads are fresh garden peas and broad beans; these are featured in my dishes on pages 364 and 455.

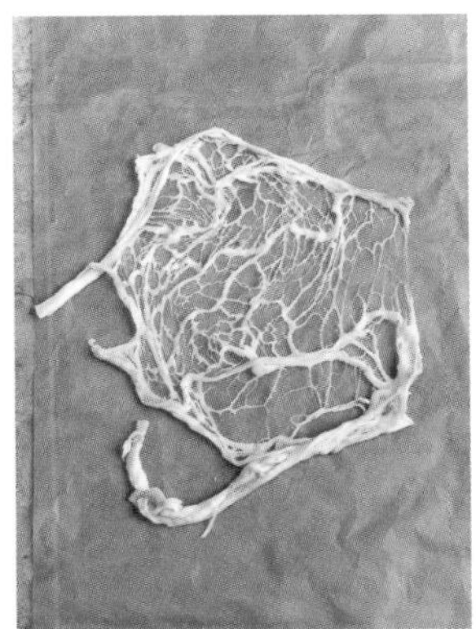

Faggots with Onion Gravy (p.459)

Caul

The caul is a thin membrane veined with fat that encases the stomach of animals. The most commonly used one is taken from slaughtered pigs. It needs to be soaked in cold water for about three hours before use, to make it flexible, then gently wiped dry with kitchen paper.

Although there is no way of preparing the caul as a dish in its own right, this piece of offal serves a useful purpose as a 'jacket' for other dishes, which it protects and lubricates with its fat. You are most likely to have seen it wrapped around butcher's faggots. It is also particularly useful for wrapping around lean pieces of meat that are to be roasted or braised – for example, a rump of beef or a chump of lamb, or a saddle of rabbit or hare.

Unlike beaten-out strips of flair fat or back fat, a caul 'jacket' does not need to be sewn up or tied up but will bind on itself if it is overlapping.

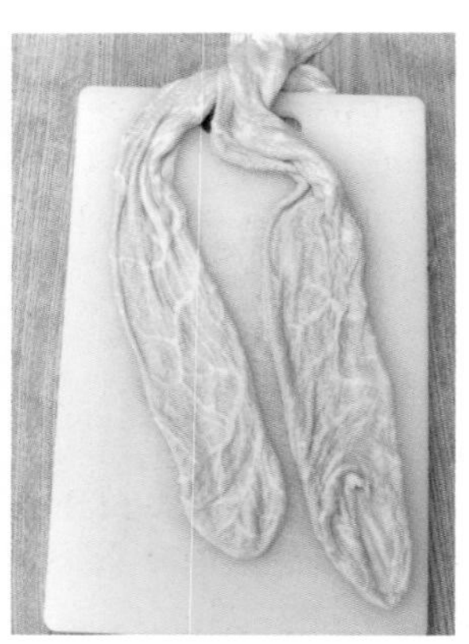

Cotechino with Lentils and Salsa Verde (p.441)

Intestines

Intestines are related to tripe (see below), both anatomically and in terms of taste and culinary use. They are, of course, the internal tubes that lead the digested food of the animal on its final journey from the stomach and back into the outside world. Needless to say, this function affects their flavour, and they are certainly an acquired taste. But, as so often, once acquired it is a taste in which enthusiasts delight to the point of revelling in it.

There is no doubt that they are more widely used, and loved, in foreign food cultures than in our own. The French make them into a powerfully flavoured sausage called the *andouillette* (challenging). The Chinese serve them crisply grilled in a sticky, sweet and spicy glaze (delicious). And in a classic Turkish *iskembecisi* (tripe house), they are served plainly boiled in an unseasoned soup, to which you then make your own judicious additions of salt, lemon juice and chilli powder (I suggest plenty of all three).

In British cuisine the most popular traditional dish made from fresh intestines is chitterlings – plaited little sausages of lightly brined pig's intestines, seasoned with plenty of pepper and traditionally fried in lard. These are now very hard to find, but one or two butchers in the West Country still sell them (see page 526). However, many of us – particularly those of us who buy good, made-in-the-shop butcher's sausages – continue to eat intestines unwittingly, as they are still the preferred natural casing of the good old British banger. They are prepared for this use by washing and salting, and come in various shapes and sizes, for making various different traditional sausages. Sheep's runners (as they are called) are for chipolatas, pig's for butcher's bangers and ox-runners for black pudding. If you want to make your own sausages, black pudding and salami, you will certainly need these natural casings. They are available by mail order (see page 529).

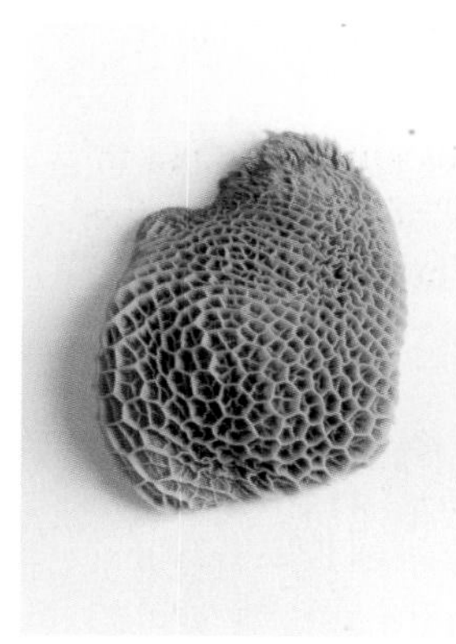

Tripe

Tripe is the stomach of an animal. Or, in the case of ox tripe, any one of the cow's four stomachs. Its curious honeycomb texture and visceral, gutty flavour make it perhaps the most challenging of all the offal cuts – beloved by enthusiasts and reviled by detractors in equal measure. (Many who profess to loathe it have, of course, never tasted it – and wouldn't dream of doing so.)

It is sad to think that most tripe lovers are probably among our older citizens, who retain an affection for it from the 'good old days'. I wonder if our taste for this offal is, with them, dying out, and in danger of being extinguished altogether. Not if I can help it!

The good and surprising news is that – thanks to our OAPs, perhaps – tripe is still available from most butchers. For some, it may be such an occasional sale that they keep it in the freezer, but that's hardly a problem, as it defrosts with dignity.

I'm guessing that a few supermarkets still stock tripe, because I have to admit it was tripe from a supermarket that was responsible for my own conversion from doubter to champion. About ten years ago, I came across a packet of ox tripe in my local Sainsbury's. On a whim, I decided to give it a go. I even followed the recipe on the packet, with a few minor alterations gleaned from Elizabeth David: I added a good half teaspoon of cayenne pepper, used beef stock instead of just water, and a few sliced carrots to boot. This, my own humble tripe *à la mode*, was a resounding success.

Compared to Continental tripe, British tripe, which is both bleached and blanched before sale, is very overprocessed, so the full intestinal aroma is considerably muted. And indeed, compared to the tripe from my own cows, which I now prepare from scratch at home, the taste is relatively meek and mild. But there will be some who regard that as no bad thing. I certainly see no need to boycott the British product. Any tripe is better than the imminently possible alternative of no tripe at all.

Giblets

Giblets is the collective term for the various items of poultry and game bird offal that were once offered with a bird as a matter of course – but now seem to be a treat that is available only from good butchers and small producers. The classic giblets comprise the neck (usually skinless), gizzard (a coarse muscle at the top of the stomach for pulverising food as it passes down from the crop), the heart and the liver.

In smaller birds (up to chicken size), the giblets are traditionally used to make a little stock, which will then bolster the gravy made in the roasting tin. I still do this whenever I have giblets, though I usually exclude the liver, which I prefer to fry and eat on toast, as a 'chef's perk', or I save them to add to the stock from the leftover roast (see pages 470-72). When it comes to well-hung game, a giblet stock can be very strong tasting, or even bitter – another acquired taste. I don't mind it fairly gamy, but occasionally, when it's turned out really bitter, I've discarded it (as 'dog's perks' – to an always grateful Dolly and Pebble).

In larger birds, such as geese and turkeys, the giblets are substantial enough to be used as a dish in their own right – usually a stew, or some kind of pâté, terrine or sausage. My own favourite giblet recipe is the stuffed goose neck in the December chapter of *The River Cottage Year.*

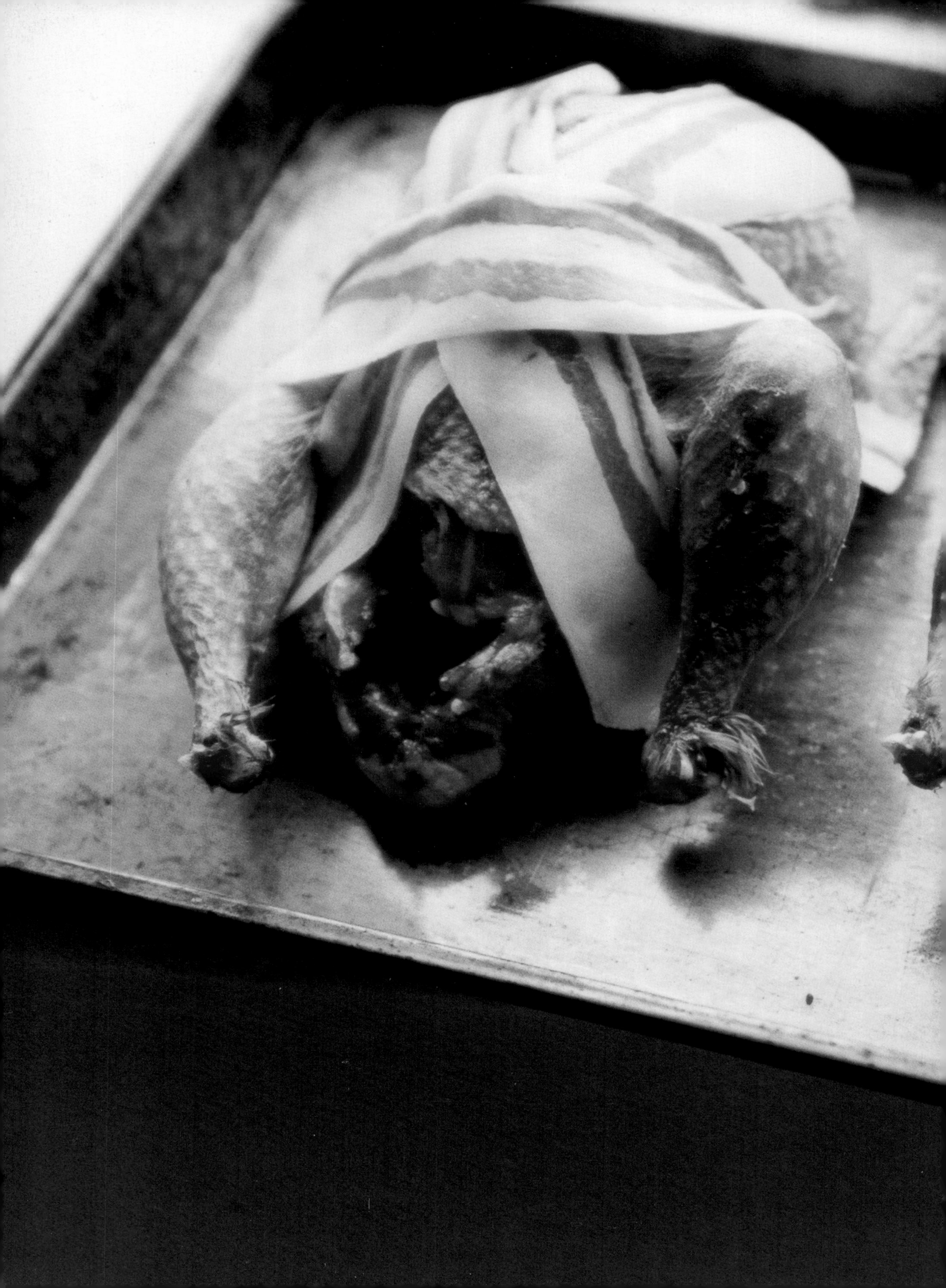

10. ROASTING

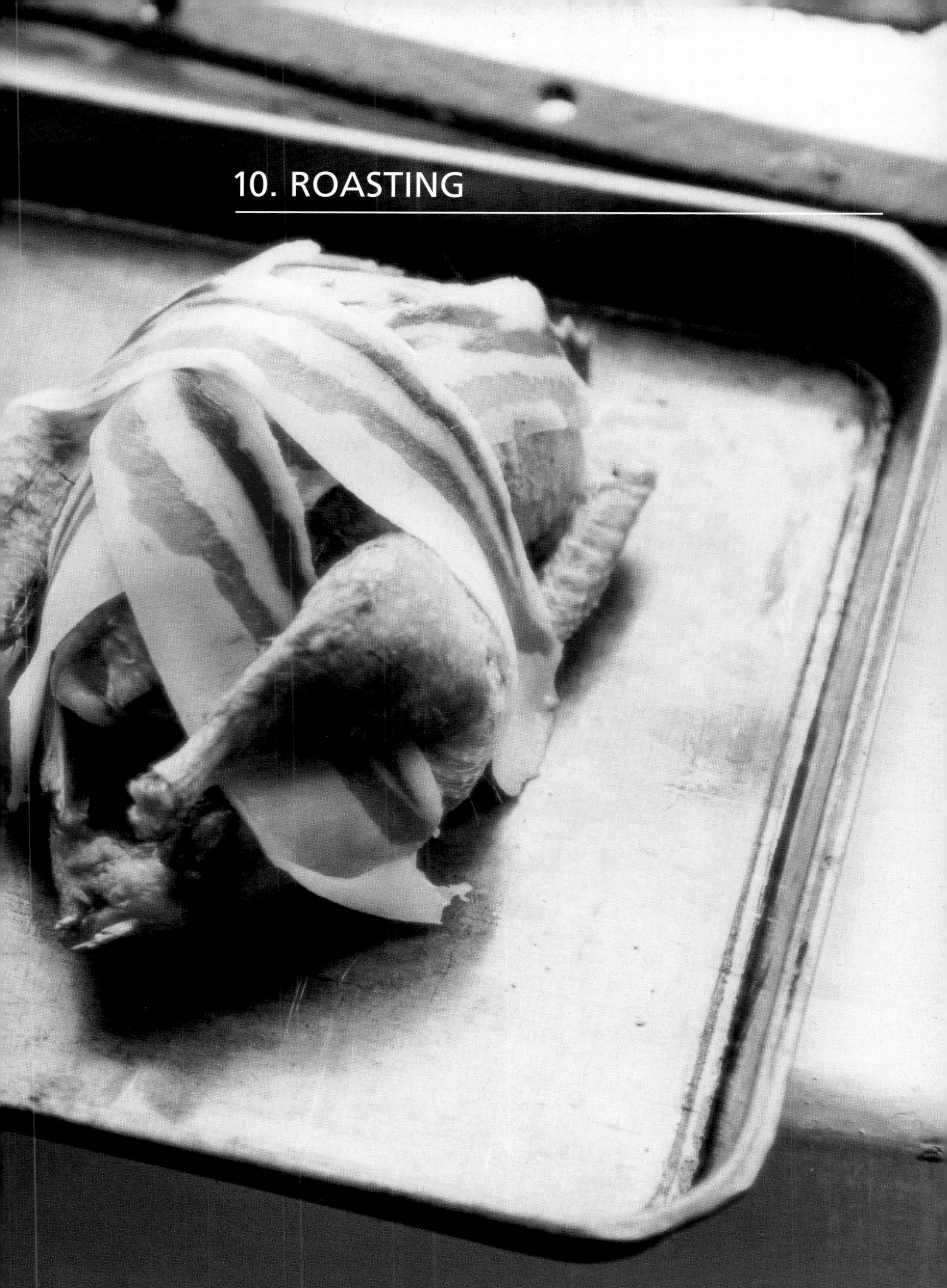

10. ROASTING

Fast and Slow Oven Cooking

This chapter comes first in the discussion of ways of cooking meat for a few simple reasons: roasting is the oldest cooking technique of all; it is, when properly understood, one of the easiest techniques to master; and it is, in my view, the most honest and delicious way there is of cooking meat.

This last thought needs a little explanation. It's hard to claim that a good roast is more delicious than an expertly made curry, a home-smoked sausage or a well-flavoured stew. In fact, it's hard to make the comparison at all. What a roast offers you, however, is significantly different from these other things. It is something pure and unadulterated: meat tasting of meat, and little else.

This makes roasting the ultimate test – not of the cook's skill (I have said roasting is easy, and I hope this chapter will help you develop lifelong confidence in your ability to roast successfully) but of the meat itself. The best roast you ever taste will be the best piece of meat you ever buy. And the best meat you ever taste will probably have been roasted. This should put you on your mettle not in the kitchen but in the marketplace. If you want to be a great roaster, then Chapter 3, Buying Meat, is probably even more important than this one.

I'll add another thought on shopping here. If you are buying meat for roasting, there is a lot to be said for choosing a piece a fair bit bigger than is strictly necessary for the number of people you are planning to feed. Firstly, it's always nice to be generous. Secondly, it may feel like an extravagance but you know that there's no chance of any leftovers being wasted (not with my final chapter, Meat Thrift, there's not). Thirdly, a larger piece of meat gives you leeway and boosts confidence. You can risk cooking, say, a rib of beef, a leg of lamb or even a whole goose with a view to serving it pink. Even if it turns out a bit too bloody next to the bone, you still have enough meat that is properly pink, medium rare or even well done, to satisfy all comers. I'm not asking you to be wildly extravagant, but being generous to your guests is also a way of being easy on yourself.

A plea for quality and generosity is the first of my three Rules of Roasting. The other two are simple matters of technique, proven over time by generations of cooks but not always fully appreciated these days. Here's a simple summary of the rules:

1. Choose suitable cuts of meat of generous size and good (ideally outstanding) quality. This means, with few exceptions, meat that has been properly hung. Give due consideration also to a joint on the bone, which has more flavour, and more interesting leftover possibilities, too.
2. Generally, roast hot and fast to begin with (I call this the 'half-hour sizzle', of which more later), then more moderately to finish cooking the meat.
3. Always rest your roast for *at least* fifteen minutes before carving it.

The last rule is perhaps the most important because it is the least observed. You may well have heard it before. And you may have dismissed it as some slightly cheffy bit of fuss that might make a small difference but is hardly going to be critical. In fact, it is beyond doubt that resting the roast changes the eating quality of the meat, leaving it more tender, juicier and therefore more flavoursome.

Recently, I've done the experiment that proves this. I roasted two small sirloin joints of beef from the same animal, off the bone, putting them in the same very hot oven, one twenty minutes later than the other. The first one came out after half an hour and was rested for twenty minutes. Then the other one came out and I carved them both straight away. The difference was quite distinct. Both joints were very rare, but in the rested joint the transition from the well-done outside to the nearly raw middle was more gradual. In the unrested joint, the mouth feel of the outer, fairly well-done slices was drier and less juicy. The first 'nice' slice – medium rare, you might call it – was chewy and a bit tough. You wouldn't have complained, because this was very good, well-hung meat. But in the rested joint the equivalent slice was something different altogether: more succulent, juicier and simply nicer to eat. Pretty much as good as it gets.

I wanted to get these rules, and that last point in particular, on page one of my roasting chapter, in the hope that as many people as possible will read it. I'll be elaborating on them later in the chapter. But first I'd like to say just a little more about the history and culture of roasting.

The Honourable Roast, Yesterday and Today

Serving a roast has long been the most inclusive, magnanimous and welcoming gesture a host can make to friends and family gathered round a table. (Even vegetarians felt the need to invent the nut roast.)

Like the breaking of a loaf of bread or the opening of a bottle of wine, the carving of a roast at the table, to share among family and friends, is as honourable a ritual today as it has been for centuries. It's hardly surprising that it happens most often on a Sunday. And no wonder, when asked in a survey what their favourite meal was, well over half the country replied 'roast dinner'. The next most popular, at less than a quarter, was fish and chips.

However, it seems to me that it isn't just your guests who are honoured by a roast. So is the animal who has died to provide it. I'll be coming to the myriad and ingenious ways of dealing with the coarser cuts of a carcass in the next chapter – most of them require slow cooking of one kind or another. But choosing a prime cut and roasting it seems to me a complementary gesture. It's like saying, 'We may boil your shins in wine and make your kidneys into pies, but this fine, lean loin, with its chine and ribs and beautifully marbled meat, we will keep this whole, season it only with salt and pepper, roast it hot, serve it bloody, and think of you.'

I don't expect everyone to share these sentiments but to me, perhaps because I raise my own meat, they are intensely felt. And I'd happily extend the notion from meat to fish, especially one I've caught myself. Bringing a whole fish to the table, rather than fillets, also strikes me as generous and civilised, and a proper tribute to the creature you are going to eat.

But back to the roast. What is it exactly, and how did it come about? We all know what roasting means. Or think we do. It's cooking something – often meat, sometimes fish and occasionally vegetables – in an oven, where it is directly exposed to the dry heat circulating all around it. A number of other factors are more or less implied in the term (though there are exceptions): the heat will be fairly fierce, at least at the beginning; fat and juices will be available for basting the roast and creating a crisp, caramelised coating (it's this, and not oven temperature or cooking time, that really distinguishes roasting from baking – think of potatoes). This is the modern understanding of the word.

It didn't use to mean that at all ...

For centuries, roasting meant cooking over, or beside, the fierce heat of an open fire. In its crudest form, as practised by our hunter-gatherer ancestors, an animal, or part of an animal, was literally thrown on the fire. It was soon discovered that a more appetising and digestible meal could be achieved by suspending the meat above or to the side of the fire and turning it occasionally. The kit for doing this evolved over the centuries from a few sticks and stones that might happen to be handy to carefully designed spits and spit rests, forged in iron and other metals.

It is a tribute to people's appreciation of good roast meat that kits for spit roasting rapidly evolved to be remarkably subtle and adjustable, even by today's standards. Levers and pulleys adjusted the proximity of the meat to the fire and raised one end of the roast higher than the other. A pair of dogs in a giant hamster wheel could keep the meat turning slowly, steadily, until it was done, quite literally, to a turn.

Over the centuries, a lot of ingenuity has gone into the art of roasting but there is no doubt that the modern oven has made it much easier. Temperature control is at the twist of a dial. Heat surrounds the meat completely, which speeds up the process. Fans keep the air moving to ensure even cooking. Clocks or digital dials with bells, buzzers and beepers remind us not to let the meat burn.

So how does all this affect the taste of the meat?

The principal difference between traditionally spit-roasted meat and meat roasted in modern ovens is that the latter will not taste of the fire. It will lack the lightly smoky, slightly woody flavour that characterises spit-roast or charcoal-grilled meat. Initially, this was undoubtedly considered a sophistication, and a virtue. But what goes around comes around, and for some time now cooks have nurtured a nostalgic longing for the taste of 'real fire' in food, and in meat in particular. These days, almost every fashionable restaurant has at least a charcoal grill, and quite possibly a wood-fired oven as well.

I don't have a problem with this. I think meat from the chargrill and the wood-fired oven can be delicious, particularly lamb and pork. But I wouldn't want the

home cook to get paranoid. If all you have to roast your meat is a basic, budget-priced conventional oven, don't panic. Provided it gets to a high enough heat (at least 210°C/Gas Mark 6 – we'll discuss this later), it will do the job fine.

In fact, with some meats it may be the best possible way to do the job. If I've managed to obtain a really stunning forerib of beef, tantalisingly marbled and beautifully aged, I would actually prefer to cook it in a regular oven rather than on a spit or in a wood-fired oven, for much the same reason as I will not be planning to smother it in garlic or herbs. All I want the oven to deliver is heat, not flavour. The flavour I'm interested in is, if I've done the shopping right, all in the meat.

Nowadays spit roasting, charcoal roasting and wood-fired ovens are specialised techniques that require time, commitment and a certain amount of fairly specialised kit. However, they are extremely worthwhile pursuits for the meat enthusiast, and for anyone who likes to eat *al fresco*, so I will be dealing with them all in Chapter 13, Barbecuing.

Having established that roasting is something you will want to do in your oven, here's how it's done.

A Theory of Perfection

You may wish to roast anything, from a snipe weighing just 100g to a 10kg leg of pork. It would be foolish to pretend that a single set of instructions will see you right in all cases. However, it would be equally silly to insist that every roast requires an elaborate recipe. What you need is a set of principles to be applied, options to be considered, and a few exceptions and special cases to be noted. This should give you the confidence to roast just about any suitable piece of meat without recourse to written instructions.

The first thing is to understand what is at stake when you roast meat. What are you trying to achieve for that leg of lamb or forerib of beef? Perfection, obviously! Few things set us salivating more than the thought, sight and smell of roasting meat. There's a good reason for this. It seems that roasting meat creates a very special set of flavours that have a remarkably universal appeal to human taste buds. The searing of meat by roasting, to create the crisp, caramelised coating I have described above, alters the cellular structure of the meat's surface, creating a completely new set of complex soluble compounds. Food scientists refer to them generically as the 'browning flavours', and are still trying to unravel their complex structure and understand the reasons for their great appeal (not least in an ongoing mission to 'bottle them' for commercial purposes).

In the past our predilection for these powerfully tempting flavours, like all our specific appetites, clearly served an evolutionary function. We are not very good at digesting raw meat but cooked meat is more acceptable to our essentially fruit- and vegetable-loving gut. So those who relish the flavour of cooked meat are likely to have less stressed guts and fewer fatal diseases of the digestive tract – a benefit they will confer on their offspring.

Of course, other cooking methods, such as frying and grilling, also produce an abundance of these appealing flavours. But it is undoubtedly an intrinsic part of the roast's appeal that it has this richly flavoured surface. So this feature must come high on our wish list of what we want from our roast.

That's the story of the surface, but what about the inside of the meat? The browning reactions cannot occur here, as the meat is too moist. But other radical changes take place as the inside of the meat heats up, and they also have consequences for our appetites. Flavour and texture appear to depend principally on the presence of moisture (essentially water) and fat. We seem to relish a state of juiciness in which the fat has liquefied, lubricating the fibres of the meat and making them easier to tear (or chew) apart, and in which the watery juices have been driven out of suspension in the muscle fibres (as they contract with the heat) but have not yet left the meat. They are, if you like, warm and flowing.

Again, from the evolutionary point of view, it is no coincidence that meat in this hot but not dry state has retained most of its nutritional value – unlike the burnt outside, whose value lies not in its intrinsic goodness but as a lure, an indicator of goodness within. Much of this goodness – natural sugars, vitamins and soluble proteins – is dissolved in the meat's juices, and is lost if they are lost. True, raw meat with no loss of moisture at all is even more nutritious than juicy, cooked meat. But it seems our decadent desire for the browning flavours has led us to a neat trade-off between nutrition and digestibility.

The evolutionary angle is perhaps a bit of a diversion. I'm not saying you should keep your roast moist because it will be good for humanity, or even for you. But the gastronomic trade-off definitely mirrors the nutritional one (as it so often does). The perfect roast will give you the best of both worlds: an irresistible, intensely savoury-sweet crust, and a wholesome, succulent, more subtly flavoured interior. The crust and the crumb. The toffee and the apple.

The loss of moisture in a piece of roasting meat is a fairly simple function of heat, over time. In theory, it could be minimised by either roasting hot for a short time or roasting at a lower temperature for a longer time. The latter, scientists agree, would be marginally more efficient in preserving overall moisture in a piece of meat but at the expense of two factors beloved of the diner: the much-vaunted roast crust and the gradation from well done on the outside to rare in the middle.

It's worth noting that long, slow roasting has its champions. Recently the chef and food writer, Heston Blumenthal, has been writing about his experiments with long cooking times at low temperatures – nor merely for traditional 'pot-roasting' cuts (see pages 213-14) but for prime roasting cuts as well. His radical recipes prescribe several hours cooking in an oven set at around, or even less than, 100°C. The idea is to produce roast meat (if it can be called that) that is very moist and tender – but not rare, and not browned. I have followed several of these recipes, and I think the technique is most successful with chicken, if you can live without the crisp skin, and pork, if you can live without the crackling (or cook it separately, though you'll need a second oven). The meat is certainly exceptionally moist and tender, but I would say that the lack of crisp-skin bonus and the much-loved browning flavours means that this is a technique for occasional experiments rather than regular roasting.

I have, though, as a result of my Heston experiments, begun to knock back my second-phase cooking time from a conventional 180°C/Gas Mark 4 to a more moderate 160°C/Gas Mark 3, and I'm delighted with the results.

So in the pursuit of the best of all possible worlds – crisp skin and browning flavours, plus moist, tender meat (sometimes rare) – I offer my personal 'best roasting practice'. It's based on a simple three-phase procedure: the Sizzle, the Cooking and the Rest.

Phase 1: the half-hour sizzle (210-230°C/Gas Mark 6-8)

In a sense, this is the easy bit. Bung just about any decent joint of meat into a very hot oven (say, 220-230°C/Gas Mark 7-8), lightly salted, and it will develop a pretty agreeable, flavoursome crust within twenty or thirty minutes.

However, if you continue to cook the meat at that temperature for much longer than half an hour you will start to damage it. Not only will your perfectly formed roast crust start to burn to unpalatable blackness but the juices will head rapidly from the centre to the surface, where they will trickle out and/or evaporate.

So although you will need that heat to create your crust, it cannot be sustained for long without doing more harm than good. For most joints, that critical time is about half an hour, so I call this high-heat phase the 'half-hour sizzle'. This may sound like a worryingly all-encompassing time frame for joints and birds that vary greatly in size, shape and substance. It is not an absolute. But it is a surprisingly reliable and effective guideline for all but the largest, smallest or oddest-shaped meats for roasting.

In theory, you could give your roast the HHS at any point during a longer cooking period at a lower temperature. But traditionally the beginning of cooking has long been favoured for the searing phase. This is largely thanks to a theory that has turned out, on examination, not to hold water (literally, as it happens). The view was that by searing the meat initially in a very hot oven you somehow 'sealed' it, preventing the juices from escaping during the rest of the cooking period. On scientific analysis, it turns out that this simply doesn't happen. The crust that forms from searing may be desirable and delicious but it is not impermeable. Moisture escapes, both as vapour and by trickling through 'cracks', and in fact is drawn from the roast particularly rapidly once the process has got going – i.e. after about half an hour.

Nevertheless, I like to include the HHS at the beginning for several reasons. Most importantly, a searing heat at the start of cooking removes less moisture from the meat than it would at the end. This is because cold raw meat, which retains moisture suspended in the fibres, will be less ready to give up its liquid to evaporation than warm meat that has already been cooking for some time and in which the juices are already 'flowing' – i.e. released from suspension. Secondly, it allows you to think of roasting as a simple three-phase procedure: the Sizzle, the Cooking and the Rest. Since the first and last of these are more or less invariable every time you roast, the only bit that need exercise your brain is the middle bit, the cooking. This is undoubtedly a great confidence booster. Finally, starting with the sizzle achieves one of the main objectives, the delectable roast crust, right at the start of cooking, along with the added bonus of filling the kitchen with the delicious smell of roasting meat sooner rather than later.

Exceptions to the rule are easy enough to grasp. Small roasts that would be overcooked, or dried out, in half an hour at that temperature are special cases. I'm thinking particularly of small joints of red meat (say, less than a kilo) that you want to serve pink: a fillet of beef or venison or a small rack of lamb, for example. For some of these roasts, there is no phase two. The sizzle, of ten to thirty minutes (depending not just on weight but on thickness), followed by the rest, is all they will need. Small game birds, such as snipe, woodcock, partridges, young pigeons, teal and doves, are another special case.

Very large roasts – big, fat legs of lamb, mutton or pork, large on-the-bone beef rib joints, whole haunches of venison etc – may merit an extension of the sizzle time to forty to forty-five minutes. Incidentally, this extended sizzle may sometimes be enough on its own to take care of a small to medium joint that you wish to serve pink. For a small leg of spring lamb, for example, forty-five minutes at the full-on sizzle, followed by a full thirty-minute rest in the open, turned-off oven, will be just enough for those who like it very rare.

The temperature I favour for the sizzle is generally 220-230°C/Gas Mark 7-8. I would lower this to 210-220°C/Gas Mark 6-7 for what I would call 'delicate roasts' – mainly this means farmed 'white meat' poultry, such as chicken and turkey, and smaller pork joints, particularly if they are not well protected by a layer of fat. Even at their best, these meats do not have much in the way of marbling fat (see page 36), and so are in greater danger of drying out. With poultry such as chicken and turkey, the skin is thin and burns easily, while the white meat is very susceptible to drying out. Farmed ducks and geese, though, with their copious layer of fat to baste them as they cook, and more robust, darker meat, are well able to stand the full 230°C/Gas Mark 8 for the full half hour.

Synthesising these exceptions is the roast chicken, which for an average-sized bird of 1.5-2kg seems to me to thrive on a slightly shorter sizzle (say, twenty minutes) at 210°C/Gas Mark 6, followed by forty minutes or so at 180°C/Gas Mark 4, followed by a fifteen- or twenty-minute rest. The recipe for Herb Roast Chicken (page 244) spells it out pretty clearly.

So that's the sizzle for you. Not a cast-iron rule but a principle that I hope will help you approach any roast with confidence and a bit of attitude: by effecting major change on your roast from the outset, at a high temperature, you take control.

Phase 2: the cooking (160-180°C/Gas Mark 3-4)

By way of experiment, try taking a big roasting joint, such as a whole forerib of beef or a large leg of lamb, give it the half-hour sizzle, whip it out of the oven and carve it straight away. On the outside it will look delectably roasted, pretty much done already, but you'll be amazed by what's happening on the inside. The first slice will show that the meat is very pink, even just below the surface. The second will be bloody as hell. And the third will probably reveal that, even just a few inches inside, the meat is quite raw and cold, as yet completely unaffected by the heat. After such a short time, even in a really hot oven, you may have achieved your roast crust, but with a big joint the actual cooking has hardly started.

A 750g fillet of beef, by contrast, may be spot on: a scant inch of doneness around the outside may be all you want, and a fifteen-minute rest would settle and gradate the meat nicely into its still-raw middle – perfect for the *bleu* brigade.

My point is that in most cases, the actual cooking of the meat really takes place after the half-hour sizzle. Sure, you've got the thing started. The heat is moving. Now you must turn the oven down to a more 'moderate' temperature. This temperature will support the continued journey of heat towards the centre of the roast but at a more modest, controlled pace, which minimises trauma to the meat. Conventional wisdom usually puts this at 180°C/Gas Mark 4, which certainly gives reliable results. In the light of Heston's observations, and my own subsequent experiments, however, I now usually go for phase 2 at about 160°C/Gas Mark 3 (and this is the temperature I suggest in my tables below).

Phase 2 is much more variable than phase 1 or phase 3, depending principally on the size of the roast. It can take between 0 (the aforementioned fillet) and 250 minutes (we're talking huge turkeys here). Where you stop on this continuum is the major decision of roasting. It depends, of course, on your personal taste (and that of your guests). It's all a matter of how you like your meat 'done'.

I can't tell you how that is (though I discuss the merits of 'pinkness' on page 225). But if you know how you like your meat I can tell you roughly how long it will take to get it there. I say roughly, because there will always be variables that are hard to account for. Ovens behave differently. Temperature dials are rarely precise. The starting temperature of the meat (is it fridge cold, say 2-4°C, or larder cold, say 7-10°C, or room temperature, say 15-20°C?) will also make a difference, the more so the bigger the joint.

Nonetheless, I can get you close, by one of two methods. You can either follow the guidelines of minutes per 500g given in table A, below, or you can use a meat thermometer, following the guidelines in table B. For larger joints – say, anything over 4kg – a meat thermometer reading will be far more reliable than a minutes x weight calculation, which will begin to fail you at this weight and over because it will prescribe an overlong cooking time. You can imagine that a 6kg forerib of beef will not be 'medium' at all after the prescribed three hours. It will be well done, if not overdone.

The reason for this (and it's obvious if you think about it) is that suitable roasting times aren't purely a function of weight but also vary according to the size and shape – particularly the thickness or diameter – of the joint. To appreciate this point, think sausages. A 20 cm-long sausage will weigh twice as much as a 10 cm-long sausage but, since they are the same thickness, it will hardly take twice as long to cook. By the same token, a ten-rib rack of pork will not take twice as long to cook as a five-rib rack, even though it will weigh around double. In fact it might only take another fifteen or twenty minutes longer to finish off. Weight is used for calculating roasting times because otherwise you'd be getting out your dividers, your parabolic curve and your calculator. Weight is simply the most convenient overall guide to size and shape, at least for a mid-range joint of, say, 2-4 kg.

Having to consult any kind of table will always irritate some cooks, who reckon they can size up a joint by eye and feel and work out its cooking time accordingly. Certainly experience may get you to a point where you don't actually have to weigh the meat and do a sum. But you should at least come to a decision about how long you're going to give it and stick with it. And don't forget to look at your watch when the meat goes in. In the kitchen, sometimes time flies and sometimes it just doesn't.

So, swallow your pride and get yourself a meat thermometer and/or check out the tables. You'll soon have them in your head. (For red meats it's easy: just think, in rough terms per 500 g, ten minutes for Rare, fifteen for Medium, twenty for Well Done – or R10, M15, WD20 minutes per 500 g.) You may notice that my times are somewhat shorter than conventional tables in other books. But believe me, I've checked them and they work – provided you take into account Phase 3 – the all-important rest.

Table A: Roasting Times (in minutes per 500 g) for Larger Meat Joints

Give your joint the twenty- (up to 2 kg) to thirty-minute (over 2 kg), or even forty-minute (over 3 kg) sizzle at 210-230°C/Gas Mark 6-8, reduce the heat to 160°C/Gas Mark 3, then apply the following guide. For extra large joints (5 kg plus), go for the shorter cooking times in brackets.

Beef (rib, sirloin and rump), lamb and venison (leg, shoulder, saddle and haunch)

Rare (very pink in the middle)	*10 (9) minutes per 500 g*
Medium (just pink in the middle)	*15 (12) minutes per 500 g*
Well done (not pink at all)	*20 (18) minutes per 500 g*

Pork

Well done (good for loin, leg and rack)	*25 minutes per 500 g*
Very well done (good for thick ends and spare rib joints)	*30 minutes per 500 g*

The juices for pork should always run clear, not pink.

Table B: Meat Thermometer Readings

The temperature given is that at which the joint should be removed from the oven. A rest of twenty to thirty minutes will then complete the roasting, raising the temperature in the centre of the meat by several degrees.

The meat thermometers I like best are the kind with a flat, round dial mounted at right angles on a testing skewer (don't buy the cheapest, though, as they are simply not accurate). The procedure for testing is to push the skewer end into the thickest part of the joint so that the point is as close as possible to the centre of the meat – but not too close to any bones, as this may skew the reading slightly. Leave it in for a good twenty seconds before taking a reading.

Beef, lamb and venison

Very rare	*45°C*
Rare	*50°C*
Medium	*60°C*
Well done	*70°C*

Pork (should never be served rare)

Medium	*70°C*
Well done	*75°C*

Table C: Roasting Times for Poultry and Game Birds

Here the times given are the total cooking times, including the sizzle. The sizzle is for up to twenty minutes at 220-230°C/Gas Mark 7-8 for dark-meat game birds, or 210°C/Gas Mark 6 for white-meat poultry. Thereafter the temperature is 180°C/Gas Mark 4. Times are for serving unstuffed game birds medium rare (just pink), and other poultry as appropriate. In each case the lower figure is for smaller specimens, the higher one for larger. Rest the meat, ideally breast downwards, for ten to twenty minutes, according to size (the larger the longer).

Snipe	*8-10 minutes*
Woodcock	*12-20 minutes (see also page 252)*
Pigeon	*15-20 minutes*
Teal and widgeon	*20-25 minutes*
Grouse	*20-30 minutes*
Partridge	*25-35 minutes (see also page 251)*
Pheasant	*30-40 minutes*
Guinea fowl	*30-40 minutes*
Mallard	*35-45 minutes*
Chicken	*45-70 minutes (test that the juices run clear) (see also page 244)*
Fat duck (farmed)	*60-90 minutes (see also pages 246-7)*
Fat goose	*70-120 minutes (see also page 247)*
Turkey	*100-200 minutes (test that the juices run clear)*

Phase 3: the rest

I begged you to take this on board at the beginning of the chapter, and with good reason. It makes such a difference. If you think you are a pretty competent roaster but don't usually bother to rest your roasts, then start now and reap the rewards – not to mention the praise. Here's the science.

The ability of meat tissue to hold water decreases as it heats up. So the hotter, outer layers of the roast will quickly expel hot juices, especially when cut. Resting a roast will lessen the temperature difference between the outside of the meat and the centre, increasing the water-holding capacity of the cooling outer layer and evening out the water-holding capacity throughout the joint. In layman's terms, you could reasonably say that the moisture 'settles back into the meat', travelling from the outside back to the centre as the temperature evens out through the joint. To achieve this most desirable effect, your roast should be rested at warm room temperature or a little above – and not in a draught that will chill the outside of the meat. Opening the oven door and turning it off is one favoured method, but only do this if you are confident that your oven cools very quickly. Otherwise you will be continuing to cook your roast, not resting it.

Resting the meat does you another great service. It helps to forgive any minor miscalculations you have made in the overall cooking time. Slightly overcooked meat will be less dry after resting, because moisture at the outside will have been drawn back into the meat. Slightly underdone meat will be less 'raw' as the warm juices are drawn back towards the middle, continuing the cooking process a little.

Slow Roasts and Pot Roasts

Rules, of course, were made to be broken. You will no doubt have heard the terms 'slow roasting' and 'pot roasting'. They both refer to methods of oven-cooking joints of meat that deploy a longer cooking time at a lower temperature. (And both pre-date Heston's low-temperature roasting experiments with prime cuts!)

In classic slow roasting, the sizzle phase is abbreviated, or dispensed with altogether, and so the magic savoury crust of the regular roast is lost. But this isn't necessarily a tragedy. The aim of slow roasting is to create a different set of virtues in the meat, sometimes using cuts that would not respond well to fast roasting – coarser cuts of beef, such as topside, silverside or rolled backrib, for example, or older, tougher game birds. Slower, longer roasting, often with the protection of added 'bards' of fat (see pages 218-20) means that these meats can still be served moist, maybe even just pink. But they will not be challengingly rare, as the grain of the meat is too coarse to make this palatable.

Sometimes the cut or joint is the same as for fast roasting: a leg or shoulder of lamb, mutton or pork, a perfectly decent plump young chicken or pheasant, a loin of young pork. But the aim is quite different: tenderness, not as in pink and juicy but as in flaking effortlessly off the bone in shreds that melt in the mouth; enhanced taste, not by the fierce caramelisation of the outside of the meat but by the gentle action of added flavours, such as herbs, spices, vegetables, fruit and wine; an accompanying sauce, or juices, that needs little enhancement or reduction, because it is finished when the meat is finished.

And this is where slow roasting becomes pot roasting – the additional ingredients go into a pot with the meat, which they at least partially, if not completely, cover. The lid may be off, on, or ajar. It is clear that we are well on the way to a stew here, and a discussion which takes place in more detail in the next chapter.

It is questionable if this is really roasting at all. But again, I'm not going to be the one to insist on rewriting the cookery dictionary. What I will say is that slow roasting and pot roasting can produce really stunning results (you may have noticed that the slow-roast Aromatic Shoulder of Pork 'Donnie Brasco' on page 231 ranks in my personal top twenty in the Alternative Recipe Index on page 532). I urge you to try them both. But in terms of practical guidelines, I feel that these are techniques where, for once, a selection of dependable – but very adaptable – recipes may be more useful than any further discussion here about principle and practice. So that is what you'll find in the recipe section that follows.

Enhancing a Roast: Tricks of the Trade

I think that takes care of the meat of the matter. Now for the trimmings, by which I mean some supplementary thoughts and tips on roasting – some general, others for specific joints and cuts – that will help make you a true master of the roast.

Preheating the oven

This is essential, if obvious. Some cookery writers make this the first instruction of almost every recipe that requires the oven. I can't quite bring myself to do that, because it seems so dreary and pedantic, but I make no apologies for putting it up front here. The tables above are based on putting meat for roasting into an oven that is very hot from the outset. As I've said, the temperature I would like you to preheat the oven to is 210-230°C/Gas Mark 6-8. If you're not convinced by your oven's performance, buy an oven thermometer and check its real maximum temperature. If you can't get it much above 200°C, then I'm afraid you're going to have trouble roasting successfully.

You should know how long it takes your oven to heat up. Don't put the meat in until the required temperature is indicated (sorry to be bossy).

Choosing a roasting tin or dish

Roasting tins and heatproof dishes come in all sizes and materials and most of them are more or less functional. All I would say is, you'll always do better to favour the robust over the flimsy – and something you can put on the hob is essential for gravy-making. That said, just go for something of roughly suitable size. In other words, don't strand a small roast in the middle of an enormous roasting tin: the valuable juices will spread too thinly, evaporate and burn, spoiling your chance of making a good gravy. And, at the other end of the scale, don't cram a roast into a tin so tightly that it ends up cooking in its own juices rather than roasting (unless you are pot roasting, when this is just the effect you are looking to achieve).

The other decision you have to make is whether or not to raise your joint above the base of the tin with a roasting rack. Many cooks insist that you should, for much the same reason as you need to avoid the too-small tin: to prevent the base of your roast from stewing in its own juices and fat. I wouldn't be so strict. Having been lazy about using a roasting rack for a number of years, I have come to accept the different taste and texture of the meat on the base of a roast as an added element of interest. It may sometimes be a little greasy, but a modicum of the 'stewing effect' creates flavour and texture – sometimes gelatinous, sometimes a bit like a confit – that can be rather wonderful, especially on pork and poultry. The contact between the meat and the tin will also generate more caramelised bits that can only do good things for your gravy.

If the amount of fat flowing from my roast is excessive (as it is sure to be with a goose or duck, and as it often is with one of my very fat legs of mutton), I can always pour some off at intervals during the cooking time.

So, I leave that one up to you, but I wouldn't be a stickler for the rack.

Seasoning and preparing the meat

All I mean by this is, have a quick think about what you have in front of you and how you would like it to be at the end of the cooking time. Then ask yourself, is there anything you should do to it before it goes in the oven to help you achieve that result?

The most basic question concerns that most basic of culinary commodities: salt. To salt or not to salt the roast before cooking has been much debated over the years. The case against is yet again concerned with preserving moisture in the meat: salt draws out water and will, the argument goes, dry out a roast unnecessarily. The case for is, of course, to do with flavour: salt, it goes, is absolutely essential to create the fully satisfying taste associated with our beloved roast crust and its much-discussed 'browning flavours'.

It is the second argument that I find most persuasive – which is not to say that the first is not valid. It is. But, in the quest for perfection, a very modest seasoning of salt over the roast will generally do more good than harm. I like to use flaky Maldon salt, which has a pleasing 'less is more' quality about it. A couple of good pinches, ground fairly fine between finger and thumb, will usually do the trick for a roast chicken or leg of lamb. You may have noticed that salt, especially flaky salt, has a tendency simply to fall off some joints – particularly those with a covering of dry skin or hard, cool fat. A light massage of olive oil or soft butter will help the salt (and other seasonings) to stick, as well as providing a little extra lubrication during the initial sizzle phase.

As always, I make a few exceptions. On small, lean roasts, such as fillets of beef or venison, or pork tenderloin, where a natural layer of fat is missing and the action of salt may be harsher and more critical, I tend not to season until near the end of cooking. A few minutes are just sufficient for the salt to dissolve into and flavour the browned surface. With game birds, where bacon is used for barding (see page 219), the salt in the bacon will do the job of seasoning the skin. Or there is the 'frothing' alternative (see page 221). As for pepper – yes, almost always, and freshly ground. But again, in moderation.

Of course, there are plenty of seasonings available beyond salt and pepper. And I have included some great recipes for roasts in this chapter that give full instructions for preparing and seasoning the meat prior to roasting. But I'd also like to give you the confidence to make these executive decisions yourself sometimes. I've spoken, perhaps a bit too piously, about the purity of the best roast beef, unadulterated by anything except salt and pepper. Of course, most meat gains, not loses, by exchanging flavours with a few well-chosen herbs and spices. You probably already stud your leg of lamb with garlic and rosemary. Why not add anchovies as well, for a change, or swap the rosemary for capers? Do you have fresh herbs handy, to make a herb butter to smear over the skin of your chicken? How about rubbing a few bruised thyme leaves and a garlic clove into your scored pork rind? What could you place in the cavity of a pheasant to help flavour and enrich the subsequent gravy? A knob of butter, a slice of onion, a sprig of thyme and a splash of cider? Give it a whirl.

Marinating

A marinade can be a useful way of flavouring meat and, to a limited extent, tenderising it. But it can't perform miracles. In particular, the action of acidic agents such as wine, vinegar and lemon juice, in breaking down the meat fibres in advance of cooking, make the meat much more susceptible to moisture loss during roasting. Briefly, what a marinade can't do is transform a piece of meat unsuitable for roasting into one that roasts well. In fact, it is more likely to do the opposite.

So, whilst the flavouring of certain roasts with herbs and spices (i.e. my Aromatic Shoulder of Pork on page 231, or the Roast Lamb on page 239) could be read as marinating of a kind, I rarely, if ever, steep meat for roasting in liquid marinades for any length of time. In particular, experience has taught me to shun any recipe that urges me to soak a whole haunch of venison in red wine for twenty-four hours before roasting it. How such recipes have ever come to be printed I don't know, as the results are unspeakably awful.

Stuffing

There are various reasons why you may want to stuff a joint of meat or a bird before roasting it, and there is one overarching reason why you may not. The last first. Any stuffing, by definition, will be at or near the centre of the meat and will therefore be the last thing to heat through and be cooked. The big question is, by the time the stuffing is cooked through, what fate will have befallen the surrounding meat? The answer, too often, is 'a pretty grisly one'. The dreaded turkey is the classic example: the cavity of a big bird may take kilos of stuffing. The cooking time required to deliver heat to the middle of the bird may be better measured in days than hours. By the time your stuffing is hot, the breast meat of the turkey will be as dry as a ship's biscuit, and barely more flavoursome.

An unstuffed bird cooks far quicker. Hot air can circulate in an empty cavity, cooking the bird from inside as well as out. As we have discussed, the loss of moisture is a simple function of heat over time: an empty bird cooks far faster and will therefore be juicier.

For this reason, I rarely stuff game birds or poultry, though I frequently make stuffings to cook and serve separately. But for those who simply love to stuff birds, two things may help you win the battle of the juices. Firstly consider pre-cooking, or at least preheating, the stuffing, and pile it in immediately prior to roasting. The heat will give you a head start. Secondly don't fill the entire cavity but only about half of it: this leaves some room for the all-important hot air to circulate, speeding up the cooking of both stuffing and bird.

For me, though, the meats to stuff are the ones you are happy to serve fairly well done: a boned-out loin or tenderloin of pork; a breast of lamb; a rolled, boned shoulder of mutton. Most importantly, the reason for stuffing should be decisive, not vague. Stuffings should contain strong flavours, chosen to do a job. A bland mush of breadcrumbs, eggs and a few dried herbs will not do it for me. Rather, think about some piquant capers to cut the fat of a lamb joint, or fruit and nuts to give tartness and texture to pork. With very lean cuts, such as the tenderloin, a fat-rich stuffing will help to lubricate the meat from within, so the longer cooking time needed to heat it through will be mitigated by what the stuffing gives back to the meat. And a stuffing should never be a mere 'filler'. It should vie with the meat itself as to which of the two you'd rather eat on its own.

These points are, I hope, well illustrated by the recipes for stuffed roasts on pages 229, 240 and 242.

Barding

The other assessment you need to make about your roast is to do with fat. And the right question is not, 'Is there too much?' but 'Is there enough?' As discussed, the presence of fat is critical to the flavour and quality of meat. In particular, fat is the roast's best friend. Its steady trickle over the surface of the roast during the cooking time performs two vital functions: it slows down the escape of moisture from inside the meat and it 'fries' the outside, crisping up the skin or caramelising the surface, to help produce our much-discussed roasted finish.

With this important work to do, there can hardly ever be too much fat. Some of my home-produced mutton and pork has a layer of fat at least 2 cm thick, and

I would never dream of trimming it before roasting. It doesn't mean you have to eat it. At the end of cooking, solid fat can be sliced off or liquid fat poured off, and anything on the plate that offends the fat-phobic diner can be left on the side.

So don't even think of trimming off the fat from your leg of lamb, sirloin or rib of beef, or loin of pork. Do, however, think of adding fat where it may be lacking. If the meat you plan to roast is not naturally endowed with enough fat to keep it lubricated during cooking, the simplest solution is to provide a thin, even layer and place it over the top of the meat. This is called barding, and butchers do it all the time, tying strips of rolled beef suet or pork flair fat on to lean pieces of beef to present them as roasting joints. Without this treatment, topside and silverside would never pass muster for roasting (and even with it, only the very best examples, from well-aged, well-marbled beef carcasses, will roast well).

Unrendered pork fat, such as back fat (see page 117), is ideal for barding. It will melt slowly over the meat as it roasts. Streaky bacon will do the same job but must be as fatty as possible. Using hard fat or bacon in this way is common practice when cooking partridges and pheasants: their white breast meat is more delicate than the darker meat of other game birds. But remove the barding for the last ten minutes of cooking in order to brown the skin.

Barding a roast may seem like a fiddle but it's probably less tedious than the attentions an unbarded roast may demand, i.e. ...

Basting

I must say, I think too much fuss is made about basting – which, as you probably know, means spooning the fat and/or juices from the roasting tin over the meat as it cooks. Most roasts really don't need to be basted. They have enough fat, either naturally or because you've put it there by barding, to 'self-baste' (a ludicrous term, I know) throughout the cooking time. Why slow things down by opening the oven door? Basting a leg, shoulder or rack of lamb, or a forerib of beef, for example, strikes me as a completely pointless exercise: the joint is almost completely covered in fat, which will run off and crisp up nicely as the joint roasts. In my experience, spooning over extra liquid fat does nothing discernible to enhance this process.

Very small roasts don't need it either. They'll cook quickly enough at a very high temperature to stay moist without basting. (A fillet of beef or venison, or small game birds such as woodcock and snipe, would benefit from a quick massage with a little olive oil or soft butter before cooking.)

Basting strikes me as worthwhile only when you want to achieve a certain finish on your roast that you wouldn't get if you didn't baste it. The main beneficiaries, for me, are the skin of a chicken and the crackling on a pork joint. The chicken should be rubbed with butter before roasting, then basted once or twice during it (see recipe on page 244). And crackling crackles better when basted, but again, a couple of times will do it.

There's one other basting scenario worth logging. In the absence of a natural layer of fat or skin (think pork tenderloin or neck fillet of lamb), basting can help create an interesting surface texture on otherwise lean meat. In this case it is particularly worthwhile to baste with the flavoursome juices of a roast as opposed to merely the fat: the result is the creation of what is called a 'glaze' – and very delicious it can be, too. A glaze will be all the better when the juices are enhanced with other suitable flavours – maybe redcurrant jelly, honey or mustard – and it will help to protect lean meat from drying out too much. Classic examples are honey-glazed roast pork or mustard-glazed roast rabbit.

When you do baste, get in and out of the oven as quickly as you can – avoid leaving the oven door open for any longer than is absolutely necessary.

Frothing

A variation on the basting theme, this is a traditional method of browning and crisping up the skin of fast-roasted game birds or poultry (and, as it happens, roast potatoes). The technique is as follows: about ten minutes before the bird is done (which may be about the same time as you remove any barding, or, in the case of a snipe, before it even goes in the oven), give it a quick baste, then a light sprinkling of well-seasoned flour. Continue roasting, and baste two or three more times, until it is browned and done. Like basting, it's a bit of a labour of love, but there's no doubt you get a great roast finish on your bird (or spud).

Making gravy

The art of making gravy is not to be taken lightly, but it's not something to panic over either. It's a chance to express yourself – without doubt an opportunity for creativity. But, more often than not, a little restraint and discipline are in order, too. And it goes without saying that patented gravy additives are not required.

I say gravy. It's a very English word, and one that many foreign cooks treat with disdain – so much so that many British cooks are now happier with words like *jus*, reduction or meat glaze. I'll stick to gravy – because at its best, it beats the hell out of any *jus*.

There is no recipe for gravy, nor should there be. Your roast is providing you with certain valuable resources. Your job is to use them well – enhance them, increase their volume if you can, but don't dilute them to insipidness or re-flavour them into oblivion.

The assets are not just the juices in the roasting tin. They are also, most particularly, the 'scrapings' – crisp, crusty bits sticking to the bottom of the tin. These are intense patches of burnt meat and/or highly reduced juices, and they are rich in the all-important 'browning flavours' discussed at the beginning of this chapter. Provided they are not so burnt as to taste bitter (and it's definitely worth tasting them to make sure), they hold the key to successful gravy. But before you go to work on them, proceed as follows:

1. Remove the meat from the roasting tin and transfer it to a warmed plate or serving tray. If you like, scrape the underside of the meat and add the scrapings to the tin.
2. Assess the amount of fat in the tin – you probably want to pour most of it away, but be careful not to lose any precious juice or meaty scrapings. If you decide to thicken the gravy with a little flour, you can afford to leave a little more fat in, as it will be blended into the gravy.
3. Assess your assets. Taste the juices: how salty are they? How concentrated? How sweet? What are the predominant flavours? What's lacking? Taste the scrapings and ask the same questions. Think about what the roast needs. A simple thin juice to add flavour and moisture? A little acidity to cut the fat? A smooth, emulsified gravy, thickened with flour? Now decide what kind of gravy you're going to make and get on with it (you haven't got all day, but you have got about twenty minutes, as the roast rests).
4. Place the roasting tin over a low hob, or on a simmering plate if you have one, and get to work on those scrapings: use the flat end of a spatula to scrape them off the tin. Rub them on the base of the tin with the spatula to help dissolve them in the juices (this is called deglazing). Add a little water or wine to help lift them. Delve into the corners, and don't waste anything. If you're going to add flour, do it now, as you deglaze. Start with no more than a teaspoon, sprinkled evenly over the tin, so it mixes in naturally as you deglaze (overdo the flour and you're forced to dilute to compensate – this is the ruination of many a gravy). Add a little more

liquid as it is needed – stock if you have it, water from cooking vegetables such as peas or carrots, if it is handy (but taste it first to make sure it is not too salty, or bitter, as cabbage or sprout water may be). Or just add plain water and/or wine. Keep tasting all the time and thinking about what might improve it.

5. Once you've deglazed all the scrapings and dissolved them as best you can, you may want to strain the gravy into a small saucepan. I often do this, as it gives me a greater sense of control: I can use a whisk to emulsify any fat, and often get away with just a tiny amount of flour. Whether you transfer your gravy to a pan to finish it or leave it in the tin, it's important that you let it boil for a minute or two if you've added any flour. This will help remove any floury taste, at the same time as settling the thickening process so you know whether you need to thin it further.

6. Finish your gravy according to your taste – and you must taste every step of the way. Most of the gravies I make are finished with nothing more than flour, water or stock, a splash of wine and a dab of redcurrant jelly, plus salt and pepper. But, for the sake of completeness, I will try and list here all the things I have used, with some success, to enhance and finish my gravies. Overall, I think in terms of the following categories:

Thickeners
Flour (needs boiling to thicken)
Butter (needs whisking in)
Cream (needs boiling to reduce)
Gravy browning (if desperate)

Looseners
Water (including vegetable cooking water)
Stock
Wine
Cider
Beer (especially stout)
Coffee (in moderation, for beef, lamb and game, but not pork)

Sharpeners
Vinegar
Lemon juice
Orange juice

Sweeteners
Redcurrant jelly (and other fruit jellies)
Apple juice
Sugar
Fruit liqueurs or spirits
Honey (good with pork)
Chocolate (good with game)
Vanilla fudge (good with pork)

Seasonings
Salt
Pepper
Chilli powder
Nutmeg
Other spices

Aromatisers
Citrus zest
Ginger (fresh grated or dry powdered)
Fresh herbs

Emergency flavour boosters

Anchovies (good with lamb)
Soy sauce (good with pork)
Worcestershire sauce (good with lamb)
A pinch of instant coffee (good with beef)
A pinch of cocoa powder (good with game)
Gravy browning (if desperate)
Stock cube (if desperate)

The list, on compilation, turns out rather longer than I'd expected! Consider these as possibilities, not prescriptions – you would probably be making a big mistake if you added more than three or four of them. Don't go overboard on the exotic flavourings unless you are really sure you want a highly flavoured 'sauce' rather than a simple, robust gravy that tastes of the meat it came from. And don't overdo wine or other alcohol: it can quickly kill the natural meat flavours in your gravy.

One final asset not to be overlooked is the extra juices that will become available as a result of carving. You will probably have made your gravy before you carve the roast. But there are few gravies that won't benefit from the last-minute addition of freshly oozed juices from the meat itself.

Above all, have fun. I *love* making gravy, and I hope you will too.

Carving and Serving

I am no expert at carving but I do know the value of a sharp knife. The sponge-like, moisture-holding properties of the roast are a factor here, too: a blunt knife will squeeze or compress the roast as you carve, and you will inevitably expel some of the valuable juices. The sharper your knife, the less pressure you need to exert to cut a slice and the less juice will be lost. If you're not a master of the sharpening steel, then one of those flexible serrated carving knives needs little maintenance and can cut like a dream – provided it's of good quality.

I think there is too much fuss made about carving roast beef into very thin slices. They may look good, and show off the skills of the carver, but they will also be prone to lose their juiciness too quickly. Very thin slices may make meat that is tough a little easier to chew, but your roast beef is going to be just perfect, so slice it generously, for more generous mouthfuls.

I would always cut chicken, lamb and pork thickly. With a leg of lamb or a chicken, I favour an approach that I suspect is rather Continental: once your guests have seen the joint or bird in all its glory, carve up pretty much the whole thing, returning the pieces/slices to the still-warm roasting tin, then taking that to the table. In this case I might not make a formal gravy at all, but instead would just check the fattiness and seasoning of the juices in the roasting tin, adjust as necessary, then let the cut pieces soak up the juices in the bottom of the tin. This is how I suggest you serve up the roast chicken on page 244.

How Pink?

I've left this controversial matter of taste to the end because, in an important sense, it's 'none of my business'. I can't tell you that you should like your meat pink and bloody just because I do. But I can tell you that, if you think you don't like it bloody, but you're not cooking the very best meat in the best way and, in particular, you're not resting it, then it's just possible you're not really giving pink meat a fair shot. Get all the parameters right and you might find yourself changing your preference from 'fully cremated' to 'bloody as hell'. Or at least to medium rare.

I say this from personal experience. I used to order my steaks medium rare, and cook roast beef 'just pink' rather than bloody. Now that I produce my own beef, and have the confidence to hang it for eight weeks or more, I like it much more underdone. I don't mind if the middle is practically raw.

My wife is even more extreme. She minds if the middle *isn't* raw. In fact, what she likes is when a good 8cm circle in the middle of the joint is absolutely fridge cold, and hasn't even felt the heat at all. Until I get to that part of the joint, I don't even bother serving her.

Raw or very rare beef is not to everyone's taste but it is, I believe, a taste that can be acquired, even worked on – a bit like sushi. It's worth acquiring, because what you then get is three different taste experiences in one roast. You have a seared, seasoned crust, where caramelised sugars and salty juices are to the fore; a ring of hot, juicy meat that gradates from medium to rare; and finally, in the centre, for enthusiasts, the steak tartare. With just a tiny dab of mustard, it really is a bit like beef sashimi.

With meats other than beef, though, I'm much more moderate. I like my roast lamb just pink – a rack somewhat pinker than a leg. And I always like a burnt bit from the outside as well. I like pigeon and the darker game birds, such as grouse and woodcock, pink – but again, only just. And I'm not happy with a chicken, pheasant or partridge, or a joint of pork, until the juices run clear.

I see I've written over 10,000 words about roasting. It's more than I meant to. But I think my exuberance is because, to me, roasting is important rather than difficult. And it's exciting rather than confusing.

I'd like to finish close to where I started – by urging you to heighten your senses when roasting. Settle for only the best meat. Cook it only with the best of intentions. Serve it only to the best people (but be forgiving). Rest it well. And make a good gravy.

May your roasts bring you much joy.

ROAST BELLY OF PORK WITH APPLE SAUCE *Serves about 8*

The thick end of the belly (last 6 ribs)

Fresh thyme leaves

Salt and freshly ground black pepper

THE APPLE SAUCE:

3-4 large Bramley apples

A squeeze of lemon juice

Grated zest (no pith) and juice of 1/2 orange

1-2 tablespoons caster sugar (to taste)

I love to roast a belly of pork because it's so fantastically forgiving. The rich seams of fat keep the meat tender and juicy, no matter how long you cook it for. So I tend to concentrate on getting the crackling right and find the rest just falls into place.

I don't like the convention of apple sauce with a very lean pork joint, such as leg or loin, because I find the tartness overpowers the delicate flavour of the meat. But for a crude, fatty cut like this, it is perfect. The citrus juice and zest keep the sauce aromatic as well as tart.

Score the skin of the belly with a sharp knife (a Stanley knife is surprisingly handy) and rub with salt, pepper and fresh thyme leaves, getting the seasoning and herbs right into the cracks. Roast in a hot oven (220°C/Gas Mark 7) for 30 minutes, then turn the oven down to 180°C/Gas Mark 4 and cook for roughly another hour, until the juices run clear when the meat is pierced with a skewer and the crackling has crackled to an irresistible golden brown. If the crackling is reluctant, whack up the heat again, as high as you like, and check every few minutes till it's done.

To make the sauce, peel, core and slice the Bramleys, tossing them with the lemon juice as you go. Put them in a pan with the orange zest and juice and a first sprinkling of sugar. Cook gently until the apples break up into a rough purée, then check for sweetness and adjust to your taste. Keep warm (or reheat gently to serve).

Remove the crackling from the pork before carving, then cut the joint into thick slices. Serve each person one or two slices with a good piece of crackling, and bring the apple sauce to the table. I like to serve this with mashed potatoes, not roast, as there's already plenty of fat and crispiness on the plate. Some simple, lightly steamed greens such as Savoy cabbage, spinach or curly kale, will help to ease your conscience as you lap up the lard.

MINCEMEAT-STUFFED PORK TENDERLOINS *Serves 6*

2 pork fillets (tenderloins)

About 2 tablespoons olive oil

Lemon juice

125g good mincemeat, preferably home-made

125g cooked chestnuts (ideally fresh, then roasted and peeled, but tinned or vacuum-packed will do)

250g well-seasoned sausage meat (or good butcher's sausages, skinned)

Salt and freshly ground black pepper

THE CINNAMON CREAM SAUCE:

200ml pork and/or poultry stock, if available (pp.474 and 470-72)

Up to 5 tablespoons double cream

1/2-1 teaspoon ground cinnamon

About 1 teaspoon redcurrant jelly (optional)

Lemon juice (optional)

You can improvise all sorts of stuffings for a pair of pork tenderloins made into a sandwich like this. Here is my 'Christmassy' version, stuffed with mincemeat – I mean the fruity kind – and a few chestnuts for good measure. The creamy sauce, spiked with cinnamon, continues the seasonal theme.

First you have to open up each tenderloin into a fairly flat, roughly even rectangle. To do this, slit the tenderloin lengthways, cutting about two-thirds of the way through the meat. Open it up, then make a couple more lengthways slits, either side of the original cut, this time cutting about half way through the meat. Using the palm of your hand, gently press and spread the meat into a rectangle. Repeat with the second tenderloin.

Place the 2 tenderloin rectangles with the rougher side (probably the cut side) facing up. Massage the surface well with a little of the olive oil and season sparingly with salt and generously with black pepper. Squeeze a little lemon juice over the meat. Spread the mincemeat, like jam on bread, evenly over the pork, half on each tenderloin. Roughly chop or crumble the chestnuts and mix thoroughly with the sausage meat. Spread this mixture in an even layer over one of the tenderloins. Place the other one on top, with its layer of mincemeat facing down.

Tie up the meat parcel with 5 or 6 lengths of string – fairly tight, but not so tight as to squeeze out the stuffing. Rub a little more olive oil all over the meat and season again. Place the parcel in the middle of a sheet of oiled foil on a baking tray and scrunch up the sides of the foil a bit so it will contain the juices as the meat cooks. But don't actually cover the meat with the foil.

Roast in a hot oven (220°C/Gas Mark 7) for 15 minutes. Baste the meat with the juices collecting in the foil, then turn the heat down to 180°C/Gas Mark 4 and cook for another 45 minutes, basting again every 10 minutes (the syrupy juices, flavoured by the mincemeat, make a lovely sweet crust on the pork). Remove from the oven when glazed and golden.

Put the meat to rest on a wooden board or warmed plate while you make the sauce. Strain all the juices from the foil into a small saucepan. If you don't have the stock, just add 2-3 tablespoons of cream and a good pinch of cinnamon and bring to the boil, whisking as you go. Taste and adjust the seasoning with salt, pepper and more cinnamon. Add a little redcurrant jelly if you think it needs sweetening, and a squeeze of lemon juice to take the edge off the richness.

For a more substantial sauce, add the stock to the roasting juices and boil hard to reduce by half. Then add 4-5 tablespoons of cream and proceed as above.

Cut the pork into slices about 1cm thick and serve 2-3 per person, arranged on a warmed plate with the sauce trickled over and, if you like, some apple slices gently fried in butter for a few minutes. And some mashed potatoes (page 518).

AROMATIC SHOULDER OF PORK 'DONNIE BRASCO'

1 whole shoulder of pork on the bone (p.117) – it will weigh about 5-8kg

5 large garlic cloves, peeled

5cm piece of fresh ginger root, peeled

2 teaspoons dried chilli flakes

2 teaspoons ground ginger

1 tablespoon brown sugar

1/2 tablespoon flaky salt

1 tablespoon sunflower or groundnut oil

1 tablespoon soy sauce

THE FIVE-SPICE MIX:

2 star anise

2 teaspoons fennel seeds

1/2 cinnamon stick

4 cloves

1 teaspoon black peppercorns

This dish gets its name because you can 'fugeddaboutit' while it cooks ever so slowly overnight in a low oven. Actually, versions of this dish have already been enthusiastically championed by both the River Café and Nigella Lawson. I include it here, shameless to be third in the queue, because not only is it a wonderful dish but it is also an incredibly elegant solution to the problem of feeding twenty or more people with minimum effort.

All I can do to claim a stake in it is offer a personalised version of the sweet spice paste (a combination of chilli, garlic, ginger and the classic Chinese five-spice mix) that is rubbed into the rind – and to give it a new, slightly silly, name. But I do urge you to try it.

Score the rind of the pork shoulder with a Stanley knife in parallel lines about 1cm apart, to a depth of 1/2-1cm (or ask your butcher to do this for you).

Grate the garlic and fresh ginger into a small bowl and mix to a paste with the chilli flakes, ground ginger, brown sugar, salt, oil and soy sauce. Pound the 5 spices in a pestle and mortar (or grind in a coffee grinder) and mix 1 tablespoonful into the paste (any left over will keep in an airtight jar; you could make larger quantities, if you like, and store).

Place the pork shoulder, skin-side up, on a rack above a large roasting tin. With your fingertips, rub just over half the spice paste into the scored rind of the pork. Place the joint in the centre of a very hot oven (230°C/Gas Mark 8) for 30 minutes (the 'half-hour sizzle'). Then remove from the oven and, using oven gloves or a thick, dry cloth, carefully turn the joint over to expose the underside. Using a knife or wooden spoon this time (the meat will be very hot), smear the remainder of the spice paste over the underside of the meat (now facing uppermost). Pour a glass of water into the roasting tin, turn the oven down to 110°C/Gas Mark 1/4 and replace the joint. Leave for anything from 16-24 hours, turning it skin-side up again, and basting with the fat and juices in the tin, about half way through. About 45 minutes before you want to eat, whack up the heat to 230°C/Gas Mark 8 again to crisp up the crackling. Keep an eye on it to make sure it doesn't burn.

To serve the pork, remove the crackled skin in a single piece and break it up to hand around your guests. Don't so much carve as scoop the tender, melting, aromatic meat on to warmed plates. Serve with a simple starch, such as noodles, plain buttered macaroni, boiled rice or even mashed potatoes. I prefer to serve a salad after, rather than greens with, the pork.

ROAST BEEF – THE FULL MONTY *Serves 10*

1 joint of aged rib of beef (3-4 ribs' worth), or aged sirloin on the bone, weighing about 4-6kg

A little olive oil or good dripping

Salt and freshly ground black pepper

This is not just a Sunday lunch, it's a celebration of all that is exciting about good meat. Now that I produce my own beef, of such high quality (he said modestly), the roast beef experience is more celebratory than ever. In fact it's about as special a meal as I can cook for close friends and family, and it now alternates with My Christmas Goose (see The River Cottage Year*) as our festive dinner.*

For me, a well-hung forerib of beef on the bone (ideally the full four ribs' worth – see page 83) is the ultimate roasting joint. Two fine alternatives are the adjoining piece of sirloin from the hindquarter, and the wing rib, both of which you can (and should) also roast on the bone.

The Full Monty is my beefy term for 'all the trimmings', which together make the roast beef experience everything it ought to be. If any of them is optional, I would say, controversially, that it is the horseradish sauce. Much as I enjoy it, I find a dab of good English mustard does much the same job. So for me, the Full Monty of trimmings is:

Yorkshire Pudding (page 517)
Perfect Roast Potatoes (page 517)
Leeks with Greens (page 523)
Beef Bone Gravy (page 516)
Creamed Fresh Horseradish (page 512)
Glazed Carrots (page 522)

Massage the whole joint with olive oil or soft dripping and season lightly all over with salt and pepper. Place in a roasting tin and put in a hot oven (220-230°C/Gas Mark 7-8). Cook for about 30 minutes, until the meat is well browned and sizzling. (If you've chosen a piece of sirloin with the fillet still attached, carve off the fillet at this point or it will get horribly overcooked. Heat it up in a hot pan later if you like, but it will be delicious at room temperature.)

Turn the oven down to 160°C/Gas Mark 3 (leave the oven door open for half a minute to help it cool quickly). Experience teaches you to know your oven and how you like your meat, but I can offer the following guidelines: after the 'half-hour sizzle', allow 9-10 minutes per 500g for very rare meat, 12-15 minutes for medium, or 18-20 minutes if you insist on having it well done. The shorter cooking times are for joints of 5kg and above.

Remove the meat from the oven. Transfer to a warm serving plate or carving tray and cover loosely with a piece of foil. Leave to rest for NO LESS THAN HALF AN HOUR before carving and serving. This is very important – see page 213.

While the meat is relaxing, you can deglaze the roasting tin to finish your gravy (page 516), put the Yorkshire pudding in the oven (page 517) and finish off the roast potatoes (page 517). To serve up, I like to carve the meat on a sideboard, putting beef, Yorkshire pudding and roast potatoes on each warmed plate, while dishes of the vegetables and boats of gravy and horseradish – as well as mustard, of course – circulate around the table.

COLD ROAST BEEF OPEN SANDWICH *Serves 8-10*

1 piece of well-hung topside of beef, weighing about 2 kg

Olive oil

Salt and freshly ground black pepper

TO COMPLETE THE SANDWICH:

Brown or white bread and butter

Green lettuce (butterhead type, not iceberg)

Mayonnaise (Hellmann's is fine)

Good English mustard or Creamed Fresh Horseradish (p.512), if you prefer

Flaky salt and freshly ground black pepper

Cold roast beef is a different animal from hot – delicious, but in a summery, picnicky kind of way. All good, rare roast beef is delicious cold but some cuts, such as topside or silverside, are actually better cold (or cured, see page 436) than hot – and so worth cooking specially for this purpose.

As to the cold beef sandwich, there is an art to it, and it should not be slapdash. Do yourself a favour and follow my instructions to the letter.

Massage a little olive oil into the beef and sprinkle with salt and black pepper. Put it in a roasting tin and place in a hot oven (220°C/Gas Mark 7) for the 'half-hour sizzle' (pages 208-9). Turn the oven down to 150°C/Gas Mark 2 and cook for a further 10 minutes per 500g. Remove from the oven, cover with foil and leave to cool at room temperature. Store in a cool larder until it is time for your picnic (or in the fridge if it's for more than 24 hours).

Prepare the open sandwich as follows: thinly slice and lightly butter some fresh bread and lay 1, or at most 2, lettuce leaves on each slice. Spread thinly with mayonnaise and add a twist of freshly ground black pepper. Lay 2 thin slices of rare roast beef on top, overlapping as necessary to fit. Smear sparingly with mustard or horseradish and sprinkle with a little flaky salt. Serve as an open sandwich – or, if you prefer, top with another thin slice of lightly buttered bread, press firmly and cut in half.

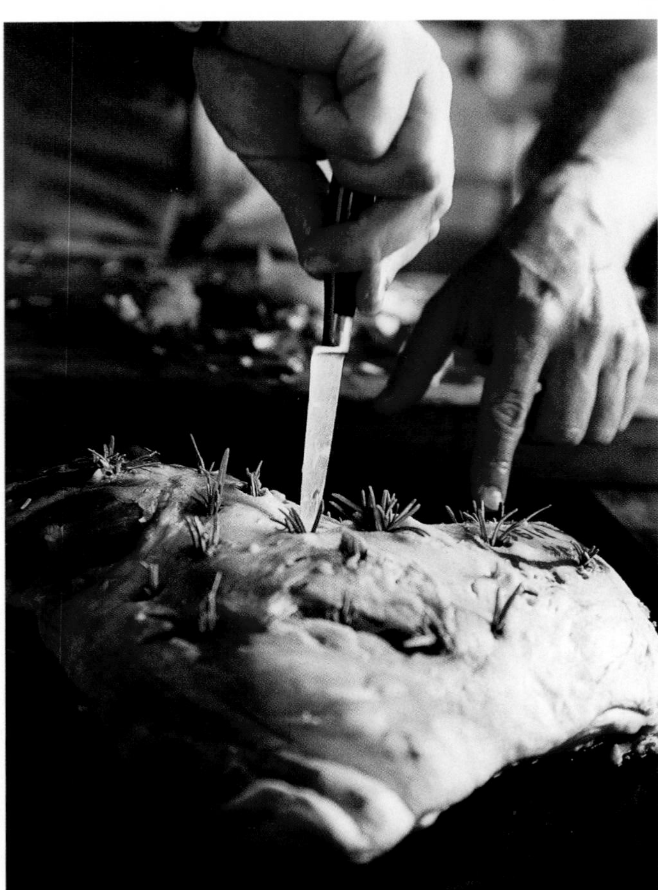

ROAST LAMB *Serves 6-10*

1 leg or shoulder of lamb, hogget or mutton, weighing 2.5-4kg

2-3 large garlic cloves, cut into thick slivers

4-5 anchovy fillets, cut into 3-4 pieces each

Several sprigs of rosemary, broken into short lengths

A little olive oil

1 glass of white wine

1 wine glass of water

Freshly ground black pepper

This is pretty much my standard procedure for roasting a whole leg or shoulder of lamb, hogget or mutton. You may balk at the idea of stuffing anchovies into the meat but don't worry about it turning out 'fishy' – it won't. The anchovies simply melt into the meat as it roasts, combining beautifully with the garlic and rosemary and lending a delicious salty tang to the juices, too.

Put the lamb in a roasting tin. With the tip of a sharp knife, make slits in the meat 2-3cm deep – say 12-15 in all. Use your finger to push a piece of garlic, a piece of anchovy and a piece of rosemary into each slit. Don't worry if some of them stick out a bit. Rub a little olive oil (from the anchovy tin, if you like) over the surface of the joint and put it in a very hot oven (230°C/Gas Mark 8) for the 'half-hour sizzle' (pages 208-9). Then pour over the glass of wine, turn down the oven to 160°C/Gas Mark 3 and roast for 50 minutes-2 hours, depending on how pink you like your lamb (if in doubt, see the table of roasting times on page 211).

About 10 minutes before the lamb is done, pour the glass of water into the bottom of the roasting tin. Remove the joint from the tin when it is done and leave to rest in a warm place for at least 20 minutes. Then adjust the juices as you like. You can either make a 'formal' gravy, thickening with flour and adding various condiments to flavour (pages 221-4). Or (and this is my preference) simply give the roasting tin a good scrape and shake over the hob, pour off some of the fat if it seems excessive, then taste and adjust the juices with a little more wine, some seasoning and perhaps a dab of redcurrant jelly. Keep the roasting tin warm, then carve the joint thickly, laying the slices back in the tin to mingle with the juices. Then pass the tin around, so people can serve themselves with meat and juice at the same time.

Accompany with roast potatoes, plus any vegetables according to the season (I love minted peas with lamb). A home-made Salsa Verde (page 514) makes a nice change from mint sauce and redcurrant jelly.

Variation

Roast Rack of Mutton Chops: Exactly the same treatment can be given to a rack of lamb chops or, better still, mutton or hogget chops, the anchovies, garlic and rosemary being stuffed into slits of varying depth made in the eye of the meat, from either end. Sizzle for about 15 minutes at 220°C/Gas Mark 7, then for another 15-25 minutes, depending on the size of the rack, at 160°C/Gas Mark 3. Let it rest for 10 minutes and it should be nice and pink in the middle.

ROLLED SHOULDER OF LAMB OR HOGGET WITH CAPERS AND ANCHOVIES *Serves 6*

1 boned shoulder of autumn lamb, hogget or mutton, weighing about 1.5-2kg

6 anchovy fillets in oil

1 tablespoon capers

2 garlic cloves

A small bunch of parsley, stalks removed

1 teaspoon mustard

A good squeeze of lemon juice

1 tablespoon olive oil (from the anchovies if you like)

1 glass of white wine

1 wine glass of water

Freshly ground black pepper

This is a lovely way to serve hogget or mutton, as the robust flavour of the meat stands up to the highly piquant stuffing. The juices will also be wonderfully well flavoured.

With your biggest knife, or a mezzaluna, chop the anchovies, capers, garlic and parsley together on a large board till all are well mixed and fairly fine. Transfer to a small bowl and mix in the mustard, lemon juice and olive oil. Season with a few twists of black pepper.

Lay your joint skin-side down and spread the mixture generously all over the inside of the meat. Roll up the joint and tie it securely with butcher's string. Place in a roasting tin and put in the centre of a hot oven (220°C/Gas Mark 7). After about half an hour, when the joint should be nicely browned, pour over the wine and water (this will give you a delicious gravy). Turn the oven down to 160°C/Gas Mark 3 and cook for a further 30-60 minutes, depending on the size of the joint and how pink you like your meat (if in doubt, see the table of roasting times on page 211). Rest for at least 20 minutes before carving.

Serve with roast potatoes or risoni (rice-shaped pasta), plus wilted greens, or Ultimate Creamed Spinach (page 523), and a gravy improvised from the juices (pages 221-4).

BAKER'S OVEN SHOULDER OF MUTTON *Serves 6-10*

1 large shoulder of mutton, hogget or mature lamb, weighing about 3-4kg

2 tablespoons olive oil

1kg onions

1kg potatoes

6 garlic cloves

1 large glass of white wine

About 500ml water or lamb stock (p.472)

Salt and freshly ground black pepper

The name of this dish refers to the tradition of leaving a Sunday roast with the local baker to cook in his cooling bread oven while you go to church to make your peace with the man upstairs. The longer the sermon, the more tender the lamb.

In more secular times, it holds its own as a great Sunday lunch dish that can be left to its own devices for several hours while you set about enjoying your weekend. Put it on first thing in the morning and you can forget about it until hunger drives you to see where it's at. By which time it will be falling off the bone into its own accompanying dish of melting potatoes and onions.

Put the mutton in a large, high-sided roasting tin, massage with some of the oil and pour the rest over. Place in the centre of a hot oven (220°C/Gas Mark 7). While you are giving it the 'half-hour sizzle', prepare the vegetables: peel and thinly slice the onions; peel and thickly slice (4-5mm) the potatoes; peel the garlic cloves and cut each into 3 or 4 pieces.

Remove the lamb from the oven and pour off a little fat if it seems excessive. Pour the wine into the tin and deglaze any crispy bits that have formed on the bottom of the tin (page 222). Scatter the garlic cloves around and then arrange the potatoes and onions around the meat in rough layers, seasoning as you go with salt and pepper. Pour over the water or stock – it should not quite cover the potatoes. Cover the whole tin with a large piece of foil, loosely tucked over the edges of the tin. Return to the oven and turn the heat down to 140°C/Gas Mark 1. Leave for about 4 hours.

Remove the lamb from the tin and set aside to rest, covering it with the foil again. Pour off a little fat from the roasting tin, if you want. Toss the potatoes around in the cooking juices and spread them evenly in the tin. Season with a little salt and pepper. Whack the oven heat back up to 220°C/Gas Mark 7 (or use the oven grill) to crisp up the top of the potatoes.

Serve the meat, which should be tender enough to scoop with a spoon, with spoonfuls of the crispy-topped, creamy-underneath, oniony potatoes. No other accompaniment is strictly necessary, but if you feel the need for extra vegetables, steam a few carrots or greens while the potatoes are crisping up.

LOIN OF LAMB STUFFED WITH APRICOTS AND PINE NUTS

Serves 4-6

1-1.5kg boned loin of autumn lamb, hogget or mutton

About 50g pine nuts

1 tablespoon clarified butter or olive oil

1 teaspoon coriander seeds

1 teaspoon cumin seeds

1 onion, chopped

10-12 unsulphured dried apricots, roughly chopped

About 50g coarse, dry breadcrumbs

A few grates of lemon zest (optional)

Salt and freshly ground black pepper

The secret of stuffing meat is to keep the flavours high and the volume low – you don't want to find a wad of bland, dough-like paste in the middle of a joint of meat, but rather a little contrasting texture and some zesty, surprising flavours.

This stuffing uses similar ingredients to a North African tagine to flavour a boned joint of mature lamb or mutton. The ingredients are pre-cooked, so the meat can still be served pink.

In a small frying pan over a medium heat, lightly dry-roast the pine nuts, tossing occasionally, until golden brown. Turn out and set aside. In the same pan, melt the butter or oil. Lightly crush the coriander and cumin seeds in a pestle and mortar (or use the back of a spoon on a wooden board) and add them to the pan, frying gently until they sizzle and pop. Add the onion and sweat until soft and translucent. If the apricots are not already moist, add them to the pan with a tablespoon of water and sweat for a couple of minutes to help plump them up.

Transfer the contents of the pan to a bowl and add the pine nuts, breadcrumbs and lemon zest, if using. Season well with salt and black pepper and mix all thoroughly together. Leave to cool a little.

Lay the boned loin skin-side down on a board and season lightly. Make an incision about 2cm deep along the eye of the meat. Press some of the stuffing into this and spread the rest evenly over the inside of the meat. Roll up the joint, with the eye of the meat at the centre, and tie into a tight parcel with butcher's string. Roast in a hot oven (220°C/Gas Mark 7) for 15-20 minutes, then turn the heat down to 160°C/Gas Mark 3 and roast for a further 20-40 minutes, according to the size of the joint and how pink you like it (if in doubt, see the table of roasting times on page 211). Leave the meat to rest for 15 minutes before slicing it fairly thickly.

There will be scant juices for a 'formal' gravy, but what there are can be deglazed (page 222) and enriched with a splash of white wine, then spooned over the meat as you slice and serve it.

Serve with boiled new potatoes or mashed old ones, according to the season.

HERB ROAST CHICKEN *Serves 4-5*

1 small but plump roasting chicken, weighing about 1.5-2kg

100g soft butter

Generous handfuls of fresh English herbs, roughly chopped

1 garlic clove, crushed

½ glass of white wine

Salt and freshly ground black pepper

A really good chicken doesn't need much embellishing – it just needs roasting. But when the herb garden starts to come good, often before the end of April in mild weather, I like to celebrate a sunny day by grabbing handfuls of fresh herbs – thyme, marjoram and chives are usually showing, parsley might come from the greenhouse – mixing them with soft butter and smearing them all over a plump spring chicken (ideally from my friends at Providence Farm – see page 136). And, if the sun continues to shine, it might be our first al fresco *meal of the year.*

It's an exercise to repeat, of course, at any point in the summer.

Take off any string or elastic trussing from the chicken, place the bird in a roasting tin and spread out its legs from the body. Enlarge the opening of the cavity with your fingers, so hot air can circulate inside the bird. It will cook quicker like that.

Put the butter in a bowl, throw in the roughly chopped herbs and the garlic and season well with salt and pepper. Mix together with your fingers, then smear all over the chicken, outside and in.

Place in the centre of a hot oven (210°C/Gas Mark 6) and leave for 20 minutes (phase 1). Then baste the chicken, turn the oven down to 180°C/Gas Mark 4, pour the wine into the tin (not over the bird) and roast the bird for another 30-40 minutes (phase 2), depending on its size. Open the oven door, turn the oven off and leave the bird for 15-20 minutes (phase 3). This is usually enough time to roast a small chicken through without burning the skin (the reason I prefer small chickens for roasting). For a bigger bird, you will have to make the necessary adjustments, adding a few minutes to each phase. You may also wish to protect the bird's skin with buttered foil for, say, the first 20 minutes of phase 2. A good test for doneness is to pierce that part of the bird where the thigh joins the breast; the juices released should run clear.

Forget about gravy. Carve the bird in the tin, as coarsely and crudely as you like (no wafer-thin breast slices, please), letting the pieces fall into the buttery pan juices and letting the fresh juices from carving mingle with the rest. Then take the tin to the table and pass it round your family or guests in the pecking order of your choosing, so they can pull out the bits they fancy. Pass it round a second time, to help redress grievances and encourage the further and fairer distribution of juices.

Accompaniments? Roast potatoes would be *de trop*. A green vegetable would probably go unnoticed. Some good bread to mop up the juices will be appreciated, while a leafy salad, produced only after your guests have demolished the chicken, might assuage a few guilty consciences.

The discovery of the roasting tin, a day or so later in a cool larder, is a joy you may not wish to share. Plunder the jellied juices, congealed bits of skin, and crusty meat tatters that cling to the carcass before you quietly make the rest, along with the giblets, into stock (pages 470-72).

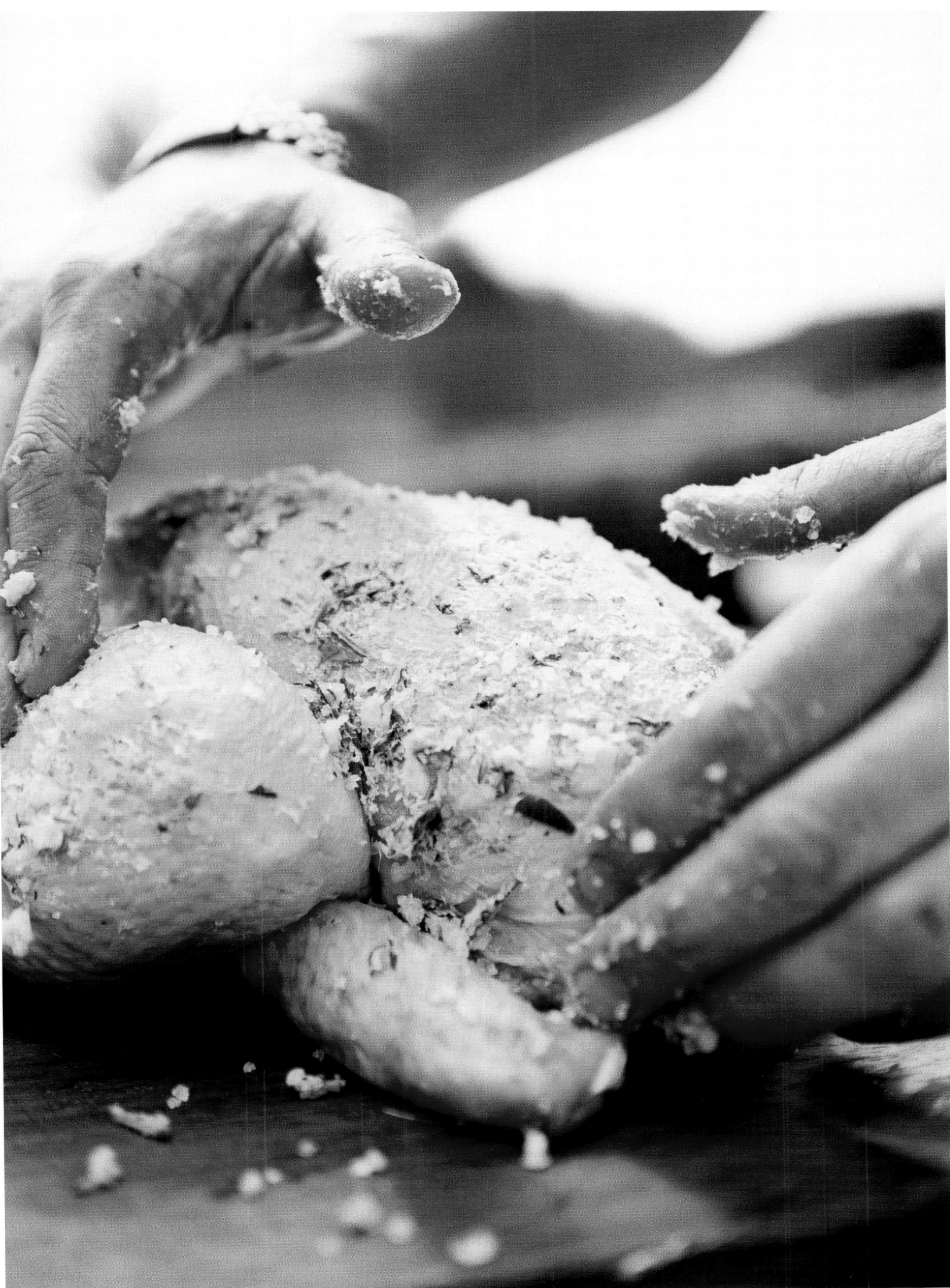

ROAST DUCK WITH BEETROOT *Serves 4*

1 large, fresh duck, free range and preferably organic, with giblets

About 1 kg beetroot, peeled and cut into chunks (or left whole if small)

1 kg potatoes, peeled, cut into roasting chunks and parboiled (p.517)

Salt and freshly ground black pepper

THE GIBLET STOCK/GRAVY:

The neck and giblets, and wing tips

1 small onion

1 carrot

1 celery stick

A little oil

1 bay leaf

1 small glass of red wine

½ teaspoon redcurrant jelly (optional)

TO ACCOMPANY:

Watercress and Orange Salad (p.523)

There's a bit of a knack to roasting a duck but it needn't be too anxiety provoking. Much of the pressure is off if you decide that you don't mind if the breast meat of the bird is not 'perfectly pink', as gastronomic purists will these days tell you it ought to be. The problem is that achieving the pink breast pretty much demands that you roast the legs separately, or at least continue to cook them after you've removed and carved the breast. Otherwise they'll be unsavourily bloody.

Better, I think, to embrace the more old-fashioned English notion of a roast duck, with the skin nicely seasoned and crisp and the meat cooked right through. Like pork, duck meat is flavoursome enough to be appetising even when a little overcooked, and the natural covering of fat that you get with a good farmed duck keeps it lubricated. The crispy skin, of course, is priceless.

The vegetables – in this case potatoes and beetroot – can be roasted around the bird in the fat that runs from it as it cooks. A little acidity is needed at some point to cut all this luscious fattiness. I like to serve the Watercress and Orange Salad (page 523) with the duck rather than after it.

Incidentally, I am grateful to the restaurateur, Stephen Bull, whose thoughts on roasting a duck I featured in an article I wrote for The Sunday Times *in 1992. His method is now pretty much my method.*

For a more modern duck dish – the breasts cooked separately and served pink – see Duck Breasts with Pineapple, Chilli and Soy on page 366.

If the duck is tied up, untruss it – i.e. cut the strings and gently pull the legs apart, away from the body. This will help the heat to get at them. Cut off the wing tips (the last bony segment) – there's no meat on them and they will boost the flavour of the giblet stock. Make this first: roughly chop up the wing tips and all the giblets except the liver (see page 199), plus the onion, carrot and celery. Fry these over a fair heat in a little oil until the meat is nicely browned and the vegetables slightly caramelised. Transfer to a saucepan with the bay leaf, cover with water (about 600 ml) and bring to a simmer. Leave at a gentle simmer for about 1¾ hours – i.e. the time it takes to cook the duck.

Now tackle the duck. Remove any obvious spare fat from inside the cavity. You can, if you like, turn the duck breast-side down on a board and press hard on the middle of the backbone until you hear a crack. This is a tip from Stephen Bull – it means that when you turn the bird breast-side up again it sits flatter in the pan, which helps it to cook more evenly. Now, using a needle, prick the skin all over the fatty parts – i.e. the breast and where the breast joins the leg. Don't prick deeper than is necessary just to pierce the skin. You want the fat to run, but not the juices from the meat. Season the skin lightly with salt and pepper.

Put the bird in a roasting tin with enough space around it to roast the potatoes and beetroot. Place in a hot oven (220°C/Gas Mark 7) for about 20 minutes, so the fat starts to run. Then turn the oven down to 180°C/Gas Mark 4, baste the bird and return it to the oven. After another 20 minutes or so, add the vegetables to the roasting tin: raw beetroot chunks (or whole if they are nice small ones) and parboiled potatoes, roughed up with a fork and well seasoned with salt and pepper. Baste the bird again.

Turn the vegetables and baste the duck every 20 minutes or so. Check the bird for doneness after about 1½ hours' total cooking time. Poke a skewer into the thickest part of the leg, close to the breast. When the juices runs clear, the bird is done. Transfer the potatoes and beetroot to a warmed dish and return them to the oven to keep warm. Tip the bird to pour any fat or juices out of the cavity into the roasting tin and transfer it to a warmed plate or carving tray.

Now fix the gravy. Carefully pour off the fat from the roasting tin into a heatproof bowl or dish (you should save and use it), leaving the brown juices in the tin. Deglaze the tin with the red wine (page 222), scraping to release any tasty browned morsels. Strain the giblet stock and the deglazed pan juices into a clean pan and boil hard to reduce them to a rich, syrupy gravy. Taste for seasoning, and add a little redcurrant jelly for sweetness, if you like.

To carve the bird for 4 people, slice between the legs and breast, then prise off the whole legs, carefully pulling the thighbone away from the body of the bird. Cut each leg in half at the joint between the thigh and the drumstick. Slice each whole breast from the carcass, with the crispy skin attached, then cut each breast into 5 or 6 thick slices. Offer each guest a few slices of breast, with either a thigh or a drumstick. Serve on warmed plates, with the gravy and roast vegetables. Serve the watercress and orange salad on side plates, with or after the duck.

SALMI OF GUINEA FOWL WITH ROAST CHESTNUTS *Serves 6*

2 free-range guinea fowl, ideally organic, with giblets if possible

A little sunflower or olive oil

1 celery stick

1 large carrot

1 medium onion

4 dozen plump chestnuts in their skins

1 bay leaf

A sprig of thyme

1 glass of white wine

1 tablepoon double cream

Salt and freshly ground black pepper

A salmi is a very specific way of cooking game and poultry and not, as some modern interpretations suggest, just a posh word for a game casserole. The key thing is that the bird in question is two-thirds roasted, then portioned up, the carcass being used to make a sauce – which is usually finished with cream. The portions are then finished in the sauce. So this does take a little while to prepare but it's worth the trouble, particularly as a dinner-party dish, as it can all be done in advance, even the night before.

This recipe serves as a generic example of how to make a salmi. Other game birds, particularly pheasant, partridge, grouse and pigeon, all make wonderful salmis. As for alternatives to the chestnuts, and flavourings for the sauce, the possibilities are endless: prunes and Armagnac, fried apples and Calvados, marsala and wild mushrooms, etc etc ...

Wipe a little oil over the breasts of the birds but do not season them at this stage. Cut up the celery, carrot and onion into 6 or 8 pieces each. Oil a roasting tin and shake the vegetables in the tin so they, too, are lightly oiled. Place the birds in the tin with the vegetables and add the giblets (i.e. neck, gizzard, heart and liver), washed and trimmed of any discoloured parts if necessary. Place in a hot oven (200°C/Gas Mark 6) and roast the birds for 30-40 minutes, until nicely browned. The juices between the drumstick and the breast should still run pink. By this time the vegetables and giblets should also be nicely coloured.

You can roast the chestnuts in a separate baking tray at the same time as the birds. Make a small slit in each one with the point of a knife and roast for about 20 minutes, until the skin is lightly charred. Peel when cool enough to handle.

Leave the birds to cool for a few minutes, then joint them. Each bird is easily divided into 4. First, gently pull the leg (i.e. drumstick and thigh) away from the body, exposing the end of the thighbone. You may be able to pull this portion clean away from the bird or you may need to cut a few little sinews with a sharp knife. Next, the breast can be sliced away from the carcass, as close as possible to the breastbone, in a portion that includes the wing. Skin all 4 portions, reserving the skin, and remove the last 2 joints of each wing, which will go in the pot for the sauce. Set aside your portions (covered and in the fridge if the dish is for the next day) and get to work on the sauce.

Tear up the carcasses of the birds with your fingers and break the bones by cracking them with a rolling pin. You are about to make an intense stock at an accelerated pace, so the smaller the pieces the better. Put the broken carcasses in a saucepan with the skin, chopped neck and other giblets, the roasted vegetables from the tin, and the bay leaf and thyme. For extra flavour, pour any excess fat out of the roasting tin, then reheat the tin on the hob and deglaze it by pouring in half the glass of wine and rubbing any burnt patches and caramelised 'scratchings' with the edge of a spatula. Pour the resulting 'gravy' into the saucepan with the rest of the wine and just enough water to cover everything (about 600 ml should be enough if everything is well packed down). Bring to the boil and simmer, at a slightly merrier pace than you normally would for a stock, for about 45 minutes.

Strain the stock through a *chinois* or heavy sieve, pressing to extract maximum juices from the carcass pieces. Then strain again, ideally through muslin or a cotton cloth, into a clean saucepan. Boil until reduced in volume by about half; you need to end up with 200-250 ml very well-flavoured stock.

You are going to use some of the roast chestnuts to thicken the sauce. Take a couple of ladlefuls of the stock and about a quarter of the chestnuts and either blend them together in a liquidiser or mash thoroughly in a small pan with a potato masher. Whisk back into the sauce, along with the cream, and bring back to a gentle simmer. If you want the sauce a little thicker, repeat the process with a few more chestnuts. Check and adjust the seasoning.

Transfer the sauce to a larger pan, if necessary, and add the guinea fowl portions. Heat through, turning occasionally to coat them well, and simmer gently for a couple of minutes. Serve on warmed plates, with the remaining roast chestnuts scattered over, and some lightly steamed greens or cabbage.

CLASSIC ROAST GROUSE

The meat of grouse has a unique, herby, heathery flavour, which leads some to regard it as the ultimate eating among game birds, while others don't much care for it. I think it's delicious, and I look forward to grouse soup (see page 507) just as much as to the roast bird.

Some people revel in well-hung grouse but I think the 'hung flavour' can end up overpowering the unique natural taste of the flesh. Two days' hanging is enough in the warm weather of August and September, seven to ten in a chilly December.

Like almost all genuinely wild game birds, the very lean meat has a tendency to dryness. Barding it with bacon is therefore particularly important. Crisply fried brown breadcrumbs are the classic accompaniment, though personally I prefer game chips – especially as I'll probably be serving the livers on fried bread anyway.

There's not much meat on the wings of a grouse, so I like to clip them off with poultry shears and add them to the stock for the gravy. The leg meat is usually a little bitter and some recipes suggest you cut off the legs and reserve them for the gravy stock, too. It's all a matter of taste. I quite like them, and leave them on.

Ideally you should make the stock in advance. Roast or fry the necks, giblets (minus the liver) and wings from the birds, plus the carrot and onion, in the fat or oil for 10 minutes, until nicely browned. Transfer to a small pan with the bay leaf, half a glass of red wine and enough water to cover by 1-2 cm. Bring to the boil and

1/2 - 1 grouse per person, plucked and drawn, the neck and giblets reserved

A little soft butter, lard or dripping

2 rashers of fatty streaky bacon per bird

Salt and freshly ground black pepper

THE STOCK/GRAVY:

The neck and giblets from the bird (minus the liver)

The wings (optional)

1 small carrot, roughly chopped

1 small onion, roughly chopped

1 tablespoon fat or oil

1 bay leaf

Red wine

Plain flour

Redcurrant or quince jelly (optional)

TO ACCOMPANY:

Game Chips (p.519), or coarse brown breadcrumbs, fried until crisp (optional)

The liver, on a piece of fried bread (optional)

Bread Sauce (p.512)

Lightly steamed greens or cabbage, or a watercress salad

simmer gently for at least an hour, then strain through cotton or muslin. Pour into a clean pan and boil until reduced by about half, so you have a cup or so of well-flavoured stock to help make your gravy (if all this sounds laborious you can skip it, but it does help make better gravy, and more of it).

Prepare the birds by smearing a little fat over the breasts, seasoning with a twist of pepper and covering them with a couple of rashers of streaky bacon. The grouse's liver is particularly good, and can be replaced in the cavity, perhaps with a couple of teaspoons of port, before cooking. Place in a roasting tin and put in the centre of a very hot oven (230°C/Gas Mark 8).

Remove the bacon after 8-10 minutes and take it out of the oven if it's as crisp as you'd like it to be. At this point you could baste the birds with any fat in the tin, but do it fast so as not to let the oven cool. About 20 minutes in total should be enough to cook most grouse through without drying them, 25 minutes for a larger bird, provided in both cases they can rest for 10-15 minutes while you prepare the gravy. The meat should be just a little pink, but if this is not to your taste, add 5-7 minutes to the cooking time.

Skim off any excess fat from the roasting tin (what little there is will be from the bacon). Place the tin on the hob and sprinkle just a teaspoon of flour into it. Scrape the base with a wooden spatula, scratching up any crispy bits and mixing them with the flour and juices. Use a small splash of wine and a little of the reserved stock to help this process and loosen the gravy. Now strain all the liquid in the roasting tin through a sieve into a small, clean saucepan. Whisk in the rest of the stock and bring to the boil. Taste the gravy, adding just a little redcurrant or quince jelly if you think it needs sweetness. Boil to reduce if you want to intensify the flavour, then season with salt and pepper as you see fit. Whisk in a little more flour if you want to thicken it. In short, fix the gravy how you like it (see pages 221-4 for further discussion).

If you want to do the liver thing, fry a small croûton of bread for each bird, scrape out the liver from the cavity of the bird and spread it, like pâté, on to the bread. Serve on the plate with each bird.

I don't generally carve grouse but serve a whole bird, or half for a more modest appetite, per person, to be tackled on the plate – fingers allowed. Serve each bird with its bacon and a handful of game chips, or fried brown breadcrumbs. Bring to the table the piping-hot gravy, bread sauce and either buttered steamed greens (such as Savoy cabbage) or a salad of watercress, rocket or other green leaves.

Variation

Classic Roast Partridge: Partridge is a delightful bird for those who don't like their game too gamy. The roasting procedure is the same as for grouse but partridge should be served a little better done, so the cooking time can be extended by 5-10 minutes. I don't usually bother with the liver. The other accompaniments – game chips, bread sauce and giblet gravy, fixed much as above – go well.

CLASSIC ROAST WOODCOCK (AND SNIPE)

Woodcock or snipe, plucked but not drawn, the head still on

A little soft butter

1/2-1 rasher of streaky bacon per bird

A little red wine and/or port

1 slice of bread per bird

Salt and freshly ground black pepper

Along with grouse, woodcock and snipe are two of the most delicious birds you'll encounter. I've repeated this recipe from The River Cottage Year *because I think it should be in the repertoire of any game aficionado. Traditionally, the insides of the birds are left in during cooking, then spread on a piece of toast on which the bird is served. This is not just a piece of macho posturing: the flavour of the intestines isn't strong at all, but creamy and mildly liverish.*

One woodcock, or two snipe, per person makes a robust starter. Supplemented with game chips and greens, the same would content many as a main course.

The only thing that should be removed from the plucked bird before roasting is the gizzard. If you are buying your birds, you could ask the butcher or game dealer to do this, but it's very easy: with the point of a sharp knife, make a small slit in the vent end of the bird. Insert your little finger and feel around. The first little hard lump you come to is the gizzard. Once you've located it, spear it with a cocktail stick or needle and gently pull it out. It will have a trail of intestine attached. Snip it off, then push the intestine back inside the cavity.

Massage a little soft butter into the breast of each bird and season with a little salt and pepper. Lay a piece of streaky bacon over the breast of each bird (half a rasher for a snipe, 2 halves for a woodcock). Tuck the head and neck of each bird (if they are still intact) under its wing and put the birds in a roasting tin. Place in a very hot oven (230°C/Gas Mark 8) and roast for 8-20 minutes, depending on how pink you like your meat: 8 minutes is about right for a medium-rare snipe, 20 minutes for a well-done woodcock. Remove the bacon after about 5 minutes, chop it fairly finely and set aside.

When the birds come out of the oven, transfer them to a warmed plate – they'll rest for about 10 minutes while you sort out the innards. Scoop these carefully out of the cavity of the birds with a teaspoon – unless the birds are very well done, they will still be quite pink and bloody. In a small frying pan, heat a little butter and add the bacon you took from the birds. Sizzle for a minute or two, then add the contents of the birds' cavities – intestines, hearts, livers, the lot – and any juices from the roasting tin. Add just a little red wine and/or port – a teaspoon or two for each bird. Bubble gently for a couple of minutes, mashing the lumpy bits with a fork, then season sparingly with salt and pepper. Take off the heat.

Make and lightly butter a small round of toast for each bird. Put a heap of the warm 'pâté' on one side of each piece of toast and a roast bird on the other. Serve at once, with the very best red wine.

Guests should be allowed – indeed encouraged – to pick up the birds and gnaw every last scrap of meat off the bone. Even the heads can be split and the tiny, pea-sized brains sucked out.

11. SLOW COOKING

11. SLOW COOKING

Stews, Braises and Pies

If roasting presents the best cuts of the best meat at their unadulterated best, then slow cooking is the complementary art of taking the coarser parts and making them wonderful by means of long and loving alchemy in the stockpot and casserole. Put another way, roasting honours meat's quality, slow cooking its versatility.

In some ways this is the most important chapter in the book – because this is the area of meat cookery in which, I suspect, most home cooks have the most room for improvement. I don't mean that to sound patronising – in fact I don't particularly mean it in terms of culinary technique at all (the principles of slow cooking are very straightforward, though they are often not fully appreciated). Rather, when it comes to slow cooking, the shortcomings of the average cook often lie in their unwillingness to explore and experiment with unfamiliar ingredients, and to appreciate the full range of extraordinary flavours and wonderful textures that are there for the taking. It seems to me that a lot of cooks, even keen ones, have a clutch of favourite recipes for, at most, half a dozen good stews or casseroles, from which they rarely depart. One of my main aims in this chapter is to encourage you to expand your personal repertoire – partly by following my recipes but also by improvising according to the principles explained below.

So, if you've never tackled the humbler meats, such as oxtail or lamb shanks, breast of mutton or scrag end of lamb, pork belly or knuckle of bacon, pigeon or rabbit, or hearts, tripe or trotters; or if you've never made a hot pot, a daube, a cassoulet, a pot-au-feu, a mole, a paprikash or a goat curry, then I hope this chapter will inspire you to try.

Another undoubted appeal of this form of meat cookery is its intrinsic economy. With few exceptions, the cuts best suited to slow cooking are the cheaper ones. I have urged you to spend more money on humanely reared meat of exceptional quality. But if the idea that you may have to pay up to twice as much for good meat from an ethically sound system of production is smarting a bit, then this chapter should help ease the pain.

For slow cooking is also the art of making something sublime and special out of something cheap and ordinary. A general rule of thumb is that you can spend less than half the amount of money on your meat (compared to the prime cuts) to feed more than twice the number of mouths – giving you at least a fourfold economy.

Even if you're rolling in cash, I think it is important, philosophically, to be a slow-cooker as well as a roaster. Nobody should hog all the prime cuts. It's bad for the soul. The best relationship you can have with meat is to know it in all its parts, and take an interest in every edible morsel it can offer you. As I have said before (and will say again), only such a holistic approach can truly assuage the conscience of the caring carnivore.

Chef Fergus Henderson has called this philosophy 'nose-to-tail eating', and in the introduction to his excellent book of that name he explains it thus: 'It would be disingenuous to the animal not to make the most of it.' I like this notion very much. I like it particularly in the context of this chapter because, as it happens, both the nose and the tail only come into their own after long, slow simmering.

Another important thing to emphasise about slow cooking is that, paradoxically, it doesn't have to be time consuming. At least, it doesn't have to take a lot of your time. Half an hour or less is often enough to prepare the ingredients, get them in a pot, and get the pot on the fire. Then, like the best wine, all you have to do is leave well alone for a small miracle to occur. Only in this case the job will be done in a matter of hours rather than years.

For the organised individual (I exclude myself here), modern technology even allows you to achieve perfection from afar. Self-contained electronic slow cookers, with timers, can turn on and off while you work, pump iron or party (no, I don't write their brochures, but I'm sure I could make a good job of it). Personally, I don't own one of these devices, but I can well see the value in one. Most of my recipes in this chapter could easily be prepared in such a machine.

The Secrets of Success

Luckily the art of slow cooking can be summarised fairly succinctly. I believe the following four rules pretty much encapsulate all the vitals:

1. Simmer slowly.
2. Add flavour.
3. Add body.
4. When necessary, add fat.

And I would add a fifth optional, but desirable, directive:

5. If time allows, make your stew the day before you serve it.

I'll take those points in order and elaborate on them:

The Art of the Slow Simmer

Everyone knows that the cheaper meats for slow cooking are, in common parlance, 'tougher' than the prime cuts for roasting, frying etc. What this actually means is that they have a higher concentration of connective tissue, and the bonds between the meat fibres are more resistant to separation. The reason for this is simple: these are the muscles that work hardest for the animals – necks that raise and lower the head during feeding, legs that carry the weight of the animal and propel it from one place to another; even tails that flick flies off their backs. All these cuts will therefore have tough sinews attaching the muscles to each other and to the tendons, and the muscles themselves will be in a state of high tension for much of the time, which will toughen the meat fibres.

The process of long, slow cooking transforms the connective tissues – and even the tendons, which are principally made up of hard, unpalatable collagen – into tender, chewable gelatine. At the same time, it slowly loosens the bonds between the muscle fibres, rendering the meat more tender and sponge-like. The slower the simmer, the more gentle this action, so that the gelatine is created and the tenderness achieved without breaking down the meat altogether, or driving too much precious moisture from the fibres.

This is the theory, and for generations the slow simmer is what the best cooks have insisted on for stews, braises and other dishes that demand long cooking times to tenderise tough cuts of meat. But it is a theory that has, like the searing-to-seal tradition (see page 208), sometimes been challenged. In this case the challengers can be confidently seen off.

The opposing argument is that the difference between slow simmering and fast boiling is a chef's fantasy, because water boils at 100°C whether it is boiling fast or slow. Whoever said that was neither a scientist nor a chef. Here's why.

It is true that the difference between fast-boiling and slow-simmering water is tiny in terms of temperature. But there is a difference of a fraction of a degree. In terms of the way that water behaves, that fraction of a degree is vital. The molecules in fast-boiling water are moving many times faster than those in slow-simmering water. You don't need to be a scientist to work that one out – you can see it with your own eyes: at the molecular level, a furious rolling boil is clearly very different from a tremulous, slow simmer.

The difference in temperature may be negligible but the difference in molecular behaviour is, visibly, radical. It's hardly surprising that the meat in the pot will be affected. Meat is almost 80 per cent water to start with, and we have already established (page 207) that the presence or absence of water (along with fat) is a key factor determining the texture and flavour of cooked meat. In the case of the fast boil, the soluble molecules of fat and water, which hold the flavourful components in suspension, are driven out of the meat at speed. The 'dry' (i.e. non-soluble) molecules that comprise the fibres of the meat will contract and tighten much quicker too. The fibres end up less relaxed, less sponge-like, and will hold fewer of the fats and juices. This is how the meat in a fast-boiled stew can end up so shrivelled and dry – sometimes the cubes that come out are about half the size of the ones that went in, and when that happens you know you've made a mistake.

In the slow simmer, by contrast, the juices will still be driven out of the meat but more slowly. And the contracting of the fibres will be less severe. The juices that leave the meat can find their way back in when the fibres have gently loosened. By then, they will have picked up many of the soluble sugars and aromatics available from the other ingredients in the stew. So, if resting is the unsung secret of roasting, then the holy grail of the stew is the gentle, trembling, barely visible simmer, where the molecules of all the ingredients are slowly dancing and mingling rather than fleeing for their lives.

There is a further factor that compounds the difference between the slow simmer and the fast boil. We have been talking about the behaviour of pure water, but the liquor of a good stew is far from unadulterated H_2O. It has various sugars, salts and compounds dissolved in it – in concentrations that will increase as the stew simmers away. Think of the liquor as a weak sugar solution and you may remember from science lessons (or, in my case, fudge and toffee making with my mum) that the boiling temperature is no longer a constant but extends either side of 100°C. The temperature of the fast-boiling liquid will exceed 100°C by several degrees. The first setting point of a boiled sugar solution, known as the 'thread', is reached at 104-5°C, and fast-boiled stew will quickly reach this temperature, where even more damage will be done to the meat. At the same time, the temperature of a very slow simmer will actually be below 100°C, as low as 96°C, in fact. These temperature differences are much more obvious, and their significance easier to grasp.

It's worth noting that when you boil a strained stock or sauce hard to reduce it and concentrate its strength, reaching these higher temperatures is highly desirable. A good sauce is effectively a light syrup. But the adverse effects of these higher temperatures on meat and other solid ingredients are well known to chefs: they will simply fall apart and become a mush. This is why stocks are always strained before reduction. Meat and other ingredients can then be returned to the reduced stock/sauce and gently heated through. You will see this process prescribed in a number of the recipes in this chapter, notably the Oxtail, or Tail and Tongue, with Rich Red Wine Sauce (page 282) and Coq au Vin (page 311).

As you may have gathered, I feel passionately about the slow simmer. And nothing makes me crosser in the kitchen than when some careless person (usually me) has forgotten a stew pot at the heating-up stage, so that it has started to boil fast. It makes me want to turn back time. I can't, of course, so I just try to curb my expletives and settle it back down to the slow simmer as quickly as I can. But however well it comes out in the end, I can't help kicking myself, and wondering what might have been.

So now that we know what we want, how do we get it? What does the slow simmer look like? Elizabeth David put it pretty nicely in her classic book, *French Provincial Cooking*, while discussing one of the ultimate slow-cooked dishes, the pot-au-feu: 'Allow to barely simmer, to tremble or shudder rather, in the centre of the pot only, for 3½ hours, keeping the heat absolutely regular.'

That pretty much does it for me. It might also be worth mentioning that, like boiling, simmering involves the rising of bubbles to the surface – but only just. The fewer the bubbles, and the longer the interval between them, the slower, and better, the simmer.

How is this achieved? We are obviously talking about the lowest heat necessary to maintain this delicate motion of the cooking liquid. With some cookers and hobs, this is itself a problem. The lowest possible setting may still be too hot, even for a substantial stockpot. Gas hobs, which I generally favour for their instantaneous delivery of heat, can be particularly tricky. What do you do if your smallest ring at its lowest setting still brings a four-litre stew to a simmer best described as 'merry' rather than 'shuddering'? Sometimes, by turning the dial back through the hottest setting and towards the off position, you can find a flame even lower than the normal low setting. If you can't get your cooker to perform this trick, then you should consider buying a heat diffuser. Usually made of steel, asbestos, or a combination of both, these are discs that sit on top of a gas ring and provide a heat-absorbing buffer between the flame and the pan. They may be pretty effective but, depending on the severity of your problem, sometimes just delay rather than prevent the over-excited simmer.

If the hob is not working for you, never overlook the option of the oven: it's often the best place for slow cooking, as anyone with an Aga, Rayburn or other range cooker where the ovens are permanently on will tell you. In most cases, a setting of 120°C/Gas Mark ½ is appropriate, and will keep your pot around perfect slow simmering temperature – provided, and this is vital, you get it to that point *before you put it in the oven*. Slow cooking in an oven is usually done with the lid on unless, as with Cassoulet for example (see page 302), you want to form a crust.

Adding Flavour

I've used the word alchemy, and there's no doubt that the best slow cooking entails the judicious combination of complementary ingredients that come together to create something that is more than the sum of their parts. Flavours will blend and homogenise. The juice (which I will refer to variously and interchangeably in the pages that follow as sauce, liquor and stock) will be a unique creation, never quite the same, even when following the same recipe. And it is usually by the taste of this juice that the dish will ultimately be judged. You simply can't have a good stew with an indifferent juice. Put another way, if forced to choose, Jack Sprat style, between the meat and the sauce, the cook who chooses the meat probably hasn't made a very good stew.

Which is not to say that the meat isn't important; it's critical. The point is that if you've got things right, the meat will by the end of its cooking time have done its vital work of giving flavour and body to the juice. It should be pretty palatable, but it will owe most of what it has to offer to the flavoured juices that, with a bit of luck, have now settled back within its tender, loosened fibres. In a sense, the meat becomes a medium for holding its own sauce – almost like pasta. You get the idea.

Meat flavours by browning and deglazing

There is one important way to ensure that the meat does all it can for the stew and that is to sear it over a high heat, thereby browning the surface. You may think I'm taking the mickey, insisting on this traditional procedure after, in the previous chapter, debunking the myth that such treatment would produce some kind of

impermeable seal on the meat. But I'm not backtracking. Searing doesn't seal but it does caramelise, burning the meat's sugars to produce those irresistible 'browning flavours' we discussed in the last chapter. On a roast they will cling to the surface crust. In a stew they will dissolve deliciously into the cooking liquid, providing one of the most important flavour components of your sauce.

The best way to sear meat for a stew is in a very hot, lightly oiled frying pan. Remember that you are looking to burn. Simply turning the meat from deep red to anaemic grey won't help. We are talking about dark brown sear marks – even a bit of black won't hurt. So use a high heat and don't overcrowd the pan, as this will quickly lower the temperature. Seal the meat in small batches. Turn it a few times to get some good colour on all sides within the space of just a minute or two, then transfer it to your cooking pot.

Don't forget that much of value is likely to be left in the frying pan – little burnt bits that have stuck to the surface. A splash of wine, stock or water, and a good scrape with a spatula, will loosen them, so they too can be added to the pot. This is called 'deglazing', and I refer to it in almost every recipe in this chapter.

Vegetable flavours for sweetness, depth and balance

I can't think of a recipe for a slow-cooked dish that doesn't have some vegetables as well as meat – at least not one that I'm tempted to cook. In some cases the vegetables may not make it to the final plate, having been strained and removed, perhaps prior to reducing the stock to make a sauce for the finished dish. But even then we should be under no illusions about their vital role. They are as sugar to sour cooking apples, or salt to bread – invisible perhaps, unsung usually, but utterly transforming.

The *sine qua non* of stock vegetables is, of course, the onion. In many recipes for stews it may be the only designated vegetable. This is because it does so much, and can just about do it all unaided. It readily offers up its mild astringency, its distinct savouriness and its robust natural sugars – and all these qualities will seep gently into any dish in which onions, whether whole, sliced or chopped almost to a purée, are simmered long and slow. Whether you're following a recipe or inventing, improvising or adapting one, if you find you have no onions, you have a problem. In fact, you'd better go and get some right now.

Second in the picking order of vegetables-to-aid-the-slow-cook would be the carrot. Its virtues are its slow-release sugars and mild, non-threatening flavour. In many cases I may not want to eat or even see a piece of carrot in my finished dish, and I will remove and discard it – feed it to the dog, even. But I am still enormously grateful for its work.

Celery completes the holy trinity of savoury stock vegetables for slow cooking. If the onion is the father and the carrot the earth(l)y son, then celery is the all-pervasive ghost: it sends out its indefinable, irresistibly rounded savouriness to the distant corners of the stew, rounding up and corralling the other flavours. Like a natural MSG, it appeals to the ESP in our taste buds.

These three flavouring vegetables have proved their worth over and over again in slow-cooked dishes from one side of the world to another.

Outside of these three, and something of a law unto itself, is the inimitable tomato. Unlike that of the trinity, the contribution of the tomato is rarely subtle. This is something whose flagrant but fragrant acidity you either definitely do or definitely don't want in your pot. Having said that, it's amazing how many classic dishes still spark a heated debate as to whether the controversial golden apple *definitely should* or *definitely shouldn't* be included. Cassoulet, paprikash, coq au vin, and even our own shepherd's pie still have fervent followers on both sides of the divide. It is my contention, however, that the tomato isn't always a sledgehammer flavouring, and can be deployed in a supporting, as well as a dominant, role, particularly where strong spices, other fruits, and rich, reduced flavours are to the fore. You'll find this out in recipes such as my Main-course Borscht (page 279), Pot-au-feu (page 284) and Citrus-braised Lamb Shanks (page 300), where tomatoes are present but in relatively subtle quantities. I hope the end results will make this point pretty eloquently.

Honourable mentions must also go to the versatile leek, which makes a pleasant complement to (and, if desperate, a save-the-day substitute for) the onion. Parsnips, turnips, beetroot and celeriac could all be seen as variations on the carrot theme, although their more radical aromatic qualities (and, in the case of beetroot, dramatic colour) restrict a cavalier, throw-it-all-in policy. Personally I like parsnips

with lamb, beetroot with beef, and celeriac with chicken and pork. Pumpkins and squashes are also 'a bit carroty', and are particularly good in spicy dishes, including curries, where they may more or less melt into the sauce.

And let's not forget the mushroom, which can be introduced to great effect whenever you want your dish to taste ... well, mushroomy.

If your meat is a given, then the above are just some of the optional building blocks you can use to construct a rich and well-rounded sauce around it. The more you use them, the better you will know them and what they can do for you. When you elaborate on given recipes and improvise new ones, these key ingredients will help you do so with confidence and enthusiasm.

Skin and Bones for Added Body

Skin and bones – and fat, which I'll discuss next – don't sound like the most promising ingredients for a stew but they are hugely important. They make me think of Marlboro Country: they are not exactly flavourful in themselves but they are undoubtedly *where the flavor is*. By this I mean they fix and support flavour. Individually, but more particularly in combination, they will give great depth to your slow-cooked dishes, as they help create a medium that naturally holds the flavours in suspension. The roles of skin and bone on the one hand and fat on the other are, respectively, to thicken and lubricate the sauce, slowing it down, if you like, so it gets the best chance to deliver its stored aromatics to your taste buds as it passes over them.

Again, there's some serious science underpinning my rather fanciful terminology, so let's have a look at it.

Like the connective tissues discussed above, both skin and bone contain high concentrations of albumen and collagen, which are converted into gelatine when boiled in water, and released gradually during the process of slow cooking. Gelatine is a fixative. In its most concentrated form it is an extremely powerful glue (gelatine made from rabbit skins was traditionally used for bonding canvas and vellum to wood, both by sailmakers and artists). Although gelatine in its pure form is colourless and odourless (as you will have observed from the concentrated culinary product in powder and leaf form), its presence in a liquid will have a strong impact on its taste. This is because gelatine increases the viscosity of any liquid in which it is dissolved, thereby trapping the molecules and tiny particles in which the flavours reside. To revert to non-scientific terminology: it's sticky, and the bits that stick to it are the tasty bits.

The viscosity of a liquid containing gelatine is a function not only of the concentration of gelatine in the solution but also of temperature. You've probably made stocks and stews that set firm like jelly when cold (if you haven't, then stick with me – you soon will). A set jelly is one of the most efficient and intense ways of delivering flavour to our taste buds, as the warmth of our mouths dissolves the bonds between the aromatic particles, so they slip slowly over the taste buds on our tongues. This is why a jelly can register the same sensation of sweetness as, say, a sugar-based drink diluted with plain water, even when it contains less actual sugar. It gets held up for longer while passing over the taste buds.

Another thing that affects the taste impact of foods is the temperature at which they are served. Taste sensations are muted at very cold or very hot temperatures (which is why a sorbet needs more sugar to generate the same level of sweetness as a purée of the same fruit at room temperature). In a warmed-up, melted jelly (which is really what the sauce of a rich, well-made stew ought to be), served not scalding hot but pleasantly warm, the trade-off between viscosity and temperature is pretty optimal for taste.

If you feel the case for gelatine has been made (I hope you do), you will no doubt wish to know the most practical ways of introducing it to your dishes. You could, of course, ladle it out from a packet with a spoon. Its mere presence would certainly add viscosity, or 'body', to the stew. But as I have said, pure refined gelatine is colourless and odourless. Impure gelatine rendered to a stock from skin, sinew and bone is far from it: it carries with it the natural flavours of the meat and bone. And provided these ingredients are fresh and untainted, their flavours are likely to be altogether desirable. So these natural, unrefined, primary sources will always be the best way to add body.

This, of course, is what making a stock is all about – and I discuss this further on page 465. So one of the best ways to add body and flavour to your slow-cooked dishes is to make the principal liquid ingredient a stock that you have prepared in advance. Ideally the stock should be made from bones of the same animal as the meat. But some stocks are more 'neutral' than others: pork, veal, chicken and, curiously, pigeon all make stocks that can be fairly universally applied, whereas lamb or mutton and most game stocks will tend to queer the taste of any other meat. Beef is fairly flexible until it reaches a certain concentration, becoming unmistakably beefy and therefore only suitable for beef-based stews and reductions/gravies that are served with steaks or roast beef.

If you don't have any stock to hand, you can simply add a bone or two to the cooking pot (bought or begged from the butcher at the same time as you buy your meat), even if it is not specified in the recipe. Roasting the bones in advance will further enhance the flavour, as the scraps of meat adhering to the bones will caramelise, increasing the levels of our treasured 'browning flavours'. The bones can be removed and discarded before the dish is served (though you may want to eat any marrow as a 'chef's perk', or at least whisk it into the sauce). The drawback of adding bones in this way, particularly big beef bones, is that your stew will require skimming regularly for the first half an hour or so of simmering, as the bones inevitably produce some scum that rises to the surface.

Some recipes have bone built in. An oxtail (page 79) will make its own rich stock without help from added bones. And the best Lancashire hot pots (page 290) and Irish stews (page 292) are made with chops, in which the natural presence of bone will do all that is needed to create a full-bodied liquor – even if water, rather than lamb stock, goes in at the start. In this case the meat is simply gnawed off the bones, which can be left on the plate – though those confident of their dental health may find that even the bones are tender enough to chew up and swallow. Other recipes may produce the necessary body without 'added' gelatine. Shin of beef, for example, with all its connective tissue and tendons, is sufficiently collagen rich, even off the bone, to generate a strong, full-bodied liquor when cooked for three or four hours. Having said that, I'd still prefer to use a shin on the bone and reap a double benefit.

The other body-boosting additive is skin. It will have to be the skin (or rind, as it's called when not made into wallets and briefcases) of a pig, as pigs are the only animals whose skins are not automatically removed at slaughter. This is not a problem, as the flavour is neutral and pork rind can be happily added to just about any other meat. The addition of pork rind to beef stews is something you will encounter in many 'old-fashioned' cookbooks, particularly where the recipes emanate from France. Elizabeth David was a big fan, and suggests it frequently in the rightly hallowed *French Provincial Cooking*. Now that I rear my own pigs, I keep a regular supply of rind in the freezer and bung it into all sorts of slow-cooked dishes. I can honestly say I can hardly think of a stew or braise that wouldn't be the better for it.

Any good butcher should let you have some rind for next to nothing. Ask yours to set some aside for you, in thick strips or squares, and keep it handy in the freezer. If you want a vivid illustration of the remarkable gelatinous properties of pork rind cooked long and slow, then check out the recipe for cotechino sausage (page 441), in which finely chopped rind is a crucial and transforming ingredient.

Often I kill two birds with one stone by using rind that is still attached to a good fatty piece of belly, either fresh or cured. The rind renders up its gelatine and the rest of the belly its unctuous, lubricious fat – which is what I'm going to talk about next. At other times the rind belongs to something that you might like to think of as a secret weapon in the battle to create body and richness in slow-cooked dishes: a pig's trotter. This is a fantastic little package of skin, bone and sinew, and even a fair bit of fat, and it can be used to great effect to enrich all sorts of stews.

A knuckle of ham or a hock of fresh pork (see page 117) is similarly loaded with appropriate goodies, and can be used in much the same way. I actually specify the trotter's inclusion in a couple of recipes (pages 282 and 486), where the gelatinous quality of the finished liquor is paramount, but you should also think about deploying it in your own improvisations. Depending on your dish you may, at the end of cooking, wish to de-bone it, chop up the meat, fat, skin and gelatinous matter (which is all edible) and stir it back into your dish for extra body. Or you may wish to remove it completely – in which case you can make a delectable snack by giving it the 'Ste Menehould' treatment described on page 295.

Fat for Richness and Flavour

I've discussed fat's critical role in 'brokering' the flavours of meat in detail in Chapter 2, What Is Good Meat? (pages 35-6). When it comes to slow cooking, fat is as important as ever. You need fat in your meat, and you need it in your liquor – not floating on top in a thick, greasy layer but, as far as possible, emulsified into a fairly homogenous, well-blended sauce.

As everyone knows, oil and water don't mix. But as we've been finding out, by the time you've finished with it the liquor in your stew or stockpot is a long way from plain old water. Think of it as a light syrup, enriched with gelatine from skin, bone and sinew, sugars and browning flavours from the meat, and more sugars and aromatics from the vegetables, herbs and seasonings. This is a medium that will take on fat. And the right level of fat incorporated into this delectable concoction is the icing on the cake – or, more aptly perhaps, the cream in the coffee.

In a well-balanced, full-bodied stew, some of the fat present will naturally emulsify into the sauce as it simmers, while some will find its way into the meat. But it can also be helped on its way. An occasional gentle stir – preferably from top to bottom rather than round the edges – will help to redistribute fat that has risen to the surface. As it slowly percolates back up to the top, some of it will be trapped between the fibres of the tenderising meat and some will be taken up by the liquor. We're talking tiny amounts in both cases, but these tiny amounts make a big contribution to the eating quality of the stew.

This assumes that an appropriate amount of fat is present in the meat you are cooking. It may well not be. There is a tendency for cooks to trim off a lot of excess fat from the coarse cuts of meat for stewing, particularly when beef is being used. Although this is clearly detrimental to our desire for fat to do its important work, it is also understandable. The fatty, gristly parts that adhere to the meat are not, at the end of the cooking time, to everybody's taste. Personally I'm pretty broad-minded about them, but even I don't want fat and sinew on every forkful. So I'm certainly not going to insist that everyone else puts up with it.

The problem is that the lean meat that remains after trimming can be very lean – lacking the natural presence of marbling fat that you would hope to find in the prime cuts. Most types of game present a similar problem, especially pigeon, rabbit, hare and venison. The meat of all of them is, to use a rather irritating modern phrase, 'virtually fat free'.

Happily there is a highly effective culinary remedy for the absence of fat: the aforementioned pork belly. You can use it in various forms: fresh or salted, as dry-cured bacon (see page 429 for how to make your own) or pancetta, or you can simply buy some good-quality streaky bacon and use that. My own preference is for salted belly – partly because I have a ready supply of the home-made product but also because I find it is a most effective way of gently salting the stew as it cooks. I prefer to use big chunks, of a similar size to the meat in the stew, because they will release their fat more slowly into the dish and they also become very tasty morsels in themselves by the end of cooking time. And of course, for the reasons discussed above, I usually leave the rind on (an exception would be a dish in which the cooking time is too short to tenderise the rind and make it pleasant to eat – a pheasant casserole, for example).

As for quantities, I am pretty cavalier with my home-made bacon. I'd happily fling in, say, 250g with a kilo of beef. This means, if you like, that roughly one in five pieces of meat in the finished stew will be bacon, not beef. That's a ratio I'm more than happy with.

Other fatty bits of pork, ham or bacon can also be used: off-cuts of Parma ham or bacon joints, cubes of raw back fat, with or without rind, the knuckle and the trotter mentioned above. But the best fat donor of them all will always be the belly of the pig. And you needn't worry about mixing pork with other meats – its flavour is highly complementary, supporting rather than upstaging them.

Other fats you may want to use in slow cooking from time to time are the soft rendered fats and liquid fats, such as lard, butter, goose fat, beef dripping, olive oil etc. These are particularly handy for oiling the pan in which you sear your meat – and whatever's left in the pan usually goes in the pot. If you're anxious that a dish you are cooking will lack fat, and you don't have the magic bacon, any of these fats can also be added 'neat' – a couple of tablespoons for every kilo of meat would be about right. They do not have the slow-release properties of pork belly and bacon fat, and will tend to rise quickly to the top of a gently simmering pot. But stirred back in occasionally, they will still leave faint but important traces of themselves behind in the liquor and the meat. Any excess fat can be skimmed off before you serve the dish.

Finally, just in case I've given the impression that I want your slow-cooked dishes swimming in gloopy fat – I don't. You should always feel free to skim off any excess fat from the surface of the dish. But do so at, or at least towards, the end of the cooking time, when the fat content will have done its work and left its mark. By this time it may be virtually invisible. But you'll taste the difference.

The Overnight Rest for Ripening

I mentioned my fifth, 'optional' rule, that ideally stews and other slow-cooked dishes should be made a day or two before you want to serve them. Of course, this isn't always practical. On the other hand, sometimes it's extremely practical – especially when you're entertaining. With the main dish knocked up in advance, the cook can relax, with little more to worry about than boiling up some noodles or rice, or baking or mashing potatoes.

There are (at least) two reasons why resting a stew for a day or two does it good. Firstly, the simple passage of time helps the dish to 'ripen' – the flavours will mingle and blend to a more pleasing harmony (highly spiced dishes will benefit particularly). Also, the action of cooling settles the texture of the meat, giving it a chance to reabsorb the well-flavoured liquor to the point of saturation. This is why, when you do reheat a stew, you should do so very gently – bringing it back to just the gentlest of simmers. (I'm probably not allowed to tell you that all you really need to do is reheat it to a pleasant eating temperature – of about 60°C – because technically that's a bit of a dodgy zone for the bug count. But that's what *I'd* do – and the reason is that if I take it much hotter than that I'm starting to lose precious liquor from my meat again.)

Even if you don't have time to leave the stew overnight, simply cooling it, leaving it for an hour or two, then reheating it will still confer many of the benefits of the full overnight rest.

And if you don't have time even to do that, then it's still a good idea to let your stew rest, covered, for half an hour or so before you serve it. To rest and cool, even by a few degrees, will help the meat to relax and reabsorb. And you may as well serve it at a temperature that will not scald your guests.

Reducing to Intensify Flavour

So, a stew is to be judged as much – or more, even – by the flavour of its liquor as by the taste and texture of its meat. But what do you do if at the end of the cooking time, when the meat is tender and ready to eat, the juice is, frankly, a little on the feeble side? Of course, if the above principles have been adhered to, this shouldn't happen. But it does. Bones and skin are not as readily available in many butcher's as they ought to be, and sometimes a stand-by stew has to be made with just water and wine as the cooking liquid rather than a pre-made stock. The resulting liquor may well be a bit lacking in oomph or, even if quite tasty, a bit thin and watery. Time to reduce.

Many amateur cooks have never reduced a stock or sauce, believing the process to be some technically demanding bit of professional cheffery. Really, there's no mystery to it. Boil any liquid that is principally water and the water will evaporate. A salt solution can be boiled back to pure dry salt, and a sugar solution to pure sugar, though this is likely to colour and caramelise. The liquor of your stew contains both sugars and salts, dissolved and osmosed from the meat and vegetables. If you boil to reduce, then the concentration of these constituents, and the aromatic flavours associated with them, will increase. The logical conclusion of reduction is a thick, Bovril-like paste which, provided you don't burn it and corrupt the flavours, can, like the branded beef extract, be reconstituted as stock by the addition of fresh clean water. It's rarely useful to go that far, but you might want to do it once as an experiment, to prove the principle. The resulting paste can be spread thinly on toast, and is the gourmet version of Marmite or Bovril. Add boiling water, vodka and Worcestershire sauce for the ultimate 'bullshot'!

Whether you're reducing stocks, sauces or the liquor from a stew, the liquid should be as 'clean' as is practically possible. If you try to reduce a stew with the meat still in it, you will drive the precious juices out of it and it will turn to mealy pap. Don't be tempted to leave bones in either, in the hope that they will continue to give up their goodness as you reduce. Boiled too hard, they will give the sauce an unpleasant, chalky taste. The best procedure is to strain the stew first through a colander to separate out the meat and vegetables, then through a fine sieve or *chinois* to filter out any small particles that might taint the flavour when boiled hard. (Chefs strain their stocks for sauce-making through muslin or a cotton cloth. They know they can then boil as hard as they like without queering the flavour or clouding that glossy, translucent sheen.)

So, strain your stew liquor into a large, clean pan that it doesn't fill by more than half – you need plenty of space as the boiling stock foams and rises up the pan. Then simply whack up the heat underneath it and boil hard. As soon as it is boiling and the water departing as steam, the process of reduction is under way. How much you reduce it is up to you. Let your taste be your guide, sampling the occasional teaspoonful (don't burn your tongue) to see how the flavours are intensifying. For most stews in need of a boost, reduction by a third or a half would be about normal. Of course, you end up with a lot less liquor in your stew. But a few spoonfuls of well-flavoured sauce are worth much more than a large puddle of insipid gruel.

You can also make some adjustments to flavours and seasonings as you reduce, adding a little more wine (the flavour of which mellows as it boils), or a dab of redcurrant jelly for sweetness. But remember that anything you add will intensify as it reduces. Be very wary of one ingredient in particular: SALT. A liquor reduced by half will be twice as salty as it was at the beginning. You should therefore never add more than the merest pinch of salt at the beginning of cooking to a stew whose liquor you are likely to end up reducing. If you're using bacon in the stew, don't add any salt at all (very salty bacon can be soaked for a few hours before being added to a stew). Sometimes saltiness alone will dictate how far you can reduce your liquor without it becoming unpalatable. And certainly you shouldn't make the final salt adjustment till you have finished reducing it.

Incidentally, and just for the record, correcting an oversalted stew, other than by dilution with an unsalted liquid (i.e. extra water or unsalted stock), is difficult and tedious. But in emergencies it can be done. The technique is to add peeled raw potatoes, which will absorb some of the saltiness as the stew continues to cook. But they'll need to be simmered for at least half an hour to have any significant effect. You can, of course, serve the cooked potatoes with your stew, if it seems appropriate.

Once you are happy with the flavour (and saltiness!) of your reduced liquor, add the meat and vegetables to the pan and return it to a gentle simmer for at least ten more minutes, to bring everything back to a harmonious whole.

Sometimes a heavily reduced, intense, almost syrupy sauce is part of the intrinsic character of a dish. Perhaps the best example in this book would be my Oxtail, or Tail and Tongue, with Rich Red Wine Sauce (page 282). The meat is removed from the dish, the flavouring vegetables discarded, and the stock strained through muslin before being heavily reduced to an intensely flavoured, syrupy sauce. The meat is then taken off the bones and returned to the sauce, heated through and served. The reduction may be as much as tenfold – over 2 litres of strained liquid, including perhaps the best part of a bottle of wine, reduced to a scant cupful (about 200ml).

One more caveat: be aware that the process of reducing accelerates rapidly as the amount of liquid diminishes. Forgetting a fast-reducing stock or liquor is fatal – suddenly it's a smoking, choking, acrid mess. Not a pretty sight, and a truly hideous smell.

If you've never tried this reducing malarky, it's something to look forward to. The effects are quite dramatic and can make you feel like a real pro!

Flour for Thickening the Sauce?

Flour has long been a popular optional addition to slow-cooked dishes, and some cookery writers ask you to toss your meat in flour before browning it for the pot almost as a matter of course. The reason is straightforward enough: it will thicken the liquor of the stew as it cooks. This may be desirable in some dishes but in others it is definitely not. And even when you're sure you want a flour-thickened liquor in your dish, you should be careful not to overdo it.

The fact is that the action of flour on the liquor of a stew is crude compared to that of gelatine or fat. Too much flour, and a sauce becomes thick and gloopy. Furthermore, unlike the process of reduction, the addition of flour does nothing to enhance. In fact it is something of a flavour-thief, masking the hard-won sugars and aromatics in a sauce to the extent that it may actually taste floury. We've all had stews that suffered from the over-liberal use of flour and we all will again. Let's not contribute to the misery by actually making one!

That's my caveat. And having issued it, I'd like to be more positive about the use of flour. In some dishes, it just is right – when you want that glossy, emulsified sauce in your Steak and Kidney Pie (page 286), for example, or when stewing beef with stout (page 288). These are English classics, and using flour to thicken a stew is often thought of as something of an English trait. But this isn't strictly true either. The French have been at it for years. Dishes like Coq au Vin (page 311) and classic civet of hare and other game usually prescribe tossing the jointed meat portions in seasoned flour, then browning them before the liquids are added and the slow cooking begins. The flour helps to bind the liquid fat with the watery juices, emulsifying the sauce as if you were making gravy. Sometimes this is just what is needed.

A couple of points to note here. It is no coincidence that these dishes are ones in which either on-the-bone joints of meat are used, rather than lean cubed meat, or a pre-made stock is prescribed as the main cooking liquid. Wine, herbs, bacon and flavouring vegetables are also present in generous quantities, and long cooking times – upwards of two hours – are anticipated. We can therefore expect a pretty rich liquor to develop – robust enough to stand up to the addition of flour as a thickener and come through undiminished. I would be much less happy to use flour in a stew where lean meat and vegetables were expected to produce a flavoursome liquor without the help of bones or a pre-made stock.

So, my rule about the use of flour to thicken stews and other slow-cooked dishes would be to ask yourself a couple of questions. Are you really looking for that gravy-like texture that flour will confer? If so, are you confident that the depth of flavour in your stock will be sufficient to withstand flour's flavour-thieving tendencies? If the answer to both of the above is yes, then turn your meat in a bowl containing two or three tablespoons of flour, ideally well seasoned with salt and black pepper. The meat should not be too wet or the flour will cake on it. Dry but slightly tacky meat will end up lightly and evenly coated, and any excess flour should be shaken back into the bowl – don't feel you have to use all the flour specified in the recipe. Browning the floured meat is essential: in a flour-thickened stew, those caramelised meat flavours are particularly precious. Also, cooking the flour at this stage means it should dissolve gently into the stew as it simmers, subtly thickening the liquor over time. If you were to place floured raw meat in the pot without browning it first you would find a gluey paste adhering to it even after two hours' cooking. Yuk.

It may come as a relief to hear that you don't have to make the flour decision at the beginning of cooking, as it can also be incorporated at the end to thicken your sauce, using what is known as *beurre manié*. This fancy French phrase refers to a simple paste made by rubbing together equal quantities of soft butter and plain flour. Use about 25g of each and add it a few crumbs at a time. It's best to strain off the stock – you can reduce it by boiling hard if you want to strengthen the flavour – then whisk the *beurre manié* into the simmering liquid. You will not gauge the full effect of each addition for a few minutes, so take it slowly, and by degrees, until you get the consistency you like. Then return the meat and vegetables to the sauce to simmer for another ten minutes or so; this should cook out any floury taste.

Potatoes, Pulses, Grains and Pasta: the Starchy Thickeners and Bulkers

Many of the classic slow-cooked meat dishes are essentially peasant pots. In the originals, the presence of any meat at all may have been scant, and something of a luxury. In the modern or bourgeois versions of such dishes, the meat content may be more generous but it is still some locally popular and intrinsically cheap bulking ingredient that gives them their distinctive character. I'm talking about the barley in the Irish stew, the macaroni in the daube, the white beans in the cassoulet, the potatoes in the hot pot, and the beetroot in the borscht.

What these dishes tend to illustrate is that the simple marriage of a starchy, bulky vegetable with a cheap, almost throwaway cut of meat can, with perhaps a few onions and a dose of spices or herbs, create a wonderful harmony that quite eliminates the need for reducing, dusting with flour, making stocks and fussing over finishing sauces. Many of them are dishes that you bung in a pot and, bar a twist of pepper and a dash of salt, they're done when they're done. Appreciation of the roles and actions of these principal starches accrues as soon as one tackles the dishes in question. Versions of all of the above, and several other classic peasant pots, appear in the recipe pages that follow.

And the Rest ...

There are, of course, hundreds of further ingredients that can be added to slow-cooked dishes: exotic tubers and roots such as manioc and cassava, a myriad of grains and pulses, fruits both fresh and dried, any number of vegetables, the entire repertoire of herbs, spices and aromatics, and most of the contents of the average off-licence (in South Africa, I hear they stew ostrich in Coca-Cola). All are at your disposal. All of them will affect the overall flavour, and many will contribute to the finished texture, too.

Over a hundred such ingredients are mentioned in the slow-cooked recipes in the following pages. The recipes work, but don't feel hidebound by them. There are infinite prescriptions for borscht, from Siberia to the Ukraine. And it is well known that no two French cooks can agree on how to make the perfect pot-au-feu. So make mine once. Twice if you really like it. Then next time make your own ...

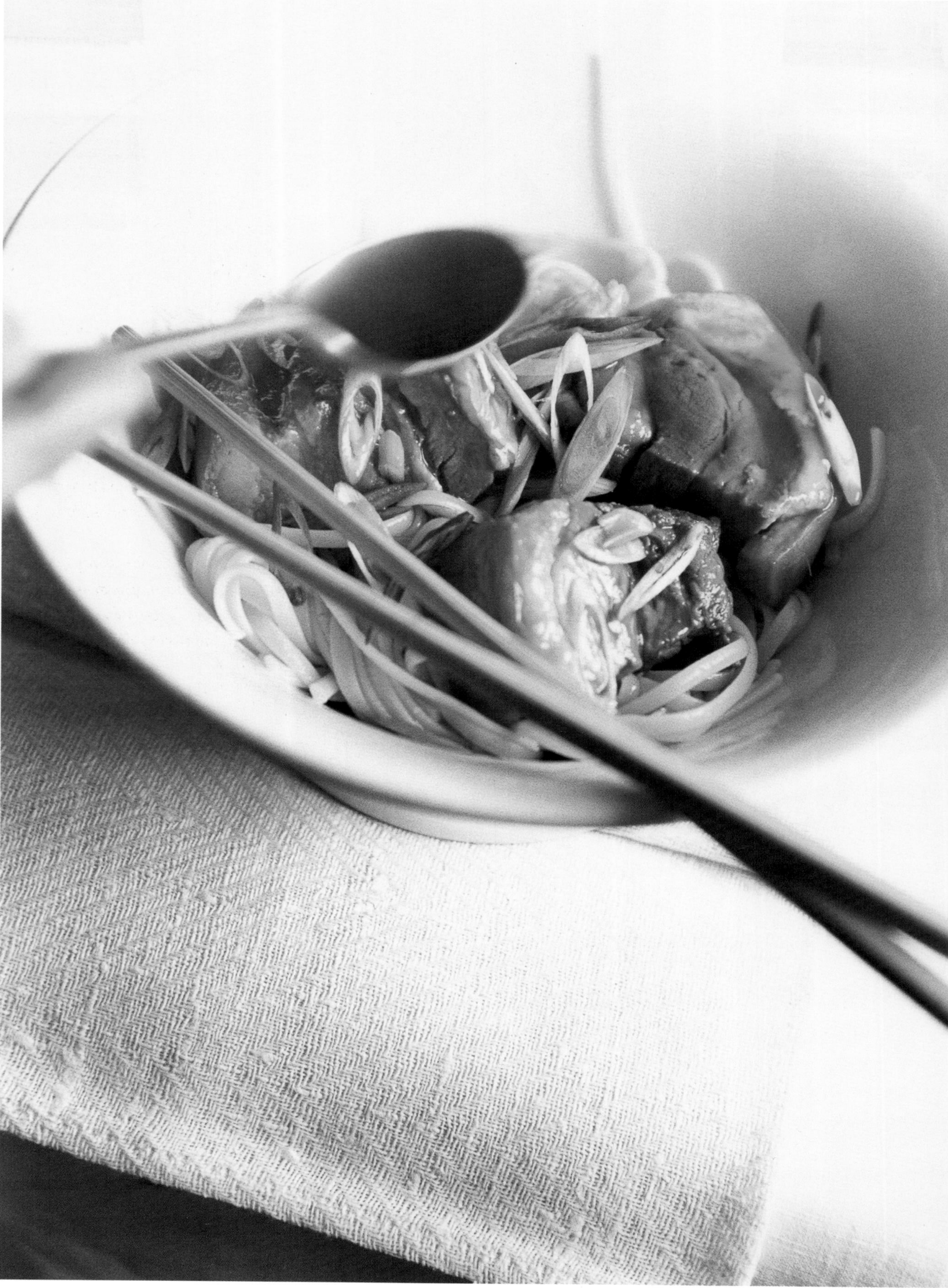

AROMATIC PORK BELLY HOT POT *Serves 6*

1.5kg pork belly, with the rind on

About 1.5 litres pork or chicken stock (see pp.474 and 470-72), if available, otherwise water

12 spring onions

100ml light soy sauce

75ml Chinese rice wine

25ml rice wine vinegar

2 tablespoons demerara (or soft light brown) sugar

3 star anise

10cm piece of fresh ginger root, peeled and sliced into rounds

A good pinch of dried chilli flakes

A fine example of the great versatility of pork belly and the slow-cooking technique, this time using aromatic oriental flavourings. This is authentic Chinese home cooking of a kind rarely found in restaurants.

Remove the bones from the pork belly and cut it into rectangular chunks, about 2.5 x 5cm. Put them in a large pan, pour over enough boiling water just to cover, then bring back to the boil. Simmer gently for about 5 minutes, skimming off the scum that rises to the surface, then drain through a colander. Rinse out the pan if necessary, return the pork to it and pour over enough boiling hot stock (or water) to cover it again. Cut 5 of the spring onions in half and add to the pan with the soy sauce, rice wine, vinegar, sugar, star anise, ginger and chilli flakes. Stir well and bring back to the boil. Reduce the heat, cover tightly and simmer very slowly for about 2 hours, turning the meat occasionally, until the pork is very tender, soft and succulent.

Remove the pork with a slotted spoon and set aside. Strain the cooking liquid into a clean pan, ideally through muslin or a fine *chinois*. Skim off as much fat as you can (but don't worry about leaving a little), then boil the stock hard to reduce and concentrate the flavours. It should be lightly syrupy and intensely aromatic, but don't over-reduce as the soy sauce may make it very salty.

Meanwhile, thinly slice the remaining spring onions on the diagonal. Return the pork to the sauce and heat through. Serve over plain noodles in warmed soup bowls, with plenty of the broth ladled over and the sliced spring onions scattered on top of the meat.

RICE PUDDING PORK *Serves 6*

2-2.5kg piece of boned loin of pork, rind and most of the fat removed

A few gratings of fresh nutmeg

2 tablespoons olive oil

50g butter

About 1-1.5 litres whole milk, hot

2 teaspoons soft brown sugar

3-4 bay leaves, ideally fresh

2-3 sprigs of fresh thyme (or a pinch of dried thyme)

Thinly pared zest of 1 lemon (no pith)

Sea salt and freshly ground black pepper

This is my take on a traditional Italian dish – pork cooked in milk – that the River Café has made into something of a modern classic. The curious, lumpy, curdled milk makes a unique but delicious sauce that I find irresistible. My additions are bay and thyme in place of the more usual sage, plus a little nutmeg and brown sugar, which effectively anglicise the dish, giving it a hint of the charms of a good rice pudding – hence the name!

Season the pork all over with salt, pepper and a little grated nutmeg. Heat the olive oil in a frying pan and gently brown the pork in it, turning it occasionally so it is lightly coloured all over. Turn off the heat and leave the pork in the pan.

Take a saucepan or casserole in which the pork will fit fairly snugly and melt the butter in it over a medium heat. Add about a third of the hot milk and all the brown sugar, stirring to dissolve. Put the pork in the pan, pour in the remainder of the hot milk until it almost covers the meat, and bring slowly to a simmer. Lightly scrunch the bay leaves and thyme to release the essential oils and add them to the pan, along with the lemon zest and another couple of gratings of nutmeg. Cover with a lid, leaving a slight gap, and cook very gently (the trembling sub-simmer I describe on page 260) so the surface is undisturbed. Cook for 1½-2 hours, during which time the milk will curdle and form a rice pudding-type crust.

Carefully remove the pork from the pan and cut it into thick slices. Spoon the crusty, milky curds from the pot, dividing them fairly between the plates, then generously spoon over the thinner, milky gravy. Serve with bread for soaking up the lovely liquor. No further accompaniment is required. Indeed, at my table, nothing else is allowed.

MAIN-COURSE BORSCHT *Serves 8*

1 kg salt pork, pancetta or bacon (p.429 for home-made), cut into 4 cm chunks, with the skin on

1.5 kg shin of beef, trimmed and cut into big chunks

50 g lard or beef dripping (for preference), or other cooking oil

2 large onions, thickly sliced

4 garlic cloves, roughly chopped

4 large tomatoes, skinned and chopped

2 tablespoons tomato purée

1 white cabbage, shredded

1 kg potatoes, peeled and cut into quarters or eighths, depending on size

5 carrots, coarsely grated

5 beetroot, coarsely grated

2 tablespoons paprika

2 litres pork and/or beef stock (pp.474 and 473)

Freshly ground black pepper

500 ml soured cream, to serve

This is an interesting alternative to the chicken-based Ukrainian borscht in The River Cottage Cookbook. *Again, it's definitely a stew, not a soup, and a great dish for large numbers. The quantities can easily be doubled or trebled.*

If you don't have any home-salted pork belly, and don't want to splash out on expensive pancetta, just buy fresh pork belly and cover thick strips of it in salt. Leave for twenty-four hours, then rinse, dry and cut into chunks.

Heat the fat or oil in a large, heavy-based frying pan and brown the pork in it first, then the beef, in batches as necessary. Transfer to a large stockpot. Turn the heat down under the frying pan and in the same fat sweat the onions and garlic until soft. Add them to the stockpot.

Add all the other ingredients (except the soured cream) to the pot, topping up the stock with a little water if needed to cover the meat and vegetables. Bring to the boil, then turn down the heat and simmer very gently, skimming off any grey scum that rises to the surface for the first 30 minutes or so. Cook for about 3 hours in all, stirring occasionally and skimming off some of the fat if you like, until the meat is completely tender. Taste and adjust the seasoning. The potatoes and other vegetables should thicken the stew as it cooks but if you want to emphasise this, spoon some of the potatoes out of the stew, mash them roughly and stir back in.

Serve in deep bowls, with plenty of soupy liquid, a big dollop of soured cream and hunks of bread (or, more traditionally, kasha – a thick porridge made by boiling buckwheat). Poached Piroshki (page 501) can also be served with this dish.

A PROVENÇAL DAUBE *Serves 6*

This is the kind of simple stew that exemplifies slow cooking at its best. A modest cut of beef, some onions, tomatoes, wine, and the all-important but often overlooked pork component, bubble together quietly for a couple of hours to produce something so much greater than the sum of its parts. There, I've almost given you the recipe. Here, to be on the safe side, are a few more details.

- *1.5kg shin of beef (or skirt or other good stewing beef)*
- *2 tablespoons olive oil*
- *250g piece of salt pork, pancetta or bacon (see p.429 for home-made), cut into 2cm chunks*
- *100g pork or bacon rind, cut into 2cm squares*
- *500ml white wine*
- *About 500ml water or light beef stock (p.473)*
- *1 onion*
- *4 cloves*
- *4 garlic cloves, bashed with the side of a knife*
- *2 bay leaves*
- *A couple of sprigs of thyme*
- *2-3 strips of finely pared orange zest*
- *2 carrots, cut into big chunks*
- *3 celery sticks, cut into 5cm lengths*
- *500g tomatoes, skinned, deseeded and chopped*
- *Salt and freshly ground black pepper*

Cut the shin into larger-than-you-would-think, not-too-boringly-square pieces, trimming off some, but not all, of the fat as you go.

Heat the olive oil in a large, heavy-based frying pan. Fry the bacon and the pork or bacon rind until lightly browned (but not crisp). Remove with a slotted spoon and place in a large casserole. In the same oil, brown the beef, in 2-3 batches, and then transfer to the casserole.

Deglaze the frying pan with a little of the wine (page 262), then add the rest of the wine, heat until it boils and pour it over the meat. Heat up the water or stock in the same way and pour that over too – enough to cover the meat by a good 2cm. Cut the onion in half and stick each half with 2 cloves, then add to the casserole along with the garlic, herbs, orange zest, carrots, celery and tomatoes. Season, going easy on the salt for the time being (remember that the bacon will give up salt to the pot). Bring to a very gentle simmer and maintain it, either on the hob over a very low heat or in the oven at 120°C/Gas Mark ½, for 3-4 hours, until the meat is completely tender. At this point the stew can be cooled and kept in the fridge for a day or two, which, as ever, would be no bad thing.

To serve the stew, make sure it is thoroughly hot – if it has been left to cool – and check the seasoning. Remove the onion (unless any of your guests fancies half an onion). Ladle the stew into deep plates or wide bowls, with plenty of the juice (which in this stew is meant to be thin and copious, rather than thick and reduced). You could serve it with potatoes – boiled, baked or mashed. Or (and I rather like this option) with macaroni or some other noodly pasta, pre-cooked and stirred into the daube a couple of minutes before you ladle it out.

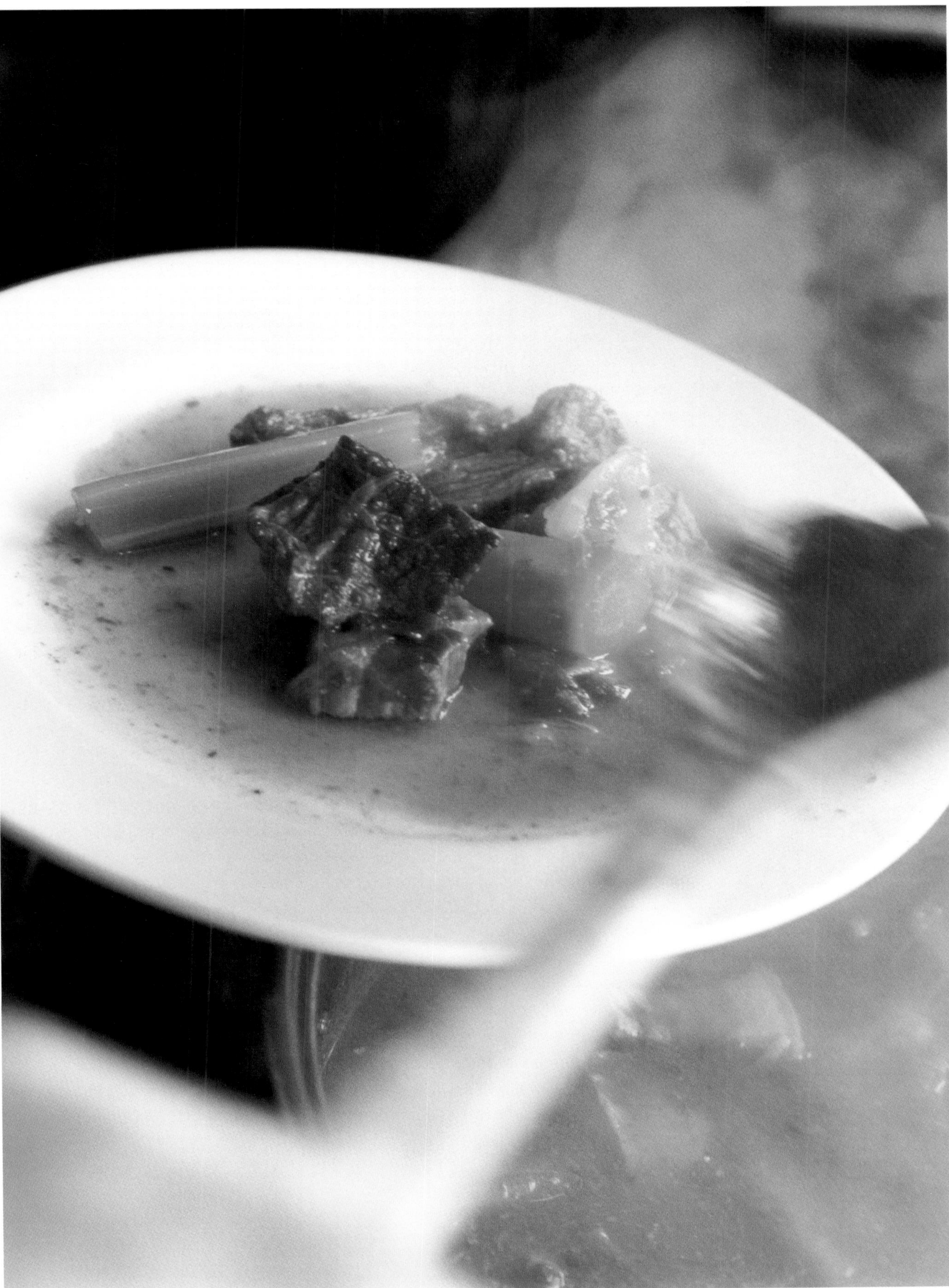

OXTAIL, OR TAIL AND TONGUE, WITH RICH RED WINE SAUCE *Serves 6-8*

1 oxtail, cut into short lengths

1 whole fresh (not pickled) ox tongue – or another oxtail!

1 marrow bone or pig's trotter (optional, but it beefs up the stock and helps set the cold version)

2 large carrots, roughly chopped

2 onions, roughly chopped

2 celery sticks, roughly chopped

1 small turnip, roughly chopped

Thinly pared zest of 1/2 orange

A bouquet of fresh herbs (bay, thyme and parsley stalks)

1/2 bottle of good red wine

Salt and freshly ground black pepper

I've always loved oxtail stew and the basic recipe for this version of it has long been a regular in my repertoire. I now often include the tongue in the pot, as the distinctly different textures of the two meats combine beautifully.

The dish also has a radically different incarnation when set in its own jelly and sliced as a terrine, to be eaten cold.

The oxtail and tongue will both benefit from a couple of hours in a plain salt and water brine, though you can omit this step if you're short of time. Then scrub the oxtail pieces under cold running water and place in a large saucepan with the tongue, marrow bone or pig's trotter, vegetables, orange zest and herbs. Add enough cold water to cover completely and bring slowly to a simmer, skimming off any brown scum as it rises to the surface (see page 190). Cover and simmer very gently (or cook in a very low oven, 120°C/Gas Mark 1/2, if you like) for at least 3 hours, until the oxtail meat is tender and coming away from the bone and the tongue can be easily pierced with a skewer.

Remove the tongue and the pieces of oxtail from the pot with a slotted spoon. Remove and discard the bone or trotter and the vegetables, then strain the stock through muslin or a clean cotton cloth into a clean pan. Add the wine and boil fiercely over a high heat to reduce. Just how much you want to reduce the sauce is a matter of personal taste. I like it fairly intense and rich, but I stop short of those very sticky reductions that seem to be *de rigueur* in expensive restaurants. When you have reached the level of reduction you require, season to taste (do not do so earlier; if you judge saltiness to be right before you reduce it, it will be far too salty afterwards). Add a few more drops of wine, if liked, to refresh the flavour.

While the sauce is reducing, remove the oxtail meat from the bones with your fingers, discarding any large pieces of fat. Peel the coarse skin from the tongue and cut the tongue into 2 cm pieces. Return the tongue and oxtail pieces to the sauce and heat through thoroughly, allowing it to bubble for a couple of minutes. Serve with mashed potatoes or, better still, Horseradish Mash (page 519) and steamed seasonal greens such as spring greens, Savoy cabbage or kale.

To serve cold

To make jellied tongue and tail (as in the picture opposite), simply ladle the finished stew, or leftovers thereof, into a suitable-sized mould (i.e. ramekins, terrine dish or pudding basin), with enough sauce to come level with the top of the meat. Cover with clingfilm or a lid and chill until set firm.

Turn out on to a plate and cut into slices. Serve with mustard, gherkins, cracked black pepper and flaky salt.

POT-AU-FEU *Serves 8-10*

At least 3 different cuts of beef, about 1.5-2kg each, for example:

A piece of brisket or flank (hindquarter or forequarter), ideally on the bone

A shin of beef, in 1-2 large pieces, on the bone if you can get it

A knuckle of veal, on the bone

An oxtail or tongue

A spare marrow bone

STOCK VEGETABLES:

For example:

4 large leeks, washed and trimmed but left whole

4 very large carrots, or 8 large ones, peeled

1 head of celery, cut into quarters

4 medium onions, peeled but left whole

4 small parsnips

OTHER FLAVOURINGS:

2 large tomatoes, halved and grilled

A bouquet garni made of 3 bay leaves and a few sprigs of parsley or thyme

Salt and freshly ground black pepper

Among the most inspiring of Elizabeth David's writings are her pages in French Provincial Cooking *demystifying the classic French stockpot dish known as pot-au-feu. My recipe is really a distilled version of hers: follow the procedure and you will get reliable results every time. You might, however, wish to have a look at the original some time.*

Pot-au-feu is a dish from the peasant hearth, and as such it is based on thrift – getting the best out of the cheaper cuts of meat, which tend to be fatty and on the bone. Indeed, in the poorest household a pot-au-feu would have been little more than plain boiled bones, with the few shards of meat attached going to the head of the household along with the marrow, and just the broth and a handful of rice or barley for those lower in the pecking order.

Today we can be a little more generous but there is no need to be extravagant: shin, leg, flank, brisket, and perhaps a knuckle of veal, plus a tail or tongue to vary the texture, are suitable cuts. If you can't get your shin or leg on the bone, buy a whole marrow bone separately, ask the butcher to saw it in half, and add it to the pot along with the meats.

Like Elizabeth David's, this recipe provides you with two dishes: a fine, beefy broth (the bouillon*) and a substantial meat course (the* bouilli*), which is eaten with the vegetables. When a marrow bone is included, slivers of the soft, fatty marrow can be served before the soup, piping hot, on toast that has been rubbed with garlic and sprinkled with coarse salt. And if there is still meat left over – which seems likely, given the quantities involved – then it's time for France's favourite leftover dish, pot-au-feu fried up with garlic and onions, for which instructions are also given below.*

As with so many slow-cooked dishes, a pot-au-feu can benefit from being made a day in advance. I should also mention that the vegetables from the pot-au-feu are very soft and mushy, which tempts some cooks, to the disapproval of purists, to discard them and cook up a fresh set, steamed until fashionably al dente, *to serve with the meat. I used to do this but my (French) wife is so irritated by it that I have 'learned to love' the mushy veg.*

Put all the meat and bones into your biggest saucepan (at least 5 litres in capacity) and pour over enough cold water to cover. Over a low heat, bring very slowly to simmering point. As you do so, a brownish scum will start to rise to the surface. Skim this off as it appears, and continue to do so for about the first 10 minutes of very gentle simmering. Once the scum is a clean white colour it can be left – it will eventually disperse. Now add all the vegetables and other flavourings to the pot, lifting the meat so that some of the vegetables fall to the bottom of the pan. Season cautiously with salt (about 2 teaspoons) and pepper. Put the lid on the pan, slightly to one side so that the steam can escape, and leave to simmer very gently,

TO FINISH THE SOUP:

250g cheveux d'ange/capelli d'angelo (angel hair) pasta, or vermicelli, alphabet pasta or risoni (rice-shaped pasta)

TO SERVE WITH THE MEAT:

Plain boiled potatoes (cooked separately)

A selection of mustards

Pickled cornichons *(gherkins)*

Gros sel *(flaky salt)*

with a few bubbles just rising in the centre, for no less than 3, and probably no more than 4 hours, until all the meats are completely tender.

Remove from the heat and lift out the meat and vegetables with a slotted spoon. (If the pot-au-feu is for the following day, cover and refrigerate the meat and vegetables. Leave the *bouillon* to cool, then chill. When chilled, the hard fat can be easily lifted from the surface.)

If you are planning to serve the pot-au-feu at once, put the meat into a warmed dish with a ladleful or two of the hot stock, then cover and keep in a warm place, such as a low oven. Carefully transfer the vegetables to another warmed dish and keep these warm in the same way. Strain the stock into a clean bowl through a sieve lined with muslin or a clean cotton cloth. Skim as much fat as you can from the top: laying sheets of kitchen paper over the surface and removing them as soon as they are saturated is a particularly effective method. Pour the clean broth into a clean pan and taste it. You could concentrate the flavour by boiling to reduce it at this stage, but if you've used enough good meat and bones it shouldn't be necessary. So, adjust the seasoning to taste and bring the *bouillon* to the boil. Add the pasta and simmer until it is cooked. Serve at once.

Then prepare the meats. If kept from the previous day, reheat slowly but thoroughly with the vegetables in a little of the *bouillon*. Remove the ribs from the brisket or flank – the meat should be so tender that the bones slip out very easily. Pick off any meat from the veal knuckle with a fork. Slice the shin meat into thick pieces. Leave the oxtail pieces on the bone but remove any very large pieces of fat. Serve everybody a mixture of the meats, with hot boiled potatoes, a selection of the hot vegetables, and a little hot *bouillon* poured over. Have on the table a selection of mustards, some pickled *cornichons* (gherkins), and, most important of all, *gros sel* (large flakes or crystals of salt).

Variations and leftovers

THE VINAIGRETTE:

1 teaspoon finely chopped shallot

2 tablespoons finely chopped parsley

1 tablespoon white wine vinegar

1 teaspoon mustard

5 tablespoons olive oil

A pinch of sugar

Salt and freshly ground black pepper

The meats cold: Some French families like to serve the *bouillon* hot but the meat cold, in which case a simple vinaigrette is made for the meat as follows:

Separate the meat from the bones while it is still warm. Cover and leave to cool. Mix together all the ingredients for the vinaigrette. Serve thin slices of the meat trickled with the vinaigrette. Accompany with 2 simple salads – one of potatoes, one of tomatoes – and with *cornichons*.

The meats fried: For some, the best of the various visits to the pot-au-feu is the final one. A sliced onion or two and a little garlic are browned quickly in some oil or fat in a heavy frying pan, then roughly chopped leftover meat is added and fried up until nicely browned and crisp. Leftover vegetables can also be included. My wife, who is entitled to dictate here as this is her very favourite dish, says that only the carrots and a little potato should go in.

STEAK AND KIDNEY PIE *Serves 6*

1kg beef skirt (ideally) or chuck steak (trimmed of gristle, but with a bit of clean fat here and there), cut into generous cubes

400g beef kidneys, as fresh as possible, cored (p.193) and cut up into forkable chunks

A little oil or fat

Up to 50g plain flour, seasoned well with salt and pepper

1 glass of red wine

1 onion, sliced

1 tablespoon tomato ketchup

1 teaspoon English mustard

1 bay leaf

About 750ml beef stock (p.473) or water

350g open-cup mushrooms, thickly sliced (optional)

Salt and freshly ground black pepper

THE ROUGH PUFF PASTRY:

200g cold butter or lard, cut into walnut-sized pieces

400g plain flour

A pinch of salt

Iced water

1 egg yolk, beaten with 2 teaspoons milk or water, to glaze

A man in a restaurant says to the waiter, 'I'll have the steak and kiddley pie, please.' 'Sorry, sir,' says the waiter, 'do you mean the steak and kidney pie?' The man says, 'That's what I said, diddle I?'

Sorry, couldn't resist.

I love this pie. I prefer it to steak and kidney pudding because you get the best of both worlds: a delicious, soggy, gravy-absorbing pastry underneath (similar to the suet lining of a pudding) and a wonderful, flaky, crispy baked-pastry crust on top. If you want, you can forget the pastry lining and just have a crisp pastry lid. But I think you'd be missing out.

The rough puff pastry is time consuming to make but it is the ultimate pastry for a fully-lined hot pie of this kind. My suggestion is to make double quantities each time and freeze the other half for your next pie. It works well after defrosting.

Tip: To check the size of your pie dish is suitable, pile in the raw meat. It should mound a good inch or so above the top of the dish. Always err on the side of too much filling. You can always make an extra mini-pie for one or two, or just have steak and kidney with a baked potato.

If I were Desperate Dan, I'd have real horns coming out of this pie. But I'll settle for a pastry decoration. The photo on pages 254-5 is more or less life size, so you can even trace around my pastry cow's head if you want to make one yourself!

First make the pastry. Toss the fat in the flour with the salt until coated, then add a little iced water and bring the dough together with your hands, adding no more water than you need to get a medium-firm dough that is not too sticky, with large pieces of the fat still intact in it. On a well-floured surface, shape the dough by hand into a fat rectangle and roll it out with a well-floured rolling pin, rolling away from you in one direction only to keep the rectangular shape as much as you can. When the dough is 2cm thick (or less), fold the far third towards you and fold the near third back over that, so that you now have a rectangle a third of the size and 3 times as thick. Give the pastry a quarter turn (90°) to the right and roll it out again, away from you, into another long rectangle. Repeat this procedure, folding and turning, at least 4 times, preferably 6 or 7. You will need to keep dusting with more flour. Should the dough become too loose or sticky (a danger in warm or damp weather), chill it in the fridge for an hour or so, then dust with more flour and resume rolling. At any rate, the finished pastry should be folded up for a final time and chilled for at least 1 hour before rolling out and using.

Now make the filling. Heat a little oil or fat in a large, heavy frying pan until fairly hot but not smoking. With floured hands, toss a couple of handfuls of the beef in the seasoned flour, shaking off any excess, then transfer to the pan and brown well on all sides. Brown all the meat like this, including the kidneys, in batches to avoid overcrowding the pan. Transfer the browned meat to a large saucepan as you go. Add an extra knob of fat between batches, if the pan needs it.

When all the meat is browned, deglaze the empty pan with half the wine (page 262), scraping up any burnt crispy bits with the edge of a wooden spatula. Add the deglazed juices and the rest of the wine to the meat in the saucepan. Heat a little more oil or fat in the now clean frying pan and sweat the sliced onion in it for a few minutes, until softened. Add to the meat, then add the ketchup, mustard, bay leaf and just enough stock or water to barely cover the meat. Stir gently. Bring carefully to a very gentle, tremulous simmer and cook for about 1½ hours, until the beef is fairly tender but perhaps not quite 'finished'. It is going to get the best part of an hour in the pie. Note that skirt may take a little longer than chuck steak.

Check the seasoning towards the end of cooking and adjust as necessary, then leave to cool. At this stage the pie filling can be left, covered, in the fridge for a day or two. Or it can be very successfully frozen. If you like mushrooms in your pie, fry them gently in a little oil for a few minutes to let the juices run, then add to the filling before you make up the pie (they will cook through in the pie).

Cut the pastry into 2 rectangles, one very slightly bigger than the other. Roll out the larger piece to about 5 mm thick and use to line a lightly greased pie dish, about 1.2 litres in capacity, right to the edge of the flat lip of the dish, trimming off excess pastry. Roll out the smaller piece so it will more than cover the top of the pie. Spoon in the meat until it is at least level with, preferably mounding just a little higher than, the top of the dish. Ladle in enough of the juices to come 2 cm short of the top of the pie – i.e. not quite covering the meat.

Brush the edges of the lining pastry with the beaten egg yolk and cover the pie with the rolled-out lid piece, crimping the edges with your thumb so the lid is well glued down to the lining. Make up any decorations with the pastry trimmings – leaves, a cow's head, your initials – and stick them on with egg yolk. Then brush the remaining egg yolk all over the surface of the pie. Make 2 X-shaped vent holes in the pastry at either end of the pie. Bake in a moderately hot oven (190°C/Gas Mark 5) for 50 minutes-1 hour, until the pastry is puffed up and golden brown.

To serve the pie, cut wedges right through the lining pastry at the bottom of the dish, so everyone (at least everyone who wants it) gets a mixture of sticky bottom and crispy lid with their pie. Serve with steamed seasonal greens, such as Savoy cabbage or sprout tops, and good English mustard. A real trencherman could no doubt manage a dollop of good buttery mash as well.

BEEF IN STOUT *Serves 8-10*

1.5kg chuck or stewing beef or shin (boneless weight), trimmed and cut into generous chunks

250g salt pork, pancetta or bacon (see p.429 for home-made), cut into slightly smaller cubes than the beef

50g butter or dripping, plus a little butter for cooking the mushrooms

500g baby onions, peeled but left whole

Up to 50g plain flour, seasoned with salt and pepper

1 litre stout, such as Murphy's

2 bay leaves

A sprig of thyme

A few stalks of parsley

250g button mushrooms

250g flat open-cup mushrooms, sliced about 5mm thick

Salt and freshly ground black pepper

TO ACCOMPANY:

Herb Dumplings (pp.519-20)

Mashed potatoes (p.518)

This is a particularly fine dish to make when you've got some good stewing beef but no stock – the stout makes a good substitute (though arguably, half stout, half stock would be even better). It's also a dish where mushrooms – too often thrown into a stew without much thought – really come into their own.

Heat the butter or dripping in a large frying pan and brown the pancetta or bacon until the fat runs. Transfer to a large casserole or saucepan. In the same fat in the same frying pan, gently fry the baby onions, shaking occasionally, until they are lightly browned all over. Transfer to the casserole. Toss the beef in the seasoned flour, shaking off the excess, and brown it in the same pan, in batches, transferring it to the casserole when it is nicely coloured.

Now pour some of the stout into the pan to deglaze it (page 262), scraping any residue from the base of the pan with a wooden spatula and tipping it all into the casserole. Pour in the rest of the stout, adding a little water only if needed to cover the meat. Add the herbs, tied into a bouquet garni, and season with salt and pepper. Bring to the boil, then set to simmer very gently, with the lid on but slightly ajar.

Cook the stew for about 2½ hours for chuck or stewing steak, more like 3 hours for shin, until the meat is completely tender. You could do this on the hob or in a very low oven (120°C/Gas Mark ½). Add a little hot water if the meat is starting to get exposed and dry out. The mushrooms go in about 1 hour before the end. Sweat them gently in a little butter till the juices have run out of them and they have 'tightened'. Add, along with the juices, to the casserole – the juices will help prevent the stew drying out.

Serve with either herb dumplings, cooked in the stew for the last 45 minutes, or creamy mashed potatoes, or both!

Variation

Beef and Stout Pie: See the recipe for Steak and Kidney Pie on pages 286-7. Make the stew as above but cook it for just 1½ hours. Use the half-finished stew as a substitute for the steak and kidney filling.

OSSO BUCO ALLA MILANESE *Serves 6*

2 hind shins of rosé veal, cut into slices about 5cm thick, skin left on (this should give you 6 good slices and a few smaller ones; the very bony end of each shin is not used but it can be used to make the stock)

Up to 50g plain flour, seasoned with salt and pepper

50g butter

1 tablespoon olive oil

2 garlic cloves, finely chopped

2 onions, finely chopped

2 celery sticks, finely chopped

1 carrot, finely chopped

1 large glass of white wine

About 450ml light stock (veal, pork or even chicken – pp.470-74)

Salt and freshly ground black pepper

THE GREMOLATA:

Finely grated zest of 1 lemon

1 small garlic clove, very finely chopped

2 tablespoons very finely chopped parsley

TO ACCOMPANY:

Risotto alla Milanese (p.520)

*You may have begun to sense my passion for slow cooking meat, and this dish demonstrates why it can be so delectable. You get tender, delicately flavoured meat, deliciously chewy skin and sinew, a bone to gnaw (*osso buco *means 'hollow bone') and a scoop of unctuous marrow, all in a single piece of meat – the shin of the veal calf, sawn in cross-section to include the bone.*

The hardest thing about this dish will be finding the veal shins. Plan in advance and get on the phone (see Directory, page 526). Ask if it is possible for the skin to be left on the shins as, like pork rind, it has a wonderful gelatinous quality when cooked long and slow. A purist (i.e. any Italian) would disagree, but I think English rosé veal (the kinder alternative to imported Continental veal – see pages 85-6) works extremely well in this dish.

Another point of contention is whether a 'classic' osso buco *should include tomatoes. So entrenched are the positions on both sides of the debate that one can only conclude that legitimate versions exist both with and without. I take sides purely on the grounds of taste: the subtleties of a good gremolata and the unctuous risotto milanese are quite lost on a dish that is already tangy with the flavour of tomatoes, so there'll be none in my osso buco.*

Dust the pieces of shin in the seasoned flour, shaking off any excess. Heat the butter and oil in a shallow casserole that is large enough to hold the veal pieces in a single layer. Add the veal and cook until browned all over, then remove from the pan and set aside. Add the garlic, onions, celery and carrot to the pan and cook until softened. Return the veal pieces to the pan, carefully arranged flat-side down so the marrow won't fall out, then pour in the wine and let it bubble until reduced by about half. Add the stock and a little salt and pepper, bring back to a very gentle simmer and cook for about 2 hours, until the meat is very tender and coming away from the bone. You can do this on the hob or in a very low oven (120°C/Gas Mark 1/2).

During the cooking time, carefully turn the pieces of veal over once or twice and, if the mixture becomes too dry, top up with a little more stock. Once the veal is tender, remove the lid from the pan, raise the heat slightly and simmer for about 10 minutes to reduce the juices a little.

Make the risotto, if you are serving it, during the last 30 minutes of the veal's cooking time (or serve the osso buco with creamy mashed potato (page 518), with a pinch of saffron infused in the hot milk).

Mix together the ingredients for the gremolata. Carefully lift the veal pieces out with a spatula and transfer to warmed plates (if the marrow falls out, pick it up with a spoon and drop it back in the empty bone once the veal is safely on the plate). Sprinkle a little gremolata over each osso buco and spoon some hot pan juices around the edge. Serve immediately, with the risotto.

LANCASHIRE HOT POT *Serves 4*

About 600g best end or middle neck mutton or lamb chops (ideally 16-20 chops)

2 lamb's kidneys, sliced into quarters and trimmed of tough core (p.193)

25g butter

Dripping or oil for frying

1 large onion, sliced

750g potatoes (ideally a firm variety, such as Desiree)

1 bay leaf

Up to 50g plain flour, seasoned with salt and pepper

2 large carrots, peeled and cut in half

3 anchovies, roughly chopped

1 1/2 teaspoons Worcestershire sauce

500ml lamb stock (pp.472-3) or water

Salt and freshly ground black pepper

This is one of the great 'peasant pot' dishes of Britain, but there's more to it than just heaving some lamb and spuds into a casserole. Not much more, but it pays to layer it up carefully (potatoes underneath, as well as on top, are a must) and to use good-quality ingredients. Winter lamb, fattier and more mature, is preferable to spring, and well-hung mutton is best of all. The kidneys are optional, in the sense that it's worth making the dish without them if you don't like kidneys, but they are certainly authentic.

Melt the butter in a pan with a little dripping or oil to stop it burning and sweat the onion in it for a few minutes, until soft but not brown. Meanwhile, peel and finely slice the potatoes (aim for 50p piece thickness). Rinse them, pat roughly dry with a tea towel and divide into 2 piles. Remove the onion from the pan with a slotted spoon and combine with one of the piles of potatoes. Place the bay leaf in a large casserole or deep ovenproof dish and cover with the potato and onion mixture, layered evenly. Season with salt and pepper.

Reheat the pan, adding a little more fat only if needed. Dust the chops with the seasoned flour, shaking off any excess, and brown in the pan in batches, until nicely coloured. Arrange the chops over the layered potatoes. Flour and brown the kidney pieces in the same way and spread them over and among the chops. Push the chunky pieces of carrot into any gaps. Scatter over the anchovies and season well with Worcestershire sauce, salt and pepper.

Bring the stock or water to the boil while you spread the remaining potato slices over the top of the meat in an even layer. Season the potatoes and pour over enough of the hot stock or water to cover them, but not by much. Cover the dish with its lid (or a double layer of foil) and place in the centre of a fairly hot oven (200°C/Gas Mark 6). After 20 minutes, turn the oven down to 140°C/Gas Mark 1 and cook for another good hour (90 minutes for real mutton chops). Remove the lid. If there is a lot of juice covering the potatoes, ladle some of it off to expose the surface (ideally the potatoes should be lightly glazed by the surface fat). Turn the heat back up to 200°C/Gas Mark 6 and cook for about 30 minutes, until the top is nicely browned (use the grill to cheat a bit if you like, but be careful not to burn the potatoes).

This is a one-pot meal. No other accompaniments are necessary (or, in Lancashire, expected). Serve up, being as fair as you can in the distribution of the crispy potatoes from the top, the chops and the kidneys, and the softer, oniony potatoes from underneath. And there's one good chunk of carrot per person.

LAMB BRAISED WITH STUFFED VINE LEAVES *Serves 6*

whole shoulder of lamb or mutton, boned and rolled

2 tablespoons olive oil

3-4 cloves

2 garlic cloves, chopped

Several good sprigs of thyme

About 250ml water or lamb stock (pp.472-3)

Zest of 1 lemon

Juice of 2 lemons

1 tablespoon chopped mint

Salt and freshly ground black pepper

STUFFED VINE LEAVES:

250g coarsely minced lamb (raw or leftover roast)

125g long-grain rice

15g butter, melted

1 garlic clove, crushed

1/4 teaspoon cinnamon

1/4 teaspoon mixed spice

A few gratings of fresh nutmeg

2 packets of vine leaves (or about 40 blanched fresh vine leaves)

TO ACCOMPANY:

Labneh (or Greek yoghurt), seasoned with salt, pepper and a tiny amount of crushed garlic, then trickled with olive oil

Pitta bread

This is the Lebanese version of a dish normally associated with Greece. I like the way it becomes a one-pot affair, the stuffed vine leaves an accompaniment to a more substantial piece of meat (in this case a boned shoulder of lamb), which is braised in the same juices. Rolling up the vine leaf parcels is a little time consuming, but it is a sociable job that lends itself to having a good natter across the kitchen table. And kids can join in, too.

Vine leaves can be bought, pickled in brine, in Greek and Lebanese delis and now in many supermarkets. But if you know anyone who has a vine (of any description), then it's lovely to make this dish with fresh vine leaves – just blanch them for a minute in lightly salted boiling water to make them pliable.

To make the stuffing, mix together the minced lamb, rice, butter, garlic and spices, then season with salt. Prepare the vine leaves according to the packet instructions. Separate the leaves and put a teaspoon of the stuffing mixture in the centre of each one. Fold in the sides so the filling is partly covered, then roll up into a tight, neat cylinder, about the size of your thumb. You should get about 35-40 parcels with this amount of stuffing.

Heat the olive oil in a large pan, add the rolled shoulder of lamb and cook, turning, until browned all over, seasoning with a little salt and pepper as you go. Place in a flameproof casserole big enough to accommodate the vine leaf parcels around the meat. Pack the stuffed leaves neatly into the casserole, around and, if necessary, on top of the lamb. Sprinkle on the cloves, garlic and thyme. Add the water or stock, then cover the meat and parcels with a couple of sheets of buttered foil, the edges tucked in (this helps you to steam and braise at the same time). Cover the pan with a lid, bring to a very gentle simmer and cook for 1½-2 hours (or in the oven at 120°C/Gas Mark ½, if you like). Then remove the foil, turn the meat over and add the lemon zest and all but a teaspoonful of the juice, plus a little more water or stock if necessary. Cook for a further hour, until the meat is completely tender.

Carefully remove the meat and the stuffed vine leaves from the casserole. Taste the juices and add a little salt, if necessary. Refresh with the last teaspoon of lemon juice and stir in the chopped mint.

Cut the shoulder meat into fairly thick slices and serve on warmed plates, with 5 or 6 vine leaf parcels per person and a few spoonfuls of the juices. Have the seasoned labneh on the table as a kind of relish, plus warmed pitta bread to mop up the juices. Indeed, if you're a dab hand with the pitta, cutlery is not strictly necessary.

MRS WHEELER'S IRISH STEW *Serves 4*

4 large lamb or mutton chump chops

4 neck chops (optional)

1 kg floury potatoes, peeled and cut in half (or in quarters if large)

2 large or 4 small to medium onions, peeled and left whole if small, cut in half if large

2 large carrots, peeled and cut into 2-3 pieces

1 medium turnip, peeled and quartered

2 rounded tablespoons pearl barley

About 750 ml water or lamb stock (pp.472-3)

Salt and freshly ground black pepper

Chopped parsley, to garnish

This recipe comes from photographer Simon Wheeler's Irish mother. It is not a subtle or complicated dish but with good ingredients it can be a very delicious one. Use large, meaty chops of mature lamb, hogget or mutton, not dainty cutlets of spring lamb. The neck chops, bonier and less meaty, are my addition. They give more body and flavour if water is being used instead of lamb stock.

Trim the chops only if they are very fatty, and certainly don't remove all the fat. Put the meat, vegetables and pearl barley in a pot with enough water or stock just to cover them. Season well with salt and pepper and bring to a gentle simmer. Cook, covered but with the lid slightly ajar, for 1½-2 hours, until the meat is completely tender. (You could do this in the oven at 120°C/Gas Mark ½.) Check and adjust the seasoning, being generous with the pepper.

Serve in warm bowls or plates, with plenty of the potato-thickened liquor and with chopped parsley sprinkled over each serving.

BREAST OF LAMB STE MENEHOULD *Serves 4*

breast of lamb
2 carrots, sliced
2 onions, sliced
A sprig of rosemary or thyme, or both
1 glass of white wine
1 glass of water
Salt and freshly ground black pepper

TO FINISH:
Dijon or English mustard
2 eggs, beaten
Dried breadcrumbs to coat
About 100g butter, melted

The breast of lamb (page 102) is the give-away cut of the animal (literally, in some butcher's shops), yet most British cooks these days have probably never got to grips with one. If that includes you, you're missing out. This dish, originally brought to our attention by Elizabeth David, is the one to make you a convert. It's something that will delight anyone who is ever excited by the words 'crispy' and 'breadcrumbs' in a recipe.

Place the breast of lamb in an ovenproof dish or casserole, cut in half if necessary to fit, with the carrots, onions and herbs scattered under and over it. Pour the wine and water over, season well with salt and pepper and cover the dish with foil (or its lid). Bake in a low oven (140°C/Gas Mark 1) for 2½-3 hours, removing the dish from the oven to turn and baste the breast 2 or 3 times, until the meat is completely tender.

Remove from the oven and leave until cool enough to handle, then slip the rib bones out of the meat by tugging them gently with your fingers. Press the boneless breast between 2 chopping boards, or 2 flat plates, with a weight on top (a few full jam jars or large tomato tins will do). Leave in a cool larder or the fridge for a couple of hours or overnight.

To finish the dish, slice the cold, pressed breast meat into two-finger-width, one-finger-length slices. Brush the slices with a little mustard, dip them in the beaten egg, and press firmly into a bowl of breadcrumbs so they are well coated. Arrange on a wire rack in a roasting tin, brush with the melted butter and place in the centre of a moderate oven (180°C/Gas Mark 4). After 15 minutes, turn on the oven grill (if it doesn't have one, whack the oven up to maximum heat) to get the lamb pieces very crisp (a touch blackened even), first on one side, then the other.

Serve on hot plates, to waiting guests, with a piquant sauce, such as Tartare (page 513), Salsa Verde (page 514), or simply Mustard Vinaigrette (page 513). To make this a meal rather than a starter or snack, extend the accompaniments to a pile of creamy mash (page 518) and Watercress and Orange Salad (page 523).

Variation

Pig's Trotters and Ears Ste Menehould: I've no idea who Ste Menehould was (all information gratefully received) but she gave her name to a town in north-east France and a culinary procedure that is nothing if not adaptable: the finishing of slow-cooked, bargain-basement cuts of meat with crumbing and crisping. Besides the lamb breast, the items that most benefit from this loving treatment are the trotters and ears of the pig. In both cases, long, slow simmering (3-4 hours) with some stock vegetables is required. Trotters will then need to be boned before pressing. Ears will do as they are. Cut them into suitable chunks and crumb and crisp precisely as above.

NDOLE *Serves 8-10*

1kg boneless mutton or stewing lamb, cut into cubes

500g salt cod, soaked in cold water for 48 hours (change the water twice)

6 tablespoons sunflower or groundnut oil

2 large onions, chopped

30g piece of fresh ginger root, grated

2 garlic cloves, chopped

2 teaspoons mild curry powder

1 fresh red chilli

600g tomatoes, skinned and chopped, or 400g tin of peeled plum tomatoes, chopped

About 1.5 litres lamb stock (pp.472-3) or water

150g pumpkin seeds

50g dried shrimps

750g (uncooked weight) bitterleaf, spinach or chard leaves, tough stalks removed (or about 400g frozen or pre-blanched bitterleaf or spinach)

Salt and freshly ground black pepper

I love this stew for its distinctive West African flavour, which comes from the combination of strong-tasting dried fish – cod and shrimps – and strong-tasting meat, traditionally goat or mutton. You'd think they would fight, but somehow they come together in happy harmony.

The authentic Cameroonian ndole, which I was taught to make by Grace Elone in the 'TV Dinners' series, includes bitterleaf – a green, leafy plant which grows, both wild and cultivated, in the region. As the name suggests, it's quite unpalatable in its raw state. Pre-prepared bitterleaf can be purchased dried or frozen in good African food shops. If fresh bitterleaf is used, it must be boiled with limestone and washed thoroughly several times before being added to the dish. Alternatively, spinach or chard can very happily be used in place of the bitterleaf.

Dried shrimps can be bought in Asian and African delis and also in many supermarkets.

Drain the salt cod, cover with fresh water and simmer for about 30 minutes. Drain and leave until cool enough to handle, then pick out and discard any bones or skin. Roughly chop the flesh.

Heat half the oil in a large frying pan and brown the mutton or lamb in it, in batches if necessary. When nicely coloured, transfer to a large saucepan. Add the rest of the oil to the frying pan and gently fry the onions, ginger, garlic, curry powder and whole chilli until the onions are soft and translucent. Then add to the meat in the saucepan.

Add the chopped tomatoes, the cooked salt cod and enough stock or water to cover the meat. Bring to the boil and simmer gently for about 1½ hours, until the meat is becoming tender.

Grind the pumpkin seeds in a pestle and mortar until they have the consistency of ground almonds. Add the dried shrimps and pound some more (or put both into a food processor and pulse to a granular paste). Stir the ground seeds and shrimps into the stew carefully and thoroughly, so they are well incorporated. Continue to simmer gently for about 20 minutes. Either add the prepared bitterleaf, chopped, or briefly wilt or blanch the spinach or chard leaves in a pan of boiling water, squeeze out most of the excess water and chop the leaves roughly. Stir into the stew, check the seasoning, simmer for just another 5 minutes, and the ndole is ready.

Traditionally this dish is served with boiled rice and fried plantains.

CURRY GOAT *Serves 8-10*

kg mutton (scrag end, hops and/or shoulder ieat)

large tomatoes, skinned nd roughly chopped

garlic cloves, bashed, hen roughly chopped

onions, finely chopped

-2 Scotch bonnet chillies, leseeded and finely chopped

A few good sprigs of thyme (or 1 teaspoon dried thyme)

A good bunch of coriander (leaves and roots)

2 tablespoons HP sauce (optional but very authentic)

50g clarified butter (or use a good cooking oil)

Salt

THE JAMAICAN CURRY BLEND:

1 tablespoon coriander seeds

1 tablespoon black peppercorns

12 cardamom pods

1 tablespoon fenugreek seeds

1 cinnamon stick

1 tablespoon ground ginger

1 tablespoon ground turmeric

The authentic Caribbean curry goat is, of course, made with goat meat. You can get goat in the UK – the male kids from milking herds are sometimes raised for the pot – but it's hard to track down. Mutton (pages 94-5), or at least older autumn lamb, makes a very acceptable alternative. Use cheaper stewing cuts. I like a mixture of shoulder meat, scrag end and neck chops, and I prefer to leave the chops and scrag end on the bone.

Every Caribbean cook has their own version of this dish and the spice combinations vary wildly. My version is based on a very dependable and delicious recipe from my friend, Lucy Pilkington.

You can buy Jamaican-blend curry powder or, more satisfyingly, you can make up a batch of your own, as described below.

To prepare the curry blend, dry-roast the first 5 spices by tossing them for a couple of minutes in a hot, dry frying pan, then pound in a pestle and mortar or grind in a coffee or spice grinder. Mix with the ginger and turmeric.

Cut the mutton into good-sized chunks (I prefer 2-3cm thick chunky slices to even cubes; think in terms of 3-4 pieces per person), trimming off only the really excessive fat.

In a large bowl (big enough to take the meat), combine 2 level tablespoons of the freshly ground spice mix with the tomatoes, garlic, onions and chillies. Strip the thyme leaves off their stalks, bruise with a knife blade and add to the bowl. Finely chop the roots and stalks of the coriander (set aside the leaves for adding to the curry at the end) and add them, too. Add the HP sauce if you like (I like).

Add the meat to the marinade, rubbing the marinade in well with your fingers. You should spend a bit of time over this, working the spices into the meat and enjoying the smell that rises from the bowl. Cover and leave in the fridge for at least 6 hours, or overnight.

Remove the meat from the seasoning, knocking off any loose bits of onion or tomato (these will be fried separately later). In a large pan, fry the meat in the butter until it is nicely browned. You'll need to do this in at least 2 batches. Transfer to a large casserole (in the Caribbean they'd use a cast-iron Dutch pot). Then fry the seasoning that you've just taken the meat out of – everything that's left in the bowl – until the onions are softened. Add to the meat in the pot. Deglaze the pan with a little water (page 262) and add these juices, along with enough extra water just to cover the meat. Add a scant teaspoon of salt. Bring to the boil, then turn it down to the gentlest possible simmer. Transfer to a very low oven (about 120°C/Gas Mark 1/2), if you like, or cook on the hob, until the meat is very tender. It will need at least 2, more like 3, hours. Serve sprinkled with the chopped coriander leaves, accompanied by plain boiled rice and fried plantains, plus mango chutney or other Jamaican pickles.

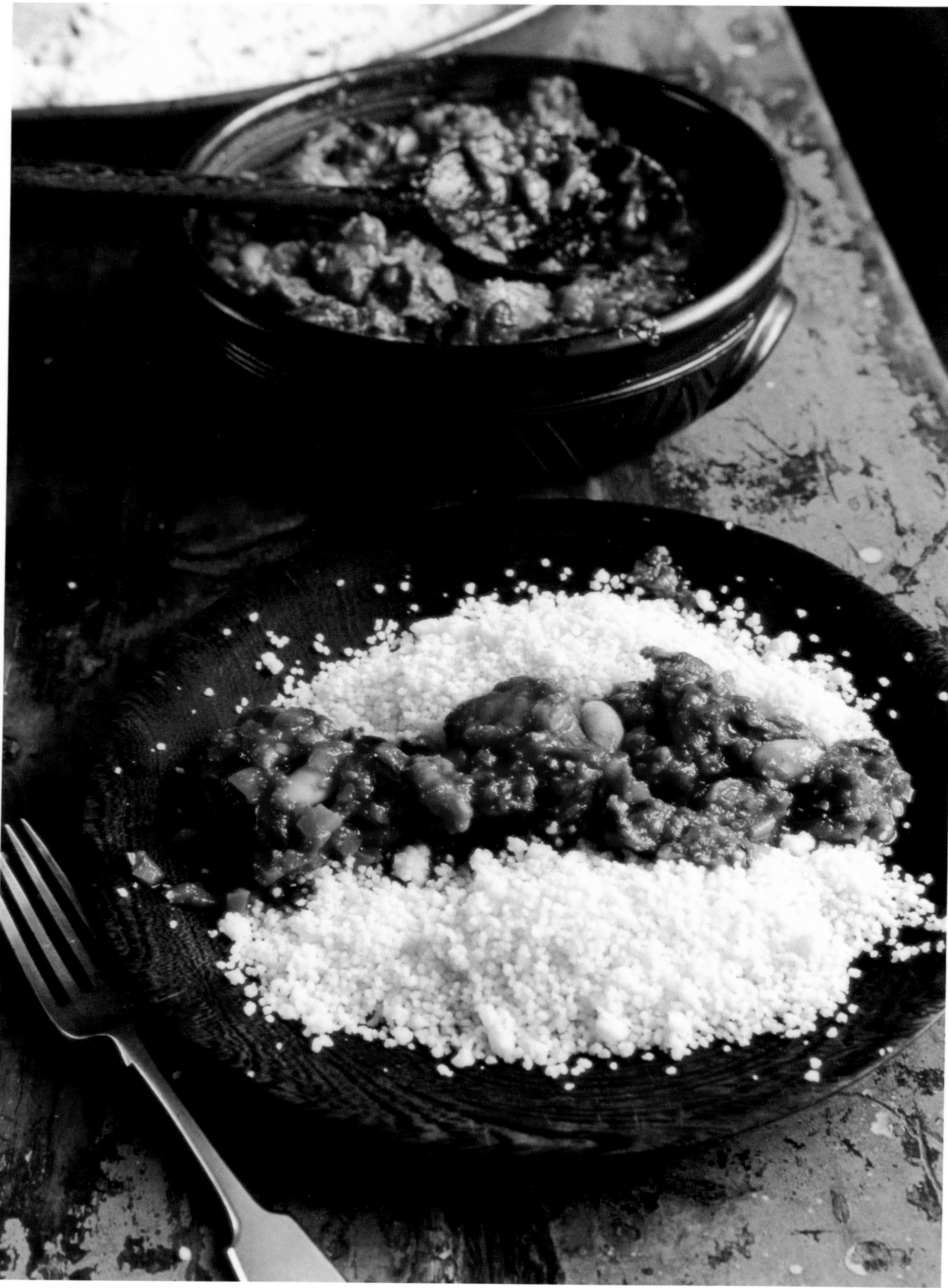

TUNISIAN LAMB WITH AUBERGINE *Serves 6*

- [illegible]kg stewing lamb or mutton, cut into large cubes (a mixture of scrag end and boned-out shoulder is good)
- 2 aubergines, cut into 5cm cubes
- 2 teaspoons fine salt
- About 4 tablespoons olive oil
- 2 garlic cloves, chopped
- 1 onion, chopped
- 2 celery sticks, chopped
- 1 leek, sliced
- 1 teaspoon cumin seeds
- 1 teaspoon coriander seeds
- 2 cloves
- 1 teaspoon ground ginger
- 2 x 400g tins of tomatoes, chopped
- About 1 litre lamb stock made from the trimmings and shoulder bones (see pp.472-3)
- 100g whole blanched almonds
- 100g unsulphured dried apricots
- A small bunch of coriander, finely chopped
- Salt and freshly ground black pepper

The wisdom of marrying lamb with aubergine is proven in a number of dishes, most notably Moussaka (page 503). From the other side of the Mediterranean comes something sweeter and spicier, where very long, slow cooking allows quite a sophisticated blend of meat, vegetables, fruit and spices to melt together beautifully. The end result is an outstanding harmony of flavours.

It's a dish that can be prepared several days in advance, and is easily expanded to feed large numbers.

Toss the aubergine chunks with the fine salt and leave in a colander to bleed. Meanwhile, in a heavy-based casserole, heat half the olive oil and brown the meat in it in batches, setting it aside when it is done. Add a little more oil if necessary, then add the garlic, onion, celery and leek and sweat until tender. Pound the cumin, coriander and cloves together in a pestle and mortar and add to the sweating vegetables with the ginger. Stir well and cook for a couple more minutes. Add the tomatoes, turn up the heat a little and simmer, stirring occasionally, until you have a thick, pulpy sauce.

Add the lamb, pour in enough stock to cover and mix well. Bring to a trembling, gentle simmer, and cook very gently, either on top of the stove or, covered with its lid, in a very low oven (120°C/Gas Mark ½), for 1 hour.

Quickly rinse the aubergine chunks and pat dry with a tea towel or kitchen paper. Heat another tablespoon or so of olive oil and stir-fry the aubergines until nicely browned. Add to the casserole with the almonds and apricots and stir everything together gently but thoroughly. Return the casserole to the heat/oven for another good hour, or longer, until both the meat and the aubergines are completely, meltingly tender.

Adjust the seasoning and stir in the fresh coriander. Leave for 15-20 minutes to absorb this last flavouring, then serve, with Couscous (page 521) or plain boiled rice.

CITRUS-BRAISED LAMB SHANKS *Serves 4*

4 lamb shanks (p.99)

2-3 tablespoons olive oil

1 carrot, finely diced

1 onion, finely diced

2 celery sticks, finely diced

A few sprigs of thyme

2 bay leaves

2 garlic cloves, finely chopped

4 tablespoons Sieved Roast Tomatoes (p.515) or 1 tablespoon tomato purée

½ bottle of white wine

250ml lamb stock (see pp.472-3) or water

Juice and finely grated zest of 1 lemon

Juice and finely grated zest of 1 orange

Salt and freshly ground black pepper

Chopped parsley, to garnish

The slow-cooked lamb shank has been one of the boom dishes of modern food culture, ubiquitous in posh restauraunts, gastro-pubs and the glossy food supplements of weekend broadsheets. Professionals love it for its effect on their profit margins but also, to be fair, because it responds so wonderfully to a long, slow bath in hot aromatic juices that it is a dependable crowd-pleaser. Home cooks should love it for the same reasons: good kitchen economy with stunning results.

The standard approach is something rich, red winey and heavily reduced – and that can certainly be very pleasant. My preference is for something fresher and zestier, and I have devised this recipe accordingly.

Heat some of the olive oil in a large casserole, add the diced vegetables and sweat, without browning, until tender. Add the thyme, bay, garlic, tomatoes, wine and lamb stock or water, along with most of the citrus juice and zest (retain a few pinches of zest and a tablespoon of each juice). Bring to the boil and then reduce the heat to a gentle simmer.

Heat a little more olive oil in a separate pan and brown the lamb shanks on all sides, seasoning with a little salt and pepper as you go. Add them to the casserole and cover with its lid. Transfer to a low oven (about 120°C/Gas Mark ½) and cook for about 2½ hours, until the meat is completely tender and falling off the bone.

Remove the shanks from the pan and keep warm while you finish the sauce. Skim off some of the fat from the surface, then taste the liquid for seasoning and to assess its intensity. Boil to reduce if you think it needs it. Stir in the reserved lemon and orange juice to refresh the citrus flavour. Serve the lamb shanks on warmed plates with a generous amount of sauce spooned over and sprinkled with a little parsley and a pinch of citrus zest. Accompany with mashed potatoes (page 518), wet polenta or (my personal favourite) some creamy beans such as butter beans or cannellini.

Variation

Citrus-braised Mallard (and Other Game): This recipe adapts fantastically to mallard, grouse, pigeon and other robust game birds that are past their roasting prime. Halve or quarter the birds according to size (you could even portion a whole Canada goose into 8 pieces), then follow the recipe exactly as above. A slightly shorter cooking time (1½-2 hours) will generally suffice.

CASSOULET *Serves about 10*

2 preserved (i.e. confit) goose or duck legs (p.451) and 3-4 tablespoons of their fat

500g fresh pork belly, cut into 3cm cubes

500g boned shoulder of mutton or lamb (or pork), cut into large cubes

675g Toulouse sausages (or coarse butcher's sausages, ideally garlicky)

1 large onion, chopped

2 garlic cloves, crushed

4 large tomatoes, skinned, deseeded and chopped

1 tablespoon tomato purée

About 150g white breadcrumbs

Salt and freshly ground black pepper

THE BEANS:

900g dried white haricot beans, soaked in cold water overnight

1 large onion, peeled and stuck with 4 cloves

2 garlic cloves, peeled

1 bouquet garni (bay, thyme, parsley stalks)

Up to 250g pork rind, cut into small squares (optional but desirable)

Cassoulet, perhaps even more than bouillabaisse or coq au vin, is one of the most controversial dishes of French gastronomy. What is beyond dispute is that it is a southern French dish of stewed white beans and various meats, which will certainly include pork in some form and usually duck or goose, and is invariably rich and hearty. The favourite points of contention are as follows:

- *The inclusion of lamb (or more properly mutton), which is considered either essential or sacrilegious, depending on your cassoulet politics*
- *The inclusion of tomatoes, which is equally hotly debated*
- *The use of breadcrumbs to create the all-important crust (regarded by some as 'cheating', as the beans will form their own crust, though less reliably)*

None of this badinage should discourage you in the least from making your own cassoulet, as most of its incarnations, if prepared lovingly with good-quality ingredients, are quite delicious. So what I provide below is merely a suggested procedure. You should feel free to depart from it, bearing in mind the above points of contention, in any direction that interests you. And once you've made a couple of cassoulets, you too can join the heated authenticity debate. But, please, don't take yourself too seriously.

Drain the beans and put them in a large saucepan with enough fresh cold water to cover them by a good 3cm. Add the onion, garlic, bouquet garni and pork rind and bring to the boil. Skim off any scum that rises to the surface, then reduce the heat and simmer until the beans are tender but still retain their shape; this will take about 1½-2½ hours, depending on the age of the beans. Top up with a little boiling water only if they are starting to look dry, but allow the liquid to thicken and become saucy towards the end of cooking. Season well with salt and pepper. Remove and discard the bouquet garni and the onion and cloves.

While the beans are cooking, melt a good 2 tablespoons of the fat from the goose or duck legs in a large, heavy-based frying pan and fry the legs in it until browned all over. Remove from the pan and repeat with the pork belly and the mutton or lamb, making sure they are well browned. Add the sausages to the pan and brown those too. Cut the duck or goose legs into large chunks and cut each sausage into 3 or 4 chunks.

Once you've browned and set aside all the meats, add the onion and garlic to the frying pan and cook gently until softened. Stir in the tomatoes, tomato purée and a little water and simmer gently for about 20 minutes, until you have a rich, pulpy sauce. Set aside.

When the beans are cooked, stir in the tomato sauce and check and adjust the seasoning (bearing in mind that the beans will draw salt from the confit). Put

roughly two-thirds of the beans and their liquid in a deep, wide pot (traditionally earthenware) and then add the meats (but not the sausages), pressing them into the beans. Cover with the rest of the beans and sprinkle over a layer of breadcrumbs, but no more than a third of them. Trickle a little more melted goose or duck fat over the crumbs and place the pot, uncovered, in a low to moderate oven (140-150°C/Gas Mark 1-2) for about 2-2½ hours. Check it occasionally and when you see that a golden crust has formed, break it up with a spoon, sprinkle over more crumbs and bake until the crust has re-formed – repeat this 2 or 3 times. If the mixture is becoming too dry, make a hole in the crust and pour in a little water.

With your final layer of breadcrumbs, press the chunks of sausage into the surface of the beans, so they too get browned and crusty in the last 30 minutes of cooking. If all has gone well, the beans will be melting and creamy, the meats completely tender and the crust deep, crisp and golden.

Serve straight from the pot, on to hot plates, trying to satisfy your guests' cravings for a little of each of the meats and a generous share of the crust. A cassoulet needs no accompaniment, save a robust and artisanal red wine, ideally from Aquitaine, the Languedoc or Cahors.

This dish is unapologetically rich, fatty and sleep inducing. I like to serve a tart and piquant salad after it, in a spirited but probably doomed attempt to awaken guests and their jaded (but sated) palates. The Watercress and Orange Salad on page 523 is worth a try.

BOLLITO MISTO *Serves 10-12*

Bollito misto (mixed boiled meats) is the Italian answer to the pot-au-feu (page 284) and, like that dish, the contents of the pot can vary from the meagre to the extravagant. With a bollito, I prefer to tend towards the extravagant, as it makes a fantastic 'feast day' meal, complete with all its trimmings – most vitally the piquant salsa verde and the jewel-like mostarda di Cremona (spiced preserved fruits), available in any good Italian deli.

The possibilities for inclusion are endless, so I'll just have to wade in and state my own preferences/prejudices. I think a bollito should have no fewer than three and no more than four different meats, so my choice would be a boiling hen, an ox tongue, a piece of beef brisket (or shin), and a cotechino sausage. I might, reluctantly, leave out the cotechino or the tongue, but never both.

Like pot-au-feu, the broth is often eaten first, as a separate course.

Put the vegetables and bay leaves in a pan large enough to hold all the meat and fill with water. Season with salt (unless the tongue is salted) and pepper and bring to the boil. (If you don't have a large enough pan to hold all the meat, divide the

1 ox tongue (ideally fresh, but salted will do, in which case soak it for 24 hours)

1 piece of beef brisket or shin, weighing about 1.5 kg

1 large free-range chicken, preferably a boiling hen

1 cotechino sausage (p.441)

3 onions, peeled but left whole

1 head of celery, cut in half lengthways

6 large carrots, peeled and cut in half

2 bay leaves

Salt and freshly ground black pepper

TO SERVE:

About 250 g tiny pasta, such as risoni (rice-shaped pasta), or broken spaghettini (optional)

Plain boiled potatoes

Puy lentils (p.520)

Salsa Verde (p.514)

Mostarda di Cremona, drained from the syrup, the larger fruits cut into halves or quarters

vegetables between 2 pans, then cook the tongue and beef in one, the chicken and sausage in the other.) The meat should be added in stages, bearing in mind the following cooking guidelines:

Tongue – 3 1/2 - 4 hours
Brisket or shin – 3 1/2 - 4 hours
Boiling hen – about 2 hours
Home-made cotechino – about 2 hours
Regular chicken – about 1 hour 20 minutes
Pre-cooked, vacuum-packed cotechino – 30 minutes

So add the tongue and beef first, then bring back to a very gentle simmer, skimming off any scum that appears on the surface. Keep the water level topped up while the meats cook, so they remain completely covered. Add the chicken and cotechino at the appropriate times and cook until all the meats are completely tender (hopefully at about the same time).

Take the tongue out of the pan first, carefully peel the skin off while it is still hot and trim off any gristle, then return it to the pan.

To serve the broth as a first course, taste and adjust the seasoning as necessary. Then pour a ladleful or two per person into warmed bowls and add some cooked pasta and the vegetables from the pot, finely sliced. Don't use up all the broth at this stage, as it's needed to keep the meats moist and warm, and to serve with them too. Offer your guests salt and pepper to season their broth as they like.

To serve the meats, have a well-warmed large, deep dish standing by, with a centimetre of hot broth ladled into the bottom. Remove the meats from the pan one at a time and slice fairly thinly, laying the slices in the dish. Return any leftover pieces to the pot to keep warm and wet. When all the meats have been sliced and laid in the dish, ladle over some more hot broth and take the dish to the table. Serve up the meats with a spoon or two of broth per person. Your guests should have hot plates, and on the table should be dishes of steaming-hot plain boiled potatoes, hot Puy lentils, salsa verde and mostarda di Cremona.

PAPRIKASH OF HEARTS, LIVERS AND TONGUES *Serves 4*

2 hearts (lamb's or pig's)

4 lamb's tongues (if available)

500g liver (lamb's or pig's)

2 tablespoons lard (or olive oil)

1kg white onions, finely chopped

1 tablespoon sweet paprika

1 tablespoon smoked paprika (if available, otherwise another tablespoon of sweet)

2 teaspoons hot paprika

200ml Sieved Roast Tomatoes (p.515), or 2 tablespoons concentrated tomato purée plus 100ml water

Salt and freshly ground black pepper

TO FINISH, AND ACCOMPANY:

Soured cream

Large, floury potatoes

Butter

This is a classic from the Eastern European repertoire, and could easily be made with plain pork (for example, cubes of boned shoulder). But for me it really comes into its own as a preparation for offal – which I'm assured by a Hungarian friend is also authentic. The last time I took two lambs to slaughter, I made it with their hearts, tongues and a bit of their liver and thought it was outstanding.

You could make this dish with any one of the main ingredients listed opposite but the combination is particularly exciting if, like me, you're a big offal fan. Lamb's tongues are often available from halal butchers, but any good butcher should be able to get them to order. All the offal should be scrupulously fresh.

Don't stint on the onions. They melt down during the long, slow cooking to form a rich, unctuous sauce. Some would say that the inclusion of tomatoes is inauthentic, but I have tried it with and without and I prefer it with.

Cut the hearts in half lengthways, trim out the coarse ventricles, and rinse well in cold water, then pat dry. Scrub and rinse the tongues and pat dry. Trim any coarse sinews off the liver and cut it into 4 equal pieces.

Melt half the lard in a heavy casserole and add the onions. Cook gently, stirring occasionally, until they are nicely softened and translucent. Add all the paprika, stir in well and cook for a couple more minutes.

Heat the rest of the lard in a separate pan and brown all the offal pieces in it for just a few minutes, turning occasionally to colour them all over. Then add them to the onions, along with the sieved tomatoes and a small glass of water. Bring to a very gentle simmer and put on the lid. Cook over the lowest possible heat or in a very low oven (120°C/Gas Mark ½) for at least 2 hours, until all the meats are completely tender. Check occasionally, turning the meat and adding a little water if it looks dry.

When the meats are cooked, replace the pot over a very low heat, if it was in the oven, with the lid removed. Take out the tongues and as soon as they are cool enough to handle, carefully peel off the coarse outer skin. Return the peeled tongues to the pot. Check the consistency of the sauce; it should be thick, unctuous and pulpy. If necessary, cook it for a few more minutes. Adjust the seasoning as necessary. You could finish the dish by stirring in a spoonful of soured cream or you could, as I prefer to do, just take the soured cream to the table to serve with it.

Accompany either with mash (page 518) or, more authentically, large floury potatoes boiled whole in their skins and then peeled. Have soured cream for the paprikash and butter for the potatoes on the table.

Marie

COQ AU VIN *Serves 4*

1 chicken, ideally a farmyard cockerel or similar

Its neck, heart, liver and gizzard, if available

50g butter

1 tablespoon olive oil

250g salt pork, pancetta or bacon (p.429 for home-made), in chunky pieces

250g small (i.e. pickling) onions, blanched and then peeled (or use medium onions, cut into quarters)

Up to 50g plain flour, seasoned with salt and pepper

1/2 wine glass of brandy

500ml red wine

500ml chicken stock (could be made from the giblets – see pp.470-72) or water

A bouquet garni of parsley stalks, bay and thyme

4 celery sticks, cut into 3cm lengths

4 garlic cloves, bruised

4 tomatoes, skinned, deseeded and finely chopped

Beurre manié *(p.273), if necessary*

250g button mushrooms (optional), sweated in a little butter

Salt and freshly ground black pepper

This is a great dish but there is no doubt that it has fallen out of favour. The reason is simple: the central ingredient – a farmyard cockerel of a certain age (nine to twelve months) – is almost impossible to lay your hands on. At least, you won't find it in the supermarket, or your average high-street butcher's.

In fact the 'coq' in question is a by-product of traditional small-scale egg-laying systems rather than meat bird production. Any eggs hatched to provide replacement laying hens will, of course, produce around 50 per cent cockerels. These cockerels, usually of the skinnier, egg-laying breeds, were traditionally hatched in the spring and allowed to scratch a living in the farmyard until late autumn or Christmas. At this point, the finest specimens might be kept on as replacements for the ruling roosters, while the others would be knocked on the head. They might be a bit scrawny and, having had the run of the yard, on the tough side but, with a diet comprising largely natural forage, by God they'd be tasty. Perfect, in fact for coq au vin.

To find such a bird you will have to be resourceful: use the Internet, explore farmers' market connections or ask anyone you know who keeps hens to put a bird by for you. Or consider some 'mainstream' alternatives: a good organic roasting chicken will be slower grown and more appropriately fed than its intensively farmed equivalent and will respond very well to this recipe, though it won't take much more than an hour to be cooked. Or you could substitute a pair of guinea fowl or a brace of pheasants, to make a dish that would no longer be coq au vin but is delicious nonetheless.

The other cunning ruse is to use the legs, wings, neck and giblets of a good free-range turkey, of which you may then roast the breast without overcooking it. The results are invariably superb.

I've made the mushrooms optional – in the sense that I don't think their absence is a reason not to make the dish, though I usually include them. Finally, do include all the giblets, if you have them. They will all end up as tender, edible morsels, to be fought over by the cognoscenti.

Joint the chicken into 4 pieces (pages 140-43) – or divide the 2 turkey legs into wing and thigh – and set aside.

Heat the butter and oil in a heavy pan and fry the bacon pieces until browned. Transfer the bacon to a flameproof casserole. Then lightly brown the onions all over in the same pan and add these to the casserole. Dust the chicken pieces lightly with the seasoned flour, discarding any excess, and brown these next, turning them several times until coloured and crisp. Pour over the brandy and, standing well back, set light to it (by tipping the pan towards the gas flame, if you are cooking on gas, or with a match if you are not). When the flames have subsided, transfer the chicken pieces and all the juices in the pan to the casserole.

Return the pan to the heat and pour in the red wine, scraping the bottom and sides of the pan while the wine bubbles. Pour the boiling wine over the chicken and then repeat the process with the stock or water (the job of deglazing is sure to be done by now, but it is good to add hot, not cold, liquid to the casserole to start the cooking). Now add the herbs, celery, garlic and tomatoes to the casserole and bring to a gentle simmer. Cover and cook over a very low heat, or in a very low oven (120°C/Gas Mark ½), for about 1½ hours (or even 2-2½ for turkey legs, or a real farmyard cockerel), until the meat is completely tender.

Strain the stock into a clean pan, leaving the meat and vegetables in the casserole, and boil the stock fast to reduce it by half, or even two-thirds, into a rich, intense sauce. If you think the sauce seems a little thin, you can whisk in a few 'crumbs' of *beurre manié*. Season to taste with salt and pepper.

Return the chicken pieces to the finished sauce, along with the bacon pieces and vegetables, plus the mushrooms if you favour them, and bring to a very gentle simmer again. Allow to bubble gently for just a few minutes before serving. Serve with plain boiled potatoes or mash (page 518).

See page 481 for the second-day, leftover version of coq au vin.

CHICKEN WITH PRESERVED LEMONS AND OLIVES *Serves 4*

1 free-range chicken, weighing 1.5-2kg, jointed (pp.140-43)

1 tablespoon olive oil

1 large onion, chopped

2 garlic cloves, chopped

2 teaspoons ground cumin

1/2 teaspoon ground ginger

1/2 teaspoon ground cinnamon

1 fresh red chilli, finely chopped (or 1/4 teaspoon cayenne pepper)

A pinch of saffron strands, steeped in 2 tablespoons boiling water

275g ripe tomatoes, skinned, deseeded and chopped

250ml stock or water

100g brown olives such as kalamata, or green olives

3 tablespoons chopped preserved lemon (use the peel only)

The liver from the chicken, if available

3-4 tablespoons chopped coriander

Salt and freshly ground black pepper

If you find yourself hankering after the bitter/salty/spicy tastes of North African cooking, this simple recipe really hits the spot. Preserved (salted) lemons are available in some delis and large supermarkets but are also easy to make yourself: cut them into 'joined quarters' – i.e. slit from end to end without cutting through either end, making a second slit at right angles to the first. Squeeze the ends of the lemon to open the slits you have made and then rub a good tablespoonful of salt into the middle. Pack as many lemons as you can into a large jar. Add an extra tablespoon of salt for each lemon and then pour over enough boiling water to fill the jar. Leave to cool before sealing, and keep for at least two weeks before use.

Heat the oil in a large, heavy-based casserole, add the chicken pieces and cook until browned all over. Transfer to a plate and set aside. Then add the onion and garlic to the casserole and cook gently until softened and lightly browned. Stir in the ground spices and chilli and cook for 1-2 minutes longer.

Return the chicken to the pan, turning to coat it in the onion and spices, and pour the saffron water over it. Add the tomatoes and stock or water and bring to a very gentle simmer. Cover tightly and cook over a very low heat for 30-40 minutes, until the chicken is tender.

Stir in the olives and preserved lemon, and the finely chopped liver if you have it, and cook for another 15 minutes. Skim off some of the surface fat, if it seems excessive. Season to taste with salt and pepper, stir in the coriander and serve – with Special Couscous (page 521) or plain boiled rice.

MOLE *Serves 8*

1.5kg pork chops (with bone), or 2 free-range chickens, or 2-3 pheasants, or a small turkey etc etc.

A little oil

1 onion, cut into quarters

2 carrots, cut into chunks

2 celery sticks, cut into chunks

2 bay leaves

About 1.5 litres stock or water

THE MARINADE:

50ml wine vinegar

50ml olive or sunflower oil

4 garlic cloves, crushed

½ tablespoon black pepper

1 teaspoon salt

1 teaspoon sugar

THE SAUCE:

2-3 dried mulato chillies

2-3 dried ancho chillies

25-50g pasilla chillies

2-3 chipotle chillies, according to heat

100g sesame seeds

50g whole raw almonds

50g whole raw peanuts

50g raisins

1 Soft Flour Tortilla (p.521), or 12 bought (unflavoured) tortilla chips

CONTINUED OPPOSITE ...

In Mexico the ultimate feast-day dish (said to have been invented by the nuns of the Puebla convent in response to a surprise visit from their bishops) is mole de guajolote. *A* guajolote *is a turkey, while* mole *just means 'sauce', but the word has come to refer to the subtle concoction of chillies, nuts and spices used in this famous dish. An authentic Mexican mole is culinary alchemy at its best – tasting like all and yet none of its constituent ingredients. And for those who like really spicy food, it's also just a great sauce, having richness, depth and complexity as well as heat. Stinting and short cuts are certainly not to be encouraged, so gather the ingredients well in advance (see the Directory, page 529, for chillies by post).*

I have never got round to the turkey version but have had great success with chicken and pork. The meat is not roasted but portioned up, marinated overnight in vinegar, garlic and black pepper, then gently stewed in a casserole until tender. The sauce is finished with the cooking liquid from the casserole.

Having heard that Mexicans also like to serve wild game birds with mole, I recently tried a pheasant mole and was delighted with the result – the mild gaminess comes through very nicely. I'm convinced that guinea fowl and partridge would also work extremely well.

Of the four chillies used, the chipotle is the hot one, and therefore the one to adjust according to your heat sensitivity.

If you are using pork, trim the chops of most, but not all, the fat. Poultry should be jointed into 4 pieces (pages 140-43). Toss well with all the ingredients for the marinade, then cover and refrigerate for at least 3-4 hours, or overnight.

Remove the meat from the marinade, reserving any liquid, wipe it dry, then heat a little oil in a large pan and brown the meat all over, in batches. Transfer to a flameproof casserole with the remains of the marinade and the onion, carrots, celery and bay leaves, plus the juices from the pan deglazed with a little of the stock or water (page 262). Cover the meat with the remaining stock or water and bring to a gentle simmer. Cook, partially covered, at a very gentle simmer, until the meat is tender (not much more than 40 minutes for pork chops but an hour or more for chicken or pheasant). Let the meat cool in the stock.

To make the sauce, dry-roast the chillies on a hot griddle or in a heavy frying pan for a few minutes, turning them occasionally. Then split them open, remove the seeds and stalk and, using the tip of a small knife, pare off the thicker veins. Rinse the chillies well, place in a bowl and pour over just enough boiling water to cover. Leave for 30 minutes-1 hour.

Meanwhile, in the same hot pan, dry-roast the sesame seeds until they begin to pop. Set aside, reserving half as a garnish. Dry-roast the almonds and peanuts until they are nicely coloured, adding the raisins briefly at the end so they puff up. Set these aside, too. Toast the tortilla until it is completely crisp, then break into small

1/2 teaspoon coriander seeds

1 star anise

1/2 cinnamon stick

12 black peppercorns

6 cloves

3 garlic cloves, peeled

2 small onions, roughly chopped

2 tablespoons concentrated tomato purée

2-3 tablespoons sunflower oil

50g very dark chocolate (at least 70% cocoa solids), grated

pieces and add to the nuts. Now put the coriander seeds, star anise, cinnamon stick, peppercorns and cloves in the pan for barely a minute, until they start to change colour and become fragrant. Transfer to a pestle and mortar and grind together (or use a coffee grinder).

Put the ground spices in a blender with the soaked chillies, sesame seeds, nuts, raisins, tortilla, garlic, onions and tomato purée, plus a couple of tablespoons of the soaking water from the chillies. Whiz up together to get a smooth paste, adding a little more water if necessary.

Heat the sunflower oil in a wide saucepan or extra-large frying pan (into which the meat will eventually fit). Fry the sauce over a medium heat for about 8-10 minutes, stirring regularly. When it is looking thick, 'toasted', and smells extremely fragrant, start adding ladlefuls of the stock from the meat, straining it through a sieve as you go. As you bring the sauce back to the boil it will thicken. You should be able to add about 1 litre of stock, and still get a thick, creamy sauce. Stir in the grated chocolate. Now add the pork chops or pieces of poultry and simmer very gently for about 10 minutes.

Eat the mole straight away or, better still, leave it to go cold, refrigerate, and reheat gently the next day. Serve garnished with the reserved sesame seeds. Plain rice, cooked pinto or kidney beans and warm Soft Flour Tortillas (page 521) are good accompaniments, plus Guacamole (page 514) and soured cream to soothe fiery palates.

RABBIT STEW *Serves 6*

2 wild rabbits, skinned and jointed (pp.171-2)

250g piece of salt pork, pancetta or bacon (see p.429 for home-made), cut into chunky cubes

1 tablespoon olive oil

1 large onion, thickly sliced

3 large carrots, cut into 4cm lengths

4 celery sticks, cut into 4cm lengths

2 bay leaves

A sprig of thyme, if handy

500ml cider

1 generous teaspoon honey

Salt and freshly ground black pepper

This is the simplest possible rabbit stew, with a thin but very tasty juice. A more luxurious way of finishing it is suggested below.

Heat the olive oil in a large, heavy-based frying pan. Gently fry the bacon until it is lightly browned and the fat runs. Transfer the pieces of meat to a casserole but leave the frying pan on the heat. Now brown the rabbit joints in the same pan, in batches, transferring them to the casserole as they are done. Finally, sweat the onion in the same pan but do not allow it to colour. Transfer to the casserole when soft and translucent. Add the carrots, celery, bay leaves and thyme to the casserole. Push everything around so it is fairly tightly packed, then pour over the cider. Add a little water if necessary to cover the meat. Add the honey and season with salt and pepper. Bring to a simmer and cook at a very low, tremulous simmer, for about 1 1/4 hours, until the rabbit is completely tender (older, tougher animals will take longer). You could cook it in a very low oven (120°C/Gas Mark 1/2), if you like, in which case put a lid on the pot.

Serve with plenty of the juice ladled over, with mashed potatoes (page 518) or small macaroni or risoni (rice-shaped pasta).

Variation

Lapin Moutarde à la Crème: For a posher, richer dish, cook as above until the rabbit is tender but not too flaky. Remove the rabbit pieces and keep, covered, in a low oven while you make the sauce. Strain the stock, first through a colander, then through muslin or a cotton cloth (the vegetables and pork don't go in this version of the dish, so save them for soup, or to fry up for supper).

In a clean pan, boil the strained stock hard until reduced to a scant 200ml. Then whisk in 200ml double cream and 2-3 tablespoons grainy mustard and boil for a couple more minutes, until thick and glossy. Taste for seasoning and adjust with salt, pepper and more mustard as you see fit. Reheat the rabbit pieces in the sauce, turning to coat them nicely. Serve on warmed plates, with any spare sauce generously spooned over, accompanied by creamy mashed potato.

JUGGED HARE *Serves 6-8*

This recipe is a classic and a great personal favourite, which I have carried over, with a few small alterations, from The River Cottage Cookbook. *It will always be an aficionado's dish but I urge the curious to give it a try. If it's any encouragement, my version is getting easier, as I've given up marinating the meat – I feel it pickles it a bit too much.*

When you order your hare, mention that you intend to jug it, and ask the butcher to save the blood for you. The hare should be hung for four or five days – more only if you like a very gamy flavour.

1 large brown hare, skinned, plus its blood (liver optional)

2 tablespoons olive oil

100g salt pork, pancetta or bacon (p.429 for home-made), cut into 2cm pieces

1 large carrot, sliced

3 garlic cloves, crushed

1 onion or 5-6 shallots, sliced

30g butter

1 rounded tablespoon plain flour, seasoned with salt and pepper

1 bottle of good red wine, such as Merlot or Cabernet Sauvignon

100ml brandy

A bouquet garni of thyme, bay and parsley

2 squares of bitter chocolate, grated (optional but very worthwhile)

Salt and freshly ground black pepper

Joint the hare with a heavy knife or meat cleaver, cutting off its legs and dividing the saddle into 5 or 6 pieces (see page 174, or you can ask your butcher to do this).

Heat the oil in a large frying pan, add the bacon and sweat for a few minutes. Add the carrot, garlic and onion or shallots and cook for a few minutes longer. Transfer the bacon and vegetables to a large, heavy, flameproof casserole (in which the hare will also be cooked).

Put the frying pan back over a low heat and add the butter. Turn the pieces of hare in the seasoned flour, then add them to the pan and fry gently, turning occasionally, until they are nicely browned. Transfer the meat to the casserole. Pour over the wine, brandy and just enough water to barely cover the meat, then add the bouquet garni. Season with salt and pepper and bring the mixture to a very gentle simmer. Cover and cook over a gentle heat, or in a slow oven (120°C/Gas Mark 1/2), for 2-3 hours. The hare is cooked when the meat is quite tender and begins to come away from the bone.

The next stage is to make a liaison of the blood and the cooking liquid. This has to be done carefully if the sauce is not to separate, but even if it does it is only the appearance, not the flavour, that will be affected. Remove the pieces of hare from the pot and put them in a warmed dish. Strain the stock through a sieve to remove the vegetables and herbs, then return it to the pan. Boil hard to reduce by about a third, then remove from the heat.

Have the blood ready in a small mixing basin. Spoon a little of the reduced stock into the blood to warm and thin it, then stir well. If using the grated chocolate, add it to the stock in the pan. Then ladle in the warmed blood a little at a time, stirring as you go. If you have the hare's liver, chop it very finely – almost to a purée – and add it to the pan. When the liaison is smooth and well blended, return to the heat and bring back to the boil. Return the pieces of hare to the pot and bring back to a gentle simmer before serving.

Give each person a couple of good pieces of hare on a nice warm plate and plenty of sauce from the pot. I always serve jugged hare with creamy mashed potato (page 518) and not much else. It's too rich and interesting to need any further accompaniment – except a top-notch claret.

12. FAST COOKING

12. FAST COOKING

Frying, Stir-frying and Grilling

If there is a number-one cliché of our age, it must be that these days, everyone's in a hurry. And of course, like most clichés, it's very largely true. Any device, service or publication that promises to shave a few minutes off the day's allotted tasks is a sure-fire winner. The problem is that nobody seems to be very sure precisely what it is we are saving time for. Perhaps so we can watch more telly?

Whatever the end use of time saved, there is undoubtedly a whole raft of daily activities that are now generally acknowledged as being worth trying to compress into a shorter time, if at all possible. Housework is one. Travelling from A to B another. And it seems hard to deny that for most people cooking and eating are also included in this category. The culture of instant calorific gratification goes way beyond the proliferation of fast-food restaurants and takeaways. It permeates the supermarkets and invades our kitchens as a stream of pre-packed meals emblazoned with the buzzwords of convenience: if it isn't 'quick', it's 'instant', and if it isn't 'easy' it's already 'ready'.

Personally, I'm determined to swim against this particular tide. My view is that those who spend more time cooking will enjoy life more, not less. I believe that time spent in the kitchen, working with real, raw ingredients, is for the most part time gained, not lost. If you are the kind of person who is inclined to congratulate yourself for having whittled the hours you pass both cooking and eating to a scant one a day, then I suspect neither this chapter, nor this book, will be telling you what you want to hear (though perhaps it's not too much to hope that you might read them and change your ways).

At the same time, I'm not so unrealistic as to imagine that most of us ever could or should wish to spend several hours every day engaged in the preparation of elaborate meals (though I often do, and I enjoy every minute of it). I applaud the chefs and food writers who have demonstrated that cooking great food from fresh ingredients of quality and integrity doesn't have to be difficult or time consuming. Most notable of these (by far) is Nigel Slater. His distinctive brand of 'high-speed real cooking', always prescribed with infectious enthusiasm, is one of the most important contributions to the literature of modern home cooking. Nobody does it better, and I would urge any Slater virgins, vegetarian or carnivore, to pop their cherry with him at the earliest opportunity.

However, much as I approve of that approach, it is not where I'm coming from. This chapter is not going to tell you how to save time when cooking meat, or how to rustle up marvellous meaty meals in minutes. Rather it is about how to understand the principles of the fast (or fast*er*) meat cooking techniques, so that they become infallible tools of your meat cooking craft. So that whether you have one of my recipes in front of you, or Nigel's or anyone else's, or whether you are improvising a recipe of your own, you approach it with complete confidence. There is no reason why you cannot expect superb results every time.

The fact is that these techniques, once mastered, and my selection of fast-cooking recipes laid out at the end of this chapter, will, as it happens, furnish you with a reasonably robust repertoire of relatively rapid recipes for meat. Hardly any of them takes longer than the proverbial half hour. Of course, that's not exactly coincidental. But neither is it the object of the exercise.

What is Fast Cooking?

Grilling and frying are the processes that are principally under review here. In fact, the two techniques are not so very different from each other in terms of both mechanics and effect, and we'll see that there is even a point (or rather a piece of equipment) at which the distinction between them becomes decidedly blurred. There is also boiling, or poaching as it is known when done with a little finesse and restraint. This is scarcely thought of by most home cooks as a way of cooking meat fast, or indeed at all – and when it's done slowly it is, of course, stewing. But with the right cut of meat and the right liquor in the pan, the results can be divine. And it's easy peasy.

And finally there's the microwave. Oh dear.

I'll come to all of these in due course, but let's start with grilling and frying.

What is a Grill?

The noun 'grill' (and the verb 'to grill') has meant various things over the centuries and I reckon a little demystification is in order to bring us up to date. Originally it superseded the term 'gridiron' to describe a framework of iron bars placed over a fire or hot coals for cooking meat and fish – basically an indoor barbecue. The grill evolved with the technology of generating heat, and with the solid-fuel, then oil-fired, range cookers of the eighteenth and nineteenth centuries came a new kind of grill – a solid plate of cast iron with raised ridges on it, which could be placed on the range to heat up. As gas took over in the twentieth century, it could be placed directly over the hob. (The word 'griddle' is often used nowadays to describe this kind of pan, though strictly speaking that's incorrect – a griddle is technically a completely flat pan with no sides, usually made of heavy cast iron. It is used less for meat and more for cooking flatbreads such as tortillas, pancakes, oatcakes and drop scones – sometimes known as griddle cakes).

Then, in the Fifties, came the 'overhead' grill. This is an adaptation of what, in a professional kitchen, would have been called a salamander: a grill configured so the flame or heating element is facing down instead of up, and intensified by reflection under a metal plate. The food is presented to this fierce wall of heat on a mesh wire rack, inside a metal (often enamelled) drip-tray that can be slid in and out beneath the flame. Domestic cookers, first gas and later electric, were developed that suspended this kind of grill above the hob, roughly at eye level.

They quickly became known as 'eye-level' grills, and by the early Seventies, pretty much every British household had one.

When I was growing up, this method of cooking was what most people would have understood by the word 'grill', and the most common phrases instructing you to grill something went along the lines of, 'Place under a moderate grill . . .' etc. Few cookers or kitchens have an eye-level grill these days but many retain some version of the overhead grill as an optional feature in the roof of the oven.

At the same time, various versions of the ridged grill are regaining popularity, the most familiar probably being one that looks like a cast-iron frying pan but has raised ridges in the base (this is the bit of kit that blurs the distinction between grilling and frying).

There is also the so-called 'chargrill', increasingly popular in restaurants and pubs all over the country. This is rarely fuelled by real charcoal but is usually gas or electric fired, with non-combustible 'faux charcoal' rocks that radiate the heat. It is not a true substitute for a real barbecue (see next chapter) but it is an effective way of grilling meat. And, for those who like to play a culinary game of keeping up with the Joneses, there are domestic versions of it, too.

These trends indicate we are at a point where the meaning of 'grill' seems to be shifting back to its original sense. But the word remains ambiguous, and in this book that's reflected by several occasions where I suggest a dish might benefit from a 'flash under the grill', and many others where I suggest a cut of meat might be suitable for cooking 'on a barbecue or ridged grill pan'. For the record, though, when talking about grilling it is to this revived, ridged, cast-iron grill that I generally mean to refer. And the adaptation to barbecue, or domestic chargrill, is also invariably an implied option.

I happen to believe that these new-old types of grill are superior to the overhead grill as a way of cooking meat, largely because there is contact between the bars or ridges of such grills and the meat. For reasons we'll discuss shortly, that's highly desirable. So if you are a die-hard eye-leveller, who feels alienated by what you may see as my retrogressive/post-modern choice of grill, then I urge you to give my perspective a fair trial. Invest £30 or so in the basic Le Creuset ridged grill pan, or similar, and you really won't look back.

What is Frying?

Whatever we mean by grilling, there is very little ambiguity in what we understand by the word 'frying'. We all know what a frying pan is, and most of us reckon we know how to use it. In particular, we feel, to be frying we must be using a pan that is, at the very least greased with, if not positively swimming in, some kind of fat or oil. When anything up to about a centimetre of oil is used, we generally say we are 'shallow-frying'. Beyond that, when hopefully we have had the good sense to switch to a much deeper pan, we must be 'deep-frying'. And when a fancy chef tells us he is 'pan-frying', then he's back in the shallow end, only with airs and graces.

A Good Frying Pan

There is a good reason why so many food writers like to refer to 'heavy' or 'heavy-based' frying pans in their recipes. Cheap, light, flimsy frying pans are a waste of time and a false economy. They heat up too quickly and unevenly, buckle easily, quickly lose their non-stick coating and soon become useless. They can also, over a high flame, heat up so quickly as to become positively dangerous.

Heavy cast-iron frying pans are a far better bet – in terms of performance and safety. They heat steadily and evenly and retain the heat well. They are less easily jogged or knocked off the hob. They can also be used very effectively for 'dry-frying' – a good way of fast cooking some lean meats that are to be served rare. (And at this point, the distinction between frying and grilling finally collapses altogether – because an oilless, heavy-based cast-iron frying pan is clearly nothing more or less than a ridgeless grill pan. Take the sides off and it becomes a griddle!) If you are looking for a good, solid cast-iron frying pan, then again Le Creuset is hard to beat – though there is now a wide choice of similar types, many of which are just as good. The only problem with such pans – and the reason why, despite their qualities, they are not generally favoured by restaurant chefs – is that they really are heavy. In a domestic setting, this solidity is a good thing, but in the fast and furious world of professional cheffing, something more manoeuvrable is required. Apart from anything else, with a heavy cast-iron pan a chef couldn't carry out that vital move that I like to call the 'cheffy toss', where, with a flick of the wrist, the entire contents of a large pan complete a 180-degree flip through the air – you've seen it on the telly a thousand times. Without the sense of superiority that this little shimmy confers, most chefs would be entirely lost.

The current chef's favourite and, I have to confess, mine, is a range of frying pans by Bourgeat, which come in about ten different sizes, from tiny to huge (see the Directory, page 529, for mail order). I currently have four and you'll see them dotted around this book in various illustrations. They are medium weight, solid enough never to buckle even at super-high heat, but light enough to handle well – I can even manage the cheffy toss in the 36 cm version. They are relatively inexpensive and don't last forever, but while they do they give excellent service. They have the best non-stick surface I have ever come across, which, after two or three years of almost daily use (and I must admit I make no great effort to avoid metal utensils), will suddenly start to fail. At which point I will simply chuck the pan – or perhaps relegate it to beach and barbecue use – and go and buy another one.

The Appeal of Frying and Grilling

With the ridged iron plate/pan confirmed as the grill of choice, personally I feel quite comfortable discussing the merits and methods of frying and grilling meat as if they were variants of the same technique (and I hope that by the end of this chapter you will too!). After all, both involve the rapid transfer of direct heat to the meat. And in both cases the heat is delivered in a flat plane – as opposed to the even, enveloping heat of an oven. This means meat that is fried or grilled is almost by definition cooked (or 'seared') one side at a time.

Together, frying and grilling are by far the most popular ways of cooking meat. I've no idea whether such statistics are available but I think it's safe to assume that meat meals prepared by some manner of frying or grilling outnumber those prepared with the use of the oven or casserole by a factor of at least five.

So why do we like frying and grilling so much? There can be no doubt whatever that a large part of the answer lies in what happens on the surface of the meat in both cases. The direct contact of the frying pan or grill ridges, and even the fierce ceiling of hot air from an overhead grill, will rapidly burn the surface of any meat, caramelising the sugars and creating an irresistible taste sensation – sometimes called, by food technologists, the 'browning flavours'. As we have already discussed in Chapter 10, Roasting (page 206), this taste is pretty much the holy grail of meat cookery.

However, browning flavours on their own do not a satisfactory meat-eating experience make. If they did, it wouldn't matter whether our roast lamb was as succulent as a peach or as dry as cardboard, or whether our grilled steak was pink and juicy or grey and mealy – as long as both were nicely browned and seasoned on the outside. Sadly, no small number of cooks seem to have reached this conclusion anyway. How wrong they are. The real pleasure of fried and grilled portions of meat, as with larger roasted joints, comes in the balance between a salty–sweet brown crust and a tender, yielding, fully flavoured interior. It's like a moist, well-made cake with a particularly delicious icing.

Achieving this ideal combination when frying or grilling is not hard, particularly if you start with meat of real quality. But nor is it an absolute pushover. The problem is that far too much frying and grilling is done on automatic pilot, whereas in fact a little premeditation is required. In this respect, it should be less like manslaughter and more like murder; it should be carried out 'with relish aforethought'.

A General Strategy for Success

These simple observations lead us to a trio of basic facts about frying and grilling, all of which may seem so blindingly obvious as to be too banal to repeat. I'm going to spell them out anyway, and I hope that you won't feel your intelligence is being insulted. They are important mainly because they are all too often taken for granted, but also because, like basic mathematical truths, they have vital consequences when more elaborate formulae are presented further down the line:

1. Flat pieces of meat are easier to fry and grill than round (or odd-shaped) ones.
2. Thin pieces of meat will cook through much quicker than thick ones.
3. A high heat will burn (or 'sear') the outside of the meat far more quickly than a low heat.

It is my conviction that all fryers and grillers would do well to keep these three observations close to the surface of their consciousness. So before you commit meat to heat, what's required is just the briefest assessment, in the light of the above facts, of what's about to happen to the piece in your hand.

For example, a fractionally more subtle observation than those above is that a piece of cold (i.e. refrigerated) meat will cook more slowly than a piece of warm or ambient meat (i.e. at room temperature). In both cases, however, the outside of the meat will sear and colour at a more or less identical rate. This is because within a few seconds, the temperature on the surface of the meat – the part that is actually in contact with the pan or grill – will be the same for both pieces. But a few millimetres under the surface, the temperature may vary by 15°C or more, as it did at the outset. With the short cooking time of, say, a rare steak, this will make a very noticeable difference to the end result. They'll look the same on the outside but you will have two distinctly different versions of 'rare' on the inside. The centre of one will still be fridge cold in the middle, whereas the centre of the other, while still just about raw, will be warm. I should say that neither is necessarily the 'correct' version – it's a matter of taste. (Though I don't know many people, other than my wife, with a taste for very rare steak with a fridge-cold middle.)

For repeated, reliable success, what you need is a good understanding of the character of the raw meat you have in your hands, and also a reasonable idea of the end result you are aiming for. For another theoretical example, consider two different cuts of lamb – loin chops and boneless leg steaks (see pages 96-9) – both eminently suitable for fast cooking, either by frying or grilling. Here's how you might approach them:

You like your lamb just pink, but not bloody, and you think this is an appropriate way to serve both these cuts – the chops perhaps a mite pinker than the steaks. You have a ridged cast-iron grill pan which you love using, because you particularly like the char-striped effect on the meat and the quasi-barbecued flavour that results. You'd be happy to use it for either of the lamb cuts. You know that the loin is one of the most tender muscles on the sheep. By contrast, the leg steaks have been cut across several muscles, all of which, being involved in legwork, are going to be a fair bit tougher than the loin. They're also about half a centimetre thicker.

In a perfect world, you'll zap the chops on a fairly high heat for a couple of minutes per side, then rest them for a few minutes before serving. The thicker, tougher leg steaks will take nearly twice as long to be slightly less pink, and will benefit from a fractionally longer rest. But at this high temperature, by the time they are done in the middle they'll be a bit too frazzled on the outside. So you decide to grill them on a lower temperature, for a fair bit longer – say, fifteen minutes in all.

Congratulations. You have thought through the fast cooking of two similar but different cuts of meat, with a clear vision of the results you wanted to achieve.

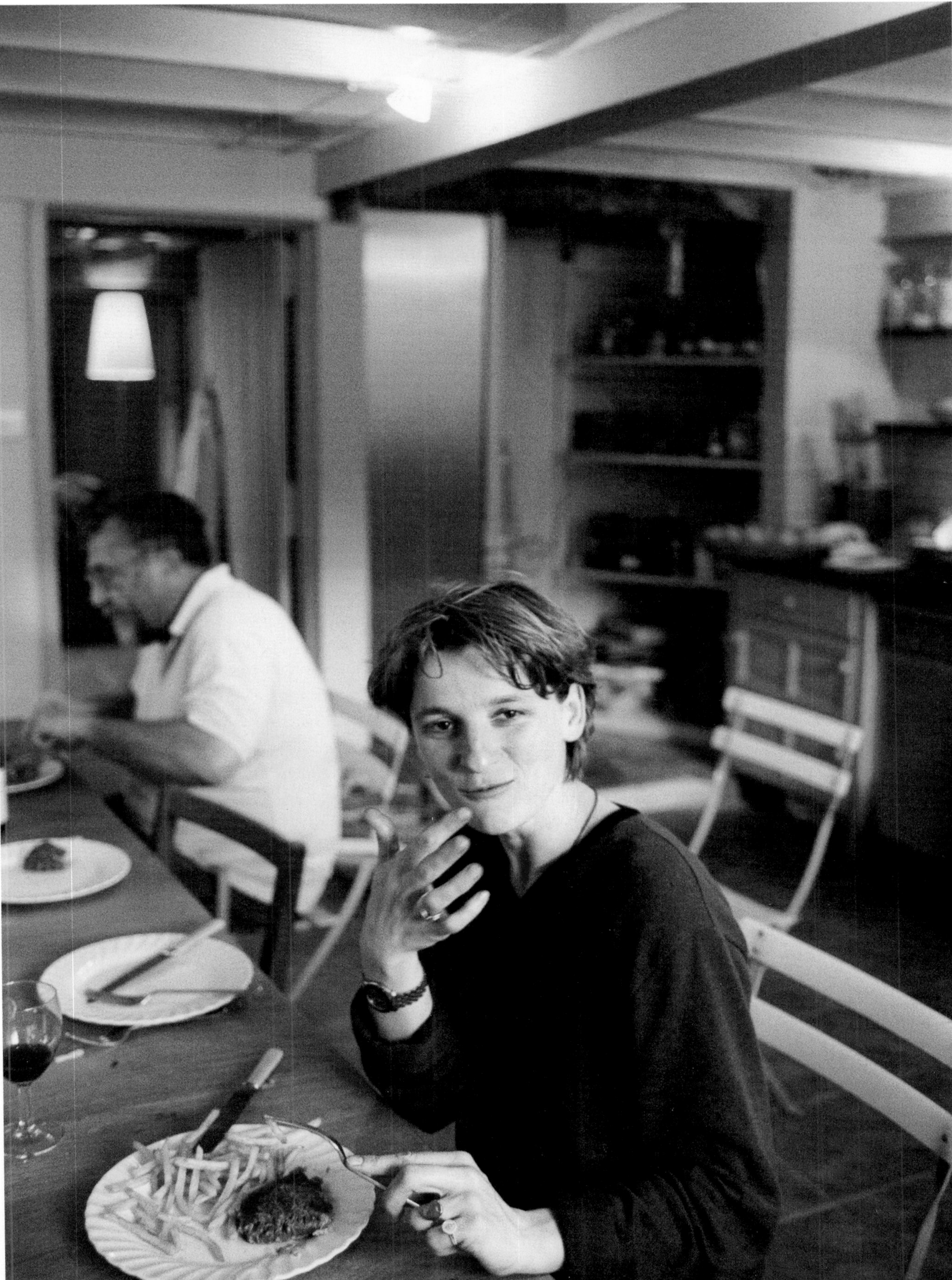

In both cases, the results are a resounding success with your guests. And because the meat in question is from a year-old hogget, hung for eighteen days, they all said it's the best 'lamb' they have ever tasted.

Imagine, though, it's not an either/or scenario. You're cooking for six people and you need both the chops and the leg steaks to feed them all well. You'd prefer them all ready at the same time, as you don't like jumping up and down from the table. And you certainly don't want to mess around with two separate pans.

Solution: you cook both chops and steaks at the slightly lower temperature. Putting the chops on a few minutes after the leg steaks, you cook them both together for the next six to eight minutes. You take them both off at the same time and rest them on a warm plate for about five minutes (while you sort out the veg, dress the salad, whatever).

Written down, I realise this sounds a bit over the top. But of course I don't imagine you'd embrace quite such an elaborate thought process. The confident meat cook would process it all in a nanosecond or two, at a pitch of thought just a fraction above that autopilot I mentioned: *'Chops tender, easy peasy, leg steaks tougher – bit tricky. Can't be arsed to do them separately, soddit, I'll fuss over the steaks, whack on the chops half way through and they'll take care of themselves. NOW WHERE'S THE CORKSCREW?'*

Time and Temperature

From the above comments, you might jump to the conclusion that I believe one of the commonest mistakes when frying and grilling meat is to cook it too quickly at too high a temperature. And you would be absolutely right. Unfortunately, the other common mistake is, inevitably, not letting the pan or grill get hot enough. Some cooks, like some drivers, can't quite bear to let their equipment get to full throttle.

Although temperatures for frying and grilling never actually get measured, and are, of course, on a continuum from gentle to extremely fierce, there are various phrases and conventions for describing the different heat levels. They are not necessarily very consistent from cook to cook, or from writer to writer, but I am ready to have a stab at describing what they look and feel like.

1. Maximum: 'smoking hot'

This is the term used to describe a frying pan or grill that is heated pretty much to maximum. Over a high gas flame or the highest setting on an electric hob it will, with all but the heaviest pan, be reached within a few minutes. After this time, this very high heat can generally be maintained with a slightly lower flame or dial setting, i.e. three-quarter rather than maximum. As the phrase suggests, at this temperature any fat or oil in the pan will be noticeably smoking – and even a dry pan or grill pan that is not scrupulously clean will smoke, too. It's worth noting that butter will be almost instantly burned black at this temperature, and the flavour of olive oil, and some other less stable oils, will also quickly spoil as it smokes. Groundnut oil and purely rendered lard or beef suet are the best fats (or, if you're cooking very rare steaks, no oil at all).

I only rarely specify this level of heat in recipes because, apart from anything else, to tell you to cook in a smoking-hot pan is to ask you to enter a realm of uncertainty. Unless I know that you have the same kind of equipment as me and, to be honest, pretty much the same level of confidence, I would be concerned for your safety.

Anyway, there are only a few cuts of meat that genuinely respond well to a smoking-hot pan or a really fierce grill. Naturally, they are the ones you will want to serve rare, as any extended cooking time will over-blacken the outside of the meat long before the middle is cooked. The cuts I have in mind are:

Steak: rump, fillet or sirloin for cooking very rare; occasionally very rare burgers made from top-quality lean meat.
Venison: fillet or medallions (i.e. boned loin slices) or loin chops.
Pigeon breasts: whole or butterflied (see page 165).
Liver: calf's, venison or lamb's (in all cases, sliced thinly for serving very pink).

And even then, some restraint is in order. In other words, unless you anticipate a total cooking time of two or three minutes at most (by which time both sides of the meat should be very nicely browned, but not yet burned), then you should consider taking your pan or grill down to the next heat level.

2. High: 'hot but not smoking'

This is an abbreviation of the instruction that would be fully written along the following lines: 'Heat a film of oil in a heavy, non-stick frying pan until very hot but not quite smoking.' And that, or something like it, is the phrase I would use to describe most high-heat frying and grilling. It's reached pretty rapidly over a high hob and is generally maintained over a medium one, though if you're loading a large pan or grill with a lot of meat you'll want to keep a higher heat under it.

It is the heat level I am comfortable with for frying most meats that are to be served rare and medium rare, though I would probably crank it up to smoking hot, as discussed above, for someone (like my wife) who likes their meat served very rare, or *bleu*, as they say in France.

Besides a very hot frying pan, 'hot but not smoking' is a pretty good description of a sensibly hot ridged cast-iron grill pan primed for the 'indoor barbecue' effect, and with that in mind, I'd extend the list of meats under 'smoking hot' above to include other meats that you might want to serve seared on the grill, and pretty pink in the middle, such as:

Lamb: chops, plain cut or better still, butterflied leg steaks (see pages 96-7), plus lean chunks of leg meat as kebabs.

Steak/beef: steaks for cooking rare or medium; marinated chunks or strips of top rump or best lean braising steak (as kebabs or for searing for a 'wrap' – see page 348). Plus burgers required rare.
Bacon: even thick rashers of bacon will cook quickly to crispness at this temperature. Keep a sharp eye on them, or cook at my 'merry sizzle' (see below).
Game/poultry: small spatchcocked or half game birds (i.e. snipe, woodcock or pigeon) or marinated breast meat, whole or kebabbed, of pigeon, duck or goose (but not chicken). Fillets of venison or hare.
Liver: all as in 'smoking hot' above, for cooking medium rare and beyond.

3. Medium: 'a merry sizzle'

'A merry sizzle' is a physical description that is easier, I think, to relate to than the deceptively abstract word, 'medium'. You might also like to think of it as the heat that will have turned one side of a burger nicely brown in a couple of minutes but still won't have burned it after five.

It's the safe, 'if in doubt' approach to almost any meat, and absolutely the right approach to the following:

Beef: burgers to be served medium or well done.
Lamb: chops, steaks and burgers to be served medium and beyond.
Pork: chops, escalopes and lean, kebabbed cubes, for at least 10 minutes, until cooked right through (see also Pan-to-Oven Frying on page 335).
Veal: chops and escalopes of rosé veal. Can be cooked *almost* pink.
Bacon: the sensible temperature for cooking bacon, unless you like it frazzled.
Game/poultry: portions and breasts of most birds – but go down a notch for bone-in chicken portions (see below).
Offal: kidneys, thicker chunks of liver, pre-cooked tongue, plus brains and sweetbreads for a Fritto Misto (see page 362).

4. Low: 'a gentle sizzle'

You could also say, 'Fry gently over a low heat.' It's just a notch up from the very gentle heat at which I sweat onions to cook them without colouring. This is not usually thought of as an appropriate temperature for frying meat but in fact the slow fry/grill is a wonderful way to cook chicken and other poultry portions. It's also the secret of perfect bangers. Meat will gradually begin to colour at this temperature, but only after at least five minutes. You can always turn up the heat at the end of cooking if you are looking for extra caramelisation, crisper skin, or both. But don't overdo it.

Sausages: you'll get away with the 'merry sizzle', especially for chipolatas, but when it comes to cooking fat butcher's bangers, the slower the better. Twenty to twenty-five minutes of slow frying should prove a revelation.

Pork/bacon: this is the best way to cook pork leg steaks, gammon steaks or thick bacon chops. Cook until lightly browned.
Poultry: like slow barbecuing (see page 381), this is the way to go for wings, thighs and drumsticks. It's also the correct temperature for chicken Kiev, if you don't have a deep-fry option.

Overcrowded Pan Syndrome (and Other Caveats)

All the above times and temperatures make a few basic assumptions about what you might call 'sound frying practice'. Probably the most important rule to bear in mind is: don't overcrowd the pan. It stands to reason that if you pile a lot of cold – particularly refrigerated – meat into a pan, it will rapidly lose heat and take some time to regain it. This means you will not be cooking at the temperature you think you're cooking at. The meat will neither sear/brown on the outside nor cook through on the inside at the rate you want. Worse still, it may start to leach a little juice, so that you are then simmering your meat in a shallow liquid and it will struggle to brown at all.

The next and related point is: make sure you preheat the pan thoroughly to the correct temperature. Again, you can't expect meat to behave predictably – cooking through and browning on the outside at the speed you anticipate – if you put it in a cool pan and bring it only slowly to the desired temperature.

With the above in mind, it makes a lot of sense to own at least two sizes of frying pan and to bring your meat to room temperature before you start cooking.

The Use of Fat When Frying

Besides temperature and timing, and aside from such niceties as marinades and complex seasonings (of which more shortly), the other main factors to consider when frying and grilling are: the use of fat; the turning and seasoning of the meat during cooking; and the matter of resting it before serving.

When it comes to frying, the use of at least some fat is more or less implicit. Yet when I am frying meat, my use of extra fat is far more scant and subtle than when I'm frying, say, potatoes. I don't want the meat to be greasy, and I certainly don't want any fat to soak into it. I simply want to create a nicely browned exterior and to push sufficient heat through the meat to get the level of 'doneness' I am after.

For most portions of raw meat to be fried or grilled – steaks, chops, burgers etc – the light 'film' of oil I mentioned earlier is appropriate. It's best achieved by pouring a trickle of oil into a frying pan that is warm but not yet at full frying temperature, then moving the pan in a rotating tilt to coat the whole of the base. Any excess oil can be trickled back into a heatproof dish kept close to the stove. You can then replace the pan on the heat and wait for it to reach the correct cooking temperature.

I like to use groundnut oil as an all-rounder or, if I have some handy, lard or dripping rendered from my own home-produced pork and beef. I prefer these

fats/oils because they can all be heated to a high temperature without burning or tainting. If you're using a solid fat, you'll naturally have to wait a moment or two for it to melt before you do the tilt and swirl.

The 'light film' approach works for frying just about any unadulterated raw meat cut, but when the meat has some kind of coating – a dusting of seasoned flour, perhaps, for liver, brains or sweetbreads, or, more substantially, a coating of breadcrumbs for a Wiener Schnitzel (page 354) or a Chicken Kiev (page 356) – then the amount of fat or oil must be increased.

Such coatings are, in a sense, a substitute for the browned exterior of plain grilled meat, so you have to get them right to make them worthwhile. To achieve the desired effect, and ensure that they become properly crisp, crunchy and golden, these coatings must absorb a little of the oil in which they are fried. Being more substantial and absorbent, a crumb coating requires more oil – say 3-5 mm depth – than a dusting of seasoned flour, for which 1-2 mm oil will generally suffice. I would also count the skin of poultry as a kind of natural coating, akin to breadcrumbs, and when frying poultry portions, I would allow a little extra slosh of oil in the pan to ensure the skin crisps up nicely.

If your crumb-coated meat is a round, deep or irregular shape (a Scotch egg or chicken Kiev, for example) rather than a Wiener schnitzel or crumbed pork escalope, or when your meat is coated in thick batter (the Spam fritter and chip-shop sausage for some reason spring to mind!), there's probably a case for considering the deep-frying option. In all cases, getting the fat temperature right is pretty critical. Too low, and the exterior is over-saturated before it's crisp; too high, and it's burnt before the interior is cooked through.

The Use of Fat When Grilling

When grilling rather than frying, no oil at all may be required, particularly if the meat has a little fat of its own that will trickle out as it cooks. However, without any lubrication, there is a risk that meat will stick to the bars or ridges of the grill. Key tactics in reducing this risk are, firstly, to make sure the grill is fully preheated to cooking temperature before placing any meat on it and, secondly, to resist the temptation to move or turn the meat on the grill for a good couple of minutes – provided that's compatible with your plans for doneness in the finished meat. This will give the grill bars time to carbonise the meat fully at the point of contact, which *should* mean it can be released without sticking. However, as a precaution, I reckon it never hurts to put a light film of oil between the meat and the heat – and when grilling I always put that oil on the meat, not the grill. Just massage a few drops of oil over the surface of the meat before placing it on the bars.

There is no doubt that some meats seem to stick on a grill more than others. Lamb and pork are stickier than beef. And one of the stickiest things you'll ever put on a grill is a slice of liver – for which the light oil massage is essential.

Turning Meat

How many times, and at what intervals, should you turn a piece of meat while frying or grilling it? In the pantheon of conventional recipe writing there are three possible one-word answers to this: 'once', 'occasionally' and 'frequently'.

My own policy, and I'm not saying this to be awkward, is 'not quite any of the above'. Assuming for a moment that we are talking about something flat – a chop or a steak – my general policy is to begin by browning it nicely, undisturbed, first on one side and then on the other, to get it to the point where I reckon it is about three-quarters done. I will then, usually in the last two to five minutes of cooking (depending on the meat in question), turn it over several times – maybe four or five – roughly every half to one minute. I think of this process as not only completing the cooking to the right level of doneness but also putting the finishing touch to the browned exterior of the meat. With this in mind, I will also usually season each side lightly with the merest pinch of salt and a twist of pepper just before each turn. The idea is to make that lightly crusted, sparingly seared surface as delicious and savoury as it can possibly be.

Towards the end of cooking, I also like to give my meat an occasional shake in the pan, again with those precious browning flavours in mind. I'm not sure that it makes a *huge* difference but it occurs to me that it might just help to dislodge from the surface of the pan some of those browned and caramelised particles, which might just adhere to the outside of the meat and enhance that crust still further.

All in all, it's an approach that serves me well. And it's easily adapted for pieces of meat that are less flat, rounded, or rough or chunky. These would require 'occasional' turning to begin with, until they are nicely browned all over, then 'more frequent' turning towards the end, during the seasoning phase.

Finally the sausage, which is probably the hardest of all things to pin down in a frying pan. A good butcher's banger will benefit from frequent, but not anxious, turning (a kind of studied, patient casualness is in order here) throughout the twenty-plus minutes of its slow sizzle.

Resting

In the Roasting chapter I urged you, even implored you, to embrace the resting ritual and marvel at what it can do for the finished texture and tenderness of your joint (see page 213 for the science). Well, the same principles are at play whenever a piece of meat is grilled or fried – albeit on a more compact scale and therefore a shorter timeframe.

The prescription, then, is the same, only less so. Pieces of fried or grilled meat should be rested but for a shorter time. I promise you that a rare grilled steak you have rested (on a warm plate for, say, five minutes) will be noticeably more yielding, and therefore more delicious, than one you slice into just seconds after it comes out of the pan. If you're at all sceptical, at least do me the favour of giving it a try – this is not a hard experiment to carry out at home.

Deglazing

There's no doubt that, whatever your technical approach to shaking and turning, some of the precious particles of burnt meat and caramelised sugars will, at the end of the cooking time, be residing not on the surface of the meat but on the bottom of the pan.

It makes a lot of sense to put them to good use and improvise a quick sauce. All that's required is a little splash of wine, water or stock, a good scrape and a stir, and maybe a modest knob of butter to give it some gloss. Don't be overambitious about quantity here. Start sloshing in large quantities of liquid and you'll quickly dilute the precious flavours to insipidity. Let your taste be the guide. It's better to offer your guests a mere teaspoon of something concentrated and delicious than a whole tablespoon of something wishy-washy and innocuous.

Deglazing the pan in this way also enforces a brief delay between removing the meat from the pan and serving it to your guests – an ideal way to give it that five-minute rest.

Incidentally, I always deglaze my frying pan but never my grill. The ridges make the whole process a bit of a nightmare and, rightly or wrongly, I'm suspicious of the effect wine will have on the well-seasoned patina of my grill – which of course, having read the instructions carefully, I never wash, only wipe or brush. (Once in a while I heat it up to maximum without cooking on it, to burn off any remnants.)

And that more or less takes care of the basic principles of frying and grilling, and therefore most fast cooking of meat. There are, however, a few variations on the theme that merit further discussion.

Pan-to-Oven Frying

Sometimes it seems like a good idea to start a piece of meat in a frying pan and then transfer it to the oven to finish cooking. It's something I find myself doing more and more. The rationale for this is that you want to ensure a nicely browned exterior but you are also concerned that a slightly extended cooking time is required to achieve the right level of doneness.

There are various cuts of meat for which this makes a great deal of sense. They tend to be the thicker, rounder and chunkier cuts of lean meat, along with large chops and poultry joints with bones in or skin covering, or both. Specifically, those that spring to mind would include a whole chateaubriand or venison fillet, a small rack or fillet of lamb, large pork chops and veal chops, whole but boneless breasts of duck or goose, and halved or quartered game birds and poultry. These are all items for which successful cooking to completion by pan or grill alone, without either burning the outside or undercooking the middle, will always be something of a challenge.

Incidentally the cheffy phrase for this procedure is 'pan-roasting' (and in order to highlight the distinction further, some chefs use the irritating term 'pan-frying' when talking about normal frying). Professionals like it because it frees up the hob and rounds out the final cooking time to something a touch more approximate and therefore more forgiving. And there is no reason at all why home cooks should not also take advantage of such latitude.

It is a particularly practical approach for anyone with an Aga or Rayburn, or any range cooker with a hot oven that is on permanently. But of course it works for any oven, provided it is properly preheated. The appropriate oven temperature is 'hot' (about 200-220°C/Gas Mark 6-7), and the right time is, of course, variable, depending on the type, size and desirable doneness of the meat. On the whole, less than five minutes would seem pretty pointless and more than twenty a little reckless.

So, once you have browned the meat in question to your satisfaction in a frying pan (usually at the 'merry sizzle' – see page 330), you can either tip the contents of the pan into a small, preheated roasting tin, or some other kind of ovenproof dish, which should then be returned to the oven without delay. Or, if it fits, and does not have a plastic, wooden or otherwise heat-vulnerable handle, you can just shove the frying pan straight into the oven. But if the latter, then please, please, *please* remember that the handle of the pan will stay hot for some considerable time after the pan has come out of the oven. I can't emphasise enough how easy it is to forget that a frying pan has been in the oven and, only seconds later, to grasp its handle with your bare hand. I know, because I do it almost every time!

A slosh of stock, wine or water in the pan just before it goes in the oven will help deliver a good *jus*, or the beginnings of a gravy, at the end of the cooking time. Remove and rest the meat while you improvise and adjust this sauce.

See the picture over the page, and for a full description of the technique, see my recipe for Pan-to-Oven Pork Chops with Garlic on page 342.

Stir-frying

Whole books have been written about stir-frying but I'm going to settle for half a dozen paragraphs. It is undoubtedly a good way of improvising some easy, tasty dishes from almost any good lean meat that is suitable for fast cooking. Here, at last, I guess we are in genuine 'rustle something up in a few minutes' territory. However, we mustn't lose sight of the basic principles. When it comes to cooking meat, the defining characteristic of a stir-fry is not that you are stirring the meat while you fry it. It's that the meat is cut into pieces that are small enough to be stirred, or shaken, around in a very hot pan and cook through in just a few minutes (ideally less than five). My crude observations 1-3 (page 325) come into particularly sharp focus here. The size and shape you cut your meat is critical. Clearly you want to brown the surface, because that's going to give you your good browning flavours, and if it is pork, duck or chicken you're stir-frying, then clearly you want to cook it right through as well. If it's good beef, say strips of rump or topside, you'll want to brown it on the outside but keep it just pink in the middle. *Ergo*, cut your beef for stir-frying a little chunkier than your pork or chicken. Think thumb-thick strips for beef and lamb, little fingers for pork, chicken and other poultry (I far prefer strips to cubes, which always remind me of advertising pack shots).

Marinating these pieces of meat before you stir-fry is generally a good idea. The browning flavours of the rapidly searing meat will be enhanced and intensified by the flavourings of the marinade. But before you rush into anything, please take a look at my section on marinades (below) for a few important caveats.

Once your meat is ready to go, which is to say, shaken fairly dry of any marinade, and your wok or, at a push, your large, heavy frying pan, is dosed with a scant tablespoon of oil that is now pretty much smoking hot, you're ready to start. Throw in the meat. Don't stir and shake constantly, just every thirty seconds or so. Then let the meat sizzle again, in contact with the pan. Beef or lamb should be browned but still a bit pink in three or four minutes, pork or poultry sizzling and cooked right through in no more than five.

The only problem, of course, is that I seem to have forgotten all about the vegetables. Actually, that was kind of deliberate. The trouble is, if you add a large pile of vegetables at the beginning, you'll never get the meat to brown and glaze properly. Pile too much into the pan and you're pretty soon not stir-frying but stewing the meat, in a wet liquor of vegetable juice, the marinade from your meat, and however much soy sauce you've sloshed into the pan. Even if you add the vegetables after the meat is done, they still release liquid, in which the browning flavours will begin to dissolve. Your meat begins to stew again. It will be tasty, but wet and overcooked.

My preferred procedure is to cook the meat alone, very quickly, as described above, then transfer it to a warm plate. Then rest the meat while you stir-fry the vegetables. This confers the same benefits as resting a roast or a steak but because the meat pieces are so much smaller, a couple of minutes does the job. Spend that couple of minutes getting the vegetables stir-fried and flavoured just as you'd like them to be – they'll benefit hugely from the browning flavours left in the pan by the meat and the marinade. Just add an extra trickle of oil and a bit of garlic at the start, then a subtle splash of soy at the end, and you'll have all the taste you could wish for – no need at all for the dreaded MSG. Then return the meat to the pan at the end, serving it over the top almost as a garnish.

I have no idea whether Oriental chefs who use a wok day in, day out would approve of my procedure. But I promise it works an absolute treat.

Marinades

Meat can be marinated prior to almost any of the cooking methods discussed in this book but it seems appropriate to discuss the merits and demerits of the process here, in the chapter about fast-cooking techniques and just before the one about barbecuing. These are the methods to which prior marinating of meat confers, in my view, the clearest benefit.

Many cooks, and too many cookery writers, are, I feel, too gung-ho about marinades. Perhaps this is because they can be used to cover a multitude of sins – both in the production of good meat and the execution of sound cooking technique. I would urge a little caution, and apply the general maxim that is true of so much cooking: it is more important to ask 'Why?' than 'Why not?' A valid answer to the first question (not the lack of an answer to the second) is required before you mix yourself a marinade.

Apart from anything else, marinades can do more harm than good, particularly to meat. Wine and other types of alcohol, lemon juice and vinegar should be used particularly sparingly, and whenever they are present the meat should not be left in the marinade too long. Personally I'm sceptical about their ability to tenderise meat. Or at least, I believe any possible benefits are negatively outweighed by the action of their astringency on the meat. If meat is left in them too long (for example, overnight), these acids will enter it, replacing its natural juices and even displacing some of its fat. Effectively, they will pickle it. This is rarely a good thing, particularly for meat that will subsequently be cooked. Heat rapidly drives the volatile acids out of the meat, leaving it without its original moisture content – and without the alcohol or acid that replaced it. Once again, the meat has become a victim of the moisture paradox, whereby meat that is wet before cooking (in this case moistened by its marinade) ends up drier at the end of it.

There are a couple of exceptions that seem to me reasonable proof of this rule. One is the Japanese teriyaki marinade, traditionally for beef. The essential flavourings are garlic, rice wine vinegar, soy sauce, sugar and sesame oil. In this case, it is entirely correct that the meat should taste ever so slightly pickled, at least on the outside. The proper end result of successful cooking – on a very hot grill or a dry frying pan, using 1cm-thick strips of good rump steak or topside – is

Right: Pork in my very versatile Indonesian marinade (see p.346). Far right: Veal chops marinating with lemon zest, rosemary and garlic (see p.380).

meat that is nicely browned and glazed on the outside, lightly pickled with teriyaki flavours for the next millimetre or two, then natural and just pink in the middle. And you don't need to marinate the meat for more than an hour to achieve that.

The use of lemon juice in some Greek marinades, usually for lamb, is another case in point. Firstly, it is slightly less of a problem than wine because relatively little of it is required to impart its distinctive citrus tang (particularly when it is used alongside strips of aromatic lemon zest). Mainly, though, it's forgivable because the whole object of the exercise is to make the meat taste seriously lemony! Whereas I rarely, if ever, want my grilled or fried meat to taste strongly impregnated with wine or vinegar.

So marinating is, for me, not so much a vain attempt to tenderise tough meat but more about imparting pleasant flavours and aromatics to good meat well chosen for the dish in hand. Most of the marinades I use are therefore pretty dry: combinations of bruised or chopped fresh herbs (rosemary and oregano are favourites for lamb; thyme and bay for pork and game), pungent alliums (most obviously garlic, but also chives, onions and shallots – all are good with all meats) and dry spices (ideally freshly crushed whole seeds – see various recipes for effective combinations). To these aromatics I add just enough oil to coat the meat generously, and just occasionally, particularly if I'm in a hurry, the merest splash of wine or lemon juice, to accelerate the transfer of these flavours to the meat.

I rarely leave meat in such a marinade for more than three or four hours, and often for less than one. The exception is what you might call 'complex marinades' for such traditional dishes as Curry Goat (page 297), Mole (page 314) and Murgh Makhani (page 355), where a deep penetration of a sophisticated spice mix is an essential part of the character of the finished dish. In all these cases the marinade works both before and during a period of long, slow cooking, at the end of which a very distinctive alchemy has transformed the character of the meat entirely.

The only other kind of marinade I use is the sticky, glutinous type that is intended to become a glaze as the coated meat cooks, particularly good on spare ribs or pork chops (see page 397).

For recipes that, I hope, uphold these principles and make sense of them, see pages 345, 346, 348, 366 and 369. Between the five of them, they pretty much describe the full extent and deployment of my modest repertoire of marinades.

Deep-frying

I've alluded to deep-frying a couple of times already. I think it's better suited, on the whole, to fish (and, of course, chips) than meat. But it has its moments in the meat repertoire – perhaps most obviously (as with fish) when a coating of batter or breadcrumbs is involved.

Deep-fried meat classics would, I suppose, include Chicken Kiev (see page 356) the Scotch egg, chicken Maryland and, of course, the aforementioned battered sausage. More esoteric items would be Spanish *croquetas* of ham and chicken and Malaysian deep-fried crispy pig's intestines. Meanwhile, my own original contribution to the canon is, I must admit, a bit of a culinary joke – meat imitating fish, or at least cephalopod (see page 345). Were it not a delicious joke, I would not have dared to include it.

The only occasion I can think of where good-quality raw meat gets the deep-fried treatment is in that curious communal meal known as a meat fondue. It's a DIY affair, fraught with all the hazards and pitfalls of heavy drinking and acting out forfeits for dropped cubes of meat, while pots of boiling oil continue to bubble away at elbow height on the table. I can only guess that the sense of shared danger and hilarious camaraderie among those who enjoy the ritual outweighs any concern about whether this is really a sensible way to cook a piece of good steak. It isn't. Cook it pink, then rest it a minute or two and you won't have done it too much harm. But if it really is good steak, you'll wonder why you didn't just fry a proper slice of it in a pan.

Suffice to say, the secret of cooking any deep-fried meat recipe successfully, whatever its merits, rests entirely on getting the temperature of the oil right, so that the outside, be it of crumbs, batter, seasoned flour or plain raw meat, does not reach the desired state of golden-brown crispness significantly before the inside is cooked. For a cooking time of twelve to fifteen minutes, sufficient to cook through a fairly substantial piece of meat (for example, chicken Kiev), that's about 160°C. For a rapid crisping of smaller morsels in two or three minutes (e.g. my Salt and Pepper Pork 'Squidlets' on page 345), it's 180-185°C.

Poaching

Poaching means cooking something fully immersed in barely simmering liquid – often plain salted water. Outside smart restaurant kitchens, poaching meat is barely heard of – though Jamie Oliver has made a good case for it, demonstrating his excellent signature dish, Barolo poached fillet steak, recently on television. In fact it is a remarkably effective way of cooking some of the best cuts of top-quality meat – fillets of beef, lamb and venison, in particular – and makes a surprising, impressive alternative to frying and grilling. It is a fast cooking technique, not to be confused with stewing, because you are using prime fillet, cooking it for just a few minutes, and serving it with a pink interior.

You wouldn't poach meat in plain water, though. A well-flavoured combination of stock and good wine gives the best results. It will sink into, and flavour, the surface of the meat, compensating for the lack of browning flavours in the absence of fierce contact heat. And, best of all, the poaching liquor can be rapidly reduced to make a fine sauce – ideally while the poached meat enjoys its well-earned rest.

Gentle poaching is also the most effective way of cooking, or pre-cooking, certain soft offals – most notably sweetbreads and brains (see pages 196–7 and 187–8).

Microwave

The first draft of this paragraph originally began, 'I'm really sorry, but I don't own a microwave.' Then I realised that I'm not really sorry at all. In fact, I'm not even a bit sorry. So I'll start again.

I don't own a microwave. And I have not made any attempt to find out if any of the recipes in this book are achievable in any half-decent form using a microwave rather than conventional cooking methods. So to try and pass on any wisdom about their deployment would be deeply disingenuous.

I will make one broad observation, based on my very limited experience of this technology. Some years ago, I lived for almost a year in a flat that did have a microwave. I could never bring myself even to attempt a roast or a stew, or to try any dish that involved placing raw meat inside the Tucker Tardis with a view to cooking it from scratch. But I did find it was very useful for simply reheating leftover soups and stews, either from chilled or frozen, and for this purpose I came to rely on it pretty heavily. It is, of course, much, much quicker than reheating conventionally over a hob. It can also be significantly less damaging to, say, a frozen stew, as impatient reheating over direct heat can easily burn the meat on the bottom even while the stew above remains a frozen lump.

I now freeze and thaw a lot of meat dishes – stews and bolognese sauces in particular. And I will admit to occasional pangs of yearning for some technological assistance in accelerated reheating – particularly when two impatient and ravenous children are looking as if they might very well end up spit-roasting the dog if I don't get their bolognese on the table soon. Such feelings are not frequent enough to precipitate action.

PAN-TO-OVEN PORK CHOPS WITH GARLIC *Serves 4*

4 pork chops (loin or chump, depending on your appetite)

1 very large, or 2 normal, whole heads of garlic

A little olive oil

200 ml white wine or strong cider

Salt and freshly ground black pepper

This is my version of one of those ubiquitous 'something with a ridiculous amount of garlic' recipes. I like it because the rind on the chops gets crisp enough to eat and the garlic cloves tender and sweet enough to eat whole.

Release all the cloves from the garlic bulb(s) but do not peel them, as the skin will protect the flesh from burning. Instead, crush them lightly with the blade of a knife.

Place an ovenproof dish, big enough to hold the chops, in the oven as you heat it to 220°C/Gas Mark 7. Heat a little olive oil in a large frying pan and add all the garlic cloves. Fry for a few minutes, then add the chops. Brown the chops on one side for just a minute, then on the other, seasoning them with salt and pepper as they brown. Remove from the pan with tongs and arrange in the preheated dish, with the fatty, bony end bits poking up into the air. The idea is that these bits will get crisp as the meaty ends braise in the pan juices. Remove the garlic cloves from the pan with a slotted spoon and scatter them over the chops.

Now return the pan to the heat and deglaze with the wine or cider, allowing it to bubble and reduce by half. Tip the contents of the pan over the chops, season well and return the dish to the oven.

Roast the chops for 15-20 minutes, basting them with the pan juices half way through cooking, if you like. When they are done, the meat of the chops should be cooked through and the thinner, fattier ends lovely and crisp. The garlic cloves, though perhaps a little blackened on the outside, should be sweet and tender in the middle, and the pan juices make an excellent gravy.

Serve each chop with a few whole garlic cloves, a couple of spoonfuls of the pan juices, some mashed potatoes (page 518) and steamed leafy greens.

Variations

The pan-to-oven method is a particularly neat and successful way of cooking all chops – lamb and veal, as well as pork. Whatever herbs or flavourings you use (and you can marinate the chops first if you like), add a little wine or stock as they go into the oven and the resulting juices can always be rustled up into a simple sauce. A couple of specific suggestions:

Veal with Lemon and Capers: Marinate veal chops with pared lemon zest, a squeeze of lemon juice, thyme and a little olive oil for a couple of hours. Then add a wine glass of water and the juice of ½ lemon as the chops go into the oven. Use the juices to make a simple sauce, adding a few capers and finishing with a little cream.

Lamb with Garlic and Anchovies: Using lamb chops, proceed exactly as for the pork chops above, but add 3 or 4 anchovies with the garlic and pan juices when the chops go in the oven.

SALT AND PEPPER PORK 'SQUIDLETS' *Serves 4*

500g pork tenderloin, or eye of loin

2 large garlic cloves, very finely chopped

1 dessertspoon olive oil

1 tablespoon flaky salt (e.g. Maldon)

1 tablespoon coarsely ground black pepper (if your mill grinds too fine, use a pestle and mortar)

2 tablespoons cornflour

At least 500ml sunflower or groundnut oil (for semi-deep-frying)

Lemon wedges, to serve

This recipe sounds barmy, and I suppose it is a bit eccentric. You may have encountered a delicious dish in Chinese restaurants called salt and pepper squid. I learned how to cook it quite recently. When I cut up my pig a few weeks ago, I suddenly had a hunch that a similar treatment would work very well for thin strips of the tenderloin. And, dare I say it, I was right.

Slice the pork tenderloin on the bias (i.e. at a 45-degree angle), about 5mm thick, to give you small, long-oval-shaped escalopes. Make 'tentacles' by making 4 or 5 cuts three-quarters of the way down each escalope (see picture). Toss these pork 'squidlets' with the garlic and olive oil and leave them to absorb it for at least 5 minutes. Meanwhile, roughly crush the flaky salt and mix with the black pepper and cornflour.

Toss the garlicky pork squidlets with the salt and pepper mixture, pressing them lightly into it so it sticks. Pour the oil into a frying pan or wide saucepan so that it is 2-3cm deep and heat until a test squidlet sizzles nicely, browning in less than a minute. Fry the squidlets in batches, for just a minute, until golden and crisp. Drain on kitchen paper, but serve as quickly as possible, piping hot, with a squeeze of lemon and/or Lemon Mayonnaise or Tartare Sauce (page 513). Eat with your fingers, which will quickly become almost as tasty as the pork squidlets.

STIR-FRIED INDONESIAN PORK (OR BEEF, OR LAMB, OR CHICKEN, OR RABBIT) *Serves 4*

The key thing here is the marinade, which is a great all-rounder. I turn to it again and again when I feel like something spicy for supper. You can use almost any meat you like provided it's lean and tender enough to be suitable for stir-frying. Pork (lean shoulder), beef (top rump or feather steak) and rabbit (boned-out saddles and thighs) would be my favourites.

I have tried adding loads of vegetables to the stir-fry but it always seems simpler, and nicer, to have just carrots and spring onions.

500g lean pork, or other meat, trimmed and cut into half-a-thumb-sized strips

2 tablespoons sunflower oil

125g carrots, peeled and cut into thin batons

6 spring onions, cut into 1cm lengths

Soy sauce

Sugar

THE MARINADE:

1 egg-sized piece of fresh ginger root, finely grated

1-3 fresh red or green chillies (to taste, and according to heat), finely chopped (or 1/2 teaspoon dried chilli flakes)

2 garlic cloves, crushed

1/4 small onion, grated

2 teaspoons coriander seeds, crushed

2 tablespoons dark soy sauce

1 tablespoon brown sugar

Juice of 1/2 lime

Mix all the ingredients for the marinade together in a large bowl, add the meat and leave in the fridge for at least 2 hours, ideally 4 or 5, but not much more or the meat will become too pickled. Remove the meat from the marinade and pat dry – drying it means it will sear and caramelise in a more satisfactory way when stir-fried. Reserve the marinade.

Heat the sunflower oil in a wok until very hot. Throw in the meat and allow it to sizzle, turning frequently with chopsticks (or tossing the contents of the wok vigorously if you are deft at that) for a couple of minutes, until nicely browned. Add the carrots and spring onions, and the juices from the marinade, and continue to stir-fry for a couple of minutes. Add a few shakes of soy sauce and a couple of pinches of sugar to help glaze the juices into a sauce. Serve at once, with plain boiled rice or instant noodles.

Variation

If you've got a barbecue on the go, or you like using the kind of ridged grill I describe on page 323, then you can mount the cubed marinated meat on bamboo skewers (soaked in cold water for 30 minutes first) and grill it for a satay version of this dish – as shown in the picture opposite. This variation goes beautifully with Spicy Peanut Sauce (page 515).

SEARED SPICY BEEF IN A WRAP *Serves 6*

1 kg rump steak, top rump or feather steak, sliced into not-too-thick steaks (about 1.5 cm)

A little sunflower oil for frying

THE MARINADE:

Juice of 1 lime

A splash of tequila (or white rum)

1 tablespoon honey or soft brown sugar

2 garlic cloves, finely chopped

1-2 small red chillies, including seeds, finely chopped

TO ACCOMPANY:

Soft Flour Tortillas (p.521)

Shredded lettuce, if you like (Cos is better than iceberg)

Guacamole (p.514)

Red Salsa (p.514)

Soured cream

Refried Beans (p.521) – optional, but makes a burrito out of it

This is perfect party food, requiring no cutlery, only hands. It's also great for kids, who can help make the guacamole and the dough for the tortillas.

Trim the steaks to exclude fat and then cut them up so that no piece is bigger than a small hand. Mix together all the ingredients for the marinade, add the meat and toss together to coat the pieces well. Leave to marinate, turning occasionally, for at least 2 hours but not more than 4.

Remove the meat from the marinade and press the pieces with kitchen paper so they're not too wet. Heat a heavy frying pan or griddle, then oil it very lightly. Throw the meat strips on to the hot pan, a few at a time. Turn after 1 minute and remove after no more than 2 or 3. They should be lightly blackened on the outside but juicy and just a bit pink in the middle (or you can take orders for 'medium', 'rare' etc from your guests).

Cut each steak into finger-wide strips. Place 4 or 5 strips of beef in an open, warm tortilla with a scrunch of shredded lettuce, a generous spoonful of guacamole and more modest ones of red salsa and soured cream. For fully fledged burritos you'll want the refried beans as well. Roll up and eat at once.

CARPACCIO OF BEEF WITH SHAVED BEETROOT *Serves 6*

About 1 kg well-aged sirloin or rump of beef, in a piece

2-3 small beetroot

TO DRESS:

A lemon wedge

Extra virgin olive oil

Flaky salt and freshly ground black pepper

This, the famous Italian variation on the steak tartare theme, is a great celebration of the best-quality raw beef. Sirloin is the best cut to use. A well-trimmed piece of rump also works.

In my opinion most restaurants slice their carpaccio too fine – on the finest possible setting of their electric slicing machine. It looks impressive, almost transparent, but dissolves too quickly in the mouth, and becomes nothing. It also allows them to get away with using lesser cuts of meat, such as topside. Since you will probably be slicing yours by hand, the thinnest slice you can achieve without making a mess of it will be about right. A couple of millimetres is ideal. But if you're a bit clumsy, don't worry. Provided the beef is good, you'll get away with it.

There are a number of ways of presenting carpaccio, according to the season. A squeeze of lemon and a trickle of olive oil are all it really needs, but salads of rocket, shavings of Parmesan, and truffle oil are all popular among chefs. I made up this beetroot version, although I doubt that I'm the first, because I love the taste of this root, and I thought the crispness would go well with the beef. And it does. In the winter months, shavings of celeriac, tossed in a mustardy vinaigrette, also make a great garnish.

You don't need as much as a kilo of beef to feed six, but a large piece is so much easier to slice. What's left will make a good-sized sirloin steak.

If your meat has been vac-packed or clingwrapped, wipe it well with a dry cloth and hang it in a cool, airy place for a day or two before you slice it. Only start slicing an hour, or less, before you plan to serve the carpaccio.

Trim any fat or sinew from the surface of the beef to give a clean cross-section of lean meat. Chill the meat for an hour or two in the freezer, so it is firm (but do not let it actually freeze). Using a long, very sharp knife – a so-called ham knife is ideal, and a fish filleting knife can also be effective – cut very thin slices across the grain of the meat. When you finish carving each slice, lay it on a starter-sized white plate. Cover each plate completely with a single layer of sliced beef, overlapping only slightly.

Wash and trim the beetroot (only larger roots need to be peeled) and slice it as finely as you can – at right angles to reveal the subtle, concentric rings of the root. To get fine shavings like those in the picture on page 351, you can use a mandoline or potato peeler. Or you can slice into fine matchsticks and make a cluster.

Arrange a rough pile of beetroot shavings in the centre of each plate. Dress at the last possible moment, with a few drops of squeezed lemon juice, a twist of black pepper, a light sprinkling of flaky salt and a trickle of olive oil. Or, if you prefer, trickle sparingly with Mustard Vinaigrette (page 513).

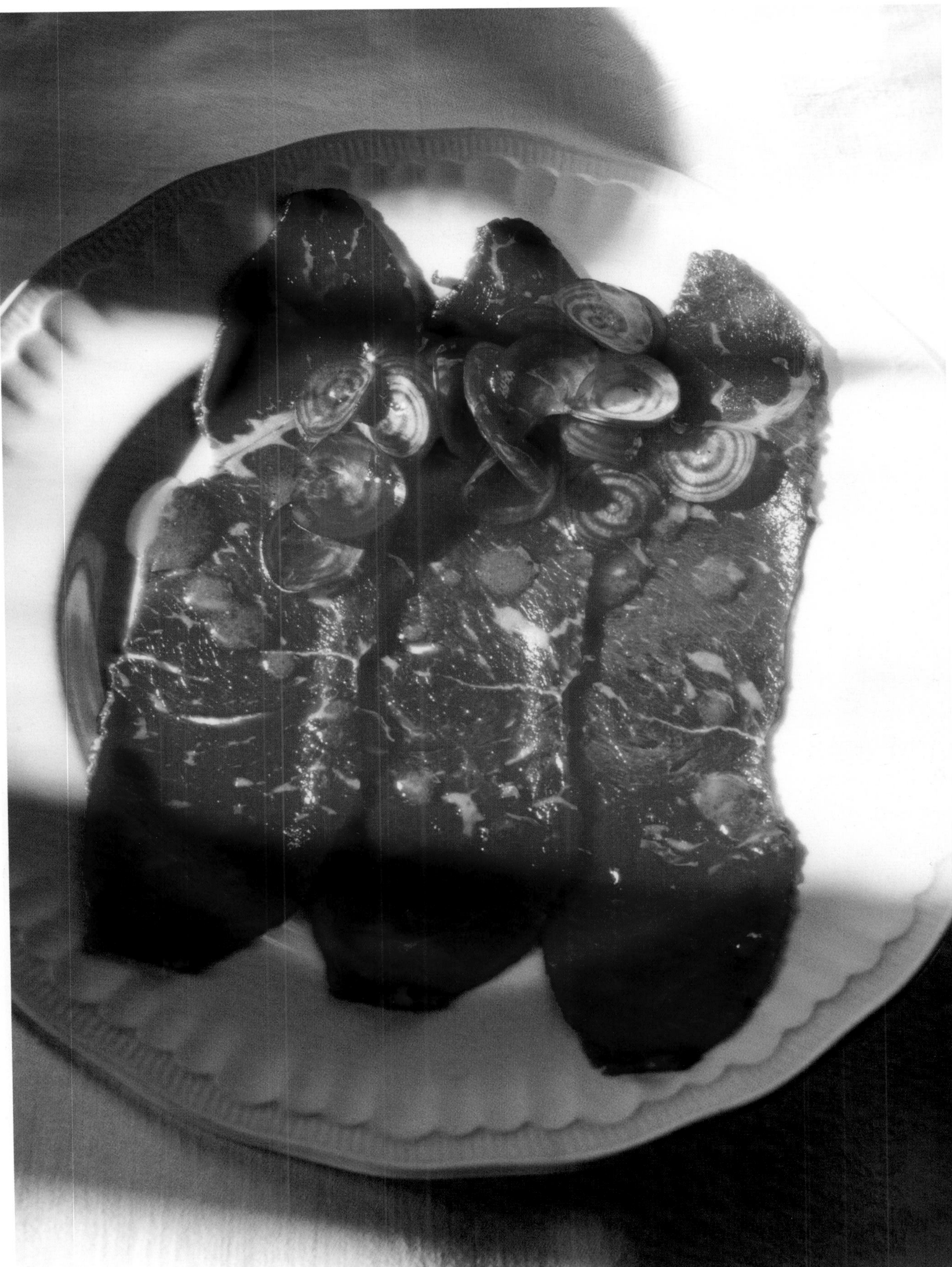

STEAK AND CHIPS

Well-aged rump or sirloin steaks (p.79), cut 3-4 cm thick, and weighing about 300-400 g each

A little clarified butter, lard or beef dripping

Salt and freshly ground black pepper

TO ACCOMPANY:

Chips (p.519)

English or Dijon mustard, or Béarnaise Sauce (p.513)

Of course, you can barbecue or chargrill your steaks but I think the chargrilled flavour is a distraction from the sheer joy of eating the very best steak. So, if I'm really confident of my meat (and, frankly, if I'm not I won't buy it), I prefer to fry them, in a little clarified butter, lard or beef dripping – but not vegetable oil.

There's no need to trim a steak: if the diner doesn't want to eat the fat he or she can leave it on the plate. Have the steaks ready at room temperature, not straight from the fridge.

Choose a medium-sized, heavy-based frying pan that isn't going to stick, and don't try to cook more than 2 steaks at a time. Take orders from your guests as to how they'd like their steaks done. Start with the longer cooking times – the very rare steaks will cook in a couple of minutes. Heat the pan, then rub a small knob of fat over to grease the surface. The pan should be hot but not absolutely smoking – hot enough to sizzle merrily when the meat hits it, and to turn a test morsel of steak nicely brown in about 30 seconds. Turn the hob down, if necessary, to maintain a steady heat.

Lay the steaks in the hot, greased pan and do not move them for at least 30 seconds. Then give the pan a little shake. After about a minute, turn each steak – regardless of how long you are planning to cook it. This will tell you how quickly it's cooking. It should already be well browned and look appetising. Season the cooked side with a little salt and pepper. After another minute, a very rare (*bleu*, as the French say) steak is ready. Just flip it once more, then season the other side and flip it again. This gives the steak a nicely seasoned surface. A steak served *bleu* is literally raw in the middle.

Longer cooking times for less rare steaks can be gauged roughly as follows (for a steak about 3 cm thick, begun at room temperature). I give an approximate overall cooking time, rather than minutes per side, because I don't think you should leave a steak for the whole of one side's cooking time without turning it. It's better to flip it every minute or so, seasoning each side very lightly just before you flip it.

Rare: 3-4 minutes
Medium-rare: 5-6 minutes
Medium: 6-8 minutes
Well done: about 10 minutes

Transfer each finished steak to a warmed plate at once and let it rest for about 3 minutes before serving. This is the equivalent of resting a joint. It doesn't take long, but it does make a difference. Serve with chips and mustard or Béarnaise Sauce (page 513), and a salad to follow. After cooking steaks, it's worth deglazing the pan with a splash of red wine. This juice can be trickled on the meat, chips, or even salad!

WIENER SCHNITZEL *Serves 2*

2 veal escalopes, weighing about 125g each

Up to 50g plain flour, seasoned with salt and pepper

100g fine white breadcrumbs

1 egg, lightly beaten with 1 teaspoon olive oil

Lard (or olive oil and butter) for frying

Salt and freshly ground black pepper

TO GARNISH:

4 thin slices of lemon (cross-sections, with all skin and pith removed)

2 anchovy-stuffed green olives, in 4 slices each

Rather like Chicken Kiev (page 356), this is something of a retro classic – yet very hard to find in a restaurant these days. Made well (and it is not difficult to make it well if you start with the appropriate set of ingredients), it is undoubtedly a treat. Because good veal is expensive, and because pan space is limited, this is a good dish to make for two.

The best (and most expensive) veal escalopes (page 86) are taken from the fillet, the next best from the eye of the loin chop. Schnitzel is usually made from cheaper escalopes, cut from the leg. But these should be cut from a single muscle, carefully trimmed and separated, then cut at 45 degrees to the grain of the meat – this helps them to spread out when beaten. These days few butchers have the time or knowledge to prepare escalopes in this way, and escalopes are often beaten out from inferior cuts of meat. They will contract and contort horribly when you try to fry them and will be tough and irritating to eat.

A good, though mildly extravagant, solution for frustrated escalope fans is to ask for veal chops and trim out the eye yourself. Freeze the bones and add to your next chicken, beef or pork stock (pages 470-74).

It has to be said that an escalope from a loin of good organic pork makes an excellent cheat's schnitzel. And talking of pork, lard is the authentic frying medium, but a combination of olive oil and butter can also be used.

Snip the edges of the escalopes with kitchen scissors to prevent them curling, then place each escalope between 2 sheets of clingfilm and bat out with a meat mallet or a rolling pin to about 5mm thick.

Spread the seasoned flour out on a large plate and the breadcrumbs on another, then put the beaten egg in a large, shallow dish. Season the escalopes with salt and pepper. Dip them in the flour, shaking off any excess, then in the egg. Finally press them lightly into the breadcrumbs so they are evenly – but not too thickly – coated on both sides.

In a frying pan large enough to cook both escalopes at once, heat enough lard (or oil and butter) to give ½-1cm depth. When it is hot enough to colour a piece of white bread pale gold in about a minute, lower the hob to maintain the heat and lay the escalopes in the pan. Cook for 2-3 minutes, until golden brown underneath, then turn and cook the other side. Remove from the pan, drain on kitchen paper, then place on warm serving plates. Decorate with 2 slices of lemon each and the sliced anchovy-stuffed olives. Serve with a seasonal leafy green salad.

MURGH MAKHANI (BUTTER CHICKEN OR PHEASANT)

Serves 6

1 organic chicken, weighing about 1.5 kg, jointed into 'small' portions (pp. 140-43)

Or 2 small pheasants, jointed

Or 1.5 kg pre-portioned organic chicken, such as thighs or legs

Or 750 g boneless organic chicken breasts

1 quantity of Tikka Marinade (p. 515)

THE TOMATO SAUCE:

2 x 400 g tins of tomatoes, chopped, and their juice

A small nugget of fresh ginger root, grated

2 garlic cloves, crushed

1-3 small green chillies, depending on heat, finely chopped

5 cloves

1 teaspoon salt

175 ml water

TO COMPLETE THE MAKHANI SAUCE:

125 g butter

2 teaspoons ground cumin

2 teaspoons tomato purée

4 teaspoons honey

150 ml double cream

1 tablespoon fenugreek

1 tablespoon lime juice

1 teaspoon black pepper

I don't cook a lot of authentic Indian food. Most of the 'curries' I make are improvised affairs. But when I filmed an episode of 'TV Dinners' with sisters-in-law and brilliant cooks, Nina and Sumita Dhand, they showed me how to make a real murgh makhani (pronounced 'merg muckney', it means, literally, butter chicken). It's similar to what many Indian restaurants would call chicken tikka masala, but this version, enriched with butter, honey and cream, is the best I've ever had – completely sublime.

Don't be daunted by the long list of ingredients. They're all fairly familiar spices. If you make up the marinade and the tomato sauce the day before, then finishing the dish is surprisingly quick and easy. You can make it with either on-the-bone portions or boneless chicken meat. And I have made it very successfully with pheasant too.

Add the chicken or pheasant pieces to the tikka marinade, mix well and leave in the fridge to marinate overnight.

Put all the ingredients for the tomato sauce in a large pan and bring to the boil. Reduce the heat and simmer gently for 20 minutes, stirring regularly, until nicely thickened. Rub the sauce through a sieve and then put on one side.

Transfer the chicken or pheasant to a roasting tin, with its marinade, cover with buttered foil and place in a hot oven (230°C/Gas Mark 8). Bake for 10 minutes, then lower the heat to 200°C/Gas Mark 6 and cook for 20-25 minutes (knock 5 minutes off each phase for boneless chicken).

To complete the sauce, melt the butter in a large pan, add the ground cumin and sizzle gently for a couple of minutes. Add the tomato sauce, bring back to a gentle simmer and cook for about 5 minutes. Add the tomato purée, honey, cream, fenugreek, lime juice and black pepper and continue to simmer gently, stirring occasionally, for about 5 minutes, until the sauce is thick, rich and creamy. Finally, add the cooked chicken or pheasant tikka. Mix well and heat right through, simmering gently for a final 5 minutes to marry all the flavours. Serve with plain boiled rice and naan bread.

CHICKEN KIEV *Serves 2*

1 small but plump free-range, preferably organic, chicken (a little under 2 kg is perfect)

50 g softened butter

2 garlic cloves, crushed to a paste with a little salt

1 tablespoon finely chopped parsley

1 teaspoon lemon juice

2 tablespoons plain flour, seasoned with salt and pepper

About 150 g dried white breadcrumbs

1 egg, beaten

Groundnut or sunflower oil for deep-frying

Salt and freshly ground black pepper

Devised in the early Sixties for the opening of the Moscow Hotel in Kiev, this must rank as one of the most famous 'modern' dishes. And its fame is entirely justified. It's not just a delicious dish to eat (the combination of garlic butter and crispy breadcrumbs is hardly likely to disappoint) but also an entertaining one: the gush of garlic butter oozing like a geyser from the centre of the chicken breast and releasing its vapours creates a wonderful moment of anticipation.

This is not a dish that is often made at home. But for anyone who likes it, and who doesn't resent a little time spent on something special in the kitchen, it's almost as much fun to cook as to eat. Make it for someone you love and admire, and they will love and admire you back. It's a comfortable dish to make for two.

You could buy boneless chicken breasts for this dish but personally I can't bear to buy anything less than a whole chicken – and I can always make a fine stock with the breastless chicken (pages 470-72). Besides, I think an authentic chicken Kiev should have the first joint of the wing attached to the breast.

If you want your butcher to joint the bird for you, ask him to give you a whole breast with the first joint of the wing attached. Otherwise joint the bird yourself at home (pages 140-43). Remove the skin from the breasts. Notice that on the inside of each breast, from close to the breastbone, is a sliver of meat loosely attached by a thin membrane. This is sometimes called the *faux filet*. Remove it carefully and set aside.

Beat together the butter, garlic, parsley and lemon juice with a pinch of salt and plenty of pepper. Divide into 2 blobs, shape each roughly into a rugby-ball shape and flatten to about 5 mm thick. Wrap in foil or clingfilm and chill to set firm.

With a very sharp knife, carefully slit each chicken breast down one side along almost the whole of its length, parallel to the grain of the meat, to a depth of about 4 cm (or as deep as you confidently can without the knife coming out the other side). The aim is to create a tidy pocket in the middle of the meat, as capacious as possible, without making any holes through which the butter could seep as the chicken cooks. Give the thick part of the breast a few firm bashes with a rolling pin to flatten and spread it a little. This will help to reduce the cooking time.

Insert the hard butter shapes into the pockets in the breasts. Don't force them, but rather trim them to fit if you have to. Use the strip of meat you saved, trimmed a little if necessary, to plug the opening to the pocket and seal in the butter.

Spread the seasoned flour out on one large plate, the breadcrumbs on another, and pour the beaten egg into a shallow dish. Coat the chicken pieces lightly with the flour, then roll them in the egg, then in the breadcrumbs. Place on a plate and chill for 30 minutes, then coat in egg and breadcrumbs again and chill again for at least 30 minutes. The double coating is extra insurance against escaping garlic butter, but also makes it doubly crispy.

The breasts need to be fried fairly gently if they are to cook through before the breadcrumbs burn. Heat the oil to 160°C in a large saucepan or a deep-fat fryer. Fry the chicken breasts, turning occasionally and very carefully, for 12 minutes at least – 15 if you can get away with it – until golden brown. Drain on kitchen paper and serve immediately.

The idea, of course, is that the hot garlic butter spurts out when you cut open the chicken. Cover any expensive silk ties or designer clothes with a napkin.

The crumb crust is quite substantial, so no starch accompaniment is strictly necessary, but a small pool of mashed potatoes (page 518) would be nice to mop up the garlic butter. You could also offer a simple green vegetable (peas, French beans or mangetout) if you like, or simply serve a seasonal leafy green salad afterwards.

Variation

If you become an enthusiast for, and an expert at preparing, chicken Kiev, you can ring the changes with the flavours you put in the butter. A version made with anchovy butter is a delight.

VENISON STEAK AU POIVRE *Serves 2*

4 noisettes of venison, taken from the back of the saddle, i.e. the loin (pp.176-7)

1 teaspoon each black, green and white peppercorns (use black only, if pushed)

A knob of butter

A little fat or oil

1 small glass of brandy

1 teaspoon redcurrant jelly

1 scant tablespoon double cream

Salt

This is more or less the classic procedure for steak au poivre but using venison rather than beef, as I think the robust flavour of venison supports the rich and piquant sauce rather better. It's a delightful dish that takes less than fifteen minutes from start to finish.

Coarsely grind the peppercorns in a mill or with a pestle and mortar and spread them out on a plate. Press the noisettes on to the pepper, one side at a time, so that they are evenly coated: you don't want a thick crust, as this would be overpowering. Aim more for a generous scattering.

Melt the butter in a large, heavy-based frying pan with a little fat or oil to prevent it burning. Fry the noisettes over a medium heat for a little over 1 minute on each side (for medium rare), seasoning with the odd pinch of salt as they cook. Just before removing them, flambé by pouring in the brandy and tilting the pan to the gas flame to set fire to it (or use a match). When the flames have died down, transfer the meat to a warmed dish while you finish the sauce.

Scrape and shake the pan to deglaze (page 334), then add the redcurrant jelly. When it has melted and the juices have reduced to a syrupy couple of tablespoons, stir in the cream. Allow to bubble and reduce a little more, then take the pan off the heat. Place the noisettes on warmed plates and pour the sauce over them. Serve with creamy mashed potatoes (page 518).

CALF'S LIVER WITH LITTLE ONIONS, SAGE AND AGED VINEGAR *Serves 4*

About 500g very fresh calf's liver

2-3 tablespoons olive oil

2 dozen baby (i.e. pickling) onions, peeled but left whole

25g plain flour, seasoned with salt and pepper

100ml aged vinegar

2 dozen sage leaves

The marriage of onions and liver is much celebrated in many food cultures, and this is just one way of achieving it. Balsamic vinegar is not the only sweet, aged vinegar of note. I recently found some delicious aged cider vinegar, from the French condiment company, Meaux, which I would highly recommend as a reliable and interesting alternative.

Cut the liver into slices 1cm thick and trim out any coarse tubes, then set aside. Heat 2 tablespoons of the oil in a large, heavy frying pan over a low heat. Add the onions and sweat gently. They mustn't take colour quickly but should brown gradually as they cook, so that after 20 minutes the outside is nicely caramelised to a dark brown colour and they are sweet and tender all the way through. Transfer to a warmed dish and keep warm in a low oven.

Add a little more oil to the pan and turn up the heat so that it sizzles. Give the liver slices the lightest dusting of seasoned flour and lay them in the pan. For liver nicely pink in the middle, turn after 2 minutes and cook the second side for just 1 minute. Transfer to 4 warmed plates while you quickly finish the sauce.

Deglaze the pan with the aged vinegar (page 334), scraping up any crusty morsels from the base as the vinegar bubbles and reduces. When you have only a scant tablespoon of sauce left, trickle it over the liver. Heat up another film of oil in the pan and fry the sage leaves, turning them as they become crispy (this only takes a few seconds).

Scatter the sage leaves and onions over the 4 plates. Serve with creamy mashed potatoes (page 518).

DEVILLED KIDNEYS *Serves 2*

4 lamb's kidneys, cut into quarters, with the whitish core trimmed out (p.193)

A little fat or oil (sunflower or olive)

1 small glass of sherry

1 tablespoon white wine vinegar or cider vinegar

1 teaspoon redcurrant jelly

A few good shakes of Worcestershire sauce

A good pinch of cayenne pepper

1 tablespoon English mustard

1 tablespoon double cream

Salt and freshly ground black pepper

A little chopped parsley, to garnish

If you think you don't like kidneys, or you're not quite sure, then this is the recipe to convert you. It's also very straightforward – it all comes together in a single pan and is ready in just a few minutes. The quantities for the various ingredients for the sauce are approximate. You should be feeling your way towards the level of piquancy you want.

Heat a little fat or oil in a small frying pan, add the kidneys and sizzle for just a minute to brown them, tossing them occasionally in the pan. Then add a generous slosh of sherry, let it bubble for a moment, and follow up with a more modest splash of wine or cider vinegar. Add the redcurrant jelly and stir to dissolve. Then add the Worcestershire sauce, cayenne pepper, mustard and plenty of black pepper. Season with a pinch of salt, take the edge off the fire with an enriching spoon of double cream and bubble for another minute or two, shaking the pan occasionally, until the sauce is reduced and nicely glossy. Taste for piquancy, and add more cayenne and black pepper if you like.

Serve with fried bread to give a bit of crunch and mop up the sauce. Alternatively, to make a more substantial supper dish, serve with plain boiled rice and a seasonal crisp green salad. Garnish with a sprinkling of chopped parsley.

FRITTO MISTO OF OFFAL WITH SAGE AND CAPERS *Serves 4*

250g cold, poached tongue (from the thick, fatty end, cooked as for Bollito Misto on p.304)

250g very fresh calf's liver

250g sweetbreads, poached (pp.196-7)

250g brains, if available, poached (pp.187-8)

About 24 sage leaves

50g plain flour

3 tablespoons olive oil

1 tablespoon capers, well rinsed and dried

Salt and freshly ground black pepper

Lemon wedges, to serve

Currently the options for this classic Italian dish are limited by the unavailability of brains – the only ones legally sold in the UK at the time of writing are pig's brains, and that probably means buying a whole pig's head and extracting them yourself. However, if you have a very good relationship with your butcher he may be able to put a few pig's brains aside for you. In taste and texture, they are indistinguishable from lamb's or calf's brains (and, I suspect, from almost every other mammal brain).

Otherwise, forget the brains for the time being. It's still a cracking dish with the tongue, liver and sweetbreads.

Cut up all the offal into generous (say, half-an-egg-sized) chunks. Finely chop half the sage leaves and add them to the flour with some salt and pepper. Toss the offal in this seasoned flour, shaking off any excess.

Heat the olive oil in a large, heavy frying pan until a piece of bread turns golden brown in it in a couple of minutes (not sooner). Maintain this temperature over a moderate heat. Fry the floured offal pieces, in 2 or 3 batches so as not to overcrowd the pan, turning them regularly, for 3-4 minutes until, like the bread, they are crisp and golden brown. Transfer each batch to a warmed dish lined with kitchen paper as they are done.

Turn up the heat, add a little extra oil if needed, then throw in the rest of the sage leaves, whole, and the capers. Sizzle for half a minute, until the sage leaves are browned and crisp, then drain them, and the capers, into a sieve. Divide the offal pieces between 4 warmed plates, re-season with pepper and flaky salt, and sprinkle over the sage leaves and capers. On each plate put a small wedge of lemon – which should be used sparingly.

Variation

Brains on Toast: In anticipation of the joyful day when brains are back in the butcher's, I want to mention the 'brains only' version of this dish. Prepared exactly as above (and illustrated opposite, made with the brains of a pair of pigs I had recently taken to slaughter), it is one of my favourite dishes of all time. Shake from the pan on to a waiting piece of toast – ideally rubbed with a little garlic and trickled with a little olive oil.

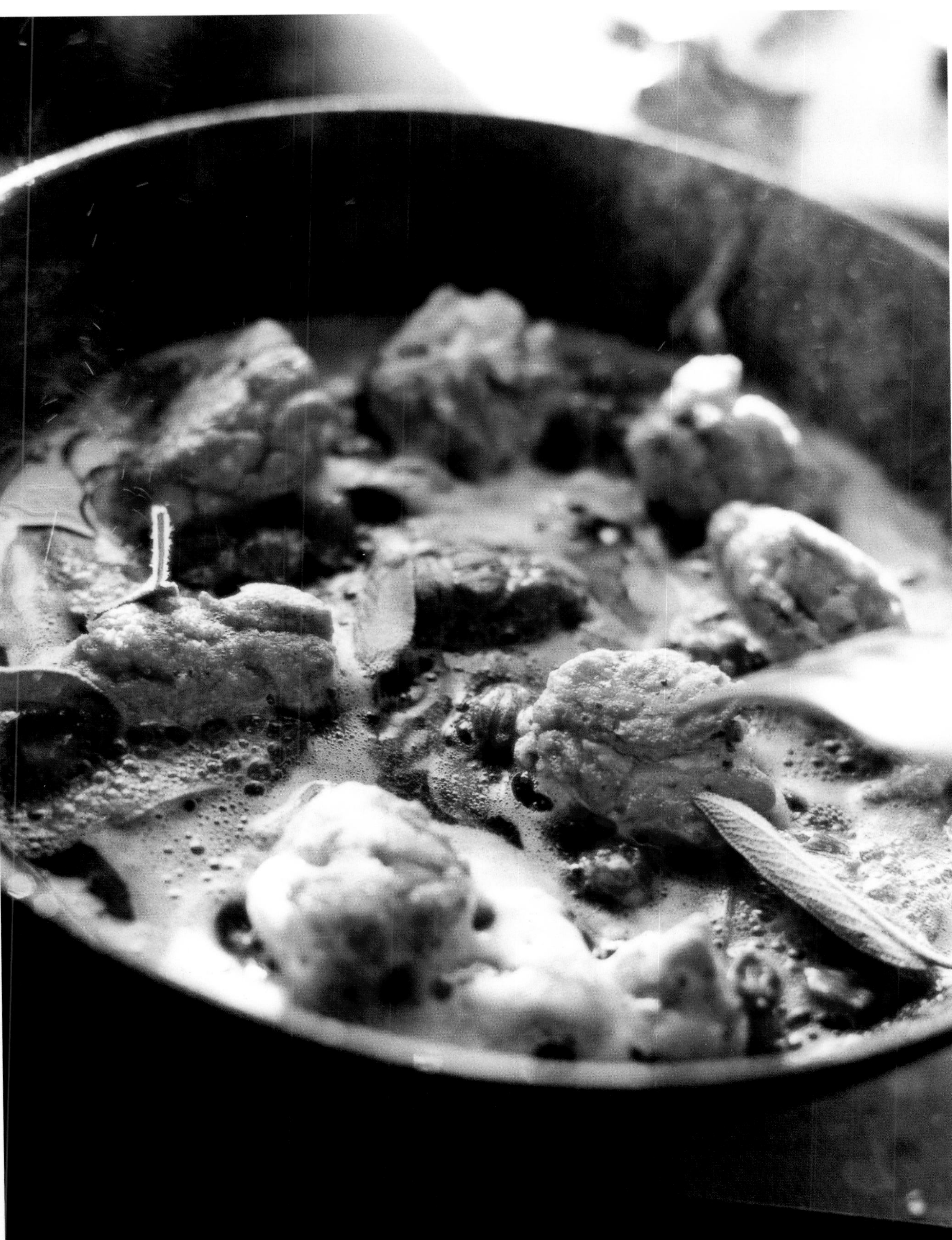

SAUTÉ OF SWEETBREADS WITH PEAS AND BEANS *Serves 2*

250g calf's or lamb's sweetbreads

1 small onion, peeled and studded with 3-4 cloves

A little plain flour, seasoned with salt and pepper

125g fresh young peas

125g small broad beans

2 tablespoons olive oil

100g salt pork, pancetta or bacon (see p.429 for home-made), diced

1 large garlic clove, finely chopped

Flaky salt and freshly ground black pepper

This is one of two dishes in the book where sweetbreads get an outing with broad beans – the other being the terrine on page 455. The combination is so good (and so popular with my wife) that it's worth ringing the changes. In this case, the sweetbreads are served piping hot, crispy on the outside and creamy in the middle. Salty bacon, sweet peas and bitter broad beans, all with a hint of garlic, make this a pretty sensational meeting of flavours and textures.

Prepare the sweetbreads as described on page 197 but add a clove-studded onion to the poaching water for a little flavour boost. Toss the sweetbreads in the seasoned flour.

Blanch the peas and beans by simmering them for just 1 minute in a pan of lightly salted boiling water. Drain and plunge into cold water (this helps to fix both sweetness and colour), then drain again.

Heat the oil in a frying pan until a small piece of bread will sizzle in it, but not too fiercely. Fry the bacon until starting to crisp up, then add the sweetbreads and continue to fry, tossing occasionally, as they brown and crisp up in the oil. Add the garlic a minute or so after the sweetbreads. When the sweetbreads are nicely browned and crisp, pour any excess oil out of the pan. Add the peas and beans to the pan and toss over the heat for a minute or so, until they are heated through. Season to taste with black pepper and flaky salt. Serve at once.

BLACK PUDDING WONTONS *Serves 4-5*

125g good-quality black pudding

125g coarsely minced pork

2 tablespoons sunflower oil

2 shallots or 1 small onion, finely chopped

3 spring onions, finely chopped

2 garlic cloves, finely chopped

A thumb-sized nugget of fresh ginger root, finely chopped

1 lemongrass stalk, outer layers removed, tender inner stem finely chopped

About 2 teaspoons soy sauce

1 packet of wonton wrappers

1 egg, beaten

Groundnut or sunflower oil for deep-frying

Freshly ground black pepper

Sweet and hot Chinese chilli dipping sauce, to serve

As a general rule, I think that making dim sum is best left to Chinese restaurants. However, I make an exception for this charming little dish, which was prepared for me by a cheeky and talented young cook, Jon Ashton, in the 'TV Dinners' series. You could call it fusion food – if you don't find that expression as irritating as I do – the culinary heritages that are fused being those of China and Lancashire!

I don't suggest you make your own wonton pastry but buy it fresh or frozen (in neat squares, ready to fold) in a Chinese supermarket, where you should also be able to get the sweet and hot dipping sauce.

Heat the sunflower oil in a frying pan, add the shallots or onion, spring onions, garlic, ginger and lemongrass and fry gently until softened. Scrape into a bowl and leave to cool for a minute. Add the black pudding, crumbling it in with your fingers, and the minced pork. Season with a few shakes of soy sauce and a few twists of black pepper. Mix all the ingredients thoroughly, using your hands if you like, to get a well-blended, sticky mixture.

Lay out the wonton wrappers on a work surface (you will need 16-20). Brush a little beaten egg along 2 edges of each wrapper. Place 2 teaspoons of the black pudding mixture in the centre of each wonton square and fold diagonally in half to make a triangle. Pinch the edges together to seal.

Heat the oil in a deep saucepan or a deep-fat fryer to 170°C (or until a test piece of wonton wrapper turns golden brown in about 2 minutes). Deep-fry the wontons, in batches of 4 or 5, for about 3 minutes, until golden brown, then drain on kitchen paper. Serve with the dipping sauce.

DUCK OR GOOSE BREASTS WITH PINEAPPLE, CHILLI AND SOY *Serves 2*

2 boneless duck breasts or 1 boneless goose breast

1/2 large pineapple

3 tablespoons soy sauce

1 teaspoon soft brown sugar or honey

3 garlic cloves, chopped

A golfball-sized piece of fresh ginger root, finely sliced

1/2-1 fresh red chilli (according to heat), deseeded and finely chopped

A few twists of black pepper

A little sunflower oil

2 spring onions, finely sliced

A little caster sugar for dusting

These days boneless duck breasts are easily bought from most butcher's and some supermarkets and are available both free range and organic. They're undoubtedly a practical product, and lend themselves to quick preparation. A more holistic approach would be to buy a whole duck or goose, use the legs to make a confit (see page 451), and the breasts for this dish.

This recipe also works well with Canada goose breasts (see page 167). And in the absence of a pineapple, the marinade can be made with the juice of a lime or half a lemon.

Peel the pineapple and cut off 2 slices about 2 cm thick. Cut these into quarters and trim off the tough core at the point of each quarter. Roughly chop the rest of the pineapple and squeeze the juice into a bowl with your fist. Discard (or eat) the remaining pulp.

Make a marinade by combining the pineapple juice (3-4 tablespoons of it) with the soy sauce, sugar or honey, garlic, ginger, chilli and black pepper. Take each duck breast and make 3 or 4 slashes in the skin (6 or 7 for a goose breast) – into the fat but not the meat. Put the slashed breasts in the marinade, turn them well to coat and leave – ideally for a couple of hours but even 10 minutes will have an effect.

Wipe the marinade off the breasts and sear them quickly in a very hot pan, greased with a little sunflower oil, to brown the meat side and start crisping the skin. Place the duck breasts side by side, skin-side up, in a small ovenproof dish in which they fit snugly. Tuck the spring onions underneath and pour over the marinade. The idea is that the meat will 'poach' in its marinadey juices, while the exposed skin crisps up in the fierce heat. Roast in a hot oven (220°C/Gas Mark 7) for 8-10 minutes (12-14 for a goose breast), until the skin is well browned and crisp. At this point the meat should still be pink.

Remove the breasts from the dish and leave to rest on a warmed plate. In a small, lightly oiled pan, fry the reserved pineapple slices, dusting them with a little sugar and turning occasionally, so they brown and caramelise. Strain all the meat cooking juices into the pan and sizzle to reduce to a syrupy sauce, tossing the pineapple pieces to coat them well. Finally, return the meat to the pan and turn a few times to coat well.

Slice the breasts, cutting through the original slashes, and arrange the pieces on warmed plates. Spoon the sauce and pineapple pieces over and around the meat. Accompany with plain boiled rice and simple steamed greens, such as pak choy or purple sprouting broccoli.

SALAD OF SEARED PIGEON BREAST WITH PAN JUICE VINAIGRETTE *Serves 4*

This dish is undoubtedly restaurant derivative, and various versions have proliferated on the menus of fashionable eateries since the mid-Eighties. It's easy to see why: quick and simple to make and plate up, smart to look at, delicious and easy to eat. Happily, it's equally a doddle to make at home.

Many butchers now sell pigeon breasts but it's so easy to slice them off yourself that it's better to buy whole, oven-ready birds. The carcasses are an asset not to be wasted, as they make great stock (page 472) and soup (page 507).

8 whole skinless pigeon breasts

2 teaspoons olive oil

A few thyme leaves (if handy)

4 plates' worth of mixed young salad leaves, e.g. baby spinach or chard, oak leaf lettuce, tatsoi, rocket, lamb's lettuce

Salt and freshly ground black pepper

THE VINAIGRETTE:

2 garlic cloves, bruised

2 tablespoons white wine

1 tablespoon white wine vinegar

4 tablespoons olive oil

Toss the pigeon breasts with the olive oil, thyme and seasoning so they are sparely coated and leave for a few minutes. Wash, pick over and spin dry the salad leaves and put them in a bowl.

Heat up a heavy frying pan until very hot and throw in the pigeon breasts. Leave for a minute before turning, then leave for another minute and turn again. Then toss in the pan for a couple more minutes. Take one of the breasts and slice it in half. If it is medium rare, i.e. nicely pink in the middle, remove all the breasts and place on a wooden board to rest. Or cook them all for another minute or two if necessary.

Quickly prepare the vinaigrette: throw the garlic cloves into the hot pan, quickly followed by the white wine, and deglaze the pan thoroughly with a wooden spatula (if in doubt, see page 334). When the wine has evaporated by half, remove the pan from the heat and add the vinegar. Then add the oil, season with salt and pepper, and swish around the pan. Remove and discard the garlic cloves, which have now done their job.

Pour half the pan vinaigrette over the salad leaves, toss well, and divide the salad between 4 plates.

Slice each pigeon breast diagonally into 4 or 5 finger-thick slices, arranging them over the leaves on each plate. Trickle what's left of the pan vinaigrette directly over the meat and serve at once.

13. BARBECUING

13. BARBECUING

Outdoor and Wood-fired Cookery

We'll never know precisely how people first learned about the effect of fire on meat, though it's safe to assume it was, like so many culinary breakthroughs, a happy accident – and one that swiftly followed the discovery of fire itself. I like to imagine a bit of 'morphic resonance' – thousands of happy accidents, involving picking up the remains of last night's antelope haunch or bison liver, discarded near the fire, and finding it curiously tender, palatable and pleasantly smoky. Soon it started to happen 'accidentally on purpose' (as we used to say at school).

However it came about, people have now been grilling, roasting and smoking their way around a smouldering fire, of wood and latterly of charcoal, for many millennia. Cynics might argue that Barbecue Man hasn't evolved much. His hide loincloth has been replaced by a plastic apron with a lacy bra and a pair of suspenders printed on it, while the subtle use of flint and dried twigs has given way to a crude slosh of barbecue lighting fluid. Otherwise he scratches and grunts his way through the barbecue ritual in much the same manner, emerging with an exaggerated sense of triumph and a blackened hunk of meat, ash coated and carbonised on the outside, raw and cold in the middle. In the modern scenario, the meat is sadly often of a chemical-industrial provenance quite unknown to our ancestors. And it frequently has the added indignity of tasting of the lighting fluid.

That's the downside of barbecuing. But it doesn't have to be like that. In fact, it should never be like that. Good barbecuing can make good meat unsurpassably delicious. The subtle seasoning of smouldering charcoal and the searing effect of hot iron bars produce an irresistible combination of caramelised meat sugars and mild smokiness, the appreciation of which, perhaps because of its primordial origins, is almost universal.

Bad barbecuing, which I fear is far more often practised than good barbecuing, is the inevitable result of impatience, latent pyromania and the subconscious desire to create an unpleasantly smoky atmosphere in which cheap but cold beer tastes better than it should. Misplaced enthusiasm for the event often outweighs respect for one's ingredients, with fatal results.

Technically there are two things bad barbecuing does to spoil good meat. The first is the direct action of flame on the surface of the meat. Instead of browning and caramelising the sugars on the surface, as we would like, flames deposit the soot of combustion on it – a black carbon coating with quite an unpleasant taste. The second problem is that of rising smoke from burning fat. Unlike wood smoke's mellow taste, fat smoke has a nasty, acrid note that spoils rather than complements the flavour of the meat. The second problem compounds the first, of course, because any fat dripping into the fire will cause flames to flare up and leave their sooty deposit on the meat.

If you want to understand exactly what's happening here, try holding a small piece of meat (nothing too precious) directly in a candle flame. You'll quickly see how the meat blackens and gets coated with a nasty-smelling (and foul-tasting, if you want to go that far) soot. Incidentally, the adverse effect of barbecue flames on meat is different from the benign effect of flambéing, in which the alcohol burns cleanly without leaving a sooty deposit.

Barbecue Solutions: Three Golden Rules

The first golden rule of barbecuing, then – and this applies to cooking over wood as well as over charcoal – is don't cook over flames, cook over embers. Resist the impulse to start cooking while your fire is still producing flames. Wait until you have a nice pile of glowing coals. In daylight, you can see when this stage has been reached because all the charcoal will have turned from black to grey, with red-hot embers peeping through. After dark, it's even easier to see when the correct stage has been reached: there will be no visible flames and the whole fire will be glowing red in the gloaming.

In the case of spit roasting, where you have to keep the fire constantly topped up to generate sustained heat for a number of hours, the first rule can be adapted: don't cook over the flames, cook to the side of them. Best of all, cook between two fires. I'll be explaining this technique in detail shortly.

The second golden rule relates to the fat problem – basically, remove the fat and you remove the problem. You'll know from previous chapters that I'm a big fan of fat, the harbinger of succulence and flavour. But its presence is to be regarded with caution on the barbecue. Yes, it's nice to have some crisp fat on the edge of your lamb or pork chops. But if you're not careful, the damage done outweighs the benefits. You don't have to cut every last scrap of fat from your meat, and in the context of the fierce heat of the barbecue, the subtle veins of marbling fat (see pages 36-8) become more precious than ever. It's the thick back fat around the edge of pork and lamb chops that you need to worry about. When it reaches a certain temperature it will start to 'render' and drip in generous trickles on to the fire, which will flare up and spoil the meat. So I usually trim it back to a modest couple of millimetres or so.

Another frequent cause of 'fat flare' is the dripping oil from marinades. Oily marinades are, of course, useful as a preparation for barbecuing meat – especially if the meat has been trimmed of its own fat to avoid a flare-up. But excess oil should always be wiped off before the meat is placed on the barbecue. Don't get too obsessive about this – a light film of oil will not hurt. In fact, it will help prevent the meat sticking to the barbecue.

If an incident of 'fat flare' does occur on your barbecue, the best response is quickly to whip off any meat that is likely to be affected and wait for the flames to die down again. If the offending piece of fat is clearly identifiable, snip it off before replacing the meat over the fire.

Adhering to the above 'best practice' becomes much easier if you take on board my third and last golden rule: be generous with the fuel medium (i.e. wood as well as charcoal). The no-flames rule means that you should not start refuelling beneath food that is already cooking. So if you want to avoid a lengthy, foodless refuelling delay mid-barbecue, begin by burning a generous amount of charcoal or wood that will settle to a thick pile of glowing embers and sustain the cooking temperature for a good hour or so. I'll say more about the vital matter of timing and temperature shortly.

Choosing a Barbecue

The above principles of good barbecuing are far more important than the kit on which you actually make your fire. And as far as the hundreds, maybe thousands, of manufactured barbecues go, I am afraid I'm no expert, and I certainly have no brands, names or models to recommend.

I'll start by telling you what I use. I had planned to build an *in situ* barbecue somewhere in the River Cottage garden during my first winter there, in preparation for an endless summer of *al fresco* dining. But there was so much else to do, I never got round to it. In May, some friends came to stay. A few of us went fishing and caught a surprising haul of early summer mackerel. They were begging to be barbecued. Casting around for something with which to improvise, I hauled up to the garden the galvanised trough I used for feeding the pigs. I decided to drill a few small holes in it with my hammer drill (actually, my wife's hammer drill) to provide some venting in order to achieve a fast and even burn. I figured a few neat holes in the side wouldn't prevent the trough continuing to function in its intended role, even after use as an emergency barbecue. But I couldn't get the drill to make any impression at all.

As I wandered about the cottage looking for an alternative fire vessel, I heard a harsh, clanking noise of metal on metal and went back outside to investigate. In a moment of over-excitement, salivating at the prospect of chargrilled fish of unbeatable freshness (and further fuelled, perhaps, by the testosterone rush that has always afflicted Barbecue Man), my friend Jerry had begun hacking at the sides of the trough with my axe. Before I could protest, he had punched a couple of neat holes in one side, an inch or two above the base. He had started, I figured, so he may as well finish. Within minutes, there were three axe-shaped gashes in each side, and Dorset's finest coppiced charcoal was being shaken into the trough. The trough burned like a dream, and the fish cooked like a dream on a couple of grills salvaged from the old electric oven I had scrapped from the River Cottage kitchen.

That was four years ago. The pig trough is still the only barbecue I have, and the only one I need. I take it to the beach, in the car when we go camping, and have even used it indoors beneath the old inglenook fireplace, where the draw was good enough to avoid smoking out the room. Last year, in a local salvage yard,

I found a heavy, cast-iron grill to replace the rather flimsy oven ones. The thick bars get wonderfully hot, and leave those irresistible charred stripes on the meat and fish I put on them. My kit is now complete, and is what I used to cook the beefburgers illustrated on page 378.

So I don't have much time for the pre-fab barbies beloved of garden centres and out-of-town leisure and DIY superstores. I'm sure some of them work well, and I'm sure some of them are close to useless. If you're shopping for one, then robustness and durability would be the chief qualities to look for – along with suitable capacity for the number of people you are likely to want to cook for (particularly bearing in mind the no-refuelling-during-cooking rule).

For those who love to improvise, the lengthways-sliced, half-oil-drum barbecue is another great favourite, and in Africa and the Caribbean no self-respecting outdoor chef would deign to use anything else. If you can lay your hands on an empty oil drum, then all you need is someone qualified to wield a disc-cutter to do the slicing. Again, a few well-spaced vent holes will help to give a fast, even burn. And since the metal is less impenetrable than galvanised steel, you may not need to resort to the axe.

Siting a permanent, brick-built barbecue somewhere in the garden still seems like a good idea, and perhaps some day I'll get round to it. When I do, I think I will model it on a simple but efficient and functional design I noticed in a friends' garden recently. Their home-built barbie is a classic brick 'altar', with the concrete fire-base a little lower than classic worktop height (about 850mm high). There is a windshield of three-brick height on three sides, with small (just 1cm wide) ventilation gaps left between all the bricks on the bottom layer. Another row of bricks, of single-brick height, right across the middle of the fire-base, divides the barbecue in half. This means you can fire up and cook on one half only when catering for smaller numbers. You can also maintain a 'hot half' and a 'medium half' to give you some options for cooking things faster or slower, or shuffling them about – a useful feature, the importance of which I'll discuss next.

Fine-tuning Barbecue Technique: Timing and Temperature

Not all meats for the barbecue require the same temperature. Some need searing over a fierce heat and will be done how you like them in just a couple of minutes: rare steaks and beefburgers, for example. You may also want to serve lamb – such as chops, kebabs and leg steaks – seared and quite pink in the middle, but ideally they will require a longer time and a slightly lower temperature than your beef steaks. Pork and chicken on the barbecue need even greater care. Neither should be pink or bloody when you serve them – but you don't want them cremated on the outside either. They'll need considerably longer on the grill at a lower temperature still.

The easiest way to raise and lower the temperature of your barbecue is simply to raise and lower the height of the grill above the fire. Most manufactured barbecues are designed to let you do this – some well, some badly. And if you are building or improvising a barbecue at home, some device for raising your grill should certainly be incorporated.

Having said that, I have a confession. My beloved pig-trough barbecue, described in glowing (naturally) terms above, incorporates no such device. If I want to raise the grill from its natural resting place directly on top of the trough, I have to gather a few bricks and pile them up at either end. As the grill is long enough to extend beyond the ends of the trough, this works pretty well. I tend to work with just two heights, high and low, which give me two temperature settings – low and high respectively. Sometimes I make the pile of bricks at one end only, so the grill is actually on a tilt, higher and cooler at one end, lower and hotter at the other.

Another useful technique for getting a variable temperature along the length of the barbecue is to do a bit of fire raking. Once your charcoal has burned down evenly, pile up the hot coals at one end, leaving them fairly sparse at the other.

These two methods for achieving a gradated temperature from one end of the barbecue to the other (or simply a hot zone and a medium zone) are useful, as they allow you to cook meats that require different temperatures at the same time, and to move meats that seem in danger of burning to the cooler zone. But they will work much better on a long, fairly narrow barbecue like mine than on the more conventional square or round one.

A more relaxed strategy is simply to allow time to adjust the temperature for you. Cook the meats that will most benefit from a fierce heat as soon as the flames have subsided. Serve them first. Then, as the temperature drops, cook the more delicate meats longer and slower, serving them as a second wave. It is in the nature of the barbecue that both cook and guest should be ready to exercise a little patience. When they are not, then trouble and disappointment are inevitable.

Finally, beware the wind factor, which can affect the temperature dramatically. On a breezy day, the rapid movement of cool air around the fire can reduce the temperature in the cooking zone considerably. You may have to lower the grill closer to the fire than usual to find the heat you are used to.

Choosing Charcoal

A great deal of the charcoal sold in the UK is of very poor quality. Imported from the tropics, it is produced from 'waste' wood, much of which is not really suitable for charcoal making at all. It doesn't burn well, and often needs a lot of help from chemical lighting fluids or paraffin firelighters to get it to burn at all. And that's not the worst thing about it. I use inverted commas round the word waste because although the wood may be surplus to the requirements of the huge timber conglomerates who cut and process the vast trees from which it is taken, it is in many cases by no means surplus to the requirements of the planet. I am talking about the by-product of deforestation – environmentally scandalous and very often illegal. Now that is a waste.

Beyond question, the best charcoal I have ever used is British-made hardwood charcoal from sustainable coppiced woodland. It is craft-made by experts using traditional techniques, from native hardwoods such as hazel, sycamore, birch, willow and hawthorn. All the wood comes from sustainable woodland management practices, such as coppicing and hedge laying. The burning of such charcoal is, in the greater scheme of things, 'carbon neutral'. This means that the carbon dioxide (the chief 'greenhouse gas') that is released into the atmosphere by charcoal making and burning is equivalent to the carbon dioxide absorbed naturally by the re-growth and replacement growth of the woods and hedges from which it has been taken.

As it happens, the burning qualities of this charcoal are quite superb. A few sheets of scrunched-up newspaper among the charcoal are all you need to get it going. It burns down to glowing coals fast and evenly, giving you cookable embers in just twenty or thirty minutes.

You do have to be slightly on the ball though. It gives about forty-five minutes to one hour of optimum cooking temperature before fairly rapidly losing its heat. So as soon as it's ready, you should get cooking. The up side, of course, is that it takes only another twenty minutes to fire up a fresh batch for another session.

British hardwood charcoal is more expensive – in terms of money, at least, as opposed to the cost to the planet – but it's worth it. If you've never used it before, I think you will find it improves your barbecuing almost effortlessly, and you will taste the difference, too.

Okay, British charcoal makers, can I have my cheque now? Seriously, if that all sounds like a blatant plug, then it's only because I think the product deserves it – so much so that you'll find various contact numbers in the Directory (page 530) for tracing a source.

What to Barbecue

This is a meat book, so I'll steer clear of the myriad joys of barbecuing fish and, indeed, vegetables. All types of meat – pork, beef, lamb, poultry and game, and some of their various offals – can be cooked successfully over the barbecue. But only certain cuts of these meats are really suitable for this kind of cooking and, as you might expect, on the whole they are the same cuts that lend themselves to other fast-cooking techniques, such as frying and grilling. The most obvious of these are steaks and chops from rumps and loins, along with cubed lean meat suitable for kebabs and, of course, minced meat for burgers, sausages and other kinds of patty.

Large joints – especially those with bones in, such as legs and shoulders of pork or lamb and foreribs or sirloins of beef – are not suitable for conventional barbecuing directly over charcoal, as they take too long and will inevitably be burned on the outside long before they are cooked through to the middle. But they can be cooked very successfully using other wood or charcoal systems, particularly

in a wood-fired oven or on a scaled-down version of the spit roast (see below for more on both these techniques).

However, smaller, boneless joints of meat, particularly those that lend themselves to being served rare, can be cooked with great success on the barbecue. Three good examples, I would say, are a piece of beef fillet, a boned and trimmed loin of lamb (or even a trimmed rack/best end from a small animal) and fillets of large (i.e. red) deer or a trimmed eye of loin from the smaller deer species (roe, sika and fallow). They need careful preparation and deft handling. But if they are turned regularly for twenty or thirty minutes over a medium heat, then rested for ten minutes or so, the results in all cases can be absolutely sublime.

I'm not going to try and give minute-accurate cooking times for all the different meats and cuts because there are far too many variables at play. But I will give my thoughts on rough strategies for success with a few of the most suitable barbecue cuts of meat, poultry and game. I'll mention a few marinades too – a popular and effective way of seasoning, lubricating and tenderising meat for a barbecue. But note that all the caveats on pages 338-40 about not pickling your meat in a marinade over-laced with booze are especially important when barbecuing, as the problem is exacerbated by the dry heat of a wood or charcoal fire. Almost all my barbecue marinades are based on oil (olive or groundnut), and I use just enough to coat rather than drench the meat, and to mediate the transfer of flavour from the herbs and spices. To avoid flare-up, I wipe off all the excess oil except for a fine coating film on the surface of the meat, which helps prevent it sticking on the bars of the grill rack. Indeed, meat that has not been marinated will benefit from a light oil massage to achieve the same effect.

Beef

Aside from the burger, which is a must (see pages 398-400 for a full discussion), I don't barbecue a lot of beef. The rump and sirloin steaks from my own beef cows, aged for a whole month, are usually fried (see page 352). It's not that they wouldn't be delicious on the barbecue. It's simply that I've put so much effort into getting them just right that I want them to taste wholly and only of themselves.

I do, however, occasionally like to barbecue minute steaks – usually slices of topside or thick flank, beaten flat with a rolling pin. Flash grilled for no more than two minutes over a very hot barbecue, crammed in a baguette with a scrunch of salad leaves and a dab of horseradish, mustard or mayonnaise, they make a superb steak sandwich.

Once in a while, I make beef kebabs. You really can't use cheap stewing meat for this. You need good, lean braising steak or even topside. I always marinate the cubes to tenderise the meat. My two favourite marinades are the very versatile Indonesian one on page 346 and a simple, teriyaki-style marinade made by combining equal quantities of soy sauce and rice wine vinegar (or cider vinegar) with plenty of grated garlic, a dash of sesame oil and a good pinch of sugar.

Veal

Being a delicate meat, veal rarely gets an outing on the barbecue but in fact, chops of rosé veal (see pages 86-7) are brilliant cooked over charcoal. I usually marinate them with lemon zest, rosemary and garlic (see the picture on page 339). They should be cooked a little more slowly than, say, lamb chops, since they are thick and you need to cook them right through. About fifteen minutes over a medium to low heat should do it.

Lamb

For me, lamb is the meat most flattered by the barbecue – so much so that I'd say there's no better way to cook a lamb chop, kebab or lamburger than over charcoal. The powerful, slightly gamy taste of lamb collides beautifully with wood or charcoal smoke, and can easily take on further aromatising, either from a herby marinade or from spices worked into minced lamb for a shish-style kebab or variations on the lamburger theme.

I don't think it's extravagant to bone out a whole leg of lamb for a barbecue. It can actually be quite a thrifty exercise. You can use the best lean meat for butterflied leg steaks (or cut it into nice lean cubes for kebabs) and the rest can all be minced up for my Souvlaki Lamburgers recipe (page 401).

I have three very simple lamb marinades, all of which are equally good for chops, leg steaks, or cubed meat to be mounted on kebab skewers: one combines lamb's classic friends, rosemary and garlic; one achieves a distinctly Greek tang with oregano, lemon juice and zest; and the other is made up of dry spices for a North African feel. Detailed instructions for all are given in the recipe section.

Pork

Pork is a slightly tricky meat on the barbecue, as once the lean cuts, such as leg steaks or chops, are exposed to the heat they quickly dry out. With so much pork being of such poor quality – overlean, flabby and tasteless – the end results can be particularly gloomy.

Personally I feel pork works best on the barbecue in just three forms – the chop (provided it comes from animals of the highest quality); the rack of spare ribs (not to be confused with the spare rib joint); and, of course, the good old sausage (along with its underrated variation, the home-made, skinless pork burger).

For both chops and spare ribs, thick 'barbecue sauce' type marinades, using sugar, ketchup, mustard and suchlike, are good because they quickly form a glaze over the meat. This not only helps to protect it from drying out but also becomes, if all goes well, a delectable, finger-licking feature of the dish when it is finally served up. My own version of this sauce is on page 397.

All these pork items, including the sausage, must not be rushed, but cooked slowly and carefully, with frequent turning and, where a glaze or marinade is used, regular basting, over the moderate heat of a subsiding barbecue. Choose good meat, and get this right, and these porky preparations shoot straight from the bottom to the top of the barbecue hit parade.

Poultry and game birds

A huge pile of torched, unseasoned drumsticks of cheap, factory-farmed chicken, blackened on the outside and still raw by the bone, is the predominant feature of many a barbecue, and stands as a grim reminder of so much that is wrong with British culinary culture, from production to consumption. Let it be a symbol of everything you must seek to avoid – in life but particularly on the barbecue.

On the other hand, start with a whole corn-fed chicken, free range or preferably organic, and joint it yourself into eight portions, as described on pages 140-43. Marinate it if you want, or simply season it well with salt and pepper and rub with a little oil. Then place over a subsiding or moderately hot barbecue. Turn frequently for at least fifteen minutes until well browned and crisp. Pile into a dish, re-season, and leave to settle for five or ten minutes. You will have created something to be keenly fought over – not lobbed into the hedge or dropped surreptitiously at the feet of the nearest (unfortunate) dog.

Other birds can also be jointed and barbecued in this way. Pheasants produce excellent-sized portions for barbecuing. Farmed ducks and geese are problematic because of the thick layer of fat that will inevitably drip and flare up on the fire. The breasts can be trimmed of fat and cubed for kebabs but this seems a waste of these birds' best assets. On the other hand, a good cull of Canada geese provided a friend and neighbour with the meat for some of the finest kebabs I ate last summer.

Furred game

Venison, rabbit and hare all deserve an occasional appearance on the barbecue. The proviso in all cases is that the meat, being so lean, has a tendency to dryness. A few hours in an oily (but not winey) marinade will certainly help.

Generally, venison can be deployed much like lamb – barbecued as chops, butterflied leg steaks and kebabs – and, like lamb, served reasonably pink. The ultimate venison barbecue treat is, as discussed above, the trimmed loin or fillet, cooked whole.

Hares and rabbits are undoubtedly tricky – a labour of love for those who regard themselves as game aficionados *and* barbecue specialists. But a saddle of either, marinated in olive or groundnut oil, then turned carefully and regularly over a moderate heat for about twenty minutes, seasoned and brushed with a little more oil (enough to lubricate but not drip) every couple of minutes, should turn out pretty divine.

The legs, on the other hand, are almost unbarbecuable – unless you use them for making gameburgers. These are a delight, and can be put together with leg meat and other trimmings from rabbits or hares, or in the case of venison, with good meat from boned-out legs and/or shoulders. In all cases, mince the game with the addition of about 30 per cent pork belly (or just work some good sausage meat into the minced game). Try seasoning with a little very finely chopped or minced onion, plus fresh parsley and thyme.

Offal

Very fresh liver, of sheep, pigs, cows or deer, can be barbecued to delectable effect. Wipe it with a film of oil first though, or it will stick horribly on the grill. Season with salt and pepper as it cooks. A slice about 2 cm thick will take four to eight minutes, depending how pink you like it. Alternatively, in true bushman style, stick a cube of liver on the end of a stick and dangle it over hot coals until lightly browned. Blow on the meat to cool it, then eat it off the stick.

Kidneys barbecue well. You can make a lovely 'mixed grill' kebab by mounting a piece of kidney, a piece of liver and a piece of sausage alternately on a skewer.

Even poultry offal has possibilities. In Brazil I once had a chargrilled skewer of chicken hearts, kidneys and livers. It was delicious. I have done the same thing at home with the same trio of offal from a rabbit. Equally fine.

Two things you probably wouldn't think of putting on the barbecue are pig's ears and tails. Yet once they have been slowly simmered until completely tender, crackling them up over charcoal to brown and blister is a brilliant way of finishing them (and a classic house special of the famous Paris brasserie, La Coupole).

Another thing you definitely wouldn't think of chargrilling is ox tongue. Fergus Henderson at St John restaurant in London surprised and delighted me with just such a dish. The ox tongue had been brined, soaked and then simmered for, I guess, about one and a half hours, until just tender. Then it was sliced and finished on the chargrill, so it came with those lovely stripes. Served with beetroot and horseradish, it was quite delicious.

No doubt there's much scope for further innovation in barbecuing offal, and indeed in using the chargrill to finish tough meats that have first been tenderised by slow cooking.

Variations on the Barbecue: Open-fire Cookery

By this I simply mean cooking over an open fire, usually made up of dead wood gathered impromptu from around the site of the fire – brushwood from the hedge or forest, driftwood from the beach, even dried-out camel dung from the desert path. In terms of culinary evolution, open-fire, or classic campfire, cookery is going backwards from the barbecue but it's none the worse for that. And if it is executed with just a small degree of skill and caution, the results can be every bit as good as the barbecue, or better. When you cook with the right wood, in the right way, the subtle, smoky flavours imparted to the meat can be sensational.

The kit required is minimal, or even non-existent – you may literally be toasting a cube of meat on the end of a stick, hand-held over the fire. Or you may take delight in whittling and arranging some contraption that suspends it for you –

brilliantly satisfying until it topples over or sets alight. Your next evolutionary step – effectively the leap from the Stone Age to the Bronze Age – is to have some kind of grill handy, and use some kind of non-flammable prop (for example, large stones) to suspend it over the fire. In this scenario you are really just building an impromptu barbecue with wood instead of charcoal as the fuel.

The principal difference between wood and charcoal as burning mediums over which meat is directly grilled or toasted is simply that wood is much less predictable, so the cook has to be more organised, reactive and on the ball. Starting with the right sort of wood is a big help. Dry, dead wood is preferable to green, growing wood, both practically as well as environmentally. And deciduous is generally preferable to evergreen – pine in particular burns with an acrid smoke that imparts undesirable flavours to your meat. Quantity is a factor as well as quality. You'll need more than a few twigs – or even a lot of twigs. A good few pieces at least 5 cm thick are essential to provide substantial heat-retaining embers, as opposed to a rapidly cooling pile of ash.

Once you've got a decent fire of dry, well-aged brushwood on the go, it's just a matter of managing it for cookability. Basically this means waiting until you have a good bed of hot embers, then perhaps raking them into a concentrated pile and prodding and poking them to avoid further flare-ups. Then on with the grill, with a few spare stones handy to raise or lower it as appropriate, and away you go. As with a charcoal barbecue, don't refuel under cooking food.

Of course, toasting and grilling are not the only way to cook meat over an open fire. And those who depend on wood as cooking fuel, either because circumstances dictate or because it is part of a chosen lifestyle, may be as adept at slow-cooking, frying and even baking as any Aga lover or gas aficionado. This is because you can, of course, use an open wood fire to heat a cooking pot or frying pan directly – including that ingenious, lidded, cast-iron pot called a Dutch oven. Again, a substantial (and therefore lasting) pile of hot embers is generally preferable to a roaring fire, though a heavy, lidded cast-iron pot can be suspended directly over flames, either standing on a high trivet or suspended from some kind of tripod.

In all such cases, the way in which heat is increased or decreased is again by lowering or raising the cooking vessel – competence, and eventually expertise, come with practice. But there is no reason at all why you cannot, if the idea appeals, cook a wonderful Pot-au-feu (page 284) in precisely the manner from which it derives its name.

Finally, you shouldn't rule out the possibility of open-fire cookery indoors. Most fireplaces can be adapted for cooking in one way or another. Anyone who has a fireplace has probably toasted a few marshmallows or roasted a pile of chestnuts. So why stop there? Replace the marshmallow with a cube of meat and you're in business. If you can rig up a grill rack close to or above the glowing embers of your fire, then you have an indoor barbecue, with as many possibilities as an outdoor one.

Pit-baking

This ingenious outdoor cooking technique, sometimes called a Maori barbecue, is used to cook large pieces of meat, or even whole small animals, such as lambs, young pigs or small deer.

There are variations on the theme, but here is one based on the traditional Maori practice. A suitable-sized pit is dug, bearing in mind the size of the meat, and a large wood or charcoal fire burned in the pit. When the fire has generated a substantial pile of hot coals or embers, these are levelled off and a fine layer of earth scattered over them. Next comes a layer of fresh leaves such as banana leaves, or sheets of wet newspaper can be used as a modern substitute. Then the meat is laid over the leaves, along with a pile of vegetables, or even fruit, that will cook with it. Another layer of leaves (or wet newspaper) goes on, and another layer of earth. Then a second fire is lit on top of the pile so that heat is generated downwards as well as up. It can take anything from four to twenty-four hours to complete the cooking, with regular stoking of the fire on top, depending on the size of the meat and the scale of the operation.

It's clearly a technique that has crossed many cultures, because the last time I encountered it was in Lapland. A huge haunch of reindeer was on the menu, in a wet paper parcel containing root vegetables and sprigs of fresh juniper. To the embarrassment of our host, it didn't work very well. Even after four hours in the pit, with a good-sized fire burning continually above it, the meat wasn't even close to being cooked through. She decided that we'd buried it too deep and hadn't put enough hot embers in the bottom of the pit. So the whole thing was done all over again and instead of dinner it became breakfast the next day. It was worth the wait, though – some of the most tender and delicious venison I have ever tasted.

Wood-fired (Pizza) Ovens

All over the world, traditional wood-fired ovens are used for baking bread and of course, in Italy, pizza. They generate a fierce, dry heat, about 240-260°C, which is perfect for bread and pizza but far too hot for cooking any meat, except perhaps to flash roast a fillet of beef. But once the baking is over and the oven slowly begins to cool, it presents an unmissable opportunity to cook all sorts of meaty things. The tradition in many cultures was for the housewives of a neighbourhood to bring joints, stews and other meat dishes to the baker and make the best use of the residual heat of his enormous oven. This is how such dishes as *gigot à la boulangère* were born. Imagine an oven starting at about 230°C and slowly cooling over about three or four hours to below 100°C. It's the perfect way to cook a leg or shoulder of lamb or mutton to melting tenderness.

Many old farmhouses all over Dorset contain traditional wood-fired bread ovens but in five years of snooping and house hunting I never once saw one restored to full working use. I vowed that if ever we ended up living in a house with a bread oven, I would restore it and use it. We did, I have, and I do. I'm still

perfecting my fire management skills but I have already had some wonderful legs of lamb out of it, including the one in the picture above.

You can now buy portable, beehive-shaped, ceramic 'patio pizza ovens' as a garden feature and a trendy alternative to the barbecue. Some are well made and fulfil their function admirably. Others aren't and do not, so take advice and shop around. Try Googling 'outdoor pizza oven' on the Internet.

Cold and Hot Smoking

Cold smoking is, in general, a way of preserving meat and fish and, of course, flavouring it. See pages 419-20 for further discussion.

Hot smoking meat, sometimes directly over an open fire, is very much a way of cooking it – often for immediate consumption. You can think of it almost as a very smoky barbecue, with smouldering wood chips as the fuel and a confined space (usually a simple metal box) keeping the smoke circulating around the meat. Poultry and game birds, especially chicken, ducks and geese, lend themselves to hot smoking, as does liver (see page 408). Hot-smoked meats can be eaten hot (i.e. immediately after smoking) or cold.

It's easy to improvise a hot smoker. All you need is a reasonably robust tin or metal box, which must not be lined with any paint on the inside. Within the tin you need some kind of rack to support the meat (or fish). Place a couple of handfuls of hardwood chips or sawdust (ideally oak or beech) on the base of the tin. Put the rack over the sawdust. Put the meat on the rack. Put the lid on the tin/smokebox. Then put the box on a moderate heat. This can be the embers of a fire, a low gas hob or a meths burner. The sawdust or wood chips will begin to smoulder inside the box, which will heat up like a small oven, cooking and smoking the meat on the rack.

The principle of hot smoking really is that simple, and practice will soon give you the knack.

A Spit Roast

There is another open-fire cooking technique, requiring a certain amount of hardware, which transforms campfire cooking into one of the most exciting and delicious forms of meat cookery there is. So I want to end this chapter by urging you to take up a challenge.

Spit-roasting a whole animal – most commonly a pig or lamb – is about as spectacular as meat cookery gets (short of stuffing a camel with a cow with a goat etc, which somehow I've never quite got round to). But it's more than just the ultimate achievement for Barbecue Man. It's a surprisingly practical way of catering for a large party (you can easily feed 100-plus with a good-sized porker). It also does full culinary justice to the beast in question: as the animal is uncut, all the juices are sealed in and this, combined with long, slow cooking, produces meat that is incredibly tender. Add to that the irresistible flavour of wood or charcoal smoke and you will understand why I think everyone should try this once. Those who do, tend to get hooked – and a spit-roast party makes a great annual event. For us, it's become a high point of the Dorset summer, with friends from far and wide pitching their tents for a night of feasting and revelry.

There are various approaches to spit roasting, with the variables being the fuel and the kind of kit that is used – firstly to manage the fire and secondly to suspend and turn the animal as it roasts. The most basic is a simple three-piece kit made of cast iron. The two spikes to support the spit are simply hammered into the ground, which must be firm enough to prevent them wobbling under the considerable weight of the spit-mounted animal. The fire, ideally of wooden logs, is lit directly on the ground. It will, of course, scorch the earth harshly, burning away any grass, so this is not recommended for lawns. The level is generally regulated by raising and lowering the meat by means of brackets or hooks on the vertical spikes, which support the spit at different heights. Or, even more crudely, on a one-height-only spit with a single bracket on top of each spike, you can simply manage the fire – building it up if it gets too cool or raking it away from the animal if it gets too hot.

The second is a more elaborate, but still quite portable, collapsible box-basket set-up, where the fire is suspended above the ground in two steel mesh baskets on short legs. This is what I now have, and what I used to roast the pig in the pictures on pages 390 and 392-3. You can see the constituent parts and how they all come together. It's particularly good for using on hard ground such as concrete and farmyards. The falling ash is easily swept up afterwards.

In either case the spit itself, on which the animal is mounted and suspended horizontally, will be roughly the same: a solid cast-iron or steel rod, 3-4cm in diameter, 2-2.5 metres in length, with holes drilled at, say, 20 cm intervals, at right angles through the rod. These holes are for the fixing skewers, of which you need five or six, that go through the animal to be roasted, through the holes, and out through the animal again, to stop it slipping on the spit as it is turned. This is an absolutely critical feature of the spit-kit, without which attempts to spit-roast whole animals are doomed to ignominious failure.

The final critical design feature, essential in either set-up, is some means of locking the spit in at least four, but preferably six or eight, different positions of rotation, so the animal can be cooked evenly all round. There are two traditional ways of achieving this. One is to incorporate a hexagonal or octagonal plate or section in the handle of the spit, and to form each of the support brackets on the vertical spike at the handle end into corresponding half-hexagons or octagons to receive it (like the head of a spanner receiving a nut). Provided both the plate and the bracket are robust and well fitted, this locks the spit very effectively in each of the positions.

The second way, which I have incorporated in my spit-kit, is to include a flat, circular plate in the handle of the spit at 90 degrees to the shaft, with a series of holes drilled around it (mine has eight). This circular plate meshes with a small square plate, with a single hole, welded on to each of the support brackets on the vertical spike at the handle end. The rotation is defined by which of the eight holes around the edge of the circular plate is matched with the hole on the support. A steel pin, on a short length of chain welded to the handle of the spit, is pushed through the two holes to lock the spit in position. It's less elegant than the first solution, but reliably robust and effective.

Ask around at farmers' markets or local farm shops and you may find you can borrow a spit-roasting kit. If you want one of your own, any good forge, blacksmith or welding workshop should be able to knock either version up for you if you provide them with a half-decent sketch (why not show them the photographs here?). Or see the Directory, page 530, for information on finding someone who can make them to order. The resulting kit should last a lifetime.

Fuel for spit roasting

I have heard of coal and coke being used as fuel for spit roasts but personally I wouldn't trust either not to impart some undesirable flavour. For me, the only choices are wood and charcoal. The former is more cost effective and the latter perhaps a little easier to manage, though it needs more frequent topping up and the charcoal (you'll need about twenty regular-sized bags) will almost certainly cost more than the pig, unless you buy direct from a charcoal maker (see page 529).

So wood is my choice, preferably well-seasoned hardwood (such as beach, oak or ash) that is nice and dry. Make a good pile of small logs well in advance, near, but not too near, the spit. It is, to say the least, a bore to have to go on a log run half way through the cooking. I speak from experience.

Choosing your animal

Advance planning is the key, and a few well-placed phone calls a month before your party will help to secure an animal of the right size. A good local butcher (the kind that remembers his or her customers' names) should be able to arrange a suitable animal for you, and may even know how to dress one for a spit roast. But buying direct from a farm will get you a better price, and many small-scale pig or lamb producers of the kind who sell at the farm gate or through farmers' markets will also know all about what you need for a spit roast.

For a pig, the most manageable size is between 35 and 50 kilos dead weight. When calculating how much you need, allow for about three to four people per kilo – depending on how many of your guests are children and how much other food is being provided. As ever, the so-called rare breeds, such as the Tamworth, Saddleback or Gloucester Old Spot, from small producers are the ones to go for: the slow-grown, close-grained meat responds so well to fire cooking and the extra layer of fat you can expect keeps everything well basted from the inside.

Ask for your pig with the head on and split up to the neck. It can either be set on the spit in a spread-eagled position (back and front legs spread out behind and in front of the body) or, my preference, in the 'sleeping dog' position – back legs tucked under its belly, front legs tucked under its chin (see pictures on pages 390 and 392). The latter is tidier and ends up shorter on the spit. The skin is less stretched and so less likely to split during roasting. But if you want it like this, you will have to ask for it, as the message has to be passed on to the slaughtermen, who need to set the carcass in this way before rigor mortis takes hold.

For a lamb, the size range is perhaps more variable, and may depend on seasonal availability. A small spring lamb might weigh 18-20 kilos, a good-sized autumn lamb or hogget nearly double that. Again, each kilo of lamb will feed three fairly hungry punters. The same possible positions – spread-eagle or sleeping dog – apply. Lambs come headless and skinless – meaning extra caution has to be taken, as the outer covering of fat can catch fire!

It's not advisable to take your meat directly from the butcher's cold room to the waiting, fired-up spit. This is because the animal will have been chilled right through to about 3-4°C, and the first couple of hours of cooking time, and fuel, will be wasted simply driving off the chill. Better to pick up the animal the day before, if you can keep it overnight somewhere where it won't be molested by opportunistic scavengers – the bath, for example. I wouldn't worry about a few flies. Even if they manage to lay some eggs on it, they won't get a chance to hatch and they'll be toasted to oblivion over the fire.

One option, which also leaves you with a bit less to worry about on the day, is to mount and skewer the pig on the spit the night before, and suspend it above an unlit fire overnight, wrapped in a large towel or sheet. By the time you come to begin the cooking, it will be at ambient temperature. But take the pig away from the fire while you are lighting it, replacing it only when the fire is well under way.

Preparing the animal

To mount either animal on the spit, the point of the spit is pushed – and let's not be too squeamish about this – through the arse, along the inside of the cavity, into the throat and out through the mouth (in the case of the pig) or the severed neck (in the case of the lamb). It does take a bit of pushing and shoving but you'll get there in the end. You then need to pass the fixing skewers through one side of the animal, through the holes in the spit, and out through the other side of the animal. You should use at least four skewers, at even intervals through the animal, to fix it securely on the spit.

The trotters or front feet can either be bound together, using strong wire, under the chin of the pig (or neck of the lamb), or bound to the last fixing skewer at the head end. The back feet, if not tucked up in the animal's belly, sleeping-dog style, can either be left hanging free or, for the full spread-eagled effect, bound to either end of an extra fixing skewer passed through an extra hole in the spit behind the animal's back end.

I don't believe in elaborate marinades or seasonings for animals to be spit roasted. All the delight and culinary excitement come in the combination of the very best meat and a well-managed fire. So I don't bother studding a whole lamb with rosemary and garlic, as I would a leg for roasting – though you could, if you had the patience. Instead, I give it a quick massage with olive oil, not so much for flavour but to help the simplest of seasonings – salt and freshly ground black pepper – to stick to the meat.

A pig merits a little more attention. If you want decent crackling – and of course you do – the skin must be scored all over. I like to do this in parallel lines, about 2 cm apart, across the shoulders, flanks and back of the pig, at right angles to the backbone all the way down. The best tool for the job is a Stanley knife or similar, with the blade retracted slightly at about 1-2 cm. You can then slash as hard as you like without any danger of going through the fat layer and into the meat. Then massage all over with a little oil and rub a few handfuls of flaky salt and plenty of freshly ground black pepper, along with a few sprigs of fresh thyme if you like, all over the scored skin, working it well into the cracks.

Some insist on basting the animal while it cooks. I don't think this is necessary with either a pig or a lamb, provided you have chosen a good animal with a reasonable covering of fat. The fat will continually drip from, and trickle over, the animal as it cooks – so why make life complicated by basting it with yet more fat?

It is possible to stuff an animal that is to be spit roasted – the entire cavity can be filled with a suitable stuffing and then sewn shut with butcher's string and a darning needle. In the hands of an expert, the results can be wonderful. But for the beginner, it's just more hard work, and an increasing likelihood that the cooking time will be misjudged (it takes forever to get the heat through the meat and into the stuffing). Once you've truly mastered the basics, you'll be able to work out the stuffed version for yourself.

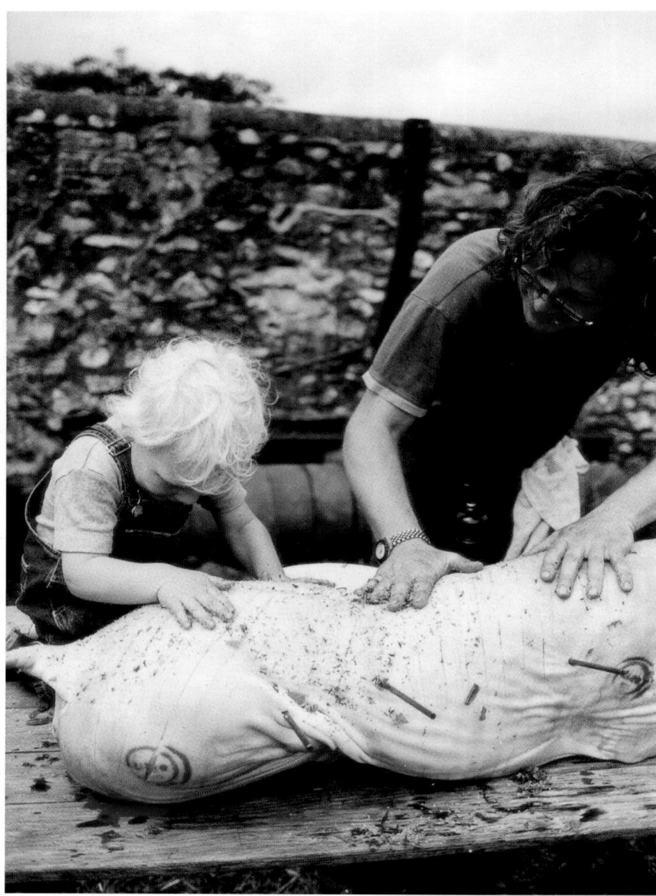

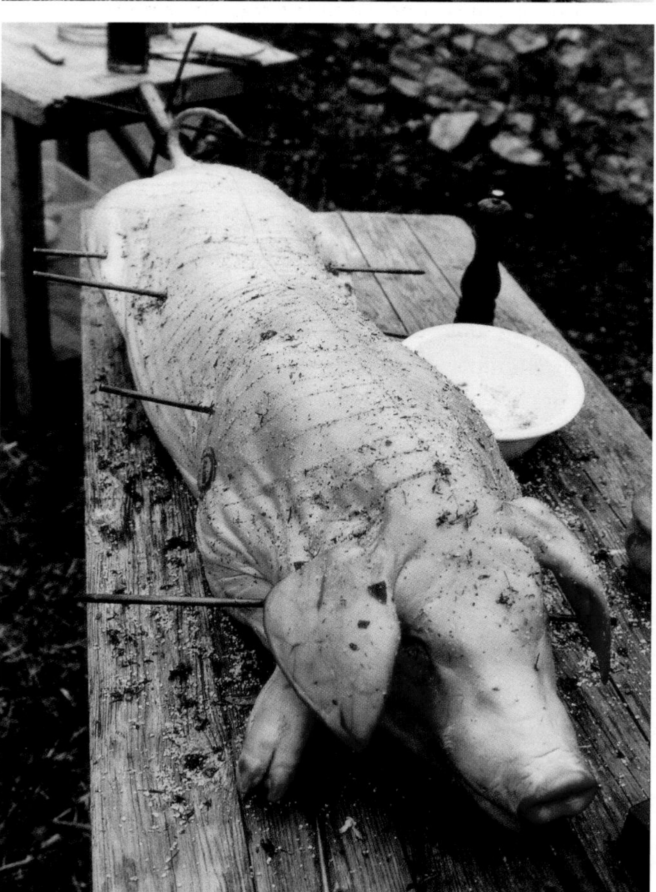

The cooking principle

You may think cooking over a spit is a fairly unsubtle, fierce kind of roasting. That is a dangerous thought, and one likely to lead unhappily to a charred outside and raw middle. It makes much more sense to think of it as a slow-cooking technique, almost as if you are poaching the creature whole in its skin. Slowly but surely over the course of a day, you are driving the heat towards the centre of the animal.

Whatever fuel or spit design you use, the cooking principle is the same: the animal is cooked by the *indirect* heat of the fire. That is to say, the flames are never directly under the animal (fat would drip into the fire and the skin would soon burn). Instead you create a column of heat along one or, better still, both sides of the animal. This is best achieved by either two parallel columns of fire (as in my suspended firebox kit opposite) or an oval ring of fire (as in the basic three-piece kit), in each case with the animal in the middle. The heat level is controlled by a combination of stoking and raking out the fire and, in the case of certain types of spit (as discussed above), raising and lowering the animal. Regular turning of the animal ensures even cooking.

The simple objective is to cook the animal right through without ever burning the outside to an unpalatable degree. With a pig, the icing on the cake is to achieve perfect edible crackling as well. This is certainly a challenge but it can be done – though I say it myself, the pig in the picture was pretty damn good (by which I mean that about 70 per cent of the available crackling was in fairly good order, the rest burned). In truth, even if you torch the crackling to inedible blackness, the meat inside should be so well protected by the skin that it will *still* be moist and delicious. But it's well worth striving for that crackling bonus.

It took me half a dozen pigs to work out the optimum procedure for pig perfection. My technique now is never to let the skin even begin to crackle until the pig is basically cooked. Then you can stoke up the fire and increase the heat to add that final, blistering, irresistible crackle. At this end stage, though, you have to watch it like a hawk, and speed up the frequency of your turns. Under this fierce final heat, crackling can go from golden perfection to charred disappointment in less than a minute.

You won't get crackling off a lamb, of course. But if you take it slow and steady you can, as well as delicious, tender meat, also have that crisp outer layer of fat brown and tasty rather than black and bitter.

In my experience, a decent-sized porker of 40-50 kilos will take at least eight hours, and it would be better to have about ten to play with. A lamb of, say, 25-40 kilos will cook a little faster – in about six or seven hours. A final tip for both animals: the thickest parts – i.e. the rump and shoulders – will naturally take longer to cook through than the loin and belly, especially as the open cavity allows hot air to circulate around this middle section. It's therefore worth trying to redress this balance by maintaining a fire that is hotter at the two ends than it is in the middle. It's easy with a bit of practice.

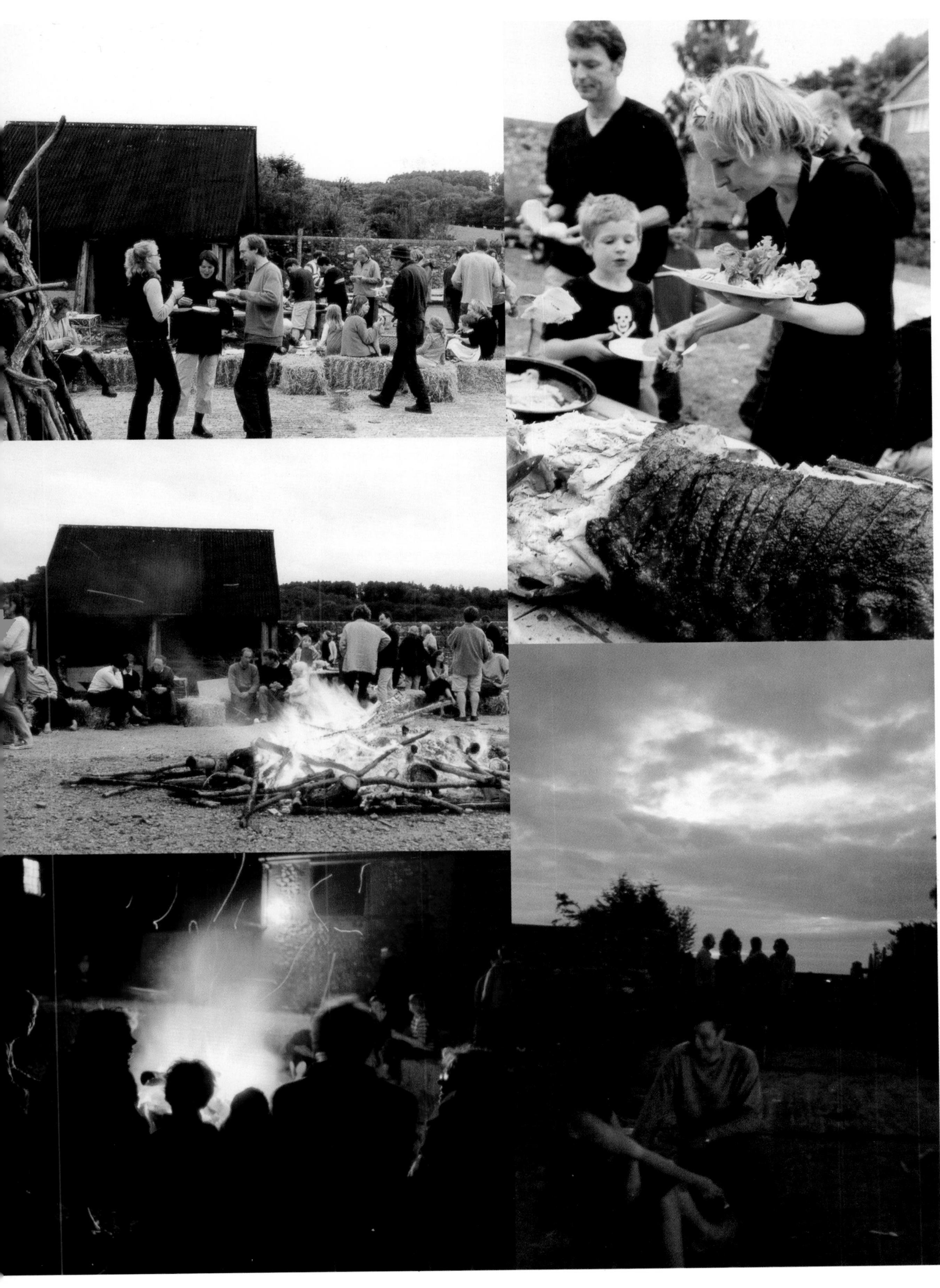

There is certainly no shame in having a meat thermometer handy to test for doneness. Push it into the thickest part of the shoulder and the rump, (anthropomorphically speaking, right into the armpit and the groin). For pork it should read about 65-70°C, for lamb 55-60°C. As ever, resting the meat is definitely a good idea. Remove it from the fire and carry it to the carving station (I suggest a hefty trestle table that you don't mind getting greasy). Leave for half an hour or so to settle, then remove all the skewers and the spit before carving.

Serving up the meat

With a pig, the first thing to do is pull off all the crackling and roughly chop or break it up. Pile it on to several plates, season with a bit of extra salt and pepper and ask a couple of trusted guests to pass it round while you carve up the meat.

I'm not going to give you technical instructions for carving – either for a pig or a lamb. Enthusiasm and a sharp knife will get you through. Just aim for thickish slices, two or three of which will go nicely into a roll or baguette. Plates, knives and forks are more trouble than they are worth when feeding this kind of food to large numbers, so some kind of sandwich is definitely the way to go, plus a few paper plates for those who just want to eat the meat with their fingers. And once you have delivered a generous amount of meat into a gaping roll or waiting plate, point the bearer in the direction of a groaning table of accompaniments, so they can fix it their way. Here are my suggestions:

With pork

Choice of pickles and chutneys (page 515)
Hoisin sauce
Good home-made mayonnaise (page 513)

With lamb

Salsa Verde (page 514)
Real Mint Sauce (page 512)
Redcurrant jelly

General

Huge pile of small new potatoes, boiled and buttered (or cold potato salad)
French bean vinaigrette
Huge salad of seasonal greens
Tomato salad (if seasonal)

BARBECUED GLAZED SPARE RIBS

1-2 racks of ribs or sticking of pork (allow about 4 ribs per person, assuming other meats are being served)

THE MARINADE:

2-3 large garlic cloves, peeled

1 level teaspoon salt

1 tablespoon English mustard

2 tablespoons soft brown sugar

2 tablespoons tomato ketchup

1 tablespoon dark soy sauce

Plenty of freshly ground black pepper (about 2 teaspoons)

2-3 tablespoons vinegar (brown rice vinegar is good)

This is barbecue cooking at its sticky-fingered best – though the dish will also work in the oven if weather doesn't permit. You can either barbecue a whole rack of ribs or subdivide the rack into smaller portions, but don't go smaller than three ribs joined together or they'll get over-frazzled. Another thing you can use is an old-fashioned butcher's cut called a sticking of pork (see page 117) – a piece trimmed off from the hand of the pork to leave a tidier joint. The sticking has some ribs attached to some deliciously fatty meat from the shoulder, and it's what you see in the picture opposite.

On a chopping board, crush the garlic and salt together with a fork to make a paste and then scrape it into a bowl. Add all the other ingredients for the marinade, the vinegar last of all, a little at a time. Mix well, adding just enough vinegar to make a thick emulsion that will coat the ribs well. Spread the marinade over the ribs so that they are well coated on all sides and leave them in a shallow dish for at least 1 hour, preferably 4 or 5. Feel free to turn and re-coat them once or twice during this time.

When the barbecue is up to speed (i.e. moderately hot, as prescribed for pork on page 380), place the ribs over the coals without wiping off the marinade. Turn frequently to avoid over-blackening, painting and dabbing them with extra marinade as you go. A certain amount of blackening is acceptable, indeed desirable in the end, but don't let it happen too soon. The ribs should take 10-12 minutes, a sticking 15 minutes or more.

Eat with fingers, gnawing every last morsel off the bone.

BEEFBURGERS

Beef silverside, rump, chuck steak or skirt (allow at least 200g untrimmed meat per burger/person)

The best (least artificial) baps or burger buns you can lay your hands on – or use sections of thick baguette

Salt and freshly ground black pepper

CHOICE OF TOPPINGS:

Sliced ripe tomatoes (lightly dressed with olive oil, if you like)

Finely sliced raw onions

Good butterhead or Cos lettuce (not iceberg), roughly torn if you like, but not shredded

Tomato ketchup (see p.516 for home-made)

Mayonnaise (see p.513 for home-made)

Dill pickled cucumbers, sliced

Thinly sliced mild cheese (I think Gruyère or Edam is better than Cheddar)

A home-made beefburger, just a bit pink in the middle, barbecue-grilled and served in a bun with your own personalised choice of toppings, is very, very hard to beat. But the burger has to be right – good lean meat, well aged, and minced not too fine. Personally I think it is not too extravagant to use silverside, topside or even rump steak for making burgers, but chuck steak (from the shoulder, often sold as braising steak) is also very good if well trimmed of any sinewy bits. And skirt, again carefully trimmed, makes excellent burgers.

I would always prefer to buy the meat and then mince or chop it myself at home. And I don't season it at all, adding salt and pepper only to the burger as it grills and again as it goes on the bun.

If using meat from the freezer (page 61), bear in mind that chilled or even partially frozen meat minces better than warm, so don't over-thaw it. Wipe the meat as dry as possible with a cloth and trim it carefully, scrupulously removing all sinew and gristle but leaving a few odd pieces of good clean fat. Mince the meat on a coarse setting, or chop it by hand with a large heavy knife until you have a coarse mince that binds together well.

Burgers should be made up as close to barbecuing time as possible. Take a generous handful of meat, weighing about 150g, and pack it into a tight ball between your hands. Flatten gently between your palms, pressing the edges in with your fingertips to make a well-bound patty.

The final shape and thickness of each patty is a matter of personal choice but there are various factors to consider – most notably, how pink do you want it in the middle and how burnt do you want it on the outside? A thick, rounded burger can give you the best of both worlds: a fairly charred exterior, rich in caramelised meat and charcoal-smoky flavours, and a centre that is still pink, or even almost raw. Another option is to have a discus-shaped burger, with a fat middle but thinner, tapered edges. The thinking behind this is that you will get a nicely charred, 'well-done' outer edge on your burger while the middle remains pink and juicy. It seems to work. Even a well-done burger should be juicy and, with that in mind, I wouldn't make a burger less than 2.5cm thick.

Lightly brush each patty with oil, then place on the barbecue over a high heat. Burgers have a tendency to stick on the barbecue grill bars, even when oiled, so a sharp spatula that can be run under them is a must (as is a rich vocabulary of child-friendly expletives, 'Burger!' being a useful example). The longer you leave the burger, the less likely it is to stick, as the charring of the meat slowly releases it from the bars of the grill. Pressing the burger down on the grill with the spatula may help to accelerate this process (and will also speed up the cooking).

Given the inevitable variation in burger thickness and barbecue temperature, not to mention personal taste, it's hard to give precise guidelines for cooking times

and turning points. But I can say that, stuck or not, I like to flip my burger after just 3-4 minutes, as I want it fairly rare. And a couple of minutes on the other side usually finish it off. My wife, who likes her burger literally raw (and I mean fridge cold) in the middle, gives it scarcely a minute on each side, but the barbecue has to be very hot. Don't forget to season lightly with salt and pepper just before you turn the burger.

What's important is to know your own kit, and your own taste, and to concentrate on the job in hand. Burgers require greater precision than other barbecue foods, because an overcooked burger is spoiled (whereas chicken, pork or sausages may be more forgiving). But once you've tamed the burger and the barbie, you'll find you are able to turn out anything from a well-done to a bloody-as-hell with instinctive ease.

When you think your burger is done as you like it, set it to rest off the heat for a minute or two while you prepare your bun and appropriate garnishes. I can't possibly tell you what you like on your burger but I can suggest some choices (see above) and I can tell you what I like. My own customised burger comprises the following stack, from the ground up, as it were:

Bun base, mayonnaise 1, lettuce, ketchup, salt and pepper 1, burger, sliced tomatoes, salt and pepper 2, mayonnaise 2, bun top.

I might occasionally go for a cheeseburger, in which case the cheese goes directly on top of the burger to encourage melting, and a few sliced onions might get a look in on top of the cheese. I never butter the bun, nor do I toast it, and the bun I prefer is a soft, flour-dusted bap made by a local baker.

Incidentally, my favourite indoor way to cook a burger is on a lightly oiled heavy-based frying pan. They tend to stick on a ridged grill pan, as they do on the barbecue, so if you are not reaping the benefit of the charcoal flavour you may as well spare yourself the grief.

SOUVLAKI *Serves 6*

1 kg boned-out shoulder or leg of lamb, trimmed and cut into large cubes (about 4 cm)

3 garlic cloves, bashed with the side of a knife

Grated zest and juice of 1 lemon, unwaxed if possible

2 teaspoons dried oregano

2 bay leaves, broken up

1 tablespoon fresh oregano (if available)

3 tablespoons olive oil

Salt and freshly ground black pepper

The unmistakable tang of the authentic Greek kebab, souvlaki, comes from the combination of lemon (zest as well as juice) with dried and fresh oregano. The dried oregano that you can buy in Greece, and in some Greek-run delis over here, seems to be very special and distinctive and is worth seeking out. The 'lamburger' version is great, too, and very child friendly.

In a large bowl, mix the lamb with all the other ingredients, but no salt yet, then cover and put in the fridge. Leave for at least 6 hours or overnight.

Divide the meat between 6 long skewers, soaked in water for 30 minutes first, if wooden. Lay them over a hot barbecue (or indoors on a ridged grill pan). Turn after a couple of minutes, then continue to turn regularly, basting occasionally with the marinade juices and seasoning with the odd sprinkling of salt. They'll take about 6-9 minutes. You can serve them just pink if you like, although the Greek style is to have them fairly well done. But don't let them dry out.

Serve with, or in, warmed pitta bread, with Hummus (page 514) and a simple tomato and onion salad, too.

Variation

Souvlaki Lamburgers: Combine exactly the same seasonings with 1kg coarsely minced lamb (or minced leftover roast lamb) and mix thoroughly together. Leave for at least an hour for the flavours to infuse. Form into patties 2 cm thick and barbecue, grill or fry in olive oil at a merry sizzle (see page 330) for 4-5 minutes on each side, till nicely browned and cooked through. Serve as for souvlaki.

INDIAN-SPICED LAMB SKEWERS *Serves 6*

1 kg boned-out shoulder or leg of lamb or mutton, trimmed and cut into 4 cm cubes

1-4 small dried red chillies (depending on size and heat)

2 teaspoons coriander seeds

1 teaspoon fenugreek seeds

1 teaspoon mustard seeds

1 teaspoon black peppercorns

1 teaspoon red peppercorns (if available)

1 tablespoon olive or sunflower oil

3 garlic cloves, finely chopped

Salt

Lamb is the ultimate meat for barbecuing, its unmistakable flavour always shining through the smoky, chargrilled taste. So here is another variation on the lamb kebab theme, this time with a dry spicing that is more Indian in style, and definitely for those who like it hot. Again, you can use the same marinade for lamb chops.

Serve with plain rice or naan bread, a good fruity chutney, and a cooling raita made by mixing plain yoghurt with a little crushed garlic, diced cucumber, salt and pepper.

Split the chillies open and remove and discard the seeds. Place in a pestle and mortar with the other dry spices and pound to a coarse powder.

Put the lamb in a bowl and mix with the oil and garlic, massaging it well so it is covered with a light film of oil. Toss thoroughly with the pounded spices and then leave to marinate for at least 2 hours.

Thread the meat on to 6 long skewers, soaked in water for 30 minutes first, if wooden. Lay them over a hot barbecue (or indoors on a ridged grill pan). Turn after a couple of minutes, then continue to turn regularly, seasoning with the odd sprinkling of salt. They'll take about 6-8 minutes to be cooked right through, but you can serve them a little pinker if you like.

Variation

Indian-spiced Lamburgers: As with souvlaki, the burger version works extremely well. Use the same quantities of seasonings for 1 kg minced lamb – but be cautious with the chillies (use ½ teaspoon dried chilli flakes, if you like). Form into patties 2 cm thick and barbecue (or fry) for 4-5 minutes on each side, till nicely browned and cooked through. Serve with the same accompaniments.

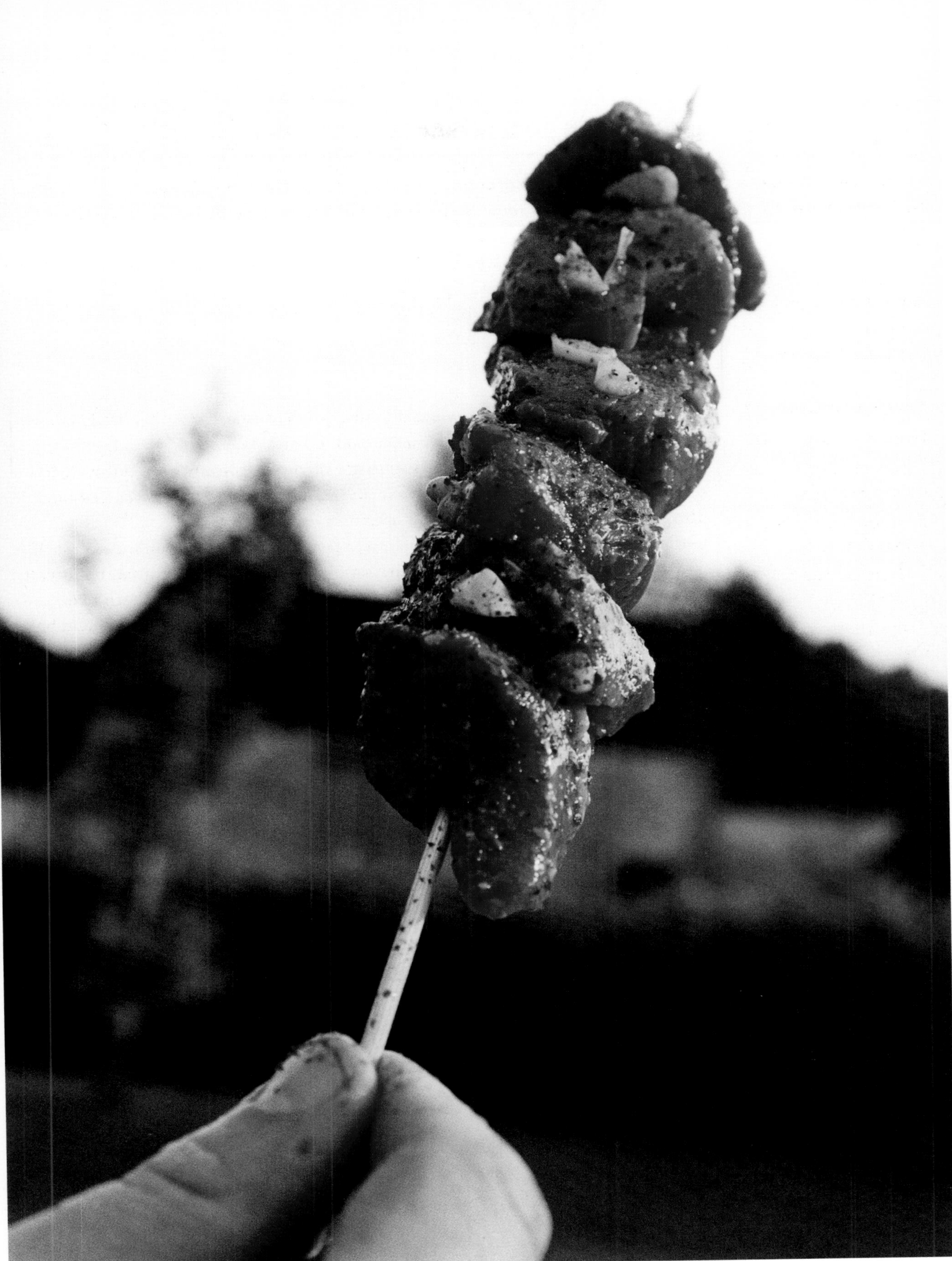

BARBECUED ROSEMARY LAMB WITH SALSA VERDE *Serves 6*

6 butterflied lamb portions, from ½ large leg (p.96), or cut up in large cubes for skewering

A dozen good sprigs of rosemary

6 garlic cloves, bashed to release the husk, then roughly chopped

2-3 tablespoons olive oil

A few good twists of black pepper

Salsa Verde (p.514), to serve

The simple procedure of chargrilling lightly marinated lamb and serving it pink with salsa verde was something I learned as a chef at the River Café. I often come back to it. Boning and 'butterflying' a leg of lamb (page 96) produces neat portions, which expose a greater surface area of the meat to both the marinade and the barbecue than straight-cut leg steaks. But if such surgery daunts you, then cutting the meat into cubes and mounting them on wooden skewers after marinating does much the same job. Or use lamb chops.

Both versions can be cooked indoors, on a ridged cast-iron grill pan.

Bruise the rosemary needles by rubbing the sprigs in your hand, then roughly strip the needles into a bowl. Add the garlic, olive oil and pepper and then the meat. Toss all together well and leave for at least 2 hours (4-6 would be good).

Remove the meat from the marinade and wipe it lightly (you don't want it dripping with oil), but leave bits of garlic and rosemary sticking to it. Place the portions (or 5 or 6 cubes mounted on a wooden skewer that has been soaked in water for about 30 minutes) over a fairly hot barbecue. Let them sear on the bars for a couple of minutes and they should turn without sticking, then turn them every couple of minutes to prevent too much blackening on one side. Depending on the thickness of the meat and how pink you want it, the butterflied pieces will take 9-15 minutes, the kebabs 6-10.

Serve with salsa verde, in a bun or split pitta bread. Or plate up more formally, accompanied by chargrilled vegetables (since you've got the barbecue going) or Ratatouille (page 522) and, perhaps, Rosemary Roast New Potatoes (page 518).

LUCY'S JERK CHICKEN *Serves 6-10*

1 or 2 whole chickens, or 2kg chicken portions, in all cases free range or organic

Lemon or lime juice

Salt

THE SEASONING:

10g each of sea salt, black peppercorns and dried pimento berries (also known as allspice)

5g mace

1/2 cinnamon stick (or 5g ground cinnamon)

1 onion, finely chopped

2 teaspoons fresh thyme (no stalks!)

4-5 bay leaves, torn into little pieces

2 Scotch bonnet chillies, finely chopped

1 tablespoon brown sugar

3 tablespoons olive oil

30g butter

Juice of 2 limes, or 1 large lemon

I asked my friend, Lucy Pilkington, for her recipe for jerk chicken and she wrote about it so compellingly and comprehensively that I reproduce her e-mail here almost verbatim. I would add only that the procedure works extremely well for pork chops and duck legs, too. And I prefer not to skin my chicken but to make a few slashes through the skin, into the meat, to help it take up the marinade.

Lucy writes, 'No one knows what the term jerk really means. It originated as a way of cooking meat, first amongst the indigenous Indians of the Caribbean (Arawaks and others) and later by the 'maroons' – runaway slaves of the Spanish and English, who became a fierce anti-slavery rebel force. Essentially the meat is slowly barbecued in spices. Most often they would jerk a whole pig but today jerk chicken is as common as pork. In Jamaica it's like the original fast food – you buy pieces of delicious jerk chicken in tin foil from guys in the street, who cook it on grilling trays over charcoal. They serve it with hard dough bread (a sweet white loaf) or 'festival' – a kind of sweet fried dumpling. In the UK you can find jerk chicken in Caribbean takeaways, but the best I've had is the chicken that's cooked at home or at a carnival.

I usually use two chickens, cut up into quarters or sometimes eighths – or for a big party I'll just do a tray of drumsticks and wings. It doesn't matter if you use rough old boiling chickens, either, as these are probably the best for cooking for a long time. What matters is that the meat should be so well cooked that it's turning dark pink – white meat is frowned on by Jamaicans!

Seasoning

There are as many different seasonings as there are people who cook jerk chicken; I've used loads. If you want to be lazy, the best jar of jerk mix is Walker's Wood, which is quite easily found in grocer's shops that stock Caribbean food – I have found it in Sainsbury's a couple of times, too. But home-made seasoning is best. It keeps in the fridge for a month, so it's a good idea to make enough to last a few batches.

The two key flavours of jerk are heat (from Scotch bonnet chillies) and spiciness (from allspice, mace and cinnamon). Scotch bonnet chillies are small, red or yellow, bell-shaped peppers found in Caribbean grocer's and often in halal butcher's. In my opinion, they are the only peppers to use – even those green chillies that are often presented as a substitute aren't powerful enough. Scotch bonnet chillies are extremely hot and should only be handled with gloves on – if you don't have any spare gloves, wrap your hands in clingfilm when chopping them or you could be in for a nasty surprise when you rub your eyes!

Brown sugar (some people use honey) and butter make the chicken nice and brown on the outside.

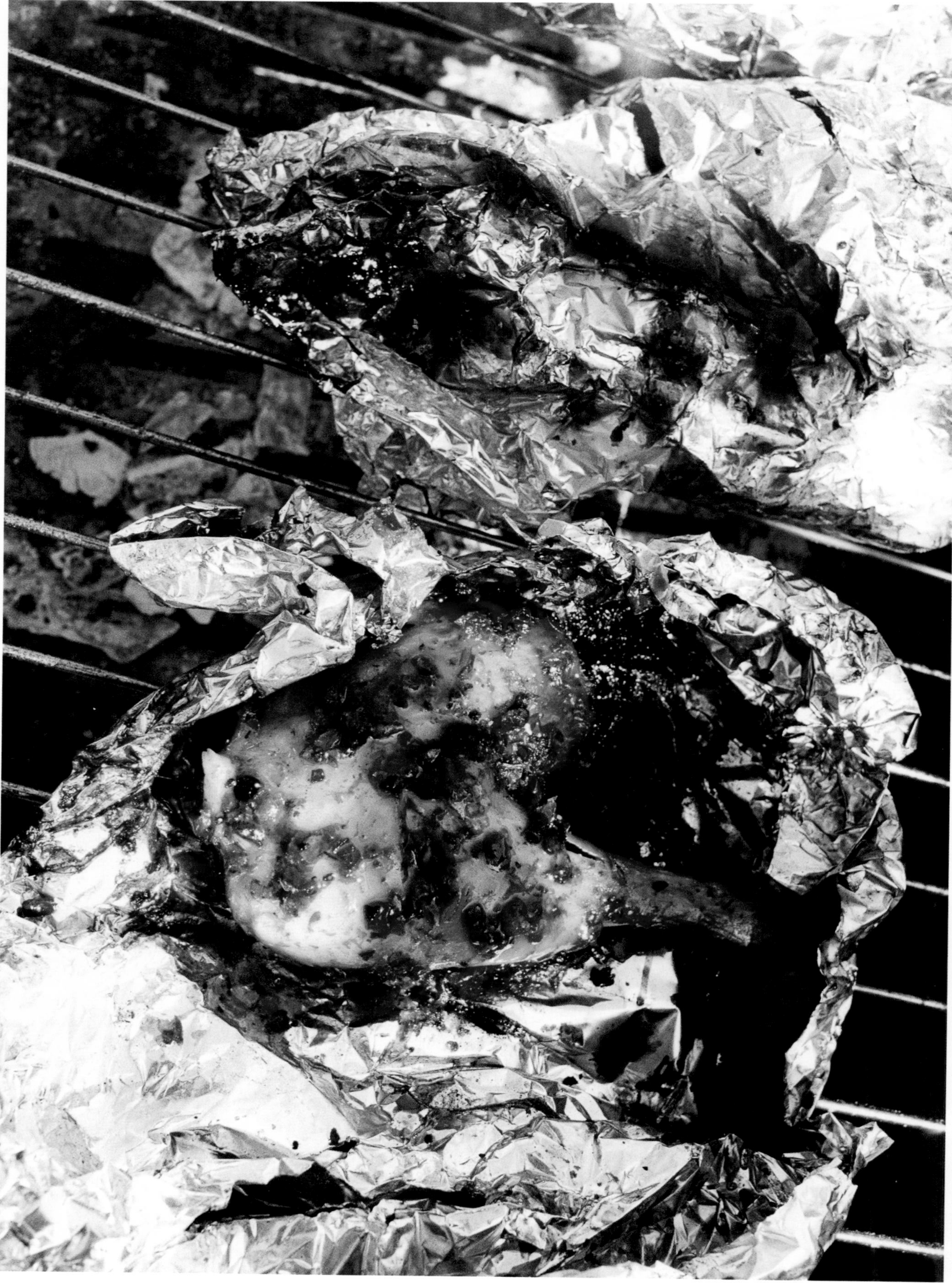

So, for the seasoning, mill the black peppercorns and pimento, grate the mace and chop the cinnamon stick. Then put them in a food processor with all the other seasoning ingredients and blend until it's a rough paste (before I had a food processor I would blend the dry stuff – black peppercorns, pimento and salt – in a pestle and mortar, then mash in the finely chopped herbs, chopped onion, and add the lime juice, oil, sugar and butter – all a bit laborious). The paste should smell and taste very lively – if it seems a bit well behaved, add more pepper, or if it's too overpoweringly hot, add more allspice, lime juice and sugar.

The chicken

Wash the chicken in water and rub it with lemon or lime juice and salt. I always skin my chicken legs, using a damp clean tea towel to get a grip and ripping the skin off from the thigh to the foot, but others like to leave the skin on. Then mix in a big bowl with the jerk paste. This is done with your hands, and takes quite a lot of kneading to make sure it's rubbed in really well.

Leave the chicken to marinate in the fridge overnight. It's never the same if you just leave it for a few hours – it needs time to work its way right into the meat, which is another reason I skin it.

To cook

Place the marinated chicken on a baking tray lined with foil and cover with a loose sheet of foil. Bake at 180°C/Gas Mark 4 for an hour, then uncover the chicken and cook for a further 45 minutes-1 hour. It should be brown on the outside, but not burnt, and very soft.

It's best done on the barbecue, though, in which case you cook it, covered, for an hour in the oven before finishing it off, uncovered, on the barbecue. Or do as they do in Jamaica, and cook it on the cooler sides of the barbecue in individual foil parcels (no need to bake it in the oven first). The parcels are slashed half way through cooking to allow the smoky flavours of the charcoal to penetrate.'

SPICED HOT-SMOKED LIVER *Serves 4*

300-400g fresh liver, in a single piece

THE SPICE RUB:

1 tablespoon salt

1 tablespoon soft brown sugar

2 teaspoons crushed or ground allspice berries

2 teaspoons English mustard

2-3 bay leaves, finely shredded

The first time I tasted this dish was in Lapland, where it was made with reindeer liver. It took me a while to improvise my own version, made with lamb's liver from my own sheep, but it was worth the effort. It also works with cow's and pig's liver. Ideally choose a clean, neatly shaped piece of liver without too many ventricles.

You need a hot smoker for this dish, which can be easily improvised, as explained on pages 385-6.

Peel off the thin outer membrane from the liver. Mix together all the ingredients for the spice rub and smear it all over the liver. Leave for at least 2, but not more than 4, hours, then wipe off completely.

Place the liver on a rack above 2 tablespoons of oak or other hardwood sawdust and a teaspoon of demerara sugar sprinkled over the base of your smoke tin. Place the tin over its burners, or on a barbecue or an open fire, and leave for about 30 minutes. Remove from the heat and set aside until the box is cool. Remove the liver and refrigerate.

Serve the chilled smoked liver cut into thin slices, with bread or toast, and a little Onion Marmalade (see page 516) if you like. Wrapped in clingfilm in the fridge, the spiced liver will keep for a couple of weeks. Vac-pack it and it will keep for a month.

Yeo Valley
ORGANIC

14. PRESERVING AND PROCESSING

14. PRESERVING AND PROCESSING

Cured Meats, Sausages, Pâtés and Terrines

People have been salting and curing animal flesh, mostly from mammals and fish, for millennia – at least ten of them. Before refrigeration, this was the only way to keep this precious commodity for any length of time without it spoiling. People quickly observed that the action of salt on meat was to draw out the liquid. And they noticed that this salted, desiccated meat was highly resistant to decay and infestation. This observation was critical to the stabilisation of human settlement. It can be no coincidence that those who became most adept at exploiting it, no doubt largely through having unlimited access to the vital raw material, soon became the most cosmopolitan civilisation on the planet – the ancient Egyptians.

Since then, every human society with access to plentiful salt has used this method of preserving meat, and as a result there are hundreds of different cured meat products around the globe. They range from English bacon and Jewish pastrami to African ostrich biltong and Hungarian donkey salami. There are thousands of regional variations in the way they are spiced and flavoured – practically every known herb and spice gets an outing in a cured meat product somewhere on the planet.

However, despite all this far-flung exotica, there are still only two basic ingredients required to preserve meat successfully, and one of them is free. They are salt and fresh air. And some of the most utterly irresistible of all meat dishes are produced by the skilful use of these, and no other, ingredients. The best air-dried hams, from Spain, Italy, Switzerland, France (and, now, dare I say, West Dorset), must surely be contenders for the (admittedly absurd) title of Most Delicious Food in the World.

Meanwhile, a rather less rarefied form of cured pork has come to symbolise, to Western culture at least, the very essence of savoury deliciousness. I may not always be ready to credit the majority with good taste in meat but even I wouldn't dispute the wisdom and rightness of the almost universal adoration of bacon – at least in communities that sanction the eating of pigs. So whether you're a gourmet or a greedy guts, the process of curing by salting, so easily taken for granted, is absolutely critical for a full appreciation of what meat has to offer the human diet. Despite being born of necessity, or perhaps because of it, an appetite for salted meat seems to have entered the human psyche as a permanent fixture. After all, it's no secret that almost every vegetarian admits they miss bacon.

Yet curiously, very few of us have any idea how to go about preserving pork, or any other meat. Although almost all carnivores eat bacon and ham with frequency, and relish (a dab of HP sauce for the former, English mustard for the latter), hardly anyone ever makes them at home, or even knows how they are made. I think this is a great shame, as the techniques are neither difficult nor time consuming. Yes, a little patience is required, as you have to wait days, sometimes weeks, for your work to come to fruition. But the actual time you spend working to make them, rather than waiting to eat them, is measured in minutes. If you've never tried it you'll probably find this hard to believe, but it honestly doesn't take more than ten minutes in the kitchen (using ingredients that, if you haven't already got in your cupboard, you can find in any corner shop) to turn a slab of good pork belly into delicious streaky bacon, or a leg from a fine rare-breed pig into a sensational ham.

Such recipes, along with those for more elaborate charcuterie, are pretty much essential in the repertoire of those who keep a few pigs for their own consumption. But I see no reason why such pleasures should be restricted to the smallholder, or even the country dweller. If you can get hold of good pork (see page 113), you can make great bacon. And here's another promise: the cured meats you make at home will be the most delicious you'll eat anywhere. Why be a slave to the clumsy, crude and chemical cures of the huge industrial pig-processors when you can do it all yourself so much better?

As you're probably beginning to guess, I really, really, *really* want you to have a go at this. And this is the reason I have included simple instructions for making your own dry-cured bacon and brine-cured ham in the recipe section of this chapter (starts on page 429, if you can't wait any longer).

Those of you who have a copy of *The River Cottage Cookbook* may already be aware of my evangelical fervour about home curing pork. And you may also know that it contains full (and, I believe, reliable) instructions for curing just about an entire pig. So, beyond the short-and-sweet bacon recipe and the brine-cured ham (which, anyway, is prepared here with my all-new-and-improved favourite brine recipe), I'm not, you'll probably be relieved to hear, going to reprise all that here. If you want detailed recipes for salami, chorizo, air-dried hams, rillons, black pudding and various fresh pork sausages, you'll know where to find them.

So in the rest of this section, my plan is to place a little less emphasis on these pork-specific charcuteries and a little more on the basic techniques of simple curing and processing, from both the British tradition and the wider culinary culture. And in the recipes that follow I will be introducing a current crop of favourites, as well as plugging a few crucial gaps in the traditional canon: rillettes of pork, the Italian dry-cured beef known as bresaola, the superb boiling sausage called cotechino, confit of goose and duck, and good old faggots – recipes that could easily have appeared in *The River Cottage Cookbook* but somehow didn't.

Incidentally, by the term 'processing' rather than 'preserving' or 'curing', I refer to those techniques that transform meat pretty radically in form and texture, partly with a view to making it keep at least a little longer but more specifically with the aim of making it more palatable, and more convenient, to eat.

These concoctions – of pâtés, potted meats, pasties and pies, for example – are some of the dishes through which a cook is best able to express his or her commitment to a holistic approach to meat – the philosophy of 'nose-to-tail' eating of which I have made so much in this book. This is because they often involve the grinding up of off-cuts and offals, the boiling and jellification of heads, tails and feet, and the all-round thrifty resourcefulness that, in bygone years, saw the good husbandry of the farmer carried through into the good housekeeping of his wife.

With some of these techniques, the simple fact of heavy seasoning and, in most cases, thorough cooking already goes some way towards improving the meats' keeping qualities. These are often further enhanced by cunning traditional ways of packing the finished dishes – in sterilised jars, covered with a layer of fat, for example – so they are protected from airborne contaminants. These days, a miniature vac-pack machine also serves the home-curer/processor in good stead.

As with preserving, the traditional techniques of processing meat are among the least exercised procedures in the modern kitchen. Making pâtés and terrines, faggots, sausages and the like is not entirely a dying art but it is an art left on the whole to professional specialists and perhaps a few enthusiastic amateurs, like me, who may just be regarded as a little eccentric. Well, we are not so mad as you might think – as you will discover if you embark on a little experimentation of your own. Some recipes – an old-fashioned raised pork pie, with a lard and hot water crust and a delicious cavity-filling jellied pork stock, for example – are indeed a time-consuming labour of love, and all the more satisfying for that. Others, such as simple pâtés, can be whipped up in minutes.

Before we get on to specific recipes, here's a brief review of the fundamental techniques – starting at the salty end, with traditional salt-based curing, moving through potting and pâté making and their various associates, and on to the processing of fresh meat into sausages and patties for boiling and frying.

Naturally I expect you to begin processing and preserving without delay. In almost all cases I think you'll be pleasantly surprised by the lack of hard labour involved. And I predict you will be utterly delighted by the results – which are sure to rank with anything you've had from the swankiest deli.

Dry Curing

Dry curing is nothing more or less than the direct application of salt to meat. Rub handfuls of salt into pork bellies once every day for a week and you have streaky bacon, ready to slice and fry. Do the same to a brisket or silverside of beef and you have classic salt beef, ready for boiling. Pack a whole leg of pork in salt, with a weight on top, leave well alone and in three or four weeks you will have a dry-cured ham. You can boil it and bake it, or hang it for a year and eat it raw.

Almost any part of any animal will have been tossed or packed or rubbed in salt somewhere in the world. In Spain and Portugal, and hence many of the countries they colonised, the tails, trotters, ears and snouts of pigs are often preserved by dry salting, then rinsed, soaked and boiled up with all kinds of other meats, both cured and fresh, to make the dish known as *cozida* – or, in Brazil, where the dish includes black beans, *feijoada*. I have taken to doing this with

these parts of my own pigs, and the resulting dish, which we usually have some time in January, is always a treat. The recipe is on page 487.

None of this is rocket science. About the only serious 'don't' of dry curing, or any curing, is 'don't let the salt have any prolonged contact with metal'. So, in choosing a vessel in which to salt your meat, think ceramic, wooden or plastic. An old wooden wine crate or extra-large plastic Tupperware box is quite adequate. Then keep the salting meat in a cool larder, outhouse or cellar, covered to ward off pesky flies (or stick it in the fridge if you can make the space). The liquid drawn from the meat by the salt will quickly turn your dry cure into a wet cure. It's best to pour this off every day before you apply fresh salt.

To the question 'how long do I cure for?' there is no simple answer. The longer you cure meat in salt, the more stable, and salty, it will become. Meats cured to the point of great longevity will, like salt fish, have to be soaked in clean fresh water, for hours if not days, to draw out the salt and make them palatable again. But the overall cure time ranges from about four days for a lightly cured 250g strip of belly to six weeks for a thoroughly cured 15kg ham or a massive slab of beef brisket.

And that's really all the information you need to begin your adventures in dry curing. Of course, there's no end of avenues to explore. A little subtle alchemy comes into play when you begin to customise your dry cure, adding to the salt such potent aromatics as bay leaves, juniper, coriander, cloves, mace and citrus zest, and such natural sweeteners as sugar, molasses or honey. There are accurate combinations prescribed for flavouring such cures from meat to meat and culture to culture. But at the same time there are no strict rules of engagement here, and improvisation is greatly to be encouraged.

Brine Curing

This is a modest technical evolution of the salting process that allows the salt to be dissolved in water, producing a salty liquor, or brine, in which the meat is completely immersed. The advantage is that the meat is thoroughly surrounded and covered by its cure.

To be effective, a brine must be sufficiently concentrated, with a high enough salt content to draw moisture from, and penetrate into, the meat. The correct concentration is, roughly, no less than 3 litres of water and no more than 4 to every kilo of salt. A good test for a brine is to put a potato in it. It should bob happily on the surface. If it sinks, the brine is too weak. It is easier to dissolve salt in warm or hot water than in cold, but it must be thoroughly cooled again before the meat is added.

Whilst a very serviceable brine can be made from nothing more than salt and water combined in the correct ratio, the flavouring of brines has, as you might expect, evolved to a fine art – even more so than with dry curing. This is achieved in part by the addition of strong herbs and spices but also by the choice of liquid, which need not be pure water. For the various English regional hams, it may be a local beer or cider, or apple juice. For Italian cured silverside of beef (bresaola), it is red wine. And many brines, like dry cures, are sweetened with sugar.

Industrial curing, of hams and bacons in particular, attempts to cure the meat 'instantly' by the direct injection of an artificially flavoured and E-number-laced brine, using thousands of tiny hollow needles. It's a doubly cynical exercise, in that it is intended not merely to save time (and therefore money) but also to bolster the water content of the product, so that when it is sold by weight the profit margins are significantly higher. The resulting bacon and gammon may look lean, moist and appealing to the unknowing purchaser, but when it is laid in a hot frying pan it rapidly contracts to expel the brine, along with most of any other residual moisture. Hence the incredible shrinking bacon effect, and the pool of scummy liquid that collects in the pan.

Traditionally brined hams, and dry-cured bacons, are far more honest and appetising products. The curing process has been subtle and slow, so that the natural contraction of the meat as moisture is withdrawn is complete by the end of the process. This means the best qualities of good pork – faint traces of fat within the lean, and a whole heap of porky flavour – are retained. Plus, what you see is pretty much what you get, in that there will be only a little further moisture loss during cooking.

By making your own bacon and hams, you will set a benchmark for excellence – standards that, once appreciated, you should never need to slip from.

Air Drying: Hams, Salami and Biltong

Air drying is not strictly a way of curing meat but of maturing meat that has already been cured, either by dry salting or in a brine. As the meat hangs in the air, it continues to dry and its natural flavours, along with any aromatics introduced into the cure, intensify over time. Most air-dried meats are intended to be eaten raw – and very thinly sliced. But in some instances – particularly if they end up unpalatably salty – they may be soaked to rehydrate and desalinate them, then used for cooking.

The most familiar air-dried meat products are probably the regional hams of Italy (Parma ham), Spain (jamón serrano), and France (jambons de Bayonne and Haute Savoie). Such hams are cured from whole legs of pork, so the air-drying process takes at least six months, and perhaps as long as two or more years. The quality of the pork, and specifically the breed and diet of the pig from which it comes, has a marked effect on the taste of the finished product. The very best Iberian hams, such as the *pata negra*, are made from a small, semi-wild kind of pig that is finished on a diet of acorns and beech mast. They are fiendishly expensive – and wickedly delicious.

Various local enthusiasts, including my friend, Victor Borg, who introduced me to the process, have proved that you don't need cool mountain breezes and acorn-fed wild pigs to make a respectable air-dried ham. The finest British-produced

pork, air dried in the finest British fresh air (damp though it may sometimes be), can still make a mean ham. The key thing is not to try and claim it as a British Parma, or a Dorset serrano. Just enjoy it for what it is. For details on air drying hams, see *The River Cottage Cookbook*.

Also familiar, and hugely popular in the UK, are many types of air-dried cured sausage, commonly known by the Italian word, salami, though they are made all over Europe and beyond, with all kinds of different meats. The ingenuity of salami making lies in its use of natural casings made from the intestines of domestic livestock. These are themselves usually preserved by salting (after thorough rinsing and scrubbing), then reconstituted by soaking to make them pliable and elastic for stuffing with minced or chopped, salted, seasoned meat. The special quality of these internal tubes is that they are robust enough to act as a barrier against airborne contaminants, yet permeable enough to 'breathe'. Natural moulds bloom on the outside of the salami but can't penetrate and spoil the meat. A fly may even lay its eggs on one, but the tiny hatched maggots simply won't get through the skin. Given a reasonable circulation of cool air, these natural casings allow steady moisture loss and gradual dehydration, until the salami reach the required state of 'ripeness' – firm, dense and richly flavoured with just a hint of residual moisture.

Once again, salt is the magic ingredient, and the magic ratio for the meat mix is 2-2.5 per cent of salt by weight – i.e. 20-25g salt for every kilo of minced meat. From a recipe point of view, this is the one constant. The best salami has about 10 per cent of finely diced fat mixed with coarsely minced lean meat, giving those pleasing pearls of white when it is sliced and served. The most popular further flavourings are pepper, garlic and wine. In Spain, huge amounts of hot and smoked paprika are used, along with garlic and sometimes fennel seeds, to produce their famous chorizo. Again, it is entirely possible, and tremendously worthwhile, to make your own salami and chorizo at home. Gratification is a little less delayed than with hams, as the process of drying takes weeks (about eight to twelve of them) rather than months. See *The River Cottage Cookbook* for instructions.

Pork is not the only meat that lends itself to air drying. Whole silversides or topsides of beef can be cured in salt, wine and spices, then hung to dry for three to five weeks, to produce the Italian cured beef known as bresaola. Imported bresaola is a popular item on the menus of many Italian restaurants. But again, it is surprisingly easy and very satisfying to make at home (see page 436).

Less familiar to us, but much beloved of the cultures that invented them, are the biltongs of southern Africa – strips of spiced, salted meat, usually more sun-dried than air-dried. Almost all the wild game of Africa, from gazelles to elephants, ostriches to giraffes, has been made into biltong. The biltong of these and other exotic species was a memorable feature of my six-month journey through southern Africa after I left college. I thought it was delicious. And it helped to sway me in favour of the controversial argument that one of the best reasons for conserving wildlife is so that it can continue to provide a sustainable food source for local populations.

Cold Smoking

If hot smoking is a cooking technique then cold smoking is, in general, a way of preserving meat and, of course, flavouring it. You can cold smoke just about every bit of a pig – to make bacon of one kind or another. But you can also cold smoke beef, lamb, poultry and game, both as lean cuts and as sausages. Most cold-smoked meats, like hams and bacon, require further cooking to become palatable; others, such as smoked spiced beef or venison, and some kinds of smoked sausage and dry-cured ham, are eaten cured and smoked, but otherwise raw.

However, smoking is not a very effective way of preserving meat unless it is salted first. And together the two techniques are more effective than either would be on its own. This is because cold smoking further reduces the moisture content of the meat (rather like air drying) and also adds further preservatives to work alongside the salt. Smoke contains, among many other complex substances, phenolic compounds that retard the oxidation of fats.

The simplest way to cold smoke meat (and this is how I cure my bacon at home) is to hang it above a gently smouldering log fire – high enough so that the temperature in the chimney is reliably less than about 35°C. A purpose-built smoker will produce a more concentrated 'box' of smoke at an even lower temperature (ideally around 25°C), and there are various simple ways to construct such a device for cold smoking at home.

Both cold and hot smoking (see pages 385-6) are techniques – crafts, really – that offer further dimensions of pleasure and satisfaction to the meat cook. Whole books have been written about the smoker's art, and most strike me as being many pages longer than they need to be. But if you want to make a start, without getting too bogged down in technicalities and temperature dials, you could do worse than look at the section on smoking in *The River Cottage Cookbook*. My introduction to the subject there is designed to give you confidence, not catatonia.

Confits of Duck and Goose

Confit means 'preserved' in French, and this technique for preserving meat involves a combination of salt and animal fat. First the meat is dry salted, much as described above, then it is cooked long and slow in rendered fat until very tender. Ideally the fat will come from the same animal as the meat. The finished confit can then be placed in a container, usually a glass jar, and completely covered in liquid fat, which is allowed to set hard around and over the meat. With this protective covering, and in a sealed jar, a confit can keep for months or even a year or two without refrigeration.

In theory, most kinds of meat could be made into confit, but the technique achieves the greatest success when applied to ducks and geese. This is because they carry so much fat that no extra is required for the cooking or covering of the meat. It's a particularly popular way of processing the meat of ducks and geese that have been raised for their fat livers – foie gras (see pages 195-6).

You can confit a whole duck or goose, jointed into four or six parts (as described for a chicken on pages 140-43), or you can use just the legs and put the rest of the bird to some other use. Making good confit is a skill that any cook should be pleased to acquire, so I've included a recipe here (page 451). And the recipe for duck or goose breasts on page 366 makes good use of the rest of the bird.

Boudins, Black Puddings and Other Blood Sausages

Many cultures have their version of the black pudding and there are probably only two ingredients common to all of them: blood and salt. The blood may be from any animal. Pig's blood is the most popular but cow's and sheep's are also used where these are the prevalent livestock. In Lapland, as you might expect, a version is made from reindeer blood.

The blood is usually mixed with some kind of cereal to stiffen and solidify it. In the UK this is generally oatmeal and/or cracked barley. In France it's traditionally breadcrumbs, in Spain and Latin America often rice. A boudin is generally enriched by the addition of cream in France and diced pork fat in the UK, while in Spain it is spiked and sweetened by raisins soaked in wine or sherry.

There is a third 'ingredient' you might say they all share, and that is the casing. As with salami, the natural intestine of an animal (usually a bullock) is used. Versions of blood pudding can be made without casings, though, and instead of being boiled in natural intestines they are baked in tins and terrine dishes, when they are sometimes referred to as 'blood cakes' or 'blood breads'.

The extent to which blood puddings are preserved by the process depends, as you'd expect, largely on the salt content. In Portugal, Brazil and the Caribbean they are sometimes heavily salted and spiced, piped into narrow casings, tied into short lengths like little chipolatas, and partially dried, so that they have a reasonable keeping quality, even without refrigeration. However, being very salty, they are not usually eaten on their own but added to big stews and peasant pot dishes so they mellow as they cook, at the same time giving up their salt to season the other meats and vegetables in the pot.

Once boiled, the natural casings are less resistant to contamination. So to help them keep longer, British black puddings and French boudins are often smeared in lard. In Italy and Spain miniature black puddings are sometimes packed in jars of olive oil. My home-made black puddings, which are only lightly salted, still keep for a good month if vac-packed and stored in the fridge.

Making black puddings at home is by no means beyond the reach of the enthusiastic amateur *charcutier*, and it is great fun. If you're interested, then I'm delighted to refer you to *The River Cottage Cookbook*.

Pâtés and Terrines

A pâté is simply a meat paste – 'paste' being the meaning of the word in French. But I doubt we would ever have developed such an enduring enthusiasm for the dish if we hadn't borrowed the name from across the Channel.

Someone, somewhere may have a better definition of precisely how a terrine differs from a pâté, and it'll probably have something to do with the traditional earthenware *terrines* in which such a dish was cooked in France. But as far as I'm concerned, a pâté becomes a terrine when it has definable chunks of meat in it. Dog lovers, though perhaps not their dogs, may appreciate that Pedigree Chum is a veritable terrine among dog foods, while Bounce (*with added tripe) is undoubtedly a pâté (sorry to lower the tone).

In the end, such definitions matter far less than the fact that both pâtés and terrines are much, much easier to make than most people think. If you have a mincing machine or a food processor, you can put together all kinds of pâtés and terrines in a matter of minutes. The simplest pâté recipes, which are invariably the best, involve nothing more complicated than mincing or processing all the ingredients to a consistency that appeals to your palate, spreading them in a suitable dish (lined with bacon, if you like – but only if you're feeling flash), covering them well and baking in a bain marie (i.e. a deep roasting tin half filled with boiling water). For some reason this straightforward procedure seems to be a well-kept secret of top chefs and housewives of a certain age. But once you've cracked it, you'll reap a whole new crop of plaudits for your culinary endeavours.

The best basis for any pâté is good fatty pork – a mixture of belly and shoulder, for example – minced fine or coarse, according to how you want it to turn out. Buying ready-minced sausage meat is, if you know it comes from a good pig, very acceptable, as is splitting open a few really good butcher's bangers. These will contain some kind of cereal binder, but that's no insult to your pâté. In fact, if you don't use sausages, there's a case for adding a little binder of your own. A handful of fine breadcrumbs (around 5 per cent of the mix) will help 'fill the cracks' and bring a pâté together nicely, particularly if you've opted for a fairly coarse texture.

After that, what other meats you add to your pâté is up to you – but there must be a *point* to it. You are looking for something that will bring real character and depth of flavour to the pâté. If all you add to your minced pork is some minced beef, then you're not really entering into the spirit of the thing. (Not that that would be an entirely worthless exercise. Good minced pork and beef, well seasoned, make a great meat loaf – but you'll enjoy it much more served hot, with mashed potato and a spicy home-made ketchup – see page 516.)

If there is a single magic ingredient for pâtés and terrines, it must be liver. Pig's liver is a useful addition to almost any pâté, though in fact which animal it comes from is less important than making sure it is very fresh. Even those who (think they) don't like liver often love pâté with liver in it (and, of course, it doesn't have to be called 'liver pâté' unless it contains a *lot* of liver). Now that I rear my own meat, and the livers of various of my livestock are available on a regular basis, I find I am knocking up new pâtés more and more.

Besides liver, the other great ingredient for pâté is game, because it also has a strong and distinctive flavour. In November every year, as the new shooting season gets under way, I have a ritual whereby I scour the four corners of my three freezers for lonely game birds from the previous season that have escaped my attention over the summer. I defrost them all, roast whatever seems most appealing, and make game pâté with the rest. For the next two or three weeks, it's a tremendous treat to have a huge game pâté on the go in the fridge, always there to provide a quick lunch or an instant snack.

Often my game pâtés metamorphose into terrines, as the breasts of birds, along with lean strips of rabbit, hare and venison or any kind of liver, make wonderful building blocks. A metaphor I've used before (and will no doubt use again) is: when making a terrine, just think of the meat as bricks, improvise some pâté-like binder as the mortar, and get on and build yourself a wall. When you come to slice it, you'll find you've constructed something even more remarkable – a slab of beautiful marble, no less. Compressing your terrine with some kind of weight while it cools after cooking is an effective way of ensuring that it doesn't crumble and fall apart when sliced, but cuts nicely and shows off that lovely layering.

It may sound a little rash but I'd go as far as to say that virtually all the best pâtés and terrines have either liver or game in them. And arguably the best of all have both. (My Terrine of Sweetbreads on page 455 is a rare exception. It's about as subtle and understated as I'd ever allow a terrine to get – and that's what makes such a wow of the broad beans that accompany it.)

Just as the meats must be distinctive, so must the seasoning. There's no room for half measures. The generous use of punchy fresh herbs is to be heartily encouraged. If liver is involved, as I sincerely hope it will be, then sage will always be an excellent choice. Thyme is a great all-rounder, and a little garlic never hurts. Wine is good but port is even better, because it packs a winey punch and adds a useful note of sweetness, without swamping the mix with unnecessary liquid. The same can be said of Calvados and brandy. In fact, now I think of it, I rarely make a pâté or terrine that doesn't include fresh herbs, garlic and either port, brandy or Calvados (or possibly all three).

There are four recipes for terrines and pâtés in the recipe section that follows but what I'm keenly hoping is that you'll realise such punctilious instructions are just there to get you started. Once you've grasped the principle of them, these delightful meat concoctions are the easiest things in the world to invent and improvise. For many, there persists some barrier of comprehension about the genre, a hunch that it's all a bit technical and tricky. Believe me, that's an illusion. Give it a firm prod with your favourite wooden spoon and it will disappear.

Haggis, Faggots, Haslet, Brawn and Potted Hough

I'm not going to spend undue space deconstructing and etymologising this quintet of Celtic/Anglo-Saxon minced meat dishes. The simple point I would make is that they are all, even if we don't quite think of them in this way, really just distinctive regional kinds of pâté or terrine. What the first two have in common principally, besides a certain gutsy charm, is that, unlike most pâtés, they are usually served hot – at least on their first outing. They may subsequently join the others on the buffet of cold platters.

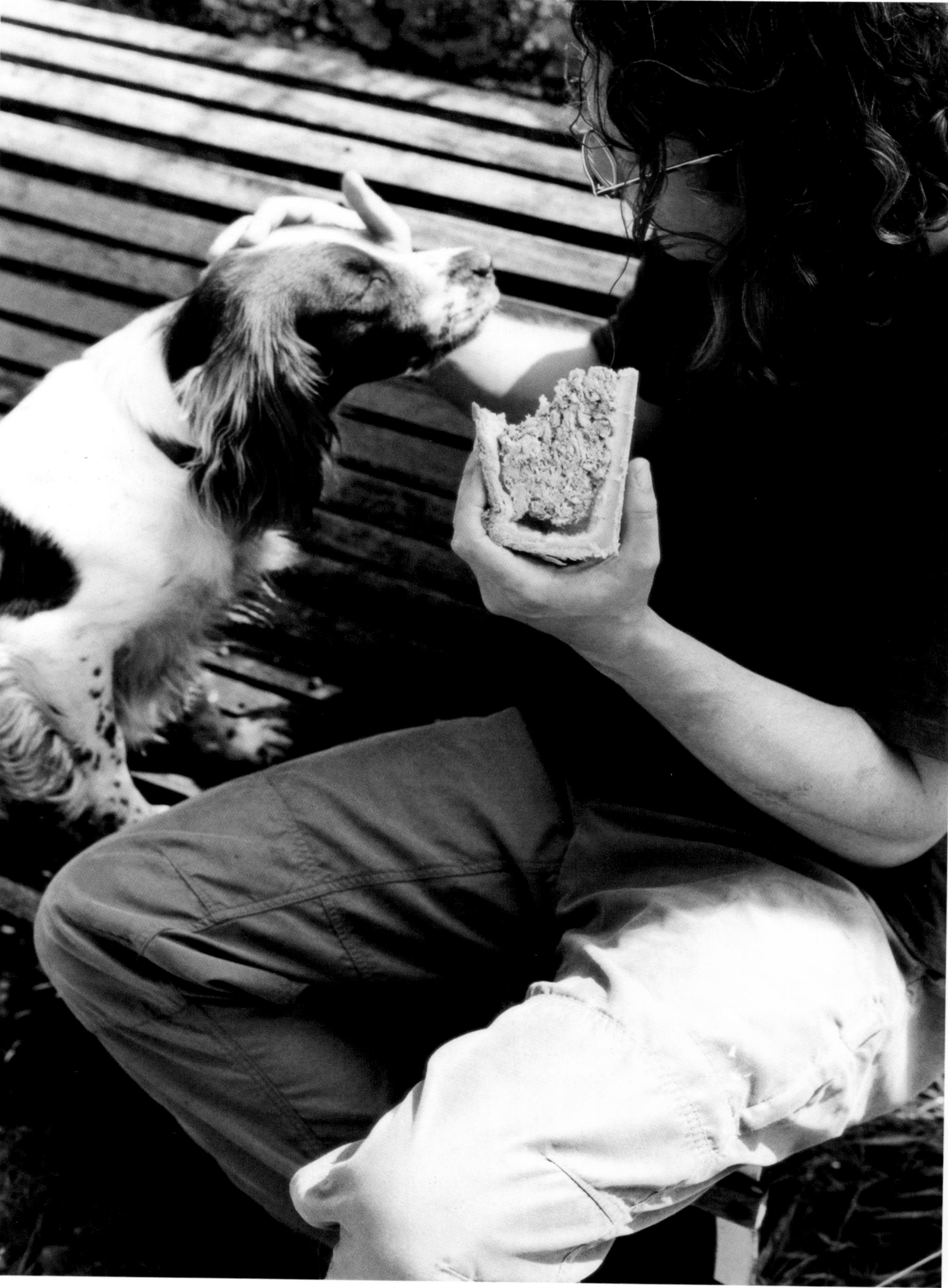

These are just some of the best-known surviving descendants of a once-populous race of regional meat dishes, in which the offals and off-cuts of the most readily available livestock were minced, seasoned, bound with some favoured cheap cereal and stuffed into, or wrapped up with, some other convenient spare part or, failing that, put in a handy crock. At their best, they are a delight, and at their worst a disgrace. I give recipes here for faggots, brawn and potted hough, which I promise are in the former camp. I confess I've passed on haslet and haggis because although I've had excellent 'in-house' versions of both from several good butchers, I've never attempted to make them myself.

Pork and Other 'Picnic' Pies

A pork pie is really a pork pâté (or arguably a terrine) that is baked not in a tin tray or ceramic dish but in an edible case of extremely robust pastry – the inimitable 'hot water crust' that is the mark of all the best pork pies. If you think about it, the pork pie is an ingenious bit of food processing – portable and durable picnic food of the highest order – that pre-dates the sandwich by several centuries. It has some keeping qualities as well. A heavily seasoned, well-made pork pie, with a good lardy crust and a jelly-filled cavity, could happily sit in a cool larder for a month without coming to any harm. And in pre-refrigeration days, no doubt it did.

The same principle of encasement is readily adaptable for many fillings, particularly veal and ham, poultry and ham, and a variety of game. This creates a whole family of what have come to be known as 'raised pies' – because of the way in which the pastry is built up inside, or outside, a deep tin or dish, and becomes self-supporting when cooked. Most controversial among them, perhaps, is the 'gala pie': you know, the one with the slice of hard-boiled egg in the middle. A butcher once explained to me that a mark of true quality in such a product is that wherever you make your slice, you should always get a circle of yellow yolk, and never just that butt-end plug of rubbery white. Apparently this is achieved by slicing the ends off all the hard-boiled eggs and laying them sliced end to sliced end to create a seemingly everlasting tubular egg. 'It shows generosity,' he said, 'that you're not stinting on the egg.' I thought of pointing out that the egg was, in the first place, surely a way of stinting on the meat. But I decided to let it go ...

I'll admit that my lavishly illustrated pork pie recipe (page 444) is probably the most time consuming in this section. You have to make the pastry, and the filling, and the jelly, then bring them together stage by stage. But it's a wonderful edible project. See how you get on with it, and if you feel you've cracked it you'll undoubtedly be able to work out any number of variations on the raised pie theme.

Fresh Sausages

Everyone loves sausages, and you can buy them just about everywhere that has a chill cabinet – including corner shops and garages. They run the whole gamut of meat quality, from sublime to unmentionable. The very worst of them – which is, of course, most of them – are made from mechanically recovered pork slurry, blasted off the carcasses of factory-farmed pigs with high-pressure hoses, then hoovered up off the abattoir floor. After being sieved and ground to an even paste, stabilised with the addition of chemical preservatives, this is mixed with cheap cereal binders (as much as 50 per cent of the final sausage), artificial flavourings and a few more preservatives to boot. It's finally squeezed into artificial casings that are crimped into sausages at the rate of several thousand an hour. Refrigerated, these have a shelf life of over a month.

On the other hand, the very best sausages are made by conscientious butchers, who use lean shoulder and fat belly, along with fresh pork trimmings from their own cutting room, a little (10-15 per cent) rusk made from dried bread, and their secret blend of herbs and spices. They won't keep for more than a week, but with a loyal clientele to support them, they won't need to.

Once again, a fine home-made sausage is by no means hard to prepare. You need a bit of kit and some nice natural casings, but it's all available by mail order. See the Directory (page 529) for the kit, and *The River Cottage Cookbook* for recipes.

Burgers and Other Patties

The burger is the most widely consumed processed meat product in the world. I've already said my piece on the perfect beefburger (page 398). The worst of them are produced, I'm afraid, much as I described the industrial sausage above – from mechanically recovered meat. But whatever the fast-food industry, in league with industrial beef farming, has done to demean the burger, and the cattle from which it comes, the burger at its best remains a triumph of good taste and design – it's simply one of the best recipes of all time.

This makes me think that if the beefburger is tragically over-exposed and over-exploited, other forms of burger or patty are woefully under-explored. Mincing good meat, flavouring it well and frying it in a flat patty makes a lot of sense. It's a great way to make inexpensive family meals that children respond to with excitement and enthusiasm. Recently I have been mincing more lamb than beef – my Souvlaki Lamburgers (page 401) are a current family favourite. And meat from rabbits, pheasants, geese and deer have all been through the mincer (usually the coarse setting) and reshaped into approximate burger form (when my son, Oscar, does the shaping, it can be very approximate).

The trick with these game meats, which tend to be lean and dry, is always to include a little minced pork – even if it's just a good sausage, split and worked into the mix. Around 20 per cent is about right to help lubricate the burger, and you'll find it brings out, rather than masks, the natural flavour of the game. Season well, including a few fresh or dried herbs and a smidgen of crushed garlic.

I have a fantasy that one day, before too long, the world will be ready for a chain of bunny burger restaurants. Maybe the menu could include pheasant nuggets with plum dipping sauce and venison sausage hot dogs.

Preserving Meat by Freezing

In a perfect world, fresh raw meat would always be preferable to frozen, and freshly made processed meats – the kind of pâtés, pies and sausages described above – would be preferable to those that have been frozen and then defrosted. Having said that, the freezer is now a fact of life, and it is a fantastically useful piece of equipment for the conscientious meat cook. For reasons I explained in detail in Chapter 2, What Is Good Meat?, good-quality extensively reared meat that has been well hung and skilfully butchered emerges from a spell in the freezer with great credit – and is far, far better eating than poor-quality fresh meat. I reckon I'm getting pretty good at looking after my meat, and I would confidently put up a joint of my own home-produced meat from the freezer against just about any meat you could find.

Of course, I would say that. But even if you don't rear your own meat, having a freezer allows you to buy half or whole lambs and hoggets and freezer packs of beef and pork from small producers who are offering the finest meat around.

It is, of course, the whole point of many preserved and processed meats that they last so long you'd barely ever think of freezing them. But it can be very useful to freeze pâtés, sausages and burgers, particularly as they are so easy to prepare in bulk, and they freeze extremely well – which is to say, of course, that they defrost extremely well. The same is true of home-cured bacon – in the unlikely event that your consumption of it is ever slow enough to make you consider the option.

Tartares and Other Seasoned Raw Meats

The processing of raw meat for immediate consumption – without any kind of preserving or heating – is a hard kind of 'cooking' to categorise. I suppose I could have put it into the Fast Cooking chapter – so fast that it never actually happened. But in the end I reckon a steak tartare – which is by far the best known of such preparations – is really a raw meat pâté, not an uncooked beefburger. (A carpaccio, on the other hand, is just a wafer-thin steak that looks so good you've decided to bypass the grill.) The other way of thinking of it, I suppose, is as a cocktail – a kind of Bloody Mary you can eat with a knife and fork.

Beef is not the only meat that can be palatable when raw. The Lebanese have several variations on the theme of raw lamb. When made with good meat, they can be superb, and I include a good example, Kibbeh Naye, in the recipe section (page 443). For all such raw meat dishes, the meat must be of the best quality, but it would perhaps be misleading to insist that it should be 'fresh'. I'd happily – joyfully – make my kibbeh from a leg of hogget hung for a fortnight, and a steak tartare from rump or sirloin that had been aged for a full month. But in both cases I'd trim the meat pretty ruthlessly to get to the kernel of delicious, unoxidised red meat in the middle.

That, of course, would leave me with a pile of crusty outer trimmings. But I have a hunch there'll be some ideas in the next chapter for dealing with them ...

HOME-CURED BACON (aka SALT PORK)

1 whole pork belly, divided into 3 equal pieces

THE DRY-CURE MIX:

About 750g coarse salt

2 teaspoons saltpetre (potassium nitrate) – optional

A few bay leaves, finely chopped

About 20 juniper berries, lightly crushed

400g soft brown sugar

25g coarsely ground black pepper

Making bacon is an essential skill for anyone who rears their own pigs, and I have discussed the subject at some length in The River Cottage Cookbook. *However, there is no reason why those without the resources to raise porkers (or, more accurately, baconers) should miss out on the fun. Making bacon is so easy, and using your home-made version such a pleasure.*

The following absurdly simple recipe produces a very versatile pancetta-style streaky bacon – strong and concentrated in flavour, a little on the salty side, and ideal for the various stews, soups and pasta sauces in this book that call for chunks of 'salt pork, pancetta or bacon'. It's also perfect for the Petit Salé recipe that follows. Smoking the bacon is optional – I smoke only about a quarter of my bacon, and still find I get through the unsmoked before the smoked.

Buy a whole belly from one side of a pig, ideally a rare-breed organic pig. It may be over a metre long, leaner and thicker at the head end and fattier but thinner towards the tail, but it divides neatly into three roughly 30cm square pieces, which are a good manageable size both for salting and for hanging and storing. Or buy the fattest bellies you can find, in single pieces of roughly a kilo.

It's hard to give exact quantities for your dry-cure mix, but the amount opposite should be about right for three pieces of belly. You may need to make up a little more cure mix, in the same proportions, after the first few days. The saltpetre's main function is to keep the bacon a nice pink colour – it's certainly optional.

The process couldn't be simpler. In a clean, non-metallic container, thoroughly mix all the ingredients for the cure with your (clean) hands. Place one piece of belly at a time on a clean work surface and just grab a handful of the dry-cure mix and start rubbing it with your fingers into all the surfaces of the meat. When it is lightly but evenly salted all over, place it in a clean box or tray, again non-metallic (wood, plastic or ceramic is ideal), and move on to the next piece of belly.

Stack the finished bellies on top of each other and leave, covered, in a cool place. Keep the leftover cure mix. After 24 hours you will notice that the meat has leached salty liquid into the container. Remove the bellies, pour off this liquid and rub the bellies with handfuls of fresh cure mix. Re-stack the bellies, preferably moving the one from the bottom on to the top.

Repeat the process daily. Your bacon will be ready after just 4-5 days, though if you cure it for longer (up to 10 days) it will keep for longer. The 4-5 day cure is perfect for breakfast rashers but you will need a proper bacon slicer to get them nice and thin.

Storing and using bacon

Bellies cured in this way should be thoroughly rinsed of excess salt, in plenty of cold water. Then pat dry, wrap in clean muslin and leave to hang in a cool, well-ventilated place such as a cellar or outhouse. Cut pieces off the belly as you need them, then rewrap and rehang. Alternatively, wrap the belly in cotton, muslin or greaseproof paper and store in the fridge. Bellies cured for more than 10 days can keep for months in this way but will tend to be unpalatably salty. Pieces cut from them can be soaked in fresh water for a few hours to counteract this. My preference is for a lighter (5-6 day) cure, which is good for breakfast rashers and general use. Any bellies that I am not likely to use within a month get vacuum-packed and go in the freezer.

Smoking

Smoking will not only add a superb flavour to your bacon but will also improve its keeping quality. Bellies salted as above for just 5 days should be rinsed and hung to dry for at least 3 days before smoking. Then hang them high in a chimney above and to the side of an open fire, or place in your home-made smoker (see *The River Cottage Cookbook*); 24 hours of near-continuous cold-smoking will do the trick. Or, if the smoking is intermittent (i.e. you are lighting the fire for a few hours each day), you can leave them for up to a week.

I have kept smoked bellies in the fridge for up to 4 months, cutting bits off when I need them. Again, wrap in muslin or paper, but never plastic. A little mould begins to appear after a while, but you can scrape it off and the bacon will be none the worse.

PETIT SALÉ *Serves 4-6*

1kg piece of home-cured belly bacon (see above), skin on

2 large carrots, roughly chopped

1 large onion, roughly chopped

4 celery sticks, roughly chopped

2 bay leaves

A few peppercorns

250g Puy lentils

Petit salé *is the French name for an unsmoked cured pork belly that has simply been boiled (when diced and fried, it becomes* lardons*). It is one of my favourite ways to honour a good chunk of home-cured bacon. The winter version is served with lentils or creamy white beans, such as haricots or cannellini. The summer version is served with peas or broad beans, or a thick purée made from either. Here's the classic Puy lentil version.*

If you know the bacon is very salty, soak it in cold water for a few hours or overnight. Drain well, place in a saucepan with the stock vegetables, bay leaves and peppercorns, then cover generously with fresh cold water. Bring slowly to the boil and simmer gently for 2-3 hours, until the meat is plump and the skin completely tender. Remove the bacon and set aside, then fish out and discard the stock vegetables.

Thoroughly rinse the lentils in cold water, put them in a pan and add the liquid in which the bacon has been cooked. Bring to the boil and simmer merrily for 12-20 minutes, until tender but with a little 'bite' remaining. Return the bacon to the pan for a minute to heat through.

Serve a pile of lentils on each warmed plate, with a thick slice of bacon on top.

A CIDER-CURED HAM

1 whole or 1/2 leg of fresh, free-range pork, on or off the bone

THE BRINE:

2 kg salt

10 g saltpetre (optional)

2 litres pressed apple juice (not from concentrate)

1 litre strong dry cider

5 litres water

1 kg demerara sugar

1 kg dark brown sugar or black treacle

20-30 juniper berries

30 g black peppercorns, crushed

10 bay leaves, crushed

10 cloves

We British love our hams, and for centuries various flavourings, such as spices, cider, beer, hops, sugar, molasses etc, have been added to a basic salt and water brine to produce highly distinctive regional cured hams. The constant is the ratio of liquid (water, cider, beer or combinations thereof) to salt, which should be 3.5-4 litres of liquid for every kilo of salt. Here is my own version of a West Country cure, using cider and apple juice.

Note: You don't have to use a whole leg (which may weigh over 10 kg), and an important consideration is whether you have a stockpot big enough to accommodate such a huge piece of meat. The quantities here are for a small boned-out leg or half a large leg. For a large leg of pork from a mature baconer, on the bone, you may need to double the quantities.

Boil all the brine ingredients together in a large pan and leave to cool. Transfer to a non-metallic brine tub and chill to 3-4°C. Place your piece of pork – also chilled, ideally to almost freezing – in the tub and submerge completely, using a non-metallic weight. Leave the pork in the brine, in the coolest place you can find, for 3 days (minimum) to 4 days (maximum) for every kilo. The maximum time is for a ham you intend to keep a long while; the minimum will suffice if you plan to cook and eat it soon after it is finished.

After its allotted time, remove the ham from the cure, wipe dry with a cotton cloth and hang it to dry in a muslin bag in a cool, well-ventilated place for 24 hours. You can then smoke it if you like: hang it high above a hardwood fire or place it in your smoker and either smoke it continuously for 24 hours or intermittently (6-12 hours a day) for about 5-7 days. Ideally the air temperature where the ham is smoking should not exceed 40°C (27°C is 'perfect' but a little variation will not hurt).

Smoked or unsmoked, this ham keeps well if you go for the maximum cure time: hang it in a well-ventilated outbuilding, or covered porch, where the draught can get to it but the rain can't, and it should keep right through the winter months. In warmer weather, hams are at risk from flies and other bugs: best get them cooked before too long. A minimum-cure-time, unsmoked ham should be kept in the fridge, wrapped in a cloth or muslin, but not plastic, and cooked within a month of curing. Don't worry if a few specks of mould appear; just wipe them off with a cloth dipped in vinegar.

Hams should be soaked in plenty of fresh water, changed every 12 hours, for 24-48 hours (depending on the length of the cure) before boiling. Bring to the boil and simmer gently for 2-5 hours, depending on size. If the water tastes very salty after the first hour of cooking, pour it away and replace with fresh boiling water.

A home-cured ham like this is ideal for both the recipes that follow.

GLAZED BAKED HAM CALIFORNIA WITH PARSLEY SAUCE

Serves 10-30

4.5-9kg ham (for example, my Cider-cured Ham opposite), ideally on the bone

1 large onion, chopped

2 large carrots, chopped

2 celery sticks, chopped

10 black peppercorns

3-4 bay leaves

5-6 sprigs of thyme

A small bunch of parsley stalks

Real Parsley Sauce (p.512), to serve

THE GLAZE:

1 generous tablespoon English mustard

250g soft brown sugar

15-20 cloves

THE SPICED PINEAPPLE:

1 large, fresh pineapple, ripe and fragrant (or buy chilled fresh pineapple rings, but not tinned)

Juice of 1 orange

50-100g light soft brown sugar

6 cloves

1 cinnamon stick

1 teaspoon coriander seeds

1 blade of mace (if handy)

A whole ham on the bone, glazed with an almost-black crust of sugar and mustard, will always be one of the most alluring and impressive things you can put on the table. It deserves very special accompaniments, including something sweet to cut the saltiness of the ham, and a real parsley sauce, creamy and soothing, to mollify the whole combination into the ultimate comfort food.

Gammon and pineapple isn't just a bad culinary joke, as was proved to me when I had lunch at the Connaught and ordered the daily special – an enormous baked leg of ham with a burnt sugary crust, served with slices of hot, spiced fresh pineapple. Even the pineapple had been caramelised with a last-minute sprinkling of sugar – and a blowtorch, I suspect.

It was wonderful, and prompted me to devise this alternative to the spiced figs accompaniment I offer in The River Cottage Cookbook. *My version forsakes the blowtorch (though by all means have a go if you're an enthusiast of that kitchen implement), gently infusing the pineapple in a spicy syrup, which, as with the figs, becomes a piquant sauce for the ham.*

Put the ham to soak in a large bucket of cold water 24-48 hours before cooking (depending on the size of the ham and the length of the original cure – i.e. saltiness). Change the water every 12 hours.

Rinse the soaked ham and place it in a large stockpot. Cover with fresh cold water and add the vegetables and peppercorns, plus the herbs, tied in a bouquet. Bring the water to the boil, then reduce the heat, cover partially with a lid and simmer very gently for 4-5 hours. If after an hour of simmering the water tastes unpalatably salty, discard it and replace with fresh boiling water – this will help to reduce the saltiness of the cooked ham.

Remove the ham from the pot and allow it to cool slightly. Meanwhile, for the glaze, place the mustard and sugar in a small bowl and mix to make a thick, sludgy paste. Carefully peel away the skin of the ham, leaving a smooth, even layer of fat over the meat. Place the ham in a large roasting tin, then score the fat layer with the point of a sharp knife in a coarse diamond pattern, but not so deeply as to go right through the fat to the meat. Spread the glaze mixture all over it in an even layer. Stud the ham with the cloves at regularly spaced intervals. Roast the ham in a moderate oven (180°C/Gas Mark 4) for 1-1½ hours, until the glaze becomes a dark, golden-brown bubbling crust.

While the ham is baking, you can sort out the pineapple and make the parsley sauce. Peel the pineapple, nicking out any persistent spiky bits on the flesh with the point of a sharp knife. Slice the pineapple into rounds 1cm thick. Using a small, sharp pastry cutter or the point of a sharp knife, stamp out the tough core of each slice, leaving you with classic pineapple rings. Save as much of the juice as you can.

Put the saved pineapple juice in a pan with the orange juice, a couple of tablespoons of water, plus the sugar and spices and stir over a gentle heat to dissolve the sugar. Simmer gently for a few minutes to make a light syrup, then remove from the heat and add the pineapple rings, turning them to coat in the syrup. Leave to cool and infuse.

Before you serve the ham, remove the pineapple rings from the pan and strain the syrup, discarding the spices. Return the pineapple and clean syrup to the pan and heat through. You can also add the strained juices from the roasting tin at this stage, but strain off the fat first and make sure they are not too salty or burnt tasting. If in doubt, leave them out.

Carve the ham while piping hot from the oven and serve on hot plates with 1 or 2 pineapple slices, a spoonful of their syrup on the meat and a generous pool of parsley sauce on the side. There won't be much room on the plate for it, but since this meal should be a feast in the best sense, have also on the table a large dish of creamy mashed potatoes (page 518), some lightly steamed cabbage tossed in butter and sprinkled with a few caraway seeds, and, if you're really going for it, some Glazed Carrots (page 522).

HAM IN HAY

1 leg of boiling ham (my Cider-cured Ham on p.432, if you like), on or off the bone and soaked if necessary

6 bay leaves

20 peppercorns

20 allspice berries

A few handfuls of hay, wetted

In The River Cottage Cookbook, *I included a recipe for lamb in hay, which has proved very popular. Then I saw that Fergus Henderson had a recipe for ham in hay in his book,* Nose to Tail Eating. *I tried it, and found it delightful – and fabulously fragrant. Here's my version (barely different from his, as it happens).*

Press the bay leaves, peppercorns and allspice berries on to the surface of the ham, then wrap it in a wet tea towel (not essential, but it helps to keep the spices close to the meat, and means you don't have to pick off bits of stewed hay later).

Choose a deep roasting tin or a large casserole, preferably with a lid (if you don't have one with a lid you can use foil). Line generously with loose wet hay, to a thickness of about 5-6cm. Place the wrapped ham in its nest of hay and cover with the rest of the hay. Pour at least 10cm boiling water into the dish. Cover with the lid, which must fit tightly, or with a double layer of foil wrapped well around the edge of the dish. Make sure there are no loose bits of hay poking out.

Bake in the centre of a low oven (140°C/Gas Mark 1) for 3½-5 hours, depending on the size of the leg. A skewer pushed into the centre of the meat should come out hot at the tip (and a meat thermometer should read at least 75°C).

Remove the ham and unwrap. Carve in thin slices and serve with mashed swede (Fergus's suggestion) and Real Parsley Sauce (my suggestion, see page 512).

BRESAOLA

3.5-4.5 kg joint of beef topside (or silverside)

THE MARINADE:

500g coarse sea salt

12 sprigs of rosemary

12 bay leaves

20 cloves

4 garlic cloves, crushed

1 tablespoon cracked black peppercorns

2 teaspoons dried chilli flakes

5-6 strips of finely pared orange zest

5-6 strips of finely pared lemon zest

1 bottle of red wine

TO SERVE:

Best-quality olive oil

Rocket or finely chopped chives

Lemon wedges, or a slice of pink grapefruit

This is the dish that answers the much-asked question (by me at any rate) of what to do with silverside and topside – two cuts that always seem to disappoint when roasted (though well-aged topside is very good cold, if roasted rare). Here they are transformed into lean, melting, mildly spiced luxury, with the classic Italian dry-cure treatment that is a relatively recent discovery in the UK. My recipe is adapted from Franco Taruschio's bresaola in his book, Leaves from The Walnut Tree.

It was my first home-made bresaola that finally persuaded me to invest in an electric meat slicer: I don't mind hacking away with a knife at one of my dry-cured hams but this just cries out to be carved 'waffer thin', as Mr Creosote would say.

Trim the outside of the meat of any fat or sinews – and remove the string if it has been trussed up by the butcher.

Mix together all the ingredients for the marinade, place in a non-metallic container into which the joint will fit quite snugly and then add the meat, turning it to coat well. Cover and leave in a cool place – the fridge, if you like. Turn the meat over twice a day for 5 days, then remove from the marinade, rinse briefly under a cold tap and pat dry with a tea towel. Wrap it in a double layer of muslin, tie up with string and hang in a dry, but cool and draughty place (such as an outbuilding or covered porch) for at least 10 days. It should be fairly hard to the touch.

Bresaola should be trimmed before slicing. Cut away the outer 5 mm from the bit you are going to slice. Slice very thinly, across the grain of the meat, like a giant salami, ideally with an electric meat slicer (see Directory, page 529, for stockists). You will notice that the outer edges of each slice are browner than the interior; this is normal, and no cause for alarm. A finished bresaola can be hung in a cool place for up to a month and used as and when you need it, but in warm or humid weather, transfer to the fridge. Always wrap in muslin or a cotton cloth, not clingfilm, so your bresaola can breathe and doesn't sweat.

To serve, spread the thin slices out over a plate (4-5 slices per person) and trickle with best olive oil. Rocket or finely chopped chives can be used as a garnish, along with a wedge of lemon (only a very few drops are needed), or even (my own eccentric version) thin slices of pink grapefruit.

Variation

Venison Bresaola and Venison Jerky: The bresaola cure works very well with venison, too. The obvious piece to use is the boned-out loin fillet. It's smaller than the usual beef joints and needs less time in the cure – about 3-4 days is enough. Then wrap and hang for 10-14 days before slicing, very thinly, as for the beef. You can air-dry it for much longer and eventually it sets very hard, like beef jerky or biltong. It can then be cut into thin shavings, or chewed off the strip, bush style. It's delicious with a cold beer.

SALT BEEF (AND PICKLED TONGUE) *Serves 10 or more*

2-3kg piece of beef (brisket, foreflank, or a whole ox tongue)

1 bouquet garni

1 carrot, chopped

1 onion, chopped

1 celery stick, chopped

1 leek, chopped

1/2 garlic bulb

THE BRINE:

5 litres water

500g demerara or light brown sugar

1.5kg coarse sea salt

1 teaspoon black peppercorns

1 teaspoon juniper berries

5 cloves

4 bay leaves

A sprig of thyme

50g saltpetre (optional)

I love salt beef – the best use of two cheap beef cuts, brisket and foreflank, that few have time for these days. In fact, I'm so keen that you should make time for it that I feel justified in reproducing this recipe, more or less verbatim, from The River Cottage Cookbook. *The 'added value' is my recipe for Red Flannel Hash on page 498.*

Some people cite silverside as the superior cut for salt beef. But I find it too lean, with a tendency to dryness, and prefer to set it aside for the Italian dry-cured beef, Bresaola (page 436).

Exactly the same brine is also suitable for pickling a tongue, which is particularly good served cold, as described below. This pickled tongue can also be used in a Bollito Misto (page 304).

Put all the ingredients for the brine into a large saucepan and stir well over a low heat until the sugar and salt have dissolved. Bring to the boil, allow to bubble for 1-2 minutes, then remove from the heat and leave to cool completely.

Place your chosen piece of beef or a whole ox tongue in a non-metallic container, such as a large Tupperware box or a clay crock. Cover the meat completely with the cold brine, weighting it down if necessary with a piece of wood. Leave in a cool place for 5-10 days (joints of less than 3kg should not be left for more than a week or they will become too pickled).

Before cooking, remove the beef (or tongue) from the brine and soak it in fresh cold water for 24 hours, changing the water at least once (you could make that 48 hours if it had the full 10-day immersion). Then put it in a pan with the bouquet garni, vegetables and garlic, cover with fresh water and bring to a gentle simmer. Poach very gently on top of the stove – or in a very low oven (120°C/Gas Mark 1/2) if you prefer. A 3kg piece of beef will take 2 1/2-3 hours. A salted tongue may take even longer. In either case, cook until the meat is completely tender and yielding when pierced with a skewer. The coarse skin of a boiled tongue must be peeled off and discarded before it is served.

Serve hot salted beef or tongue carved into fairly thick slices, with lentils, beans, Horseradish Mash (page 519) or boiled potatoes and either Creamed Fresh Horseradish (page 512) or good English mustard. Both are excellent cold, and the tongue in particular makes the following delicious cold platter.

Variation

Cold Tongue with Lentils and Green Dressing: Carefully slice the cooked tongue to about 1cm thickness and lay the slices over some cooked Puy lentils (see page 520) that have been left to cool. Trickle Salsa Verde (page 514) over the tongue and serve. A very good 'picnic' version of this dish can be made by dicing the tongue into small cubes and tossing it together with the lentils and dressing. It can then be easily transported in Tupperware!

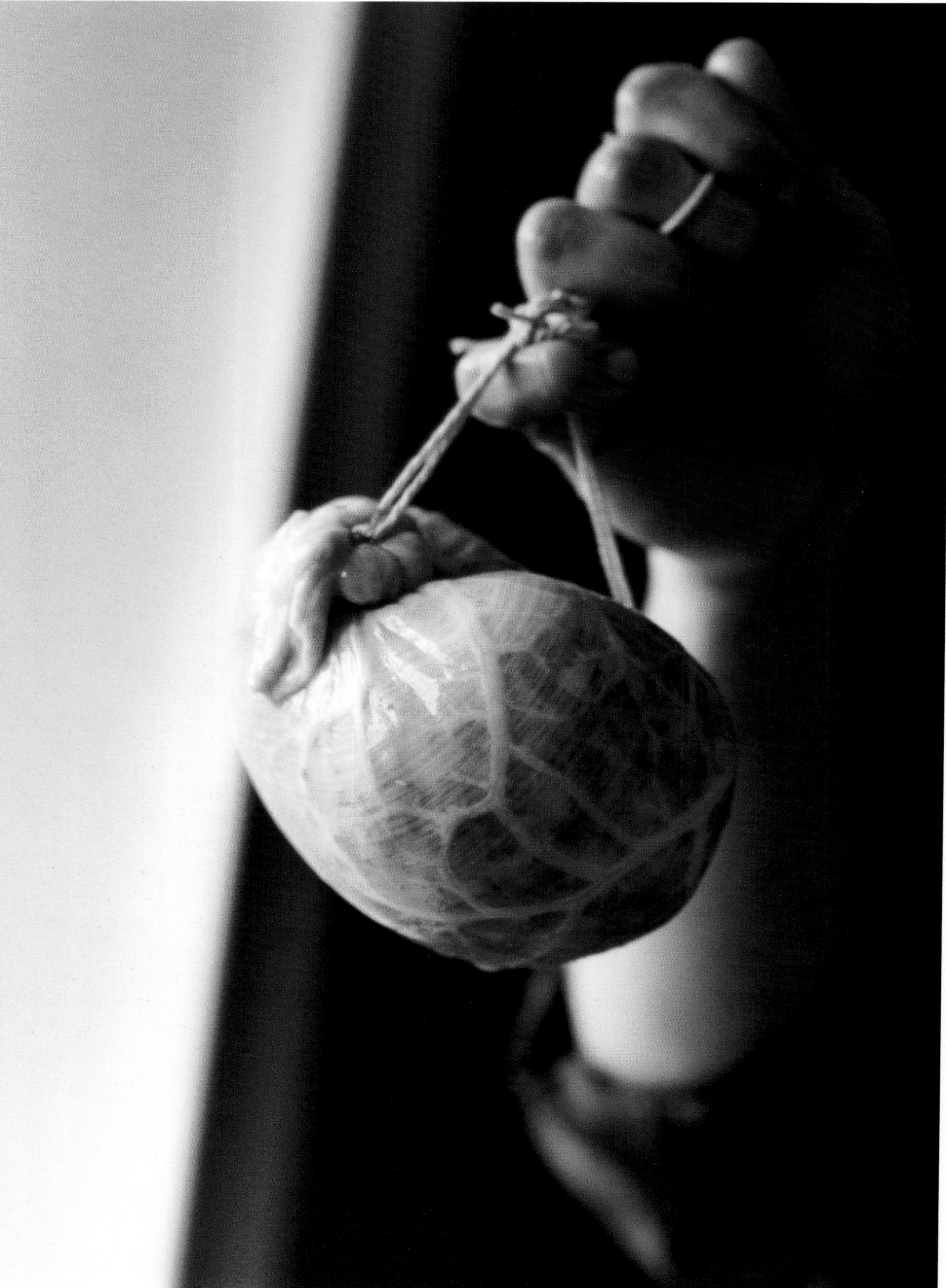

COTECHINO WITH LENTILS AND SALSA VERDE *Makes 3-4*

Natural sausage casings (see Directory, p.529) – ox-middles (5-10 cm wide) for a salami-style cotechino or ox-bung (about 15 cm) for a haggis-style cotechino

1 kg fairly lean pork shoulder

400 g back fat or fatty pork belly (or a combination)

600 g pork rind

50 g fine salt

10 g saltpetre (optional)

1 glass of red wine

2 garlic cloves, finely chopped

1 teaspoon freshly ground black pepper or mixed peppercorns

A few gratings of fresh nutmeg

1/2 teaspoon ground cinnamon

1/2 teaspoon ground cloves

A good pinch of ground mace

1/2 teaspoon dried thyme

4 dried bay leaves

The cotechino is a very distinctive Italian cured boiling sausage, whose unique sticky-salty quality is created by including finely chopped pork rind in the meat mix. For years I had only ever tasted the vacuum-packed, factory-made version you can buy in Italian delis. They're pretty good. Then I ate one made by chef Mauro Bregoli at his restaurant, The Old Manor House, in Hampshire. It was outstanding. I have since learned to make my own cotechino, and there are few of my 'pig products' that I look forward to with more relish.

Cotechino is traditionally served with lentils or beans and salsa verde, but also plays a vital role in Bollito Misto (see page 304).

Note: The pork, fat and rind are easier to process if very cold or even partly frozen.

Before you get to work on your cotechino mix, put the casings to soak in a large bowl of fresh water. Slosh them about to rinse off the salt, then run the tap through the inside of them to flush them clean. When they are slippery, flexible and thoroughly rinsed of salt, they are ready to use.

Coarsely mince the pork. Ideally the back fat should be finely diced into 'petit pois' sized cubes by hand but you can get away with pulsing it in a food processor or coarsely mincing it. If you're using belly, just mince it. The pork rind must be finely chopped, by hand or in a food processor, not minced. Now combine all the ingredients in a large basin, mixing thoroughly with your hands.

Fill the sausage casings following the instructions with your sausage machine, or by hand using a plastic funnel, until you have sausages about 25 cm long, tightly packed and double knotted with butcher's string at both ends.

Hang the cotechini in a dry, airy place, such as a draughty outbuilding or covered porch – they shouldn't touch each other. They are good for boiling any time after about 5 days but perhaps at their best at around 15-20 days. By about 40 days they will be pretty dry and hard. If you want to keep them any longer, they should be vac-packed or clingfilmed and refrigerated, when they will keep for another month or so. Or freeze them to keep indefinitely.

To cook a cotechino, completely immerse the sausage in a pan of fresh cold water and bring to the boil. Simmer gently for about 1 1/2 hours for thin ones (i.e. stuffed middles) or 2 1/2 hours for fat ones (i.e. stuffed bung). Cut into thick slices and serve on a bed of warm lentils (page 520) with Salsa Verde (page 514) and, if you can get them, the Italian spiced fruits called mostarda di Cremona.

STEAK TARTARE

About 150g rump or sirloin steak per person

THE TRIMMINGS:

1 raw egg yolk per person ***(including me)***

Some shallots, finely chopped ***(1 good teaspoon)***

Some salted capers (preferable to vinegar-pickled, but these will do), rinsed and roughly chopped ***(1/2 teaspoon)***

Some gherkins, finely chopped ***(not for me)***

Some flat-leaf parsley, finely chopped ***(a good shake)***

Dijon mustard ***(not for me)***

English mustard ***(about 1/4 teaspoon)***

Worcestershire sauce ***(3 good shakes)***

Tabasco sauce ***(4-5 drops)***

Tomato ketchup ***(1/2 teaspoon)***

Salt ***(just a pinch)***

Freshly ground black pepper ***(3-4 good twists)***

TO ACCOMPANY:

Chips (p.519)

Or Melba Toast (p.522)

No apologies for carrying this recipe over from The River Cottage Cookbook. *It's one of the greats – provided you start with the very finest beef you can lay your hands on. For me, it's one of the treats I look forward to when I take delivery of a well-hung side of my own home-reared beef.*

My non-prescriptive version of the dish allows each diner to fix his or her own, using a selection of classic flavourings. But this time I thought I'd let you know how I like mine (see bold quantities in brackets, opposite), even if it does mean owning up to the not absolutely authentic (and previously unmentioned) smidgen of tomato ketchup.

Trim the meat of all fat (except marbling) and sinew, then process or mince it finely. Another traditional way to do it is to scrape the meat with the blade of a knife – but I find the resulting texture is *too* fine-grained, and almost pâté-like.

Shape the meat into patties, one per person, and place on serving plates. Make a dip in each patty and tip the egg yolk into it. Place all the other ingredients in individual bowls and take to the table. Encourage everyone to mix their own. Serve with chips, or Melba toast.

KIBBEH NAYE *Serves 4-5 as a starter*

About 500g lean lamb (weight after trimming)

50g bulgar wheat

1 small onion (or 2 shallots)

2-3 tablespoons best-quality extra virgin olive oil

2 good pinches of cayenne pepper

A few drops of lemon juice

About 1/2 teaspoon salt

A small bunch of parsley, finely chopped

TO SERVE:

Pitta bread

Cos lettuce

Fresh radishes

Black olives

I love this dish, a kind of Lebanese lamb tartare, and have found it is best made with mature lamb or hogget. Don't buy lamb mince, which will be made with all the ropy trimmings, but go for half a leg, or leg steaks or chump chops, and trim out any sinews, then mince it (or pulse in a food processor) yourself.

Cook the bulgar wheat by simmering it gently in a fraction over twice its volume of lightly salted water. After 12-15 minutes, when almost all the water has been absorbed, turn off the heat and put a lid on the pan. Leave to cool and absorb the rest of the water.

You can either grate the onion or, if you fancy your knife skills, chop it very finely into pinhead dice (this gives just a little more texture). Finely mince the lamb, or pulse it in a food processor. It should be a fairly smooth paste. Transfer to a bowl and beat in the onion, 1 tablespoon of the olive oil, the first pinch of cayenne, lemon juice (no more than a few drops) and salt.

Some recipes tell you to beat in the bulgar with the rest of the ingredients, but I like the version where the lamb paste is pressed on to a plate in an even layer and the bulgar wheat is spread on top, then lightly pressed into the lamb. You can use 1 large plate to pass around, or prepare individual servings on small starter plates. Chill for an hour or so before serving.

Finish by trickling with the remaining olive oil, then scatter over the parsley, and the final pinch of cayenne. Eat with hot pitta bread and undressed Cos lettuce leaves, radishes and olives.

A RAISED PORK PIE *Serves 10-12*

1kg pork shoulder, cut into 5mm cubes

250g fresh pork belly, minced (or fatty sausage meat)

250g salt pork, pancetta or streaky bacon (p.429 for home-made), finely chopped

12 sage leaves, finely chopped

Leaves from 2 good sprigs of thyme, chopped

1 teaspoon salt

1 teaspoon coarsely ground black pepper

1 teaspoon ground white pepper

1/2 teaspoon ground mace

A good pinch of cayenne pepper

1 bay leaf

250ml good pork stock that will set to jelly (p.474)

THE HOT WATER CRUST:

100g lard, diced

100g butter, diced

200ml water

550g plain flour

1 1/2 teaspoons salt

2 medium eggs, beaten, plus 1 egg, beaten, to glaze

I only recently made my first raised pork pie, for the television series I presented, 'Treats from the Edwardian Country House'. I thought it was going to be terribly hard, with its unfamiliar pastry (the hot water crust) and liquid stock that has to be poured into the cavity to make the jelly. But our superb food researcher, Hattie Ellis, trawled old recipe books and came up with this synthesised version. It's easy, and it works brilliantly. Deeply satisfying.

Make the hot water crust pastry first. Put the lard, butter and water in a saucepan and heat gently until melted; do not let it boil. Put the flour and salt in a mixing bowl. Make a dip in the centre and add the beaten eggs, stirring them gently around with a knife so they are half mixed with the flour. Pour in the melted fat and water and mix together to form a soft dough; add up to 50ml extra warm water if it is too dry. Knead gently, adding more flour if it is too sticky to handle. Wrap in clingfilm and chill for 1 hour.

For the filling, mix all the meats with the herbs, salt and seasonings (except the bay leaf), so they are thoroughly combined.

Now assemble the pie. Cut off a generous quarter of the pastry and keep in the fridge, for the lid. On a floured surface, roll out the rest of the pastry into a 30cm circle a good centimetre thick. Use this to line a 20cm springform cake tin, pressing the pastry into the sides and flattening any overlap with your fingers. It should come 6-8cm up the sides of the tin.

Fill with the seasoned pork mixture and push the bay leaf into the middle of it. Roll out the reserved piece of pastry into a circle about the size of the tin. Brush the edges of the lining pastry with a little beaten egg, and lay the pastry lid on top of the pie. Crimp the edges together so they are sealed. Cut a 1cm diameter hole in the centre of the pastry lid.

Place the pie in a moderate oven (180°C/Gas Mark 4) and bake for 30 minutes. Reduce the temperature to 160°C/Gas Mark 3 and bake for a further 1 1/4 hours. Carefully release the side of the tin and remove it. Brush the top and sides of the pie with beaten egg and cook for another 15 minutes to set the glaze. Take the pie out of the oven and allow to cool. It will have shrunk slightly in the oven, creating a cavity that is traditionally filled with jellied stock. It's a bit like filling a car with petrol, but requires a slightly more delicate touch. Do it when the pie is still just a little warm. Warm the jellied stock until it is pourable, but not hot. Carefully lift the edges of the centre hole of the pastry with the tip of a knife, making sure you have good access to the cavity. You can use a small funnel for this or, better still, a 'turkey baster', with a squeezy rubber bulb on one end. Tilt the pie from time to time to help distribute the stock, then try and get a little more in. Stop when the stock begins to overflow from the hole. Leave the pie to cool, then put it in the fridge. It will keep for about 2 weeks. Serve with English mustard, pickles and salad.

MEXICAN-STYLE CHORIZO

500g pork shoulder
250g pork belly
15g salt
2 garlic cloves, crushed
3 tablespoons wine vinegar
1 teaspoon freshly ground black pepper
2 teaspoons cayenne pepper
2 teaspoons sweet paprika
1 teaspoon ground coriander
A few gratings of fresh nutmeg
1/2 teaspoon dried thyme

CHORIZO OMELETTE:
2 eggs
A pinch of salt
1 teaspoon butter
1 medium potato, cooked and cut into 2-3cm cubes
2 tablespoons fried chorizo mix

Chorizo is most familiar as a Spanish sausage (see pages 418-19) but in Mexico the definition of it is more flexible than that. The mixture of highly seasoned minced or finely chopped pork can just as well be kept in a bowl in the fridge as in a sausage skin, and is extremely convenient as a stand-by and for garnishing all sorts of dishes. It's a system that can be adopted, with much pleasure and satisfaction, over here. Bear in mind that the spicing is likely to be personal to each household, so the combination opposite should be taken only as a guide.

Finely chop the pork shoulder until the biggest pieces are pea-sized. Or coarsely mince it if you prefer. Coarsely mince the pork belly. Combine the meat with all the other ingredients, mixing thoroughly with your hands. Transfer to a sealed Tupperware dish and refrigerate. Leave for at least 24 hours before using. Every couple of days, pour off any salty liquid that leaches out and add an extra pinch of salt. Keep for up to 2 weeks.

To serve, heat a little olive oil in a pan and add a tablespoon or two of the chorizo mix, according to your needs. Stir-fry it, breaking it up with the edge of a spatula, for 5-7 minutes, until you have crispy, pea-sized crumbs of meat.

Chorizo Omelette (serves 1): The chorizo mixture can be used to spice up all manner of things. A delicious place to start is with a simple omelette.

Beat the eggs and salt together with a fork. Heat the butter in an omelette pan. Gently fry the potato until it is starting to colour. Pour the beaten eggs into the pan, over the potatoes. As the egg starts to set around the edges, push the edges back into the centre to allow more of the runny egg to fall back and set. For me, this omelette is ready when the bottom is lightly browned, most of the edge is set firm, but the surface is still a bit wet and eggy. And I don't turn it over. You, of course, might have different ideas.

Sprinkle the hot chorizo pieces over the omelette and serve at once.

Other suggestions

Chorizo with Shellfish: Clams, mussels and oysters, hot or cold, raw or cooked, combine wonderfully with fried chorizo. Just sprinkle it over as you serve them.

Chorizo with Broad Beans: Toss just-picked, lightly steamed broad beans with a sparing amount of fried chorizo, a trickle of olive oil and a squeeze of lemon juice.

Nachos: Tortilla chips (page 522) topped with fried chorizo and grated cheese, melted in a hot oven, then guzzled in front of a good DVD on a widescreen telly and washed down with a cold beer, is, for those of us who rarely get to the cinema these days, the ultimate in home entertainment.

PORK RILLETTES *Makes just over 1kg*

500g pork shoulder

500g pork belly, rindless

300g home-rendered pork fat (from flair fat or back fat – see p.117) or bought lard

100ml water

3 sprigs of thyme

2 bay leaves

3 cloves

A pinch of mixed spice

A few gratings of fresh nutmeg

Salt and freshly ground black pepper

Rillettes – shreds of highly seasoned pork (or duck or goose) preserved in their own fat – are one of the great inventions of the French charcutier. *They are hard to find in the UK but very easy to make at home. The secret is the long, slow cooking of the meat in fat, so it doesn't crisp up and brown but just melts and falls apart. If you're a fan, you really should give them a try. It is preferable to render some good-quality pork fat yourself than to use lard.*

Cut the pork shoulder into thumb-size strips, along the grain of the meat. Cut the pork belly into slices 1cm thick. Place the rendered fat and water in a wide, heavy saucepan over a very low heat and add the meat. Tie up the thyme, bay and cloves in a small square of muslin and add to the pot. Cook very slowly, so the liquid is just trembling, not bubbling, for at least 4 hours. This can be done either on the hob (where you can keep an eye on it) or in a very low oven (120°C/Gas Mark ½). Turn the meat occasionally, just to check nothing is sticking to the bottom of the pan.

The meat is cooked when it is completely tender, still only lightly browned, and can easily be dragged into shreds with 2 forks. When it has reached this stage, remove from the heat and leave to cool for a while. When *tiède* (a little warmer than room temperature), remove the muslin bag and shred the meat with 2 forks and the occasional bash from a wooden spoon. Carefully add the seasonings as you go – mixed spice, nutmeg, salt and pepper – tasting and adjusting until it's just right.

When the meat is finely and evenly shredded, transfer the rillettes to a large bowl, cover with a piece of paper greased with pork fat and refrigerate. They are best after they have been left to ripen for a few days in the fridge. Serve either chilled or at room temperature, or gently warmed until the fat runs, according to your taste. Accompany with fresh crusty bread and *cornichons* (small pickled gherkins), which are essential to cut the fat. I like my rillettes cold from the fridge with a warm baguette.

Rillettes can be kept in the fridge (or even a cool larder) for up to 6 months if you pack them in jars or Tupperware boxes with no air pockets and cover the surface with a good 5mm of clean rendered fat.

Variation

Goose, Duck and Rabbit Rillettes: Besides pork, the most popular rillettes are made from goose, duck and rabbit, often combined with pork. They are all delicious. The easiest way to create these classic variations is to substitute the boned-out meat of the relevant creatures for the pork shoulder and to use goose or duck fat instead of pork, if you can get it. Then proceed precisely as above.

PRESERVED DUCK OR GOOSE LEGS

2 large duck or goose legs

25g rock salt

1 teaspoon freshly ground black pepper

2-3 sprigs of thyme

2-3 bay leaves, broken

6 garlic cloves, crushed

2 tablespoons olive oil

About 750g rendered goose or duck fat, or lard at a pinch

I love this dish – confit, *as the French call it. Having a jar just sitting in the larder, bursting with savoury potential, makes me salivate every time I see it.*

A whole duck or goose can be jointed and preserved but it is more common to use just the legs. The legless carcass can then be roasted, as it is in my special Christmas recipe (see The River Cottage Year*). Or the breasts can be cut off and used in all kinds of recipes. One of my favourites is a distinctly non-French dish using fresh pineapple, chilli and soy sauce –* *see page 366.*

Removed from the fat in which they are stored, the confit legs are traditionally crisped up in a hot oven and served with lentils or beans. I made a delicious summer version of this the other day by tossing shredded, crispy shards of home-made goose confit with just-picked broad beans from the garden. Outstanding.

Generally one leg of duck will serve one person as a generous main course, and a goose leg will just about do two. But if you're shredding and tossing, as with the broad beans, one duck leg will serve four and a goose leg just about stretch to six. Confit is also an essential ingredient in the classic Cassoulet – *see page 302.*

Mix together the salt, pepper, thyme, bay leaves and garlic and rub them thoroughly into the skin and meat of the legs. Leave for 48 hours in a tray or dish in the fridge, giving the legs another salty massage after 24 hours. Take out and scrape off all these seasonings and reserve.

Heat the olive oil in a heavy pan over a moderate heat and brown the legs thoroughly, skin-side down first and then all over. Put the legs into an ovenproof dish in which they fit as snugly as possible, adding the seasoning scrapings and enough rendered fat to cover, or almost cover, the meat. Then cook in a low oven (150°C/Gas Mark 2) for about 2 hours, until the meat is nearly falling off the bone. If the legs are not quite covered by the fat, turn them carefully 2 or 3 times during cooking. Remove from the oven and leave to cool.

To preserve your confit legs, put them in a large Kilner jar or similar, or into a plastic tub with a lid, and pour over enough warm, liquid goose or duck fat to cover them completely and seal the meat from the air. Leave until the fat has set hard, then cover with the lid. Thus preserved, the confit will keep for several months in a cool larder or even longer in the fridge. Or simply smeared in fat and wrapped in clingfilm, they will still keep for a good couple of weeks in the fridge. When the confit is to be served, remove the legs from the container and scrape off most – not all – of the fat (rendered and filtered, it can be used again). Place the legs skin-side down in a baking tray. Put into a very hot oven (230°C/Gas Mark 8) for 5 minutes, then drain off the melted fat. Return to the oven, skin-side up, for 5-10 minutes, until piping hot and crisp.

Serve with beans or lentils and accompany, or follow up, with a crisp salad. The Watercress and Orange Salad on page 523 cuts the fat beautifully.

RICH LIVER PÂTÉ *Makes 2 x 500g or 1 x 1kg pâté*

750g fresh liver

1 large onion, finely chopped

A knob of butter

150ml whole milk

1 tablespoon double cream

100g breadcrumbs

250g minced pork

A splash of port

A few sage leaves, chopped

Leaves from 1 sprig of thyme, chopped

A pinch of ground mace

A pinch of cayenne pepper

1/2 teaspoon salt

Streaky bacon rashers, stretched with the back of a knife, to line the dishes (optional)

Freshly ground black pepper

This delicious pâté can be made with any liver at all, from rabbits to reindeer and chickens to chinchillas … which of course I've never tried. I often make it with the very fresh liver of my pigs, lambs and cattle on the day I take them to slaughter. They're all a little different, but it works every time. You can ring the changes with the alcohol and herbs, but port and sage are good all-rounders.

Pick over the liver, trimming and discarding any tough membranes or coarse ventricles, and chop roughly. Sweat the onion in the butter until soft and translucent. Warm up the milk with the cream, add the breadcrumbs and leave to soak for 5 minutes.

Put all the ingredients except the bacon rashers into a food processor and pulse for several bursts until thoroughly mixed. (You can make it as coarse or smooth as you like. I ring the changes, and sometimes even remove half of it while still coarse to make one pâté, then whizz the rest until pretty smooth to make another.)

Pile the mixture into 1 large (or 2 medium) terrine dish(es), which can be lined with stretched rashers of bacon if you like, or just greased with a little butter. Cover with a lid or a double layer of buttered foil. Place in a roasting tin and pour enough boiling water into the tin to come half way up the sides of the dish. Put in a moderate oven (160°C/Gas Mark 3) for 1 1/4-1 3/4 hours. The pâté is cooked when it comes away from the side of the dish and is firm to the touch.

Remove from the roasting tin and press with a weighted board, or similar, while cooling. Serve with toast. This pâté can be kept in the fridge for at least a week, and freezes well.

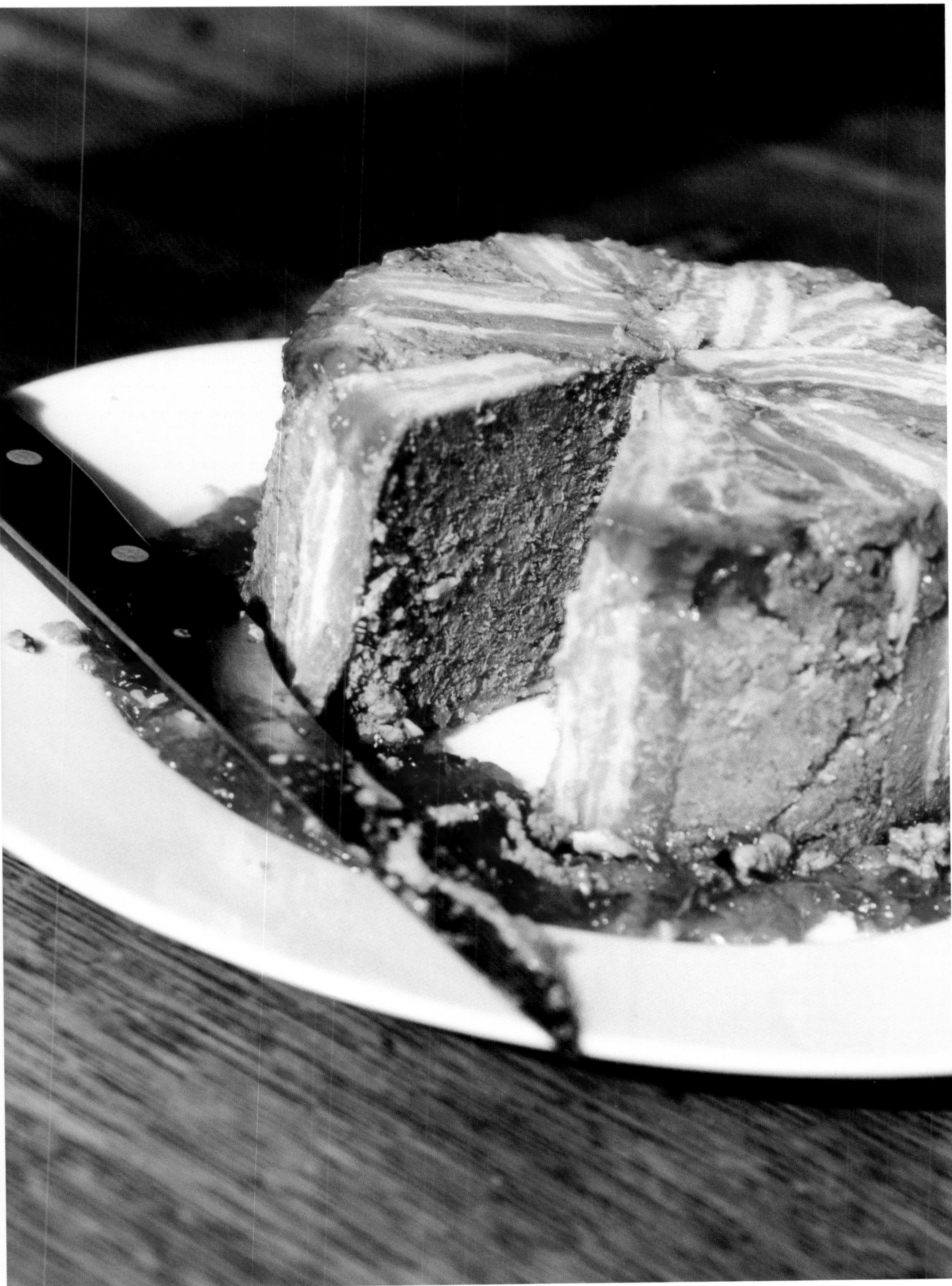

TERRINE OF SWEETBREADS WITH A BROAD BEAN PURÉE

Serves 8

500g calf's or lamb's sweetbreads (pp.196-7)

1 bay leaf

10 thinly sliced streaky bacon rashers, stretched with the back of a knife

THE FORCEMEAT:

250g minced pork (you could use skinned butcher's sausages)

1/2 egg, beaten

25g white breadcrumbs, soaked in a little milk

1 tablespoon port or Madeira

A few sage leaves, finely chopped

A sprig of thyme, finely chopped

Salt and freshly ground black pepper

THE BROAD BEAN PURÉE:

250g large broad beans (shelled weight), plus a few baby broad beans to garnish, if liked

1/2 garlic clove, grated

A squeeze of lemon juice

1-2 tablespoons olive oil

This is a very 'cheffy' dish, which I devised to please and, I admit, impress my wife, who loves sweetbreads and broad beans. I include it for two reasons. Firstly, to show that such concoctions, fancy and scary though they may sound, are not at all difficult to make successfully at home – think bricks and mortar (see page 423). Secondly, I happen to think it's quite delicious.

Poach and pick over the sweetbreads as described on page 197.

To make the forcemeat, mix the minced pork with the egg, breadcrumbs, port or Madeira and herbs and season well with salt and pepper.

Now assemble the terrine. First grease your terrine dish (a loaf tin will work too) and line it with a bay leaf, then the bacon rashers. Spread a 1cm-thick layer of forcemeat over the bottom of the terrine. Then arrange about a third of the sweetbread pieces in a layer on top, pressing them firmly into the forcemeat. Repeat with another 2 layers of forcemeat and 2 more of sweetbreads. Don't worry about making these layers too precise and even. Just make sure there is plenty of 'mortar' (forcemeat) around your 'bricks' (the sweetbreads). Finish with a thin layer of the forcemeat, and wrap any loose ends of bacon back over the terrine. Cover with a double layer of buttered foil, and the lid of the terrine dish if it has one.

Put the terrine dish in a bain marie (i.e. a roasting tin with enough boiling water to come half way up the sides of the dish) and place in a moderate oven (160°C/Gas Mark 3) for about 1½ hours. The terrine is cooked when it comes away from the side of the dish and is firm to the touch. Remove from the oven and leave to cool a little. Then press with a weighted board, or similar-sized dish, and leave in a cool larder or fridge overnight.

To make the purée, simmer the broad beans in salted water for 8-10 minutes, until completely tender. Drain and leave until cool enough to handle, then slip the dark green kernels out of the grey-green skins, which can be discarded. Use a fork to mash the kernels with the grated garlic, a squeeze of lemon juice and a little salt and pepper. Then beat in enough olive oil to give a thick, glossy purée. You could make this purée in a food processor.

To serve up the dish, first turn the terrine out on to a board: run a thin, sharp knife blade around the sides and then prise it carefully out of the dish, with a pair of forks if that helps. With a very sharp knife, carefully cut it into slices about 2cm thick (1 slice per person). Place each slice in the centre of a small plate, with a generous spoonful of the purée on the side. Garnish with a few raw, just-picked, baby broad beans, if you have them.

POTTED HOUGH *Serves 8-10*

1kg shin of beef (boneless weight)

1 marrow bone, sawn in half

1 pig's trotter (optional)

2 large carrots, peeled

1 bay leaf

1 large onion, peeled and studded with 6 cloves

About 1/2 teaspoon ground mace

A pinch of cayenne pepper (optional)

A pinch of ground ginger (optional)

Salt and freshly ground black pepper

This is a pleasantly spiced version of corned beef, and makes an excellent picnic dish. Hough is the Scottish word for leg, or shin, of beef but you can use other cheap cuts of meat, such as foreflank or brisket (you will need to discard some of the excess fat on these). The inclusion of a pig's trotter helps to set the jelly.

Put the meat, bone and trotter in a stockpot with the carrots, bay leaf and the onion studded with the cloves. Cover with cold water and bring to a gentle simmer. Skim off the grey foam that rises to the surface, then simmer very gently for 3-4 hours, until the meat is completely tender. Remove the meat from the pan and, when cool, cover and refrigerate. Remove and discard the bone and vegetables from the liquid (but keep the pig's trotter). Leave the stock in the pan to go cold – in a cool larder or fridge (ideally overnight) – then remove the fat that has set hard on the surface.

Warm the stock so it is liquid again, then strain it through a sieve lined with muslin or a cotton cloth. Boil hard until it has reduced by about half and tastes well flavoured and beefy but not too rich.

Put the cold beef, along with the meat and skin from the pig's trotter, through a coarse mincer. Transfer to a large basin and moisten with a couple of ladlefuls of the stock. Season well with the spices, salt and black pepper, mixing in thoroughly and tasting as you go. When you're happy with the seasoning, pile the minced meat loosely into a terrine dish or pudding basin(s), or individual ramekins. Ladle over a little more stock – just enough to cover the meat and set as a thin layer of jelly – and put in the fridge to set.

Traditionally potted hough is served cold with pickled beetroot. In the summer I also like it with boiled baby beetroot and/or new potatoes. You can turn it out of its dish by dipping it briefly in warm water and slipping a knife round the edge.

PIGEON PÂTÉ *Serves 4-6*

6 whole pigeons

50g butter

2 tablespoons olive oil

1 onion, chopped

1 large garlic clove, chopped

1 small glass of port

1 egg

100g sausage meat (or about 2 good butcher's sausages, skinned)

1 teaspoon redcurrant jelly

A sprig of thyme

A pinch of ground mace

50g whole pistachio kernels (optional)

2 bay leaves

About a dozen streaky bacon rashers, rind removed

Salt and freshly ground black pepper

For anyone who shoots pigeons in any quantity, this is a wonderful recipe to have down pat. And for anyone who just likes great pâté, it's well worth buying the pigeons. If you can't get them with their livers, then buy 2 or 3 chicken livers to replace them.

The pigeon carcasses could be roasted and used to make Game Soup (page 507).

Pluck and draw the pigeons (page 162) and then cut off the breasts, along with any other meat you can easily trim from the carcass. Locate and save the livers and hearts. Cut each breast into 3 or 4 pieces.

Heat half the butter and oil in a frying pan, add the onion and garlic and fry until soft and translucent. Remove from the pan. Add the rest of the butter and oil to the pan and turn up the heat a little. Quickly fry the pigeon meat, livers and hearts until they are nicely browned all over. Remove from the pan and set aside to cool. Deglaze the still-warm pan with the port (page 334), then pour the deglazing juices over the meat. Transfer to a food processor, add the egg, sausage meat, redcurrant jelly, thyme and mace and season with salt and pepper. Process until fairly fine but still textured. Mix in the pistachio kernels, if using, by hand.

Place the bay leaves shiny-side down on the bottom of a terrine dish or a small loaf tin. Stretch the bacon rashers on a board with the back of a heavy knife. Then line the dish with the rashers of bacon, leaving enough hanging over the sides to cover the top of the pâté. Pile the mixture into the dish, then fold over the loose ends of bacon. Cover with its lid (or a double layer of buttered greaseproof paper secured with a rubber band).

Place the dish in a bain marie – i.e. a deep roasting tin filled with enough hot water to come about half way up the sides of the terrine dish. Bake in a moderate oven (180°C/Gas Mark 4) for about 1¼ hours. The pâté should be starting to shrink away from the edges of the dish. Remove from the roasting tin and press with a weighted board, or similar, while cooling.

When completely cool, run a knife between the terrine dish and the bacon, then invert the dish on to a plate or board to turn out the pâté. Serve in slices, with warm bread or toast and perhaps some chutney. A few days 'ripening' in the fridge will improve the flavour of this pâté.

FAGGOTS WITH ONION GRAVY *Serves 6*

About 250g fresh pig's liver

About 250g fresh fatty pork scraps, or coarse sausage meat

1 fresh pig's heart, split in half and rinsed

About 100g ham or bacon scraps

About 100g fresh breadcrumbs or oatmeal

A few sage leaves, finely chopped

A few thyme leaves, finely chopped

A good pinch of ground mace

A good pinch of ground allspice

Caul fat or streaky bacon rashers, for wrapping

Salt and freshly ground black pepper

Onion Gravy (p.517), to serve

Traditionally faggots were improvised by butchers, and home cooks, using whatever bits of pork offal and bacon off-cuts came to hand. Inevitably, individuals honed their recipes and different butchers became famous for their distinctive style – much of the art is in the spicing. The thing that almost all faggots have in common is their lacy wrapping of caul fat (see page 197). These days not all butchers sell this but you can make faggots without it – wrap them in flattened streaky bacon instead.

Good faggots are a wonderful thing, and worth making from scratch. Feel free to improvise on the recipe below, according to what comes to hand.

Roughly chop, then coarsely mince all the meats and combine in a bowl. Add the breadcrumbs or oatmeal, plus the herbs, spices and some salt and pepper and mix together thoroughly. Shape the mixture into 6 balls. Wrap each in a square of caul fat – cut large enough to overlap, it will bind on itself. Or stretch rashers of streaky bacon with the back of a heavy knife, making them as long and wide as you can, and wrap the faggots in these. Two rashers per faggot should do it, one crossed over the other at right angles.

Flatten the balls slightly and place in a baking tin or other ovenproof dish in which they fit together fairly snugly. Bake in a moderate oven (180°C/Gas Mark 4) for 50-60 minutes, basting once or twice with the fat and juices that run from them. They will be slightly shrunk and nicely brown when done. Serve at once, with onion gravy. Split Pea Purée (page 520) and/or mashed potatoes (page 518) make good accompaniments.

Faggots can be left to cool and kept in the fridge for up to a week, then reheated gently in the gravy to serve. They are also delicious cold – cut into cubes with a little English mustard to dab on them. And a faggot sandwich – with white bread and brown (i.e. HP) sauce – is highly recommended.

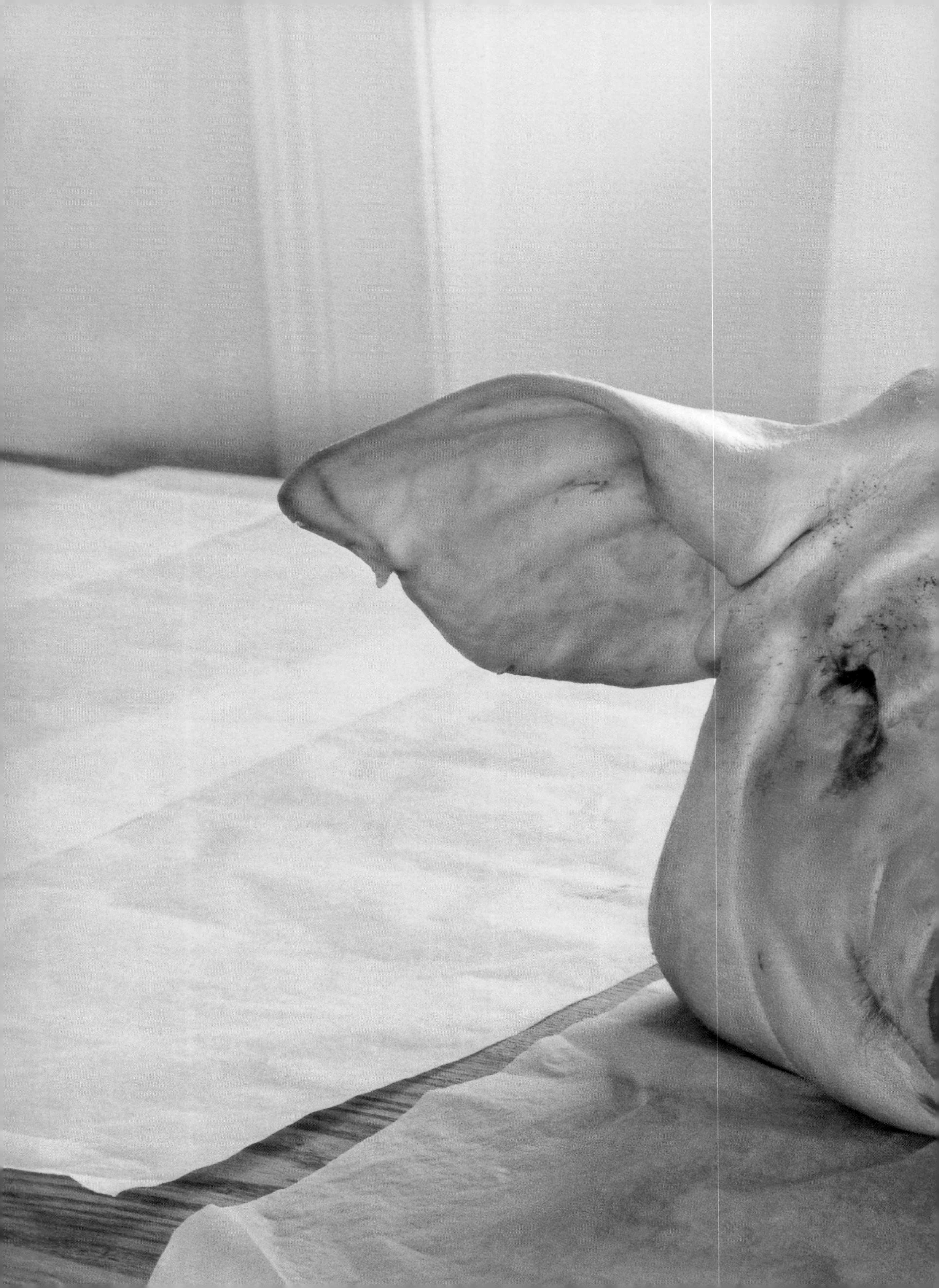

15. MEAT THRIFT

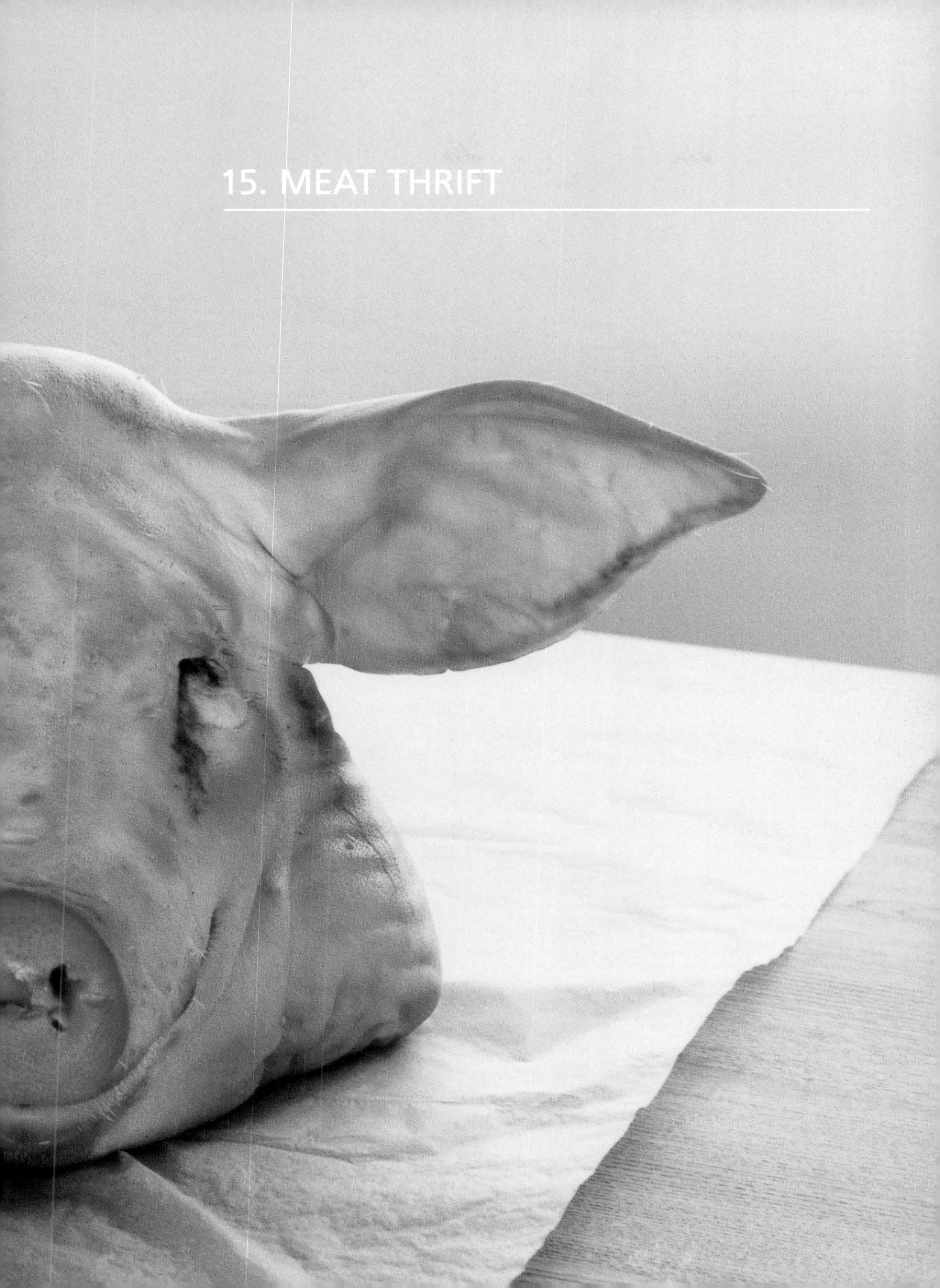

15. MEAT THRIFT

Stock, Soups and Leftovers

If the word 'thrift' has negative associations for you, then banish them now. If 'parsimonious', 'mean' and 'frugal' pop up in your mental Thesaurus, it's time to forget them. Replace them immediately with 'imaginative', 'resourceful' and 'thorough'. These are the adjectives that best describe the outlook of the complete meat cook, as he or she assesses the full spectrum of available meat cuts and the endless possibilities they present.

Meat thrift is all about respect. Respect for the animals that have died to feed you. Respect for the farmers who have (assuming you've chosen your meat well) worked tirelessly to keep those animals healthy and contented, so their meat is as good as it can be. And respect for the whole history of animal husbandry and meat gastronomy – endeavours that until recently scorned any practice that was wasteful of the livestock on which they depended.

These days, a total lack of respect pervades almost the entire business of meat production. As I have argued throughout this book, the possibility of reclaiming these lost values rests with you, the consumer. And if you're not for them, then I'm afraid you must accept that you're against them.

The commitment to be thrifty and resourceful with meat should become second nature to the enlightened cook, but there are two key moments in the chain of consumption when it is actively expressed. Firstly, when deciding what meat to buy as you set about planning a meal. Secondly, when that meal is over but the meat is not finished, and you wonder what can be done with the leftovers.

Thrifty Meat Shopping

To uphold the principles of thrifty meat consumption requires a commitment to diversity and creativity – but that doesn't mean you have to be extravagant or profligate. Quite the contrary.

If you are even moderately well off and can afford good meat, there's no excuse for dabbling with factory-farmed rubbish at all. But splashing out on prime roasting and grilling cuts of organic beef, lamb and pork isn't, on its own, the solution either. The best thing you can do for both the welfare of meat animals and your own pleasure in the kitchen is firstly to find a source, or sources, of responsibly, respectfully farmed meat, and secondly to make a commitment to using the whole gamut of available cuts from (and in the case of the pig, including) nose to tail. If you're interested enough in good meat to have come this far, why not go the whole hog? Make an active commitment to explore those thrifty dishes that have served the 'peasants' of the world so well. These are invariably among the most delicious dishes of any food culture – necessity being the mother of invention and all that.

Of course, knowledge of such dishes is indispensable to those on a tight budget – it always has been. But these days it is clear that there are two ways of saving money when it comes to buying meat. The 'modern' way is to head straight for the section of the supermarket where low prices reflect low standards and a complete lack of concern for welfare (we're talking two-for-one deals on mass-produced chickens and 'economy' packs of frozen minced beef). The 'old-fashioned' approach is to know what to do with certain cuts of meat that are inexpensive even when taken from the best possible carcass – shin of beef, scrag end of lamb or belly of pork, for example. Such thrifty practice has always been in the best interests of good farming, good cooking and good conscience. Those who embrace it do the whole business of meat production a big favour.

In the end, even when it comes to an extravagant treat – steak, for example – the reformed bargain hunter may discover the 'less is more' perspective that favours a well-aged, well-marbled rump steak sliced to order by a trusted butcher over a bumper pack of pink, wet, immature, pre-cut sirloins in the supermarket. Because it's only a treat if it really is a treat.

The great thing about raising your own meat and dividing up whole carcasses for storing in the freezer is that you quickly learn to work your way around the different cuts. Reach for the prime cuts too often and you are left with a freezer full of 'tricky bits'. However, once you've learned that those bits are not really so tricky after all, and are easily transformed into some of your favourite meals, then whatever you pull out of the freezer (you could do it blindfolded, as an interesting exercise in culinary creativity), you know you're in for a treat.

The same lessons can be learned if you buy half or quarter animals direct from the best producers and keep them in the freezer. In the end this good, thrifty use of every cut on a whole, quality carcass is what makes sense for every household, wherever it is on the economic scale.

I accept that not everyone has the freezer space to embrace this policy without compromise. But you can still shop in tune with the principle it upholds, ringing the changes with the different cuts each time you visit the butcher's. Here is a quick checklist of what might be considered the thriftiest cuts for each of the three main meats, and the thriftiest creatures from the whole array of poultry and game. For ideas on what to do with them, refer to the discussion of the cuts in each of the relevant chapters in Part One: Understanding Meat. See also my Cheap But Very Cheerful list in the Alternative Recipe Index (page 534): as most of the recipes at the end of this chapter deal with the impending subject of leftovers, many of the recipes that are thrifty 'from scratch', as it were, appear elsewhere – particularly in the Slow Cooking chapter.

Thrifty beef cuts (see pages 78-84)

Shin; brisket; forequarter flank/short ribs; skirt; oxtail; beef bones for stock; offal – ox heart, tripe (pages 192, 198-9)

Thrifty lamb cuts (see pages 95-103)
Scrag end; shanks; shoulder; breast; offal – tongue, heart, liver (pages 186, 192, 194-6)

Thrifty pork and bacon cuts (see pages 116-21)
Head (including ears and cheeks, sometimes available separately); tails; knuckle/hand (especially of bacon, aka ham hocks); trotters; belly; offal – heart, kidneys, liver (pages 192-6)

Thrifty game
Pheasants, in season November to January (page 163); pigeons, all year round (pages 164-5); rabbits, especially in summer and autumn (page 169-72)

Thrift with Leftovers

Some of my favourite meat dishes are made from leftovers. The point that is perhaps not made often enough is that most of them are all the better for it. A shepherd's pie made from scratch with fresh minced lamb will never come close to one put together from a leftover leg or shoulder of roast lamb.

Professional chefs have all sorts of tricks for recycling leftover meat. Even in the best restaurants, this is a fundamental part of the difficult economics of the business. Yet they often seem to regard the reappearance of meat ingredients from one day's menu to the next as a shameful secret, to be covered up at all costs. Personally, I would prefer them to take the opposite approach and make a feature of it. If I had my way, all restaurant menus would have a section openly devoted to dishes made from leftovers – as part of a fixed price 'Thrift Menu', for example.

You should have no qualms about using leftover meat. Not to revisit the cold roast with a view to squeezing another meal out of it would be a travesty on three fronts: a blunder in basic home economics; a missed opportunity to eat what is, in my house at least, often one of the most enjoyable meals of the week; and, not least, a posthumous insult to the animal from which the joint came.

A good knowledge of strategies and recipes for cooking with leftovers should also inform your choice of meat in the first place. You may plump for a whole shoulder of lamb rather than a pack of chops when only four or five are to be fed, in the certain knowledge that the family will get at least one further meal from it in the days that follow. Or you may buy a whole chicken rather than a pair of boneless breasts to share with your partner, in the expectation that it will provide you both with very different suppers for three or four nights in a row.

Even so, you never quite know how much meat will be left after the first sitting. This means the further culinary possibilities of leftovers must be assessed after, and not before, they have been left over. Only then should you start weighing up their potential. Probably the first thing to assess is how much decent lean meat you have left and how much of 'the rest'. Have you got enough skin, bones and less obviously appealing bits and pieces to think about making a stock?

Making Stocks

A stock is a flavoured liquid made by cooking together vegetables, herbs and other flavourings, which usually include the skin and/or bones of meat or fish. Stocks are generally used as a basis for soups, stews and sauces, and the most rewarding meat stocks are the ones made from a decent pile of bones. You can start from scratch, using fresh raw bones acquired specifically for the purpose. Or you can make a stock with leftover cooked meat and bones. Or – and here is how many of the best stocks are made – you can combine the two.

Stocks whose meat and bone content derives entirely from leftovers (the vegetables, of course, should always be fresh) fall into two basic quality categories – first and second class, if you like. I would define a first-class stock as one good enough – that's robust and concentrated enough – to make a fine soup, or perhaps, when reduced, a substantial sauce, with only modest assistance from further added flavours. A second-class stock, put together perhaps from a more modest collection of leftovers, is one that will never quite stand up on its own but will nonetheless provide a useful boost to another dish – such as the one you are putting together with the meat left over from the same joint.

Realistically, the only joints and roasts likely to provide you with enough bones and bits to make a first-class stock are whole poultry and game birds and, at a pinch, a whole forerib or sirloin of beef, saddle of lamb or venison, or extra-long rack of pork. On the other hand, stocks made from scratch, using fresh bones acquired specifically for the purpose, should, if you play your cards right, always be first class.

As a general rule, stocks made from mixed meats don't work very well. The combined flavours taste somehow unnatural, like mixing tea and coffee. Lamb tastes so distinctively lamby that you wouldn't want a dish that made a feature of any other meat to include lamb stock. The exceptions to the 'don't mix' rule are pork and veal bones, which may be considered more or less neutral, and added to stock made from any other type of meat bones. That's why a pig's trotter or a calf's shin is a useful addition to almost any stock, especially if you want it to set as a jelly. Combinations of pork and poultry bones, or pork and game, make particularly fine stocks.

General rules of stock making

The success of any given stock depends on making the best use of what's available on the day. However, there are a few general rules that will help to put all your stocks in pretty good order. But before any of these comes a certain state of mind, not least a degree of pride in your work. One way to achieve this is to imagine that you are making a fine stew of which, when it is finished, you will only be allowed to serve the liquor. Think of every conceivable way to make the flavour deep and intense, yet clean and clear. Know what you're adding, and why you're adding it. That's the basic attitude that informs all five of my golden rules for stock making:

1. Be generous with the vegetables and other aromatics – in quantity and quality
A well-made stock requires a sweetness and balance of flavours that it simply won't get from skin and bones alone. Onions and carrots have a high sugar content and pleasing flavours that balance each other well, and are therefore the *sine qua non* of stock vegetables. If you have neither, or even only one, don't even start making a stock (though leeks could just about understudy onions in an emergency). Wait until you have got some in – even freezing your bones and other meaty bits, if necessary.

Beyond this double act (Laurel and Hardy?), celery is highly desirable but not, in my view, essential. Other aromatic root vegetables – parsnips and celeriac spring to mind – are very nice to include but shouldn't be allowed to dominate.

All vegetables for stocks should be as fresh and perky as you'd like them to be in a stew. Browning or shrivelled outer leaves of leeks, for example, will impart a slight flavour of old cabbage to your stock. Bendy carrots with mildew spots won't do either – though they might just be salvaged by vigorous peeling and trimming. Do not use vegetables that have been cooked. All their best assets – their flavours and sugars – are already spent.

Peelings, outer leaves and vegetable scraps can be included, provided they pass quality control, but they will not be enough on their own. You'll need whole carrots and onions – at least two medium or one very large of each (and ideally double that) for every whole chicken carcass or, say, 1kg of beef or lamb bones, and corresponding 1-1.5 litres of water.

When it comes to herbs, I'd use fresh – thyme, parsley (the stalks alone are fine) and bay are good all-rounders – or none at all (except perhaps a dried bay leaf). Most dried herbs, stewed for the length of time it takes to make a good stock, will impart a tired taste – like bad herb tea.

2. Pack it all tight
A single tea bag in a huge teapot will not make anyone a decent cup of tea. By the same token, you can't miraculously increase the capacity of your stock to feed and please by simply adding more and more water. So, pack the bones and other meaty leftovers fairly tightly with the vegetables in a saucepan of a suitable size – together they should at least half fill it. It will certainly help if you chop up or break the larger bones and cut the vegetables into small chunks. Then use as little water as you need to cover everything in the pan. But keep it all covered – just – throughout the cooking time, by topping up with boiling water occasionally, as necessary. Bits of bone left high and dry sticking out of the pot will not be surrendering their flavours to the stock, and that's a waste.

Incidentally, the best pots for stock making are heavy-based stainless steel or Le Creuset-style enamelled cast iron, though you can use any robust saucepan that can hold a gentle simmer over a low flame (see below). It's a good idea to have at least two options – 'large' (about 10-12 litres capacity) and 'medium' (about

3-4 litres). I'm not sure where the scientists have got to in the debate about aluminium cookware and Alzheimer's – but then I haven't had any aluminium saucepans in my kitchen for years.

3. Find the 'tremulous simmer' – and keep it going

I've described this very gentle simmer, whereby a few bubbles just tremble the surface every few seconds or so, several times already in this book – and I've just done it again. It is important, and never more so than when making stock. Boiled any harder than this, stocks will not merely become cloudy, they may well release and emphasise some undesirable flavours – a kind of chalkiness trapped deep in the bones, or even some ammonia-like notes associated with over-boiled meat.

Once you've found this gentle simmer, keep an eye on the surface of the stock for the first ten to twenty minutes. If any grey or brown scum appears, like small patches of dirty bubble bath, skim it off with a slotted spoon. This will help to keep your stock clean – in terms of transparency and also taste. Once the bubbles in the scum are clean white, not grubby, you can stop skimming.

The tremulous simmer can be maintained in a low oven, rather than on the hob – 110-120°C/Gas Mark 1/4-1/2 is about right. Here the pan should have the lid on, to prevent too much evaporation.

If you're knowingly knocking up a second-class stock, for immediate use, then two hours at this gentle pace will release most of the flavour you can expect. If you've laid down the foundations – plenty of good bones and fresh veg – for a first-class version, then you should give it about four or five hours (if it's an extra large stockpot – 10-litre capacity or more – you can happily leave it overnight). Beyond that, you're never going to squeeze any extra flavour out of your bones and vegetables, and any further cooking only risks tainting the fine flavours you've managed to capture.

4. Taste and adjust accordingly – boil to reduce if necessary

At the end of the cooking time, strain the stock. Ideally do this twice – once through a colander to sift out the big stuff, then through a fine sieve or *chinois* to remove the smaller particles. If you're saving the stock for later use, let it go completely cold – either in the fridge or a cool larder, or even, in winter, outside. Then any fat that has rendered into the stock will set hard on the top and is easily removed.

But above all, *taste* it – at the earliest opportunity (i.e. *before* it gets cold). This way you know what you've ended up with. If you feel the flavour is weaker than you'd hoped, or than you need for the recipe you have in mind, then you have the option of rapid boiling to reduce the volume (through evaporation) and thereby concentrate the flavour. But before you do this, be sure to strain the stock one final time, this time through cotton or muslin, and return it to a scrupulously clean pan. Once it's free of all small particles, you can boil it as hard as you like without the risk of spoiling the flavour.

How much you reduce it is up to you, and of course depends on what end use you plan for it. But you might like to think of a stock in terms of three levels of increasing concentration, starting with ...

Well-flavoured water: This is the concentration of a good second-class stock or a light first-class one, intended to be added to, but not the entire flavour source of, a stew or soup. When a recipe calls for 'a litre of stock or water', be pleased that it is this, and not plain water, that you have to hand. If, however, it calls for 'good strong stock' or similar, think in terms of reducing it by half or even two-thirds, until you have ...

A potent brew: This describes a stock that would stand up unadulterated as a punchy consommé or sippable broth. It is also a very sound basis for a robust stew or soup, where you want the meat flavours to run deep in the liquor. On the other hand, it's probably too strong for a light, fresh vegetable soup, which may end up tasting a bit heavy and meaty. It's likely to set as a light jelly when cold – or a very firm jelly if a pig's trotter has been involved.

If you've followed my Rules 1-3 above, starting with a good collection of bones, then such a strong stock may be achievable without further reduction. But if you really are looking to serve it as consommé or broth, you might want to boil it down a little further – by up to a third, say. Taste as you go, and stop when it's right.

If you want to make your stock even more concentrated, it is either because you are in the business of turning it into a sauce or because you want to keep it, frozen probably, in very concentrated form. In this case you may boil it away to anything between one-fifth and one-tenth of its current volume (that's one-thirtieth of its original volume), until what remains is best described as ...

An intense reduction: This is highly concentrated, dark brown or almost black, intensely flavoured (and, one hopes, delicious). You may detect a certain stickiness on the lips when it's sipped off the edge of a teaspoon. Cold, it will undoubtedly set as a firm, almost rubbery jelly.

With the right finishing (usually wine and some suitable seasonings), this is a posh, cheffy sauce in its own right. Otherwise it can be poured into ice-cube trays and kept in the freezer, to be used like stock cubes – only far better than anything you can buy in the shops. It can then be diluted to either of the two concentrations described above (from whence, of course, it came) and used accordingly. If, like me, you make and freeze a lot of stock, reducing it right down is pretty much essential to save freezer space.

5. Never add salt to a stock

You don't know at what final concentration you will be using your stock (see rule 4, above). So, add salt to the dish you make with the stock, not to the stock itself.

Besides these general principles of stock making, a few meat-specific notes are in order. I'll start with chicken stock – probably the stock most frequently made by home cooks generally. Well made, it is worthwhile and versatile – a very useful thing. Badly made (as I'm afraid it often is), it is a complete waste of time.

Chicken stock

Call me old-fashioned – I'll take it as a compliment anyway – but I think it a culinary crime to roast a whole chicken and not make a stock afterwards. A good chicken stock is any number of great meals waiting to happen. It takes fifteen minutes at the most to put together the stock, thirty seconds to strain it into a bowl at the end, and then it's waiting in the fridge, pregnant with possibilities, ready to assuage family hunger in all kinds of elegant ways.

Nigella Lawson has written that you should never make a chicken stock with the leftovers of only one roast chicken, but bag up the carcasses in the freezer until you have at least two, preferably three. She has a point. It is certainly nice to work with a generous amount of raw materials when making stocks. But it is undoubtedly possible to make a good litre of first-class, deeply flavoured chicken stock from a single bird – enough to make a very worthwhile soup or risotto for four people. I know, because I've done it countless times.

Here's how a single-carcass chicken stock gets made in our house. Once everyone's had their fill of the roasted bird, the plates get cleared and anything on them remotely chickeny – skin, bone or flesh – gets scraped into a bowl and put on one side (in a cool larder or fridge) along with the carcass. I've seen some people throw wing and drumstick bones off finished plates straight into the bin, then proceed to make a stock with just the main carcass – as if it was somehow bad manners or unhygienic to use bones that may perhaps have been nibbled by human teeth. Well, different people have different ideas about manners, but in my book it's bad manners to the chicken to consign any of its bones to the bin until they have given up their fine flavour to my stock. As for hygiene, the stock will be simmered at around 100°C for at least two hours. Your family or guests would have to be carrying some pretty extraordinary germs (anthrax springs to mind) for them not to be annihilated by this process.

When I have ten minutes, I'll get the chicken carcass out and quickly pick over it, pulling off any good meat with my fingers and putting it aside for separate consideration. I will then tear the carcass apart into fairly small pieces and cram these, along with all skin, bones, fat and any jelly or scratchings from the roasting tin (everything, in fact, except the saved meat), into one of my smaller stockpots. Besides these leftovers, there is one more magic ingredient that transforms a chicken stock and that is the neck, which I always save for the stock and like to add fresh. In the absence of a neck, a fresh wing or two will have much the same effect – occasionally, packs of organic chicken wings can be found at farmers' markets, good butcher's, and even Waitrose. You can add the heart and gizzard too, assuming you have the full set of giblets, but not the liver, which can give a slightly bitter flavour (I usually fry it with a little garlic and mash it on toast). You can make a perfectly good chicken stock without them, but these fresh ingredients will contribute what you might think of as the Jewish flavours, transforming a light, toasty stock into a rich, chickeny broth. Unfortunately a factory-farmed bird invariably comes without giblets. But then you haven't got this far in the book without kicking the plastic chicken habit yet – have you?

By way of stock vegetables I will add, as an absolute minimum, a large onion, a large carrot, a bay leaf and a few peppercorns. Ideally, though, I'll make it two of each, and also add any of the following: a couple of celery sticks, a nugget of peeled parsnip or celeriac, half or a whole leek, a sprig of thyme and a few parsley stalks. I'll cut all the vegetables into chunks and pack them fairly tightly with the torn-up chicken, so that no more than 1.5 litres of fresh clean water, and preferably a little less, is needed to cover everything. If you use whole vegetables, and don't bother to break up the carcass but put it into a larger pot, it may take 3 litres of water or more to cover it all, and you will have a correspondingly insipid stock. Of course, it can be reduced later. But somehow a heavily reduced chicken stock is never as good as one that has that distinctive, chickeny richness from the moment you take it off the heat.

I'll bring the water to that 'tremulous' simmer and let it cook, uncovered, for an absolute minimum of three hours – better still, four or five. I'll top it up occasionally, and check it never bubbles more vigorously than that gentle simmer. Or I might put a lid on and cook it in the slow oven of the Aga for a similar amount of time. Then I'll gently strain the stock through a fine sieve, leave it to cool thoroughly and chill it in the fridge. The fat will set and can be scraped off the top, though I don't usually bother unless it is excessive.

My favourite way of consuming a chicken stock of this kind is a tribute to its quality. It's served as an unthickened broth, with just a few little extras. I will bring it back to the boil, season it to taste with salt, and add perhaps a handful of small pasta, rice or pearl barley, some young peas from the garden, and maybe some finely chopped chicken meat saved from the carcass. The variety and quantity of your additions will determine whether the resulting soup is a snack, a starter or a full-blown supper.

As it happens, I made just such a broth last night. My additions were a couple of handfuls of miniature pasta bows, a small bag of broad beans from the freezer and some ribbons of my own bacon, which I fried briefly with a little garlic, then added to the stock. I considered including fried matchsticks of home-made chorizo but decided against, because the stock had such a good flavour I reckoned it didn't need any more help. We had friends to supper and I served the broth as a starter, to be followed by a light main course of sausages, lentils and salad. Another time, with a bit more pasta and veg thrown in, it would, with a slice of toast apiece, comfortably have done the four of us for supper.

You can, of course, make a chicken stock with a raw carcass, if you have one to hand – for example, if you have removed the breasts to make Chicken Kiev (page 356). Simply roast the bones at 200°C/Gas Mark 6 for about fifteen minutes, until nicely browned, then proceed as above.

Game stock

A brace (or more) of leftover roast pheasant or partridge makes a very good basis for a stock. In fact, all other game birds make good stock, too – with the occasional, and unpredictable, exception of some waterfowl, whose stock may end up a bit fishy (particularly if the bird tasted a bit fishy in the first place). Pigeon carcasses make an excellent stock, almost beefy in intensity, and easily good enough to use in sauces and consommé-style outings.

In all cases, proceed as for chicken stock, above. When a game stock turns out well, it makes one of the most delicious consommés. It also has an uncanny affinity with parsnips – and a creamy parsnip soup made with game stock is a real winter favourite of mine.

For a particularly rich and delicious game soup, see the recipe on page 507.

Lamb stock

Lamb and mutton bones do not make an especially good all-purpose stock. It tastes too distinctively 'sheepy' to underpin a vegetable soup or a risotto. However, if you're making lamb or mutton soups and stews, then lamb or mutton stock is just the right liquid medium on which to base them.

Most of my lamb stocks are of the second-class variety, made in accordance with the rules above and using the bones and any leftover juice or gravy from a roast leg or shoulder. In both cases I crack the main bone in half to get it into a smaller pan, so I need less water to cover it and come out with a tastier stock at the end. Shanks and shins, from legs and shoulders respectively, are both invaluable sources of body and lambiness. Make sure you retrieve either from the plate of whoever has been given the privilege of gnawing it, and pop it in the pot.

I usually make this lamb stock with a view to boosting my shepherd's pie or moussaka, and for this purpose it will require some pretty drastic reduction – from, say, 1 litre to 200-250ml – to give the chopped leftover lamb a decent flavour boost without making it too wet.

If a leftover lamb dish is not immediately on the cards, though, I'll freeze the stock until I'm next making a lamb- or mutton-based stew, such as my Lancashire Hot Pot (page 290), Irish Stew (page 292) or Citrus-braised Lamb Shanks (page 300).

The only time I make a more substantial 'first-class' lamb stock, from scratch, is when Ray and I have been butchering a carcass for the freezer, in which case we save all usable bones. I'll roast half of them for ten to twenty minutes at 200-220°C/Gas Mark 6-7 and leave the other half raw, to give a balanced combination of caramelised browning flavours and fresh cooked lamb flavours.

A litre or two of the resulting stock usually gets an immediate outing as richly flavoured mutton broth. If this is the plan, the breast of lamb, with its ribs running through it, will also go in the stockpot. Pearl barley, split peas, sliced carrots and leeks are cooked in the clean, strained stock until tender, then shredded meat from the breast, and any other worthwhile morsels picked from the bones, are added back in at the end. The remaining stock goes into the freezer.

If you're ordering a half-lamb box for the freezer, it's worth mentioning that you'd like any extra available bones, then you can make a first-class lamb stock, and mutton broth, of your own. If you want to be really thrifty (and why not?) then whenever you buy a boned-out leg or shoulder, don't forget to ask your butcher for the bone that came out.

See also my procedure for Cheaty Mutton Broth (page 477), which makes a similar soup from a leftover roast.

Beef stock

As I've already mentioned, the only roast beef joints that will give you enough bones to consider making a stock are a whole forerib, wing rib, or sirloin on the bone. They won't make a lot of stock but they will make a good, compact one – if you follow my rules.

However, once or twice a year (whenever Ray and I butcher a whole side of beef), I make a huge quantity of beef stock. Chefs traditionally make a distinction between beef stocks made with raw bones and those made with cooked. I long ago decided that it must surely be possible to have the best of both worlds, and so I generally make my beef stock with a combination of the two. The four enormous marrow bones (two from each leg of the side of beef), sawn in half, stay raw. The other smaller, less evenly shaped bones, mainly bits of sawn chine and rib, get roasted in a very hot oven for about twenty minutes. I cram as much as I can into my huge 80-litre stockpot, along with a couple of kilos each of carrots, onions and celery and about twenty bay leaves! In the end – after a night of gentle simmering – I have about 20-30 litres of good, strong stock.

I'm inclined here to add a number eleven to my top ten signs of a good butcher on pages 51-2: a good butcher should always be able to provide you with fresh beef bones for making stock. With a little help from such a butcher, you can make an excellent scaled-down version with just one whole marrow bone (ask for it to be sawn into four or five short lengths) and another kilo or so of other rough beef bones. A butcher who has no bones is suspect to say the least.

Beef stock is worth freezing in highly concentrated form – a cube of it can be dropped neat into a bolognese, or it can be diluted with wine and water to form the basis of any good beef-based stew.

See also my recipe for Pot-au-feu (page 284), which, besides various cuts of delicious boiled beef, should provide you with one of the best stocks, or technically *bouillons*, you'll ever taste.

Veal stock

Veal stock is traditionally the 'posh stock' of restaurant kitchens. Chefs like it because it has good body and gelatinous properties but a light flavour that is not overpoweringly beefy. In that sense, it is, like pork stock below, 'neutral' and can be successfully combined with other stocks. It can therefore be used in all kinds of dishes, and particularly as the base of intense sauces and reductions.

The most delicate veal stock (known to chefs as *fond blanc*) is made with raw bones but you can make a richer (beefier, if you like) version with roasted bones, or a combination of the two. In all cases the procedure is as for beef stock, above.

Pork stock

You don't hear or read much from English chefs or food writers about pork stock. It's a shame, because the bones from good pigs make a really fine and highly versatile stock – as every Chinese chef knows. Most pork joints are boned out and rolled – which means that a good butcher, or a small producer who butchers his or her pork and takes it to the farmers' market, should be able to provide you with plenty of bones, if you ask nicely. You may even get them for nothing.

I always roast pork bones for stock making, but not too much. They should be nicely browned and crisp looking, but not blackened – about ten to fifteen minutes in a hot oven does it. If you want a stock that sets to jelly, bung in a pig's trotter. And, if you have only a few pork bones, they can be usefully added to any other stock you are making.

You may not be familiar with pork stock but it's far from daunting. Just think of it as chicken stock, for which it makes a suitable substitute in almost any recipe. In fact, one of the most appetising and savoury of all stocks is made from a combination of roast pork bones and roast chicken carcasses.

Ham stock

You would rarely set out to make a ham or bacon stock. But the liquor that is left over from boiling a good whole ham on the bone, or even a couple of knuckles of bacon, is certainly very tasty. Its uses are limited mainly by the level of its saltiness. If it isn't too salty, it makes a good base for many vegetable soups. And even if it's quite salty, you might still be able to pull off some kind of pea and ham soup, either with fresh or dried peas or a combination of the two. This is because the sweetness and mealiness of the peas is quite forgiving of the salty tang of the ham. A little pasta, rice or diced potato simmered in the same pot will help knock back the saltiness still further.

Using Up a Leftover Roast

The most common leftover meat scenario is the half-eaten roast – a substantial joint of pork, beef or lamb, or a whole chicken, turkey, duck, goose or game bird(s) of one kind or another.

Once you've exercised (or rejected) the stock option, what remains is a pile of meat. It may be overdone or underdone, in big pieces or small, fatty or lean, gristly or clean, or, most likely, some or all of the above. The first thing to say is that there really are no hard-and-fast rules about the best way to use up leftovers. They provide the best raw (or, rather, cooked) materials for quirky culinary experiments. Cold sausage and marmalade sandwich? No problem! Leftover chicken fried with garlic, peanut butter and soy sauce – it might just work! Lateral thinking and improvisation are absolutely the order of the day.

But before you attempt to hijack your taste buds with such crazy combinations, don't overlook the easiest second meal of all. I'm hoping that you've already decided that from now on you'll be buying only meat of the very best provenance. The best hot roast meat becomes the best cold roast meat. And if you like cold roast meat, as most of us do from time to time, then it's an effortless way to enjoy it. Personally, one of my favourite things to eat is cold roast pork with a little flaky salt and pepper and a dab of mayonnaise.

Once you've passed over the cold option or, indeed, indulged it and found there is still some meat to spare, you're back in improvisational snacks and suppers territory. And that's one of the most fun places to be in the kitchen. It's tempting just to say, 'Enjoy yourself!' and leave it at that. But, in the hope that you might find some jumping-off points from my own experiments, here are a few ideas for the commonest cold cuts. (These are offered in addition to my favourite leftover 'classics', which are described in more detail in the recipe section that starts on page 484.) Oh, and before we proceed, a brief ...

SAFETY NOTICE: You will no doubt be aware that there are some hygiene issues involved when making dishes that involve reheating cold cooked meat. I take the view that if you're handling leftover meat that you're confident is safe to eat cold, then you're not going to make it unsafe just by tossing it in a frying pan for a few minutes or dropping it into a hot soup for immediate consumption. However, if you're using cooked meat to compile pies, such as shepherd's pie, or patties, such as rissoles, then you should make sure they are thoroughly cooked through (that is re-cooked through) and not left hanging around for ages in places – be they ovens, worktops, hostess trolleys(!)* or sideboards – that are best described as 'warm'.

Leftover roast chicken

Chicken and olive fry-up: Roughly chop the chicken, a clove of garlic and a dozen stoned olives. Slice half an onion and mash a couple of anchovies. Sauté everything together in a frying pan with a little of the oil from the anchovies until the chicken is getting crisp and the onion lightly coloured. Add cooked pasta, or cooked Puy lentils, or both, and toss all together. I like to serve this with a dressed tomato salad. This also works as a cold dish, in which all the ingredients are combined in a salad bowl, not a frying pan.

Easy chicken croquettes: Chop the chicken fairly small and mix with a roughly equal quantity of coarse fresh breadcrumbs. Mix in enough beaten egg to get a sticky but spoonable mixture, and season well. Shallow-fry spoonfuls in hot oil, turning occasionally, until golden and crisp.

Chicken with peas, pasta and bacon: Improvise a simple pasta sauce, a kind of 'chicken carbonara', with bacon, peas, egg, cream and chicken. Toss with your favourite pasta and serve with grated Parmesan or Cheddar.

Leftover roast game

My recipe for Game Soup on page 507 makes the question of what to do with the leftover carcasses of roast game birds a bit of a no-brainer. If there are really substantial pieces of meat on the birds, the chances are they will be delicious cold. Or they could be incorporated into a pâté or terrine (see pages 421-3 for some principles of improvisation). But to be honest, in my house, pretty much every game bird carcass that comes out of the kitchen is picked fairly clean before it returns there.

Leftover roast beef

Refried 'eye of roast' medallions: This second bite at the cherry of delicious rare beef only works from a cold roast forerib or sirloin, cooked nice and rare. Trim off all the outer, well-done meat (to be used elsewhere, e.g. for meatballs, below), leaving you with the lean eye of the loin, which should be rare on the outside and very rare in the middle. Slice across the grain of the meat into as many 2 cm-thick medallions as you can get from the piece. Then flash-fry at extremely high heat for barely a minute on each side. Rest for a few minutes, then serve.

To boost the flavours on the crust of the meat, you can, if you like, marinate the medallions for an hour or so (try the teriyaki marinade on page 379 or my Indonesian marinade on page 346), or simply rub them with garlic.

Cold beef 'Bloody Mary' tartare: Another variation on a classic, using cold, cooked rare beef instead of raw. Slice the leftover roast beef into thickish slices (about 5 mm). Trim off the outer, well-done edges, then cut the slices into 1 cm strips. Make a dressing like a super-concentrated Bloody Mary, from a couple of tablespoons of tomato juice, a dash of Worcestershire sauce, lemon juice, horseradish and Tabasco – as spicy or mild as you like. Toss with the beef strips and leave to macerate for half an hour before serving – with buttered brown bread or toast and a simple salad.

Meatballs: Mixing raw and cooked meats is meant to be one of the cardinal sins of health and hygiene. Meatballs are a rare exception – provided they are to be cooked thoroughly in a sauce. Excellent meatballs can be made by mixing minced leftover roast beef with raw sausage meat – either plain or from good butcher's sausages, split open with the skin discarded – or even minced bacon. Fry gently until nicely browned all over, then cook through in a tomato sauce. Serve with spaghetti (or see page 491 for the full-blown version).

By the same token, you can also mix coarsely minced cooked beef with coarsely minced raw beef to make a fine bolognese (see page 497). The browning flavours on the outer crust of the roast beef do wonders for the sauce.

Leftover roast lamb

I utterly adore a good shepherd's pie (page 504) and I'd have to eat roast legs and shoulders of lamb more often than I do before I'd consider any other use of the leftovers. However, you do need a fair bit of meat to make it worthwhile. If that's not forthcoming, I might go for something along the following lines:

Shepherd's pie hash: In this quick-fire version, less meat is needed. Cut the lamb into cubes and fry gently in oil with a little garlic and a sliced onion until the onion is softened. Add diced cooked potatoes, turn up the heat a little and fry together until the lamb, onion and potato are all getting a bit crisp. Season well, with salt, pepper and Worcestershire sauce, and eat straight from the pan. You can also use cooked rice or pasta instead of diced potato.

Cheaty mutton broth: Put everything that remains of the joint in a saucepan, along with 2 large peeled onions and 2 large peeled carrots. Cover with water, but only just. Simmer gently, or cook, covered, in a low oven, for 1 hour. Then add a few handfuls of pearl barley (or a mixed pulse soup mix that includes it) and/or a couple of peeled potatoes cut into cubes, and simmer for another hour, or until the pulses are tender.

Remove the bone and any loose meat. Pick off all the available meat and chop it roughly, returning it to the pan. Fish out, slice, and return the onions and carrots, too. Add a handful of fresh or frozen peas, if you like. Simmer for a few more minutes, check the seasoning and serve.

Cold lamb in minty yoghurt dressing: Pull and slice the cold meat from the bone, trimming off and discarding excess fat and coarse sinews. Tear or slice the lamb into finger-sized strips. Make double quantities of the yoghurty version of my mint sauce (see page 512) and toss with the lamb. Leave to macerate and chill for at least half an hour, then serve. I like to eat it with plain cold rice, lightly dressed with a little olive oil and a squeeze of lemon juice.

Leftover roast pork

The curious thing about leftover cold roast pork is that, in terms of possible usage, it is almost exactly the same as cold roast chicken. That's not to say it tastes the

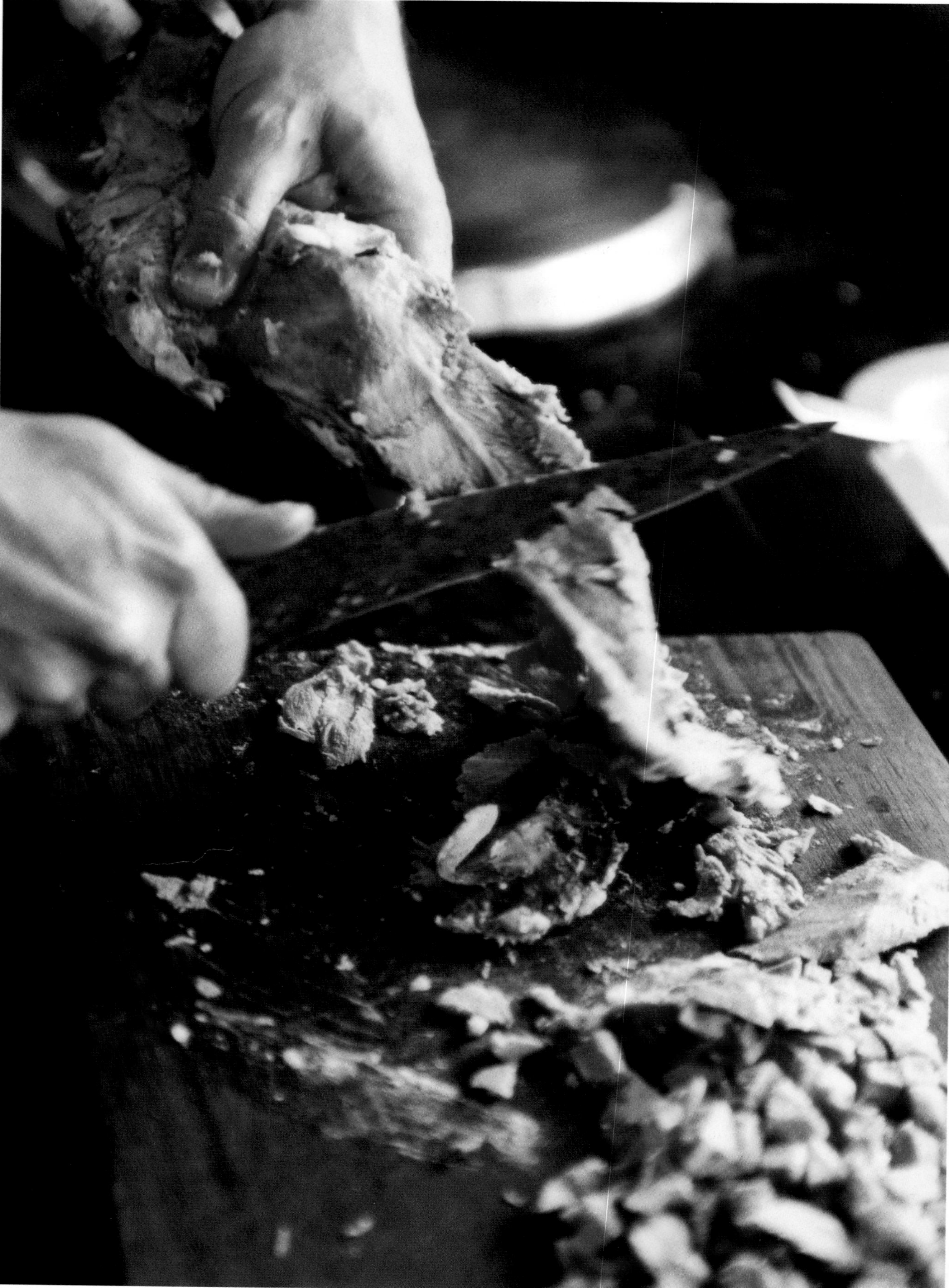

same – it doesn't. But it is similarly versatile, and can be used in all kinds of simple combinations.

You can start by trying all three of my suggestions for chicken (above) with pork. And you can continue by assuming that my three suggestions for cold pork, below, will also work with chicken.

Pork tonnata: The classic veal tonnata works just as well (or even better) with pork (or chicken or turkey). My less than classic, but very delicious version involves mixing a tin of tuna (in oil, not brine), flaked, with a tin of anchovies, roughly chopped, 2-3 tablespoons of mayonnaise (preferably home-made), a good squeeze of lemon juice and a few gratings of zest. Smear it over thick slices of cold roast pork. Sprinkle with capers, but only if you like capers (I do).

Tartiflette: This is a leftovers version of the Alpine classic. You could use ham or bacon instead of pork. Fry cubes of cooked pork with sliced onions and diced cooked potato until all are getting nicely browned and crisp. Add a dollop of double cream and shake in the pan to coat everything. Lay generous slices of a good melting cheese over the top – you could use Gruyère, Taleggio, raclette, tomme, or even dolcelatte. Place in a very hot oven or flash under a grill, until melted and bubbling.

Refried pork sandwich: This is greedy – but, astonishingly, even better than a bacon sandwich. (I realise some people will argue that that is, by definition, not possible. But don't side with them until you've tried it.) Fry slices of cold roast pork, the fattier the better, in very hot olive oil, maybe with a crushed clove of garlic, for 1/2-1 minute on each side. Take 2 slices of very fresh bread, or lightly grilled toast. Spread one with mayonnaise, the other with ketchup, and put a slice or two of refried pork between them. Lettuce and sliced fresh tomato are optional – i.e. for wimps.

Leftover ham

In a sense, there's no such thing as leftover ham. Or, put another way, you could say that ham is permanently left over. The whole point of ham, clearly, is to sit around looking tempting, daring you to resist. I rarely can. I'll smear it with mustard and slap it on buttered bread. Cut a slice and eat it with a fried egg. Or scrambled. Or poached. Or I'll just pick at it, on and off all day, and eat it with nothing at all.

I think I can say, somewhat extravagant though it might sound, that in almost any improvised dish of leftovers, be it a sandwich or a soup, a stir-fry or a hash, a risotto or a pasta dish, a smattering of chopped ham will do more good than harm. And I'm going to leave it at that. Except to add that small amounts of ham work particularly well in the guise described below.

Scant pickings: leftover meat as a 'spice'

Most of the above improvisations require at least a generous handful of leftover meat for even a one-person portion. But when your joint has fed a large number of mouths and the remnants are pretty meagre, a dish as substantial as a shepherd's pie, or even a good plate of cold beef sandwiches, may be out of the question. Is the scant 100-200g of meat you could salvage really worth bothering with?

It certainly is. And it may even be the making of a meal for four, not because of what it can contribute in term of calories or quantity, but because of what it can do in terms of taste and texture. Think of it as a little like the Mexican-style chorizo I describe on page 446 (the one that doesn't get made into a sausage but is used sparingly, almost as a textured seasoning). You can achieve just the same effect with almost any leftover cold meat – because a little of those much-loved browning flavours goes a long way.

Whether it's ham, lamb, pork, chicken or beef, the procedure is pretty much the same. Chop the meat into very small 'shards' (about ½-1cm). Fry quickly in a little hot oil with a clove or two of finely chopped garlic until well browned and crisp. For just the last minute or so of cooking, a few drops of soy sauce (or, in the case of lamb and chicken, perhaps Worcestershire sauce) and even the tiniest sprinkling of sugar will help to finish it off with a sweet and salty glaze. Oriental chefs know well the value of such a garnish on a plate of fried rice or noodles. But these little crispy, highly seasoned 'meat croûtons' can be sprinkled over almost anything: a soup or a salad or a stir-fry of fresh vegetables, an omelette or scrambled eggs, a bowl of plain pasta, a buttery baked potato, or a pile of creamy mash. In all cases the effect is the same: an instant hit of highly seasoned taste and texture that will transform a stopgap supper.

Leftover Stews

Compared to leftover joints of roast meat, leftover stews may seem unpromising. The French in general, and my wife in particular, would strongly disagree. They have a pretty generalised procedure which may not sound very convincing, but I can testify that it offers guaranteed deliciousness every time. Classically it's done with Pot-au-feu (see page 284) but it works well with other beef-based daubes, stews and casseroles, and for lamb and venison, too. I call it fried stew.

Start by removing the meat from the sauce of the stew and roughly chop or shred it into smaller pieces. For, say, a meagre two-persons' worth of meat, peel and finely slice (not dice) a large onion, and peel and cut into smallish batons one very large or two or three medium carrots. Melt a little fat or oil in a frying pan and fry the onion and carrots at a merry sizzle – they should be allowed to colour slightly as they fry, but not too much or too fast.

When the carrots are getting nicely browned and the onion starting to crisp a little, throw in the chopped meat. Turn up the heat just slightly and continue frying, shaking and stirring the pan occasionally, so that the meat starts to brown as well. Keep going for a few more minutes, until meat, carrot and onion are all well browned and crisp, without quite being burnt. Then and only then you can moisten the dish by adding a tablespoon or two of the sauce from the stew and perhaps a small splash of wine. Stir and reduce rapidly for another minute, so the meat and vegetables are just glazed rather than wet. Then serve at once, with plain buttered pasta, rice or mashed potatoes.

Stew into soup

I have one other strategy for leftover stews, which I tend to exercise if there is plenty of liquor left but not much in the way of meat. Essentially it gives the stew a second outing as a kind of 'big soup', or minestrone, with pasta and/or rice and/or pearl barley. The important thing is to include some robust fresh vegetables – carrots, onions, beetroot (if in season), maybe some peas or a few mushrooms – so the soup doesn't become too insipid, and even then not to dilute the soup with too much water. (If you happen to have good stock of the same meat as the stew, then you can extend the soup even further.)

At one time or another I have expanded stews and casseroles of practically every meat – beef, lamb, venison, poultry and game – into variations on the big soup theme. You can, of course, tailor your additions to the kind of meat that your stew is based on. Tomatoes go well with beef, broad beans or even tinned beans with lamb, and mushrooms with poultry and game.

One of the best 'stoups' (or should that be 'stewps'?) I ever made was with a leftover Coq au Vin (page 311). I took all the meat off the bones, chopped it up and returned it to the liquor. I stirred into it a generous amount of cooked risoni (those tiny pasta pieces that look like unnaturally perfect grains of rice), and so this particular stewp ended up as a sort of pasta-chicken risotto thing. The consensus, as so often with leftovers, was that the second outing was even better than the first. Stewpendous, in fact.

A stewp is never the same twice, of course, and that's a large part of its charm. But I can produce some basic stewp guidelines. Here's a description of the basic procedure, by way of encouragement.

First, remove any leftover meat (discarding any bones, if necessary) and vegetables, chop all fairly fine and return to the liquor. Finely chop an onion and/or a leek and cut a carrot or two, a beetroot if handy, or maybe a couple of tomatoes (skinned) into small dice. Sweat all these in a little butter for a couple of minutes, then pour in enough water to cover by barely a centimetre. Simmer for a few minutes, until the carrots are tender but not mushy. Cook your broken spaghetti or small pasta or pearl barley or rice in a separate pan of rapidly boiling water, then drain when tender. Combine, in whichever pan seems sensible, the leftover stew, the simmered vegetables and perhaps a little of their (now flavoured) cooking water, and the pasta/barley/rice. Heat through, taste and season, taste and season, then serve.

Odds and Sods: Puy Lentils with Everything

There are as many leftover meat dishes as there are meat dishes (which is a slightly scary thought). So there is much I have not had time or space to discuss. What about leftover tongue, beefburgers, sausages, liver, pâtés, pork pies ... and indeed, what about leftover leftovers?

I have a magic formula, a kind of default recipe for all cold, cooked meat leftovers, which serves me in pretty good stead. I cook a load of Puy lentils in plenty of boiling water until they are just tender but still *al dente*. I drain them and toss in a little olive oil. I make up a version of my Mustard Vinaigrette (page 513), adding, if handy, plenty of chopped parsley and/or capers. I cut up the meat – any of the above, and sometimes unlikely combinations of two or more of them. When the lentils are completely cold, I toss them with the chopped meat and vinaigrette, so that everything mingles.

It is a combination that rarely disappoints, and can even be rather swanky and sophisticated. Which can't be bad.

Leftover Raw Meat

Certain ways of preparing raw meat – including boning out legs of lamb, for example, or trimming a piece of rump steak for making tartare (you may remember, I promised we'd get to that) – inevitably leave one with small but not insignificant piles of raw meat trimmings.

Of any given pile, I tend to ask myself: is there enough good, lean, non-sinewy meat here to be worth chopping or mincing to make some kind of burger or patty – even if it's only enough for Oscar and Freddie's supper? If yes, then that's what I'll do. A version of the beef/lamburger may well be in order.

If no, presumably because it's too coarse, then I'll go on to consider whether there's enough real substance, in terms of skin and sinew, to make it worth adding to some future stockpot.

And if I can't quite squeeze it into either of the above categories, I know a couple of fine dogs who will be only too happy to take care of it for me. Some might call that extravagant rather than thrifty. But when every bit of meat that comes into your kitchen is put to good use in one way or another, then the distinction between these notions is not as clear as it might have once seemed. And that's a rather amazing thing.

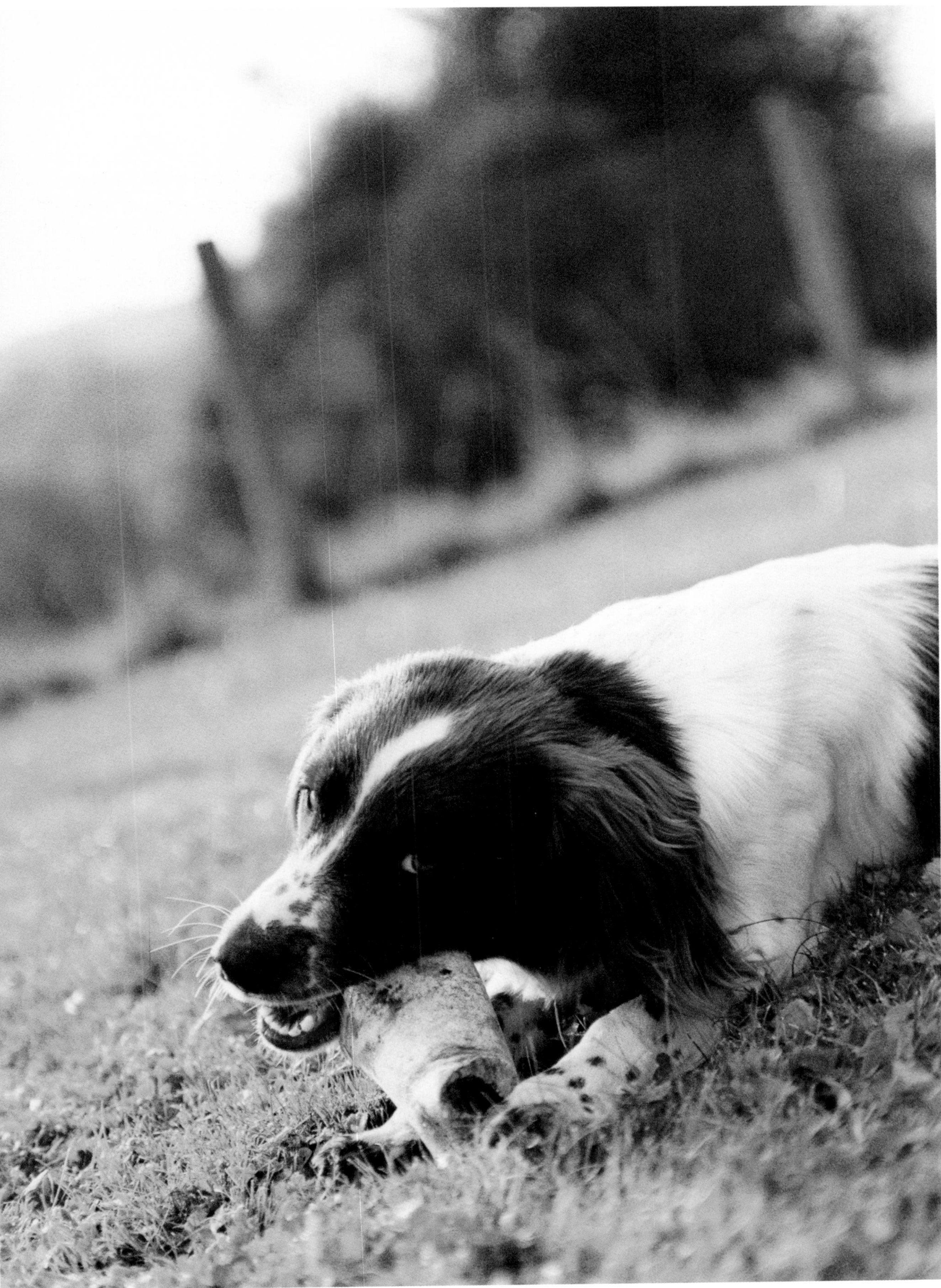

BOSTON BAKED BEANS *Serves 8*

400g piece of salt pork, pancetta or unsmoked streaky bacon (see p.429 for home-made)

500g dried white haricot beans, soaked in plenty of cold water overnight

50g soft brown sugar

3 tablespoons black treacle

1 tablespoon English mustard

4 cloves

8-10 pickling onions, peeled but left whole (or 2-3 small onions, cut into quarters)

Salt and freshly ground black pepper

I love this recipe, which doesn't feature meat in a big way but illustrates beautifully something I am often trying to explain: that the role of meat in a dish need not always be central to be vital. Sometimes it is a lubricant, sometimes it's almost a spice. In this case, the bacon acts as both. You could discard it at the end of cooking, as it will have done its most important job. I wouldn't, though, as it's rather delicious.

Drain and rinse the beans, then put them in a flameproof casserole with enough fresh water to cover them by about 5 cm. Bring to the boil and boil hard for at least 10 minutes. Lower the heat to a gentle simmer, cover and cook for about 1 hour, until the beans are tender but not completely soft. Remove from the heat.

Cut the bacon into 5 cm cubes, leaving the rind on, and add to the beans. Stir in the brown sugar, black treacle and mustard. Press each clove into an onion and add, with the extra onions, to the pot. Season with pepper, but no salt at this stage as the bacon will make it salty. If necessary, add a little hot water so that the beans are covered.

Replace the lid on the casserole. Place in a low oven (140°C/Gas Mark 1) and bake for about 3 hours. Then remove the lid and drag some of the bacon chunks to the top. Return, uncovered, to the oven, for a further hour. This helps to brown the bacon and thicken the sauce.

Check the seasoning, then serve the beans on their own, with crusty bread (or on toast), as a snack or light meal. Or serve with sausages and mash. These baked beans will keep in a sealed jar or Tupperware container in the fridge for 2 weeks.

BRAWN *Serves about 10*

1 pig's head, quartered

2 pig's trotters

2 onions, peeled and quartered

A large bundle of herbs – parsley, bay leaves, thyme and marjoram

A muslin bag of spices (1-2 teaspoons each of cloves, coriander seeds and mixed peppercorns)

A handful of chopped parsley

Juice of 1/2 lemon

Salt and freshly ground black pepper

Everyone who wishes to embrace the holistic, 'nose-to-tail' approach to meat should buy a pig's head once in a while and make a brawn. This classic dish, which I first described in The River Cottage Cookbook, *uses all the meat from the head of the pig, including the tongue, cheeks and ears. The natural gelatine in the bones of the head should be enough to set the brawn in its own jelly, but adding a couple of pig's trotters will make sure.*

Cut the ears away from the head and scrub them thoroughly under a warm tap (pigs have ear wax too). Remove any bristles with a razor or tweezers. Then place with the quartered head in brine (see pages 416-17) for 24 hours.

Place the quartered head, ears, trotters, onions, bundle of herbs and bag of spices in a large stockpot. Cover with water and bring slowly to a gentle simmer. For the first 30 minutes of cooking, skim off any bubbly scum that rises to the surface. Cook, uncovered, at a very gentle simmer for about 4 hours altogether, until all the meat is completely tender and coming away from the bones. Top up the pan occasionally as the water level drops.

When cooked, lift out the meat and leave until cool enough to handle. Pick all the meat, skin and fat off the head bones (it should fall off quite easily). Peel the coarse skin off the tongue and discard. Roughly chop all the bits of meat, including the fat and skin and the tongue, and toss together with the chopped parsley and the lemon juice. (Everything except the bone and bristles can go into a brawn, but if you want to make it less fatty, just discard some of the really fatty pieces at this stage.) Season to taste with a little salt and pepper.

Remove the herbs, onions and spices from the cooking liquor and strain it through a fine sieve or, better still, muslin. Stir a few tablespoons of this gelatine-rich liquid into the chopped meat to help the brawn set as it cools. Pile the mixture into terrine dishes (1 large, or 2 or 3 small ones), or a pudding basin. Place a weighted plate or board on top and put in the refrigerator to set.

A brawn can be turned out of its mould on to a plate to serve. Serve cold, in slices, with pickles and gherkins. Or make a delicious *salade de tête*: cut the brawn into 2 cm dice and toss with cold cooked Puy lentils (page 520) and a Mustard Vinaigrette (page 513). The finished brawn will keep in the fridge for a couple of weeks. It also freezes well.

Fried brawn

Brawn is also delicious fried up and served hot. Put a couple of slices in a pan and melt gently over a low heat. Pour off a little of the excess fat, then turn up the heat so the meat begins to fry. Add a little garlic, if you like, and when most of the shreds of meat are nice and crisp, serve with mashed potatoes (page 518) and/or warm lentils, perhaps some cabbage, and mustard on the side.

FEIJOADA *Serves 12-20*

ESSENTIAL:

About 2 pig's trotters, split lengthways (and ideally dry-salted for 12-48 hours, see recipe)

About 500g green gammon and/or 500g fresh pork shoulder, cut into cubes

About 250g smoked pork belly, pancetta or bacon (p.429), cut into 3cm cubes

About 250g spicy Portuguese (or Spanish) chorizo, cut into 2cm chunks

About 250g fresh pork sausages

OPTIONAL EXTRA MEATS: (2 or 3 of the following, if you can get them; up to 250g of each)

Pig's tails, salted, as for trotters, in short lengths

Pig's ears, salted, as for trotters, thickly sliced

Spare rib, cut into short lengths and salted, as for trotters

Salt beef (brisket), in chunks

Morcilla (small Spanish black puddings), left whole

Lomo (spiced cured loin of pork), in chunks

CONTINUED OVER ...

This is the national dish of Brazil and, having spent six months in Rio de Janeiro in 1984, aged nineteen, I have a great fondness for it (as I do for many Brazilian things). Originally it was a dish for slaves and peasants, made from any odd bits of pig or cow that could be scavenged from the kitchens of their masters, then salted to preserve them until enough had been accumulated to stew up with the staple of their diet, dried black beans. Now it serves as a more elaborate celebration of Brazil's multicultural heritage, including the best of Portuguese charcuterie, such as chorizo (spiced sausages) and lomo (cured loin rubbed with paprika).

Recently, while reporting for Radio 4's 'The Food Programme', I watched the owner of the Brazilian Touch Café in Oxford Street, London, prepare an authentic feijoada from scratch. He included no less than twelve different types of meat. It was a great feijoada, but I don't think such exuberance is necessary to produce a really worthwhile and authentic dish. What you need is a balance of the gelatinous (trotters, ears or tails), the fatty (pork belly), the spicy (chorizo sausages) and the lean (gammon and shoulder of pork). After that there is any number of optional extras (see my list below) but none is essential.

Of the all-important trimmings, the only tricky one to find is the farofa (cassava flour). However, it can be bought in some Portuguese or Brazilian-run delis – such as Lisboa in London's Golborne Road, where you will also find chorizo, lomo and, on Fridays and Saturdays, salted trotters, ears, tails, snouts and ribs, all ready for your feijoada. In the absence of farofa, you can use dried brown breadcrumbs finely ground in a food processor.

All in all, this is a great party dish for a rabble of friends with adventurous palates. Ideally it should be prepared the day before you plan to serve it.

Two or three days ahead of time, put the split pig's trotters (and tails, ears and ribs, if using) into a non-metallic bowl and sprinkle thoroughly with salt. Cover and refrigerate for 1-2 days. The night before cooking the dish (ideally 2 nights before serving it), lift the meats out of the bowl, discard the liquid and rinse the meats thoroughly in cold water. Cover with fresh cold water and leave to soak overnight. (You can omit this salting process and use fresh trotters, tails, ears and ribs, if you like, but you should simmer them on their own for about half an hour before transferring them to the main dish. This means you can leave behind any scum.)

Also the night before, soak the gammon, and any salt beef that you are using, in fresh water, leaving them overnight. Thoroughly rinse the beans and put them to soak separately overnight, in enough fresh cold water to cover by at least 10cm.

The next day, allowing at least 5 hours for the overall cooking time, put the beans and their soaking liquid into a casserole large enough to hold all the ingredients, with the bay, parsley and thyme tied up in a bundle. Top up with enough cold water to cover by 5cm. Bring to the boil and boil hard for 10 minutes.

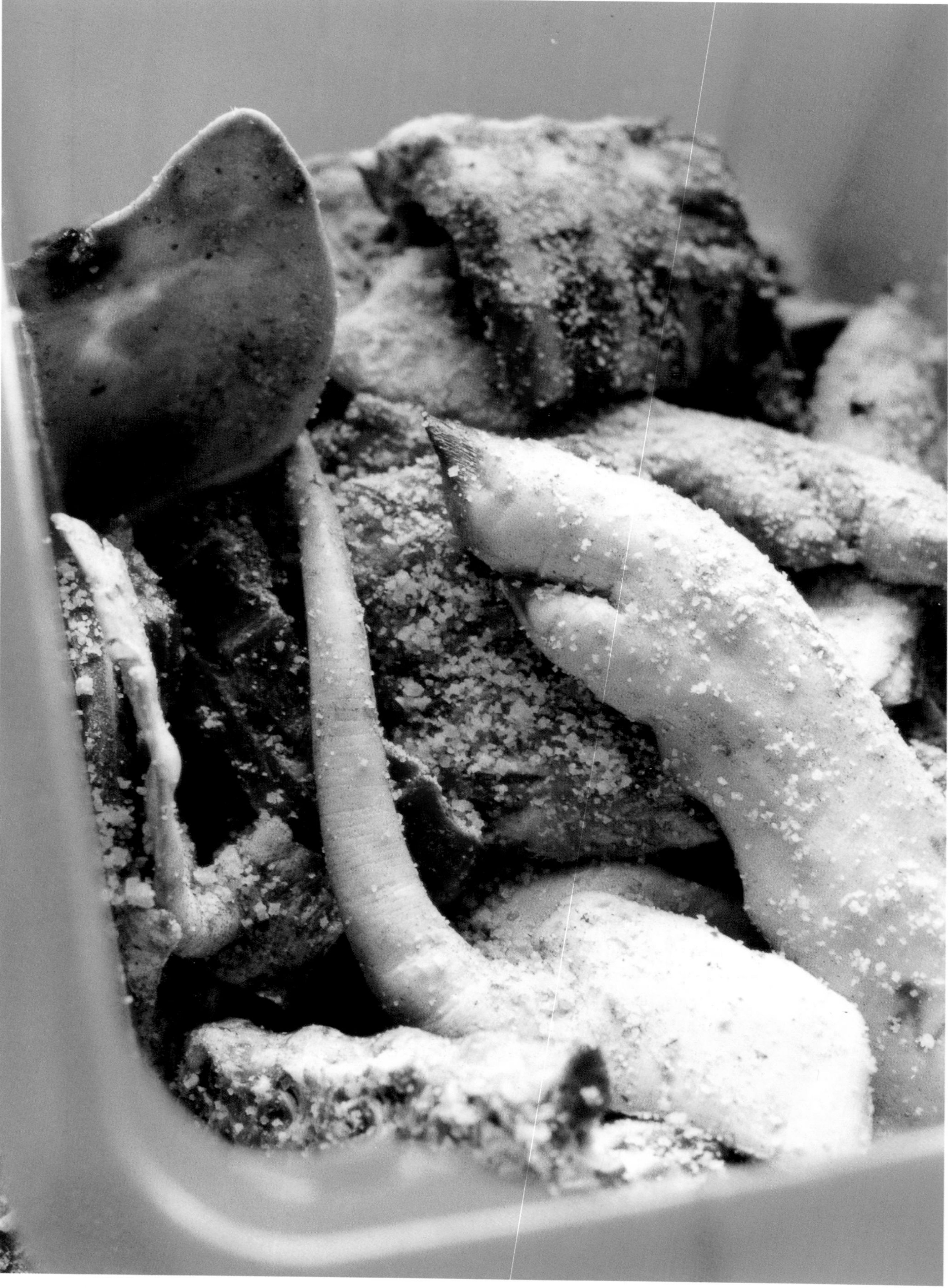

OTHER INGREDIENTS:

1 kg dried black beans (or use black-eyed beans, but not kidney beans, which are too big)

2 bay leaves

A bunch of parsley stalks

A few sprigs of thyme

25 g lard or 2 tablespoons sunflower oil

2 large onions, finely chopped

4 celery sticks, finely chopped

2 garlic cloves, finely chopped

4 large tomatoes, skinned, deseeded and chopped

Salt and freshly ground black pepper

TO ACCOMPANY:

Plain boiled rice

Steamed greens (ideally kale)

Piri piri (chilli sauce)

3 oranges

Farofa (toasted cassava flour), if available, or very fine dried brown breadcrumbs

Add the drained pig's trotters, along with the tails, ears, ribs and salt beef, if you are using them, then simmer gently over a low heat, covered, for about 1 1/2 hours.

Now melt the lard or oil in a heavy pan and brown, in batches, the cubes of smoked pork belly, gammon and/or shoulder and the chorizo. As they are done, transfer each meat to the pot of simmering beans and mix in. Brown the fresh sausages, too, but do not add them to the pot yet, just set them aside. By the time you've done this, the beans/trotters etc will have had about 2 hours.

In the fat that remains in the pan, gently sweat the chopped onions, celery and garlic. When soft and translucent, add the tomatoes, cook until you have a soft, pulpy sauce, then set aside. Continue to simmer the beans and meats gently, stirring occasionally and adding a little water if the beans at the top are being left high and dry.

After another hour or so (i.e. 3-3 1/2 hours overall), add the browned pork sausages, each cut into 3 or 4 pieces. Also at this stage, if you are using them, remove and cut up the salt beef into large chunks, then return it to the pot, and add the morcilla and lomo.

By now the beans should be very tender. Ladle about a mug's worth of beans into the pan containing your pulpy tomatoes and onions. Heat gently, mashing the beans into the sauce as you go. When you have a thick, pasty sauce, stir it back into the main pot, mixing thoroughly. Simmer for another half an hour or so. Taste the beans. They should be completely soft and yielding, and pretty salty, having taken on the salt from the meats. Add a little black pepper if you like. The liquid should now be thick and saucy. If it isn't, remove and mash some more beans and stir them back in.

At this point you can serve the feijoada or leave it to cool, keep it overnight and reheat it gently the next day. If you're trying to sell this dish to the squeamish, then you might want to pull out the trotters and cut them into more manageable (and less recognisable!) chunks, then stir them back into the dish.

The correct accompaniments for feijoada are plain boiled rice and steamed greens (usually kale), which are both served on the side. On the table should be a bottle of chilli sauce (Portuguese piri piri sauce is authentic but Tabasco or any good chilli sauce will do), to be applied according to your taste, and some slices of orange, on a plate. These are used to refresh the palate occasionally between salty, creamy, beany mouthfuls. Finally you should offer a bowl of farofa. It is sprinkled directly on the feijoada to create a crisp, granular texture. Fine brown breadcrumbs, toasted until hard and crisp, make a very acceptable alternative.

CHINESE-STYLE SPARE RIBS AND PIG'S TROTTERS

Serves 6, or more as part of a bigger Chinese spread

4 pig's trotters

500g spare ribs of pork, in short lengths of 2-4 rib width

2 tablespoons sunflower oil

5cm piece of fresh ginger root, grated

4 large garlic cloves, finely crushed

50ml dark soy sauce

100ml light soy sauce

50g light brown sugar

100ml brown rice vinegar, or cider vinegar

150ml pineapple juice, ideally fresh (apple juice works as a back-up)

Salt

This is the third book in which I have included a version of this recipe, and I keep honing and improving it. I make no apologies for labouring the point, as it's the surest way I know of converting doubters to the joys of pig's trotters – though serious doubters could use only spare ribs, doubling the quantities. Thanks again to Rose Billaud, who first showed me how to make it.

Make sure that you remove all the hairs from the trotters – shave them with a razor if necessary.

Using a meat cleaver, split each pig's trotter into 4 or 6 pieces (i.e. once down the middle and once or twice across). Your butcher could do this for you.

Heat the oil in a large, heavy-based pan, add the pig's trotters and spare rib pieces and fry until browned. Add the ginger, garlic and a little salt and continue to fry to release the aromatic flavours. Add the soy sauces, sugar, vinegar, pineapple juice, and just enough water to cover. Bring to a gentle simmer, cover with a lid and leave to cook until the trotters are tender (about 2-2½ hours). Stir occasionally, and make sure the liquid is not too low.

When the trotters are cooked, remove all the meat (i.e. trotters and ribs) from the pan with a slotted spoon and put in a bowl on one side. Continue to simmer the cooking liquid gently until it has reduced to a rich, syrupy consistency. Return the meat to the pan and heat through in the sauce.

The dish can be served immediately, though the flavour will continue to improve if it is left overnight in the refrigerator. The meat can then be eaten cold, in the jelly in which it has set, or reheated.

Serve with plain boiled rice and simple stir-fried vegetables (crunchy French beans with carrot and spring onions), or as a course in any Chinese-style banquet. Eating with the fingers has to be allowed, as does spitting out any knuckly pieces of bone from the trotters! The brave will want to eat the spare ribs bones and all.

PASTICCIO *Serves 8*

1 litre Rich Tomato Sauce (p.513)

1/2 glass of red wine

500g penne pasta

1 litre Best Béchamel Sauce (p.512)

200g piece of Parmesan cheese, freshly grated

3 Italian mozzarella cheeses (not the fake Danish stuff)

Basil leaves, roughly torn

A little olive oil

Butter

THE MEATBALLS:

About 500g minced beef (fresh or leftover)

About 500g minced pork (i.e. coarse sausage meat)

About 250g minced veal (optional)

1 egg, beaten

1 tablespoon olive oil

1 small onion, finely chopped

2 garlic cloves, finely chopped

50g Parmesan cheese, freshly grated

A pinch of cayenne pepper

A dash of lemon juice

A few sprigs of herbs, such as oregano, parsley and basil, chopped

Olive oil for frying

Salt and freshly ground black pepper

This is Mafia food, Goodfellas or Sopranos style – a huge pile of pasta, meatballs, tomato sauce and cheese, baked in the oven until crisp on the top and unctuous in the middle. In an Italian house the meatballs would be made from scratch, using fresh pork, beef and veal. I sometimes do this but I also find that leftover roast beef, combined with coarse sausage meat, makes excellent meatballs. I also think, though I possibly risk a concrete overcoat for saying so, that the veal is superfluous: the combination of beef and pork is the thing.

If you want something a little less elaborate, it is well worth making up the meatballs, simmering them for half an hour or so in the tomato sauce and serving them over plain buttered spaghetti, with a bit of Parmesan on the side.

Combine all the ingredients for the meatballs except the oil for frying and mix thoroughly. Roll the mixture into small (top-of-your-thumb size) meatballs, laying them on a tray as they are ready.

In a large frying pan, heat a little oil and fry the meatballs in batches, turning or shaking them occasionally, for 10 minutes or so, until nicely browned. As they are ready, transfer them to a bowl containing the tomato sauce. When you've finished cooking the meatballs, deglaze the pan with the red wine (page 334) and pour this juice into the tomato sauce, too.

Cook the pasta in a large saucepan of boiling salted water, draining when still nicely *al dente*. Mix thoroughly with the béchamel sauce.

Grease a large casserole dish with a little olive oil or butter. Spread about a third of the penne and béchamel mixture over the bottom. Sprinkle over a generous layer of grated Parmesan, about a quarter of what you have, and then ladle over a layer of meatballs in tomato sauce. Make a layer of mozzarella slices (one whole cheese's worth), topped with some roughly torn basil leaves, seasoned with black pepper and trickled with a little olive oil. Repeat the layers, starting with the next third of pasta and béchamel, and then complete with a third layer. The final layer of mozzarella should be dotted with butter and sprinkled with the last quarter of the Parmesan. At this point the dish can be chilled and kept for a day or two before you serve it.

Bake, covered, in a moderate oven (180°C/Gas Mark 4) for 30 minutes – or 40 if it's been in the fridge. Remove the lid and cook for a further 15-20 minutes, until the top is crusty and golden brown. This dish needs no accompaniment, as you can imagine. But you might wish to follow it with a seasonal leafy green salad.

FLYING TOAD IN THE HOLE *Serves 4*

I've always loved toad in the hole and have always felt that, on the whole (!), the meat-baked-in-batter concept is under-explored. This recipe aims to glamorise the dish a touch, while in no way compromising its earthy, trencherman appeal. The posh gravy is optional but makes it into a definite dinner-party winner.

2 pheasant breasts, cut in half (or 4 pigeon breasts)

4 fat butcher's sausages

2 large, plump prunes

3 streaky bacon rashers

1 tablespoon olive oil

THE BATTER:

125g plain flour

1/4 teaspoon salt

A few twists of black pepper

2 medium eggs

1 egg yolk

150ml milk

150ml water

THE GRAVY (OPTIONAL):

About 500ml clear game stock, ideally made from the pigeon bones (p.472)

About 1/4 bottle of red wine

(Or serve the Onion Gravy on p.517)

Choose a roasting tin or flameproof dish into which the breasts and sausages will fit with plenty of space for the surrounding batter.

First make the batter. Put all the ingredients in a food processor, with the plunger removed to help aeration, and pulse for about five 10-second bursts until you have a smooth batter. Alternatively, put the flour and seasoning in a large mixing bowl, beat in the eggs and yolk, then whisk in the combined milk and water by degrees, until you have a smooth batter the consistency of single cream. Leave the batter to rest for at least 30 minutes before using.

If you are making the gravy, do that in advance, too. Ensure that the stock is quite clear. If in doubt, warm it through and strain through a piece of muslin or a cotton cloth. Add the wine and boil hard to reduce it to an intensely flavoured sauce with a light, syrupy consistency. Season with salt only at the end.

Take the pieces of pheasant breast and make 2 or 3 parallel slits about 2cm deep in each one. Cut each prune into 4 or 5 slices, discarding the stones. Cut one of the streaky bacon rashers into thin strips. Push a piece of bacon (the fattier the better) and a sliver of prune into the slits in the breasts. Cut the remaining 2 rashers of bacon in half and flatten and stretch each half with the side of a large knife. Then wrap each piece of pheasant breast in the stretched half rasher.

Pour the oil into your chosen dish and place in the centre of a hot oven (220°C/Gas Mark 7) to heat through for about 10 minutes. Then add the sausages and wrapped breasts – they should sizzle in the oil. Start them cooking in the oven for a few minutes, then turn them browned-side up and push them around so they are more or less evenly spaced in the tin. By now the oil should be very hot. Pour the batter over and around the sausages and breasts and return the dish to the oven. Cook for at least 15 minutes, but probably not more than 20, until the batter is puffed up and a deep golden brown.

Give each person a slab of the batter, with a sausage and a breast in it, and a spoonful of the rich gravy. Have buttered cabbage or other greens to accompany.

Variation

Another great addition to toad in the hole, which you can use as well as or instead of the pheasant breasts, is kidneys. Use whole lamb's kidneys, half pig's kidneys, or trimmed calf's kidneys cut into suitable chunks. Prepare exactly as for the pheasant breasts.

PICADILLO *Serves 4-6*

250g coarsely minced beef

250g coarsely minced pork

1 tablespoon wine vinegar or cider vinegar

1/4 teaspoon salt

1/2 teaspoon sugar

A few twists of freshly ground black pepper

1 tablespoon dripping or olive or sunflower oil

1 onion, finely chopped

2 garlic cloves, very finely chopped

1 small red pepper, finely chopped

1-3 fresh Mexican chillies (jalapeño for mild heat, habanero for fierce heat), deseeded, rinsed and finely chopped

50g flaked almonds

50g raisins

50g stoned green olives (pimento-stuffed if you like), roughly chopped

250ml beef or pork stock (see pp.473-4)

125ml Sieved Roast Tomatoes (p.515) or 1 tube concentrated tomato purée

This is the Mexican equivalent of the Italian ragu *– an all-purpose, mildly spiced meat sauce made with minced pork and beef. It's a great family staple, and especially good for kids. It can be eaten with soft tortillas or tortilla chips (pages 521-2) and various Mexican trimmings, used as a filling for empanadas or, less authentically but very agreeably, with pasta, baked potatoes or just good crusty bread and butter.*

Picadillo is one of the dishes that have been hijacked, with the addition of red kidney beans, to become the Tex-Mex chilli con carne. A recipe for, and discussion of, this much-abused dish follows this one.

As always, a coarse, home-made mince will give you a much better result than the paste you get from most butcher's and supermarkets. A very good picadillo can be improvised from leftover pork, beef, or a combination, but if you're starting from scratch, here's how:

Put the meats in a large bowl and season them with the vinegar, salt, sugar and pepper, mixing well together. Leave to stand. Heat the dripping or oil in a large, heavy frying pan and sweat the onion, garlic, red pepper and chilli for about 10 minutes, until the onion is soft and lightly browned. Add the meat to the pan and cook, turning it over, until well browned. Transfer to a casserole or large saucepan, add all the other ingredients and mix well. Bring to a very gentle simmer and cook, partly covered, for about an hour, stirring occasionally. Add a little more water or stock if the mixture starts to look dry (though the finished picadillo should not be too wet).

Picadillo is best left to cool, refrigerated for a day or two and then gently reheated. Serve as a filling for soft tortillas (pages 521-2), or as a dip for tortilla chips (home-made or bought), with as many of the following accompaniments as you can muster: Guacamole (page 514), Red Salsa (page 514), Refried Beans (page 521), soured cream and grated cheese (Caerphilly and Wensleydale are good but Edam or mild Cheddar will do).

CHILLI CON CARNE *Serves 8-10*

1 kg coarsely minced beef

500g shoulder of pork, cut into 1 cm cubes

250g spicy chorizo sausage, cut into 1 cm cubes

500g dried red or black kidney beans, soaked in cold water overnight (or 1 kg tinned beans, rinsed)

4 tablespoons olive oil

2 large onions, chopped

1-5 fresh green chillies, deseeded and finely chopped

2 tablespoons malt, wine or cider vinegar

2 teaspoons dark brown sugar

2 x 400g tins of plum tomatoes (ideally made up into the Rich Tomato Sauce on p.513)

250 ml beef or pork stock (pp.473-4) and/or the cooking liquid from the beans

1 cinnamon stick

2 bay leaves

1/2 teaspoon dried oregano or marjoram

1-5 tablespoons chilli powder

Salt and freshly ground black pepper

Discussing the authenticity or otherwise of recipes for chilli con carne is, in a sense, moot because it is by its nature an inauthentic creation – a bit like the ploughman's lunch. It's really an American bastardisation of at least two Mexican dishes, the Mole (page 314) and the Picadillo (opposite). And now it has been further bastardised, to the point of banality, by the English, and the English pub in particular, which serves a second-rate bolognese laced with chilli powder and bulked with a few tins of kidney beans and calls it chilli con carne.

My attempt to restore some dignity to the dish can hardly lay claim to aboriginal correctness. Suffice to say that I have seen pork shoulder, chorizo sausage and cinnamon cited in various recipes that all seem committed to something more interesting and culturally rich than the napalm bolognese. My recipe, synthesising theirs, works. I hope it will be the best chilli con carne you have ever had. And it is a great party dish. I won't even disapprove if you serve it with baked potatoes instead of tortillas. But please don't call it authentic.

The '1-5' quantities for the fresh chillies and chilli powder range from mildly hot to blow-your-head-off. It's up to you to adjust as you like it. I find about 1 1/2-2, in each case, is quite hot enough for me, and I do some of the adjustment at the end with the dried chilli powder.

If using dried kidney beans, drain and rinse them after soaking and put them in a large pan of fresh water. Bring to the boil, boil hard for 10 minutes, then simmer gently for up to 2 hours, until completely tender. Reserve some of the cooking liquid, especially if you don't have any stock.

Heat a little over half the oil in a large frying pan and brown all the meats in batches, then transfer to a large casserole or stockpot. Add the rest of the oil to the frying pan and sweat the onions, on a slightly lower heat, until soft and translucent. Add to the meat, along with all the other ingredients except the beans, and not too much salt at this stage. Bring to the boil and simmer gently, stirring regularly and adding a little extra stock or water if ever it looks dry. Cook for at least 1 hour, maybe 1 1/2 hours, until the pork is tender and the sauce nicely amalgamated. Add the beans for the last 20 minutes or so, and taste and adjust the heat and seasoning towards the end of cooking.

Serve with tortillas (pages 521-2), either soft or fried as tacos, Guacamole (page 514) and soured cream. Or, of course, with buttered baked potatoes.

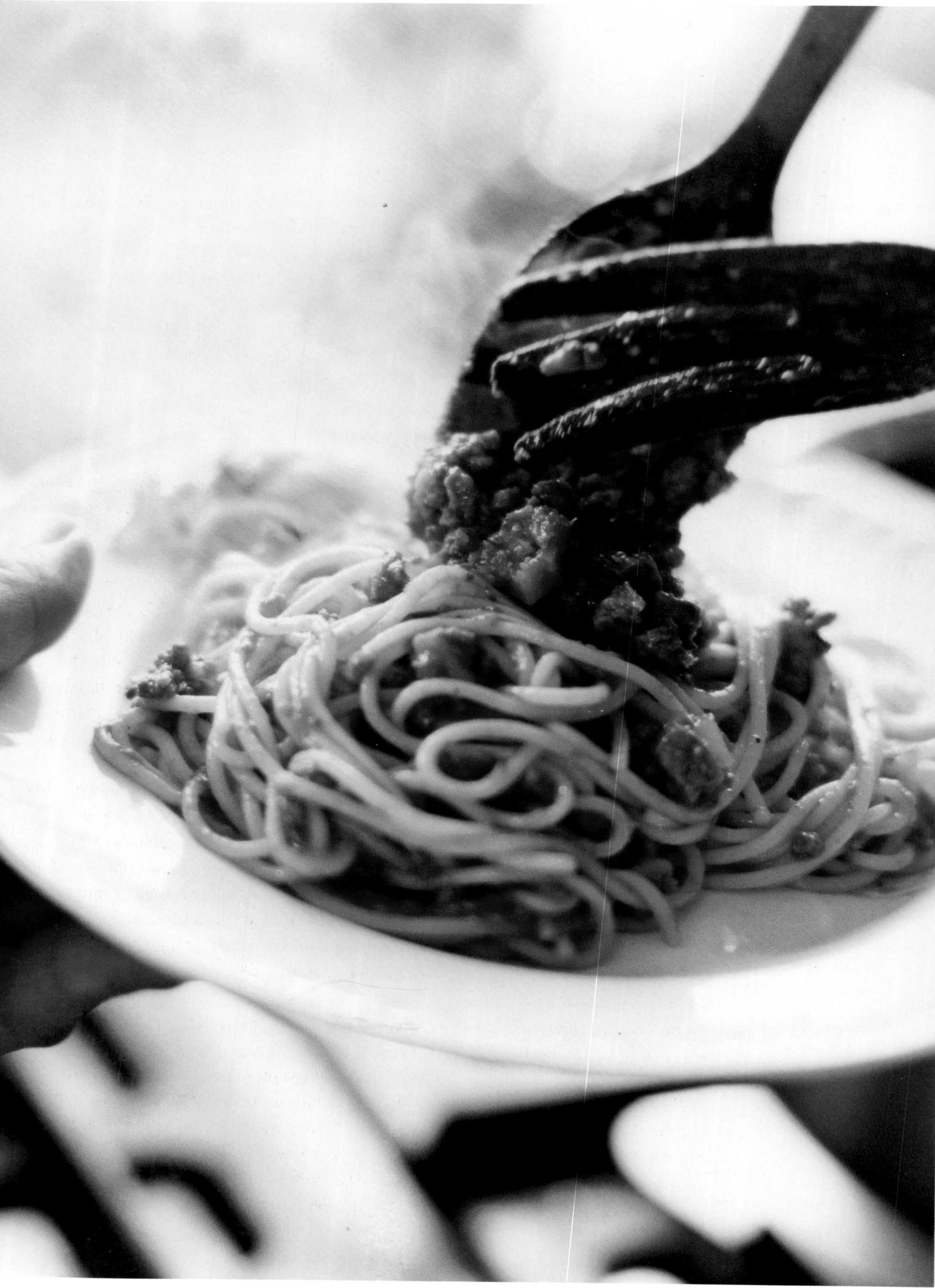

SPAGHETTI BOLOGNESE *Serves 6*

1kg coarsely minced beef

250g salt pork, pancetta or streaky bacon (see p.429 for home-made), finely diced

4 tablespoons olive oil

1 glass of red wine

2 large garlic cloves, finely sliced

500g onions, finely chopped

400g tin of plum tomatoes

250ml tomato passata (sieved tomatoes) or Sieved Roast Tomatoes (p.515)

300ml beef or pork stock (pp.473-4), or water

2 bay leaves

A few sprigs of herbs, such as thyme, basil, parsley, marjoram or oregano, if available

1 tablespoon cream or a large knob of butter (optional)

Salt and freshly ground black pepper

TO ACCOMPANY:

500g spaghetti or linguine

A knob of butter

Fresh Parmesan cheese

Bread

In the UK, spaghetti bolognese is perhaps the best loved, and certainly one of the most widely eaten, Italian pasta dishes. But it is not always the most lovingly made. It is often thrown together in a hurry, and rarely cooked as long as is necessary to mellow the sharp acidity of the tomatoes and produce a properly rich and melting texture and a luscious blend of flavours.

It's thrifty, because you can use the cheapest cuts of beef, minced, or even leftovers from a roast – though a good bolognese will always contain at least some fresh beef. The other essential ingredient is some kind of fatty pork – usually finely diced streaky bacon or pancetta but air-dried ham trimmings and even sausages or sausage meat can be used.

In a large frying pan, heat half the olive oil over a medium heat and fry the bacon in it so the fat runs. Add the beef and brown it – if you don't have a very large frying pan, do this in several batches – then transfer it to a good-sized casserole. The idea is to make sure that some of the meat is properly browned, as in lightly burned, not just 'greyed' by this process. You want those caramelised browning flavours to come out into the sauce. When you've browned the last batch of meat, deglaze the pan with the red wine (page 334) and add these juices to the casserole.

Now wipe the frying pan out with a wad of paper towel, add the rest of the olive oil and heat gently. Add the garlic and onions and sweat until the onions are soft and translucent. Add the tomatoes and passata and turn up the heat so the mixture bubbles merrily. Stir regularly, breaking up the tomatoes with a spatula or spoon. You are making a quick tomato sauce here, which gives a much better result than simply tipping the tomatoes into the meat. When the tomato sauce has reduced and thickened a little and the tomatoes are nicely broken up, add it to the meat, along with the stock or water, and the bay leaves tied in a bouquet with any other herbs you are using. Season with plenty of pepper and ½ teaspoon of salt.

Bring to a gentle simmer and cook, uncovered, for at least an hour, stirring occasionally. The finished sauce should be thick, rich and unctuous (i.e. not just mince in a thin liquid with little bits of tomato and onion floating around). You can cook it for up to 2 hours, if you like. For extra richness, finish the sauce by stirring in the cream or butter.

Boil the spaghetti or linguine in plenty of well-salted water and drain when still just *al dente*. Return to the pan and toss with a knob of butter. There are 2 ways to serve up the dish. The tidy English way: pile a big nest of spaghetti on to each plate and ladle a pool of sauce in the middle. And the Italian way: toss the spaghetti with the sauce in the pan till thoroughly mixed up and serve ready sauced. I prefer the latter, though it may be less pretty.

Pass a hunk of Parmesan around the table, with a grater. Offer bread to mop up the plates. Then serve a simple leafy green salad afterwards.

RED FLANNEL HASH *Serves 6*

About 500g leftover salt beef, or corned beef

About 250g cooked (not pickled) beetroot

About 250g cooked potatoes

2 onions, sliced

Dripping or oil

Cayenne pepper (optional)

A fistful of parsley leaves, finely chopped

Freshly ground black pepper

Named after the famous New England red flannel cloth, this is a traditional American way of using up salt beef or corned beef. It's certainly very red, and very tasty, a hearty supper for a hungry brood.

The quantities here assume you have a pretty huge frying pan – if not, cook the mixture in two batches, or in two frying pans simultaneously.

Cut up the beef, beetroot and potatoes into 1-2cm dice and place them in a large bowl. Sauté the onions in a good knob of dripping or a film of oil in a large, heavy frying pan for about 10 minutes, until tender but not too browned, then add the salt beef, beetroot and potatoes. Mix everything together thoroughly in the pan, seasoning well with black pepper and with cayenne if you like.

Fry without shaking or turning until the underneath is starting to get brown and crispy. Then turn with a spatula and fry some more (it's like cooking bubble and squeak). Keep frying to brown, then turning, until it's all looking nicely browned and crispy.

Garnish with a scattering of parsley, and serve with Wilted Spinach (page 523) or other leafy greens, and strong mustard, Worcestershire sauce and/or tomato ketchup (see page 516 for home-made ketchup).

PIROSHKI *Makes about 24*

About 250g leftover lamb, beef or poultry, finely chopped or coarsely minced

1 tablespoon sunflower oil

1/2 teaspoon coriander seeds, crushed

1/2 teaspoon cumin seeds, crushed

1 small onion, finely chopped

1 garlic clove, crushed

A little stock, gravy, wine or water

Salt and freshly ground black pepper

THE DOUGH:

225g plain flour

1 teaspoon baking powder

1/2 teaspoon salt

2 eggs

2 tablespoons vegetable oil

A little beaten egg, to glaze

SUGGESTIONS FOR FURTHER MEAT FILLINGS:

Leftover oxtail stew

Meat from a roast, minced or finely chopped, highly seasoned, and mixed with a little gravy from the roast

Seasoned sausage meat mixed with chopped cooked chestnuts and/or apples, and/or sautéed onions

Chopped pheasant mixed with bread sauce

Chopped chicken mixed with anchovies

Chopped pork or chicken mixed with peanut butter (just try it!)

The Russian word 'piroshki' simply means 'little pies', and in Russia they are traditionally served with drinks, or as a side dish with soups such as borscht. Improvised fillings can be made with all kinds of things, including potatoes and onions, cabbage, and various meats, either leftover or fresh.

I usually make piroshki when I have leftover lamb or chicken. Fresh dill is one authentic seasoning. But so are cumin and coriander, which I use here.

Piroshki can also be poached, like a kind of fat ravioli (see below). The great thing about the authentic Russian pastry dough described here is that it can be used for both the poached and the baked version. But you can use just about any pastry to make piroshki, including the hot water crust described for my Raised Pork Pie (page 444) and the rough puff I use for my Steak and Kidney Pie (page 286).

First make the dough: sift the flour, baking powder and salt into a bowl and make a well in the centre. Whisk the eggs with the oil and pour into the well in the flour. Using a wooden spoon, gradually draw in the flour, then beat until smooth, adding just a trickle of cold water if you need it. The dough should be fairly soft but not sticky. Turn it out on to a lightly floured work surface and knead for 5-10 minutes, until smooth and elastic. Lightly oil the bowl, put the dough back in, then cover and leave for about an hour.

Meanwhile, make the filling. Heat the oil in a pan, fry the spices in it for a minute or so, then add the onion and garlic and cook gently until softened. Stir in the meat, season with salt and pepper and cook for a few more minutes, so the meat is nicely browned. Add a little stock, gravy, wine or water to moisten just a little, check the seasoning, then take off the heat and leave to cool.

Knead the dough again for a minute or two, then roll it out as thinly as possible (no more than 2-3mm thick) and cut out rounds with a 7-8cm plain cutter. Place a little of the filling on each one, slightly to one side, then fold in half to make a tiny pasty, wetting the edges and pinching them together to seal. Turn the corners in a bit, to give a gentle crescent shape.

Lay the piroshki on a greased baking sheet, glaze with a little beaten egg and bake in a moderately hot oven (190°C/Gas Mark 5) for about 15 minutes, until golden brown. Serve warm.

Variation

Poached Piroshki: Poach the piroshki in very gently simmering water, a few at a time, for about 5-7 minutes, until the dough is cooked through and doesn't taste floury (i.e. test one). Remove with a slotted spoon and drain on kitchen paper, then place in a warmed dish and trickle with melted butter. Divide the piroshki between warmed serving plates, put a dollop of soured cream on each plate and sprinkle over a little paprika. Or poach in clear stock and serve as a soup.

PASTILLA *Serves 2*

About 100g leftover cooked meat

1 tablespoon icing sugar

1 teaspoon ground cinnamon

50g flaked almonds, toasted

50g butter

2 eggs, lightly beaten

A small bunch of parsley, finely chopped (optional)

A small bunch of coriander, finely chopped (optional)

4 sheets of filo pastry

Salt and freshly ground black pepper

THE STOCK:

Leftover poultry, game or meat bones

1 onion, roughly chopped

1 leek, roughly chopped

2 carrots, roughly chopped

2 bay leaves

4 cinnamon sticks

1 large glass of red wine

This is my 'leftovers' version of a wonderful North African recipe, traditionally made from scratch with doves or pigeon. The fully fledged version is in The River Cottage Cookbook. *It works well with leftover game and poultry (duck and goose especially), and also with lamb, venison or rabbit. The combination of eggs, meat, spices and nuts sounds curious but it is quite wonderful.*

If you have enough leftover meat you can make a big pie, but otherwise I like to make individual filo parcels. Obviously quantities depend on how much meat you have left over. The recipe here is about right for a couple of good-sized parcels.

Make the stock well in advance. Put the poultry carcasses or meat bones in a pan with all the other stock ingredients except the wine and add enough water to cover. Bring to the boil, skim off any scum from the surface and then simmer gently, uncovered, for at least 2 hours. Strain the stock, ideally through cotton or muslin, into a clean pan, add the red wine and boil hard until reduced to an almost syrupy consistency. You should be left with a scant 50ml (about 3-4 tablespoons).

Now make the filling. Chop or break the meat into rough shards. Mix together the icing sugar, ground cinnamon and toasted almonds. Heat half the butter gently in a small pan, add the eggs and stir frequently to scramble them gently. Take off the heat while still pourable and mix in the chopped parsley and coriander, if using, and some salt and black pepper.

Melt the rest of the butter and brush some over the surface of a baking sheet. Spread one sheet of filo pastry over the baking sheet and brush with more melted butter. Place another piece of filo over that and brush again. Put half the meat in the centre of the filo sheet and trickle over half the reduced stock. Then spoon over half the scrambled eggs and sprinkle over not quite half the almond and sugar mix. Fold the filo sheets corner to corner over the filling to make a triangle. Fold the 45-degree corners across the filling bulge, one over the other, then roll up the parcel towards the top, 90-degree angle, so you have a sausage shape. Make the second parcel in the same way (or you can make lots of mini parcels). Reserve just a little of the icing sugar mix.

Bake the pastilla parcels on the greased baking sheet in a moderately hot oven (200°C/Gas Mark 6). After about 6-7 minutes, when the tops are crisp and golden, take the baking sheet out and turn the parcels over. Put back in the oven for another 5 minutes or so, until they are crisp and golden brown all over. Dust the finished parcels with the reserved icing sugar and almond mixture. Serve at once, still piping hot.

MOUSSAKA *Serves 4*

About 750g leftover roast lamb, coarsely minced or finely chopped

2 large or 3 medium aubergines, cut lengthways into slices 5mm thick

2-3 teaspoons salt

3-4 tablespoons olive oil

1 large onion, finely chopped

2 garlic cloves, crushed

1 teaspoon ground cinnamon

2 tablespoons tomato purée

1 small glass of red wine

Any gravy/juices left over from roasting the lamb

1 tablespoon chopped parsley

Salt and freshly ground black pepper

THE TOPPING:

2 eggs and 1 extra yolk

150ml milk

250g Greek yoghurt

A pinch of paprika

50g kefalotyri cheese (or use a 50/50 mixture of Parmesan and Gruyère), grated

I love moussaka, and I particularly like to make it with leftover roast lamb, as the roasting of the meat gives a depth of flavour that is hard to achieve with raw meat. If it's a leftover leg roasted with anchovies and rosemary (page 239), then so much the better – you will find these flavours blend rather than offend. This recipe has an authentic, custardy top, rather than just a cheesy béchamel.

Lightly sprinkle the aubergine slices with the salt and leave in a colander to bleed for half an hour or so (while you proceed with making the lamb sauce).

Heat about half the olive oil in a large frying pan, add the onion and cook gently for about 10 minutes, until softened. Raise the heat a little, add the lamb and cook, stirring, until both onion and meat are lightly browned. Then stir in the garlic, cinnamon, tomato purée and wine. Let the mixture bubble for a minute or two, then add any gravy or lamb juices you may have and/or a wine glass of water. Season with salt and pepper and simmer for about 30 minutes, until it becomes a rich, moist sauce, adding a little more water if it dries out too much. Adjust the seasoning to taste and stir in the parsley.

Briefly rinse and pat dry the aubergine slices, then brush them on both sides with the remaining olive oil. Place on a baking sheet and roast in a hot oven (200°C/Gas Mark 6) for about 15 minutes, until brown and tender. Season with black pepper.

To make the topping, lightly whisk the eggs and egg yolk together in a large bowl. Bring the milk to boiling point and pour it on to the eggs, whisking constantly. Mix in the yoghurt, paprika, a pinch of salt and a twist of black pepper, then stir in the grated cheese.

Brush a large, rectangular ovenproof dish or roasting tin with olive oil and arrange about a third of the aubergine slices over the base. Cover with half the meat sauce, then another third of the aubergines, then the other half of the meat sauce. Add a final layer of aubergines, pour the yoghurt sauce over the top and bake in a moderate oven (180°C/Gas Mark 4) for about 35-40 minutes, until golden brown on top. Leave for about 10 minutes before cutting into squares to serve.

SHEPHERD'S PIE *Serves 4-6*

500g leftover roast lamb

1 tablespoon olive oil

1-2 onions, chopped

1-2 carrots, finely diced

1 garlic clove, chopped

Any juices or gravy saved from the joint, and/or concentrated lamb stock made from the bone

1/2 glass of red wine

1 tablespoon tomato ketchup

1-2 teaspoons Worcestershire sauce

Up to 1kg creamy mashed potatoes (p.518) – be careful not to make it too runny

Salt and freshly ground black pepper

Shepherd's pie is by its nature an improvised dish, but nevertheless it is one to approach with a certain amount of care and respect – because when you make a good one it's one of the most delicious things on the planet.

I used to mince the meat but now I prefer to chop it fairly coarsely, so the individual pieces are roughly pea sized. The texture of the finished pie is then more robust and satisfying. I often go to the trouble of making a little stock from the roasting bone (simmer for two hours with an onion and a carrot, then strain and boil until reduced to a scant cupful). I don't add tinned tomatoes – this is not lamb bolognese – but use ketchup and Worcestershire sauce to get a sauce that is rich and piquant.

Roughly chop the meat into pea-sized pieces. Use a food processor if you like but be careful to stop whizzing before you turn it into pâté. Heat the olive oil in a large frying pan or wide saucepan that will accommodate everything. Sweat the onions, carrots and garlic in the oil until the carrots have softened slightly. You can let the onions brown just a little.

Add the meat and fry gently until nicely browned. Add the gravy or stock, plus the wine, ketchup and Worcestershire sauce, then season with salt and pepper. Simmer gently for a few minutes, adding a little water if the mixture looks dry. Taste for seasoning and add a little more ketchup, Worcestershire sauce, salt or pepper, as you see fit. Simmer gently for another 20-30 minutes, until the meat is tender and the flavours well blended. Do a final taste for seasoning and adjust as necessary. Again, add a little more water, or wine, to loosen the mixture if you think it needs it. I like it well lubricated but not soupy.

Put the meat in a pie dish and pile the mash on top, covering the meat completely. Use a fork to rough up the surface of the mash (you can chill or freeze the pie at this point, for reheating later). Bake in a fairly hot oven (200°C/Gas Mark 6) for 25-45 minutes – depending on whether the pie is warm or chilled when it goes in – until the mash is nicely browned on top and the sauce is bubbling up around the edges. Serve at once, ideally with minted peas.

FRIED CHICKEN WITH POTATOES AND ANCHOVIES

Leftover chicken

Cooked potatoes (boiled or roast)

½-1 small tin of anchovies, drained

2 tablespoons olive oil

2 garlic cloves, roughly chopped

A few spring onions or 1 medium onion, finely sliced

Chopped parsley (optional)

This is a hot, fried version of a favourite cold salad that I described in The River Cottage Cookbook, *and I must say it's a struggle to decide which I prefer. Other possible additions include bacon, black olives, capers and sun-dried tomatoes.*

Cut up the cold chicken, but not too small. Roughly chop the cooked potatoes. Chop ½-1 tin of anchovies, according to the amount of chicken you have and how much you like anchovies.

Heat the olive oil in a frying pan and throw in the chicken, potatoes, anchovies, garlic and onions altogether. Toss and fry for 5-10 minutes until the chicken, potatoes and onions are all getting nicely browned and crisp. Serve at once, sprinkled with chopped parsley if you're in a fancy mood.

CORONATION CHICKEN *Serves 4*

About 400g leftover chicken, turkey or pheasant, cut into thick, boneless slices

2 tablespoons good, spicy fruit chutney

1 tablespoon good Madras curry paste (or powder, at a pinch)

100g Greek yoghurt

100g mayonnaise (p.513)

TO SERVE:

25g flaked almonds, toasted till golden

Chopped chives, coriander, or both, if handy

One of the world's least fashionable dishes, I would suspect. However, with a lovingly made sauce (Hellman's and curry powder don't quite do it on their own), it remains a very nice way to serve up cold poultry in a salady, summery fashion. Try it with pheasant some time, too.

Mix together the chutney, curry paste, yoghurt and mayonnaise in a large bowl, then add the cold meat and toss together. Chill for a couple of hours.

Just before serving, spread the dressed meat out on a platter and scatter over the toasted almond flakes and chopped herbs.

GAME SOUP *Serves 4*

Carcasses of at least 4 roasted game birds (and/or a hare)

2 tablespoons dripping or sunflower oil

100g salt pork, pancetta or streaky bacon (see p.429 for home-made), diced

2 large carrots, chopped

1 onion, finely chopped

2 celery sticks, chopped

A splash of brandy

1 small glass of port

1 large glass of red wine

1 litre chicken or pork stock (pp.470-72 and 474) – not game

2 tablespoons Sieved Roast Tomatoes (p.515) or 1 tablespoon concentrated tomato purée

2 garlic cloves, bruised

2 bay leaves

A few sprigs of thyme (or 1/2 teaspoon dried thyme)

1 tablespoon mildly spiced fruit chutney

100g pearl barley, rinsed in cold water

Salt and freshly ground black pepper

In his book Roast Chicken and Other Stories, *Simon Hopkinson offers a recipe for grouse soup, and it has become one of my favourite soup recipes (from one of my favourite cookbooks). Unfortunately, I don't have '4 grouse carcasses' burning a hole in my fridge nearly as often as I'd like to. But I do find that other game – pheasants, partridges, pigeons, mallard, the occasional woodcock or hare – come my way quite often. And so I have taken to improvising bastard versions of the Hopkinson recipe. It's never the same game, and therefore never the same soup, twice. But it rarely disappoints.*

Pigeon is always a good addition, as, like grouse, it has an underlying beefiness that keeps the soup robust. Mallard, on the other hand, can sometimes make it taste a bit fishy. A version in which I included the remains of a roast saddle of hare was quite sublime – up there with the four-grouse version. You can always stockpile game carcasses in the freezer until you have a promising combination.

Roughly chop the game carcasses into small pieces. Heat the dripping or oil in a large, heavy-based pan and fry the bacon in it for a few minutes until nicely browned. Add the vegetables and continue cooking until they too are lightly coloured. Add the chopped carcasses and stir for a few more minutes. Meanwhile, bring the 3 alcohols and the stock to the boil in another pan. Pour them over the game and vegetables and add the sieved tomatoes or tomato purée, garlic, bay leaves, thyme, chutney, a pinch of salt and a few twists of pepper. Add a little water if it is needed to cover the game. Lower the heat to a very gentle simmer and cook for a good 1 1/4 hours.

Strain the soup once through a colander and a second time through a fine *chinois* sieve, or muslin. Pour it into a clean pan, bring back to the boil and add the pearl barley. Simmer for 20-30 minutes, until the pearl barley is tender. Adjust the seasoning to your taste and serve.

BACON, SAUSAGE AND BLACK PUDDING PILAF *Serves 4*

Up to 250g salt pork, pancetta or bacon (p.429 for home-made), diced

Up to 250g cooked sausages, roughly chopped

Up to 250g butcher's black pudding, roughly chopped or crumbled

1 tablespoon olive oil

1 onion, finely chopped

500g cooked basmati or other long-grain rice

Ground mace or nutmeg (optional)

Salt and freshly ground black pepper

This is a scrummy stand-by supper dish, which you can make with just bacon and sausages but is even better with black pudding as well. I often make it with home-made black puddings I have frozen, as the texture is always a bit crumbly anyway. If you're starting with uncooked sausages, fry them first and chop them up, then add the bacon and proceed as below.

In a large pan, gently fry the bacon in the olive oil until it is starting to crisp a little. Add the onion and sweat until soft, golden and translucent. Add the sausage pieces and black pudding and turn up the heat a little, so they both crisp up and the onions start to take a little colour (you can burn them brown, but don't burn them black). Then throw in the cooked rice and heat through, tossing the pan occasionally, until everything is well mixed and nicely hot. Taste, and season as you like with salt and black pepper, and maybe a pinch of mace or nutmeg. Serve at once. I have been known to top it off with a fried egg.

THAI PORK DUMPLINGS

For every 100g finely minced fresh pork, chicken, duck or a combination, you will need some, most or all of the following:

1 dessertspoon lightly beaten egg white

2 teaspoons nam pla (Thai fish sauce)

1 tablespoon chopped coriander leaves

A small nugget of fresh ginger root, grated

1/2 garlic clove, grated

1 lemongrass stalk, bashed with a hammer

A pinch of salt

These are a lovely way to use up fresh pork or poultry trimmings, or to spin something exotic out of a couple of uncooked sausages that are nearing chuck-out status. They are also well worth making from scratch.

Combine all the ingredients, including the meat, in a bowl and leave for a couple of hours, if practical. Then carefully pick out the strands of bashed lemongrass – the flavour will be in the mixture but you don't want the scratchy slivers in your dumplings (at least I don't).

Form into little thumbnail-sized balls and poach in gently simmering water for 5-6 minutes. Drain and serve on plain boiled rice, with soy sauce to splash on.

VALENCIAN PAELLA *Serves 10–12*

1 small chicken or guinea fowl, jointed (pp.140-43)

1 rabbit, jointed (p.172)

1 wild duck or pheasant, jointed (pp.140-43)

4 tablespoons olive oil

2 large onions, chopped

1 green pepper, finely sliced

1 red pepper, finely chopped

250g runner beans or long green beans, cut into 5cm lengths

A good sprig of rosemary, needles stripped and chopped (optional)

1 large tomato, skinned and chopped

2 garlic cloves, finely chopped

1 teaspoon paprika

750g Spanish paella rice (or American long-grain rice, but not basmati)

1-2 pinches of saffron strands

16-20 snails, tinned, vac-packed or fresh

250g cooked butter beans

Salt and freshly ground black pepper

I first came across this very meaty version of the famous Spanish rice-based dish when I presented the series, 'TV Dinners', for Channel 4. The cook who prepared it, Dave Hayward, has a Spanish mother, and together they made a convincing case that this 'inland' paella from Valencia pre-dates the better-known seafood version by several generations. Whatever the history, it's certainly great for a party.

I have found it works best when I use a whole chicken, a whole rabbit and a whole duck, then joint them into about eight pieces each (pages 140-43). But you could scale the dish down, buying boneless breast meat (about 250g of each) and using pre-made stock, or even a stock cube, instead of plain water.

You could omit the snails, but I think it would be a pity as they add earthiness and a peasanty authenticity. You can buy cooked snails, tinned, frozen or vac-packed, in many good delis and specialist food shops. Or you can collect your own English garden snails, which are smaller but quite edible. You'll need about twice as many. Purge and prepare them as described in The River Cottage Cookbook.

The quantities below are designed for a proper 60cm paella pan so, if you don't have one, you will need at least a pair of large frying pans. Otherwise attempt the scaled-down version, as suggested above.

Heat the oil in the pan, swirling it over the base as it heats, then add all the meat. Fry, turning regularly, for 5-10 minutes, until all the pieces are nicely browned. Add the onions and stir-fry for a couple of minutes, then add the peppers, green beans and rosemary and stir-fry for a couple of minutes longer. Add the tomato and garlic and fry for 5 minutes, stirring occasionally. Add the paprika and stir it into the mixture, to heighten the colour and season the dish.

Pour on enough cold water to cover the meat and vegetables – about 1.5 litres (with a paella pan, the tradition is to add water until it comes up to the rivets of the pan). Then add the rice. In Spain the rice is poured across the paella pan in the shape of a cross. You have enough when your rice cross comes a little above the level of the liquid. Add the saffron and season with plenty of salt. Add the snails and the butter beans. Stir to mix everything together and colour the rice with the saffron. Cook for about 20 minutes over a heat that allows the liquid to bubble gently, until the liquid has been fully absorbed and the rice is completely cooked (i.e. not chalky in the middle). If the liquid has been absorbed before the rice is cooked, add a little extra hot water. Stir occasionally if you like, but leave well alone for the last 10 minutes, so a crust can develop.

Check the seasoning: an undersalted paella may taste bland. Don't worry if the rice starts to stick to the bottom of the pan – it's meant to. The crisp scrapings from the bottom, known as *socarrat*, are something the guests should be fighting over! Hand out forks so they can eat straight from the paella dish. Alternatively, serve on plates, trying to be fair with the meat, the snails and the *socarrat*.

THE TRIMMINGS

THE TRIMMINGS

BEST BÉCHAMEL SAUCE

Makes about 600ml

1 carrot
½ onion
1 celery stick
1 bay leaf
500ml whole milk
50g butter
50g plain flour
Salt and freshly ground black pepper

Grate the carrot, onion and celery and place them in a saucepan with the bay leaf and milk. Bring to the boil, then take the pan off the heat and leave to infuse for about an hour. Strain out the vegetables and bay leaf, then put the flavoured milk in a clean pan and reheat gently, but do not allow it to boil.

Melt the butter in a separate pan and stir in the flour. Cook this roux gently for a couple of minutes, then whisk in the milk, a third at a time, to get a nice smooth sauce. Let it simmer very gently for 5 minutes. It should have a pouring consistency, like double cream – if it is too thick, thin it with a little more hot milk. Season to taste with salt and pepper.

Variation: Real Parsley Sauce
Make the béchamel sauce above. Finely chop a good bunch of parsley (about 100g leaves when stripped from the stalks) and stir into the sauce just before serving.

BREAD SAUCE *Serves 8*

1 small onion
4 cloves
500ml milk
1 bay leaf
125g fresh (or slightly stale, but not rock hard) bread, torn into small pieces (or, of course, breadcrumbs)
50g butter, cut into small pieces
Salt and freshly ground black pepper

Peel the onion, cut it in half and stud it with the cloves, then put it in a pan with the milk, bay leaf and a twist of black pepper. Bring to the boil, then take off the heat. Add the bread, cover and leave to infuse for at least an hour.

Finish the sauce shortly before serving: fish out the onion, cloves and bay leaf and stir over a low heat until simmering gently. Simmer for 2-3 minutes. Turn off the heat, and stir in the pieces of butter. Adjust the seasoning and serve hot, at the table, in a sauce boat.

CREAMED FRESH HORSERADISH

Serves 8-10

About 100g fresh horseradish root
2 teaspoons good vinegar (aged if possible)
1 teaspoon English mustard
A pinch (no more) of sugar
125g crème fraîche
A pinch of salt
A twist of black pepper

Peel and finely grate the horseradish. Combine it with the vinegar, mustard and sugar, mix well and leave to macerate for 10 minutes. Mix again. Stir in the crème fraîche and season to taste with salt and pepper. Don't keep for more than a couple of days.

REAL MINT SAUCE *Serves 4-6*

A good bunch of mint
1 tablespoon cider vinegar
1 tablespoon olive oil
½ teaspoon sugar
½ teaspoon English mustard
Salt and freshly ground black pepper

Strip the leaves off the mint sprigs and chop them finely, but not too finely. Put them in a jam jar with the vinegar, oil, sugar, mustard, a good pinch of salt and a few twists of black pepper and shake until combined into a thick sauce. Taste and adjust the seasonings if necessary.

Variation: *You can turn this into a richer, more unctuous sauce by stirring in 3 tablespoons of plain yoghurt. Delicious with barbecued or roast lamb.*

MUSTARD VINAIGRETTE

Makes 150ml

2 teaspoons English mustard
1 small shallot, very finely chopped
1 teaspoon sugar
2 tablespoons cider vinegar
120ml olive oil
Salt and freshly ground black pepper

Put all the ingredients in a jam jar with a lid and shake together until thick and emulsified.

MY CHEATY MAYONNAISE

Makes 300ml

My cheaty recipe includes a small spoonful of bought mayonnaise, which helps to stabilise it.

2 egg yolks, at room temperature
1 heaped teaspoon good-quality bought mayonnaise
100ml light olive oil
200ml sunflower or groundnut oil
A squeeze of lemon juice
Salt and freshly ground black pepper

Put the egg yolks and bought mayonnaise in a small mixing bowl and whisk until combined. Pour both oils into a jug and trickle them, as thinly as possible, on to the egg yolks, beating constantly with a balloon whisk. Once the mayonnaise has taken, you can increase the flow to a steady trickle. It should be very thick and emulsified by the time you've finished adding the oil.

After you have added about half the oil, loosen the mayonnaise with a squeeze of lemon juice. Season to taste with salt and pepper, plus a little more lemon juice, if necessary.

Variation: Lemon Mayonnaise
Add the finely grated zest of 1/2 lemon to the egg yolks and season with extra lemon juice at the end.

Variation: Garlic Mayonnaise
Beat 1/4-1/2 finely grated clove of garlic into the finished mayonnaise. Leave for at least an hour to mellow and ripen.

BÉARNAISE SAUCE *Serves 4*

3 tablespoons wine vinegar
5 peppercorns
1 small bay leaf
1/2 shallot, finely chopped
1 sprig of tarragon, plus 1 teaspoon chopped tarragon
1 sprig of chervil, plus 1 teaspoon chopped chervil (optional)
150g unsalted butter
1 large egg yolk
Salt and freshly ground black pepper

Put the vinegar, peppercorns, bay leaf, shallot, tarragon sprig and chervil sprig, if using, in a small pan and bring to the boil. Simmer until reduced to about 1 tablespoon of liquid, then strain into a small bowl.

Melt the butter over a low heat. Put the egg yolk into a bowl and mix in the vinegar reduction, then whisk in the warm butter a little at a time until you have a loose, mayonnaise-type consistency. Mix in the chopped herbs, season to taste with salt and pepper and serve straight away.

TARTARE SAUCE *Serves 4*

2 generous tablespoons mayonnaise (ideally home-made – see above)
1-2 hard-boiled eggs, finely chopped
1 tablespoon roughly chopped parsley
2-3 gherkins, finely chopped
2 teaspoons capers, finely chopped
1 teaspoon English mustard

Combine all the ingredients thoroughly in a small bowl.

RICH TOMATO SAUCE

2 tablespoons olive oil
2-3 large garlic cloves, crushed
2 x 400g tins of peeled plum tomatoes
30g butter
Salt and freshly ground black pepper

Heat the olive oil in a large, heavy-based frying pan or shallow casserole and throw in the crushed garlic. Let it sizzle for a moment, but before it takes any colour add both tins of tomatoes with all their juice. As the tomatoes come to the boil, break them up with a wooden spoon. Simmer the sauce hard, but not too hard, stirring regularly, until it becomes thick and pulpy (make sure it doesn't stick to the bottom of the pan). Only when the sauce is finished should you adjust the seasoning with salt and black pepper, otherwise it will become overseasoned as it reduces. Stir the butter into the sauce just before serving.

SALSA VERDE (GREEN HERB SAUCE)

Serves 4

1 small garlic clove
A good bunch of flat-leaf parsley, trimmed of coarse stalks
About 15-20 basil leaves
Leaves from 3-4 sprigs of tarragon
4-5 anchovy fillets
About 1 teaspoon capers
About 1 teaspoon mustard (Dijon or English)
A pinch of sugar
A few drops of lemon juice or vinegar
2-3 tablespoons extra virgin olive oil
Freshly ground black pepper

Finely chop the garlic on a large chopping board. Then add the herbs, anchovies and capers and chop all together until the ingredients are well mixed and fairly fine in texture. Transfer to a bowl and mix in a little mustard, sugar, lemon juice or vinegar and black pepper, plus enough olive oil to give a glossy, spoonable consistency. As you add these last ingredients, taste and tweak the mixture till you get something you really like.

This sauce is best made immediately before serving but it will keep for a few days, covered or in a jar, in the fridge.

RED SALSA *Serves 6*

2 large red peppers
500g ripe tomatoes
1/2 red onion, finely chopped
1 garlic clove, very finely chopped
1-2 green chillies (to taste and according to strength), deseeded and finely chopped
Juice of 1/2 lime
A squeeze of fresh orange juice
1 teaspoon sugar
4 tablespoons chopped coriander
Salt and freshly ground black pepper

Roast the peppers whole in a fairly hot oven (200°C/Gas Mark 6) for about 20 minutes, until blackened all over. Place in a bowl, cover with a plate and leave until cool enough to handle. Peel and pick off the charred skin and discard, along with the seeds. Roughly chop the flesh.

Pour boiling water over the tomatoes and leave for 30 seconds, then drain. Peel off the skin with the point of a sharp knife and scoop out the seeds. Finely chop the seedless, skinless tomato flesh and mix with the chopped red pepper. Add all the other ingredients and mix well together, being careful to use only enough chilli to achieve the heat level you like. Chill the salsa until needed. It will keep for at least a week.

GUACAMOLE *Serves 6*

4 ripe but firm tomatoes, skinned, deseeded, and finely chopped
2 tablespoons lime juice (lemon if pushed)
1/2 teaspoon caster sugar
1 garlic clove, crushed to a paste with a little salt
A trickle of olive oil
2 large, ripe avocados
About 1 teaspoon chilli sauce or 1/2 small, hot chilli, finely chopped
Salt and freshly ground black pepper

Mix together all the ingredients except the avocados and chilli and leave to mingle for about half an hour. Peel and stone the avocados, scraping the inside of the skins to get all the dark green bits. Mash the avocado flesh with a fork, then add the tomato mixture and keep mixing until you get a thick, not quite pourable consistency. Add enough chilli to give the desired heat strength and adjust the seasoning to taste.

HUMMUS *Serves 6-8*

425g can of chickpeas, drained
2 garlic cloves, chopped
4-6 tablespoons olive oil
4 tablespoons tahini paste (optional)
Juice of 1-2 lemons
1 tablespoon chopped parsley or coriander
Salt and freshly ground black pepper

Optional flavourings:
Cayenne pepper
Ground cumin
Ground coriander

Put the drained chickpeas, garlic, 2 tablespoons of the olive oil, and the tahini, if using, in a food processor and blend until smooth. Add the juice of 1 lemon, plus 2-4 more tablespoons of olive oil, depending on the consistency you want – for kebabs, it should be a pourable sauce. Blend again, then taste and season with salt and pepper, more lemon juice if necessary, plus whichever of the optional flavourings you fancy: a good pinch of cayenne pepper, or 1/2 teaspoon or so of ground cumin and/or coriander. Transfer to a bowl, add the parsley or coriander and mix well.

SPICY PEANUT SAUCE *Serves 4-6*

1 onion, finely chopped
2 garlic cloves, crushed
1 tablespoon groundnut or sunflower oil
1/2-1 fresh red or green chilli (to taste and according to heat), finely chopped (or use chilli sauce from a bottle)
2-3 tablespoons dark soy sauce
1 tablespoon brown sugar
125 g crunchy peanut butter
Juice of 1/2-1 lime

Gently cook the onion and garlic in the oil until soft and lightly browned. Add the rest of the ingredients and mix well, then let the sauce bubble and thicken in the pan. Taste and adjust the flavour by adding more lime juice, chilli or soy, according to your preference (personally I like plenty of lime). Add a little water to get a nice, 'pourable but only just' consistency. This sauce will keep for a week in a sealed jar in the fridge. If reheating it, you may need to add a little more water.

TIKKA MARINADE

1 teaspoon salt
2 tablespoons plain yoghurt
1 tablespoon lime or lemon juice
2 tablespoons garam masala
2 teaspoons chilli powder
2 teaspoons ground coriander
2 teaspoons ground mixed spice
2 teaspoons ground fenugreek
A golfball-sized nugget of fresh ginger root, grated
4 large garlic cloves, finely chopped
1-2 tablespoons sunflower or groundnut oil
2-4 green chillies, depending on size and heat, finely chopped

Mix all the ingredients together in a large bowl. This marinade is essential for Murgh Makhani (page 355) and can also be used as an all-purpose marinade for boneless lamb and poultry, which can then be put on bamboo skewers and cooked on a barbecue or, classically, in a tandoor.

SIEVED ROAST TOMATOES

Slice plenty of good, ripe tomatoes in half, spread them out on a baking tray, cut-side up, scatter with a few roughly chopped cloves of garlic and trickle with olive oil. Roast in a moderate oven (180°C/Gas Mark 4) for about 40 minutes, until soft, crinkled and lightly browned. Then rub them through a sieve to remove the skin and pips.

RIVER COTTAGE CHUTNEY

You can use this recipe as a template for chutney experiments, substituting other fruits and vegetables according to seasonal availability. Try, for example, pumpkin instead of marrow, plums or grapes instead of tomatoes, chopped dried apricots instead of sultanas, etc.

1 kg marrows or overgrown courgettes, diced
1 kg tomatoes (red, green or a mixture), skinned and diced
500 g cooking apples, peeled, cored and diced
500 g onions, peeled and diced
500 g sultanas
500 g light soft brown sugar
600 ml white wine vinegar
About 2 teaspoons dried chilli flakes, according to your heat preference
1 teaspoon salt

For the spice bag:
25 g dried ginger pieces
12 cloves
2 teaspoons black peppercorns
1 teaspoon coriander seeds

Tie up all the ingredients for the spice bag in a piece of muslin. Put it in a large, heavy saucepan with all the rest of the ingredients and bring slowly to the boil, stirring occasionally. Simmer gently for 2-3 hours, uncovered, stirring occasionally to ensure the chutney does not burn on the bottom of the pan. The chutney is ready when it is rich, thick and reduced; if you draw a wooden spoon through it, the mixture should part to reveal the base of the pan.

Pot up the chutney while still warm (but not boiling hot) in sterilised jars (see below) with plastic-coated screw-top lids; these are essential to stop the vinegar interacting with the metal. Leave to mature for at least 2 weeks – ideally 2 months – before using.

Note: To sterilise jars, just put them through a cycle of the dishwasher and leave them until dry. Alternatively, you can wash them thoroughly in hot soapy water, rinse in fresh hot water, then put them to dry in a low oven for at least half an hour.

HOME-MADE TOMATO KETCHUP

3kg ripe tomatoes, roughly chopped
4 onions, sliced
1 large red pepper, seeds and white membrane removed, chopped
100g soft brown sugar
200ml cider vinegar
1/4 teaspoon dry mustard
A piece of cinnamon stick
1 1/2 teaspoons whole allspice
1 1/2 teaspoons whole cloves
1 1/2 teaspoons ground mace
1 1/2 teaspoons celery seeds
1 1/2 teaspoons black peppercorns
1 bay leaf
1 garlic clove, peeled and bruised
Paprika or cayenne pepper to taste (optional)
Salt

Put the tomatoes, onions and red pepper in a large, heavy pan and simmer over a medium heat, stirring occasionally, until very soft. Push through a coarse-meshed sieve and return to the pot with the sugar, vinegar and mustard. Tie the cinnamon, allspice, cloves, mace, celery seeds, black peppercorns, bay leaf and garlic in a square of muslin and drop it into the stew.

Bring the mixture to the boil, then reduce to a slow simmer. Cook, allowing the mixture to bubble gently, stirring often and carefully, for 20-40 minutes. The time taken will depend on how juicy your tomatoes are but in any case continue to cook until it is thick and pulpy. Taste a couple of times while it is cooking and remove the spice bag if the flavour becomes too strong.

Season to taste with salt and paprika or cayenne, if using, then leave to cool. Pour the ketchup through a funnel into suitable bottles and seal. Stored in the fridge, this ketchup will keep for a month. If you bottle it in sterilised jars while still warm (see page 515), it should keep for a year.

ONION MARMALADE

5 tablespoons olive oil
1kg large white or red onions, halved and thinly sliced
1 teaspoon sugar
Balsamic vinegar to taste
Salt and freshly ground black pepper

Heat the oil in a large pan, add the onions, then cover and cook over a low heat until the onions are greatly reduced in volume and completely tender – this can take up to 1 hour. Sprinkle with the sugar, raise the heat to medium and cook uncovered, stirring regularly, until the onions are golden brown and all the liquid has evaporated. Season with salt and pepper, then stir in 1 tablespoon of balsamic vinegar – the onions should taste sharp/sweet. Simmer for a few minutes longer, then taste and adjust the seasoning, adding more vinegar if necessary. Leave to cool. It will keep, covered, in the fridge for 2 weeks.

BEEF BONE GRAVY *Serves 10*

This is not really a gravy but a classic stock reduction (page 469) from a beef bone stock that can be prepared well in advance. It's boosted with the roasting juices from a joint of beef to give the ultimate gravy for Roast Beef – The Full Monty (page 232).

At least 2 litres good, clear beef stock (page 473)
1/2 bottle of red wine
Salt

If you have any doubts about the clarity of the stock, warm it through until hand-hot and free flowing, then strain it through a cotton cloth or muslin.

Put the stock in a clean, heavy-based pan at least 4 litres in capacity, add the wine and boil hard to reduce, skimming off any rising deposits occasionally. As it becomes darker and more concentrated, taste regularly. It will cry out for salt but do not add any yet, as the saltiness will concentrate as you continue to reduce. Stop reducing when you have a rich, concentrated beefy sauce that is lightly syrupy but not too sticky. Only at this point should you season, to taste, with salt.

Finish the gravy at the last minute by adding the deglazed pan juices from your roasting tin or frying pan, but exclude as much fat as you can and check that the juices are not too salty. Then strain at least through a fine sieve, if not muslin. A brisk whisk will help to emulsify the two sauces.

You can keep the gravy, chilled as a jelly, in the fridge for up to a week. Before serving, gently warm it until not quite boiling and 'refresh' with a small splash of the wine you're going to drink with the beef.

ONION GRAVY

To make a classic onion gravy for serving with faggots or toad in the hole, gently sweat 1kg finely sliced onions in a little oil until very tender and sweet, then stir them into the Beef Bone Gravy (see above).

YORKSHIRE PUDDING *Serves 10*

I am indebted to David Wallington, of the Whiteleaf Inn at Croyde, North Devon, who gave me these instructions for Yorkshire pudding almost ten years ago. They have never failed me.

250g plain flour
1 teaspoon salt
4 medium eggs, plus 2 egg yolks
300ml milk
300ml water
2 tablespoons olive oil

Put all the ingredients except the oil in a food processor, with the plunger removed to help aeration, and pulse for about five 10-second bursts until you have a smooth batter. (Alternatively, put the flour and salt in a large bowl, beat in the eggs and yolks, then whisk in the combined milk and water by degrees, until you have a smooth batter the consistency of single cream.)

Rest the batter for at least half an hour before making the pudding. At any rate, you should not put the pudding in the oven until you have removed the beef and set it to rest. This serves as an excellent way of ensuring you carry out this vital exercise of relaxing the meat. You can then turn up the oven, which may or may not still contain the roasting potatoes, to 220°C/Gas Mark 7.

I like to make a single Yorkshire pudding in a big roasting tin, then slice it, rather than create individual puddings. It looks better and feels more generous. Choose a roasting tin or ovenproof dish about 40 x 25cm, pour in the olive oil and heat it in the oven for at least 5 minutes, and no less. (If a few drops of batter don't sizzle when dropped in the tin, return it to the oven for another 5 minutes.)

Pour the batter into the hot, sizzling tin, return it to the oven and leave for 20-25 minutes, until the pudding is well puffed up and golden brown.

MY FAVOURITE STUFFING *Serves 8*

This is a rich chestnut and celery stuffing for poultry or pork. I particularly like it with turkey, in which case I added the chopped liver of the bird. Of course, as discussed on pages 217-18, I would never actually stuff a turkey, but this cooks well in a separate dish.

500g fresh chestnuts
1 small onion, finely chopped
1 head of celery, chopped
25g butter
12 plump prunes, stoned and roughly chopped
1 tablespoon chopped parsley
50g fresh breadcrumbs
The turkey's liver, trimmed, washed and finely chopped (optional)
1 egg, beaten
Salt and freshly ground black pepper

Make a small slit in the skin of each chestnut, then blanch or roast them to ease peeling. Peel off both the tough outer skin and the thin, brown inner skin, then simmer in unsalted water for 15-20 minutes, until completely tender. Drain the chestnuts and leave to cool, then place in a basin and break them up roughly with a fork – they should be crumbled rather than puréed.

Over a medium heat, sweat the onion and celery in the butter for a few minutes, until softened, then add the prunes, chestnuts and parsley. Season with salt and pepper, mix well and cook for a few minutes longer. Remove the pan from the heat.

When the mixture has cooled a little, mix in the breadcrumbs, liver, if using, and egg until all the ingredients are well combined. Use this mixture to stuff a loin of pork (page 229). Or, if serving with poultry, pile the mixture into an ovenproof dish and bake for 30-35 minutes in a moderate oven (e.g. with the turkey at 180°C/Gas Mark 4), until nicely browned and crisp on top.

PERFECT ROAST POTATOES

This is not so much a recipe as a few tips for achieving the desirable crisp-but-not-black outside and fluffy interior that we all know we love.

Choose a floury variety of potato, such as Cara, Maris Piper or King Edward, and cut fairly small – egg size, if you like. Parboil in gently boiling salted water for about

8 minutes – stop before the potatoes are cooked right through. Drain and leave to cool completely, then scratch roughly with a fork and season with a little fine salt. Only roast the potatoes round the joint if there is plenty of fat in the tin – at least 5 mm – and plenty of room. Better to preheat the oil (goose fat or lard if you have them, sunflower or groundnut if you don't) in a separate tin, adding any fat from the roasting tin just before the spuds go in. Do not add the potatoes till the oil is sizzling hot. Baste or turn them carefully as soon as they go into the tin, so they have a light coating of oil from the start.

Roast the potatoes for the last 45 minutes of your joint's cooking time, turning at least once. If they look as if they could use a bit more browning/crisping, leave them in after the joint has come out to rest and whack up the heat (if you are serving them with roast beef, you will need to increase the heat for the Yorkshire pudding anyway; see page 517).

Drain well and keep in a warm oven, uncovered, and not too piled on top of each other. Season again, with salt and pepper, before serving.

ROSEMARY ROAST NEW POTATOES

Serves 6-8

1kg new potatoes, or other waxy potatoes such as Charlotte or La Ratte
Duck fat, goose fat or olive oil
8 plump garlic cloves, lightly bashed
3 sprigs of rosemary
Salt and freshly ground black pepper

Peel the potatoes (or scrub them thoroughly) and cut them in half if large. Place in a large pan of boiling salted water and simmer for 5 minutes. Drain the potatoes and let them dry off in a colander for a few minutes. Meanwhile, in a fairly hot oven (200°C/Gas Mark 6), heat enough fat or oil in a large roasting tin to give a depth of about 5mm.

Add the potatoes to the hot fat, together with the garlic and 2 of the rosemary sprigs. Turn carefully to coat them in the fat, season with a little salt, then return to the oven and roast for about 40 minutes, until the potatoes are golden and tender, turning them half way through. Drain well on kitchen paper, season with salt and pepper, then snip a little rosemary from the remaining sprig over the potatoes and toss well. Serve immediately.

SOME THOUGHTS ON PERFECT MASH

The creamiest, smoothest mash of all is achieved by having the potatoes as dry as possible when mashed up with a generous amount of hot milk and butter. The 'floury' potato types are best, as they give up their moisture easily to produce soft, crumbly flesh. Such types include King Edward, Caesar, Cara, Desiree, Pentland Javelin and Wilja.

Some chefs (the Roux brothers, apparently) like to bake rather than boil the potatoes, which they dust with fine salt first, to get them as dry and crumbly as possible. The flesh is then scooped out of the skins, sieved into a pan of bubbling hot milk and butter, or even cream and butter, and whisked until smooth. Such mash is indeed heavenly, and not too troublesome to prepare – at least you don't have to peel the potatoes. But not everyone wants to turn the oven on just to make mash.

Another good tactic is to boil the potatoes in their skins in very well-salted water. Choose roughly similar-sized potatoes so they all cook at the same rate. The moisture in the potatoes is drawn out by a process of osmosis. When they are thoroughly tender, drain them in a colander and leave to steam until just cool enough to handle. Then the skins are easily peeled off with your fingers. Break up the potatoes roughly with a fork, to allow more of the moisture to steam off. After a couple of minutes' more steaming, the potatoes can be sieved, or pressed through a potato ricer into a pan of hot milk and butter as before.

Potatoes peeled and then boiled are more likely to become waterlogged and are harder to time: undercook them and you will have hard, waxy pieces in your mash; overcook them and they will take up more water as they break up in the pan. But assuming you get them about right, they, too, will benefit greatly from 'steaming off' in a colander before mashing. While the potatoes are draining, heat some butter and whole milk in the pan they were cooked in. Then return the spuds to the pan and mash thoroughly or, better still, crush them back into the pan through a potato ricer or rub them through a sieve. Then beat or whisk thoroughly until smooth and creamy.

Always heat the butter and milk almost to boiling point before mixing with the potatoes. I like to infuse some freshly ground black pepper, and sometimes the merest pinch of nutmeg, in the hot milk for a few minutes before the potato goes in. Taste and carefully adjust the seasoning again before serving.

The amount of butter and milk you use will determine the final texture of the mash. You can choose to have anything from a super-rich, almost pourable purée (serve sparingly with fried black pudding for a fab starter) to a more traditional, stiffer mash that you can pile high next to your bangers or on top of a shepherd's pie. For a regular 'side-order' mash, I like about 125g butter and 250ml whole milk for 1kg potatoes.

HORSERADISH MASH

Add 2 tablespoons of freshly grated horseradish root to the hot milk and butter (see above), then leave to infuse with a lid on for about half an hour. Do this in a separate pan just after the potatoes have gone on, and by the time they are cooked the horseradish flavour will be fully infused. Then proceed as discussed above.

CHIPS *Serves 4*

4 large, floury potatoes, such as Caesar, Maris Piper, Desiree or King Edward
At least 2 litres groundnut oil for deep-frying
Sea salt

Peel the potatoes and cut them into fairly thin chips (I hate to say it, but McDonald's size is about right). Put the chips into a large bowl of cold water and swish them around to remove some of the starch, then drain well and dry on a tea towel.

Heat plenty of oil to 140°C in a deep-fat fryer or a large, deep saucepan. Put a batch of chips into a frying basket (but it shouldn't be too crowded) and lower them into the oil. Fry them for about 5 minutes, until the chips are soft and flabby but not coloured: to test them, remove a chip and squash it between your fingers – there should be hardly any resistance. Drain on kitchen paper and fry the remaining chips in the same way.

This can all be done well in advance – several hours if necessary – then just before you want to serve the chips, heat the fat to 190°C and fry the chips, again in batches, until crisp and brown. This should take only about 2 minutes. Drain well on kitchen paper, sprinkle with sea salt and place in a serving dish in a low oven to keep warm while you cook the rest.

GAME CHIPS *Serves 6*

If you don't have time to make game chips, you can always use good-quality potato crisps, heated briefly in a moderate oven, instead.

3 medium-sized floury potatoes
Groundnut oil for deep-frying
Sea salt

Peel the potatoes and cut them into the thinnest possible rounds – a mandoline is useful for this, and a potato peeler also works. Place them immediately in a large bowl of cold water and leave to soak for 20 minutes to remove excess starch. Drain well and dry thoroughly on a tea towel.

Heat some oil to 190°C in a deep-fat fryer or a large, deep saucepan. Add the potato slices, a handful at a time, and fry for 2-3 minutes, until crisp and golden brown. Drain on kitchen paper, sprinkle with sea salt and serve immediately (or you can keep them warm in a low oven for 10 minutes or so, but not much more).

HERB DUMPLINGS
Makes 12 large dumplings

115g self-raising flour
115g fresh white breadcrumbs
115g suet
1 small bunch of chives, finely chopped
1 small bunch of parsley, finely chopped
Leaves from a few sprigs of thyme, finely chopped
2 eggs
Salt and freshly ground black pepper

Put the flour, breadcrumbs, suet, chopped herbs and some seasoning into a large bowl, mix thoroughly and then make a well in the centre. Beat the eggs lightly with a fork and pour three-quarters into the well. Mix with a fork, bringing the dry ingredients into the centre, to form a soft dough. Take over with your hands, working the dough until smooth and adding the rest of the egg if it seems too dry. Do not knead more than is necessary to bring the dough together. Divide the dough into quarters, then make 3 round dumplings from each quarter.

Dumplings should be cooked on top of your stew, with the lid on, for the last 25 minutes of cooking time. Arrange them, if possible, so that they do not touch each other. If there are too many for the size of your pot, then an extra batch can be cooked separately in a steamer.

RISOTTO ALLA MILANESE *Serves 6*

1.5 litres chicken stock
80g butter
1 small onion, very finely diced
40g beef marrow, if available, diced (or use pancetta)
400g arborio rice
1 small glass of dry white wine
1 large pinch of saffron strands, infused in 4 tablespoons hot water
30g Parmesan cheese, freshly grated, plus extra to serve
Salt and freshly ground black pepper

Put the stock in a pan and bring to the boil, then turn it down to simmering point. Heat half the butter in a large, heavy-based pan, add the onion and the marrow or pancetta and cook gently for 6-8 minutes, until the onion is soft but not coloured.

Turn the heat up to medium, add the rice and stir for 2 minutes, until it is well coated in the butter. Add the wine and simmer until it has been absorbed. Pour in a ladleful of the hot stock and stir until it has almost all been absorbed by the rice, then add another ladleful of stock. Continue to add the stock at intervals in this way, stirring all the time.

After about 15 minutes, add the saffron liquid, then proceed with the remaining stock. When the rice is done (about 18 minutes after you started adding the stock), it should be tender but still a little al dente *and the mixture should be moist but not runny. Remove from the heat, season with salt and pepper, then beat in the remaining butter and the Parmesan cheese. Serve immediately, with extra Parmesan if you like.*

SPLIT PEA PURÉE *Serves 6*

350g green split peas
1 onion, finely chopped
1 carrot, finely chopped
1 celery stick, finely chopped
1 small leek, chopped
A sprig of thyme
1 bay leaf
50g butter
A pinch of caster sugar
Salt

Soak the split peas overnight in plenty of cold water. Drain, rinse and put into a saucepan with the vegetables, herbs and enough water to cover. Bring to the boil, then reduce to a simmer and cook until tender. Drain off the water, discard the bay leaf and thyme, and put the peas and vegetables, with the butter, through a mouli-légumes, sieve or food processor (although the latter makes a less interesting texture). Now season to taste with the sugar and some salt. Heat through before serving, thinning the purée with a little hot water if it is very stiff.

LENTILS FOR COTECHINO, TONGUE etc
Serves 6

250g Puy lentils
2 tablespoons extra virgin olive oil
1 garlic clove, finely chopped
1 small onion, finely chopped
1 celery stick, finely chopped
Salt and freshly ground black pepper

Rinse the lentils, put them in a pan with at least 1 litre of cold water and bring to the boil. Simmer for about 15 minutes, until nearly tender but still al dente*, then remove from the heat and drain.*

Heat the oil in a pan and sweat the garlic, onion and celery in it until soft. Add the lentils and a splash of water and season with salt and pepper. Cook for 5-10 minutes, adding the odd splash of water as necessary, until the lentils are tender and the water has been absorbed. Check the seasoning, trickle with a little extra olive oil if you like, and serve.

COUSCOUS *Serves 6*

300g couscous (the quick, pre-cooked type, which is what most shops sell now)
350ml hot water or light stock
25g butter
Salt and freshly ground black pepper

Put the couscous in a large bowl, pour over the water or stock, then cover and leave for 10 minutes. With a fork or your fingers, gently fluff up the couscous, separating the grains. Stir in the butter and season to taste. The couscous can be prepared in advance and then reheated, covered, in a fairly hot oven (200°C/Gas Mark 6) for 10 minutes or so.

SPECIAL COUSCOUS *Serves 6*

300g couscous
50g raisins
350ml hot water or light stock
1/2-1 teaspoon harissa paste, to taste
4 tablespoons olive oil
1 onion, finely sliced
25g butter
25g flaked almonds, lightly toasted
1-2 tablespoons black olives, stoned and halved
2 tablespoons chopped coriander
1 tablespoon chopped mint
Lemon juice, to taste
Salt and freshly ground black pepper

Put the couscous and raisins in a large bowl. Mix the water or stock with the harissa, then pour it over the couscous, cover and leave for 10 minutes. With a fork or your fingers, gently fluff up the couscous, separating the grains. Stir in the oil and some salt and pepper.

Fry the onion in the butter until soft and golden. Add it to the couscous with the almonds, olives, herbs and a good squeeze of lemon juice, then fork through until everything is well mixed. Taste and adjust the seasoning with more salt and pepper, harissa or lemon juice.

REFRIED BEANS
Serves 6

400g dried black beans or red kidney beans, soaked in cold water overnight and then drained
2 garlic cloves or 1/2 onion, peeled
1 small onion, finely chopped
3 tablespoons vegetable oil
2 green chillies
4 tablespoons lard or dripping (or use vegetable oil)
Salt and freshly ground black pepper

Put the soaked beans in a large pan and add enough cold water to cover them by about 8cm. Add the peeled garlic cloves or onion, bring to the boil and simmer until the beans are completely soft – this can take up to 2 hours. If the beans start to look dry, top up with boiling water.

When the beans are nearly done, fry the chopped onion in the oil in a separate pan until golden. Add to the beans, with the oil, and then add the whole chillies. Season well with salt and pepper and simmer for 20 minutes. Drain off excess liquid and leave the beans to cool.

You can serve them like this as an accompaniment to stews, or make refried beans. To do this, heat the lard or dripping in a large, heavy-based frying pan and gradually mix in the beans, mashing them with a potato masher or a fork as you add them. Keep stirring the beans as they fry, making sure they do not stick to the pan. Cook until they form a thick, lumpy mass and nearly all the moisture has evaporated, then adjust the seasoning and serve. They are good with a little Mexican-style Chorizo, browned in a separate pan as described on page 446, stirred in.

SOFT FLOUR TORTILLAS
Makes about 24

100g plain white flour
500g *masa harina* (Mexican maize flour) – if you cannot get hold of any, use all plain flour
1 teaspoon salt
75g lard (optional, but it makes the dough a bit more forgiving, especially if using all plain flour)
Up to 500ml warm water
1 teaspoon sunflower oil (if needed)

Sift the flour, masa harina *and salt into a bowl, then rub in the lard. Stir in enough warm water to form a soft but not sticky dough (you probably won't need all the water). Turn out and knead on a floured surface for about 10 minutes, until smooth and elastic. Put the dough into a clean bowl, cover and set aside to rest for 1 hour.*

Take an egg-sized piece of dough and roll into a neat ball. With the base of your palm, press it on a lightly floured surface into a circle about 20 cm in diameter and no thicker than a 10-pence piece. Alternatively you can press it in a lightly floured tortilla press – a tool designed specially for the job. If the pressed or rolled tortilla has ragged edges, the dough is too dry. Add a few drops of water and knead a little longer. A dough that sticks when being rolled or pressed is too wet. Add a little more masa harina *or white flour and knead again.*

Make the remaining tortillas in the same way, then cook them one at a time on a preheated dry, heavy-based frying pan until the underside is flecked with pale brown spots and bubbles appear on the surface. This should take about a minute (if the spots appear too quickly and are black rather than brown, the pan is too hot). Turn the tortilla and cook the other side, pressing down the bubbles with a rolled-up tea towel for about 40 seconds. You can grease the pan very lightly with the sunflower oil.

Keep the tortillas warm by wrapping them in a clean cloth when they are cooked. This also helps to soften them if they are a bit brittle. They can either be eaten straight away or stacked, cooled, wrapped in clingfilm, refrigerated and reheated later – ideally within 48 hours. Or they can be frozen in a sealed bag for up to 6 months. Reheat them in the same way they were cooked, in a hot, dry pan.

Tortilla chips

Leftover tortillas can be deep-fried, either whole, halved, or cut into 6 triangles to make tortilla chips.

MELBA TOAST

The standard way of making Melba toast is to toast the bread lightly on both sides, then remove the crusts, cut each piece of toast horizontally in half to make 2 very thin slices, and put them in the oven until brittle. However, you can cheat by slicing white bread as thinly as possible and putting it in a hot oven for a few minutes, until it starts to brown.

RATATOUILLE *Serves 4*

Olive oil
4 garlic cloves, finely chopped
About 250 g aubergine, cut into 2 cm cubes
About 250 g small courgettes, sliced 1 cm thick
About 250 g sweet cherry or Sungold tomatoes, whole
About 250 g onions, cut into fairly thick slices
A few basil leaves, torn
Salt and freshly ground black pepper

Place 4 small pans over a medium heat and cover the base of each with a little olive oil. Add a clove of chopped garlic to each pan, and one of the vegetables. The aubergine takes a little longer than the others, so start that first, if you like.

Cook the courgettes until tender, then turn up the heat a little to brown them lightly. The aubergine, when finished, should be completely soft and tender, almost creamy. The tomatoes should be wrinkled and sweet but still just about holding their shape. And the onions should be soft, sweet and lightly caramelised. Season the vegetables towards the end of cooking and remove each pan from the heat when you are happy with it. When all the vegetables are ready, toss them gently together in a large pan and heat through for a few minutes, then add the torn basil leaves.

GLAZED CARROTS *Serves 8-10*

75 g butter
1 kg carrots, peeled and sliced on the diagonal
2 teaspoons caster sugar
1/2 teaspoon salt
About 300 ml good jellied chicken or beef stock (pages 470-73)
Freshly ground black pepper
Chopped fresh parsley, to garnish

Melt the butter in a wide saucepan and add the carrots, sugar, salt and enough stock to come half way up the carrots. Bring to a simmer, then cook gently, uncovered, shaking the pan occasionally, until the carrots are just tender. Remove the carrots with a slotted spoon, transfer to a warmed dish and keep warm. Raise the heat under the pan and boil the liquid rapidly until it has reduced to a rich, shiny glaze. Return the carrots to the pan and turn to coat them in the glaze. Adjust the seasoning and serve sprinkled with parsley.

WILTED SPINACH *Serves 4*

This simple cooking technique works well with other leafy greens, too, such as chard, kale and Brussels tops.

1kg fresh spinach
A good knob of butter
Salt and freshly ground black pepper

Wash the spinach and strip out the coarse central stalks. Put the leaves into a large pan with the water still clinging to them, plus a tablespoon or so of extra water. Push them around over a medium heat until just wilted. Stir in the butter and season to taste with salt and pepper. Serve immediately.

ULTIMATE CREAMED SPINACH

Serves 4

500g fresh spinach
250ml whole milk
1 small onion, grated
1/2 carrot, grated
1 bay leaf
Freshly grated nutmeg
50g butter
25g plain flour
Salt and freshly ground black pepper

Wash and trim the spinach, stripping out the coarse central stalks. Bring a large pan of salted water to the boil. Blanch the spinach in 3 or 4 batches, putting a good handful of leaves into the rapidly boiling water and stirring them in. Bring back to the boil and boil for just 1 minute. Remove the leaves from the water with a small sieve or slotted spoon and refresh in cold water. Then squeeze with your hands to extract as much liquid as you can before roughly chopping the spinach.

Put the milk in a pan with the onion, carrot, bay leaf, a few gratings of nutmeg and a couple of twists of black pepper. Bring almost to boiling point, then leave to infuse for 10 minutes. Strain into a warmed jug, discarding the herbs and vegetables.

Melt the butter in the pan (you don't need to wash it) and stir in the flour to get a loose roux. Cook this gently for a couple of minutes, then add half the warm, seasoned milk and stir in. When the sauce is thick and smooth, stir in the rest of the milk. Bring to the boil and simmer gently for just a minute. Then stir in the chopped spinach. Heat through until thoroughly hot, but don't let it bubble for more than a minute. Taste and adjust the seasoning with salt, pepper, and a touch more nutmeg if you like. Serve at once, ladled generously into large warmed bowls. You can, if you like, serve with grated Parmesan, Gruyère or even Cheddar, but I think it's a purer, more spinachy dish on its own.

LEEKS WITH GREENS *Serves 8-10*

4 leeks, finely sliced
A little butter
1 Savoy cabbage or 1kg winter greens or Brussels tops (or a mixture), roughly shredded
Salt and freshly ground black pepper

Sweat the leeks in a little butter for 6-8 minutes, until tender. Meanwhile, lightly steam the greens over boiling water for about 2 minutes. Drain well, toss with the leeks and season to taste with salt and pepper. The leeks should be soft and the greens still quite crunchy.

WATERCRESS AND ORANGE SALAD

Serves 4-6

2 large bunches of watercress, washed and spun dry
4 oranges
1 tablespoon olive oil (or walnut oil, if handy)
Salt and freshly ground black pepper

Trim the large stalks from the watercress, put the sprigs into a shallow serving bowl and set aside.

Slice the peel off the oranges, removing every trace of white pith. With a sharp serrated knife, cut out each segment from between the membranes, dropping the segments into a bowl as you go, and turning the membranes over like the pages of a book. Squeeze the leftover membranes of one orange over a small bowl to provide about a tablespoonful of juice. Add the oil and some salt and pepper and whisk well.

Scatter the orange segments over the watercress and trickle over the dressing. Toss well and serve.

DIRECTORY

DIRECTORY

Here is a personal selection from the many producers of humanely reared, extensively farmed meat in the UK – sadly there simply isn't the space to list them all. You will probably find more suppliers in your area, including ones that do farm gate sales. All producers and shops listed below offer a mail-order service unless otherwise stated.

GENERAL

Brown Cow Organics: Perridge Farm, Pilton, Shepton Mallet, Somerset BA4 4EW
Tel/fax: 01749 890298
www.browncoworganics.co.uk
Winner of the Soil Association's Best Beef award for 2003, Brown Cow's richly flavoured, well-hung beef comes, unusually, from a dairy herd of Guernseys. Also available are Kelly's turkeys, bacon, sausages and their own bresaola, cured in wine and spices.

Cedar Walk Farms Ltd: Unit 8, Leighton Lane Industrial Estate, Evercreech, Shepton Mallet, Somerset BA4 6LQ
Tel: 01749 830800; fax: 01749 831000
www.cedarwalk.com
Accredited as a butcher by the Rare Breeds Survival Trust, Cedar Walk produces excellent pork from Gloucester Old Spot pigs that are free to root around in woodland. Also suckler beef, hung for 4-7 weeks, and lamb hung for 2 weeks. Slow-grown poultry available, plus game, offal, bacon hocks, trotters, Bath chaps and dry-cured bacon.

Eastbrook Farms Organic Meats Ltd: Eastbrook Farm, Bishopstone, Swindon, Wiltshire SN6 8PW
Tel: 01793 790460; fax: 01793 791239
www.helenbrowningorganics.co.uk
Award-winning organic meat, some from rare breeds; rosé veal is a speciality, including shins for osso buco. Also dry-cured bacon, sausages and, occasionally, ducks.

Farmer Sharp: Diamond Buildings, Lindal-in-Furness, Cumbria LA12 0LA
Tel: 01229 588299; fax: 01229 583496
www.farmersharp.co.uk
A cooperative of Lake District farmers producing lamb, wether and mutton (hung for 1, 2 and 3 weeks respectively) from Herdwick sheep. Also Galloway beef and rosé veal. A range of smoked and air-dried mutton products is planned. Need proof of their farming credentials? Andrew Sharp's great-uncle was Beatrix Potter's shepherd.

Graig Farm Organics: Dolau, Llandrindod Wells, Powys LD1 5TL
Tel: 01597 851655; fax: 01597 851991
www.graigfarm.co.uk
This award-winning enterprise works with a group of farmers across Wales to offer a vast range of organic or free-range meats and other products. Choose from well-hung chickens, rare-breed pork (including trotters and other offal), beef, game, Welsh mountain lamb and mutton, and even goat.

Happy Meats: Bank House Farm, Stanford Bridge, Worcestershire WR6 6RU
Tel: 01886 812485; www.happymeats.co.uk
Happy Meats' rare-breed pigs are raised in small family groups on an additive- and GM-free diet. Also grass-fed rare-breed beef and lamb, wild venison and other game. Bacon and game can be smoked in their own smokehouse.

Heal Farm Meats: King's Nympton, Umberleigh, Devon EX37 9TB
Tel: 01769 574341; fax: 01769 572839
www.healfarm.co.uk
Rare-breed meat reared to high welfare standards, including Gloucester Old Spot, Tamworth, Berkshire and Saddleback pigs, North Devon cattle, Shetland and Ryland lamb, Bronze turkeys and various Devon-cross chickens. Rosé veal sometimes available. Butchery is done on farm.

Higher Hacknell Farm: Burrington, Umberleigh, Devon EX37 9LX
Tel/fax: 01769 560909
www.higherhacknell.co.uk
A friendly mixed organic farm, offering well-hung South Devon beef, lamb and chickens at reasonable prices. Bronze and white turkeys available at Christmas.

Hindon Organic Farm: Nr Selworthy, Minehead, Somerset TA24 8SH
Tel/fax: 01643 705244; www.hindonfarm.co.uk
Winner of the Soil Association's Producer of the Year 2003 award, Hindon Farm sells organic Aberdeen Angus beef, lamb and Gloucester Old Spot pork.

Longwood Farm: Tuddenham St Mary, Bury St Edmunds, Suffolk IP28 6TB
Tel/fax: 01638 717120
An organic farm doing all its butchery on site, Longwood produces pork from Saddleback and Duroc pigs, well-marbled South Devon and Galloway beef, traditional Suffolk lamb and slow-grown chickens.

Marshfield Beef and Lamb: Field Farm, Ayford Lane, Marshfield, Chippenham, Wiltshire SN14 8AB
Tel: 01225 891397; www.marshfieldorganic.com
A Soil Association-registered farm producing superb Hereford and Aberdeen Angus beef, hung for 21-28 days, plus Dorset lamb and, occasionally, mutton. They refuse to vac-pack their products, as they believe the quality of the meat suffers. Farmers' markets and local deliveries only.

Northfield Farm: Whissendine Lane, Cold Overton, Nr Oakham, Rutland LE15 7QF
Tel: 01664 474271; www.northfieldfarm.com
Accredited as a butcher by the Rare Breeds Survival Trust, Northfield Farm offers beef from naturally reared cattle, hung for 4-6 weeks. Also rare-breed lamb and pork, plus home-cured bacon, poultry and, occasionally, veal.

Providence Farm Organic Meats: Crosspark Cross, Holsworthy, Devon EX22 6JW
Tel/fax: 01409 254421
www.providencefarm.co.uk
Superb organic pork, lamb, beef and poultry – including guinea fowl, ducks and geese – all reared on the farm. Recently started producing small batches of rare-breed table chickens, including Ixworths, Sussex and Cornish Game. They have been showered with awards, including the Soil Association's Best Poultry award for their chicken in 2003.

The Real Meat Company: Warminster, Wiltshire BA12 0HR
Tel: 0845 762 6017; www.realmeat.co.uk
The Real Meat Company has a strict code of welfare standards which result in fine meat. Particularly recommended are its slow-grown chickens and well-aged beef. Phone for details of branches; mail order also available.

Sheepdrove Organic Farm: Warren Farm, Lambourn, Berkshire RG17 7UU
Tel: 01488 71659; fax: 01488 72677
www.sheepdrove.com
This organic mixed farm produces well-hung beef from South Devon and Aberdeen Angus suckler herds, plus lamb, mutton, pork and slow-grown chickens. Useful small items include lardons, chicken 'stockpot bags' (carcasses for making stock) and pots of organic chicken livers.

Somerset Farm Direct Ltd: Bittescombe Manor, Upton, Wiveliscombe, Taunton, Somerset TA4 2DA
Tel: 01398 371387; fax: 01398 371413
www.somersetfarmdirect.co.uk
Top-quality, traditionally reared lamb, poultry and game, plus superb mutton, straight from the farm. All the meat has been properly hung and prices are reasonable.

Somerset Organics: Gilcombe Farm Shop, Gilcombe Farm, Bruton, Somerset BA10 0QE
Tel: 01749 813710
www.somersetorganics.co.uk
Besides a good variety of organic meat from selected Somerset farms (beef, lamb, pork, chicken and duck), Somerset Organics specialises in game, and will try to get hold of anything in season for you.

Swaddles Green Farm: Hare Lane, Buckland St Mary, Chard, Somerset TA20 3JR
Tel: 0845 456 1768; fax: 01460 234591
www.swaddles.co.uk
Organic beef, lamb, pork, chicken and duck, plus venison. The oak-smoked back bacon was a winner in the Soil Association's Organic Food Awards 2003.

Weatherall Foods Ltd: Crochmore House, Irongray, Dumfries DG2 9SF
Tel: 01387 730326; fax: 01387 730682
www.blackface.co.uk
Excellent selection of game in season, including grouse, teal, woodcock and snipe – and game sausages. Also heather-bred Scottish Blackface lamb, mutton (October only) and haggis, pork from Iron Age pigs (a Tamworth/wild boar cross) and Bronze turkeys.

Welsh Hook Meat Centre: Woodfield, Withybush Road, Haverfordwest, Pembrokeshire SA62 4BW
Tel: 01437 768876
www.welshhookmeats.co.uk
Winner of several Soil Association awards, including Best Pork in 2003, the Welsh Hook Meat Centre supplies well-hung organic and non-organic meat and poultry from Welsh farmers. Halal meat also available.

SPECIALISTS

The Ark Chicken Company: 39 Ellerhayes, Hele, Devon EX5 4PU
Tel/fax: 01392 860430
Traditional free-range poultry from slow-growing breeds, including chicken, geese, turkey, quail and corn-fed guinea fowl. The birds are housed in moveable arks (also available for sale), which means they can be regularly moved on to fresh pasture.

Border County Foods: The Old Vicarage, Crosby-on-Eden, Cumbria CA6 4QZ
Tel: 01228 573500; fax: 01228 573501
www.cumberland-sausage.net
Austen Davies's sausages, including yard-long Cumberland sausage, contain nothing but

free-range rare-breed pork and seasonings, while his black pudding is made with fresh English pig's blood (most producers use dried imported blood). Also dry-cured bacon, pig's cheeks, serrano ham and pancetta.

Devon Foods Ltd: Knightswood Farm, Bluebell Lane, Cullompton, Devon EX15 1RW
Tel: 01884 32816; www.devonfood.co.uk
One of the few suppliers of certified organic chicks in the UK, Devon Foods will provide you with chicks or point-of-lay poulets if you fancy keeping a few hens yourself. Their slow-grown, rustic birds are also supplied wholesale to butcher's and farm shops – contact them for details of outlets.

The Ellel Free-range Poultry Company: The Stables, Ellel Grange, Nr Lancaster, Lancashire LA2 0HN
Tel: 01524 751200; fax: 01524 752648
www.ellelfreerangepoultry.co.uk
Small producers of traditionally reared birds, including guinea fowl, geese, Bronze turkeys and Poulet de Bresse chickens (the only producer of this famous breed outside France). All birds are sold with giblets in and hung for 5-10 days, depending on size.

Fuglemere Rare Breeds: 48 Northcroft, Slough, Berkshire SL2 1HR
Tel/fax: 01753 642029
Well-flavoured lamb from small, lean primitive breeds such as White-faced Woodland, Portland and Norfolk Horn. Mutton is available in season. Also, Longhorn beef, hung for 3 weeks.

Goodman's Geese: Walsgrove Farm, Great Witley, Worcester, Worcestershire WR6 6JJ
Tel: 01299 896272; fax: 01299 896889
www.goodmansgeese.co.uk
Well-hung free-range geese, fed a natural diet with no additives and growth promoters, available from late September to Christmas; Bronze turkeys also available.

Goose Slade Farm: East Coker, Yeovil, Somerset BA22 9JY
Tel: 01935 863735; fax: 01935 864470
Free-range geese fed on a natural diet of corn and wheat, dry-plucked and then hung for 7-10 days. Most direct sales are through the farm shop but Phil and Liz Dunning are happy to arrange delivery if required.

Guildhall Deli (formerly The Cooked Meat Shop): 8 The Guildhall Markets, Bath
Tel: 01225 425640
Sells Bath chaps and chitterlings, along with other traditional cooked meats. No mail order.

Hill End Farm: Brinkworth, Chippenham, Wiltshire SN15 5AZ
Tel: 01666 510261; fax 01666 510780
Joe and Ro Collingborne started to produce rosé veal at their dairy farm to prevent male dairy calves being shot (see page 85). The calves now stay on the cow for 4-5 months and are reared in a large, straw-bedded barn. Farm gate sales, or delivery can usually be arranged.

Ian and Denise at Heritage Prime: Shedbush Farm/National Trust, Muddy Ford Lane, Stanton St Gabriel, Bridport, Dorset DT6 6DR
Tel: 01297 489304; fax: 01297 489531
www.HeritagePrime.co.uk
Heritage Prime's wonderful rare-breed pork, lamb, beef and poultry are not just organic but biodynamic (described as organic plus). If you want cuts such as hams, heads or bellies prepared for your charcuterie experiments, ask for a half or quarter 'piggy box'. By appointment only.

Kelly Turkeys: Springate Farm, Bicknacre Road, Danbury, Essex CM3 4EP
Tel: 01245 223581; 01245 226124
www.kelly-turkeys.com
Superior Bronze and Black turkeys that wander through woodland by day and sleep in open-sided barns at night. Renowned for their flavour, the birds are hung for at least 10 days.

Langley Chase Organic Farm: Kington Langley, Chippenham, Wiltshire SN15 5PW
Tel: 01249 750095; www.langleychase.co.uk
Winner of the Soil Association's Best Lamb award in 2003, Jane Kallaway rears a closed flock of the primitive Manx Loghtan lamb – a very rare, slow-growing breed with distinctively flavoured dark flesh. Mutton, sausages and burgers also available.

Little Warren Farm: Fletching Common, Newick, East Sussex BN8 4JH
Tel: 01825 722545
Winners of the Soil Association's Best Veal award in 2003, Jim and Diana Murray produce organic veau sous la mère *– their calves suckle their mothers for 6 months. Organic beef also available. Buy at the farm or, for mail order, contact Guy Sparkes, 24 Old Dover Road, Blackheath, London SE3 7BY; tel: 020 8355 8597.*

Peele's Norfolk Black Turkeys: Rookery Farm, Thuxton, Norwich, Norfolk NR9 4QJ
Tel/fax: 01362 850237
The original home of pure-bred Norfolk Black turkeys. James Graham's grandfather saved the breed from extinction in the Fifties and the free-range birds are still reared according to the same programme, with a feed of oats and

barley grown on the farm. They are slaughtered at around 8 months and Mr Graham is happy to prepare them to customers' specifications.

Pentre Pigs: Pentre House, Leighton, Welshpool, Powys SY21 8HL
Tel: 01938 553430; www.pentrepigs.co.uk
A small, enthusiastic producer of traditional free-range Berkshire, Tamworth and Kune Kune pigs. Whole and half pigs available, plus the usual cuts, bacon, sausages and offal (including cheeks, heads and trotters).

Piperfield Pork: The Dovecote, Lowick, Berwick-upon-Tweed TD15 2QE
Tel: 01289 388543
Succulent, full-flavoured pork from a closed herd of free-range Middle White pigs, fed a special mix of cereals and beans that varies according to each pig's needs. Also sausages and dry-cured bacon, gammons and hams.

Seldom Seen Farm: Billesdon, Leicestershire LE7 9FA
Tel: 0116 259 6742; fax: 0116 259 6626
Specialises in free-range Embden-cross geese, and also supplies Bronze turkeys and a three-bird roast – consisting of boned-out pheasant, chicken and goose, one inside the other, with pork and orange stuffing.

Wild Beef: Hillhead Farm, Chagford, Devon TQ13 8DY
Tel/fax: 01647 433433
Perhaps not quite wild, but these native breeds of cattle are raised in as natural an environment as possible, roaming on the moor with their mother for the first year of life and feeding on wild flowers, herbs and bilberries as well as grass. The meat is hung for 4 weeks.

Wild Meat Company: Low Road, Sweffling, Saxmundham, Suffolk IP17 2BU
Tel: 01728 663211; www.wildmeat.co.uk
A huge variety of top-quality game available, including harder-to-find birds such as teal, snipe and widgeon. Also wild venison, hung for 2-3 weeks (or to customers' requirements).

MISCELLANEOUS INGREDIENTS

Cool Chile Co: PO Box 5702, London W11 2GS
Tel: 0870 902 1145; fax: 0870 162 3923
www.coolchile.co.uk
Dried chillies by mail order, plus a wide range of Mexican ingredients, including masa harina.

Natural Casing Company Ltd: PO Box 133, Farnham, Surrey GU10 5HT
Tel: 01252 850454; fax: 01252 851284
Supplies natural casings for everything from chipolatas to hog's pudding. Also saltpetre.

Peppers by Post: Sea Spring Farm, West Bexington, Dorchester, Dorset DT2 9DD
Tel: 01308 897892; fax: 01308 897735
www.peppersbypost.biz
Fresh chillies in season (late July–early December) from Michael and Joy Michaud's Dorset farm. Varieties include poblano, serrano, habanero, jalapeño and cayenne.

EQUIPMENT

P. H. Hardwill Ltd: Hurst Works, Blackdown, Beaminster, Dorset DT8 3LE
Tel: 01460 30661; fax: 01460 30173
This is where I went for my spit-roast kit. They are steel fabricators but will happily build a spit-roast kit to your specification. Mail order not available.

Natural Casing Company Ltd
Stocks filler nozzles to fit various mincers. *See above for contact details.*

Nisbets: 1110 Aztec West, Bristol BS32 4HR
Tel: 01454 855551; fax: 01454 855565
www.nisbets.co.uk
Mail-order supplier of professional catering equipment, including stockpots, terrine dishes, chef's knives, mincers, meat thermometers and electric meat slicers. Sells the Bourgeat range of frying pans at reasonable prices.

A. W. Smith & Sons: 82-88 Sherlock Street, Birmingham B5 6LT
Tel: 0121 622 2137/3684; fax: 0121 666 6680
www.awsmith.co.uk
Suppliers of industrial catering equipment, including excellent hand-cranked sausage-making machines, plus small, industrial mincing machines – expensive but, in my kitchen at least, essential! Also great prices on quality cook's and butcher's knives.

HARDWOOD CHARCOAL

www.allotmentforestry.com
This website aims to increase the use of local woodlands products in gardens and allotments. Search by county to find suppliers of sustainable hardwood charcoal in your area.

The Dorset Charcoal Company Ltd: Tudor Cottage, Pidney, Hazelbury Bryan, Dorset DT10 2EB
Tel: 01258 818176; www.dorsetcharcoal.co.uk
Supplies barbecue charcoal from sustainable local sources, plus logs and kindling.

Graig Farm Organics
Besides a wide range of meat, Graig Farm sells local hardwood charcoal from a selection of broadleaf trees. *See page 526 for contact details.*

USEFUL ORGANISATIONS

www.bigbarn.co.uk
Aims to put consumers in touch with local food producers, thus encouraging them to buy direct and take an active interest in local food and farming.

Compassion in World Farming (CIWF): Charles House, 5a Charles Street, Petersfield, Hampshire GU32 3EH
Tel: 01730 264208; fax: 01730 260791
www.ciwf.co.uk
Campaigning organisation aiming to bring an end to factory farming and the long-distance transport of animals worldwide.

The Food Commission: 94 White Lion Street, London N1 9PF
Tel: 020 7837 2250; fax: 020 7837 1141
www.foodcomm.org.uk
A completely independent, non-profit organisation campaigning for the right to safe, wholesome food and providing independently researched information. Members receive a quarterly magazine.

The Game Conservancy Trust: Fordingbridge, Hampshire SP6 1EF
Tel: 01425 652381; fax: 01425 651026
www.gct.org.uk
Promotes the conservation of game in the British countryside and advises on practical management techniques.

Guild of Q Butchers: PO Box 26139, Dunfermline, Fife, Scotland KY12 7WJ
Tel: 01383 432622; fax: 01383 432626
www.guildofqbutchers.co.uk
All members are independent butchers who undergo annual inspections to ensure standards are maintained. Contact the Guild for details of specialist butchers in your area or mail-order suppliers.

National Association of Farriers, Blacksmiths and Agricultural Engineers: The Forge, Avenue B, 10th Street, Stoneleigh Park, Warwickshire CV8 2LG
Tel: 024 766 96595
Can put you in touch with blacksmiths in your area if you are looking for someone to build a spit-roast kit.

The National Farmers' Retail and Markets Association: PO Box 575, Southampton, Hampshire SO15 7BZ
Tel: 0845 230 2150
www.farmshopping.com
www.farmersmarkets.net
Recently merged from The Farm Retail Association and The National Association of Farmers' Markets, this trade organisation helps farmers and retailers sell their produce direct. Contact it for details of your nearest farmers' market or for a list of farm shops and local suppliers.

www.organicbutchers.co.uk
A nationwide directory of organic meat suppliers – lists butchers, farm shops, farm gate sales and mail order.

Rare Breeds Survival Trust: National Agricultural Centre, Stoneleigh Park, Warwickshire CV8 2LG
Tel: 02476 696551; fax: 02476 696706
www.rare-breeds.com
Charity aiming to conserve Britain's native livestock heritage. Phone for details of rare-breed meat suppliers in your area.

www.rivercottage.net
A website I set up to encourage discussion about food, where it comes from and why that matters. Includes edible projects, recipes and recommended producers.

www.shelfordfeast.co.uk
The ancient feast of Shelford was revived in 1996. Its website gives a fun and interesting perspective on organising a barbecue for large numbers, with lots of tips on building the kit for spit roasts and pit barbecues. Recipe ideas range from grilled sardines to stuffed camel and Samuel Pepys' recipe for spit-roasting a whole deer.

www.slowfood.com
For anyone who's ever despaired at the relentless advance of fast food, Slow Food is an Italian-based international organisation of 'eco-gastronomes' wishing to preserve artisan foods and regional traditions. Local groups, or 'Convivia', have recently been set up in the UK. For details, phone 0800 917 1232.

The Soil Association: 86 Colston Street, Bristol BS1 5BB
Tel: 0117 929 0661; fax: 0117 925 2504
www.soilassociation.org
Campaigns to raise awareness about the benefits of organic food and farming, and gives support and advice on growing and producing organic food. Publishes The Organic Directory *(£4.95), which gives details of your nearest producers.*

BIBLIOGRAPHY

GENERAL

Blythman, Joanna: *The Food We Eat (Michael Joseph, 1996)*

Budiansky, Stephen: *The Covenant of the Wild: Why Animals Choose Domestication (HarperCollins, 1992)*

Davidson, Alan: *The Oxford Companion to Food (Oxford University Press, 1999)*

Eyton, Audrey: *The Kind Food Guide (Penguin Books, 1991)*

Mason, Laura, with Brown, Catherine: *Traditional Foods of Britain: A Regional Inventory (Prospect Books, 1999)*

McGee, Harold: *McGee on Food and Cooking: An Encyclopedia of Kitchen Science, History and Culture (Hodder, 2004)*

Rogers, Ben: *Beef and Liberty (Chatto & Windus, 2003)*

FOOD POLITICS

D'Silva, Joyce and Tansey, Geoff (eds): *The Meat Business: Devouring a Hungry Planet (Earthscan, 1999)*

Rowell, A: *Don't Worry (It's Safe to Eat): The True Story of GM Food, BSE and Foot and Mouth (Earthscan, 2003)*

Sams, Craig: *The Little Food Book (Alastair Sawday Publishing, 2000)*

Schlosser, Eric: *Fast Food Nation: What the All-American Meal is Doing to the World (Allen Lane, 2001)*

SOURCING INGREDIENTS

Brown, Lynda: *The Shopper's Guide to Organic Food (Fourth Estate, 1998)*

Litchfield, Clive: *The Organic Directory (Green Books, with the Soil Association, 2002)*

Stein, Rick: *Guide to the Food Heroes of Britain (BBC Books, 2003)*

The Authentic Food Finder *(The Write Angle Press, 1998)*

West Dorset Food Links Local Food Directory: *(free brochure giving information on local farmers, food processors and small retailers; for similar publications in your area, enquire at your local reference library)*

COOKERY

Bissell, Frances: *The Real Meat Cookbook (Chatto & Windus, 1992)*

Blumenthal, Heston: *Family Food: A New Approach to Cooking (Penguin, 2003)*

David, Elizabeth: *A Book of Mediterranean Food (John Lehmann, 1950); French Country Cooking (John Lehmann, 1951); French Provincial Cooking (Michael Joseph, 1960); Spices, Salt and Aromatics in the English Kitchen (Penguin Books, 1970)*

Davidson, Silvija: *Loaf, Crust and Crumb (Michael Joseph, 1995)*

Del Conte, Anna: *Gastronomy of Italy (Pavilion Books, 2001)*

Fearnley-Whittingstall, Hugh: *A Cook on the Wild Side (Michael Joseph, 1993); Cuisine Bon Marché (Macmillan, 1994); The River Cottage Cookbook (HarperCollins, 2001); The River Cottage Year (Hodder & Stoughton, 2003)*

Gray, Rose, and Rogers, Ruth: *The River Café Cookbook (Ebury Press, 1995); The River Café Cookbook Two (Ebury Press, 1997)*

Grigson, Jane: *Charcuterie and French Pork Cookery (Michael Joseph, 1967); The Observer Guide to European Cookery (Michael Joseph, 1983)*

Grigson, Sophie: *Sophie Grigson's Meat Course (Network Books, 1995)*

Hazan, Marcella: *The Classic Italian Cookbook (Macmillan, 1980)*

Henderson, Fergus: *Nose to Tail Eating (Macmillan, 1999)*

Hopkinson, Simon, with Bareham, Lindsey: *Roast Chicken and Other Stories (Ebury Press, 1994); The Prawn Cocktail Years (Macmillan, 1997)*

Lawson, Nigella: *How to Eat (Chatto & Windus, 1998)*

Leigh, Rowley: *No Place Like Home (Fourth Estate, 2000)*

Ortiz, Elisabeth Lambert: *The Book of Latin American Cooking (Robert Hale, 1984)*

Roden, Claudia: *Mediterranean Cookery (BBC Books, 1987); The Book of Jewish Food (Viking, 1997)*

Roux, Albert and Michel: *The Roux Brothers' French Country Cooking (Sidgwick & Jackson, 1989)*

Schwartz, Oded: *Preserving (Dorling Kindersley, 1996)*

Seymour, John: *The Complete Book of Self-Sufficiency (Dorling Kindersley, 1998)*

Taruschio, Ann and Franco: *Leaves from The Walnut Tree (Pavilion Books, 1993)*

The Good Cook series (Pork/Beef/Lamb/Offal), (Time Life books, o/p)

Larousse Gastronomique (Hamlyn Publishing, 1988)

ALTERNATIVE RECIPE INDEX

Organised by mood and inspiration to help you plan a meal, this index is the browser's way into the cookery elements of this book. The idea of the lists below is to reflect the way I feel a lot of home cooks actually set about planning their cooking – casting around for a suitable dish to fit the occasion in question. I also felt it would be a fun exercise for me, to get some insight into my own subliminal mental grid reference of meat recipes. I was right. I have enjoyed myself thoroughly.

As I set about this amusing task, it became clear that several recipes would appear more than once – and so they should. In theory, I suppose, the recipe with the most entries could be classed as some sort of 'champion' of the book. I won't tell you what it is here. But I might inaugurate a little discussion of it on our website – *www.rivercottage.net.*

1. CELEBRATIONS

All good meat is a celebration – of life, of our landscape, perhaps of British agriculture at its best. But some dishes have an extra flag-waving element that makes them fit for very special occasions – Christmas perhaps, or a birthday party. For me these tend to be dishes that have some ritual to them, that have a long tradition, from whatever culture, or that reverentially take a piece of meat of the highest quality, cook it simply and put it centre stage with a strong supporting cast of 'trimmings'.

2. SHEER COMFORT

I think of these recipes as creating a warm glow among a table of eaters – perhaps just immediate family or close friends – not only in the eating, but also in the anticipation. There's nothing formal here. Think Sunday suppers and trays in front of the telly.

3. OFFALLY GOOD

These are the dishes for enthusiasts of 'spare part' cookery – a farmyard Frankenstein's fantasy list. They offer some of the most interesting and varied tastes and textures in the pantheon of meat cuts. They also serve as a kind of checklist to help you develop and keep your pledge to the 'nose-to-tail' philosophy of ethical meat consumption.

4. IMPRESS YOUR FRIENDS

Perhaps this is a slightly silly list. I hope every dish in this book would 'impress your friends'. The ones I have chosen are simply those that I feel may earn you an extra eyebrow raise and a toast to the chef – perhaps because they are a little unusual or unexpected, a touch 'cheffy', or because, like the steak and kidney pie, they are well known, much talked about, but only rarely delivered at their outstanding best.

Duck or Goose Breasts with Pineapple, Chilli and Soy (p.366)
Spit-roast Pig (p.386)
Spiced Hot-smoked Liver (p.408)
Cotechino with Lentils and Salsa Verde (p.441)
Terrine of Sweetbreads with a Broad Bean Purée (p.455)
Piroshki (p.501)
Game Soup (p.507)

5. À DEUX

These are treats to cook for your partner when you're feeling romantic, extravagant, excited or all three. Some of them may be a little labour intensive – too much trouble to consider for feeding a large number, perhaps. But as little labours of love for dining à deux*, they are perfect. Not everyone will agree, but for me a lot of raw meat and offal dishes seem to fall into this category. Perhaps it's because they somehow emphasise carnivorousness, and therefore perhaps carnality.*

Mincemeat-stuffed Pork Tenderloins (p.229)
Loin of Lamb Stuffed with Apricots and Pine Nuts (p.242)
Classic Roast Grouse (or Partridge) (p.250)
Classic Roast Woodcock (and Snipe) (p.252)
Osso Buco alla Milanese (p.289)
Carpaccio of Beef with Shaved Beetroot (p.349)
Steak and Chips (p.352)
Wiener Schnitzel (p.354)
Chicken Kiev (p.356)
Venison Steak au Poivre (p.357)
Calf's Liver with Little Onions, Sage and Aged Vinegar (p.358)
Fritto Misto of Offal with Sage and Capers (p.362)
Sauté of Sweetbreads with Peas and Beans (p.364)
Black Pudding Wontons (p.365)
Salad of Seared Pigeon Breast with Pan Juice Vinaigrette (p.369)
Steak Tartare (p.442)
Kibbeh Naye (p.443)
Preserved Duck or Goose Legs (p.451)
Pastilla (p.502)

6. ALL SPICED UP

For lovers of punchy aromatics and/or a hefty dose of spice, and for those who can't seem to quit smoking, these are the dishes to awaken the most jaded of taste buds. In most cases the heat factor is a variable that you can manage, by adding more or less chilli or hot paprika.

Aromatic Pork Belly Hot Pot (p.277)
Curry Goat (p.297)
Paprikash of Hearts, Liver and Tongues (p.308)
Chicken with Preserved Lemons and Olives (p.313)
Mole (p.314)
Stir-fried Indonesian Pork (or Beef, or Lamb, or Chicken, or Rabbit) (p.346)
Seared Spicy Beef in a Wrap (p.348)
Murgh Makhani (p.355)
Barbecued Glazed Spare Ribs (p.397)
Indian-spiced Lamb Skewers (p.402)
Lucy's Jerk Chicken (p.405)
Spiced Hot-smoked Liver (p.408)
Mexican-style Chorizo (p.446)
Picadillo (p.494)
Chilli con Carne (p.495)
Thai Pork Dumplings (p.508)

7. RIVER COTTAGE CLASSICS

The following recipes all appeared in one of my last two books, *The River Cottage Cookbook* and *The River Cottage Year*. I reproduce them here, in a few cases with some small alterations born of recent experience, for two obvious reasons: first, you may not have copies of those books; and secondly, this book would have felt incomplete without these dishes.

Oxtail, or Tail and Tongue, with Rich Red Wine Sauce (p.282)
Jugged Hare (p.317)
Home-cured Bacon (p.429)
Salt Beef (p.438)
Steak Tartare (p.442)
Brawn (p.486)
Chinese-style Pig's Trotters (p.490)

8. FEEDING A CROWD

When you have twenty or more hungry guests to feed, then big roasts or big pots are the order of the day. The following dishes either intrinsically feed large numbers, because of the sheer weight of meat, or can easily be expanded to do so. I've also ruled out anything prohibitively expensive or time consuming.

Aromatic Shoulder of Pork 'Donnie Brasco' (p.231)
Pot-au-feu (p.284)
Lamb Braised with Stuffed Vine Leaves (p.291)
Curry Goat (p.297)
Tunisian Lamb with Aubergine (p.299)
Cassoulet (p.302)
Spit-roast Pig (p.386)
Glazed Baked Ham California with Parsley Sauce (p.433)
Ham in Hay (p.435)
Boston Baked Beans (p.484)
Feijoada (p.487)
Pasticcio (p.491)
Spaghetti Bolognese (p.497)
Moussaka (p.503)
Valencian Paella (p.509)

9. ONE-POT WONDERS

These are dishes, usually casseroles, stews or braises of one kind or another, that may have lengthy cooking times but are nonetheless easy to prepare, because everything goes in one pot, then on the hob or in the oven, until it's done. When finished, they are generally complete meals – give or take, in one or two cases, a baked potato or a pile of pasta on the side.

Rice Pudding Pork (p.278)
Main-course Borscht (p.279)
A Provençal Daube (p.280)
Beef in Stout (p.288)
Lancashire Hot Pot (p.290)
Mrs Wheeler's Irish Stew (p.292)
Ndole (p.296)
Cassoulet (p.302)
Chicken with Preserved Lemons and Olives (p.313)
Boston Baked Beans (p.484)
Spaghetti Bolognese (p.497)

10. CHEAP BUT VERY CHEERFUL

These are my 'thrift specials' – not so much meals made from leftovers as dishes that use the give-away cuts of meat to excellent effect.

Aromatic Pork Belly Hot Pot (p.277)
Lancashire Hot Pot (p.290)
Breast of Lamb Ste Menehould (p.295)
Citrus-braised Lamb Shanks (p.300)
Paprikash of Hearts, Liver and Tongues (p.308)
Rabbit Stew (p.316)
Petit Salé (p.430)
Salt Beef (p.438)
Pork Rillettes (p.447)
Potted Hough (p.456)
Boston Baked Beans (p.484)
Brawn (p.486)
Chinese-style Spare Ribs and Pig's Trotters (p.490)
Flying Toad in the Hole (p.492)

11. PICNIC/AL FRESCO SPECIALS

The heading says it all: portable cold food and easy barbecue cooking of the highest order.

Cold Roast Beef Open Sandwich (p.236)
Beefburgers (p.398)
Souvlaki (p.401)
Indian-spiced Lamb Skewers (p.402)
Barbecued Rosemary Lamb with Salsa Verde (p.404)
A Cider-cured Ham (p.432)
Bresaola (p.436)
Cold Tongue with Lentils and Green Dressing (p.438)
A Raised Pork Pie (p.444)
Pork Rillettes (p.447)
Rich Liver Pâté (p.452)
Potted Hough (p.456)
Pigeon Pâté (p.458)
Brawn (p.486)
Coronation Chicken (p.506)

12. CHILD FRIENDLY

When it comes to cooking and eating, I don't like discriminating against the younger generation – I particularly don't like the concept of a children's menu (Kiddies Korner!) in restaurants. As if the under-tens don't have the capacity to appreciate good ingredients and subtle flavours. However, where home cooking is concerned, there are some recipes that lend themselves to family meals (i.e. meals including kids, plural) more than others. This is either because they can be put together at short notice with a minimum of fuss, or because there is some ritual in the preparation or eating that children will especially enjoy.

Herb Roast Chicken (p.244)
Lamb Braised with Stuffed Vine Leaves (p.291)
Pan-to-oven Pork Chops with Garlic (p.342)
Seared Spicy Beef in a Wrap (p.348)
Barbecued Glazed Spare Ribs (p.397)
Beefburgers (p.398)
Souvlaki (p.401)
Indian-spiced Lamb Skewers (p.402)
Boston Baked Beans (p.484)
Flying Toad in the Hole (p.492)
Picadillo (p.494)
Spaghetti Bolognese (p.497)
Red Flannel Hash (p.498)
Piroshki (p.501)
Shepherd's Pie (p.504)
Fried Chicken with Potatoes and Anchovies (p.506)
Coronation Chicken (p.506)

MY PERSONAL TOP TWENTY

I'm not sure how wise it is to do this, and I wouldn't swear this is the right order, but here goes:

1. Roast Belly of Pork with Apple Sauce (p.226)
2. Shepherd's Pie (p.504)
3. Classic Roast Grouse (p.250)
4. Steak and Chips (p.352)
5. Oxtail, or Tail and Tongue, with Rich Red Wine Sauce (p.282)
6. Steak and Kidney Pie (p.286)
7. A Raised Pork Pie (p.444)
8. Fritto Misto of Offal with Sage and Capers (p.362)
9. Steak Tartare (p.442)
10. Jugged Hare (p.317)
11. Roast Lamb (p.239)
12. Spaghetti Bolognese (p.497)
13. Glazed Baked Ham California with Parsley Sauce (p.433)
14. Aromatic Shoulder of Pork 'Donnie Brasco' (p.231)
15. Roast Beef – The Full Monty (p.232)
16. Devilled Kidneys (p.361)
17. Cassoulet (p.302)
18. Bollito Misto (p.304)
19. Classic Roast Woodcock (p.252)
20. Chinese-style Spare Ribs and Pig's Trotters (p.490)

INDEX

Page numbers in *italic* refer to the illustrations

HUGH'S ACKNOWLEDGEMENTS

I've written this book over four years in collaboration with a team that has shown fantastic enthusiasm and amazing patience from start to finish. My editor, Richard Atkinson, has seen the project grow in scale with few signs of alarm, and has given me his unconditional support at every stage. He has also brought his excellent judgement to bear on the text and production and convinced me for the third time in a row that I simply could not wish for a better editor. Simon Wheeler must feel he's photographed every meal I've eaten for the last five years, and yet his perspective on meat, both raw and cooked, is fresh and exhilarating at every turn. His pictures seem to have appetite as well as attitude, and I don't know how he does it. Paddy Cramsie has had to design this book across a constantly shifting schedule and in the end to an absurdly unrealistic deadline. Yet not only has he managed to delight a committee of unbridled nit-pickers (myself included) with his clear vision and elegant solutions, he has remained the very definition of calm and charm throughout. My copy editor, researcher and chief recipe tester, Jane Middleton, has become an indispensable support, not only as a rigorous and constructive critic of my recipes and my prose, but also as a sounding board for my ideas and argument. I hold her opinion of my opinion in the highest esteem.

I would also like to thank Ray Smith for butchering my animals so skilfully and sharing his knowledge so generously; Bryan Johnson for his ever-dependable assistance and always impeccable judgement in the kitchen (including possibly the best chips of all time); Portia Dean and Derryck Strachan for further invaluable kitchen support and helpful comments on my recipes. And thanks for help with specific recipes to Ivan Samarine, Lucy Pilkington, Victor Borg and Mrs Wheeler.

On the home farm front I'd like to thank Bernie James for his exemplary husbandry and skilled stockmanship of our own animals. If only all meat lived so well. Thanks also to Frank and Nicola Greenway for all their help, advice and agricultural troubleshooting.

For giving their time and sharing their knowledge, and supplying me with some of the finest meat, poultry and game (and occasional antidotes of fish), I would like to thank all of the following: Pammy and Ritchie Riggs of Providence Farm; Ian and Denise Bell at Heritage Prime; Peggy Darvill at Lake Farm; all at Eastbrook Farm; Robert Hayball and Chris Rowe of the Smoky Hole Shoot; Trevor Symes at Snell's; Jan and Ben Andrews; Pat Carlin; Nick Fisher; Julian Kennard and the Worsel Gunners. And thanks to David Lanning at Lloyd Maunder for his honesty and openness about modern poultry farming.

At Hodder, I'd like to thank the entire team for reacting so positively to this project at all stages. I'm especially grateful to Jo Seaton, Al Oliver and Briar Silich. And thanks to John Mitchinson for getting the ball rolling.

I'd like to thank Leigh Goodman for bringing some sense and structure to my diary and helping to make publicity and press seem less like work and more like play.

Thanks to everyone at Keo Films and rivercottage.net for their continued support, and particularly Andrew Palmer, Zam Baring and Rob Love for past adventures and future possibilities.

And thanks to my friend and agent, Antony Topping, for continuing to give a remarkable impression of someone who still thinks it's a pleasure to work with me. It's certainly a pleasure to work with you.

Thanks to Mum, Dad, Soph and Nick for your past, present and future support. It's always a pleasure to feed you and be fed by you, literally and metaphorically.

Lastly, and firstly, I'd like to thank Marie, Oscar and Freddie, for everything.